29.95 test
10.00

BUILDING THE RULE OF LAW

BUILDING THE RULE OF LAW

Jennifer A. Widner
University of Michigan

W. W. NORTON & COMPANY
NEW YORK • LONDON

The text of this book is composed in Electra
with the display set in Fenice Bold
Composition by Tom Ernst
Manufacturing by Maple-Vail Book Manufacturing Group

Library of Congress Cataloging-in-Publication Data
Widner, Jennifer A.
    Building the rule of law / by Jennifer A. Widner
        p. cm.
    Includes bibliographical references and index
    ISBN 0-393-05037-8
    1. Nyalali, Francis L. 2. Judges—Tanzania—Biography 3. Judicial power—Tanzania.
    KTT11.N93 W53 2001
    347.678'014'092—dc21
    [B]

                                                                    00-056609

W. W. Norton and Co., Inc., 500 Fifth Avenue, New York, NY 10110
www.wwnorton.com

W. W. Norton and Company Ltd., 10 Coptic Street, London WC1A 1PU

1 2 3 4 5 6 7 8 9 0

To my parents, Joan and Ralph Widner,
whose values, enthusiasm, and patience
made this book possible

To my aunt, Barbara Kennedy,
whose keenness for research helped during difficult passages

and

To the judges and magistrates this book is about

Contents

Preface

THIS BOOK IS about the separation of powers, judicial independence, and the rule of law. For a variety of reasons, I have departed from the conventional language in which these themes are discussed these days. The pages offer insights of general importance, but they also convey the story of a chief justice, Francis Nyalali, his court in Tanzania, and his counterparts in neighboring countries of Africa. Although the underlying social science scaffolding will be evident to some readers, I hope the portrait of a man and his times makes the ideas more accessible to a wider audience.

The historian Barbara Tuchman once described biography as "useful because it encompasses the universal in the particular. It is a focus that allows both the writer to narrow his field to manageable dimensions and the reader to more easily comprehend the subject."[1] I echo these sentiments, though this book does not offer a definitive biography by any means. There are important substantive and stylistic reasons for following Tuchman's advice.

First, there is new interest in the crafting of institutions. This interest has its roots partly in the policy concerns of our times. It also responds to evidence that at critical junctures in history or in special settings, human behavior is far more a product of calculation and strategy than of stable routines, attitudes, or characteristics. Where before social scientists searched for broad covering laws, they now focus more on choice and bargaining.[2]

A focus on crafting necessarily concentrates the attention of social scientists on individual men and women. To understand the outcomes of negotiation, it

---

[1] Barbara Tuchman, *Practicing History* (New York: Ballantine Books, 1981), p. 81.
[2] For example, with respect to the study of courts and politics, see Lee Epstein and Jack Knight, *The Choices Justices Make* (Washington, D.C.: CQ Press, 1998).

is important to know the preferences and tastes of those involved, the ideas that inform their assessments of risk and reward, and the options that they consider. Thus, to pinpoint the effects of general mechanisms or processes, students of politics need to draw on insights available only through interviews and other forms of ethnographic investigation, including biography. In this sense, the decision to write the book as a study of a man and his times is uncontroversial.

The stylistic choice addresses another problem too. Social science writing has an unfortunate tendency to assume away the quandaries, hand-wringing, indecision, and mistakes of real-world decision making. Biography is humble in a way social science models often are not. It takes into account when someone was undecided, lacked information, did not care, suffered coercion, forgot, or later thought he or she had made a mistake. In so doing it defines more accurately the scope for human creativity. It helps illuminate how general insights apply.

Finally, the focus on a man and his times is also partly a function of the state of knowledge. One of the fundamental problems encountered in carrying out the research for this book was the shortage of basic description, a critical resource for thinking about causes and effects. African legal scholars are prolific writers, and they have contributed heavily to the study of substantive legal doctrine. Foreign law teachers who worked in Africa during the 1960s and 1970s also have made vital contributions to the understanding of rules and institutions. But on the subject of contemporary legal institutions and their problems, there is little in the way of written documentation, outside of consultant reports. These circumstances make a case for a book that presents "the big picture" in a form accessible and useful to a diverse readership. The "man and his times" approach helps convey material without which further investigation cannot take place.

For those who are interested in the sources of the information presented in these pages, let me also offer a few words. Elite interviews were central to the book. They illuminated whom judges considered important to the future of the courts and why; provided information about the goals different actors sought to attain; and yielded insight into the costs, benefits, and risks of different courses of action. The former chief justice of Tanzania, Francis Nyalali, was kind enough to grant many long interviews on the record, and his account, combined with the views of other members of the Tanzanian bench and bar, constitute the core of the book. The perspective gained from these conversations helped provide points of departure for interviews with judges and lawyers in other countries. Some of those interviewed would not offer remarks for attribution, while others did. I used the reflections they provided mainly as general guidance in choosing which issues to explore in greater depth. In three countries—Uganda, Tanzania, and Botswana—the interviews embraced not only senior judges and justice officials but also magistrates working in rural areas.

In trying to ascertain general trends in the perceived independence of the courts as well as patterns in the popular use of the courts, I resorted to other methods. In a subset of the countries in the region, I conducted two types of surveys. One study was based on a random sample of members of the bar, whose views I requested in a written survey containing mainly close-ended questions. Other information came from a larger study based on a multistage area sample of households, both rural and urban. The surveys took place between September 1995 and May 1996.

For other types of cross-national analysis, I used data from the International Country Risk Service, Freedom House, Interpol, and similar sources. For example, statements about prison conditions and the frequency of specific types of human rights abuses come from my own coding of the U.S. State Department *Human Rights Reports* and from analysis of that information. The sources are footnoted in the text, but the original data and tables have been removed to preserve the flow of the text.

In some instances I used participant observation to help enlarge my own understanding of the issues at hand. I took the notes for selected phases of the U.S.-Africa Judicial Exchange, a program jointly sponsored by the Superior Court of the District of Columbia, the American Bar Association, and the National Judicial College. The position of note taker enabled me to learn from judges and lawyers on two continents and to build a more casual relationship with some of the judges than would ordinarily have been possible. It also allowed me to observe trials and mediations firsthand.

As with any book of this type, there remains considerable room for investigation and comment. Many important and interesting problems of comparative law are addressed only fleetingly. And there are great opportunities for elaboration about the way people use courts and other elements of the legal process. My hope is that scholarly readers in Africa and elsewhere will use the book as a point of departure. I trust that their own contributions will permit a much better account of the subject a few years from now.

Acknowledgments

SOMETIMES AUTHORS HOLD onto manuscripts longer than they should, not just because of the press of business but also because the project itself is so absorbing. This book has opened new horizons and created new intellectual friendships.

My first debt of gratitude is to the people the book is about: Chief Justice Francis Nyalali, who retired from his post a few months before this book appeared in print, along with the members of the bench and the bar in Tanzania, Uganda, Botswana, Zambia, Malawi, and Zimbabwe. Judges, magistrates, and lawyers in these countries patiently answered questions and reflected on their work. These pages represent their collective effort. Not everyone interviewed will agree with everything said. Inevitably there will be some differences in interpretation of events and personalities. I hope the statements I have made are accurate and fair for their time and context.

Much of the satisfaction I derived from this book has come from conversations with African authors on law and legal institutions. I owe special thanks to Joe Oloka-Onyango, Ibrahim Juma, Bojosi Otlhogile, Tiyanjana Maluwa, and Chris Maina Peter, for the illumination they provided. The book also benefited enormously from the wisdom imparted by scholars who have dedicated much of their time and energy to law in Africa, especially the writings of William Twining, Anthony Allott, Robert Seidman, Yash Ghai, Patrick McAuslan, James Paul, and John Hatchard.

Many people moved the project forward. The book started as a glimmer of an idea in 1994, during a conversation with Rozann Stayden, then of the American Bar Association. Remembering the discussion, Stayden telephoned a year later and asked whether I would tag along as part of an exchange program involving American and African judges. Would I go to "judge school," help out, and take the notes? I jumped at the chance. The only hurdle, Stayden said, was that I would have to pass muster with Judge Nan R. Shuker, of the Superior Court of the

District of Columbia. The formidable Judge Shuker provided the tutelage, advice, and personal enthusiasm that moved the project from glimmer to completion. The hours spent in Judge Shuker's company and in the corridors of the superior court were invaluable. Although this book probably falls short of their standards, not least in the length of time it has taken to prepare, these pages would not read as they do without the assistance Stayden and Shuker offered. Judge Susan R. Winfield, attorney Harlow Case, and alternative dispute resolution specialist Melinda Ostermeyer also provided invaluable counsel in the early stages.

The sudden and unexpected impetus the project received from the U.S.-Africa Judicial Exchange meant that the research had to coexist with other obligations. I owe thanks to the Fulbright program for allowing me to detour occasionally from the research that it funded, in order to spend time conducting interviews and surveys for this project. Dr. Kiki Munshi, then stationed in Tanzania, was especially thoughtful. She provided occasional harbor and intriguing conversation. She negotiated transportation to far-flung regions in return for service as a workshop leader.

The book's unusual beginnings also meant that the project proceeded in reverse of the usual order. That is to say, my formal introduction to much of the subject matter came only after my practical introduction. Jeffrey Lehman, dean of the University of Michigan Law School, took my request to study law seriously and went out of his way to help someone who was not on his faculty. I will be forever grateful for the opportunities he created. He opened the door to a world that is unfortunately unfamiliar to too many social scientists. His gesture influenced not only this book but also many other aspects of scholarship and life. Other members of the law school were equally gracious and open-minded. The faculty allowed me to participate in their courses and cheerfully renewed a conversation with history and philosophy. The library staff members helped to find obscure publications and to renew my carrel permit when absent-mindedness set in, as it often did. Throughout, the law school was a model of what an excellent academic institution should be.

The most delicate and valuable gift an author can receive is thoughtful criticism. Several people spent many hours reading, prodding, and arguing, and this brief acknowledgment cannot capture their real contribution. They persevered through the tortured prose of the initial draft and made each successive version better than the last. Any errors that remain are mine.

A. W. Brian Simpson, of the University of Michigan Law School, showed himself a model scholar in yet one more way, somehow finding time in an impossible schedule to read every word, retrieve references, and provide a link to European thought. In addition to the many valuable comments he provided, his humor, erudition, and humanity infused membership in a community of scholars with new meaning and helped instill a sense of proportion and history. I cannot thank him enough.

Donald Herzog, also of the University of Michigan Law School, turned his deft logic to an early draft. His quest for greater engagement of some of the intellectual questions at the core of the manuscript was invaluable. His exhortations against the dizzying dispatch of conceptual issues, combined with his enthusiasm for local color, contributed greatly to the character of the book. The text would be very long indeed if I had responded successfully to all of his concerns!

The late William Burnett Harvey provided direction and historical pointers early in the development of the manuscript and turned his careful lawyerly eye to every page of a middle version. He disagreed with much and forced me to respond. Although I have replied only incompletely, the account is the better for his reflections. Bryant Garth, of the American Bar Foundation, tried to keep me from being too conventional and pointed out causal relationships a newcomer to the study of courts might not have seen. Rick Messick, of the World Bank, offered many leads to comparative material and brought his own lively interest in the subject matter at a time when my own energies were flagging. Jack Knight, at Washington University, and Robert Bates, at Harvard University, read the manuscript for W. W. Norton and contributed suggestions from a social science perspective. Their enthusiasm brought a sigh of relief, and their comments were thought provoking, as always.

W. W. Norton editor Roby Harrington gave the manuscript a chance. The book is about an issue of global importance in a context too often neglected. Roby could see possibilities when others could not, and he did not even balk too much at the length. I am most grateful. The care he, Rob Whiteside, Mary Babcock, and their fellow editors lavished on the manuscript was a wonderful contribution.

I am also very fortunate to have a family of avid readers. My parents, Joan and Ralph Widner, and my aunt, Barbara Kennedy, reviewed multiple drafts, rising above and beyond the call of duty. They argued with me about everything from the accessibility of the first chapter, to substantive concerns and verb tenses. For several years they tolerated holiday invasions of paper and Post-it notes, as well as the temporary loss of their kitchen table. They cheerfully acquiesced in my detours to the Library of Congress during family visits to Washington. And their common sense provided an important beacon. They were also almost always right.

My final debt is to the two organizations that helped provide time, free from the heavy teaching and service demands that normally make "real work" impossible during the academic year. The U.S. Institute of Peace and the John D. and Catherine T. MacArthur Foundation jointly sponsored a writing leave. I am deeply grateful and hope the results meet with their approval.

Jennifer A. Widner
University of Michigan
Ann Arbor

Note on Names and Terms

THIS BOOK speaks to people in many different parts of the world. African lawyers and judges usually are conversant with the terms used in the United States and England, but lay American readers see the names and terms that appear in the text less often. Therefore, a glossary appears after the concluding chapter. It contains specialized legal terms and selected foreign words. Most of the African names and terms in this book are phonetic. If there is an accent, it generally falls on the second syllable.

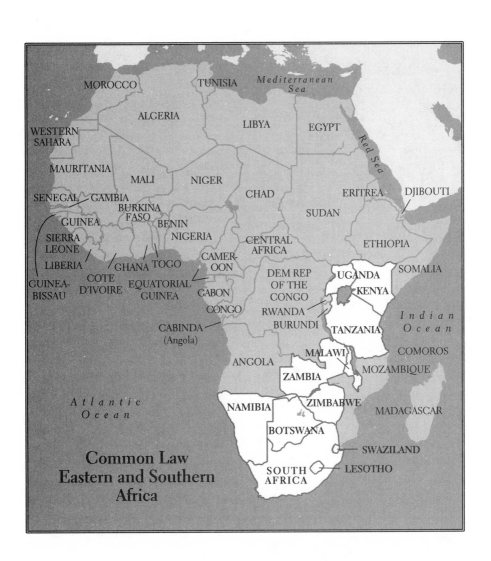

Common Law Eastern and Southern Africa

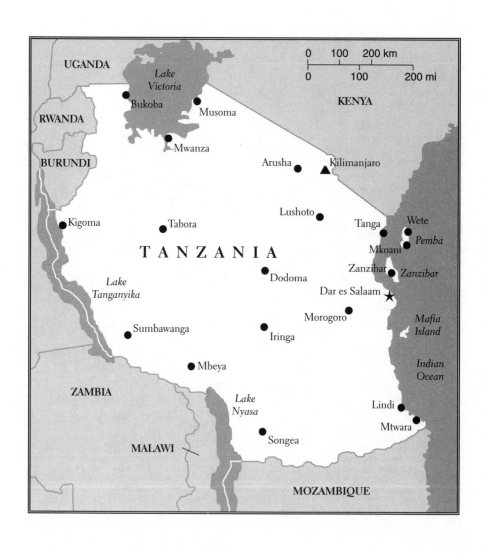

BUILDING THE RULE OF LAW

Introduction

IN THE EARLY months of 1999, a drama about the separation of powers played itself out in Zimbabwe, in southern Africa. On January 12, Zimbabwe military personnel arrested and tortured two journalists, Mark Chavunduka and Ray Choto, who had written about an alleged coup attempt. The action violated the constitution, which required that civilians be tried in the country's common law courts. A Zimbabwean lawyer applied for a writ of habeas corpus on behalf of the journalists. When the court granted the application and required that the journalists be brought before a magistrate, the permanent secretary in the Ministry of Defence, Job Whabira, initially refused to comply. Chief Justice Anthony Gubbay was overseas. Four Supreme Court justices wrote to the president and asked him to offer an explanation. The president replied by calling for the resignation of the judges and by suggesting that Western influence lay behind the objections. Zimbabwean citizens took to the streets to protest the military's actions.

The public outcry drew attention to two important values the executive branch threatened. One was the rule of law. Public officials should obey the rules prescribed in the constitution and the statutes. Civilians accused of crimes should have a fair hearing before an impartial court. The second value was judicial independence, or at least the kind of independence that arises from the separation of powers. To have the opportunity to have one's grievances heard before an impartial judge requires that courts be insulated from partisan political influence in particular cases. Political leaders should not be able to force judges from office just because they don't like the decisions rendered. The implied threat in Zimbabwe outraged members of the public because it raised the specter of a court subject to political whim.

The incident provided a metaphor for the changes that started to take place in Africa, Russia, and other parts of the world, at the close of the twentieth century. Thirty years earlier, many people in developing countries either considered courts to be the agents of political leaders or thought them frail, without the power of the sword or the power of the purse behind them. At the end of the century, infringements of judicial independence, as represented by the military action in Zimbabwe, generated street protests as well as foreign censure. The public relationship to the judiciary appeared to have changed and with it, the institutional position of courts and law. The protest in Zimbabwe was emblematic of trends throughout the region and in other countries.

This book tells a general story about how people construct a new institutional order. It is about the struggle to establish the separation of powers, the independence of the judiciary, and the rule of law in common law Africa, where conditions seemed especially difficult at the century's end. It is about why courts in some countries gained greater independence from presidents and legislatures, while in others partisan political influence affected the disposition of individual cases. It is about the way men and women who occupied similar positions in neighboring countries and in other places and times have addressed the same kinds of choices. And it is about a man whose career exemplified the struggle of many people to enhance the independence of the courts and broaden their popular acceptance, the Honorable Francis L. Nyalali. During his long tenure as chief justice of Tanzania, Nyalali was in frequent contact with his counterparts in Uganda, Kenya, Zimbabwe, Malawi, Botswana, Zambia, and other countries within the region and in other parts of the globe. His career provides an especially important window on an era and the challenges it posed.

A CRITICAL JUNCTURE

Judicial independence is the focal point of this story, although it takes its place alongside a broader concern for building the rule of law. The subject commands attention for a variety of reasons. One is that in many African countries, as in other parts of the world, ordinary people have started to make greater use of the legal system to resolve disputes. A 1995 study polled households in Tanzania and found that 6 to 8 percent of the people interviewed said their families had used the magistrates' courts in the previous year.[1] There were comparable find-

---

[1] United Republic of Tanzania, Presidential Commission of Inquiry against Corruption, "Service Delivery Survey: Corruption in the Police, Judiciary, Revenue and Lands Service," Survey financed by the World Bank and carried out by CIET International on behalf of the Commission, (Dar es Salaam, Tanzania: Presidential Commission of Inquiry against Corruption, July 1996) p. 11.

ings from research carried out in Uganda and Botswana at about the same time. These surveys asked whether a member of the household had been a party to a case in the magistrates' courts during the previous five years. In the least litigious areas, 14 percent of respondents answered yes. Where land competition was intense, the proportion rose to 45 percent.[2] There was also scattered evidence that use of the courts was increasing. For example, in Tanzania, the numbers of cases filed in the High Court climbed steadily from 1985 through the mid-1990s. During this period, people filed about one thousand more cases each year than they had the year before. To ordinary people worried about access to land, matrimonial disputes, violence at the hands of police or neighbors, the legality of drumming during festival periods, or even the identity of the rightful heir to a local throne, the impartiality of the courts mattered.

Judicial independence gained importance for other reasons as well. The 1990s represented a critical juncture. Changes in the scale of social and economic life, new political rules of the game, and the agendas of aid donors all converged to create a historical turning point, a propitious time to redefine the position of the judiciary.

Growing popular use of the courts corresponded with changes in the rules that governed political life, which put the spotlight on the judiciary. Beginning in 1989, a wave of political change swept much of the African continent. The fiscal crises of African states had bred popular dissatisfaction and helped push incumbents to create new opportunities for participation. Two-thirds of the countries in the region moved toward multiparty competition. Politicians began to turn to the courts to define and uphold fair campaign practices. Separation of powers and judicial independence acquired new significance.

Changes in policy ideas also helped build momentum for a renewed focus on justice systems. Structural adjustment policies designed to increase reliance on markets and reduce economic distortions often failed to generate growth or improve standards of living. Bemused by the limited impact of these policies, donor countries and the multilateral aid agencies turned their attention to the challenge of creating "an enabling environment" for entrepreneurs. Hernando de Soto's book, *The Other Path*, drew attention to bottlenecks businesses encountered as a result of complex systems of regulation and poorly drafted laws.[3] Delay, ineffectiveness, and partisanship in the courts also attracted concern as possible drags on commerce and investment. A new "law and development movement" was already under way in Latin America; in the 1990s, it began to take hold in the transition countries of eastern and central Europe, central Asia, and Africa. Judicial independence came more sharply into view.

Third, although its impact was still very limited, economic liberalization

[2] Jennifer Widner, Public Attitudes Surveys, 1995–96.
[3] Hernando de Soto, *The Other Path* (New York: Harper & Row, 1989).

slowly began to reduce the points at which the judiciary and the other branches of government were at odds with each other. The 1960s and 1970s belonged to a period of history in which governments in developing countries, as in Europe, took a more active role in economic affairs. Even where decision makers favored reliance on markets over centralized investment plans, price controls, and public ownership of enterprise, the shortage of domestic entrepreneurs with large amounts of capital meant that governments often played a large part in efforts to generate growth. However, the inevitable conflicts between employers and employees, investors and shareholders, and suppliers and contractors took on a political cast when the government was a party to all disputes. In this context managing litigation posed special challenges for the courts. The circumstances invited infringement of judicial independence. Whatever its other merits or demerits, privatization of public enterprises potentially reduced the numbers of such encounters, as well as their toll on the relationship between the branches. As one commentator wrote in connection with parallel situations in Eastern Europe, "The state cannot enforce the law consistently and even-handedly if it thinks of itself as a surrogate parent for its citizens, as bearing the ultimate responsibility for their welfare."[4] Liberalization relieved this pressure. It both lowered the stake executive branch officials had in controlling the courts and created a nascent private sector constituency for an independent judiciary.

Finally, "outsider crime" had become an increasingly difficult problem for many Africans during the 1980s. In the past, wrongs against society were usually wrongs against a small community by one of its members. Troublemakers were easily identifiable. People knew their families. They could hold kin responsible for compensating victims and preventing further disruption. Ostracism and exile were serious threats because individuals depended on families and social networks for support. By contrast, in the late twentieth century, improvements in transportation, the spread of small arms, and the growing presence of international drug syndicates made crime a more serious problem for ordinary Africans. The governments of southern African countries reported rising rates of homicide, assault, and theft during this period, and their residents expressed increasing worry about the safety of person and property.[5] Because criminals had started to come from outside the community, people looked for new solutions to replace the approaches they had used earlier, approaches that often depended on the ability to mobilize pressure from kin and friends. Vigilante groups were one. The police and the courts were another, provided big men could not buy verdicts for troublesome colleagues and kin.

---

[4] George P. Fletcher, "The Rule of Law," in *Basic Concepts of Legal Thought* (New York: Oxford University Press, 1996), p. 17.

[5] These data are reported in detail in Chapter 17.

TERMS OF REFERENCE

Both rule of law and judicial independence had attracted attention in the late 1950s and early 1960s, although then, as now, the terms were difficult to define. In the popular imagination, *rule of law* usually connoted the antithesis of disorder, vigilantism, corruption, abuse of power, and arbitrariness. Lawyers distilled three important elements from this mix. One concern was for predictability and publicity. No one should be punished or disadvantaged by the retrospective application of a new standard; rules should be uniform across activities of a similar type; laws should be public, not secret, so that people could reasonably know them. A second concern was for "due process," the opportunity for a fair hearing. To have one's story heard by an impartial adjudicator was an entitlement that lay at the foundation of most justice systems, including those in Africa. Third, the concept of the rule of law also contained an appeal to a sense of fairness not satisfied by a "law of rules" based solely on adherence to statutes and careful attention to procedure. Content or substance mattered too.[6] As the example of apartheid in South Africa brought home forcefully, predictability and due process did not promote a sense of justice in the presence of abhorrent statutes.

The concept of the rule of law figured importantly on the agendas of international conferences involving African judges and lawyers as new countries appeared on the world map. The International Commission of Jurists, a distinguished Geneva-based nongovernmental organization, sponsored meetings in New Delhi, Lagos, and other capitals. The commission's statement from its New Delhi conference in 1959 noted, "The rule of law to most lawyers means . . . rather more than certainty of the laws and of their enforcement. It is conceived rather as a body of principles, institutions, and procedures which can be separated from the more controversial political and social issues and which are found and self-evident in any legal system worthy of the name."[7]

Like *rule of law*, the term *judicial independence* attracted attention, and it too had several meanings. To cultivate impartiality, judges were expected to avoid handling disputes in which they had ties with any of the parties. They

---

[6] For a helpful discussion of different definitions of *rule of law*, see William Burnett Harvey, "The Rule of Law in Historical Perspective," *Michigan Law Review*, 59 (1961), pp. 487–500; William Burnett Harvey, "The Challenge of the Rule of Law," *Michigan Law Review*, 59 (1961), pp. 603–613; Ruti Teitel, "Paradoxes in the Revolution of the Rule of Law," *Yale Journal of International Law*, 19 (1994), pp. 239–247; Fletcher, "The Rule of Law," pp. 11–27; and Jeremy Waldron, "The Rule of Law," in *The Law* (London: Routledge, 1990), pp. 29–55.

[7] International Congress of Jurists, *The Rule of Law in a Free Society*, A Report of the International Congress of Jurists, New Delhi, India, January 5–10, 1959 (Geneva: International Commission of Jurists, 1959), pp. 54–55.

should rescue themselves when necessary to prevent conflicts of interest. Second, pressure from fellow judges could breach impartiality unless channeled through certain accepted means. In common law countries, doctrines favoring respect for precedent were one such source of pressure, and the risk of reversal on appeal, another. But it was a third sense of the term judicial independence that attracted the greatest attention, mid-century as well as in the 1990s. A pillar of impartiality was insulation of the courts from political pressure to decide particular cases in certain ways. This kind of concern was associated in many jurisdictions with the separation of powers. For example, judges should not be subject to dismissal, the loss of salary or pension, or harassment from the executive or the legislature in retaliation for decisions they make. One American scholar usefully labeled these different meanings of judicial independence "party detachment," "individual autonomy," and "political insulation."[8]

From the mid-1960s through the early 1980s, both rule of law and judicial independence fell out of favor in some parts of the world. In many countries, the 1960s bred an effort to conceive of a separate "socialist legality." Although in theory this way of thinking provided for an independent judiciary to resolve disputes, in practice the courts were often effectively subordinate to other branches of government. In some places officials called for judges to become accountable by adopting the ideology of the party in power. Said one judge, "Socialism was sung as a song. And we had to sing it."[9] The new ideas provided a cover for administrators who felt frustrated that fellow citizens did not always want to do what fledgling governments wished them to do. It offered a way to hold off potentially embarrassing inquiry into problems that often had started as simple mistakes by people who lacked the resources or the training to do their jobs as well as they hoped.

The end of the twentieth century brought renewed concern for judicial independence as an important source of the rule of law. Across the globe, judges and lawyers met to try to hammer out new guidelines. The International Commission of Jurists published the Siracusa principles of judicial independence,[10] a long list of standards that addressed the very many ways people might exert or feel pressure to decide a case in a particular way. They began

[8] Owen Fiss, "The Right Degree of Independence," in Irwin Stotzky, ed., *The Transition to Democracy in Latin America: The Role of the Judiciary* (Boulder, CO: Westview, 1993), p. 55. For other thoughtful treatments of judicial independence from an American perspective, see the special issue on judicial independence, *Southern California Law Review*, 72, 2 (1999); Owen M. Fiss, "The Limits of Judicial Independence," *University of Miami Inter-American Law Review*, 25 (1993), pp. 57–67; Martin H. Redish and Lawrence C. Marshall, "Adjudicatory Independence and the Values of Procedural Due Process," *Yale Law Journal*, 95 (1986), pp. 455–476; and Philip B. Kurland, "The Constitution and the Tenure of Federal Judges: Some Notes from History," *University of Chicago Law Review*, 36 (1969), pp. 665–698.

[9] Justice Robert Kisanga, interview with author, Dar es Salaam, Tanzania, May 31, 1996.

[10] International Commission of Jurists, "Draft Principles on the Independence of the Judiciary (Siracusa Principles)," *CIJL Bulletin*, 25/26 (April–October 1980), pp. 59–71.

with terms of appointment and dismissal. But they did not stop there. They went on to identify other direct forms of influence, such as bribery and harassment, as well as intervention in the judicial process, such as control over the assignment of cases to individual judges. They focused on whether the executive branch plays a formal role in administrative matters that affect judges' own fortunes—for example, in the determination of salaries, hiring, promotions, and transfers. They drew attention to the removal of cases from the jurisdiction of the courts and their placement in parallel tribunals that do not safeguard due process, as well as failure to enforce judgments. Scholars and policy makers began to monitor performance with respect to these standards and to refine the lists still further.[11]

Concerned about the rule of law, lawyers in Africa, as in other parts of the world, increasingly spoke of judicial independence in a larger sense too. Legal scholar A. W. Brian Simpson captured this sentiment when he wrote that "formal independence—freedom from the sack, freedom from suit, and freedom from the grosser forms of pressure such as massive reduction of salary—is something essentially negative." There is more to the concept, he suggested. "Judicial independence also involves the idea that the judiciary will operate as a check or restraint upon the executive, and make their contribution to the business of government by championing the virtues associated with the rule of law, of openly administered justice, of rational decisions in conformity with professional tradition. . . ."[12] He tried to advance a positive notion of independence. In the ranks of practicing professionals, the oft-heard belief that judges should avoid being "executive minded" captured a similar idea.

Some might still object that the concepts of rule of law and judicial independence were inspired by Western values and of little significance for those who had inherited other civilizations and traditions. But the street protests in Zimbabwe and similar demonstrations in other parts of the region suggested otherwise. Capturing the new sentiment in Africa in the mid-1990s, Tanzania's chief justice, Francis Nyalali, observed that ". . . independence of the judiciary, impartiality of adjudication, fairness of trial, and integrity of the adjudicator are so universally accepted that one may reasonably conclude that these principles are inherent to any justice system in a democracy." He continued, "[T]here is no doubt that these same principles are part of the African dream, resulting from the liberation struggle against colonial and racial oppression. They need not . . . be expressly stated in our constitutions or statutes. They are inherent to

[11] For a notable example, see Anthony N. Allott, "The Independence of the Judiciary in Commonwealth Countries: Problems and Provisions," pp. 71–99, in *Report of the Tenth Commonwealth Magistrates' and Judges' Conference*, Victoria Falls, Zimbabwe, August 22–26, 1994 (London: Commonwealth Magistrates' and Judges' Association, 1994).
[12] A. W. Brian Simpson, "The Judges and the Vigilant State," *Denning Law Journal*, 1989 (1989), p. 147.

the statehood which came into being when our respective countries became politically independent."[13]

INAUSPICIOUS CIRCUMSTANCES

Even though judicial independence came to occupy a more prominent place in the concerns of many Africans during the 1990s, there could be little doubt about the difficulty of the institution-building task ahead. Broad trends, such as economic liberalization or the legalization of opposition political parties, might help create demand for courts that were independent of partisan influence in particular cases. But the "supply side" mattered too. Could existing institutions and their leaders respond? Did reformers have the vision and the political skills to make a difference? The innovators faced some tough challenges.

One of the most striking difficulties arose from the lack of resources most courts faced. In common law jurisdictions, the law includes not only the statutes but also precedent, the rulings of the highest court. Judges are supposed to know how their colleagues on the bench have interpreted the law or filled in gaps and ambiguities. In countries where courts lacked money to publish important decisions, the law was hard for magistrates, judges, and litigants to know. In some instances, the statutes themselves were unavailable too. Because judges and magistrates in different courts applied different rules, equality before the law suffered. Further, the variation made it difficult to monitor the exercise of political pressure. Were differences in the ways judges decided similar cases linked to the lack of a "legal literature" and consequent inability to know the law, to differences in the facts, or to influence by local politicians and administrators? Usually it was hard to say. Finally, these problems impeded the development of the law in a manner congruent with local norms.

Scarcity of resources affected efforts to build judicial independence in other ways too. Police often lacked transportation to crime scenes and conducted investigations late, after the evidence had disappeared or grown stale, if they inquired at all. Inadequate investigation often led magistrates and judges to dismiss cases. These actions sometimes provoked strong words from the authorities and community members. The temptation to retaliate, to pressure a magistrate, or to try someone outside the courts would then grow. For these reasons, infringements of judicial independence at the local level, especially in poorer, more remote areas, often presented a more serious challenge than con-

[13] Francis L. Nyalali, "Speech on Corruption Delivered at the Opening of a Seminar Organized by the Danish Association for International Cooperation at Mwengo," Usa-River, Arusha, Tanzania, November 14, 1995.

troversial cases involving politicians, at the higher levels of the court. Usually the latter were fewer and farther between, and frequently governments grudgingly went along with highly visible verdicts they did not like.

Magistrates and judges in rural areas also agonized over a related problem. Often state attorneys were less well trained and less prepared than the lawyers who represented defendants in criminal trials or private parties in civil cases. The common law judge was not supposed to help litigants argue their cases or to adopt the kind of investigative role played by the *juge d'instruction* in countries with civil law systems. Yet magistrates and judges alike spoke often of the difficulty in which they found themselves when the community's interest was poorly represented by public prosecutors. They experimented with more active roles, walking and sometimes crossing the thin line between getting stories and evidence out on the table, on the one hand, and acting as prosecutors or serving political interests, on the other.

Another set of challenges resided in the deep legal pluralism that characterized most African countries. Customary and religious laws, state law, and international law coexisted alongside one another. In rural areas, people usually took disputes to customary forums first, before they went to court, if they went to court at all. They lived most aspects of their everyday lives according to the procedures and rules developed within their cultural communities. State law recognized this pluralism, and most African constitutions made family life, personal status, succession, and inheritance the domain of the customary. These arrangements were practical. They helped maintain a measure of continuity between sensitive aspects of law and local norms. Nonetheless, deep legal pluralism potentially posed difficulties. Clashes between the rules embodied in different types of law could lead to confusion and dissatisfaction with the courts.

"For people to appreciate what we judges do," Nyalali observed, "they must think the common law speaks to their situations and their needs, too. In a diverse society like Tanzania, with many legal traditions, we need to integrate the principles of customary law with our statutes, the common law, and the ideals behind our new constitution. If we don't, people will not use the courts and will not defend them. They will think we judges live in a different world from the one they inhabit."[14] A public constituency for the courts would only emerge when ordinary people appropriated the law as their own. Although the integration of a country's legal systems could not take place overnight, most considered it important that the courts gradually reconcile the customary laws with each other, with common law principles, and with the terms of new constitutions and international covenants. For this reason, some judges felt that the real action at the end of the century lay with family law, and especially with matters that affected the equality of women.

[14] Francis L. Nyalali, interview with author, March 17, 1996.

Finally, these were intemperate times. Land pressure, greater exposure to economic fluctuations, crime, and even political party competition correlated with the increased popularity of witchcraft and vigilantism, which clashed with the fundamental ideas on which the judicial system rested. Due process, integral to the rule of law, usually played little part in these practices. Curtailing vigilantism and witchcraft was a difficult matter, however. Vigilantism often sprang up because the reach of the police and the courts was too limited to provide security of person or property. In witch murders, the defendants often truly believed that the victims would cause supernatural harm. When courts convicted vigilantes or witch murderers, they risked the ire of citizens who lacked other means to protect themselves or who did not fully share the principles at the core of the common law.

STRATEGIES

Building independent courts was a step toward strengthening the rule of law. Under the circumstances that prevailed in most parts of Africa, as well as in the transition countries of eastern Europe and central Asia, it was a difficult step indeed. But the magnitude of the task did not deter people from trying. By the mid-1990s, there were early signs of success in many places, although variations across countries remained and there was still much to do. The judiciary in Botswana long had a reputation for independence, and with an occasional exception, it maintained its strength during the 1990s. In Tanzania, lawyers observed that the judiciary had grown more independent between the mid-1980s and the mid-1990s. Canvassed in 1995–96, three-fourths of the members of the Law Society, the bar association, said they thought that the court enjoyed greater independence than it had a decade before.[15] In Uganda, earlier governments had made chief justices victims of violence, but by the late 1990s, the Ugandan court also enjoyed an enhanced reputation. In surveys, 79 percent of lawyers said the court was more independent than it had been a decade before. Although there were no numbers to provide systematic evidence, lawyers believed that roughly the same was true in Malawi. By contrast, during the same period the reputation of Kenya's judiciary, once strong, appeared to suffer. Some controversial and highly visible decisions led people to question whether the judiciary there was immune from partisan influence in particular cases. And in Zimbabwe, a court long known for its independence as well as for its eloquent decisions, found itself embattled.

Of course, getting a reasonably accurate measure of independence was difficult. Independence was both directly unobservable and multidimensional.

[15] Jennifer Widner, Law Society Surveys, 1995–96.

One approach was to take the Siracusa principles, the list of criteria the International Commission of Jurists drew up in 1980; collect information on each of the indicators in the list; and compute an index or score for each country on an annual basis. Unfortunately, for many countries the information necessary to assess performance in this way was simply unavailable. English legal scholar Anthony Allott, a longtime friend of Africa, initiated such an effort in the 1990s, but he confessed it would be slow going.[16] It was important to have accurate information not only about appointment procedures and rules for dismissal but also about harassment, bribery, rotation and transfer, and many other matters far less easy to monitor.

Usually casual observers employed a second strategy for determining how independent a court is. They tried to count the proportion of cases the government lost. In the periods in which the government prevailed more often, the courts were considered less independent. Although this way of thinking had a certain intuitive appeal, it also had serious flaws. Judges may rule in favor of the government for any number of reasons, and looking only at outcomes of cases provided no means for determining which decisions were really the result of partisan influence and which were the product of poor preparation by counsel or of the underlying facts of the cases. Nonetheless, there was surely something interesting in the increasing numbers of human rights rulings against governments in Africa during the late 1980s and 1990s.

A third approach was to allow those who had most contact with the judicial system, the lawyers who argued cases in the courts, to offer their own evaluations of trends in their countries. Surveys of members of the bar could be used to help estimate the direction of change within a country and the frequency of certain kinds of practices. Like its alternatives, this approach was also imperfect: The lawyers interviewed could employ different metrics and reference points in their responses, making comparisons across countries difficult. But these surveys of "expert attitudes" were usually more feasible than the alternatives, under the circumstances.

What had happened to produce the pattern of institutional performance casually observed across countries, as well as the trends within countries that the surveys discerned? Academic authors often observed that courts had neither the power of the purse nor the ability to take up arms. Therefore, they concluded that judges must play little role in building independence. Pondering other times and places, they suggested that sometimes the other branches of government might find it in their interest to delegate authority to independent courts. For example, in countries with competitive party systems, politicians would certainly have a material reason to want courts that were not subject to

[16] Allott, "The Independence of the Judiciary in Commonwealth Countries: Problems and Provisions," pp. 71–99.

partisan influence! Independent courts could deter incumbent politicians from abrogating the rights of critics to speak, to move about, and to associate by offering redress in instances of abuse. They might also play an important role in adjudicating election petitions, and they could help increase the fairness of campaigning and voting.

Theoretically, then, legislators in a competitive multiparty system had a stake in an independent judiciary. And so might executive branch officials. Corruption within the public sector bureaucracy was a serious drag on economic growth and on fairness around the globe. But closely monitoring the behavior of civil servants was very expensive. An alternative to close supervision was to let citizens take complaints to independent courts and get the courts to enforce the rules.[17]

These viewpoints did not fully capture the African experience. Although the region entered a period of political change in the late 1980s, when efforts to build independent courts began, competitive multiparty systems still lay in the future, and the incentives competition might have provided to politicians simply weren't there. Moreover, in countries like Tanzania, Zimbabwe, Uganda, and South Africa, the judges themselves were visible actors on the stage, just as John Marshall was in the founding years of the American republic. Tanzania's chief justice, Francis Nyalali, felt the kinship with his American forerunner keenly. Standing next to the statue of John Marshall in the U.S. Supreme Court, Nyalali once volunteered, "This is the man I most admire." He observed that he confronted some of the same kinds of challenges Marshall had faced. Both men accorded importance to the role of the bench in forging judicial independence than did the university professors.

So what was really going on in Africa at the end of the century? The academic theorists weren't entirely wrong. Increases in independence usually started with a temporary "deal" between the executive and the judiciary. There was an initial delegation of authority from the executive branch, or sometimes from the legislature. The reasons were idiosyncratic. The need to root out corruption in the ruling party, never a pleasant task for the man in charge, led some heads of state to think an independent court a good idea, at least temporarily. Alternatively, new leaders sometimes came to office on a campaign to restore justice and the rule of law—and found that they had to deliver on the promise by respecting the jurisdiction of the court. Concern for historical image also

[17] Three examples of judicial independence as a product of delegation are William M. Landes and Richard A. Posner, "The Independent Judiciary in an Interest Group Perspective," *Journal of Law and Economics*, 18, 3 (December 1975), pp. 875–901; Salzberger, "A Positive Analysis of the Doctrine of the Separation of Powers, or: Why Do We Have an Independent Judiciary?" *International Review of Law and Economics*, 13 (1993), pp. 349–379; and James Rosberg, "The Rise of an Independent Judiciary in Egypt," Ph.D. dissertation, Department of Political Science, Massachusetts Institute of Technology, Cambridge, 1995.

could serve as a motivator, as could fear of what an opposition party might do if it won power and the court could not serve as a check and a balance. The logic of delegation partly accounted for the trends people observed.

But one of the truisms of life that crosses cultural boundaries is, "You can't trust a politician." If the "deals" or pacts to respect judicial independence depended on the continuing good will of those in political power, they would be ephemeral indeed. The commitments were unreliable and the arrangements, unstable. So judges tried to lock in the new independence in several ways. In this very general, nonpartisan sense, they were political actors.

For example, courts tried to reduce the number of points at which pressure could be brought to bear or improve the flow of information to enhance monitoring. Judicial reformers introduced case-flow management committees, individual calendar systems, streamlined rules of procedure, and access to alternative dispute resolution. These changes slowly made courts more user-friendly. They also helped chief justices enhance the flow of information and the salience of reputation within the court itself, enabling them to monitor more effectively the points at which the independence of the judiciary broke down.

Chief justices also began to explore ways to reduce the susceptibility of judges and clerks to pressure from politicians and executive branch officials. One was to enhance the importance of professional reputation. Judges and magistrates needed to care about their reputations for fairness and impartiality. They had to care about the management of the courts they helped to run. Chief justices began to publicize criteria for promotions, where before the routes to advancement in the judiciary were virtually unknown. They sought to resurrect the judicial conferences that had once brought magistrates and judges into more frequent contact with one another and had encouraged people to tend their professional reputations. They supported the publication of decisions in law reports, not just to make this element of the law available to people, but also because the prospect of seeing one's arguments in print was a spur to clear reasoning.

Having important and vocal constituencies was critical for sustained independence. The courts needed friends who could keep political leaders from reneging on their grants of independence to the judiciary. But in most African countries, as in developing countries in other regions, "natural constituents" were few and far between. Foreign investors could settle their disputes in California or other jurisdictions, by writing such provisions into their contracts with public agencies or subcontractors. Local investors were usually too vulnerable to pressure and too few in number to make much difference. In the short run, then, many courts reached out to the international community, if not as a temporary guarantor, then as a helpful source of scrutiny.

Domestic constituencies took more time to build. Some judges saw hope in the legalization of opposition political parties. Like the academic authors, they reasoned that wary of each other, political parties would rapidly find it convenient to support an independent court that could handle election disputes impartially and prevent winners from completely overturning the legislative agendas of losers every four or five years. The judiciary would gain greater protection under multiparty systems than under single-party states, the judges hinted. In several countries, members of the bench played important roles in facilitating the transition to multiparty rule, in an extrajudicial capacity.

The larger project was to help ordinary citizens see the courts as useful, important, and an institution worth protecting. Tanzania's Chief Justice Nyalali observed, "[T]he ultimate safeguard is really public opinion." Judges cannot force the military back into the barracks. Nor can they run for seats in parliament. "The people have to value an independent judiciary and be willing to defend it."[18] Throughout the region, judges echoed this view that the best safeguard of judicial independence was public appreciation. If people used the courts and cared about them, they might take to the streets to defend them, as they did in Zimbabwe. Although some observers might have deemed the Zimbabwe incident as a sign of decline, others watched the public response and thought it augured a new age of civic engagement in Africa. The Zimbabwe situation showed that the glass was half full, not half empty, they argued.

In pursuit of this larger ambition, friends of the court and even the judges themselves began to try to build a new legal culture. Some chief justices encouraged fellow judges and lawyers to write columns on legal issues for the newspapers. They supported legal literacy programs. They sometimes took to the airwaves themselves, via radio. And occasionally they pursued more unusual and exotic gambits.

The effectiveness of the judicial system mattered for constituency building, just as it did for internal control and cohesion. Nyalali commented that "to win public affection, we, the judges, must do our jobs well. The courts must work. People must feel they can resolve disputes satisfactorily and in a reasonable amount of time. If they do, then the people will support us. It is really the quality of justice that determines whether we remain independent."[19] Citizens had long expressed dissatisfaction with delay, confusion, and corruption in the judiciary. To build alliances, chief justices had to rescue the courts from public disapproval.

In all of these endeavors, the substantive law—the content of statutes and decisions—mattered. Enforcement of legislation widely considered unjust could jeopardize popular approval and acceptance of the courts as an institution. Some judges try to construe statutes in ways that blunted the provisions that clashed most severely with widely shared standards of fairness. Others felt

---

[18] Francis L. Nyalali, interview with author, notes included in Jennifer A. Widner, "The Quality of Justice: Report on the U.S.-Africa Judicial Exchange," prepared for the U.S. Information Agency (Washington, D.C.: Superior Court of the District of Columbia in conjunction with the American Bar Association and the National Judicial College, July 1995), mimeograph.

[19] Ibid.

unempowered to play such roles. Clarity of drafting also influenced levels of judicial independence. Both elected legislators and executive branch officials could take offense if judges implied that legislation was ambiguous and sought to clarify the meaning of the language, or if the courts used powers of judicial review to strike down bills inconsistent with constitutional provisions. Bad drafting sometimes placed the judiciary on a collision course with the other branches of government. Inherited precedents sometimes constrained courts in ways that undermined the appearance of impartiality or that conveyed an impression of institutional weakness. The story of reform is intimately bound up with the substance—the content—of the rules themselves.

It was tempting to suggest that there was a formula. Institution-building strategies focused attention on a short-term pact or deal with the other branches of government. Judges tried to make this pact endure by increasing internal control and accountability, and by building constituencies.

But real life always injected variation. Bargaining or statecraft played a central role. The results the various tactics produced were contingent on the behavior of many people, and that made it difficult to lay out a precise sequence judicial institution building should follow. Moreover, the tactics judges pursued modified their environment, rendering the tasks and challenges slightly different for latecomers than for the first experimenters. The appearance of a "wave" of reform throughout the region was partly a function of the changing opportunity structure the labors of the pioneers created. Thus, there was no single "right way" to do things. Chief justices could achieve enduring higher levels of independence by combining tactics in various ways, as local conditions permitted.

Another dimension of reform impeded the search for a magic formula. In the long run, history probably will show that in the early days, the personal examples the judges set were important. In South Africa, Zimbabwe, Tanzania, and other countries, judges often became role models from whom both officials and ordinary people took their cues. Speaking at the bicentennial celebration of the birth of Chief Justice John Marshall, Henry Hart captured this challenge perfectly. In words Nyalali would appreciate, he observed, "It is a delusion to suppose . . . that if only you can prevent the abuse of governmental power everything else will be all right. The political problem is a problem also of eliciting from government officials, and from the members of society generally, the affirmative, creative performances upon which the well-being of the society depends."[20] In building institutions, the character of leaders mattered. The models judges provided for their countries helped set the tone of change and provided a way to make the values implicit in the rule of law part of everyday life. In this respect, some succeeded more than others did.

[20] Hart as quoted in Harvey, "The Challenge of the Rule of Law," pp. 611–612.

A MAN AND HIS TIMES

This study of a man and his times illuminates the process of institutional change. It chronicles the experiences of courts in building separation of powers in common law eastern and southern Africa, using the story of the Honorable Francis Nyalali and the Tanzanian judiciary as a point of departure. Nyalali was first appointed to his country's highest judicial office in 1976. By the time he stepped down in February 2000, he had become the longest-serving chief justice of his day. His experiences provide a window for understanding the interaction between judges, politicians, and publics throughout the African region and the consequences for judicial independence and the rule of law.

The court over which Nyalali presided sits in Dar es Salaam and serves the country of Tanzania, on Africa's Indian Ocean coast. At the end of the twentieth century, Tanzania was part of a narrow zone of relative peace on the African continent. That zone encompassed parts of Uganda and Kenya to the north, as well as Zambia, Malawi, Zimbabwe, Botswana, South Africa, and Namibia to the south. It was flanked by a zone of severe conflict: repeated genocide in neighboring Rwanda and Burundi; persistent civil war in the Sudan and Angola; war in Mozambique until 1992; and disintegration in Somalia and the Democratic Republic of the Congo, the former Zaire. Tanzania, Malawi, and Zambia, as other countries in the region, hosted thousands of refugees, who were ever-present reminders of why rule of law was important.

At first glance, the basic indicators did not seem to augur well for Tanzania. Its gross domestic product, a measure of national wealth, was among the lowest in the world, and it harbored great ethnic and religious diversity. If poverty and diversity are sources of violence, then Tanzania should have been a difficult case indeed. Yet, paradoxically, it enjoyed greater stability than many of its neighbors. The countries least favored were those where two, three, or four cultural blocs dominated and where economic inequality was extreme, while Tanzania's extraordinary diversity and its comparatively low levels of inequality seemed to push people to enter into relatively peaceful coexistence. Since its independence, the country had witnessed no coups or widespread civil unrest, save a military mutiny quashed in 1964.

The country's past was fairly typical of the history of its African neighbors. Many different groups migrated into the area, beginning in about 1000 A.D. and continuing well into the late 1800s. There were early trading ties among these communities as well as with foreigners who settled on the coast. The Omanis long managed a Persian Gulf slave trade, older but smaller than its Atlantic counterpart. Their networks reached far into the interior. They built spice plantations on the islands, including Zanzibar, and developed a business in gold, ivory, and other commodities.

Germany claimed the mainland, Tanganyika, as a colony during the Great Powers' scramble for Africa, in the late 1800s. It lost control in World War I, when the League of Nations named the territory an international mandate, held in trust by Britain. For all intents and purposes, Tanganyika became a British colony. Similarly, Zanzibar, once controlled by the Omanis, then a British protectorate, moved gradually under British colonial office control. Tanganyika gained independence through a negotiated settlement in 1961, and Zanzibar followed in 1963. In 1964, the two territories formed a union, the contemporary United Republic of Tanzania.

The colonial histories of the other countries that feature in the story shared many of the same characteristics. Both Kenya and Uganda were British colonies. So were Malawi, Zambia, and Zimbabwe. Botswana, too, fell under the British umbrella, although the extent of the colonial presence was not nearly as great in its dry, desert expanses as in the countries that attracted settlers. In all of these countries, as in most of Africa, independence came through negotiation. Although punctuated by isolated incidents of violence, nationalist resistance to colonial rule had proceeded along relatively peaceful lines in most places. By the late 1950s, independence was an idea whose time had come. Nationalist leaders and colonial administrators sat across from one another at long tables to hammer out terms. Written constitutions, sometimes with bills of rights and sometimes without, were usually part and parcel of the arrangements worked out, although they usually were cut from the same mold. The transfer of power took place without significant disruption, except in Zimbabwe, where white settlers issued a unilateral declaration of independence and plunged the country into civil war, and in South Africa, where majority rule did not arrive until 1994.[21]

The common law tradition prevailed in this region at the time of independence. In its general outline, the courts and the law reflected the English heritage. Precedent, or the past rulings of the highest courts, had the status of law. The role of the judge was much the same as it was in places like India, Ireland, England, the United States, Canada, and Australia. Resource scarcity, legal pluralism, and other conditions made the African situation distinctive, however, and the challenges they created are one of the main subplots of this book.

THE ORGANIZATION OF THE BOOK

The succeeding chapters fall into three main parts. The opening chapters provide a context. They begin in the early years of Chief Justice Nyalali's career

---

[21] For the purposes of this study, the eastern and southern African region includes Uganda, Kenya, Tanzania, Malawi, Zimbabwe, Zambia, Botswana, Namibia, South Africa, Lesotho, and Swaziland. Mozambique, a former Portuguese colony, is a civil law jurisdiction. Madagascar, off the coast, is also a civil law country, based on the French model.

and sketch the background and training of judges at the time of independence, the organization of the courts, the origins of the law, and the cracks in the rule of law that appeared in the 1970s. They set the stage. The middle chapters explore the steps Nyalali and other chief justices from neighboring countries took to try to build separation of powers and heighten judicial independence. They profile the critical junctures that occurred in the mid-1980s and the opportunities they created for institution building. They focus on organizational reforms designed to increase internal control and accountability and build constituencies. The last chapters profile some of the more difficult challenges courts in Africa face—for example, deciding how to define the powers of community security organizations in the absence of a viable police force and how to address problems like witchcraft. The conclusion sketches the "rules of thumb" that emerged from the experience of judges in the region.

The subject matter of these chapters is global. Judges in Africa sought to blend practices and principles in local law with institutions and ideas drawn from other regions. They occupied a world stage, befitting the magnitude of the challenges they faced. The lessons they have to offer have significance beyond the communities they serve.

CHAPTER TWO

Origins

AN IMPORTANT ELEMENT of the rule of law is the ability to have one's grievances heard before an impartial judge. There may be few universals in life, but dispute resolution that is even-handed and detached, yet still accountable, is a virtue that appears to be widely prized. Across cultures, communities respect people who have the requisite habits of mind, even if the forms of dispute resolution vary. And in a world where states exercise considerable influence on everyday life, the impartiality so cherished is partly a function of insulation from partisan political pressure in particular cases.

But the independence of mind that favors impartiality also has a more positive aspect. It is not just freedom from coercion or temptation. It is also a recognition of the importance of giving the actions of the other branches of government a sober second thought, of restraining practices that violate the dignity of community members, and of "championing the virtues associated with the rule of law, of openly administered justice, of rational decisions in conformity with professional tradition. . . ."[1]

Although institutional design is of central importance for independence, the attitudes imparted through upbringing, training, and early experience are also vital. For instance, in some parts of the world, family connections between judges, lawyers, and politicians long favored "executive-mindedness." The same dynasties dominated all three spheres. Information, preferences, general outlooks, and favors passed between members and limited the insulation from political pressure. In Africa, family ties proved less of a bond between the judiciary

---

[1] A. W. Brian Simpson, "The Judges and the Vigilant State," *Denning Law Journal,* 1989 (1989), p. 147.

and the other branches. But the conventional wisdom among lawyers was that the training many of Africa's first judges received and the intimidation they faced in their early careers conspired to bring about a similar frame of mind. If the courts provided little protection to individuals and communities in the years after independence, they argued, it was a product of a British tradition of restraint, imparted through early judicial training, and of practical inexperience.

The life of Francis Lucas Nyalali, later Tanzania's third chief justice, together with the experiences of his peers, provides a window on judges' origins and their significance for judicial independence in an African context.

MUSOMA

In 1965, young Francis Nyalali was called to the bar at Lincoln's Inn, in London. England's Inns of Court, legal fraternities, provided training for many young Africans and Asians who aspired to build new national legal institutions in countries that had just become independent. An urgent demand for new lawyers in these territories moved the British government to fund graduate training as part of its foreign technical assistance programs. The Inns provided a venue.

Years later, Nyalali remembered the eagerness with which he looked forward to the moment of his graduation and return home. His degree was a step toward participation in building his country, then called Tanganyika. Independence had arrived four years earlier, and all hands were needed. For a young man, the cause was noble and exciting. Nonetheless, Nyalali felt his first obligation was to explain to his parents just how he intended to transform his new degree, the product of their hard labor as well as his own, into something that would support a family.

Nyalali tried hard to articulate his aspirations to his mother, Salome Madiya, an especially important figure in his life. He drew an analogy. "Do you remember Judge Carter?" he asked. Sir William Morris Carter had served as chief justice of Tanzania from 1920 to 1924 and had spent many years as president of the Court of Appeal of East Africa. He adjudicated cases along the central rail line, moving across the country by train. He handled mainly capital cases and frequently sentenced people to death. Local residents quickly invented a play on words in two languages, changing "Carter" to "Kata." In Kiswahili, the verb *kata* means to cut up, divide, reduce, decide, or bring to an end, an apt characterization of Judge Carter's job description. Nyalali recalled that the image elicited a quizzical look from his mother. Yes, she understood what the role entailed, but exactly how was this ambition consistent with his nationalist ideas?[2]

In 1966, upon his return, Nyalali won appointment as a resident magistrate,

[2] Francis L. Nyalali, interview with author, March 21, 1996.

a position that required him to hear both criminal and civil cases as well as supervise three tiers of junior magistrates, few of whom had any formal legal training. Almost immediately the opportunity to ponder the fit between politics and professional obligations asserted itself. The court handed out location assignments to its new officers. Everyone eagerly awaited news of postings. Would it be a job in a remote area or somewhere near the capital? A court where one spoke the language of the community or not? A place with a bad reputation or a good one? When Nyalali's turn came, his spirits sank . . . Musoma. Among the young recruits, there was a handful of positions no one relished. They were known to be difficult. The court had to be especially careful in selecting people to send to these spots. Musoma was one.

In the northwestern part of the country, on the shores of Lake Victoria, Musoma had three big counts against it as a post in which a new magistrate might succeed. First, the leader of the country's nationalist movement, the "founding father," Julius Nyerere, came from there. Now president, Nyerere would probably watch what took place in his home area with great attention. Worse, people would feel they had a special privilege, and every time someone lost a judgment, he or she would likely appeal to the political authorities in Dar es Salaam. Then there was the community's reputation. The Kuria and the Zanaki, the president's people, were renowned throughout the country as warriors. Well before the colonial era, they had shown themselves prone to fight, if not among themselves, then against others. And, of course, given these talents, in years past the government had recruited heavily in the area to fill the ranks of the police and the army.

Nyalali's first thought was to resign. All in all, one could not imagine a worse spot to serve as a beginning magistrate. In this environment, political and social pressure likely would prove intense. Nonetheless, pride pushed Nyalali to swallow his reservations. He went where he was told to go, but with the caveat that he would go into private practice after six months if he was refused a transfer.

The initial fears were never realized. When his private deadline expired six months later, Nyalali decided he really did not want to leave. He enjoyed the open, frank style of the people who lived in the area. "They would tell you directly what they thought about you!," he recalled. "I was then, and remain, uncomfortable with those who say nice things but disagree off stage. With these people I thought I was safe, they were so up front!"

Aware that local dissatisfaction with the judiciary stemmed from the frequent dismissal of cases, one of Nyalali's first steps was to try to figure out why magistrates had thrown out disputes and attracted local ire. He found that people only accustomed to village life were very uncomfortable in town and especially in court. These settings were wholly unfamiliar and quite daunting. Witnesses often failed to appear, in order to avoid the ordeal.

Inspired by a personal interest in organizational problem solving and goaded onward by the enthusiasm of youth, Nyalali decided to take the magistrate's court on circuit, as an experiment. In most African countries during the colonial period, the high courts traveled, periodically setting up shop in district capitals as the early English court had done centuries before and as American judges had done after the Revolution.[3] High courts in Africa continued this practice in the independence period, the petrol supply for vehicles permitting. Nyalali thought it would help to extend circuit duties to the resident magistrates out in the districts, too. He wanted the resident magistrate to go on the road, hearing cases out in the villages as the primary court magistrates did. Fewer cases would be dismissed if the courts went to the people instead of vice versa, he reasoned. Now people in his district would not have to travel the long distance to Musoma and endure town life. He kept careful track of expenses, right down to the depreciation of the vehicle he used, in the hope of making a case that the change in practice not only would reduce dismissals, but also would save money.[4]

The community Nyalali served reciprocated with its affection. People appreciated the young magistrate's responsiveness, and they found they could live with the other unfamiliar procedures and principles he asked them to follow. They did not try to go over his head and telegraph the president's office. On the contrary, when news of a transfer to Kigoma, on the country's western border, came through in 1967, something surprising happened. "People visited the president when he came to the area, on leave," Nyalali remembered. "Normally they told him to get rid of the public servants assigned to their area, and administrators lived in perpetual fear, although I don't think he ever acted on the lists they gave him. This time, a delegation of elders said they wanted to block the transfer. I laughed when I was told about it. I said, 'It doesn't work that way. Matters of transfer of magistrates are the responsibility of the chief justice. The president has more important matters to attend to. He won't entertain the idea.'"

Three weeks later, a telegram arrived from Dar, from the registrar of the court. It read: "Transfer to Kigoma canceled. Letter of explanation to follow." Nyalali recalled worrying. "What have I done?," he wondered. Sometime later, the local administrator found him and told him that when the president arrived for his next leave, he was to meet him at the airport. "The president came and I was in the reception group and was introduced to him. He asked, 'How is court business?' A very young magistrate, I eagerly told him how many cases were filed and pending, and I mentioned that people did not always accept decisions. He replied, 'You'll get used to it!' I thought he wasn't very interested. Later I realized he must have followed my career in a general sense, but it was a long time until we met again."

---

[3] American Supreme Court justices had circuit duties until 1891, although they were relieved of many of these burdens with the appointment of nine circuit judges in 1869.
[4] Francis L. Nyalali, interview with author, May 29, 1996.

In those early months as a new magistrate, Nyalali quickly discovered many of the fundamental challenges with which he and his judicial colleagues all across common law Africa would be forced to contend throughout their careers. There were inevitable contradictions between the role of the courts inherited from a colonial past and long-standing local custom. There were difficulties in blending tradition with new ideas and practice. It was often hard to protect against the many subtle social gestures that people tried to employ to subvert a judge's independence and tempt him to succumb to fears and pressures, real or imagined.

The hallmarks of Nyalali's style showed themselves early in the face of these challenges. He quickly saw the utility of responding creatively to challenges with which he was presented. He grasped the necessity to make the courts more accessible. He did not shy away from taking the initiative or from pursuing reform.

P. Telford Georges, the country's first chief justice, proved supportive. He received and read Nyalali's reports about his experiment in "taking the courts to the people" by going on circuit within his region. He also entertained lengthy discussions when the young magistrate attended seminars in the capital. But not everyone agreed that a magistrate should try to experiment, as Nyalali had. The role of the judge was a matter for debate in these early years. It was uncertain how much initiative a junior member of the bench could safely pursue and still win promotion later.

SCHOOL TIES

The young Magistrate Nyalali could point to himself as typical of the first generation of African judges. Born in 1935, Nyalali came from the countryside bordering Lake Victoria, near Mwanza. His parents, Lucas Makali and Salome Madiya, were both Sukuma people. His father divorced his mother when he was three, and Nyalali went to live with his grandparents. Although his home community was patrilineal and gave custody to the father and his father's parents, Nyalali was his mother's only child, and his relatives remained open to her. Nonetheless, although Nyalali remained devoted to his mother, she was rarely present, and the other children would taunt him, in quarrels, calling, "Your mother is not here!" and "Your mother was sent away!" He developed an early reserve and a careful, deliberate demeanor in defense, habits that served him well in a judicial career, later. His grandfather, an important medicine man, singled him out to help pick wild herbs he needed in his work.[5]

The community was semipastoral. People raised goats and cattle at the same

[5] Ibid.

time that they tended grain crops. Responsibilities for household and community functions were allocated according to age. Nyalali's cohort or "age-grade" gradually was introduced to the knowledge necessary for survival and success. They were assigned first to look after the goats and sheep, then the calves, and finally the herd of cattle.

In this region, there was no thought of school. Families needed the boys to look after the livestock, and book learning was foreign. If the colonial authorities tried to pressure parents to send children to study reading and writing, they would enroll the sons of distant relatives and keep their own sons at home.

Formal education came by chance. At eleven, Nyalali had risen to become top herdsboy. But just a short time later, he was injured in a storm so severe its winds pushed the cattle and their attendants into the papyrus swamp at the edge of the lake. Possibly the cattle, frightened, stampeded. Nyalali only remembered coming back to consciousness after a fall. He resolved that he would leave this way of life. He recalled once having heard someone say that if a boy was registered in school and a relative tried to take the child away and put him to work in the fields, the authorities would follow up and take him back. In a bid for freedom, he secretly registered himself at the local primary school.

Within six months of starting primary school, eleven-year-old Nyalali had moved from grade one to grade three. He excelled. After four years, he sat for the exams to enter junior secondary school and earned the best marks of any student in the primary schools around the lake. He won admission but again encountered a lack of interest on the part of his family.

Continuing in school looked a remote prospect. Secondary schools were boarding schools, usually at some distance from most of the communities they served. They charged fees. Nyalali's family saw no reason to pursue formal education, and Nyalali could not afford the fees on his own. "I had the idea that children from families unable to pay should be exempt from fees," he remembered. "I must have heard that somewhere." Exemptions came from the district commissioner, however, and it was inconceivable that his relatives would go to see the man themselves. The district commissioner was an officer of the colonial government, a European. "They were terrified by the might of the British Empire. These were people you wanted to stay away from, they thought!"

Fear of going home and looking after cattle gave teenage Nyalali the courage to contemplate visiting the district commissioner himself. Nyalali summoned all his resources and traveled to Mwanza, a small commercial center on the lake shore, seeing the town for the first time in his life. "I felt the same way witnesses feel when they come to town for the first time," Nyalali remembered. He approached the administrative buildings and saw guards. He would have to get past them. He realized that in his school uniform, he must have appeared a pathetic sight! "I persisted, and when the guards said, 'Go away!,' I yelled and caused a commotion. The district commissioner heard the noise and peered through the window." He saw that the boy refused to budge and told the guards to let him in, to see what was the matter.

Nyalali greeted the district commissioner formally, as he did his teachers. He explained that he had the top score on the tests for junior secondary school but could not pay the fees. The district commissioner listened and seemed receptive, but he said the local chiefs would have to authenticate the story. He sent Nyalali home to get a letter from the chiefs.

The Sukuma possessed a complicated system of small kingships whose power was checked by village councils of elders.[6] Nyalali approached the chief in his village. The chief listened. He understood that the school fee problem was not really a matter of poverty; Nyalali's family could have sold a cow to raise the money. But he also knew the boy was doing well, and he wanted someone from the area to go to school. He wrote a letter, which construed the facts a bit differently than they were. It read: "Nyalali comes from a poor family that doesn't own even a single hen!"

By the time the district commissioner granted the exemption, the school year was already three months under way. Nyalali had difficulty at first but after two months was again at the top of the class. He broke the school record in the final examinations and was allowed to go on to the senior secondary school at Tabora, a distinguished institution that trained many of those who would rise to become important figures after independence. His classmates elected him a prefect.

Looking back to that time from his position as chief justice, Nyalali observed that what the judges of the 1990s had in common with one another and with other new political elites was not a particular social background, nor a tradition of involvement in the legal profession, but school ties. Almost everyone who was later of political consequence went to one of three schools. Tabora was one.[7] The same pattern held true in most of the other countries in the region. For example, in Kenya, Alliance High School produced a high proportion of the new leaders. These schools created ties of friendship among those they trained. They also aimed to create leaders. "We were told we were the cream of the crop," Nyalali recalled. They tried to make students feel they were special.

Some of the teachers also tried hard to force students to shed their identities, or their ties with their homes. "In my eighth year, there was an incident. An old German priest who taught religion at the school asked me my name, and I said 'Nyalali.' He was furious and fumed, 'I don't want this barbaric name!' I gave him 'Francis' instead, but I was very upset and never quit thinking about it." Nyalali reported that he almost gave up Christianity at the time, although later in life he was a devout Catholic. "We lost our roots. Now, people would proba-

[6] Ralph A. Austen, *Northwest Tanzania under German and British Rule: Colonial Policy and Tribal Politics, 1889–1939* (New Haven: Yale University Press, 1968), p. 13.
[7] Francis L. Nyalali, interview with author, July 19, 1997.

bly call us black white people; there is even a term for it in Kiswahili, *muzungu mweusi!* Later we retraced our steps, however."

Nyalali commented that his own Catholicism took root before he went to school. His father and relatives were Catholic converts. But religion became important to him personally only after 1949. In his teenage years he desperately wanted to continue his formal education. The uncertainty about whether he would be able to pay the fees, coupled with a deep desire not to drop out, prompted a more serious turn toward religion. He found certainty and solidarity, assurance and help. Catholicism was something to cling to, and it took root.

School ties mattered in many ways. Decades later, during an investigation of corruption in the judiciary, Nyalali remarked that the public was mainly concerned about the lower levels of the court. They had no complaint with the judges of the Court of Appeal, whose behavior Nyalali ascribed to their common experience at the Tabora school. He maintained that the school's teaching and the reputational pressures the network of peers created encouraged graduates of his generation to toe the line.[8] For later generations, the significance of school ties was altered. There were more schools available, and teaching placed less emphasis on civic values and religion.

Upon graduation from Tabora, Nyalali won admission to the university. At the time, Makerere University in Kampala, Uganda, served the region. In the late 1950s and early 1960s, Makerere was nicknamed "the Harvard of Africa," for the liveliness and cosmopolitan character of its intellectual community. It trained many of East Africa's future scholars and leaders. It was also home to the influential magazine of opinion, *Transition*. The magazine carried the writing of cosmopolitan literati-to-be: Okot p' Bitek, Ngugi wa Thiong'o, Paul Theroux, Gunnar Myrdal, Dennis Brutus, Ali Mazrui, and Ifeanyi Menkiti. Years later it would figure importantly in debates about judicial independence.

The headmaster at Tabora wanted Nyalali to pursue medicine because he had strong examination scores in the sciences, and the university advisers urged the same. As others of his day, however, Nyalali became interested in politics. While Nyalali was a student at Tabora, Julius Nyerere had visited, Nyerere recently had founded Tanganyika's nationalist movement, and he urged the young men of Tabora to join him. Nyalali was inspired. At Makerere, his peers from other countries were similarly motivated to enter politics, and Makerere was brimming with excitement. In 1953, students had founded the Makerre College Political Society, whose members went on to lead the anti-colonial struggles in many countries and then to staff newly independent governments. Instead of medicine, Nyalali chose to concentrate in history. Makerere University did not teach law, which he preferred, and history came closest, he reasoned.

[8] Ibid.

Nyalali quickly entered student politics, won election as president of the Students Guild, and almost failed academically. One of his friends was Benjamin Mkapa, who also was involved in the student movement and who eventually would become president of Tanzania.

Nyalali's origins and education resembled those of many other judges in English-speaking Africa. For example, Enoch Dumbutshena, who later served as chief justice of Zimbabwe, was born at a mission station in an area about fifty miles from his country's capital and lived the rural life during his youth.[9]

In these early years, there was no discernible pattern in the social backgrounds and views of the people recruited to serve in new national judiciaries. "The majority went to school only by accident," Nyalali observed. Basic education was largely free, and there were scholarships at the secondary school level which would cover one-third to one-half of the fees. In some cases governments paid the full tab, including university training. Thus, financial disability did not necessarily bar pursuit of a legal education. Only in the 1980s and 1990s did cost sharing create a risk that those less well off would be unable to acquire the skills needed to join the bench or the bar.

JUDICIAL EDUCATION

The coming of independence sharply increased the demand for lawyers in Africa. Britain departed from the continent more quickly than many nationalist leaders anticipated. When Julius Nyerere had visited Tabora Secondary School and spoken with Nyalali and other students about assuming responsibility for the direction of the country's affairs, he thought in terms of twenty-five years, not seven. The new governments needed law graduates immediately to provide drafting skills for attorney generals, serve as public prosecutors, supply counsel to public corporations, negotiate treaties, and staff the judiciary. Yet, few trained African lawyers were available in the eastern and southern parts of the continent. At the time of independence, the bar in most countries was mainly European and Asian. Tanzania had only two African lawyers outside government. Botswana also had two, one of whom was still completing his studies. Kenya had six.[10] Uganda had twenty African lawyers, almost all of whom were in government service and had not joined the private bar.

There were few existing institutions to help supply the demand. This predicament quickly attracted the attention of outsiders. In England, in 1960–61, the gov-

[9] Enoch Dumbutshena, *Zimbabwe Tragedy* (Nairobi, Kenya: East African Publishing House, 1975), p. 33.
[10] Walter B. L. Kapinga, "The Legal Profession and Social Action in the Third World: Reflections on Tanzania and Kenya," *African Journal of International and Comparative Law*, 4, 4 (1992), p. 876.

ernment appointed Lord Denning to inquire into African legal education needs.
Lord Denning was an English judge who became something of a legal folk hero.
He was considered a bit naïve by fellow lawyers in his own country, vain, but cour-
teous. He had acquired a reputation as a "maverick" judge by adopting some relatively new approaches to legal interpretation and by taking a very active role in
institutional affairs. The "Denning Report," formally the Report of the Committee
on Legal Education for Students from Africa, made extensive recommendations
about the establishment of law faculties and bar courses.[11] It won Denning a
devoted following in Africa, although, in an irony of history, toward the end of his
career he attracted official censure for racist remarks.

It was in this context that Nyalali pursued the study of law. The British government financed his graduate education through the Overseas Technical
Assistance Program. Because there were no degree-granting law faculties in East
Africa at the time, he would have to travel abroad, either to Fort Hare in
apartheid South Africa, where Nelson Mandela had studied, or to India, Great
Britain, or the United States. In these years, when nationalists sought equal treatment for Africans under the law, India lost favor as a place to learn, on the
grounds that its law was a pale version of the common law, streamlined to ease
control by colonial powers. Although the U.S. system shared with emerging
African countries a written constitution, which England did not have, American
decisions could only be treated as advisory or persuasive in common law Africa,
while much English precedent had the status of law. Thus, England had a special cachet.

Nyalali went to read law at Lincoln's Inn in London. During much of the
twentieth century, aspiring barristers, the lawyers who argue cases before the
court, learned their trade by joining an Inn, reading law, associating with practicing judges and lawyers over meals, and passing an examination administered
by the Council of Legal Education, which offered optional supplementary lectures.[12] The council lectures broached a number of legal subjects, but they did
not provide the combination of systematic study of law and legal practice usually found in university programs in common law countries today.

The training the Inns provided was expedient. It helped meet the sudden
demand from Britain's former overseas territories. Generally a two-year enterprise, preparing for the bar in this way was less expensive and faster than training
to be a solicitor. Solicitors, the lawyers who do not appear before the court and
who carry out much of the practical work of the profession, typically acquired
more substantial training in university programs or through apprenticeship.

[11] United Kingdom (Great Britain), Lord High Chancellor's Office, *Report of the Committee
on Legal Education for Students from Africa* (London: Her Majesty's Stationery Office,
January 1961).
[12] For a more extensive description and analysis, see L. C. B. Gower, *Independent Africa—
The Challenge to the Legal Profession* (Cambridge, MA: Harvard University Press, 1967).

Moreover, neither the Inns nor the Council of Legal Education provided instruction in important subjects such as customary law. More enterprising students joined classes at the School of Oriental and African Studies to make up for this deficiency. Others would have to acquire this background later. Finally, while qualification at the Inns of Court, through reading law, was normally the precursor to an apprenticeship, such practical opportunities were rarely available to foreign students on their return home.[13] African graduates had to employ the skills they had learned immediately, without further tutelage.

Nyalali quickly discovered a landlord in a London neighborhood who took in students. In his first experience outside of East Africa, he found the mix of personalities challenging. His housemates were Nigerian. Then, as now, the differences in personal style between the quiet reserve of East Africa and the more expressive West African flamboyance sometimes produced friction. Although united in a common political cause, the students from Tanzania and those from Nigeria tended to go their separate ways. Eventually Nyalali moved out and rented a flat in the Holborn area. He became a member of a local pub and found that he was able to build friendships with people there. "It was a healthy discovery," he remembered. "People were outgoing and helpful. They were very different from those I encountered under colonial rule."[14]

Nyalali's contemporaries, the men who became chief justices in other countries, traced similar paths, although some acquired more formal classroom training in law than Nyalali did. Enoch Dumbutshena, who served on the courts of Zimbabwe and Namibia, attended Adams College in Natal, South Africa, followed by the University of South Africa and then Gray's Inn. Annel Silungwe, from Zambia, went to the University of Zambia and then to the Inner Temple, another Inn. Akinola Aguda, who later served as chief justice of Botswana and Swaziland, attended the London School of Economics and then won a law degree from the University of London.

LEGAL EDUCATION IN AFRICA

Nyalali's successors had other options. In the early 1960s, the University of Dar es Salaam opened a law school that would serve the East Africa region. Western countries and private foundations made grants to help create the law faculty, supporting the travel and salaries of temporary law teachers from other parts of the Commonwealth. U.S. assistance was formalized through a program called

[13] Neville Rubin, "The Content and the Methods of Legal Education in Africa," in A. Bockel, Y. P. Ghai, J. Imbert, et al., *Legal Education in Africa South of the Sahara*/La Formation juridique en Afrique noire (Brussels: International Association of Legal Sciences/Établissements Émile Bruylant, 1979), p. 52.
[14] Francis L. Nyalali, interview with author, July 19, 1997.

SAILER—Staffing of African Institutions of Legal Education and Research. With Ford Foundation funding, the program sponsored faculty members from the United States to teach in visiting positions on new African law faculties or to serve as temporary deans, and SAILER screened applicants to the Fulbright Law Teachers in Africa competition. It also established fellowships to help African students study in the United States. In 1967, these activities were folded into the portfolio of the International Legal Center in New York.[15] Britain created similar opportunities and incentives to lure faculty from major Western universities to help establish law faculties at Dar and other "magnet schools" in Ghana and Ethiopia.[16]

The roster of those who taught in Africa included a wide range of personalities and views. For example, the first dean of the law faculty at Dar was A. B. Weston, described by a colleague as "an unconventional Australian," who "appreciated the strengths but mocked the weaknesses of traditional British methods."[17] Some of the other faculty included Issa Shivji and Yash Ghai, East Africans of Asian descent; Akilagpa Sawyerr, a Ghanaian legal scholar; James Read, William Twining, and Patrick McAuslan from England; and Robert Seidman and William Whitford from the United States. A cavalcade of young foreign lawyers helped staff similar programs in other countries. Patrick Atiyah, later at Harvard, got his start in the Sudan in the late 1950s. James C. N. Paul and Jacques Vanderlinden shared the deanship at Hailie Selassie University in Ethiopia. William Burnett Harvey and A. W. Brian Simpson served on the faculty of law at the University of Ghana. Many of the first recruits coauthored books and articles with one another and went on to have distinguished academic careers.[18] As

[15] John Seaman Bainbridge, *The Study and Teaching of Law in Africa* (Hackensack, NJ: Fred B. Rothman & Co., 1972).

[16] Chapter 10 discusses the history and contributions of the "law and development movement" in greater detail.

[17] Sol Picciotto, "Law, Life, and Politics," in Issa Shivji, ed., *Limits of Legal Radicalism: Reflections on Teaching Law at the University of Dar es Salaam* (Dar es Salaam, Tanzania: Faculty of Law, University of Dar es Salaam, 1986), p. 39.

[18] Many of the people involved in these early assistance programs achieved scholarly renown later. Issa Shivji and Yash Ghai wrote prodigiously in later years. Shivji chaired an important commission to reform land tenure in Tanzania and invested considerable energy in holding the law faculty together through the challenges that lay ahead. Yash Ghai eventually moved to Hong Kong and wrote about human rights law in Africa and Asia. Akilagpa Sawyerr, once vice chancellor of the University of Ghana, carried out extensive research on court interpretation of customary law. James Read and Patrick McAuslan continued their research on important aspects of African law and legal institutions throughout their careers. Read played a central role in sustaining the *Journal of African Law*. William Twining produced books on a wide range of topics, from the problems of newly independent countries, to a biography of Karl Llewellyn, a distinguished American legal thinker. Some of his own reflections on this period appear in a book called *Law in Context* (Oxford: Clarendon, 1997). Patrick Atiyah became known for his work on contracts and on legal theory. William Burnett Harvey coauthored the contracts casebook used in many American law schools. James Paul continued

promising African law students appeared, they swelled the ranks of these faculties. In Tanzania, Costa Mahalu, Chris Maina Peter, Barthazar Rwezaura, and Mgongo Fimbo, among others, played a central role.

When the Tanzanian program opened for business in 1961, it offered a three-year undergraduate concentration in law, based on the English model. The curriculum included many of the subjects taught at the instructors' home institutions. For example, the first year included a course titled, "Constitutions and Legal Systems of East Africa," as well as courses in contracts, criminal procedure, criminal law, and legal method. Classes on torts, land law, and administrative law were the main offerings in the second year. Students were also required to choose among several additional classes, which taught international law, Islamic law, and commercial law, as well as shorter courses on criminology and other topics. The third year emphasized civil procedure and evidence, supplemented by more choices from the list of electives. Not all the courses listed were offered each year because of shortages of faculty.

Appropriate texts and local legal materials were almost nonexistent at first. William Twining remembered arriving in the Sudan, where he held his first teaching post, and realizing that English precedents made little sense to his students, for whom the conflicts portrayed in the casebooks seemed wholly foreign. Law reports from the Sudan and other African jurisdictions tended to divert attention to unusual situations, cases in which parties had the resources to appeal, and away from the disagreements most common and most important on the ground.[19] At Dar es Salaam, faculty member Sol Picciotto recalled that the faculty gradually developed their own materials, which they circulated as stenciled handouts.[20] A few of these eventually found their way into compendia cheaply printed by local publishers, such as the East Africa Literature Bureau. William Burnett Harvey, a former University of Michigan Law School faculty member who had served as dean of the Faculty of Law at the University of Ghana, spent a year as a Fulbright Scholar at the University of Nairobi in 1971–72 and compiled a set of readings in *An Introduction to the Legal System in East Africa*. The volume was still used and available in bookstores in the 1990s.[21]

Later, as African faculty members assumed posts in the new law schools, several began to produce their own casebooks and texts. Their Western counter-

---

his relationship with grassroots organizing in Africa, as did Robert Seidman. They also taught at American universities. Brian Simpson became a distinguished legal historian, based first at the University of Chicago and then at the University of Michigan.

[19] William Twining, "The Camel in the Zoo," in Issa Shivji, ed., *Limits of Legal Radicalism: Reflections on Teaching Law at the University of Dar es Salaam* (Dar es Salaam, Tanzania: Faculty of Law, University of Dar es Salaam, 1986), pp. 17, 19.

[20] Sol Picciotto, "Law, Life, and Politics," p. 39.

[21] William Burnett Harvey, *An Introduction to the Legal System of East Africa* (Nairobi, Kenya: East African Literature Bureau, 1975).

parts also took their experience home, and produced a Law in Context textbook series.[22]

By the end of the 1960s, the concept of regional magnet law schools succumbed to political tensions between countries. Programs sprang up at other institutions. For instance, Makerere University, in Uganda, established a three-year undergraduate law degree in 1968, just four years after the University of Dar es Salaam launched its regional program. Nairobi followed in 1970.

The authors of the Denning Report had worried that foreign legal education would not provide sufficient acquaintance with the statutes, precedents, and institutions students would encounter upon entering practice. It recommended both specialized bar courses and some form of apprenticeship. These needs remained even after the creation of local law schools. With some outside help, several countries acted on the first concern by setting up new bar courses designed to address the nuances of national law. They offered preparation for the national exams required for entry into the legal profession. For instance, in 1963, the Kenyan legislature created the Kenya School of Law, under control of the attorney general, to provide a bar course for aspiring advocates and judges with degrees from other countries or with at least an "0-level" certificate.[23] In 1970, Uganda created the Law Development Centre, which provided both paralegal training and a bar course for students with prior degrees from the universities in Makerere, Dar, Nairobi, Zambia, or the United Kingdom. Zambia insisted that graduates of the University of Zambia law program pursue an additional short course at its Law Practice Institute. By contrast, Tanzania created no similar program.

The demand for apprenticeships was harder to meet. For the most part, the African men and women who entered the judiciary as resident magistrates or judges in the 1960s had little or no practical professional experience before they assumed their first jobs.[24] Outside of South Africa, there were no clinics and clerkships initially. There were few opportunities for the kind of apprenticeship common in industrial countries, where young lawyers usually work as associates in firms for several years before becoming partners or striking out on their own. The University of Dar es Salaam tried to create an apprenticeship in 1973–74, met through government service. A one-year internship rotated students between the office of the attorney general, the magistrates' courts, and other institutions.[25]

---

[22] See William Twining, *Law in Context: Enlarging a Discipline* (Oxford: Clarendon, 1999), pp. 36–62.

[23] Tudor Jackson, *Guide to the Legal Profession in East Africa* (London: Sweet & Maxwell, 1970), p. 7.

[24] For a forceful statement, see Yash Ghai, "Legal Education in Kenya and Tanzania," in A. Bockel, Y. P. Ghai, J. Imbert, et al., *Legal Education in Africa South of the Sahara/La formation juridique en Afrique noire* (Brussels: International Agency of Legal Sciences/Établissements Émile Bruylant, 1979), pp. 272–273.

[25] Medard R. K. Rwelamira, "The Tanzania Legal Internship Program: A New Horizon in Legal Education," *African Law Studies*, 15 (1977), p. 32.

In later years, African lawyers sometimes criticized the legal training the first generation of judges received. One claim was that the British tradition of judicial restraint and strong deference to the legislature had hamstrung the courts' ability to build a rule of law. By contrast with American judges, who exercised considerable powers of judicial review and turned this authority to the protection of individual rights during the 1950s and 1960s, British judges had less clear authority to challenge the constitutionality of a law or practice. Powers of judicial review existed, especially in administrative law, but they were different from the explicit authority many new constitutions granted and from the powers available to the U.S. court. In England it also was common to apply the principle of *stare decisis*, the policy of standing by decisions of higher courts or applying precedent to future cases with similar facts, to many aspects of a decision, not just to the holding, the *ratio decidendi*, as was true in the United States.[26] Moreover, the legal culture of the bench and the bar meant that the interests of government and the word of officials often carried more weight than they might have at other times and places.

A second, related concern was that the training most judges received neglected some essential skills. For example, newly independent African countries had written constitutions. While American lawyers and judges were accustomed to working with such a document, British judges and lawyers were not. England had no written constitution, although principles embodied in important historical documents and decisions had similar status. The country's accession to regional and international human rights documents conferred the equivalent of a written bill of rights, but it took many years for jurisprudence to begin to define the authority of these provisions.

Yet it is not evident that training was the most significant limitation on the emergence of independent judiciaries or judges who valued independence in its positive sense in the early years. Many new judges and lawyers were aware that English jurisprudence was itself changing. For example, the man most often quoted and admired by African law students was Lord Denning, who was scarcely part of the tradition of restraint. Denning annoyed many of his fellow English judges by arguing that the courts had an obligation to use their powers of interpretation to clarify ambiguous phrases or fill gaps in the laws to "do justice." In appreciation of Lord Denning's approach, the students at the new law program in Dar es Salaam initially called their student organization the Denning Law Society. Moreover, the Westerners who helped establish the first law schools and taught the early generation of African lawyers were a diverse lot

[26] William Burnett Harvey, "A Value Analysis of Ghanaian Legal Development since Independence," unpublished manuscript in "A Selection of Lectures and Informal Talks on Law and Universities and the Communities That Usually Tolerate and Sometimes Support Them," collection of papers in the estate of William Burnett Harvey, Boston, MA, 1999.

who came to be known more for their unconventional styles than for their conformity with British philosophies of legal interpretation in the 1950s. If anything, one scholar suggested, they returned home to enlarge legal thinking and become "academic leaders of broader approaches."[27] Further, constitutional matters arose infrequently in the early years, by contrast with the late 1980s and 1990s. The bulk of the caseload was fairly mundane. Most complaints provided little opportunity for eloquence about basic rights or other fundamental constitutional principles.

Perhaps the greater lacuna in the training of many judges lay in the fact that their preparation had mirrored that of the English barrister, the courtroom performer, not that of the solicitor responsible for most of the everyday legal work. The confidence that comes from a solid, detailed knowledge of more common matters might have stood the first judges in better stead and made them less vulnerable to what community leaders thought.

Finally, a powerful, but neglected reason for executive-mindedness was that new judges and their friends in political office had just struggled together to win independence. The nationalists monopolized the label "progressive." Activism on behalf of basic rights could seem to interfere with the bold plans of new governments. Only hard experience would prod many judges and lawyers to act on the values implicit in the rule of law.

For the first thirty years after independence, a judge's training and jurisprudential skill usually mattered less than sheer bravery. Although there were some remarkable decisions, just as there were others that set back the rule of law, the heroes of the era were often not the continent's greatest legal minds but the judges who had an extra dose of personal courage and organizational savvy.

---

[27] Twining, "The Camel in the Zoo," pp. 23–34.

CHAPTER THREE

The Courts

THE COURT FRANCIS Nyalali joined as a young magistrate would have appeared familiar to anyone from a common law country. There was nothing exotic about the institution, from a Western view. Yet differences in design and context helped make judicial independence hard to achieve. Nyalali's own story highlighted the practical difficulties.

Newness was one source of ambiguity. Chief justices had to develop a working relationship with politicians and civil servants, nearly all of whom were unfamiliar both with their jobs and with the role of the judiciary. In Tanzania, that challenge initially fell to Chief Justice Telford Georges, who was born in Dominica in the Lesser Antilles, left the bench in Trinidad and Tobago for Dar es Salaam in early 1965, and served in Tanzania until 1971. Georges threw himself into the job, learning Kiswahili to communicate with ordinary people, who spoke no English, and listening intently to the views of the new corps of young magistrates.[1] He also spent considerable time trying to establish a rapport with political leaders and to instill an understanding of the courts. Fond memories of his efforts still attracted comment in the mid-1990s, not only from Nyalali, who would later occupy the same post and face the same problems, but also from members of the Law Society and administration.

Another source of ambiguity came from the legacy of colonial rule. Earlier, the common law courts tended to operate one way in London and another on the edges of the empire. Before World War I, there was considerable enthusiasm for placing increased judicial power in the hands of the colonial adminis-

---

[1] R. W. James and F. M. Kassam, *Law and Its Administration in a One Party State: Selected Speeches of Telford Georges* (Nairobi, Kenya: East African Literature Bureau, 1971), pp. 1–6.

tration and for tailoring law and procedure to perceived local needs. The roles of the magistrates and the district officer, a civil servant, were often one and the same. After the war, the English judiciary on duty abroad began to oppose this arrangement. Judges argued for the separation of powers. They urged that if authorities wanted local populations to embrace the idea that the courts were impartial, then it was inadvisable to vest both judicial and executive power in colonial functionaries. They accused the colonial office of creating the wrong impression. But it was only in the 1950s that colonial administrators lost most of their judicial role. And even then, it was common practice for judges to draft ordinances on behalf of the attorney general and the legislature and for the chief justice to stand in for the governor when he went on leave.[2] Indeed, chief justices usually sat on the governor's executive committee and substituted for the governor when he traveled abroad. Further complicating the picture was the fact that as late as the 1950s, judges in the colonial territories did not have security of tenure and held office at the pleasure of the crown,[3] even if safeguarded by specification of the few grounds on which a dismissal might occur.

Resource scarcity intensified the challenges new judges and magistrates faced in their first years on the job. Shortages of everything from statute books to office space forced judges to rely on executive branch officials and local big men in ways that could compromise the ability to be impartial.

These challenges gave content to the claim that bravery and organizational savvy meant as much or more than the quality of the legal mind in the early postindependence period.

STRUCTURE

The structure of the new court systems shared many features, across countries. In Africa, the statutes pertaining to magistrates and judges generally established a four- or five-tier system. At the lowest level, new governments established primary courts with limited original jurisdiction to hear petty civil cases and misdemeanors. In many countries, they could apply customary law as well as the statutes and precedents that together constituted "state law." The magistrates who presided did not have law degrees, and in most countries representation by

[2] For a more extensive discussion, see Henry F. Morris and James S. Read, *Indirect Rule and the Search for Justice: Essays in East African Legal History* (Oxford: Clarendon, 1972), pp. 79–104; and Y. P. Ghai and J. P. W. B. McAuslan, *Public Law and Political Change in Kenya* (Nairobi, Kenya: Oxford University Press, 1970), pp. 125–175.
[3] The relevant case is *Terrell v. Secretary of State for the Colonies* (1953) 2 Q. B. 482. See discussions in Sir Kenneth Roberts-Wray, *Commonwealth and Colonial Law* (New York: Praeger, 1966); and A. D. E. Amissah, "The Role of the Judiciary in the Government Process: Ghana's Experience," *African Law Studies*, 13 (1976), pp. 4–30.

legal counsel was not allowed. People had to represent themselves. A second-level magistrates' court handled cases involving slightly more money or more serious crimes, usually those carrying potential sentences of up to two years. Magistrates grade II, as they were usually called, had slightly more training but did not need university degrees. At the third level, magistrates had to be lawyers. The courts over which they presided had original jurisdiction in civil cases involving still more money and in criminal cases carrying penalties up to ten years in prison. These courts also accepted appeals from the lower levels. Counsel could be present.

Typically responsibility for supervising the magistrates' courts resided in the High Court, a court of unlimited civil and criminal jurisdiction whose judges had law degrees and sometimes had practiced as advocates before joining the bench or had served as judges in other jurisdictions. Most high courts held sessions both in the capital and on circuit. They created High Court stations in important secondary towns, to increase accessibility.

The Court of Appeal, sometimes called a Supreme Court, constituted a fifth tier. In most instances, courts of appeal initially operated on a regional basis, as they did in the colonial period. For instance, in 1962, the colonial-era Eastern African Court of Appeal became the Court of Appeal of East Africa, part of a regional organization, the East African Community. Each country determined separately whether the Court of Appeal's decisions constituted binding precedent or persuasive authority, but whichever choice a country made, the Court's law reports were widely read and followed by lawyers after independence. Political tensions disrupted the East African Community and led to the creation of national courts of appeal in the 1970s. A parallel West African Court of Appeal enjoyed a brief existence until Ghana, Nigeria, and Sierra Leone withdrew.[4] In the south, Botswana, Swaziland, and Lesotho shared a court of appeal until the 1980s. The same kind of arrangement existed in the West Indies.

Administrative responsibility for the courts typically lay with the chief justice (in Tanzania, the *jaji mkuu*) and a team of senior judicial officers, usually including a deputy chief justice *(jaji kiongozi)* or principal judge. Other judges from the Court of Appeal and High Court often managed special tasks, such as continuing judicial education. The day-to-day operation of the court fell to the chief registrar and subordinate court registrars, the counterparts of clerks of court in the United States.

The terms of appointment to the bench varied. In the industrial democracies, where there are systems of checks and balances in place, there is almost always some provision for the participation of elected officials in judicial selection. Heads of state generally have the power to propose candidates for high judicial office after consultation with members of the bar and the chief justice.

---

[4] Briefly noted in Roberts-Wray, *Commonwealth and Colonial Law*, p. 431.

Legislators may possess the power to review and confirm proposed appointments, to ensure that the choice of the executive meets with the approval of a legislative majority or a supermajority. For example, often two-thirds of the national assembly or of the upper chamber, in a bicameral system, must show their approval to confirm a nominee. In a few instances, as in some state court systems in the United States, judges are popularly elected.

In Africa, in the early years, appointment processes varied by country and by level of the court. Partisan politics entered to varying degrees. In Uganda, Kenya, and Tanzania, the president appointed the chief justice and was not required to consult anyone or obtain legislative confirmation. At the level of the High Court and the Court of Appeal, the chief justice recommended candidates for appointment by the president. Still farther down the ladder, at the magistrate level, a judicial service commission consisting of the chief justice, a judge, and two other members selected by the minister of justice played a central role in the appointment process.

At the lowest echelons, the primary courts, magistrates often reported to the ministries of justice or local government, not to the judiciary. In Tanzania, statute placed the power to appoint these magistrates, the most junior personnel, in the hands of the Special Judicial Service. This special commission shared control of appointments and promotions with local boards that included the regional commissioner (a political appointee) as well as the district magistrate and resident magistrate for the area.

In the late 1980s and 1990s, judicial service commissions began to play a greater role in the appointment process throughout the region. Commenting on this development years later, when he was chief justice, Nyalali said, "For quite some time, I was uneasy about the process we used for selection of candidates and for appointment to both the High Court and the Court of Appeal. Since the president knew very little about the legal profession, the constitution seemed to me to confer too much influence upon the chief justice," whose advice the president would follow. The Tanzanian constitution was amended in the 1990s to involve the Judicial Service Commission in the appointment of judges to the High Court and Court of Appeal. Even then, Nyalali remained concerned. "My reservations persisted even after the constitution was changed in the early 1990s," he remembered.[5] "I therefore devised a system which required the chief justice to seek names of legal practitioners suitable for appointment to the High Court from representatives of a broader set of legal institutions." Whenever a vacancy on the High Court occurred, the chief justice would write to the heads of the High Court zones, the dean of the Faculty of Law, the president of the Law Society, the attorney general, and the chief corporation counsel, among others, inviting them to suggest names for consideration by the Judicial Service Commission. This practice was entirely adminis-

[5] Francis L. Nyalali, personal communication, September 1998.

trative; it was not required by the constitution. But it quickly became popular, and it was accepted by the Judicial Service Commission and by the president.

Because of the shortage of African lawyers, most courts filled some or all of their senior positions with judges from other parts of the Commonwealth, on a contractual basis. Because of their larger and older legal professions, the West Indies and Ghana supplied many personnel. England, India, Sri Lanka, and South Africa were other important sources. South African opponents of apartheid found that service in neighboring jurisdictions enabled them to pursue the profession for which they were trained without appearing to support a legal system they found unjust.

The security of tenure granted most other judges did not extend to those on contract. Some members of the bar conjectured that expatriate judges were more cautious than others, as a result. And judges on contract sometimes professed the need for restraint. An American scholar reported a conversation in which an expatriate member of the East African Court of Appeals, "when taxed with the legalistic quality of that court's opinions, . . . said that to address openly the policy questions which were at issue would lead to the withdrawal of politically sensitive cases from the court of jurisdiction."[6] Yet expatriate judges in several countries made quite courageous decisions, while plenty of judges born and bred in the countries they served showed deep caution.

PROCESS

How would a lawyer coming before the new African common law courts have brought a case in the courts? Rules of procedure and evidence came from England by way of India, in most countries. Streamlined codes were devised for India in the late 1800s, to tailor the common law to the perceived needs of a foreign setting. In the colonial period, these codes won adoption in eastern and southern Africa. Independence governments proposed few changes.[7]

Above the lowest grades, courtroom decorum or custom also was shaped by the same conventions that prevailed in England or the United States. The choice of "uniform" in court was what one would have found in other parts of the Commonwealth. The powdered wigs and long robes, which deprived the judges of their individual identities and leant the proceedings a special, impartial character, proved popular. African courts adopted them, and efforts to incorporate local themes provoked opposition. In a gesture that recalled the actions of U.S. Chief Justice John Marshall, Tanzanian Chief Justice Georges

---

[6] Robert B. Seidman, "Judicial Review and Fundamental Freedoms in Anglophonic Independent Africa," *Ohio State Law Journal*, 35 (1974), p. 841.
[7] Henry F. Morris, *Evidence Law in East Africa*, Law in Africa Series No. 24 (London: Sweet & Maxwell, 1968).

tried to discard the scarlet and ermine of the English robes. Though he came from the West Indies, Chief Justice Georges was often considered "more Tanzanian than the Tanzanians themselves," and this initiative was consistent with his general style. However, while John Marshall's pointed personal adoption of republican black eventually attracted a following in the new United States,[8] in Tanzania there was public outcry. "People thought the court was insufficiently institutionalized, and they thought it important to keep the symbols the robes represented," Nyalali reflected years later. The court compromised, adopting black for Court of Appeal proceedings and red for High Court criminal proceedings or an appeal from a court martial.[9]

At the upper levels, proceedings were generally in English, which provided a convenient *lingua franca* in settings where litigants often spoke mutually incomprehensible languages. In Tanzania, Kiswahili shared the status of an official language with English. It was preferred at the lower levels and useful in the upper courts.

The language problem was serious in all African judiciaries. Throughout the continent, ordinary people usually mastered at least two or three languages. A rural person negotiated everyday life in his or her mother tongue and the language of at least one neighboring community. Sometimes younger people, traders, or men who had done military service also acquired a European language such as English, French, or Afrikaans, or another language that could serve as a regional *lingua franca*. In parts of East Africa, such as Tanzania, Kiswahili, a trading tongue based partly on Arabic, served that purpose. Facility with a language such as English or Kiswahili usually diminished the farther people lived from the capital city.

This linguistic diversity increased the scope for misunderstanding and for miscarriages of justice. The Tanzanian situation exemplified the difficulties. The first mix-ups often occurred when a case was filed. Out in the countryside, private individuals, almost always unrepresented by counsel, were free to make both civil and criminal complaints. They did not have to involve the police if a crime was involved, as they did in urban areas. But in the parts of Tanzania where the grasp of Kiswahili was more limited, people did not always distinguish the word for a criminal case, *jinai*, from the word for a civil case, *madai*. If a clerk processed a complaint hurriedly, he might misunderstand and mischaracterize the issues. Moreover, when the case came to trial, the language of the proceedings would inevitably privilege the expressive skills of some parties over others.[10]

---

[8] Jean Edward Smith, *John Marshall: Definer of a Nation* (New York: Henry Holt, 1996), p. 285.
[9] Francis L. Nyalali, interview with author, July 19, 1997.
[10] Frederic Lee Dubow, "Language, Law, and Change: Problems in the Development of a National Legal System in Tanzania," in William O'Barr and Jean O'Barr, eds., *Language*

Even in the higher courts, where both English and Kiswahili were official languages, there were risks of a mistake in translation. In appellate decisions during the 1990s, judges occasionally took issue with the translation of words. For example, Nyalali recalled an appeal in which the applicant spoke no English and he could not follow his lawyer's statements. "I directed counsel on both sides to make their oral submissions in the common language of the ordinary people of Tanzania, that is, the Kiswahili language, so that the appellant could follow and understand what was being said in his case." The effect was dramatic and decisive. "After counsel for the appellant had ended his submission, the appellant raised his arm indicating that he had something to say. I allowed him to do so. He proceeded to address the court in Kiswahili on a point of evidence which his lawyer had missed." Later, when members of the court sat alone in conference to consider judgment, the intervention made personally by the appellant turned out to be the decisive point in the appeal. The appeal succeeded.[11]

Inevitably, there was considerable demand for interpreters, who were paid a nominal fee for their services, when needed. Often the court pressed administrative staff members into service in this capacity. Nyalali recalled that in earlier days there were "many colorful stories . . . about famous or infamous court interpreters. They could make or unmake a case, since neither the presiding judge nor the magistrate nor the lawyers were familiar with Kiswahili or the local vernaculars."[12] Given the level of linguistic diversity, a court composed solely of judges born in the country solved only part of the problem.

JURIES AND ASSESSORS

In a departure from the common law courts of the Western democracies, the institution of the jury was conspicuously absent in Africa. In countries with jury systems, the judge has the responsibility of applying the law, but juries take over the task of deciding the facts. Peers weigh evidence to estimate states of mind, what a party knew or could have known, and whether adequate consideration of alternative courses of action took place, among other things. In this way, a jury system helps reduce the gaps between the perceptions of an

---

and Politics (The Hague: Mouton & Co., 1976), pp. 96–97. See also A. B. Weston, "Law in Swahili—Problems in Developing a National Language," *Swahili*, 35, 2 (1965), pp. 2–13; and Barthazar Rwezaura, "Constraining Factors in the Adoption of Kiswahili as a Language of the Law in Tanzania," *Journal of African Law*, 37, 1 (1993), pp. 31–45.
[11] Francis L. Nyalali, "Cross-cultural Perspectives of the Proof Process: The Tanzanian Experience," Paper presented at the annual meeting of the Society for the Reform of Criminal Law, Vancouver, Canada, August 3–7, 1992, p. 2.
[12] Ibid., p. 3.

unelected judiciary and those of community members. However, jury systems also suffer from several disadvantages, including the possibility of corruption, increased expense, and the possibility that peers might nullify the law thereby making the legal system unpredictable. Although juries caught the fancy of revolutionary governments in Europe, during the 1700s and early 1800s, they quickly disappeared from all countries except England, Denmark, Belgium, and a few Swiss cantons. The Americans remained deeply committed to them.

In Africa, there was fleeting experience with jury systems. In the early 1800s, the British had waxed enthusiastic about using juries in the empire. They had introduced the system into the Cape Colony, later South Africa, on the grounds that lay participation in trials would reassure inhabitants that the colonial government would not take their property or abrogate their rights without due process of law.[13] They also initiated jury systems in Sierra Leone, Ghana, the Gambia, and Nigeria. The institution was less popular in East Africa, where only Kenya, Zanzibar, and what was then Southern Rhodesia (later Zimbabwe) accepted the system. And in Kenya and Rhodesia juries were available only for Europeans. Growing concern about the litigants' ability to manipulate jurors led to the curtailment of the civil jury in the 1860s in most of these countries. At the time of independence, juries found few proponents. Ghana chose not to continue the system.[14] In 1969, South Africa abolished juries too.[15]

Space for the incorporation of lay opinion instead came through the inclusion of "assessors" in aspects of the trial. The function of assessors differed across courts.[16] In England, the role was akin to that of the expert witness, used to advise the court when special knowledge was required. In some parts of common law Africa, including South Africa, and at the higher levels of the court, assessors performed similar functions. By contrast, at the lower levels of the court, the assessor played a part more like that of a jury and sometimes assumed some of the functions of a judge as well. Originally, "their role, though somewhat similar to that of the jury, was different in the sense that the assessors were not judges of facts, but were simply advisers on the facts,"[17]

---

[13] Ellison Kahn, "Restore the Jury? Or 'Reform? Reform? Aren't Things Bad Enough Already?'" (multipart article) *South African Law Journal*, 108, 4 (1991), p. 677.

[14] See R. Knox-Mawer, "The Jury System in British Colonial Africa," *Journal of African Law*, 2, 3 (1958): 160–163; and J. H. Jearey, "Trial by Jury and Trial with the Aid of Assessors in the Superior Courts of British African Territories," *Journal of African Law*, 4, 3 (1960); 5, 1 (1961); and 5, 2 (1961).

[15] Dirk van Zyl Smit and Norma-May Isakow, "Assessors and Criminal Justice," *South African Journal on Human Rights*, 1, 3 (1985), p. 219.

[16] On the history and use of assessors, see Morris and Read, *Indirect Rule and the Search for Justice*, p. 188; Sir John Gray, "Opinions of Assessors in Criminal Trials in East Africa as to Native Custom," *Journal of African Law*, 2, 1 (1958), pp. 5–18; and R. W. Moisey, "The Role of Assessors in the Courts of Tanzania," *East African Law Journal*, 3, 4 (1967), pp. 348–353.

[17] Nyalali, "Cross-cultural Perspectives of the Proof Process," p. 10.

Nyalali observed. Assessors could put questions to witnesses, as long as the judge thought them proper.[18] In some countries, they gained the latitude to apply the law to the facts, as well. At the conclusion of the trial, they were required to offer opinions on the general issue, either alone or in combination with answers to specific questions.

The use of assessors persisted after independence. The main reason was that in a plural society, "what was common knowledge locally was not necessarily common knowledge throughout the country," Nyalali commented.[19] Moreover, the idea of popular participation in the judicial process was attractive even to those who felt that juries were impracticable.

In Tanzania, assessors grew to have a very important role at the lowest levels of the court. The Magistrates Courts Act of 1963, which inaugurated the country's new court system, said that when a matter involved a rule of customary or Islamic law, the magistrate could sit with assessors, but the opinions of assessors were only advisory, not binding. A year later, the law was amended to make the presence of assessors mandatory in all proceedings in open court, at the lower levels. By 1969, the arrangement had altered further. At the primary court level, the magistrate sat with two assessors, each of whom had a vote in the verdict. The matter before the court was to be decided by the majority.[20] This arrangement was similar to the "mixed courts" of Germany's civil law system, in which a professional judge and two lay judges decided cases involving smaller crimes.[21]

Although all the countries used assessors in the 1960s, most did not make the assessors' views binding the way Tanzania did at the lower levels of its court.[22] In Uganda, for example, the magistrate could override the assessors' opinions provided he recorded his reasons. In South Africa, a majority of a mixed bench, consisting of a judge and two assessors, determined matters of fact, but the

---

[18] Gray, "Opinions of Assessors in Criminal Trials in East Africa as to Native Custom," p. 5.

[19] Francis L. Nyalali, interview with author, March 17, 1996.

[20] Neville Rubin and Eugene Cotran, eds., *Annual Survey of African Law*, 1969 (London: Frank Cass, 1973), p. 137.

[21] In Germany, this system was considered preferable to a jury system, which was expensive and time-consuming to run and which made use of elaborate exclusionary rules, which members of the public often considered too generous to the defendant. Decisions made by "mixed courts" in Germany were subject to trial de novo, on appeal. For a description, see John Langbein, "Mixed Court and Jury Court: Could the Continental Alternative Fill the American Need?" *American Bar Foundation Research Journal*, 1 (1981), pp. 195–219.

[22] Note that the Tanzanian use of assessors in this period was at odds with the principles the distinguished jurist T. O. Elias enunciated in the 1990s. Among these principles, he wrote, were "that jurors, but not assessors, are judges of fact; that it is no part of the assessors' duty to decide as to the guilt or innocence of the accused because they are not required to return a verdict as jurors are; and that their advisory opinions need not be unanimous." T. O. Elias, *Judicial Process in the Newer Commonwealth* (Lagos, Nigeria: University of Lagos Press, 1990), p. 20. The literature on the role of assessors encompasses many conflicting perspectives. These appear to be linked to the fact that there are relatively few comparative studies of what assessors do in practice, as opposed to theory.

judge alone decided matters of law. The general trend also was to limit the kinds of cases in which assessors played a role, so that in Kenya, for example, by the 1990s, assessors were only used in criminal cases involving capital offenses.

Methods for selecting assessors also varied across countries. In Tanzania, in the early years, assessors tended to be respected older members of the community, retained on a monthly basis. By 1972, regulations for the appointment of assessors stipulated that each court district choose from a panel of at least thirty approved members nominated by the Branch Executive Committees of the ruling political party, the Tanzania African National Union (TANU), and cleared by the District Executive Committee.[23] Assessors ranged widely in age and background, and many acquired nearly permanent status. They increasingly were identified in the public mind as "assistant magistrates," and they often sought such professionalization.[24] By contrast, in Uganda parties had the opportunity to strike names from the list of people from which the court might draw. In South Africa, assessors were generally lawyers or former magistrates who nominated themselves. Judges chose among them.[25] In Botswana, assessors were selected from among qualified headmen, subchiefs, or chiefs.

Later, during the reform period of the 1990s, many suggested that the courts should stop using assessors, especially as they often could not pay for the services, and the assessors instead survived on contributions from litigants. Nyalali expressed mixed emotions about this proposal. On the one hand, credibility was something that was hard for outsiders to evaluate, and magistrates and judges were usually "foreign" to the localities in which they worked.[26] On the other hand, whereas assessors had once been community elders, the newer lists from which the court could draw were often dominated by the party faithful.

Although in the independence era, there was never much interest in jury systems either on the part of legislators or on the part of judges, juries did one thing that assessors could not do. Because they remove much of the responsibility for the final verdict from the judge, in tense social or political situations they relieved some of the risk and danger associated with the judicial role. Much later, during a tour of the Superior Court of the District of Columbia in the United States, a group of African judges asked where the judges' armed guards stood. The guide replied that there were no guards standing near the judge, and the man who posed the question asked what was to keep a defendant or an angry party to a civil case from taking matters into his own hands. Chief Justice Nyalali, a member of the group, turned to the jury box and com-

---

[23] Rubin and Cotran, *Annual Survey of African Law*, 1970, pp. 130–131.

[24] Moisey, "The Role of Assessors in the Courts of Tanzania," p. 349.

[25] Smit and Isakow, "Assessors and Criminal Justice," p. 223.

[26] Francis L. Nyalali and the then *jaji kiongozi*, Justice Barnabas Samatta, interview with author, August 19, 1995.

mented, "But the real decision makers are over there!"[27] In theory, how much easier it would be to build independence, he observed, if the judicial process allowed for a greater lay role in the determination of fact. Judge and jury then would share responsibility, and officials or ordinary people dissatisfied with the outcome of a trial might be less inclined to retaliate.

For the most part, in the 1990s the objections to jury systems outweighed the advantages in the minds of judges and elected officials alike. Only Malawi decided to experiment, on a limited basis. In its 1994 constitution, it provided for juries of peers in capital cases. By the end of the century, the results of the experiment remained unclear.

LABYRINTHS

Even where it existed, structural protection of independence provided new magistrates and judges little help in threading their way through the mazes of potential conflicts of interest presented by real life. Remoteness and resource scarcity created dependencies and fears that often were difficult to negotiate. The introduction of new role definitions for district administrators, who had wielded judicial power in the colonial era, also created friction between the branches of government in rural areas where it was least controllable.

The kind of independence the legal community calls "party detachment"— insulation from the influence of socially powerful litigants—was usually the first to be challenged. Once appointed to a post, a magistrate or judge had to arrange his affairs to ensure that he was both "of the community," in the sense that he understood general issues and problems, and apart from people who might come before him or who might have an interest in the outcome of a particular case. This twin task was a difficult one to fulfill in small communities anywhere in the world. In newly independent Africa, without a general public awareness of the role the judge was supposed to play, the challenge was greater. Ties of blood and marriage brought extensive social obligations. Resource scarcity also mattered.

Getting started often created the first set of problems a magistrate or judge encountered. Where there was little housing, the impersonal mechanism of the market could not be used to minimize social dependencies. A magistrate's landlord could occupy a position of considerable power if he could terminate a lease in response to an unfavorable court decision. Where transportation was also scarce, as it was in most places, it was easily rationed according to the number of favors one could grant. Until the 1990s, to minimize these problems, most gov-

[27] The exchange took place during a tour of the court in May 1995. The author was present at the time. "Notes from U.S.-Africa Judicial Exchange," May 1995.

ernments provided judges with housing, utilities, and a vehicle with a driver. In a few places, senior magistrates were included in this arrangement as well. But lower-level magistrates were left to the mercy of the communities they served.

Pensions and retirement opportunities were another potential source of influence over the behavior of judges in Africa's weak economies. Until the end of the century, pensions were often a small proportion of salary, because governments did not automatically adjust them for inflation. Where alternative job options were few, judges and magistrates often worried about how they would provide for their families later in life. The desire to keep options open—for example, to remain on the list of those who might head a commission of inquiry—could produce reluctance to rule against the government or against important politicians.

There were other delicate ways to bring pressure to bear or make displeasure known. One magistrate in Uganda related a story about a predecessor who ruled against the town government in a decision. The courthouse was a short distance from a main road, but the track that led to it was deeply rutted and badly in need of regrading. In apparent retaliation for the magistrate's decision, the town authorities removed the road from the list of those to be repaired, rendering the courthouse nearly inaccessible. When a new magistrate arrived to replace the old one, the road was miraculously regraded.

Even architecture militated against judicial independence. Only in a few countries did the lower courts have their own facilities. Magistrates and judges alike worried that members of the public would take cues from the physical layout of the court and thus perceive the judiciary and the executive as one. In Botswana, magistrates long shared premises with police and the local administration. The same was true in parts of other eastern and southern common law countries. One Ugandan judge said he once presided over cases in a courtroom accessible only by walking through the police office and the prosecutor's office. Rents in local government offices could be raised or agreements revoked to protest decisions.

The biggest challenges were often social. As a resident magistrate already fairly high up in the hierarchy and based in a district center, the young Nyalali was protected from many of the pressures faced by those who lived in the villages they served. He was not immune, however. And he encountered some of the challenges very quickly, though in ways that eventually proved innocuous.

In a part of the world where the kinship ties and obligations people recognize range far beyond the nuclear family, most judiciaries maintained at least an informal policy of locating an officer away from his or her home community and away from the spouse's birthplace too. But unlike many magistrates, Nyalali was single when he entered the judiciary. And his situation potentially gave rise to a problem.

New to the community, with a pledge to refrain from too great an involvement in its affairs, Nyalali was content simply to devote himself to his job at first. Besides, the fierce reputation of the people in the Mara district made him suspect that a local marriage would not work. Family pressures built, however. Salome Madiya, Nyalali's mother, told her son to find a wife. Nyalali's new acquaintances in the other government services conspired to help out.

The regional commissioner reassured him, "People from Musoma are fine; I know a good family with a daughter you should meet. . . ." Another acquaintance said he too knew of a perfect woman, who was soon to attend teacher training school. Still a third said, "I know just the girl, but she is sick in hospital now, so we will have to visit." The regional commissioner was the first to provide an introduction, and the two men visited the parents, catching only a few words with the girl herself, by local custom. Afterward, when the regional commissioner spoke with Nyalali's other friends, everyone realized that each had the same woman in mind: Loyce Phares. They conspired to arrange a meeting out of the sight of Loyce's parents, by having Loyce's temporary job moved from the regional administration block to the magistrate's court. Within a month of meeting, in 1968, Loyce and Nyalali went their separate directions, she to teacher training school in Morogoro, in the central part of the country, and he to a new assignment in Tabora.

Eventually, Loyce secured a post at a school in Tabora, and the two married without having to face the potentially challenging social pressures that a sudden, extensive kin network could create for a young magistrate.[28] Loyce later observed that not all social pressures were handled so easily. "People did not always understand that the magistrate's job was to apply the law. Often what they did not like was the law, but they confused the law with the person making the decision."[29] She remarked that once when Nyalali had heard a sensitive case in Dar, a litigant had attempted to poison the children. The safety of the four sons and daughters—Emmanuel, Victor, Karoli, and Loulou—was a worry for the Nyalalis. Loyce pointed out that at least the judiciary had an informal policy of moving magistrates and their families after big cases, to protect them. Variants of this policy existed in other countries in the region as well. While members of the public viewed the transfers as evidence of political influence or reprisals within the judiciary, chief justices and registrars had to balance the risk of such criticism against the welfare of their officers.

Building friendships was a problem too. All the adults in the family had to watch their words carefully, to avoid giving the appearance of favor to anyone who might be a party to a case before the court. In the small communities in which most magistrates worked, interpersonal relations were especially delicate. In big cities, there would usually be another magistrate who could hear a

[28] Loyce Phares, interview with author, May 29, 1996.
[29] Ibid.

case, if a party turned out to be a friend, a child's playmate's parents, or the landlord and it was necessary to recuse one's self. In rural areas and secondary towns, someone from a neighboring jurisdiction would have to be brought in. That required time, and it trespassed on people's patience.

Loyce recalled those early days as difficult. "People would try to use you," she said. "One had to be polite, not dismissive, but without giving anything away." "Most of the time I stayed indoors. I tried to understand my position by imagining myself a magistrate without the power to charge." She got to know the other magistrates and their families and helped teach the younger wives "how to be careful and how to cope with their husbands' roles."[30]

FROM TABORA TO MZUMBE

In common law countries, the doctrine of *stare decisis* provides an accepted means of securing accountability to the law and helps ensure uniformity and stability. Quality control is also possible through the appeals process. People who think a judge has misunderstood the law, misapplied the law, or committed a mistake can ask a higher court to review the case. Outside of these forms, judges are supposed to refrain from influencing one another's decisions. They may share information about what the law says or seek advice on procedure, but a judge is not supposed to bring pressure on another to handle a case a particular way. But as in any heirarchy there were many subtle ways for colleagues to express displeasure and rid themselves of someone with whom they disagreed.

Now settled in Tabora, Nyalali continued to take the courts to the people, as he had started to do at Musoma. The region was dominated by the Nyamwezi people, who had developed a reputation as traders in the 1800s, transporting copper and ivory from as far away as Katanga, in the Democratic Republic of the Congo, to the Indian Ocean. Historically they had built ties with the Omanis, who had colonized the coast, and their trading partners established an outpost for Islam in the community. Christian missionaries had also settled there by the 1880s and created the schools so many leaders attended. By Nyalali's time, most people had taken up farming, and the region was known for tobacco production.

Nyalali's experiments met with a divided reception. Some judges and fellow magistrates approved, while others did not. Chief Justice Georges appeared deeply interested. At one point, he arranged to pause for a day while en route to Kigoma and met with Nyalali at his house to discuss administrative reform. They spoke for five hours. Nyalali remembered his interlocutor as a man of formidable intellect, with a genuine interest in the problems of the people and the institution.

[30] Ibid.

But shortly thereafter, there were troubling signs that not all was well. Nyalali received news of yet another transfer, this time to teach lay magistrates at the Institute of Development Management at Mzumbe, in Morogoro. The junior ranks of any hierarchy tend to worry about the significance of changes in assignments and tasks. In the judiciary, promotions, rotations, and transfers generally are protected from political interference, by giving the authority to make these decisions to judges and not to civil servants or politicians. But it was still possible for judicial officers to signal their displeasure with a colleague by influencing his appointment to an undesirable location, instead of rotating magistrates according to some sort of impersonal selection process. Already, by the late 1960s, junior personnel had decided that assignment to an undesirable place, a "punishing station," was a sign of disfavor. The magistrates thought they had detected a clear pattern. Their colleagues who were considered "problems" were posted to the south of the country, to Lindi or Mtwara, both reachable only by very poor roads, or to the magistrates' school at Mzumbe, which took them out of active judging.[31]

Nyalali's first thought was that his experiments had met with disapproval. His interpretation was not necessarily correct. Chief Justice Georges faced an immediate need to train an effective corps of primary court magistrates; he said he thought Nyalali was an innovator, and someone with imagination was essential to overhaul the program. Nyalali was unpersuaded, however. He asked that to save face with his colleagues the court first post him to Morogoro, the district in which the Mzumbe Institute of Development Management was located, and then transfer him to the school.

Years later, in speaking about these events, then–Chief Justice Nyalali's voice still betrayed the uncertainty and frustration of this period. He relived Chief Justice Georges's attempt to reassure him. Georges had said, "Someone who is punished may be given a chance to develop maturity." Was teaching itself bad? It provided an opportunity to mold magistrates.[32] Everyone would suffer from a half-hearted effort.

If the other punishing stations in the south were remote places, with very poor road access, Morogoro was the opposite. Centrally located at an important

---

[31] Throughout eastern and southern Africa, lay training for the lower levels of the judiciary generally took place in vocational schools like the one at Mzumbe. Uganda originally trained magistrates at a special school in Entebbe, until it constituted the Law Development Centre in 1968. The Kenya Institute for Public Administration offered an eleven-month program for people who aspired to be magistrates.

The Ford Foundation took a special interest in supporting these programs to help countries accommodate to changes introduced when the post of district commissioner was divided and its judicial functions were located in the courts. For example, in civil law Zaire (now called the Democratic Republic of the Congo), Ford helped found the École Nationale de Droit et d'Administration (ENDA) where the famous opposition politician Étienne Tshisekedi directed the program.

[32] As recounted by Francis L. Nyalali, interview with author, May 30, 1996.

crossroads where the routes to Dar and to Iringa, Mbeya, and Zambia intersect, news from many parts of the country would arrive quickly and there would be frequent visitors. The bustling market town also enjoyed a beautiful location. The steep sides of the Uluguru Mountains formed a beautiful backdrop and created a microclimate with an abundance of flowering plants. An avid gardener, Loyce could only have enjoyed this spot.

In the 1960s, Tanzania's training program for primary court magistrates taught the essentials of procedure, evidence, criminal law, and customary law.[33] Initially, the program was considerably shorter than those offered in other countries. Someone already serving as a magistrate enrolled in a three-month course, while new magistrates stayed at the Institute of Development Management for six months. By the 1990s, the course had lengthened to nine months, and outside evaluators recommended still further expansion to two years.[34]

As Chief Justice Georges predicted, Nyalali found that the work was absorbing. He discovered that the syllabus was, in his words, "horrible." "I told the CJ that the syllabus needed change, and I made a lot of recommendations, including proposals to clear up mis-statements of the law." At least as important, from the perspective of his own development, was the experience of having to read, speak, and think in Kiswahili. Nyalali had acquired his own education in English. He had a lot of learning to do to acquire the specialized Kiswahili law vocabulary required, and teaching forced that endeavor to proceed apace. As one of his first steps in office, Chief Justice Georges had financed the preparation of a Swahili law dictionary, which came in handy. "The time at Mzumbe enabled me to think about the law directly in Swahili," Nyalali recollected. "Before that, I had to think first in English, then in Swahili. The fluency I acquired served me well in difficult moments later."[35]

BUKOBA

Nyalali's experience at Mzumbe did not last long. In the late 1960s, the judiciary came under fire for a number of problems, including delay. A backlog of cases and an apparently tactless and overwhelmed magistrature had sparked public outcry in Bukoba, in the northwest, across Lake Victoria from Nyalali's original post at Musoma. The coffee and tea growers of Bukoba had a reputa-

[33] Tudor Jackson, *Guide to the Legal Profession in East Africa* (London: Sweet & Maxwell, 1970), p. 44.
[34] United Republic of Tanzania, Tanzania Financial and Legal Management Upgrading Project (FILMUP), "The Legal Sector in Tanzania: Interim Report of the Legal Task Force," unpublished report, Dar es Salaam, Tanzania, June 1995, pp. 26–27.
[35] Francis L. Nyalali, interview with author, May 30, 1996.

tion for litigiousness. "People loved going to court for the entertainment!," Nyalali commented. "As a result, the cases continued to pile up." Chief Justice Georges decided he had to replace the resident magistrate and deal with the congestion in the court. He turned to Nyalali, who had improved the rate of disposition of cases at each of the posts where he had served.

After a brief stay in Dar, to consult, Nyalali went out to see what could be done. First he sat down with the magistrates in the region and spoke with them. He reminded them that "all public servants are servants. In the colonial period, the court was seen as a way to terrorize people. In independent Tanzania, magistrates had to change that image, by treating people with respect. For example, an elderly witness had to be given a chair"[36] instead of being forced to stand, as was the practice. They had to work harder to dispose of cases. Nyalali also announced that he was inaugurating an information-gathering system. Every two weeks magistrates grades II and III would have to prepare a record indicating the status of their cases—how many were filed and how many were decided.

The first news from the new reporting system was discouraging. "We discovered that by working hard for two weeks, we finished 'x' number of cases. Of course, people would file fresh cases in the same period, and those would be 'y.' But 'y' was always greater than 'x,' and the backlog kept growing. We couldn't reduce the load! Just working hard was having no impact."

The next step was to make better use of the magistrates' workday. The limited availability of courtrooms meant that in areas with two or more magistrates, only one person at a time could hear cases. Nyalali proposed a shift system. One magistrate would work during the day, and another would hear cases in the evening, until 10:00 P.M. "The police were not happy with this arrangement, but the public could see that we were trying to serve them," Nyalali recollected.[37]

Nyalali next examined the types of disputes that brought people to court. Most cases were about trespassing on land, or other matters that easily could have been solved out of court. People appeared to be bringing cases for the fun of it, to tell stories. "I looked at the law and found that in the Criminal Procedure Code there was a provision regarding frivolous cases. It was possible to convict the accused but also to fine the complainant if the matter should have been handled out of court. We used that section." Nyalali waited for the High Court to overturn his judgment on appeal or to intervene. No reversal materialized. For the first time, the court decided more cases than were filed. "In the villages, people still remember that year. They laugh. The word was, 'If you go to Bukoba, you don't know whom Nyalali will fine, so let's settle it here!'"[38]

[36] Ibid.
[37] Ibid.
[38] Ibid.

Nyalali also began to develop a keen appreciation for the delicacy of the relationship between the judiciary and the other branches of government. If the courts performed their job poorly and people protested, then political officers were tempted to step into the void and assume functions that were properly judicial. That was happening in many parts of the country. Local leaders of the ruling political party sometimes established their own courts to hear cases.[39]

Charges of inefficiency could be abused, unfortunately. People who wanted to punish the magistrate for an unpopular decision or keep a particular judge from hearing a case sometimes lodged unfounded complaints about delay to win the transfer of a magistrate. Moreover, the mere allegation of bad management could serve as a publicly acceptable pretext for ousting the jurisdiction of the courts entirely. As Nyalali realized, the only way to protect the institution was to improve performance, keep careful records for documentation purposes, and try to inculcate a legal culture that made people hesitant to interfere with the jurisdiction of the courts.

[39] Rubin and Cotran, *Annual Survey of African Law*, 1969, p. 139.

Pluralism and Legitimacy

A MURAL GREETS people who ascend the public staircase in the High Court and Court of Appeal in Dar es Salaam. In vivid colors, the painting depicts the different sources of law important for Tanzania. One scene shows the resolution of a dispute by village elders. Another shows a Muslim *kadhi* court. In a third, colonial-era police chase a man and take him before an administrative officer. In a fourth, an African lawyer argues a case before an African bench in a European-style courtroom.

A version of the mural could have appeared on a court wall in almost any other part of the world. That the law was not all local, that it drew elements from many systems, did not make Tanzania unique. Nor did it make Africa so. Laws and legal systems mixed and spread both by imposition and by imitation. Colonialism had imposed statutes and procedures, but at the time of independence and thereafter, law reform commissions eagerly borrowed from other countries, as they fashioned responses to new legal problems or rethought some of the colonial-era statutes.

In some parts of the world, transplanted rules or codes, or even entire foreign systems of law, won wide adoption and presented few conflicts with existing legal principles.[1] But in Africa, norms from very different systems were uneasily juxtaposed, and race or ethnicity played a large role in determining which rules applied to which people. Most of those who were asked to respect the state law

---

[1] For a general discussion of the problem of legal transplants, see the writings of Alan Watson, *Legal Transplants: An Approach to Comparative Law* (Charlottesville: University Press of Virginia, 1974) and *Legal Origins and Legal Change* (London: Hambledon Press, 1991).

had no hand in choosing the rules that would govern them. As a result, the perceived conflict between systems of law often loomed large.

When then-Magistrate Nyalali visited the capital on his way to new posts, the mural on the High Court wall would remind him of the avid discussions taking place in legal circles about "the problem" of pluralism. By the mid-1950s, African and English jurists largely agreed that integration of different systems of law was an important aim. New countries in Africa should seek first to harmonize and eventually to unify competing legal norms. The practical demands this challenge created were considerable, and the regional law conferences of the 1960s tended to focus on these goals in an effort to share ideas and experiences.[2] In 1963, with the help of the Ford Foundation, the important African Conference on Local Courts and Customary Law brought together a large, international group of lawyers and scholars in Dar es Salaam to discuss the subject.

Legal pluralism created three main difficulties for judicial independence. First, where the existence of alternative legal norms entailed the creation of parallel tribunals, such as completely separate customary courts, it could be difficult to carve out a place for the state courts in the popular political imagination. Judicial independence had importance only for people who anticipated that they might use the state courts. The courts would have no salience whatsoever for people who resolved all of their disputes in other ways and thought that they and their neighbors could continue to do so. Common law magistrates and judges had to win some indefinable minimum share of the market for disputes if they hoped to cultivate public support.

Second, where parallel justice systems existed, it was possible for politicians and other litigants to shop for a forum in which they could win a case. Forum shopping is a common practice in most of the world, but jurists usually try to limit the opportunity for lawyers to engage in it when the motive is to find a sympathetic judge or a more favorable body of law, instead of avoiding delay in a congested court. The possibility of controlling the assignment of a case to a judge undermined impartiality. It opened up the prospect of political manipulation, not necessarily of the judge, but of the judicial process. And it threatened the legitimacy of all dispute resolution, not just the common law courts.

Finally, legal scholars and judges were concerned that where people accepted one set of legal norms in their everyday lives, yet found their disputes adjudicated according to the terms of another, the perceived injustice would cause disaffection.[3] Yet where there was deep legal pluralism, the task of inte-

---

[2] The relationship between customary law and European law was the focus of international conferences in London (1956 and 1960), Dakar (1962), Dar es Salaam (1963), Venice (1963), and Ife (1964). See T. W. Bennett and T. Vermeulen, "Codification of Customary Law," *Journal of African Law*, 24, 2 (1980).
[3] A contemporary treatment of these themes appears in Gordon R. Woodman, "Legal Pluralism and the Search for Justice," *Journal of African Law*, 40, 2 (1996), pp. 152–167.

gration would have to proceed in phases to preserve fairness, some argued. In the short term, it meant both defining spheres of influence, where necessary, and determining how to resolve conflict between laws or norms in ways that would win hearts and minds. In the long run, it meant finding and developing shared principles and procedures.

That the courts appear to be "just" was an important objective made less easily attainable by deep legal pluralism. How did the jurists perceive the choices open to them?

THE COMMON LAW

At the time of independence, for most of the countries of eastern and southern Africa state law was a version of the English common law. In a general sense, the common law referred to a legal tradition that treated the precedents embodied in judicial decisions as law alongside the statutes and the doctrines of equity. In discussions among lawyers, it also meant the part of that tradition that was "judge-made" law—the principles, reasoning, "tests," and criteria embodied in the rulings of upper courts.

Reception statutes adopted in the colonial period, and usually ratified after independence, effected the transfer of laws from one country to another. For most of the countries in the eastern and southern Africa regions, this legislation stated that the statutes of general application, the common law, and doctrines of equity in force in England on a prescribed date would have force in the new location. The colonial government would "receive" them and use them as the law in force. Once established, these traditions acquired a life of their own through legislation and the development of a body of local precedent.[4]

Yet there was still some mixing of the major international legal traditions. If English history had produced comparatively greater faith in judges than the continental tradition had, that confidence had not always extended to those who served in the colonies. In the early colonial era, judges and magistrates were often district officers who had little legal training, operating in areas where they were often avowedly unfamiliar with local norms. In administrative circles a consensus developed that some guidance was necessary to help them in their jobs, especially with regard to interpretation of local traditions. "Codes," including the codification of customary law, had considerable appeal, although they typically were associated with the civil law tradition.

---

[4] On reception statutes see Robert B. Seidman, "The Reception of English Law in Colonial Africa Revisited," *Eastern Africa Law Review*, 2, 1 (1969), pp. 47–86; and on the general topic in a European context see Alan Watson, *Sources of Law, Legal Change, and Ambiguity* (Philadelphia: University of Pennsylvania Press, 1984).

These matters first arose in the context of India in the 1800s. There, responsibility for design of the legal system fell to a group of men who held views not widely shared in official circles back in England. The philosopher-cum-political economist, Jeremy Bentham, considered a bit of a crank by the cognoscenti, offered his help. In England, Bentham had championed efforts to rationalize the law. Indeed, it was he who coined the term *codification*.[5] His views met with rejection in London, but they gained currency abroad, partly because of the important role of administrators in resolving disputes in the early years. For example, Lord Macaulay, who wrote the Indian penal code, had generally opposed Bentham's utilitarian ideas at home, but he shared the philosopher's thoughts on law in the colonies.[6] Another Bentham protégé, James Fitzjames Stephen, played a major role in drafting additional statutes, which he hoped would provide administrators with a clear and sensible set of rules and curtail both the exercise of discretion by judges and opportunities for manipulation by lawyers. He wrote at the time, "Well-designed legislation is the only possible remedy against quibbles and chicanery. All the evils which are dreaded . . . from legal practitioners can be averted in this manner."[7]

Several of the Indian codes won adoption unmodified in Africa, where they prevailed over English precedent on the matters they addressed. Typically, the Indian penal code and the evidence and procedure codes were part of the package. As a result, the "English law" of Africa was different from what was practiced and taught in London; matters subject to the common law in England often were regulated by statute abroad—and frequently by laws that simplified or altered principles found in precedent.

In southern Africa, including Botswana, Zimbabwe, Lesotho, Swaziland, and Namibia, as well as South Africa, the Roman-Dutch legal tradition, part of the civil law family, coexisted alongside the common law. Although judicial institutions operated much as they did in the English common law tradition, and although significant portions of commercial and constitutional law, evidence, and procedure bore the English stamp, the courts in these countries could draw on concepts from the civil law when they chose.[8]

The English common law continued to hold several attractions at independence. One of the most important was largely emotive. What most of the nationalist movements sought was equal treatment under the law. They wanted the same law that applied to the citizens of the colonizer to be applied to

---

[5] Sanford Kadish, "The Model Penal Code's Historical Antecedents," *Rutgers Law Journal*, 19 (1988), p. 522.
[6] Eric Stokes, *The English Utilitarians and India* (Oxford: Clarendon, 1959), p. 191.
[7] As quoted in Bijay Kisor Acharyya, *Codification in British India*. Tagore Law Lectures, 1912. (Calcutta: Banerji & Sons, 1914), p. 101.
[8] H. J. Erasmus, "Roman Law in South Africa Today," *South African Law Journal*, 106, 4 (1989), p. 669.

Africans. In the settler colonies of East Africa, the resort to the Indian codes had provoked resentment among some, including many Europeans, who felt these laws inferior and outdated. Most of the codes simplified procedures and shed safeguards present in English law. The criminal code incorporated elements of Hindu and Muslim law and thus was tailored to India, even though some claimed it misstated the principles in these traditions.[9] In some areas, codes from Queensland, considered closer to English law, replaced the Indian codes. But throughout the region, new African judges were inclined to share the view that a greater role for the common law was important, both to secure parity and to permit gradual adaptation to social and economic change.

There were other practical reasons why preserving space for the common law and leaving some matters to judges to decide seemed sensible. Developing new statutes to replace those in place at the time of independence or drafting comprehensive sets of rules would require considerable expertise, time, and money. All were in short supply. In the 1960s, with only a few trained African lawyers, governments would have to import drafters from other countries. That surely would provoke concern about the degree to which legislation would reflect local aspirations, norms, and principles. Careful review of existing laws and revision or reform was a process certain to take several years at least, if experiences in industrial countries with similar exercises were any guide. The money these efforts would require had urgent competing uses.

Although in theory, new leaders could decide to adopt a different tradition, in practice, no one bothered to think in such grand terms. Dramatically changing the character of a legal system was an expensive and difficult thing to do, and there was already too much on the post-independence agenda. As a result, where the French had established a presence, a distrust of judges, part of the French revolutionary tradition, followed. Most of the accouterments of the civil law tradition came along too, including a preference for comprehensive codes and the belief that judges should have as little capacity to interpret and make law as possible. Where the English moved in, with their slightly greater trust in the judiciary and their affection for custom, the courts were given a bit more latitude, and precedent had the status of law, alongside legislation and administrative rulings.

In the end, most of the countries of eastern and southern Africa settled on incremental change. New legislatures ratified the earlier reception statutes. The codes that existed at the time of independence usually continued in effect until legislatures got around to revising them, which they were able to do only piecemeal.

Thus, laws that originated in Europe would continue to be part of the living tradition in Africa. Years later, when Nyalali became chief justice, he noticed

---

[9] Acharyya, *Codification in British India*, pp. 40–41.

that all the photographs and portraits of colonial-era judges had disappeared from the walls of the court. He considered that odd. Tanzania's experience was linked with the histories of other communities through the common law. Although there was much that did not merit celebration, it was important for people to remember the many currents that had come together to create the rules and norms they lived by. "I had the staff find the pictures in the basement and dust them off. Then we hung the portraits on the walls again. We need to confront our history and learn what it has to tell us, not pretend that it did not happen."[10] Later, in a famous land case, he wrote, "An understanding of our country's past is crucial to a better understanding of our present," and added that it helped a society avoid repeating mistakes.[11]

CUSTOMARY LAWS AND THE COMMON LAW

The common law tradition existed alongside a number of legal systems, some of local origin, but others, such as *shari'a*, also of foreign provenance. The common law bore similarities to aspects of these other systems. Arguably, it was itself a type of customary law, although it was written down whereas local customs were not. Legal scholar A. W. Brian Simpson, an early dean of the Faculty of Law at the University of Ghana, once suggested that the common law and customary systems shared many characteristics. The common law "consists of a body of practices observed and ideas received by a caste of lawyers, these ideas being used by them as providing guidance in what is conceived to be the rational determination of disputes," he wrote. "The ideas and practices which comprise the common law are customary in that their status is thought to be dependent upon conformity with the past, and they are traditional in the sense that they are transmitted through time as a received body of knowledge and learning."[12]

In what ways, if any, were African legal systems different in their general character from the common law? Few subjects in the study of African law attracted as much attention, confusion, and debate during the twentieth century as this one. The stereotype of customary law as a set of unwritten rules passed down through the generations gradually had yielded to other conceptions—and often to new overgeneralizations. Empirical investigation revealed considerable variety. In many systems, dispute resolution consisted mainly of

[10] Francis L. Nyalali, interview with author, March 16, 1996.
[11] *Attorney General v. Lohay Akonaay and Another*, Court of Appeal of Tanzania at Arusha, Civil Appeal No. 31 of 1994, 2 LRC 399.
[12] A. W. Brian Simpson, "The Common Law and Legal Theory," in Alison Dundes-Renteln and Alan Dundes, eds., *Folk Law: Essays in the Theory and Practice of Lex Non Scripta* (Madison: University of Wisconsin Press, 1994), pp. 133–134.

procedures designed to facilitate negotiated settlement. In others, adjudication through the application of rules to a set of facts was more common. Thus, in some settings, dispute resolution was largely consensual while in others it more closely resembled impersonal application of rules by a neutral third party on the model of a court.[13] In very general terms, the customary law differed from the common law mainly in the kinds of institutional and political arrangements that governed its development, its concomitantly more local character, and the fact that it was not written down but had to be remembered.

At the time of independence, most people relied on customary law and on customary forums for resolving disputes, or on informal means of dispute resolution. They asked kin, neighbors, or elders and headmen to help resolve common conflicts, such as matrimonial disputes, vandalism by wayward youth, and the occasional brawl. In some instances, they turned to the chairmen of that ubiquitous social club, the drinking group. Even in the mid-1990s, the fragmentary evidence available suggested that most village and neighborhood disputes were handled informally or in old ways, not through the common law courts.[14] These studies also revealed that most people thought these forums effective for resolving the kinds of matters taken to them.

Islamic law differed from customary systems in several respects. Like the English common law, it was imported. It arrived in East Africa with Arab and Persian traders before the twelfth century. These traders established more than thirty major towns on the Indian Ocean coast. They also created ties inland that traversed much of East Africa and drew ivory, slaves, and other commodities. After a turbulent period from about 1500 to 1650, when the Portuguese battled for control of the trade routes, the Omanis reestablished Arab hegemony until the British displaced them. In law, the influence of the Persian Gulf persisted, even after trade diminished.

In most of eastern and southern Africa, the Muslim communities that took root in successive waves of migration and trade brought diverse beliefs, not a single system of legal and religious thought. The new brotherhoods, schools, and sects won growing numbers of converts in the twentieth century. Intermarriage and social interaction probably explained part of the increase. The English colonizers also aided the expansion by according more power and prestige to the emirs or sultans on Africa's Indian Ocean coast than to indigenous inhabitants, a gesture that led some ordinary people to convert. Conversion sometimes also signified resistance to English colonial rule. Initially, the Shafi'i school of law prevailed, alongside the smaller Hanafi, both

---

[13] For one source on what distinguishes a court from other forums for dispute resolution, see Martin Shapiro, *Courts: A Comparative and Political Analysis* (Chicago: University of Chicago Press, 1987).
[14] Jennifer Widner, Public Attitudes Surveys, 1995–96.

part of the Sunni tendency within Islam. Sufism spread somewhat later in Tanzania and in East Africa, more generally.[15]

Under Islamic law, the *kadhi* courts were the first to hear a dispute. Western sociologists such as Max Weber once deemed that religious values, politics, or other beliefs drove decisions in these courts, instead of the formal rationality that allegedly prevailed in European legal systems. In Western academic discourse, the term *kadhi*, or *qadi*, usually became a synonym for partisanship or bending to community pressure. For example, the American jurist Justice Felix Frankfurter once casually proclaimed, "This is a court of review, not a tribunal unbounded by rules. We do not sit like a Kadhi under a tree dispensing justice according to considerations of individual expediency."[16] Later, careful comparison suggested that the assumed differences in the way judges made decisions in *kadhi* courts and local-level common law courts were largely illusory.[17] *Kadhi* courts appeared to place more emphasis on the personal attributes and backgrounds of litigants at a time when Western courts tried to deemphasize these things and to focus on what happened in a single event. However, in practice judges in the lower levels of most courts of general jurisdiction often took the personal attributes into account and also tried to effect reconciliation, or convince the parties to bargain with each other, before moving to trial. Moreover, the *kadhis* applied principles across cases, even if these usually reflected local standards of fairness, and they followed certain consistent lines of inquiry. The court was not arbitrary, as the Western use of the term often implied.

Under Islam, judges typically have little discretion to develop the law.[18] The law is supposed to rest on the legal pronouncements of the Koran and the traditions embodied in the *hadith*, the stories or traditions that became fundamental texts by the tenth century. Judges confine themselves mainly to the application of these legal rules to the facts of an individual case. Points of unsettled law can be referred to higher authority within each legal school, whose senior members could issue opinions, or *fatwas*. This process of appeal operates much as a dispute about a religious matter within Catholicism might be referred to Rome.

In most parts of Africa, Islamic law had a special status, different from cus-

---

[15] J. N. D. Anderson, *Islamic Law in Africa* (London: Frank Cass, 1955), p. 133; Jamal J. Nasir, *The Islamic Law of Personal Status* (London: Graham and Trotman/Kluwer, 1986); Ira M. Lapidus, *A History of Islamic Societies* (Cambridge: Cambridge University Press, 1988); August H. Nimitz, Jr., *Islam and Politics in East Africa: The Sufi Order in Tanzania* (Minneapolis: University of Minnesota Press, 1980).

[16] *Terminiello v. Chicago*, 337 U.S. 1, 11 (1949).

[17] For example, see the study of *kadhi* courts in Morocco by Lawrence Rosen, *The Anthropology of Justice: Law as Culture in Islamic Society* (Cambridge: Cambridge University Press, 1989); the book review by Sally Engle Merry, "Review of Lawrence Rosen's *The Anthropology of Justice*," *Columbia Law Review*, 91 (December 1990), pp. 2311–2327; and Susan F. Hirsch, *Pronouncing and Persevering: Gender and the Discourse of Disputing in an African Islamic Court* (Chicago: University of Chicago Press, 1998), pp. 116–125.

[18] An interesting treatment of this subject appears in Martin Shapiro, "Islam and Appeal," *California Law Review*, 68, 2 (1980), pp. 350–381.

tomary law. Nyalali observed that "Islamic law . . ., by reason of its world-wide religious validity, cannot be integrated with customary law."[19] On the mainland it applied to family matters only, as it did in other countries of the region. But on Zanzibar, Islamic law applied more broadly to all matters not covered by statute. In 1964, when Tanganyika united with Zanzibar to form the United Republic of Tanzania, the union agreement created a special court for the predominantly Muslim island. Zanzibar retained its own chief justice and its own court system. *Kadhi* courts acquired exclusive jurisdiction in aspects of personal law or family law, such as marriage, divorce, and inheritance, with appeals made to the Zanzibar High Court, which comprised one judge sitting with four sheiks.[20] For other matters, Zanzibar continued to operate its own parallel system of common law courts, which mirrored the organization of courts on the mainland but made reference to Islamic law, except where statutes governed. The exact terms of the relationship between the courts, repeatedly modified, always appeared ambiguous.[21]

For new governments, the policy question was how to meld these very different legal systems—customary, religious, and common law—into a shared set of norms without creating injustice. People developed settled expectations on the basis of one or another system of law. They built their life plans in the faith that the rules they had known would continue in force. To ensure fairness, reformers had to avoid retrospective application of new standards, as well as sudden changes that were hard for the people affected to learn about.

THE CHALLENGE OF INTEGRATION

New leaders had several decisions to make. The first concerned the status of customary law. Should new governments continue to recognize the customary law or should customary law be abolished or limited? Second, how would disputes be heard? Countries could entrench legal dualism by creating parallel court systems, allocating citizens to different forums based on ethnic heritage. They could allow a limited right of appeal from customary forums to state courts, the common law courts. Or they could abolish formal customary adjudication of disputes in integrate the customary courts into the state court sys-

---

[19] Francis L. Nyalali, "Speech on Legal Reform for Democracy in Tanzania," Delivered at the Centre of African Studies, School of Oriental and African Studies, University of London, London, England, October 5, 1994.
[20] United Kingdom, Overseas Development Administration, "Draft Report on the Tanzanian Judiciary," Report of a commission chaired by Mark Bomani (London: Overseas Development Administration, 1994).
[21] Rainer Michael Bierwagen and Chris Maina Peter, "Administration of Justice in Tanzania and Zanzibar: A Comparison of Two Judicial Systems in One Country," *International and Comparative Law Quarterly*, 38 (April 1989), pp. 395–412.

tem. The third set of choices concerned the method judges in the state courts should use to choose which customary system applied in any given case. What principles should govern the choice of law that applied in a dispute? The fourth set of choices focused on the best way to recognize the principles and rules in customary law, if and when the need arose. Allowing the state courts to consider expert testimony and other evidence, and then to devise their own statements, was one option. Codifying customary laws and turning them into statute was another possibility. Periodically restating the customary laws was a third alternative for providing guidance to judges.

With little hesitation, most countries quickly imposed some important limits on the application of customary law. For example, customary law would not apply to criminal offenses. In an era of increasing mobility, it would be too easy for someone to run afoul of a local provision of which he or she had no knowledge and face restrictions on liberty or other stiff penalties. The sentiment at early African judicial conferences mirrored the antipathy many American legal reformers had once felt toward "common law crimes"—defined mainly through court decisions of which newcomers might be unaware.[22] There was broad agreement that socioeconomic change made a general, written criminal code essential, for the sake of justice.[23]

Moreover, few customary systems dealt extensively with commerce, administration, and many other aspects of contemporary life. In these areas, governments had few qualms about saying that national legislation would apply. It was mainly in the land law, some aspects of noncontractual liability or tort ("delict," in Roman-Dutch southern Africa), and personal and family law—inheritance, succession, marriage, and divorce—where people had formed stable expectations and customary principles remained important.

Integration of the Courts

Preservation of legal dualism won little support in the independence era.[24] Separate customary courts were deeply unpopular with nationalist movements,

---

[22] Concern about "common law crimes" in the United States was a powerful motivating factor behind one of the first American code proposals, advanced by Edward Livingstone for the state of Louisiana, a civil law enclave, in 1826. Kadish, "The Model Penal Code's Historical Antecedents," p. 525.

[23] William T. McClain, "Recent Changes in African Local Courts and Customary Law," *Howard Law Journal*, 10 (1964), pp. 187–226; and *Record of the Proceedings of the African Conference on Local Courts and Customary Law*, Dar es Salaam, Tanganyika, September 8–18, 1963 (Dar es Salaam, Tanganyika: Faculty of Law, University of Dar es Salaam, 1964), pp. 24–25.

[24] Unification had taken place much earlier in the civil law systems of Francophone Africa. The belief of common law jurists was that this policy had come at the price of sacrificing "African elements" or principles of law. See McClain, "Recent Changes in African Local Courts and Customary Law," pp. 187–226; and Taslim O. Elias, *Judicial Process in the Newer Commonwealth* (Lagos, Nigeria: University of Lagos Press, 1990).

which wanted equal justice for all. In later years they also attracted scathing criticism from scholars for having deepened and perpetuated ethnic differences and distracted people from problems of poverty, which should have mattered much more. Legal professionals disliked them because they created an opening for forum shopping and undermined the perceived impartiality of the justice system as a whole, in consequence.[25]

But this modernist consensus masked significant practical problems. The state-run common law courts were often distant, and they were expensive to use. The procedures were unfamiliar to the majority of people. Thus, even where legislatures decided that disputes under customary law should be heard in the common law courts, the need for community forums, or for "bringing justice to the people," remained. Access to justice was a continuing concern, and the preservation of customary courts or equivalent institutions helped solve that problem.

New legislatures responded to these dilemmas in a variety of ways. Tanzania eliminated "native courts" at the time of independence and allowed disputes about customary obligations to be heard in magistrates' courts. The government also created Arbitration Tribunals.[26] In these neighborhood tribunals, five lay mediators, community members, sought to resolve disputes with reference to customary law. They emphasized compromise and settlement.

Uganda and Kenya eventually moved to an integrated system too, while Zambia and Zimbabwe created special courts, managed by the ministry of justice instead of the judiciary, to hear customary law matters, though with the possibility of appeal to a district court. The Botswana government allowed its long-established system of customary courts, staffed by chiefs and headmen, to continue, but circumscribed its jurisdiction and permitted appeal to the common law courts. By contrast, Malawi set up a system of traditional courts, staffed by appointees of the minister for justice, which remained outside the administrative purview of the judiciary. In 1969, it eliminated all appeal from these courts to the common law system.[27]

Much later, in Uganda, the government of Yoweri Museveni created local council courts to restore some of the functions once played by customary courts. These "resistance council courts," later called "local council courts," were staffed by elected representatives of a village or community. They had jurisdiction to hear petty disputes, and they were considered important because they created a forum

---

[25] *Record of the Proceedings of the African Conference on Local Courts and Customary Law*, p. 12.

[26] The government substituted Ward Tribunals for Arbitration Tribunals in 1985 and created a right of appeal to the primary courts and finally to the district courts on points of law.

[27] See Boyce Wanda, "The Role of the Traditional Courts in Malawi," in Peter Nanyenya Takirambudde, ed., *The Individual under African Law*, Proceedings of the First All-Africa Law Conference, October 11–16, 1981 (Kwaluseni, Swaziland: University of Swaziland Department of Law, 1982), pp. 76–92

that was accessible, inexpensive, and easily understood. In practice, some worked well while others did not. Joe Oloka-Onyango, a member of the Makerere University law faculty, wrote that in the "RC courts," ignorance of the law and bias were troublesome, most charged fees even though they were supposed to be voluntary, and women's interests often suffered.[28] Judges also grew concerned that in practice the RC courts often took on serious matters outside their jurisdiction, which brought them into conflict with the courts of judicature. As elsewhere, the relationship of the common law courts to these parallel systems remained ambiguous and fraught with tension. Nonetheless, for many types of problems, the RC courts provided a convenient, quick, cheap way to resolve a dispute.

Choice and Conflict

When common law courts heard cases brought under customary law, how would judges know what the relevant customary system was? And in cases where it wasn't clear which legal system should apply, what guidelines should judges follow?

In 1963, participants in the African Conference on Local Courts and Customary Law suggested there were three ways to solve this problem. The first was to lay down statutory rules directing the choice of law. The second option was to draft a statute which stated that the most "appropriate" law should apply and to offer courts very general guidance which judges should follow in making these determinations. The third was to let the courts work it out by themselves.[29]

Variations on the second option won widespread adoption, although a few countries, such as Kenya, went different routes. In the early years, the race or ethnicity of the parties mainly determined which law would apply.[30] But later, legislators and judges began to modify these grounds. Courts began to take into account the lifestyles of the parties, the place where the problem arose, the kind of transaction involved, and other considerations.[31] The model of private international law again offered a guide. In private international law, when litigants come from two different countries, the choice of law is based on a judgment about the system of law the parties "would consider reasonable to apply in the circumstances of the case."[32] Many African courts also began to focus on "reasonable expectations under the circumstances," instead of making an automatic link to a body of law based on determination of ethnic origin.

---

[28] John-Jean Barya and Joe Oloka-Onyango, "Popular Justice and Resistance Committee Courts in Uganda," Report for the Centre for Basic Research and the Friedich Ebert Foundation, Kampala, Uganda, 1994, passim.

[29] Proceedings of the African Conference on Local Courts and Customary Law, pp. 39–40.

[30] T. W. Bennett, "Conflict of Laws—The Application of Customary Law and the Common Law in Zimbabwe," International and Comparative Law Quarterly, 30 (January 1981), p. 67.

[31] Ibid., p. 87.

[32] Ibid., p. 66.

Acceptance of this system was not universal. In the closing years of the century, for example, judges interpreted the practice of visiting relatives in home areas as implicit acceptance of the community and its customary laws. They reasoned that the man or woman who stayed in town and did not return home had severed ties with kin and that state law therefore should govern his or her actions. But feminist lawyers argued that people should not have to surrender what they viewed as the "good aspects" of their heritage, the practice of visiting relatives, in order to escape the customary law and participate in national life under the common law. They urged alternative guidelines.[33]

These choice of law problems provide insight into the reasons why chief justices expressed particular concern about the effects of legal pluralism on judicial legitimacy. A distinguished South African expert on customary law, T. W. Bennett, remarked that the "discretion to decide which system of law to apply carries greater responsibility than courts usually bear." The risks of creating injustice were considerable. Bennett offered a telling example, the more poignant because of the frequency with which like fact patterns arose throughout eastern and southern Africa in the 1990s. "If a man were to have intercourse with an unmarried woman against her will, and to use violence to achieve this end, such action might well be considered to be criminal under the common law and delictual [subject to the law of torts] under customary law." He continued, "In the former instance, the common law of rape would be applied and, if the accused were convicted, he would face capital punishment." By contrast, "[i]f customary law were applied, he would be required to pay damages."[34]

These difficulties were common. In Botswana, as elsewhere, the choice of law affected the rights a person had and the defenses available. Under customary law, a girl's father could sue for damages caused by the seduction of a daughter. Roman-Dutch law recognized the same tort, but the woman, not the father, was the party who had standing to sue. Therefore, it was possible for the defendant to be sued twice, once by the father in customary law and once by the woman in the Roman-Dutch common law.[35]

Judicial Development, Codification, and Restatement
If state court judges were expected to apply customary law, then how would they know what the customary rules were? Much debate focused on this problem.

---

[33] Monica Muhoja, a leader of the Women's Legal Aid Centre, Tanzania, interview with author at the annual meeting of the African Society for International and Comparative Law, Harare, Zimbabwe, July 1999.

[34] Bennett, "Conflict of Laws—The Application of Customary Law and the Common Law in Zimbabwe," pp. 73–74.

[35] Bojosi Othlogile of the University of Botswana Department of Law, interview with author, Ann Arbor, Michigan, Spring 1998.

One option was to let the judges do the work. That is, courts could try to identify or recognize the pertinent customary law provisions that applied in a particular case. Judges and lawyers usually begin by drawing an analogy. They asked how they would learn about the substance of a foreign law if faced with a case where the rules from another country applied. The most common response in that kind of situation was to bring in an expert witness to testify about the law and to "prove" the law in this way, as a matter of fact.[36]

But as in any trial that uses expert witnesses in the United States or England, questions of partisanship inevitably arose. It was difficult to ensure a "fair" or impartial assessment of the law. Experts were not always unbiased. A third alternative was to refer to texts and codes drawn up by scholars and lawyers. In the colonial period, anthropologists and lawyers had studied the disposition of cases in many communities and had written down the rules that guided judgments. There were also official studies conducted by the anthropological research branch of the chief commissioner's office, often based on reports from elders.

There was one final way in which the courts could recognize a rule of customary law. In *Angu v. Attah*, England's Privy Council, which long heard appeals from colonial courts and some of their postcolonial successors, stated that although all rules had to be established first by calling witnesses and proving the law as fact, if a rule had been proved in this way many times over, the court could simply take judicial notice.[37] In parts of West Africa, it appeared that judges sometimes would consider proof in court on only one other occasion as sufficient. In other words, they started to treat proof of customary law as they would precedent. Scholars worried that this practice might well produce increasing divergence between the "lived" customary law and the caricature of custom the courts used in the interests of efficiency and predictability.[38]

There were few empirical studies of the actual practice magistrates and judges followed to recognize principles of customary law. Casual observers and

---

[36] Robert Seidman, "Rules of Recognition in the Primary Courts of Zimbabwe: On Lawyers' Reasonings and Customary Law," *International and Comparative Law Quarterly*, 32 (October 1983), p. 882. When independence leaders got wind of this analogy, they were scandalized. Why should the norms of a country's own peoples be considered "foreign law," or be treated simply as "fact"? Ghana's Kwame Nkrumah spoke out in an opening ceremony at the Faculty of Law at the University of Ghana in 1962, announcing, "There is a ringing challenge to African lawyers today. African law in Africa was declared foreign law for the convenience of the colonial administration. . . . African law had to be proved by experts." He went on, "But no law can be foreign to its own land and country, and African lawyers, particularly in the independent African states, must quickly find a way to reverse this judicial travesty." Kwame Nkrumah, first president of Ghana, as quoted in McClain, "Recent Changes in African Local Courts and Customary Law," p. 212.

[37] Gordon Woodman, "Some Realism about Customary Law—The West African Experience," in Alison Dundes-Renteln and Alan Dundes, eds., *Folk Law: Essays in the Theory and Practice of Lex Non Scripta* (Madison: University of Wisconsin Press, 1994), p. 85.

[38] Ibid., p. 90.

the one or two scholarly studies extant suggested that proof of customary law was often a bit looser than the official procedures required. Among the bases for choice were "previous decisions of the superior courts on questions of customary law; personal knowledge of the judges; judges' opinions of what was reasonable; and assertions by litigants when not effectively challenged."[39]

All these methods were open to the same criticism. David N. Smith, an American legal scholar who participated in some of the early "law and development" scholarship in Africa, hazarded the guess that when magistrates applied "customary law" by consulting texts, they inevitably ended up applying an older, outdated version. Moreover, because of their reliance on these sources, they tended to favor rural values instead of urban. By contrast, he found that in urban "customary" forums or neighborhood courts, if litigants came from two different cultural backgrounds, presiding officers tended to start with the facts, look for common principles in the two traditions, and in the process of making the decision, mold an "urban common law" that responded to new situations.[40] Differences rapidly developed between judicial customary law and the customary law people used in their communities to resolve disputes.

An alternative to these methods was to transform the customary law into statute — that is, to codify the customary laws of a country. In plural political systems, where legislative elections were freely contested, this option seemed the more democratic approach. But it harbored dangers of its own.

Proponents of codes could point to experiments in the United States, where states evolved their own rules and created a complicated legal patchwork. In the years just before the first meetings on codification of customary laws in Africa, many of the brightest American legal minds urged the creation of criminal and commercial codes in the United States. They argued that codes would enhance the clarity and predictability of the law. They worried about the messiness of the common law, judge-made law, which sacrificed uniformity and predictability for flexibility. They also believed that codes would shift power from unelected judges to democratically elected legislatures, which would be able to make important policy decisions about which elements of custom or common law to enshrine in statute. Finally, they thought the process of formulating the codes would provide an opportunity for revision and reform in the light of changing social and economic circumstances.[41]

In these American discussions the critics of codification also weighed in.

---

[39] Gordon Woodman, "Customary Law, State Courts, and the Notion of Institutionalization of Norms in Ghana and Nigeria," in Anthony Allott and Gordon R. Woodman, eds., *People's Law and State Law* (Dordrecht: Foris Publications, 1985), p. 147.

[40] David N. Smith, "Man and Law in Urban Africa: A Role for Customary Courts in the Urbanization Process," *American Journal of Comparative Law*, 20 (1972), pp. 240–242.

[41] Frank Remington, "The Future of the Substantive Criminal Law Codification Movement: Theoretical and Practical Concerns," *Rutgers Law Journal*, 19 (1988), pp. 867–895.

They worried that the objective of clarity was unachievable. The difficulty of envisioning all the possible circumstances that might arise in the real world meant that the rules the codifiers laid down would inevitably prove too broad or too narrow. It was better to let a judge make adjustments in the application of statutes and past decisions, they felt, than to constrain judicial decision making in ways that might produce unfairness. Judge-made rules were also more flexible than authoritative codes, which would require periodic, expensive overhauls.

If anything, the advantages of codification were more muted in African contexts, and the disadvantages were more serious. Customary law was "living law." It changed constantly. In some countries ordinary people implicitly acknowledged this characteristic by prefacing their statements of the law with the phrase, "during my times."[42] But codification inevitably froze the law and limited its adaptability. Moreover, some systems of customary law more strongly resembled mediation than they did adjudication, and it was difficult to identify hard-and-fast rules. Decisions were negotiated settlements. The law was "process," not a set of rules.

The arguments against codification were even stronger, because the recording techniques gave pride of place to interpretations of custom held only by a few, instead of being representative of the common understanding in the community. The recording process usually entailed interviews with chiefs and consultation with special panels of local experts organized by district governments. What customary law was alleged to say depended very much on who was asked to participate.[43]

Finally, although codification could increase the public's ability to know the law in theory, its practical application in Africa easily might have the opposite effect. As one customary law expert later pointed out, traditionally learning about the customary law was part of informal childhood education.[44] When governments tried to codify customary laws and reformed the laws as part of their enterprise, ordinary people might find it very difficult to learn what the new laws said. Low literacy levels and the inevitable problems of making legal materials available would severely limit publicity and cause injustice. Reflecting on choices confronting countries in French-speaking Africa, legal scholar Jeswald Salacuse worried that when countries such as Côte d'Ivoire sought to simultaneously unify and modernize family laws by imposing a set of common principles, the result could be "fantasy law, harsh social dislocation, and even the general discrediting of the legal system in the eyes of the people."[45]

[42] Bojosi Othlogile of University of Botswana Department of Law, interview with author, Ann Arbor, Michigan, Spring 1998.
[43] Martin Chanock, *Law, Custom, and Social Order* (Cambridge: Cambridge University Press, 1985), pp. 21–22.
[44] T. W. Bennett and T. Vermeulen, "Codification of Customary Law," *Journal of African Law*, 24, 2 (1980), pp. 209–210.
[45] Jeswald W. Salacuse, "Modernization of Law in French-Speaking Africa: Fantasy or Revolution?" *African Law Studies*, preliminary issue (January 1969), p. 72.

In some countries, such as Tanzania and Ethiopia, governments decided the benefits of codification outweighed the difficulties. They offered several reasons. To spur economic activity, amid increasing rates of urbanization and geographical mobility, uniformity in the law seemed important. Stable expectations about the norms that would govern transactions would lead theoretically to high levels of investment and more expansive trade across regions.[46] Often customary laws appeared to constrain women's participation in economic life and reduce the "human capital" available. Finally preserving customary law untouched seemed likely to draw attention to cultural differences and to divide people.[47]

Codification and unification received support in Tanzania, where Hans Cory, a sociologist long engaged in recording the customary laws of different groups, was hired to prepare the groundwork. Cory consulted local politicians and party members.[48] District boards helped develop the texts. Although Cory died before the project was complete, the documents provided the basis for a new statute, the Local Customary Law Declaration, which effected a partial unification of customary laws.[49] Years later, Nyalali observed that "this codification process, coupled with judicial precedents, had the effect of transforming the various customs of the indigenous people of Tanzania into an indigenous common law of Tanzania."[50]

The debate about the pros and cons of codification led other countries to consider "restatements" as an alternative. By contrast with a code, which usually is given statutory form, a restatement would have no binding force in judicial decision making. Prepared by a team of highly respected practitioners and legal scholars, it examined the welter of statutes and court decisions on a topic and arranged the rules, principles, tests, and reasoning they contained in a single document, clearly stated, with commentary on ambiguities, variations, and trends. Restatements were easy to consult and could have persuasive authority in a judge's decision. They helped supply the needs of the new courts while preserving some of the flexibility of the customary law.

Legal practitioners in the United States already had made extensive use of

---

[46] Bennett and Vermeulen, "Codification of Customary Law," p. 207.

[47] Eugene Cotran, "The Unification of Laws in East Africa," *Journal of Modern African Studies*, 1, 2 (1963), p. 214.

[48] This process is described in detail in McClain, "Recent Changes in African Local Courts and Customary Law," pp. 187–226; and Hans Cory and M. M. Hartnoll, *Customary Law of the Haya Tribe*, Cass Library of African Law, No. 7 (1945; reprint London: Frank Cass & Co., 1971).

[49] Rwezaura, "The Integration of Marriage Laws in Africa with Special Reference to Tanzania, p. 141.

[50] Francis L. Nyalali, "Cross-Cultural Perspectives of the Proof Process: The Tanzanian Experience," Paper presented at the annual meeting of the Society for the Reform of Criminal Law, Vancouver, Canada, August 3–7, 1992, p. 11.

restatements. There, the task of research was vested in a nongovernmental organization, the American Law Institute (ALI), founded in 1923. The ALI tapped a select group of lawyers to help draft the restatements in each area of the law. Each restatement took a decade or more, and often the law had altered so significantly by the end of the period that a new restatement was commissioned shortly after the completion of its predecessor. Private philanthropies, such as the Carnegie Corporation and the Rockefeller Foundation, underwrote the cost.

The process of consultation the ALI put in motion offered an avenue for public participation in the development of the law, and the texts provided a means of communicating a fairly technical, complex body of information. However, the ALI also attracted criticism for some of its projects.[51] The power of moneyed interest groups to influence proceedings caused worry from time to time. Similar concerns arose about the appropriateness of a private legislative body formulating rules about matters of importance to the general public. One study suggested that the structure of the ALI also produced a strong bias toward the status quo.[52] On balance, however, assessments of the ALI tended to be positive. The restatements won places on lawyers' bookshelves and in judges' chambers.

Without foreclosing the possibility of codification, with the help of private foundations, a team of scholars from Africa and England established a Restatement of African Law Project, modeled on the efforts of the ALI and financed by the Nuffield Foundation. The original aim was to cover sixteen countries and to restate customary laws regarding personal status, the family, inheritance and succession, and land.[53] In 1959, under these auspices, teams from the School of Oriental and African Studies, based in London, began to impanel chiefs to ascertain and record customary law in many countries. After independence, these efforts continued. In the late 1960s and 1970s, for example, Botswana had a program for recording Tswana law.[54] During the 1980s and 1990s, there were over five restatement projects going on in South Africa.[55] In the late 1990s, Namibia embarked on a related venture.

More cognizant of the difficulties involved than most people, Nigerian legal

---

[51] For an overview, see the Symposium on the American Law Institute, which appeared in the *Hofstra Law Review*, 26 (Spring 1998).

[52] Alan Schwartz and Robert E. Scott, "The Political Economy of Private Legislatures," *University of Pennsylvania Law Review*, 143, 3 (January 1995), pp. 595–654.

[53] William Twining, "The Restatement of African Customary Law: A Comment," *Journal of Modern African Studies*, 1, 2 (1963), p. 221.

[54] Neville Rubin and Eugene Cotran, *Annual Survey of African Law*, 1969 (London: Frank Cass, 1973), p. 212.

[55] Anthony N. Allott, "International Developments in Customary Law—The Restatement of African Law and Thereafter," in Republic of Namibia, Law Reform and Development Commission, *The Ascertainment of Customary Law and the Methodological Aspects of Research into Customary Law, Proceedings of a Workshop* (Windhoek, Namibia: Law Reform and Development Commission, February/March 1995), p. 5 of executive summary.

scholar and jurist Taslim O. Elias sought to frame guidelines for both restatement and codification programs:

1) The investigator must remember from the outset that there is a clear distinction to be made between law and custom . . . perhaps it is better to say whether the particular practice is recognised by the majority of the local community as binding on all and sundry, or whether it is merely conventional or permissive.

2) Equally, the investigator will need to assure himself that some watered-down versions of English or a European law which Native Authorities have been remitted to administer are not passed off on him as customary law. It is not that the two should not finally fuse together; it is that they must first be distinguished in the stage of investigation.

3) In the process of collecting his data, the investigator will often come up against conflicting versions of the customary law of a given community, whether these are contained in court records or given by informants. . . . To whatever the divergence may be attributed, it is the investigator's duty to arbitrate between any two or more views of what the customary law on certain disputed issues may be.

4) Another pitfall that must be avoided is to assume that a community with an apparently homogenous body of customary law has a uniform set of rules governing its members without exception. . . . It is of first importance to recognise that customary law may vary from place to place within the same territory and accordingly to watch and record the discernible 'law regions.' . . . The general as well as the particular principles of even a homogenous body of customary law must be recorded if a true picture of the whole legal community is to be obtained. . . .

6) Some colonies in British Africa . . . gave statutory powers to the chiefs to declare, as and when necessary, what they considered to be the customary law within their areas of jurisdiction. The trouble here is of a two-fold nature. The first is that, in far too many cases, these chiefs concurrently exercised executive and judicial functions and it may often be difficult to know whether the law they declare is *de lege lata* [the law as it is] or *de lege ferenda* [the law as it ought to be]. The second is that, as chiefs, they may tend to be . . . the least competent to make an effectual synthesis of the old and the new rules of conduct in a fast-changing social and economic scene. . . .[56]

Elias urged others to resist the idea of a code in favor of a legal textbook, along the lines of a restatement.

Most countries also had legislation that permitted rejection of customary law

---

[56] T. O. Elias, "The Problem of Reducing Customary Laws to Writing," in Alison Dundes-Renteln and Alan Dundes, *Folk Law: Essays in the Theory and Practice of Lex Non Scripta* (Madison: University of Wisconsin Press, 1994), pp. 323–325.

rules under certain conditions. One such consideration was "repugnancy to natural justice." Some statutes contained, instead, the requirement that laws conform with "justice, equity, and good conscience" or equity, natural justice, and public policy.

These phrases had a very long and curious history. Although they arrived with English law, they were not English in origin. The architect of the English Reformation, Thomas Cromwell, borrowed them from the continental civil law tradition. He acquired the phrase during his study of Roman law and he put it to use on behalf of the lower house of parliament in its pleading to revise rules which were "against all justice lawe equite and good conscience."[57] The phrase gained a further lease on life as part of the common law tradition by way of the British East India Company. The company chose to continue the civil law system installed by earlier Portuguese settlers in its Indian posts and applied this standard to all the foreigners who plied their trades in the region.[58]

For understandable reasons, at the time of independence, there was a groundswell of support for revoking the repugnancy provision. There was something condescending about a judge determining that a rule with which people had lived, and presumably found acceptable, was "repugnant." Therefore, at the African Conference on Local Courts and Customary Law in Dar es Salaam, in 1963, participants resolved that the clause should be discarded and established a preference that problematical rules of customary law be altered not by courts, but by the legislature through statute. Nonetheless, most elected assemblies maintained the repugnancy provision or its equivalent. For example, in Tanzania, where the Local Customary Law Declaration had the status of subsidiary legislation, the courts were able to ignore provisions where these violated general principles of law.[59]

Usually the repugnancy clauses and their replacements permitted the courts to strike down customary rules that contravened the principles of natural justice. Although a vague term from the perspective of most laymen, *natural justice* to lawyers and judges embraced principles felt to be fundamental and widely shared. These principles were largely procedural and concerned the requirements for due process or fair trial. They included the rule that a judge has a duty to hear both sides of a case before making a decision; that judgments should be supported by reasons; that no one should be a judge in his own

---

[57] As quoted in J. Duncan M. Derrett, "Justice, Equity and Good Conscience," in J. N. D. Anderson, ed., *Changing Law in Developing Countries.* (New York: Praeger, 1963), p. 128. For a good general explanation of repugnancy clauses, see also William Burnett Harvey, *An Introduction to the Legal System in East Africa* (Nairobi, Kenya: East African Literature Bureau, 1975), pp. 522–525.

[58] Ibid., p. 129.

[59] Barthazar Rwezaura, "The Integration of Marriage Laws in Africa with Special Reference to Tanzania," in Jamil M. Abun-Nasr, Ulrich Spellenberg, and Ulrike Wanitzek, eds., *Law, Society, and National Identity in Africa* (Hamburg: Helmut Buske Verlag, 1990), p. 141.

cause;[60] that criminal trials should be heard continuously, without protracted adjournments; that criminal trials should be conducted in the presence of the accused;[61] and that "ordeal by poison" offends basic notions of fairness. Rules were not to be abandoned simply because they caused hardship but instead because they violated these aspects of procedural justice.[62]

The "repugnancy clause" was rarely invoked either during the colonial period or after independence. A quick review of the legal literature shows its occasional use to strike down substantive rules. Usually this use of the clause was limited to customary practices that ordered nonconsensual personal relationships, imposed liability on one for the deeds of another, or inflicted punishment or death on the basis of a personal attribute instead of a criminal state of mind. These instances included those where a person was compelled to enter into a marital union against his or her will;[63] where debts were paid with infant girls;[64] where property of one member of a family was seized to satisfy claims against another member; where guardians were absolved of responsibility for wards; where a father was considered liable to have his cattle seized to provide his son's bridewealth; and where a family was granted the right to take back a daughter or sister and her children from her husband in order to compel him to pay her bridewealth.[65]

LEGITIMACY AND INDEPENDENCE

Judges worried about the effects of legal pluralism on popular acceptance of the state courts and on the willingness of people to stand up for an independent judiciary for three main reasons. One was that the existence of alternative legal norms might make it hard to draw peoples' attention to the state courts. The common law and the courts might be labeled "foreign" or inauthentic. Second, the existence of parallel forums could create opportunities for forum shopping and for political manipulation of cases. Governments could try to take opponents to customary courts, where due process concerns were less pro-

---

[60] T. W. Bennett, "The Interpersonal Conflict of Laws: A Technique for Adapting to Social Change in Africa," *Journal of Modern African Studies*, 18, 1 (1980), p. 84.

[61] Henry F. Morris and James S. Read, *Indirect Rule and the Search for Justice: Essays in East African Legal History* (Oxford: Clarendon, 1972), p. 176.

[62] Akilagpa Sawyerr, "Customary Law in the High Court of Tanzania," *Eastern Africa Law Review*, 6, 3 (1973), p. 272.

[63] Bennett, "The Interpersonal Conflict of Laws," p. 85.

[64] Ibid., p. 176.

[65] Sawyerr, "Customary Law in the High Court of Tanzania," p. 271. *Bridewealth* is a payment by a husband-to-be to the bride's family. Historically it often took the form of cattle or livestock, although it also might have included items like blankets and other household goods. Today, it is sometimes a money payment.

nounced. Finally, experts worried that conflicting legal norms would lead to distrust of all systems of law and all dispute resolution.

The effects of pluralism on the acceptance of the common law courts would remain high on the list of chief justices' concerns as the end of the twentieth century approached. For example, in South Africa, the problem of defining the "right" relationship between the customary law and the common law entered the negotiations over the country's new constitution and became the subject of many studies and protracted negotiations thereafter. Namibian jurists put the same issue on the agenda of their country's Law Reform and Development Commission and urged that its World Bank–financed legal capacity building program help address ways to ascertain customary law.[66] After it eliminated separate traditional courts in the 1990s, Malawi also sought to draw the customary law into the common law system.

But reformers and ordinary people did not always see eye to eye. In Botswana the late Chief Justice Mololeki Mokama floated the idea of unifying the state courts and customary courts in his country. A 1994 Botswana government report commented that "[i]f confidence in the administration of justice is to be built up, an integrated system of courts must be a vital consideration." It recalled the comment of an earlier chief justice to the effect that ". . . a dual system weakened both systems, one section of the community develops confidence in one system and cares little for the others. If multi-racialism is to have any meaning, all persons in the country should be subject to and have access to, the same tribunals. That is what is envisaged in the Constitution."[67]

In response, a 1996 Commission of Inquiry into the Judiciary in Botswana put the issue on its agenda and carried out conversations around the country to canvas views. The findings surprised the judiciary. One member of the commission said that people seemed to prefer to keep the existing system as it was. "They liked the idea that they didn't need lawyers to use these courts. They also liked the lay participation and wondered whether anyone who wandered in would be allowed to speak if the courts were integrated."[68] In particular, they asked, "In the proposed system, 'Can we stop a lawyer and ask our own questions? We don't know these lawyers. They come for the hearing and then they go away!'" The chiefs felt the proposed reforms threatened their birthright, because hearing disputes was the bulk of their work. The issue became quite sensitive.

---

[66] Republic of Namibia, Law Reform and Development Commission, *The Ascertainment of Customary Law and the Methodological Aspects of Research into Customary Law: Proceedings of a Workshop* (Windhoek, Namibia: Law Reform and Development Commission, February/March 1995).

[67] As quoted in Republic of Botswana, Directorate of Public Service Management, Office of the President, Report on the Administration of Justice (draft), August 1994, p. 35.

[68] Bojosi Othlogile, of University of Botswana Department of Law, interview with author, Ann Arbor, Michigan, Spring 1998.

Many years later, reflecting on Tanzania's experience, Chief Justice Nyalali commented, "Obviously, in order that law may serve as a crucial bond between the people within the nation state, it has to be law which is common to all the people and has to be reasonably known to a reasonable number of people." But he pointed out that the laws closest to people's everyday lives, the customary laws and Islamic law, were not common to all the people:

> During the first half of the 1960s a programme of codification of customary law was undertaken for the purpose of making it more certain. With the benefit of hindsight, it may now be said that the programme was flawed. It was mistaken in that it put a great emphasis on codification of the rules of customary law rather than on the broad principles underlying such rules. History has shown that the codified rules did, in due course of time, become unacceptable to changing society and were ignored by the people, who evolved new customary rules in line with new circumstances. Had the exercise of codification dealt with broad principles, the courts would have been able to apply the principles to new circumstances in the manner the English Customary Law was developed by English courts. Since the majority of the people of Tanzania, particularly the rural population, still respect their customary laws, it is incumbent on us to establish a new programme to codify the common principles underlying African customary law in Tanzania. Once that is done, it would be for the Tanzanian courts to articulate and apply those principles to specific cases and changing times.[69]

Nyalali tried to explain what he meant by codifying *principles*. "By general or common principles which underlie African customary law, I mean those basic norms which define the relationship between individuals," he suggested. He offered a provocative example. "Under the customary law of inheritance, it is recognized that the actions of ancestors are a factor in the lives of the present generation, whose actions are also a factor in the lives of the next generation. Consequently, heirs inherit not only the assets of a progenitor but the liabilities as well—the liabilities being passed on from generation to generation like the national debt!"[70]

---

[69] Francis L. Nyalali, "Legal Reform for Democracy in Tanzania," *Lawyer* (Journal of the Law Society of Tanganyika, Dar es Salaam) (September–December 1994), p. 7.
[70] Francis L. Nyalali, personal communication, October 1998.

Challenges

SEVERAL DRAMATIC CHANGES threatened to make life considerably more diffi-cult for the new national courts in eastern and southern Africa during the 1960s and 1970s. These had a more immediate effect on judicial institution building, especially on judicial independence, than the problems of legal inte-gration did. Emboldened by the prospect of self-government and by brave new social experiments, many officials and party members took the law into their own hands and reacted with consternation and anger when their efforts met resistance in the courts. New ideas about the proper role of judges, often pro-moted under the rubric of "socialist legality," found an attentive audience. Demands for political accountability gained more currency than notions of independence or impartiality did.

This general picture disguised variation. Botswana remained immune from these broad trends, the exception in this sphere as in so many others. Judiciaries in Zambia and Kenya experienced fewer difficulties in the early years, although some of the same tendencies manifested themselves there later. In Tanzania, Uganda, and Malawi, judicial legitimacy suffered severely. The question was why.

Establishment of new governments is never an easy task. When people seek to define roles and rules, power is hotly contested. Nyalali observed that the chief justice's role "was always a balancing act." John Marshall, the American jurist that Francis Nyalali came so much to admire, had struggled mightily with politicians who took aim at the courts. Later, when he became chief justice, Nyalali read Jean Edward Smith's biography, *John Marshall: Definer of a Nation*, and found striking parallels. The Marshall Court had faced numerous threats to its jurisdiction, and its judgments sometimes were explicitly ignored, in public demonstrations of defiance. At the time of *Marbury v. Madison*, the famous decision that created the basis for judicial review in the United States, the independence of the judiciary was in doubt. Congress had canceled the Supreme Court's 1802 term, and there were calls for impeachment of the justices. Marshall and then President Thomas Jefferson did not get along. The decision said that Marbury, a man to whom Jefferson wished to deny a commission as a justice of the peace, was legally entitled to his commission, which the previous administration had granted him. That stance would no doubt have angered Jefferson. But the decision went on to say that the Constitution provided the Supreme Court no original jurisdiction in the case. It could not act on Marbury's complaint. And that part of the decision appeared to mollify the president. The important bits of the opinion that created the basis for judicial review were all in dicta, the parts not central to the holding. The court chose to respect these dicta as binding authority in later judgments. American jurists and legal scholars have wrestled with this decision, which was "political" but not partisan. It helped define the relationship between the branches of government that would come to prevail in the United States. Thus, the difficult times of the 1970s and 1980s in Africa paralleled some of the challenges the American court faced at its founding too.

Nyalali watched the struggle to define the institutional authority of the courts from a new post. By 1971, political developments had sown the seeds of chaos in relationships between workers and enterprise managers. Strikes and lockouts spread throughout the country. The Permanent Labour Tribunal seemed unable to effect enduring resolution of these disputes, and there were even fears that its chairman would be locked out of his office. The president sought someone who was responsive but firm. He remembered Nyalali, who had won the respect of people in Musoma years before, and asked the judiciary whether he could be seconded to the tribunal. Chief Justice Telford Georges, who shortly was to make way for a Tanzanian-born successor, agreed to the president's request, and Nyalali took up a new post for the period 1971–74.

BOLD EXPERIMENTS

Throughout eastern and southern Africa, the assumption of powers of self-government initially produced a tug-of-war between public institutions much as it had in John Marshall's United States. The exhilaration induced by independence bred an aggressive assertiveness. People vied with one another for authority over nearly every aspect of life, from the high politics of the relationship between the branches of government to the "small arms wars" waged through argument and gossip to determine control over village development activities.

Institutions could not be created by the pen alone. Jurisdictional boundaries were established through constant haggling and maneuvering at the grassroots, punctuated by occasional intervention from the top when the threat of chaos loomed too large. Even at the highest levels, however, "judicial independence" and "separation of powers" often remained fairly abstract until experience gave these terms color and meaning.

The structure of the political system was inauspicious for the development of independent courts. Throughout Africa in the 1960s and 1970s, there was a shift toward one-party rule. In 1965, Tanzania opted for a single-party system. At the district level, parliamentary elections pitted ruling party members against each other. At the presidential level, voters could cast their ballots for or against the single name listed. The candidate ran unopposed. Malawi and Zambia quickly followed Tanzania to one-party rule. Kenya became a de facto one-party state, although it did not ban opposition until 1982. In Uganda, two main political parties dueled at the polls periodically but remained in the background during long periods of military rule and civil strife. In Zimbabwe and South Africa, minority white governments held a lock on power. Only in Botswana did the multiparty system envisioned at the time of independence sustain itself.

In the absence of lively competition between political parties, members of parliament had no material stake in an independent judiciary. In the West, independent courts and multiparty politics frequently developed in tandem. The ideas may have evolved in some places as different solutions to the same kind of problem, the control of arbitrary executive or legislative authority. But another possible reason for the correlation was that campaign fundraising in a competitive party system would be difficult, if not impossible, if the next legislature could simply ignore the statutes of its predecessor. No one would donate money to help a candidate if the person's achievements could be reversed on whim by the next government.[1] And candidacy itself would be dangerous if compliant courts could convict opposition candidates without cause. Theoretically, then, party competition gave politicians a material incentive to check executive encroachment on judicial functions. Without competition, politicians' individual attitudes toward the courts mattered much more. Whether the head of state accepted the principle of judicial independence and ensured that his ministers and officers in the field followed suit was key.

Bold governmental initiatives aggravated the troubles facing new judicial systems. All of the newly independent countries in the region faced the task of improving standards of living or generating "development," that most enigmatic of aspirations. During the 1960s, new leaders offered an array of strate-

---

[1] William M. Landes and Richard A. Posner, "The Independent Judiciary in an Interest Group Perspective," *Journal of Law and Economics*, 18, 3 (December 1975), pp. 875–901.

gies. On the other side of the continent, Ghana's Kwame Nkrumah and Côte d'Ivoire's Félix Houphouet-Boigny had faced off in a policy contest nicknamed the "West African Wager." Nkrumah advocated the creation of state-owned farms and increasing national control of industry in order to protect Ghanaians from "neocolonialism." He argued that allowing foreign businesses and governments to participate in the country's economic affairs inevitably would distort policy in favor of those who owned capital and put ordinary people at a disadvantage. Next door, in Côte d'Ivoire, Houphouet-Boigny took issue with that claim and chose to lure funds from abroad through a mixed program that included government investment in enterprises, tax holidays for foreign businesses, and participation in a monetary union linked to the French franc. Similarly, Tanzania and Kenya articulated dramatically different policies. Kenya's policy makers sought to generate high rates of economic growth, which they believed would trickle down to small farmers, and they combined this approach with an emphasis on self-help development, while in Tanzania, President Nyerere laid out an intriguing plan for a distinctively "African" agrarian socialism.

Fondly referred to as "Mwalimu" (the teacher), Nyerere was an erudite man of the left who once translated Shakespeare into Kiswahili and claimed fluency with the works of Karl Marx, the problems of Appalachia, and a wide range of global issues. He worried that market-based economic systems would exacerbate inequality, breed jealousy and tribalism, and ultimately impede development. He felt that capitalism, with its distinction between "workers" and "employers," bred an idle class of privileged people. The idea that some could "sit back" and make money on the work of others sat poorly with local values. "In the traditional African society everybody was a worker," he wrote. "The organization of traditional African society . . . was such that there was hardly any room for parasitism." He observed that "[t]hose of us who talk about the African way of life, and, quite rightly, take a pride in maintaining the tradition of hospitality which is so great a part of it, might do well to remember the Swahili saying, '*Mgeni siku mbili; siku ya tatu mpe jembe*'—or, in English, treat your guest as a guest for two days; on the third day give him a hoe."[2]

Idle wealth arose from the institution of private property, Nyerere argued. The ability to accumulate assets through purchase of title or deed held, for him, the prospect of a "landlord class," not unlike that constituted by the British settlers who had moved into Tanzania. To treat land as a commodity—something that could be bought and sold—was to say that an individual could deny access to the means of survival to other members of the community. He wrote, "In traditional

[2] Julius K. Nyerere, "*Ujamaa*—The Basis of African Socialism," in *Freedom and Unity: A Selection from Writing and Speeches, 1952–65* (Dar es Salaam, Tanzania: Oxford University Press, 1966), p. 165.

society, . . . nobody starved, either of food or of human dignity, because he lacked personal wealth; he could depend on the wealth possessed by the community of which he was a member."[3] In precolonial times, people shared burdens equally, and they also shared the fruit of their labor equally, he argued.

If allowed to spread, Nyerere suggested, market-based capitalist systems would sow the seeds of inequality, communal strife, instability, and poverty in Africa. In the context of a plural society, the pursuit of material interest and the scramble to get a larger share of the social pie inevitably would lead to discord among different cultural communities. Political instability would result. Poverty would rule. To avoid this turn of events, he wrote, Tanzanians "must walk, while others run." Equality would have to come before growth.

At the same time, Nyerere did not envision a simple effort to recapture old ways of life. Africa could not resuscitate forms of organization long gone, he said. Instead, he embarked on an effort to retrieve fundamental values that persisted from this earlier era, and he fashioned new institutions and policies to support them. He articulated this program under the name of *ujamaa*, the Kiswahili word for "kinship" or "brotherhood," built on the root word for family.[4]

The main elements of *ujamaa* were laid out most clearly in the Arusha Declaration of 1967. Nyerere sought to promote self-reliance through disengagement from the world market and ordered an end to trade and foreign investment. He advocated nationalization of key sectors of the economy vulnerable to "parasitic behavior," such as the banks. He announced "Operation Maduka," an effort to abolish middlemen, especially the private traders who dealt in the basic commodities farmers needed to survive. In urban areas, the program entailed reduction in the salaries of urban officials and the promulgation of guidelines to inspire a new work ethic. In rural areas, sweeping changes restricted individual ownership of land and possession under customary law. Instead, the government announced provisions for a system of communal land tenure, under which people were to work the land in common and to divide the proceeds among themselves. People would move into new *ujamaa* villages, to which the government could provide schools, water, and medical services more cheaply than it could if households were separated by considerable distances. Places where famine and floods posed routine problems were targeted first.[5] For several years, this project proceeded without any enabling legislation,

---

[3] Ibid., p. 164.

[4] American readers will recognize *ujamaa* as one of the seven principles of Kwanzaa, a holiday that originated in the United States. The seven principles have Kiswahili names and express noble concepts. Political life in Tanzania during the late 1960s and 1970s tried to put many of the same ideas into practice. That all did not end well says nothing about the principles, which are laudable, and much about the difficulty of trying to put them to work.

[5] United Republic of Tanzania, *Report of the Presidential Commission of Inquiry into Land Matters* (Shivji Commission), vol. 1, *Land Policy and Land Tenure Structure* (Uppsala,

until the Rural Lands (Planning and Utilization) Act of 1973 granted the president unrestricted discretionary power to declare a part of the country a "specified area" and to empower the regional administration to regulate land use.

Teamwork between the country's single political party, the Tanzania African National Union (TANU), and government would put the new policies into effect. The party organized the populace into a system that grouped every ten households into a cell. Cell leaders performed a variety of functions and reported on their communities to higher authorities. Party activists worked side by side with government officials to help move people into villages and ensure adherence to the new cooperative ethic.

With the benefit of hindsight and subsequent changes in development policy thinking, the Arusha Declaration appeared to rest on excessively optimistic assumptions about the capacities of government and an underappreciation of material self-interest as a motivating factor in human behavior. The ordinary people the measures were meant to serve complained about the social dislocations involved, especially the loss of family land. Communal production proved unpopular in many parts of the country, and equipment maintenance, soil conservation, respect for work hours, and other aspects of farm life declined. Economic growth suffered.

The declaration attracted worldwide attention and substantial enthusiasm. Foreign policy makers in the United States were critical. But the American consulting group McKinsey & Company reportedly drafted some of the plans for organizing villages, and the program attracted interest and quiet support from several Scandinavian countries.[6]

Although President Nyerere remained committed to judicial independence in theory, the ambitiousness of the task he had set for the government was destined to create difficulties for the fledgling national courts. Dramatic changes in the law or in government practices inevitably created bigger caseloads for the courts, as people tried to determine what the changes really meant. Bigger caseloads often meant more delay. Magistrates with only a few months' training found it hard to respond to the workload and the new issues raised in the cases brought before them. A rising crime rate aggravated the problem.[7]

In Tanzania, as in other countries, misunderstandings about the proper role of the judiciary complicated the situation further. At the local level, administrators and party officials sometimes thought that it was the courts' responsibility to

---

Sweden: Scandinavian Institute of African Studies and Ministry of Lands, Housing, and Urban Development, United Republic of Tanzania, 1994), pp. 42–43.

[6] McKinsey & Company neither confirms nor denies its participation and has a policy of not answering inquiries about whether it has worked for clients, public or private.

[7] United Republic of Tanzania, Judicial System Review Commission, *The Report of the Judicial System Review Commission* (Msekwa Report) (Dar es Salaam, Tanzania: Judicial System Review Commission, 1977), p. 28.

enforce government policies or party initiatives. They did not recognize that the rule of law required civil servants and elected officials, as well as ordinary citizens, to respect the law. They asked magistrates to levy fines against those who did not participate sufficiently in community self-help development projects, even though the legislature had never defined the behavior as illegal and never prescribed a penalty. They demanded enforcement of actions to oust people from land needed by village development committees, though no law gave the development committees the power to take the land. Nor had any act of the legislature authorized the movement of people into *ujamaa* villages.[8] Cooperatives were banned, and people were detained, without reference to any statute.[9]

The courts declined to hear complaints that had no legal basis, and resentment grew.[10] When the courts said there was no legal cause of action, party officials and administrators grew angry. And if magistrates sought to take public policy into account in their decisions, to curry favor with officials, members of the public felt the courts sided too much with the government.

For people trying to make a "beautiful revolution," it was obviously frustrating to find that there were constraints on the means one could pursue. Even the president remonstrated that "[t]here is a separate hierarchy and system of command for the judiciary, and once a man is appointed it is extremely difficult to displace him. These things are intended to help secure impartiality. But they must not do more. They must not lead to the belief that a judge can be, or should be, 'neutral' on the basic issues of our society. . . . Otherwise their interpretations may appear ridiculous to that society, and may lead to the whole concept of law being held in contempt by the people."[11]

"The idea of separation of powers did not make much sense to people," or at least to local office holders, Nyalali remembered. As a result, frictions at the grassroots level sometimes reached upward to the president's office. "People felt the president should have all the power. They would take judicial matters to him. He would say, 'But I don't have the power,' and people would not believe him."[12] Ideas mattered. Where people did not understand that the courts were supposed to be independent of executive influence, the pressures on both the executive and the judiciary built to substantial proportions. "Mwalimu had trouble translating liberal ideas into practice, because many of

[8] Francis L. Nyalali, "Legal Reform for Democracy in Tanzania," *Lawyer* (Journal of the Law Society of Tanganyika, Dar es Salaam) (September–December 1994), p. 6.
[9] Issa G. Shivji, "The Rule of Law and Ujamaa in the Ideological Formation of Tanzania," *Social and Legal Studies*, 4, 2 (June 1995), p. 162; and Nyalali, "Legal Reform for Democracy in Tanzania," p. 6.
[10] Frederic Lee DuBow, "Justice for People: Law and Politics in the Lower Courts of Tanzania," Unpublished dissertation, Department of Sociology, University of California at Berkeley, 1973, p. 238.
[11] Julius K. Nyerere, "The Judiciary and the People," *Freedom and Socialism* (Dar es Salaam, Tanzania: Oxford University Press, 1968), p. 110.
[12] Francis L. Nyalali, interview with author, May 29, 1996.

the people he was dealing with had no schooling. He was one of the few graduates. They could understand him when he tried very hard to communicate, but he was a busy man and he could not pay attention to everything," Nyalali commented.[13] Control of officers in the field was always difficult but especially so under these circumstances. Contempt of court through nonenforcement of judicial decisions was common.[14]

The sense that the courts were unfair also may have stemmed from changes in the law and law enforcement. There was a tendency to criminalize ordinary practices that interfered with the implementation of a government policy.[15] Where there was no legal basis for a civil suit, local officials sometimes filed criminal charges such as sedition against a recalcitrant villager.

Finally, there was some evidence that customary and informal dispute resolution also lost legitimacy in the face of competition with the political party and the ten-cell system. A researcher on the ground at the time observed that "with few exceptions, wherever there are cell leaders their most consuming function is to hear disputes."[16] A survey found that most people preferred mediation of land disputes by cell leaders to clan meetings.[17] This shift in preferred forum may have resulted from a belief that traditional conflict resolution by elders was unfair, but equally it may have stemmed from a sense that the party was supreme and that elders were less able to carry out their roles as a result.

FIRST STRUGGLES

In response to growing restiveness about the performance of public institutions in general and the courts in particular, the Tanzanian government took several steps. First it set up the Permanent Commission of Inquiry, which served as an ombudsman of sorts.

Normally ombudsmen are independent officers of the legislature with the mandate to investigate complaints against public officials or departments. They have the ability to investigate complaints about human rights abuses, illegal behavior, or maladministration and to make recommendations for addressing problems they identified. They can criticize and publicize, but not prosecute.

In Tanzania, the commission was appointed by the president to investigate charges of abuse of power against government officials, except those in the offices of the president and the head of state of Zanzibar. It reported to the

---

[13] Ibid.
[14] M. K. B. Wambali and C. M. Peter, "The Judiciary in Context: The Case of Tanzania," in Neelan Tirachelram and Radhika Coomaraswamy, eds., *The Role of the Judiciary in Plural Societies* (New York: St. Martin's Press, 1987), p. 137–138.
[15] Shivji, "The Rule of Law and Ujamaa in the Ideological Formation of Tanzania," p. 154.
[16] DuBow, "Justice for People: Law and Politics in the Lower Courts of Tanzania," p. 191.
[17] Ibid., p. 196.

president. Although the commission was not allowed to review the substance of judicial decisions, it did have authority to investigate magistrates' conduct and problems of court administration, such as delay.[18] In the first years, there were more complaints against the primary courts than against any other single agency of government.[19]

The government response was to try to increase supervision of the lower judicial ranks and to create new, more political forums for dispute resolution. In 1971, the party and government created special local boards with the power to appoint magistrates and pursue complaints against the lower-level courts. Finally, some of the political party branches created their own courts and heard cases outside the judicial system.[20]

In Uganda, the struggle to define institutional power was different and more deadly. Instead of the courts being drawn into a jurisdictional contest by friction at the grassroots, the main challenge came from the top of the government hierarchy. In 1966, then-President Milton Obote detained several of his cabinet ministers. The court ruled in favor of the ministers, who had petitioned for release, whereupon the government recharged the detainees under emergency power regulations. The legislature quickly indemnified the executive, and when the detainees appealed again, the court retreated and ruled for the government. In looking back on these events, one legal scholar observed, "The Court did not question the passing [of the Act which indemnified the government] . . . nor the fact that it was both of retrospective application, and that it was directed against specifically named individuals."[21]

The position of the courts deteriorated rapidly after that point. Successive legislative enactments granted the president supremacy and indemnified him against all court proceedings, and prevented the court from granting relief to citizens in cases brought against the government, where injury occurred as a result of efforts to maintain law and order. Parallel tribunals proliferated,[22] especially under the legendary dictator Idi Amin.

THE JUDICIAL RESPONSE

In Tanzania, the judiciary responded to these developments in several ways. Occasionally a judge chastised the administration for its behavior. For example,

---

[18] Bernard Frank, "The Tanzanian Permanent Commission of Inquiry—The Ombudsman," *Journal of International Law and Policy*, 2 (1972), passim, pp. 255–279.

[19] DuBow, "Justice for People: Law and Politics in the Lower Courts of Tanzania," p. 237.

[20] James S. Read, "Human Rights in Tanzania," in Colin Legum and Geoffrey Mmari, eds., *Mwalimu: The Influence of Nyerere* (London: James Currey, 1995), p. 134.

[21] Joe Oloka-Onyango, "Judicial Power and Constitutionalism in Uganda," Working Paper No. 30 (Kampala, Uganda: Centre for Basic Research, January 1993), p. 3.

[22] Ibid., passim.

in response to efforts to block enforcement of court judgments, Judge J. K. Mnzavas observed, "One of the things that distinguishes Tanzania from other One-Party states is the independence of its judiciary; should one now commence, as the Honourable Regional Commissioner, to block and interfere with court orders which are not of his liking we will, I am afraid, be sinking to the level of a Banana Republic where judges can be dismissed at whim and where judgments are written by rulers. None of us would like such a situation to develop in Tanzania."[23]

Concern for accountability figured importantly in Chief Justice Georges's strategy to enhance the legitimacy of the courts. The English legal tradition emphasized the need for judicial restraint and deference to the legislature. Georges thought that the conditions that prevailed in the new country made it especially necessary for magistrates and judges to interpret the laws with strong regard for public policy. He worked to ensure that judges understood that independence was "not being safeguarded to set them apart from the people. Its purpose was really to enable them better to serve the people of whom they were a part. Judicial independence would hardly survive where it appeared to encourage the growth of judicial arrogance."[24] Courts could lose touch with the societies they served. Georges pointed to the disparate experiences of Americans with their courts. Georges noted, "The role of the Supreme Court of the United States of America in leading the fight for equality for black Americans has tended to build up the case for a venerable and impartial Court, giving the lead where public opinion lags behind. . . ." But only two decades earlier, the court had fallen out of step. Georges suggested, "It should not be forgotten . . . that President Roosevelt had to threaten to pack the same Court in order to secure vital economic measures to remedy the great depression."[25] In the early part of the century the U.S. Supreme Court had struck down many laws that sought to regulate working conditions, create minimum wages, and set some limits on the powers of big business. These decisions paid no heed to the vast changes in the character of the American economy and society.

Georges felt that public opinion was critical, without control of the purse or the sword. "In the final analysis," he wrote, "the only real safeguard is an alert public opinion, quick to show its resentment when restrictive measures are proposed which are not reasonably justifiable in a democratic society."[26] It was

---

[23] Judge J. K. Mnzavas as quoted in David V. Williams, "State Coercion against Peasant Farmers: The Tanzanian Case," *Journal of Legal Pluralism*, 20 (1982), p. 97.
[24] Honorable Philip Telford Georges, personal communication, October 14, 1996.
[25] Philip Telford Georges, "Traditionalism and Professionalism," in R. W. James and F. M. Kassam, eds., *Law and Its Administration in a One Party State: Selected Speeches of Telford Georges* (Nairobi, Kenya: East African Literature Bureau, 1973), p. 49.
[26] Ibid., p. 49.

important for judges to engage the issues of the day, and to pay attention to the changes taking place in social organization and economic life.

Georges espoused a less isolated role for judges. He wrote about his own views. He urged judges to respond to missteps on the part of the administration or party by explaining the basis for their concerns. And he encouraged judges to join the party, in order to help explain the role of the courts and to show that the judiciary would not be obstructionist. Reasonableness commanded respect, and the route to authority lay in explanation.[27]

Georges took this perspective quite far. In a set of essays reprinted later, he struggled to define the role of a judge in a one-party system. "The concept of the judge as a neutral, belonging to no party in the multi-party democracy, can have no meaning here," he wrote. "If he stands aloof seeming to play the a-political role which is supposed to be his, his motives will doubtlessly be suspect. A new way must be found."[28] Georges saw parallels in the situation of elected state court judges in the United States and in the "English lawyer politicians appointed to the Bench." He remarked that ". . . it was difficult to believe that political convictions or prejudices acquired over a life-time . . . can suddenly be jettisoned." He placed hope in the "sense of professional integrity and professional competence [to] secure some objectivity in the handling of legal affairs, despite political commitment."[29]

But Georges also emphasized the need for professional solidarity. Courts were accountable first and foremost to the law itself, and the rules for promoting judicial independence were geared toward that goal. Georges held regular meetings of judges and magistrates. He hoped these conferences would help build professional ties. He suggested that although there was nothing to prevent "attempts at interference in the administration of justice," it was possible to "create the situation where the judicial officer can successfully withstand such interference with full confidence that his resistance will not lead to his being punished."[30] In a world where magistrates lived and worked in remote areas, this aspiration sometimes may have seemed a bit utopian.

George's court also used other tactics to prevent infringement. One was to transfer magistrates when they experienced trouble. An American research associate on the law faculty at the university in Dar found that primary court magistrates rarely presided in a location more than 1.4 years and observed that that rate had declined to less than a year by the later 1960s.[31]

Looking back on this period, Chief Justice Georges recollected thinking that the court could have faced more difficult challenges than it did. Unlike neigh-

---

[27] Georges, "The Role of Judges and Magistrates," p. 78.
[28] Georges, "The Courts in the Tanzania One Party State," p. 27.
[29] Ibid.
[30] Georges, "Traditionalism and Professionalism," p. 54.
[31] DuBow, "Justice for People: Law and Politics in the Lower Courts of Tanzania," p. 246.

boring countries, Tanzania's constitution contained no bill of rights. And Georges suggested that in the period of the one-party state, "It was . . . helpful . . . that the Constitution did not set out a legally enforceable Bill of Rights. . . ." He noted that the country's founding documents did contain general principles which the judges could use in educating the public about a "fair and well ordered society." By contrast, he felt that a justiciable bill of rights might have led to many suits against the new government, and for the courts, "[t]o have sought confrontation at that stage would have been impolitic."[32] He expressed caution, fearing a backlash.

Where the infringement of judicial independence was severely threatened, personal negotiation between institutional leaders often worked best. Georges considered then-President Nyerere accessible, as did Nyalali when he assumed the post years later. By contrast, chief justices in other countries often found contact with their presidents hard to develop. In the event of an action that encroached on judicial authority, it was possible to approach the head of state. Georges commented, "The resolution of these issues was always such as to contribute to the development of an independent judiciary protected from political interference."[33] Similarly, Nyalali observed that the president "would listen if I said I thought a decision would be unconstitutional. . . . He's that sort of person. When he confronted a constitutional objection, he backed away."[34] Nyerere was "always open to private discussion and debate."[35]

The chief justices of the region concurred that under the circumstances that prevailed in Africa, it was extremely important for a chief justice to be religiously civil and to communicate with presidents often. The more contact, the fewer the surprises. The less to distract from the message, the easier it was to persuade. In these years of flux, when neither political culture nor procedures nor interest groups safeguarded the separation of powers and judicial independence, the tone of the interpersonal relationship influenced the amount of space a chief justice had in which to experiment and to disagree.

Nyalali recalled a situation that arose later, after he became chief justice. The president had come under so much pressure from local party officials who objected to the courts' handling of a case that he felt he had to intervene. He discussed the matter in a cabinet meeting and then tried to dismiss a magistrate. Nyalali learned of the incident inadvertently. The magistrate had been called to the State House, the president's office, but he went to the High Court first and explained to the registrar that he had been summoned. The registrar picked up the phone and called the chief justice. "This would have been a

---

[32] Georges, "Traditionalism and Professionalism," p. 49.
[33] Philip Telford Georges, personal communication, October 14, 1996.
[34] Francis L. Nyalali, interview with author, May 29, 1996.
[35] Philip Telford Georges, personal communication, October 14, 1996.

breach of independence. The President appoints and promotes, although these functions are delegated to the Judicial Service Commission. However, the power to discipline lies wholly with the Commission."

"I thought the consequences would be serious," Nyalali recalled. "I got his secretary on the telephone and found that a radio broadcast about the dismissal was already planned. When I said the action violated the constitution, the secretary was alarmed. I obtained an audience with the president." The two men met at the president's private home, where the surroundings were less formal.

"Mwalimu must have sensed my mood. He asked, 'What have you heard?' I explained. I saw the president was visibly moved. He asked me, 'What shall I do?'"

"I said it would be appropriate to bring the matter before the Judicial Service Commission. We would investigate and we would give an appropriate sanction if the situation demanded."[36]

But other observers were less charitable in their assessments of the early 1970s. Said one member of the law faculty, "The President was ordering hundreds of undergraduates to be sent down and hundreds of farmers to be detained without any lawful authority; and his example in the violation of the law was followed by numerous others at all levels of the government and the party."[37] Another remarked that there was "[t]oo much timidity and mediocrity." A third observed that "[j]udicial silence and/or acquiescence to executive excesses and violation of legal powers partly contributed to the erosion of the legitimacy of the judiciary as custodian and fountain of peace...."[38]

MWONGOZO

In the early 1970s, in his post as chairman of the Permanent Labour Tribunal, Francis Nyalali was constantly in touch with what went on in the judiciary. A judge or magistrate assigned to work in the tribunal (later known as the Industrial Court) remained in the employment of the Judiciary Department, although payment of salary and similar benefits was the responsibility of the tribunal. Colleagues continued to see one another. Nonetheless, the assignment kept Nyalali busy and somewhat removed from the kinds of pressures others faced.

The new post gave Nyalali an opportunity to study the psychology of dispute

[36] Francis L. Nyalali, interview with author, May 29, 1996.
[37] Yash P. Ghai, "Legal Radicalism, Professionalism, and Social Action: Reflections on Teaching Law in Dar es Salaam," in Issa Shivji, ed., *The Limits of Legal Radicalism: Reflections on Teaching Law at the University of Dar es Salaam* (Dar es Salaam, Tanzania: Faculty of Law, University of Dar es Salaam, 1986), pp. 28–29.
[38] Sufian Hemed Bukurura, *Judiciary and Good Governance in Contemporary Tanzania: Problems and Prospects* (Bergen, Norway: Christien Michelsen Institute, Development and Human Rights Studies, September 1995), pp. 2–3.

resolution in an informal, hands-on way, and proceed with his interest in adapting the courts to the needs of the country. Just as the changes in policy had led to a lot of jockeying for power in the rural areas, *ujamaa* had prompted workers to challenge employers, waiving the recently issued party guidelines, the Mwongozo or green book, in their hands. Clause 15 of the guidelines read, "There must be a deliberate effort to build equality between leaders and those they lead. For a Tanzanian leader it must be forbidden to be arrogant, extravagant, contemptuous and oppressive. The Tanzanian leader has to be a person who respects people, scorns ostentation and who is not a tyrant. He should epitomise heroism, bravery, and be a champion of justice and equality."[39] In the workplace, Clause 15 inspired a new assertiveness and a certain amount of chaos. The government faced conflicting pressures. Nationalization had put many enterprises under government control, and the spate of strikes threatened not only to slow economic growth but also to create a political crisis. A senior officer at the Ministry of Labour observed that "[i]ndustrial disputes . . . have reached a stage where the Government can no longer tolerate them" and remarked that the leaders of many workers' committees were creating disputes and taking the law into their own hands.[40] The tribunal was supposed to resolve these conflicts and keep the country's economy on course.

Under law, workers and management were supposed to follow a series of steps to settle their differences. At the enterprise level, the first step was for a workers' committee to meet with management to try to define and solve the problem that produced unhappiness. If no agreement was reached at that level, then higher authorities came into the picture. If the dispute was about disciplining an employee, the case would go to a conciliation board, under the Security of Employment Act, and if that intervention failed, the minister for labour would hear the dispute. There were no parallel arrangements for handling arguments about terms and conditions of service, if they were not resolved at the labor-management meeting. Most often, employees appealed to the political party to intervene or to the National Union of Tanganyika Workers office. Both bodies could set up ad hoc investigations, but they lacked training in investigation, they were often partial, and they had no legal authority to make settlements binding. Although empowered by statute to create an intermediate machinery for hearing such disputes, the minister for labour had not acted to do so.[41] As a result, strike actions, other worker protests, and employer lockouts reached the Permanent Labour Tribunal often after considerable delay, when people were frustrated and hot tempered.

---

[39] Mwongozo Clause 15 as quoted in Francis L. Nyalali, *Aspects of Industrial Conflict: A Case Study of Trade Disputes in Tanzania 1967–1973* (Dar es Salaam, Tanzania: East African Literature Bureau, 1975), p. 13.
[40] As quoted in K. F. Ileti, "Post-Mwongozo Workers' Disputes in Tanzania: Two Case Studies," *Eastern Africa Law Review*, 7, 2 (1974), p. 168.
[41] This account paraphrases Nyalali, *Aspects of Industrial Conflict*, pp. 3–7.

In *Aspects of Industrial Conflict*, a slim volume he wrote toward the end of his tenure to explain the operation of the tribunal, Nyalali set forth the rudiments of the system. With respect to wages, the law was very specific about what workers could and could not be granted. The Permanent Labour Tribunal Act of 1967 described ten different considerations the legislature had taken into account in devising rules. These included the need to maintain a high level of domestic capital accumulation, the aim to develop payment-by-results schemes to help increase labor productivity, the creation of incentives for workers to develop experience and skills, interest in increasing the competitiveness of local enterprises compared to foreign businesses, and maintenance of a favorable balance of payments. Also to receive attention were two workers' concerns: maintenance and expansion of employment opportunities and prevention of erosion in wages through "unnecessary and unjustified price increases." The president could add other directives.

A long list of guidelines contained in a White Paper followed from these various goals. They included the proviso that wage and benefit increases should not exceed 5 percent per year, except where effective payment-by-results systems had been implemented. The 5 percent increase was not automatic, and the guidelines specified the considerations the court had to take into account, including rates of pay in other industries and services, the likely effect on prices and employment, and whether the request included a proposal for increasing productivity. The average increase in earnings should not exceed the average increase in labor productivity for the whole group of employees affected. For the most part, the guidelines were those one would find in a management plan for a firm in an industrial country. The main exception was the allocation of bonuses, which originally was tapered so that those paid the least received the highest bonus in proportional terms. This requirement was altered later to read that any surplus over the enterprise's annual approved target would be divided equally among all workers concerned.

Nyalali thought that more was at stake in the wave of strikes than standards of living. "I had the feeling that workers in Tanzania felt humiliated," Nyalali recalled. "They resented being seen solely as tools of production. If they won respect from leaders in industry, they would be willing to accept the court's decision."[42] If they did not feel that respect was forthcoming, they would agree to nothing, and the country's economy would be in jeopardy.

Nyalali first spoke with the minister for labour to see whether he could reorganize and refurnish the court's offices. "We managed to get one room well furnished—a waiting room for the workers. I also created a fund to buy tea and bread." He continued, "When the workers arrived, we would show them into our waiting room and on the pretext that the chair was just finishing the previ-

---

[42] Francis L. Nyalali, interview with author, May 30, 1996.

ous case, we would ask them to be seated and we would serve tea, while they waited. By the time we started to talk, their mood had changed."[43]

When the discussions began, Nyalali insisted that the parties start by reviewing their positions and their reasons for thinking their demands should be met. "We spoke about their own organization and the choices they faced." Nyalali would listen, then explain the law in Kiswahili, the language most of the workers spoke, instead of English, in which many felt uncomfortable. If the law did not permit the enterprise to accede to the demands the workers made, Nyalali would explain carefully what to do if the workers did not like the law. Negotiations became more civil, and the parties almost always accepted decisions. "It was a formative stage for me," Nyalali recalled. He learned how important respect was in effecting agreement, and he acquired skills in settling cases to supplement his training as an adjudicator.

In 1974, after four years in the public spotlight at the Permanent Labour Tribunal, Nyalali moved back to the judiciary proper. He was promoted to the position of High Court judge and sent to Arusha, an important High Court station in the north of the country, at the foot of Kilimanjaro. Arusha was a prized post. The town was pleasant and bustling. Seven years earlier, it had hosted the conference that had formally inaugurated Tanzania's unique brand of African socialism. In the decades to come, it would be home to other important meetings and events, including the gatherings of the East African Community, the peace negotiations among the countries of Africa's Great Lakes Region, and the International Criminal Tribunal for Rwanda. Nyalali should have been pleased with his new post. Instead, he grew increasingly worried.

---

[43] Ibid.

The Nadir

AFFAIRS TOOK A decided turn for the worse in the 1970s. In Tanzania, Uganda, and Malawi, the institutional status of the courts declined still further, although it remained relatively stable in countries such as Kenya and Botswana. The rule of law collapsed, as governments began to engage extensively in preventive detention, often with little regard even for the weak limits statutes imposed on the practice. Frustration with the courts grew. On the one hand, politicians and civil servants objected to the restrictions judges and magistrates placed on their behavior. On the other hand, members of the public criticized the courts as ineffective and increasingly corrupt.

In the short run it was difficult to mobilize resistance to these trends. Judges often mounted only a weak response, caught between practical difficulties and a legal heritage that provided few resources for fighting some of the worst excesses. The bar had little leverage as a lobby for independent courts in the countries where the problems were worst. And the law scholars who spoke out sometimes faced retribution.

JUDGES IN THEIR OWN CAUSE

The Tanzanian government was eager to appoint someone born in the country to the post of chief justice, and Telford Georges, who was from Dominica, moved onward at the end of 1971, after having served six years. Most of the promising Tanzanian candidates were still too inexperienced, and Georges had lobbied unsuccessfully for the temporary appointment of another non-Tanzanian. After six years, there would be a larger pool of Tanzanian candidates with experience, he argued, and a foreign appointee could be replaced, since he would serve on contract, as Georges had.

George's advice was for naught. The president appointed a Tanzanian, Augustine Saidi, from the High Court, as Georges's successor. The announcement met with a very cool reception from the bench, whose members felt Saidi lacked the ability to stand up to authority in defense of his judges. Discord erupted almost immediately over the new chief justice's aggressive embrace of political party ideology. Some of his colleagues thought he was "more of a politician than the politicians." He made no secret of his own policy preferences and remarked to the press that the interests of the greatest number should prevail.[1] He announced that he would personally handle all cases involving *ujamaa* villages. At least one justice of appeal dissented from this edict and refused to comply.[2] The vice president had to be called in to help mediate a solution.

Saidi's tenure marked a period of declining judicial legitimacy and low morale. Saidi had no special relationship with the president and therefore found it difficult to intervene to prevent a problem from developing into a full-scale infringement of the court's jurisdiction. Instead of contacting the president directly, he went through ministers, signaling his subordinate status to all. Party officials and administrators took advantage of that, and the status of the judiciary declined.

The legislature moved to increase its control over the courts. It did this, mainly by increasing the vulnerability of lower-court proceedings to party control. For example, it began to recruit assessors not from among local elders but from the ranks of the young party cadres. This practice may have enhanced party control, but it also lowered resistance to corruption. "An assessor couldn't ask for a bribe from a neighbor, but when a party functionary was installed as assessor, the community link was broken," Nyalali later observed.[3] Reputation among family and kin no longer mattered. Thus, ironically, some of the government's purported efforts to make the lower levels of the judiciary more responsive to the policies of the legislature may have aggravated the problem of arbitrariness it perceived.

Other measures enhanced executive control over the judiciary. For example, under an amendment to the Criminal Procedure Code, the director of public prosecutions won the right to appeal a case to the High Court on a matter of

---

[1] As reported in Harrison George Mwakyembe, *Tanzania's Eighth Constitutional Amendment and Its Implications on Constitutionalism, Democracy and the Union Question*, Juristische Schriftenreihe 58 (Hamburg: Die Deutsche Bibliothek/Deutschen Akademischen Austauschdienstes, 1998), p. 140.
[2] Chris Maina Peter and M. K. B. Wamali, "Independence of the Judiciary in Tanzania: A Critique," *Verfassung und Recht in Übersee*, 21, 1 (1988), p. 77.
[3] Francis L. Nyalali, interview with author, August 19, 1995.

either fact or law, even when the accused won an acquittal in the lower court. Although this provision became common in Africa, it was unusual elsewhere because it exposed an accused person to double jeopardy.

Looking back on this period, Nyalali later remarked, "There were certain things [Mwalimu Nyerere] . . . could not deliver. Under those conditions it was easy to be a dictator. Liberalism was an uphill task. When everything was said and done, some of us think the president could easily have been more a dictator than he was."[4] A member of the Law Society concurred. "Mwalimu had two faces, and within himself, he saw the conflict. Although he did not kill, he could be a very tough man. Still, he always thought about the underdog, and very few African presidents think about the man in the street. It is comforting to think your leader is trying."[5]

If rule of law had reached a low point in Tanzania, in Malawi conditions were similar, and in Uganda, the attack on the judiciary was still more severe. Ugandan Chief Justice Benedicto Kiwanuka was killed for his objections to government interference in the courts.[6] Different heads of state removed four subsequent chief justices by unconstitutional means too: Udo Udoma, Dermont Sheridan, Samson Wambuzi, and George Masika. High Court judges and magistrates also found themselves in trouble. The man who became principal judge in the 1990s, Jeremiah Herbert Ntagoba, went into exile in 1981. He had heard a defamation case brought by a man who was then vice president. The man lost the case and sent soldiers to the judge's residence. Ntagoba fled with his family and ended up first in Kenya, then in Zimbabwe.[7] A chief magistrate was shot. Other magistrates ended up in jail. One endured two years under house arrest, beginning in 1981, when the government pressed treason charges, simply because he was believed to be sympathetic to an opposition political party.[8]

New laws also gave the military broad judicial powers. The Armed Forces (Powers of Arrest) Decree of 1971 gave soldiers powers of arrest with respect to a wide range of crimes. Two years later, in 1973, new laws permitted trials of civilians in military tribunals, including trials for treason and offenses against the government.[9]

Looking backward, Peter Kabatsi, later Uganda's solicitor general, observed

---

[4] Francis L. Nyalali, interview with author, May 29, 1996.
[5] Member of the Law Society, interview with author, May 1996.
[6] Joe Oloka-Onyango, "Judicial Power and Constitutionalism in Uganda," Working Paper No. 30 (Kampala, Uganda: Centre for Basic Research, January 1993), p. 46.
[7] Principal Judge J. Herbert Ntagoba, interview with author, Kampala, Uganda, February 1996.
[8] Magistrate, interview with author, Kampala, Uganda, February 6, 1996.
[9] Neville Rubin and Eugene Cotran, eds., *Annual Survey of African Law*, 7, 1973 (London: Rex Collings, 1977), p. 126.

that after Yoweri Museveni became president in 1986, the army continued to meddle in court cases. It took several years to reestablish jurisdictional boundaries. "Some of the senior army officers started to respect the courts when they themselves got in trouble. We took an interest in the court martials. Generally, those weren't arbitrary; the judges in the military courts were lawyers too. Sometimes they overdid it, however, and we took the cases on appeal and granted bail. These days if the military doesn't respond to a writ of habeas corpus, we leak that to the press, quietly."[10]

Views from a distance often said what those more directly involved could not. Justice Vincent Crabbe, originally from the West Indies, served as a contract judge in Africa in the years after independence and went on to launch a program in legislative drafting for parliamentarians. As a young judge in Ghana, his life had once been threatened. "It led me to write a will!" he joked grimly. "People generally had great respect for judges in the early days. But then a number of things happened. The military boys altered perceptions. The status of the judiciary declined when they took over. Then the rule of law collapsed, and the judges were contaminated. The public learned that there were people in the judiciary who would give in, and they wouldn't trust the institution anymore."[11]

PREVENTIVE DETENTION

Not all of the challenges to judicial authority were extralegal. The case of preventive detention provided a window on the way the substance of the law could compromise institutional integrity too. Bad laws and bad drafting could make institution building much more difficult.

Throughout the Africa region, new governments frustrated by the difficulties of development and ill at ease with criticism resorted to vaguely defined powers of preventive detention. Like sedition acts and seditious libel provisions, preventive detention laws were all part of the package of colonial legislation new leaders retained in the independencence era. England had evolved provisions for detention in response to political problems first in Bengal and later in Ireland in the 1870s, where it had proved hard to win a conviction from an Irish jury.[12] With the advent of World War I, in 1915, the government in

[10] Peter Kabatsi, solicitor general, interview with author, Kampala, Uganda, November 8, 1995.
[11] Justice Vincent Crabbe, interview with author, Washington, D.C., May 1998.
[12] For the history of preventive detention laws, see A. W. Brian Simpson, "Round Up the Usual Suspects: The Legacy of British Colonialism and the European Convention on Human Rights," *Loyola Law Review*, 41, 2 (1995), pp. 629–711; and A. W. Brian Simpson, *In the Highest Degree Odious: Detention without Trial in Wartime Britain* (Oxford: Clarendon, 1992).

London put in place new regulations. These remained on the books after the war ended and found their way into the law of the colonies as a result. Ghana led the way by reenacting preventive detention legislation in 1958, a year after independence. Others followed suit.

Detention laws allow the arrest and imprisonment of a person before that person has actually done anything harmful to society. Moreover, confinement takes place by administrative action, without a court order or a public hearing, and for a specified period after a person is detained, the laws oust the jurisdiction of the courts. For these reasons, public security acts that contain detention provisions have attracted wide disapproval from the international legal community. During the 1960s and 1970s, they were nonetheless commonplace.[13]

Most countries in eastern and southern Africa had detention laws on the books. In Malawi, Zimbabwe, Uganda, and Kenya these were enshrined in the constitution, which spelled out in limited detail the ways in which detention could be employed. In South Africa, Zambia, Swaziland, and Tanzania, the legislation had no specific constitutional authorization.[14] Detention provisions often appeared under several different laws and under emergency powers acts.

Interpretation of detention laws varied by country and over time. In Swaziland, Tanzania, Malawi, Uganda, and Kenya, courts were generally unwilling to exercise review of detention orders.[15] Fear of a political backlash may have played a role in this practice, but the law itself seemed to many judges to dictate this result. The 1939 English precedent of *Liversidge v. Anderson*[16] shaped jurisprudence in Africa on this point. In *Liversidge*, the House of Lords decided that as long as there was a valid detention order from the secretary of state that said there were reasonable grounds, the courts could not inquire further. Years later, the position was reiterated by the English courts by Lord Denning in *R. v. Secretary of State ex parte Hosenball*, a deportation case, in 1977.[17]

The English precedent was well known in African legal circles. It was cited as persuasive authority in the controversial 1966 Ugandan case, *ex parte Matovu*, which received considerable attention in African law reviews at the time. Michael Matovu was detained under Uganda's Emergency Powers (Detention) Regulations of 1966. He challenged the detention on several

[13] On the general principles involved, see Simpson, *In the Highest Degree Odious*, and Andrew Harding and John Hatchard, eds., *Preventive Detention and Security Law: A Comparative Survey*, International Studies in Human Rights (Dordrecht: Martinus Nijhoff, 1993).

[14] Steven Greer, "Preventive Detention and Public Security: Towards a General Model," in Andrew Harding and John Hatchard, eds., *Preventive Detention and Security Law: A Comparative Survey*, International Studies in Human Rights (Dordrecht: Martinus Nijhoff, 1993), pp. 26–27.

[15] Greer, "Preventive Detention and Public Security," p. 31.

[16] *Liversidge v. Anderson*, 1942 A.C. 206.

[17] Noted in Simpson, *In the Highest Degree Odious*, p. 419.

grounds. On the issue of whether the Emergency Powers Regulations conferred overly broad discretionary powers on the president and his ministers, the court disclaimed jurisdiction to consider the exercise of power by the minister, commented Tanzanian legal scholar Yash Ghai.[18] It cited *Liversidge* approvingly. In 1970, in *Re Ibrahim*, another Ugandan case, the court echoed this view. The Kenyan court followed the same approach in *Ooko v. Attorney General*.[19] The Tanzanian courts effectively did the same until 1985, when the preventive detention law was amended to allow a detainee to petition the court on any grounds.[20]

In the late 1980s and the 1990s, the trend began to reverse. Decisions in Zimbabwe helped break the previous pattern. Zimbabwe informally institutionalized strong judicial review of detention orders during the 1980s and 1990s. And in the late 1980s, the South African courts resurrected Lord Atkin's dissenting opinion in *Liversidge* and began to assert more control.[21]

In common law eastern and southern Africa, detention laws served many ends. In the early 1960s, they were occasionally invoked to control killings and looting associated with sects. Thereafter, their use rapidly expanded. In 1966, Kenya detained a labor leader for sabotaging good relations between labor and management as well as the government's labor policy.[22] In Malawi, government officers detained people so that they might conduct criminal investigations (then Acting Chief Justice Richard Banda nullified one of these orders in 1983 and other justices followed suit).[23] Zambia extended the application of its preventive detention laws to economic crimes, including drug trafficking, in the 1980s.[24] Similarly, the Zimbabwe government sought to use detention to prevent economic sabotage. South Africa employed states of emergency and detention laws to detain thousands of people during this same period. One estimate placed the number of people incarcerated there under preventive deten-

[18] Yash P. Ghai, "Matovu's Case: Another Comment," *Eastern Africa Law Review*, 1, 1 (April 1968), p. 70; and also Robert Martin, "In the Matter of an Application by Michael Matovu," *Eastern Africa Law Review*, 1, 1 (April 1968), pp. 61–67.
[19] Joe Oloka-Onyango, "Police Powers, Human Rights and the State in Kenya and Uganda: A Comparative Analysis," *Third World Legal Studies*, 1990 (1990), p. 23.
[20] K. S. K. Lugakingira, "Personal Liberty and Judicial Attitude: The Tanzanian Case," *Eastern Africa Law Review*, 17, 1 (1990), p. 120.
[21] The dissent is used as persuasive authority in *Minister of Law and Order v. Hurley* as explained in J. Sarkin-Hughes, "South Africa," in Andrew Harding and John Hatchard, eds., *Preventive Detention and Security Law: A Comparative Survey* (Dordrecht: Martinus Nijhoff, 1993), p. 211.
[22] *P. P. Ooko v. Republic of Kenya*, unreported, as discussed in J. B. Ojwang, "Kenya," in Andrew Harding and John Hatchard, eds., *Preventive Detention and Security Law: A Comparative Survey* (Dordrecht: Martinus Nijhoff, 1993), p. 113.
[23] B. P. Wanda, "Malawi," in Andrew Harding and John Hatchard, eds., *Preventive Detention and Security Law: A Comparative Survey* (Dordrecht: Martinus Nijhoff, 1993), p. 124.
[24] Melvin Mbao, "Zambia," in Andrew Harding and John Hatchard, eds., *Preventive Detention and Security Law: A Comparative Survey* (Dordrecht: Martinus Nijhoff, 1993), p. 279.

tion legislation, between 1963 and 1986, at 7,820 and the number held under emergency powers at over 40,000.[25]

In Tanzania, the resort to preventive detention was greater than it was in most other countries. In addition to the country's Preventive Detention Act of 1962, several other laws permitted detention without trial for varying periods. The Regional Commissioners Act of 1962 allowed a regional commissioner to detain people provided he brought the person before a magistrate within forty-eight hours. In the 1980s, the Human Resources Deployment Act even permitted the arrest and detention of unemployed people before repatriation to rural areas.[26] Moreover, the original legislation stipulated that no detention order could be questioned in court. The country had no bill of rights in its constitution until much later, so it was more difficult for a lawyer to draft a complaint that someone's fundamental rights had been violated than it was elsewhere.[27]

The judiciary chose not to interpret the Preventive Detention Act as totally excluding judicial review. In 1976, the court held that it could inquire into adherence with the procedures laid out in the legislation, even if the substance of the order remained beyond the court's reach.[28] Effectively, the court adopted a subjective test of reasonableness. All that was required was that the president be satisfied that the person threatened peace and order. The legislation contained no standards to guide and check the president's decision.

Within the legal community, opposition to the law was widespread. For example, in the early 1970s, state attorneys voiced their concern, upon finding that officials had started to use preventive detention in lieu of criminal proceedings.[29] On several occasions, the court pointed out the very wide latitude the law gave the government, calling the legislation "draconian."[30] One justice remarked, "I am afraid that even 'disappearance in the night' that dreaded phenomenon of the police state could find fertile soil and be made a reality by this provision."[31] However, the courts argued that they were mainly restricted to consideration of adherence to proper procedure.

The president was clearly torn, as related by High Court Judge Kamugumya Lugakingira, many years later. The judge recalled a passage from *Freedom and Unity*, a collection of the president's speeches. There, Nyerere wrote, "The principles of individual freedom and the rule of law require that no person be

---

[25] J. Sarkin-Hughes, "South Africa," p. 210.
[26] Chris Maina Peter, "Tanzania," in Andrew Harding and John Hatchard, eds., *Preventive Detention and Security Law: A Comparative Survey* (Dordrecht: Martinus Nijhoff, 1993), p. 248. See also Chris Maina Peter, "Incarcerating the Innocent: Preventive Detention in Tanzania," *Human Rights Quarterly*, 19 (1997), pp. 113–135.
[27] This subject is the centerpiece of Chapters 7 and 8.
[28] James S. Read, "Human Rights in Tanzania," in Colin Legum and Geoffrey Mmari, eds., *Mwalimu: The Influence of Nyerere* (London: James Currey, 1995), p. 140.
[29] Ibid.
[30] Peter, "Tanzania," pp. 249–250.
[31] Ibid., p. 249.

arrested and held without quickly being convicted of illegal actions. But we know that we cannot always get the proof necessary for conviction, especially in cases of subversion, corruption, and intrigue. Yet if we adhere to the principles of the rule of law, without any exception, our young democracy—and these principles themselves—may be the sacrifice."[32]

During succeeding decades, because of the breadth in the use of preventive detention across the globe, the international community moved gradually to formulate standards for preventive detention laws in order to limit the violence done to human rights. Advocating the total abolition of these statutes appeared unrealistic, and the "model law" approach seemed more likely to curb the worst excesses. In the 1990s, Andrew Harding and John Hatchard, at the University of Zimbabwe, convened legal scholars from different parts of the globe, including many parts of Africa, to devise a set of norms.[33] They evolved several main tenets, which they argued should govern such legislation: (1) The constitution should set forth the circumstances under which it was possible to invoke detention legislation and the limitations that should be placed on use of such laws. (2) The constitutional provisions should stipulate that the judiciary has the power to review preventive detention orders, procedures, and the manner of detention, just as the courts have power to review other administrative acts. (3) Grounds for detention should relate to national security and law and order, not to economic or criminal acts. (4) The authority to detain had to be vested in a minister answerable to the legislature, not in lower officials. (5) The detention order must be served on the person detained within seven days of arrest, and it must bear the minister's signature. (6) The order also must state the grounds on which the detention was necessary and detail the allegations that led to the issue of the order. (7) The person detained must have "early and regular access to counsel of his choice, or failing any choice, to competent counsel selected by the appropriate legal professional body, and at the expense of the state." (8) All detention orders should be subject to review within two months of issue and they should lapse after six months.[34]

The standards also set out guidelines for judges for handling detention cases. The norms included rigorous enforcement of all procedural restrictions on detention. The advisers who convened urged that failure to observe any restriction should be regarded as invalidating the detention.[35] In scrutinizing the reasonableness of the government's grounds for detention, the judges were encouraged to

---

[32] Julius Nyerere as quoted in Lugakingira, "Personal Liberty and Judicial Attitude," pp. 114–115. The quote comes from Julius K. Nyerere, *Freedom and Unity* (London: Oxford University Press, 1967), p. 6.

[33] The standards are set forth in Andrew Harding and John Hatchard, "Introduction," pp. 1–22, in Andrew Harding and John Hatchard, eds., *Preventive Detention and Security Law: A Comparative Survey* (Dordrecht: Martinus Nijhoff, 1993), pp. 7–10.

[34] Ibid.

[35] Ibid., p. 10.

look carefully and critically at the allegations of fact (something courts in England had not considered they had the power to do). In evaluating the facts, they were supposed to use an objective test, not a subjective standard. That is, the perception of the minister or the person with decision-making authority was not what mattered. The question was not, did the minister or the arresting agent believe he had grounds for using the detention law? Instead, the court had to ask whether a reasonable person would have thought that the facts implied that the individual detained would cause imminent harm to law and order or public security. The "objective," reasonable-person standard was a familiar device in countries with common law traditions. Many branches of the law determined liability by asking whether someone had acted reasonably—in other words, engaged in behavior that was rational, honest, fair, moderate, and what an ordinary person in the same or similar circumstances would have done.

The Zimbabwe court eventually went a step farther and specified that the grounds should be "(1) such as prima facie warrant detention, (2) sufficiently detailed to enable the detainees to make a meaningful representation to the tribunal, and (3) based upon information which is considered reliable."[36] Finally, the government had an obligation to inform judges of each detention within twenty-four hours, and judges would have the right to meet with each detainee.

THE BAR

Whether aggressive executive branch officials can erode the independence and legitimacy of the courts depends at least partly on what well-positioned interest groups and public opinion will let them get away with. Typically the people most concerned about the impartiality and effectiveness of the judiciary are the members of the bar who have to argue cases before magistrates and judges. If the forum is partisan, then winning an argument does not depend on the skill or specialized knowledge of the advocate, the assets in which lawyers trade. Instead, social and political connections determine outcomes, and legal skills have little worth. Thus, to people who want their professional competence to matter, an impartial forum is important. And for these reasons, where the bar itself is large and well organized, one might anticipate higher levels of judicial independence to follow.

This conventional wisdom fared poorly in the Africa region. At first glance, rule of law and respect for the courts during the 1970s did seem to mirror the strength of the legal profession, as measured in the size and liveliness of the

---

[36] John Hatchard, "Zimbabwe," in Andrew Harding and John Hatchard, eds., *Preventive Detention and Security Law: A Comparative Survey* (Dordrecht: Martinus Nijhoff, 1993), p. 301.

bar. For example, in Botswana, where government officials demonstrated high respect for the judiciary, it was also true that the bar had unusual qualities. Although not organized into a law society that could act as a lobby group, advocates saw one another routinely at Lobatse, the seat of the court, or in Gaborone, the capital. Information circulated easily because of the small size of the population, which totalled just over a million people. Many of the advocates who practiced in front of the courts were also keen court watchers; they were often South Africans who played a role in the antiapartheid movement. And access to published decisions of the courts was more widespread than it was in other countries.

In Kenya, where public policies gave the private sector a greater role in the economy than it had in many other African countries at the time, the bar was larger than it was in socialist neighbors. Its members met routinely. In the early years, its officers spoke out on matters of interest to the profession.[37] But the fragility of the bar as a nonpartisan organization became readily apparent in the 1980s and 1990s, when the government sought to intervene in law society elections and harass advocates who spoke out on the subject of multiparty democracy. Many continued to voice their views, but they did so at considerable risk.

The Tanzanian bar remained relatively small. At the time of independence, most of its members were Asian, and many had left by the 1970s. For advocates, the policies embraced by the Arusha Declaration eliminated or constrained private business activities, and opportunities for the practice of law dwindled accordingly. In 1970, the legislature created the Tanzania Legal Corporation, which hired lawyers of Tanzanian birth to provide services to new public enterprises. The agency quickly expanded its services to members of the public as well, usurping much of the remaining work for private lawyers.[38] The status of the Tanganyika Law Society diminished thereafter.[39]

Looking back on the period from the 1990s, a Law Society official commented, "Lawyers faced hard times after 1965." "No African president likes lawyers," he continued. "We tell people what they can do and what they can't do. No president likes that."[40] Many of the most experienced lawyers had left, and "there were hardly any models; there was no one to learn from." Only in

[37] Yash P. Ghai, "Law and Lawyers in Kenya and Tanzania," in Clarence J. Dias, ed., *Lawyers in the Third World: Comparative and Developmental Perspectives* (Uppsala, Sweden: Scandinavian Institute of African Studies, 1981), p. 149.

[38] United Republic of Tanzania, Tanzania Financial and Legal Management Upgrading Project, "Final Report on the Attorney-General's Chambers and Other Government Legal Offices" (Dar es Salaam, Tanzania: Financial and Legal Management Upgrading Project, 1995), p. 133.

[39] The Law Society maintained the name "Tanganyika Law Society" because its ranks were limited to those who practiced before courts on the mainland.

[40] Official of the Tanganyika Law Society, interview with author, Dar es Salaam, Tanzania, May 22, 1996.

the late 1990s did the Law Society begin to play a more active role in public policy matters.

In neighboring Uganda, the position of lawyers was complicated by threats of violence and governmental instability. One district magistrate commented that out of his law school class of 1976, one member was forced into exile, one joined Yoweri Museveni's rebel movement in the bush, and five were arrested by the government in the five or so years after graduation.[41] Members of the Law Society surveyed in the 1990s said that in this climate there was little they could do to act in defense of the courts or to participate in other public policy issues. The Law Society started to take a more active role again only after Museveni's government came to power in a rebel struggle in 1986. The advocates suggested that signs of new executive branch openness created opportunities for the bar to play a larger role.[42] The Law Society's activities followed the overtures of the head of state, not vice versa. For example, in 1991, aided by the more open political climate six years after the struggle ended, the society announced it was starting a Justice Ben Kiwanuka Memorial Lecture to commemorate the chief justice who was assassinated in the Idi Amin era.[43]

In all countries, the capacity of the bar to act on behalf of judicial independence suffered from additional limitations, many of them economic. The absence of a big demand for private legal services meant that many lawyers were often unable to accept cases on behalf of indigent clients.[44] Similarly, habeas corpus applications grew unpopular because they were not remunerative and they could attract political pressure. The head of Botswana's law faculty suggested that even in his country representation in criminal cases was so financially unrewarding that defendants often went without adequate counsel, a concern many American lawyers shared about their own country, though on a different scale.[45]

Without an organized active bar, advocates feared the consequences of criticizing the courts themselves. They knew they would have to appear before the judges at whom their comments were directed. They worried about the reaction and its implications for their abilities to secure a fair hearing. When the bar would not speak on behalf of the group, individuals had to stake their personal reputations, and many chose not to do so. There was anonymity and safety in numbers and organization.

[41] Magistrate, interview with author, Masaka, Uganda, February 6, 1996.

[42] Jennifer Widner, Uganda Law Society Survey, January 1996.

[43] Uganda Law Society archives, Law Society offices, Kampala, Uganda. Note of June 18, 1991.

[44] Yash Ghai and others have made this point. See Ghai, "Law and Lawyers in Kenya and Tanzania," p. 170.

[45] Bojose Othlogile, University of Botswana, Department of Law, interview with author, Ann Arbor, Michigan, spring 1988.

THE INTELLECTUAL AGENDA

Africa's new intelligentsia was also a source of potential influence on behalf of the courts. In industrial democracies, discussion of court decisions, court management, and the relationship between the branches was an important function of universities and the press. The protection of academic freedom and of press freedom provided shelter for a range of views and for information gathering. Usually judges were uncomfortable discussing decisions, policies, or ideas with people who would appear before them in the courthouse, and vice versa. But legal scholars could engage the flaws and merits of opinions in a more rarified atmosphere without advancing or jeopardizing the interests of a client.

In the ideological hothouse of the 1960s, scholars in Africa's new universities sometimes found it difficult to play this role. Decolonization took place amid the Cold War, and law was quickly drawn into the field of battle. The Soviet Union and other countries offered their own alternative to the legal traditions brought by colonial powers. Forged from elements of civil law systems, as well as arguments and rationales drawn from social science,[46] "socialist legality" sought to maximize the legislative authority of ruling parties and strictly limited the role of judges in interpreting terms and filling gaps in statutory schemes. Introduction of new, comprehensive legislation for regulating wide areas of human activity was part of this movement, which placed an almost religious faith in the capacity of human minds to envision the range of fact patterns that could arise in a rapidly changing world.

Most of the proposals remained rhetorical, but the movement did shape elite attitudes toward judicial institutions in some countries and altered intellectual currents in some of the universities. Although the new doctrines provided for an independent judiciary to resolve disputes, the institutional arrangements in the Soviet Union and the Eastern Bloc often implied subordination of the courts to other branches of government. Judges were subject to legislative recall. The legislature could overrule judicial decisions in particular cases.[47] And there was no judicial review of administrative actions. China and Southeast Asia offered some variations on the theme but roughly conformed to this pattern. In theory and in practice, the new ideas were at odds with the belief that the judicial process should be insulated from partisan influence in individual cases.

During the mid- to late 1960s, "socialist legality" appealed to many new gov-

---

[46] Mary Ann Glendon, Michael Wallace Gordon, and Christopher Osakwe, *Comparative Legal Traditions: Text, Materials, and Cases* (St. Paul, MN: West Publishing, 1985), passim, pp. 672–703.
[47] Ibid., pp. 683–684.

ernments struggling to acquire the ability to direct social and economic change. The courts often appeared to frustrate important government initiatives, which sometimes included expropriation of property, forced movement of people, or incarceration of those who opposed a program or withheld their cooperation. Judges seemed to get in the way by insisting on things like fair hearings and compensation at market value. They also demanded that police adhere to evidence codes, that people be arrested only on reasonable suspicion, that accused persons be brought before the court in a timely manner, and so on.

The new legal ideas promised relief. In Egypt, 'Ali Sabri, the secretary general of the Arab Socialist Union, took the lead in projecting this approach.[48] He argued that judges should participate in the policy work of government, applying the law and helping to draft new legislation to advance the political objectives of those in power. The notion of separation of powers should be abandoned, and in his country judges should be members of the Arab Socialist Union, he contended. Political leaders took action against the judiciary to enforce the new point of view. Eventually, two hundred judges were removed from office. Similar ideas and innovations attracted attention in Ethiopia, Tanzania, Mozambique, Somalia, Libya, and Guinea, although they were never implemented to the same degree. They gained a toehold in many other countries.

Ironically, the countries where Western assistance to law faculties was greatest were also those where these new ideological currents caught on most strongly: Ghana, Tanzania, and Ethiopia. All presented difficult environments for legal liberals. Politicians had turned away from the multiparty Westminster parliamentary systems negotiated at the time of independence and concentrated power in the presidency and in a single political party. Many were abandoning the pluralist aspirations of Western industrial democracies.

On the other side of the continent from Tanzania, Ghana was a case in point. Political tensions had mounted in Ghana in the early 1960s. By the fall of 1963, there had already been two attempts on President Kwame Nkrumah's life. The government had grown increasingly nervous.

The law faculty became one of the casualties, injured but not destroyed. William Burnett Harvey, better known to his own countrymen as author of an important contracts casebook, had moved to Accra from the University of Michigan to assume the deanship of the Ghana Law School in 1962. Conor Cruise O'Brien was then the vice-chancellor. The law faculty was in a period of ferment. With O'Brien's assent, Harvey sought to alter the curriculum to supplement lectures with the case method and class discussion. There was some resentment toward this change and toward the presence of foreign personnel, as well as factional maneuvering that attracted the attention of Ghana's Special

---

[48] Nathan J. Brown, *The Rule of Law in the Arab World: Courts in Egypt and the Gulf* (Cambridge: Cambridge University Press, 1997), pp. 86–89.

Branch. At a speech in October 1963, Nkrumah launched an attack on the law faculty and urged that it be "Ghanaian-ized," although the majority of the faculty were already Ghanaian scholars. A wing of the political party pushed for Harvey's dismissal. Nkrumah bowed to the pressure.

A delicate situation grew more so as the months passed. In late 1963, a special court, composed of the chief justice and two other members of the Supreme Court, convened to hear an important treason case. The court convicted members of the political opposition but failed to deliver verdicts against two former ministers. The party newspapers expressed outrage and laid responsibility at the door of the law faculty and the training it provided. The chief justice was dismissed two days after the judgment. The defendants were later retried by another court and sentenced to death. The government proposed to amend the constitution to revoke judges' security of tenure in office, making continued service contingent on the president's pleasure. In January 1964, Harvey was ordered deported.[49]

International intellectual currents and internal political difficulties affected the law faculty at the University of Dar es Salaam too. When the school first started, several members of the faculty had sought to teach "law in context." They moved away from reliance on English law texts, incorporated mimeographs of local court cases into their teaching, and developed classes that exposed students to economic issues relevant to the countries they would serve.

But soon the government interjected a more political note into academic life and into these new endeavors. In 1966, leaders sought to introduce a national service requirement for university students in order to draw them into the life of the country and prevent class distinctions from developing. When the proposal met with protest, the police moved in and three hundred students were expelled.[50] Although shocked by the display, university professors took the gesture as a signal to encourage teaching in line with the new policies of the country. An academic planning committee instructed the lawyers that "[l]aw should be taught in accordance with our socialist policies."[51] It also stipulated that "[c]ontacts should be made with law institutions in Socialist countries."

As a result of these demands, the law faculty introduced a first-year course on social and economic problems of East Africa and opened a law clinic. It also

---

[49] This account comes mainly from William Burnett Harvey, "Ghana, The Curtain Falls," Unpublished manuscript in "A Selection of Lectures and Informal Talks on Law and Universities and the Communities that Usually Tolerate and Sometimes Support Them," Collection of papers in the estate of William Burnett Harvey, Boston, MA, 1999.

[50] Sol Picciotto, "Law, Life and Politics," in Issa Shivji, ed., *Limits of Legal Radicalism: Reflections on Teaching Law at the University of Dar es Salaam* (Dar es Salaam, Tanzania: Faculty of Law, University of Dar es Salaam, 1986), p. 40.

[51] Costa Mahalu, "Three Decades of the Law in Context Approach," in Issa Shivji, ed., *Limits of Legal Radicalism: Reflections on Teaching Law at the University of Dar es Salaam* (Dar es Salaam, Tanzania: Faculty of Law, University of Dar es Salaam, 1986), p. 88.

invited a series of East German legal scholars to lecture. These measures were perceived as fairly "soft," however. Commented one faculty member later, "The German academics had very limited knowledge of the inherited Tanzanian legal system. The subject they taught, an optional one, had no direct relevance. . . ."[52]

Through the mid-1970s, pressure built further. Many of the Western scholars fell under a shroud of suspicion. Others entered into hot debates about what and how to teach in order to be consistent with party ideology. A party youth league branch formed, along with a more militant student group, the University Student Africa Revolutionary Front. Both demanded a further shift to the left. An early leader of the more militant group was Yoweri Museveni, ironically the man who fifteen years after his graduation would wrest Uganda from a period of disastrous misrule, win accolades from the World Bank, and (sometimes grudgingly) rebuild the courts.[53]

Divisions appeared. Some of the radical lawyers "thought it was bourgeois to file *habeas corpus* applications," said Yash Ghai. Ghai shared many of the leanings of his colleagues, but he also had a keen sense of the practical difficulties of lawyering and a fundamental respect for law.[54] The particular brand of radicalism that swept Africa devalued the rule of law and crippled fledging governments in their dealings with outsiders. "We were producing lawyers with a (socialist) conscience, a great deal of indignation, a smattering of the social sciences and firm theoretical perspectives on the law," he commented. "We were not teaching them the skills of a negotiator or a draftsman."[55]

The problem was much the same in the neighboring civil law country, Mozambique. As a visitor to the law faculty there in the early 1980s, prominent South African lawyer and antiapartheid activist Albie Sachs noticed the discontent with law graduates who "couldn't write out contracts, they couldn't handle problems of internal discipline, they couldn't deal with international trade, they couldn't create a robust, new legal precedent that corresponded to the needs of the new society."[56] People had no confidence that the law was there to protect their interest. Instead, socialist legality protected a few.[57]

Even in the early stages, in the late 1960s, these trends ignited public argu-

[52] Ibid., pp. 88–89.

[53] J. Kanywanyi, "Twenty-five Years of Teaching Law in Dar es Salaam," *Zimbabwe Law Review*, 7 (1989–90), pp. 45–46.

[54] Yash Ghai, "Legal Radicalism, Professionalism, and Social Action: Reflections on Teaching Law in Dar es Salaam," in Issa Shivji, ed., *The Limits of Legal Radicalism: Reflections on Teaching Law at the University of Dar es Salaam* (Dar es Salaam, Tanzania: Faculty of Law, University of Dar es Salaam, 1986), pp. 28–29.

[55] Ibid., p. 30.

[56] Albie Sachs, "Two Dimensions of Socialist Legality: Recent Experience in Mozambique," *International Journal of the Sociology of Law*, 13 (1985), p. 140.

[57] Ibid., p. 139.

ments about judicial independence. In 1968, Makerere University–based *Transition* magazine, always a forum for regional debate during this period, carried two articles by Picho Ali,[58] a man on the staff of then President Milton Obote's office in Uganda. In 1966, Obote had launched a "move to the left." Picho argued that the changes constituted a revolution and that the courts had to uphold the new laws and policies, not the old. He objected to the behavior of an expatriate contract judge who had ruled differently than the president had hoped he would in a case. He wrote that "[the law was designed to] punish those elements who attempt to destroy the stability of some of the states of the continent. But because we have a judge—an expatriate judge—who thinks that the law should be interpreted exactly in the way it is written without being guided by the aims and objectives . . . such a law is supposed to serve."[59] He continued, "Law is . . . to defend the gains of our revolution and to be the legal expression of our attitudes of mind on various problems. Accordingly, ideological considerations have a part to play in legal decisions." The climax was the claim that "[i]deological parity gives . . . new content to independence of the judiciary in the sense that the judiciary accepts the aims and objectives of our state."[60]

The articles attracted much comment in letters to the editor. In a letter to the magazine entitled, "The Fact That We Hate Apartheid Should Have No Relevance in the Way We Punish Traffic Offenders," Abu Mayanja, a Ugandan politician, asked whether governments had a right to intervene in individual cases, and he objected to the manipulation of court proceedings for ideological purposes. He queried whether a visitor from South Africa cited for a traffic violation should be imprisoned for the views of his government. He also chastised the Obote government for the incoherence of its program. "In my view, talk of ideological commitment would have meaning in a state like Tanzania which has mapped out for itself a recognizable ideology, but none at all when applied to Uganda."[61] There was no real program in place, he argued, and the government had retained most of the colonial statutes and made use of them to restrict participation by the people. Another writer decried the absence of checks and balances in Uganda and quoted Thomas Jefferson's words in caution. "Let Thomas Jefferson have the last word," he wrote. Remember, "'It is better to keep the wolf out of the field than to trust to drawing his teeth and claws after he shall have entered.' President Obote may be . . . a conscientious

---

[58] Picho Ali, "The 1967 Republican Constitution of Uganda," *Transition*, 7, 34 (1968), pp. 11–12; and Picho Ali, "Ideological Commitment and the Judiciary," *Transition*, 7, 36 (1968), pp. 47–49.
[59] Ali, "Ideological Commitment and the Judiciary," p. 48.
[60] Ibid., p. 49.
[61] Letters to the Editor, *Transition*, 7, 37 (1968), p. 15. See also Abu Mayanja, "Government's Proposal for a New Constitution of Uganda," *Transition*, 6, 32 (1967), pp. 20–25.

President, but what guarantee do we have against a moron 'wolf' who might enter after him?"[62]

The exchange created its own courtroom drama. The magazine's editor and one of the letter writers were arrested on sedition charges. The magistrate found both innocent,[63] and the rapport between the judiciary and the executive worsened.

THE COLLAPSE OF LEGITIMACY

By the mid-1970s, widespread dissatisfaction with the Tanzanian courts and a perceived collapse of the rule of law inspired the creation of a special commission of inquiry, chaired by Pius Nsekwa, chief executive secretary of the Tanzania African National Union (TANU). The commission's report described the concerns that had guided the review in this way:

> In order to guarantee human dignity and equality, our proposals must not be such as will violate the basics of the Rule of Law, namely, that there should be no discrimination based on colour, religion, or sex; that there should be no arbitrary use of power; that the state should be governed in accordance with laws passed or authorized to be passed by the people or their lawful representatives; that no person should be punished for an act or omission which is not an offence created by law; that no person should be condemned without being afforded an opportunity to be heard; that no person should be tried and/or punished by a body other than a court of law or authority constituted by law for that purpose.
>
> •••
>
> The Rule of Law is an expression, in practical terms, of human dignity and equality. Since human dignity and equality cannot come about without their being accompanied by justice, the law wherewith justice in a given situation is determined should itself be just.[64]

---

[62] Peter Medad Muliro, Letters to the Editor, *Transition*, 7, 35 (1968), p. 13. Muliro's paraphrase of Jefferson is almost completely accurate. In *Notes On Virginia*, Q. XIII, 1782, Jefferson wrote, "The time to guard against corruption and tyranny is before they shall have gotten hold of us. It is better to keep the wolf out of the fold, than to trust to drawing his teeth and talons after he shall have entered." See Andrew A. Lipscomb and Albert Ellery Bergh, eds., *The Writings of Thomas Jefferson, Memorial Edition*, vol. 2 (20 volumes) (Washington, D.C.: Thomas Jefferson Memorial Association of the United States, 1903–4), p. 165.

[63] J. F. Scotton, "Judicial Independence and Political Expression in East Africa—Two Colonial Legacies," *East African Law Journal*, 6 (March 1970), p. 1.

[64] United Republic of Tanzania, Judicial System Review Commission, *Report of the Judicial System Review Commission* (Msekwa Report) (Dar es Salaam, Tanzania: Judicial System Review Commission, 1977), p. 25.

After making an initial request for public views, the commission started to tour the country to meet people face to face. It discovered that people were not only dissatisfied with the courts but also highly critical of the police, whose behavior had elicited fewer complaints to the Permanent Commission of Inquiry than the courts had. The authors of the report commented that "people cited lax, corrupt, and dishonest and partial investigators; they cited collusion by investigators with criminal and suspicious characters, and they said that many investigators mistreat complainants by either ignoring their complaints or harassing them unnecessarily."[65] The legitimacy of the justice sector as a whole had collapsed; so had the rule of law.

It began to seem that the words of the nationalist struggles would only come alive with hard experience. In the 1960s and 1970s, few members of the political elite in most countries had much acquaintance with law. Judicial independence was not part of the common sense or accumulated wisdom most new politicians brought to their roles. That was true in many parts of the world in some measure. The tension between accountability and independence was irresolvable and always bred disappointment among some, who were then tempted to abandon the ideal. Even in the late 1990s, elements of the religious right in the United States called for the impeachment of six of the justices of the U.S. Supreme Court because they did not like the substance of the court's decisions. Justice Anthony Kennedy, a centrist, was motivated to remind Americans of the basic concepts that guided the country's political life. One of the differences was that in Africa, fewer powerful constituencies were convinced of the importance of an independent court and were prepared to act to defend those views.

[65] Ibid.

CHAPTER SEVEN

Openings

BY THE MID-1970s, morale on the Tanzanian bench had reached a low point. Complaints about extralegal action by regional administrators heightened tension between the executive and the judiciary. Popular discontent with the courts appeared to run strong. Chief Justice Saidi's relationships with the other judges were strained. The final blow came with the news that Saidi was involved in a dispute in an *ujamaa* village. Saidi had joined the commune in a display of fidelity to the policies of the ruling party. When a conflict arose in the commune, he had one side arrested and moved to sit in judgment himself. He said he would preside as a magistrate, as he had in other disputes about land. There was a public outcry. "I was then a judge in Arusha," Nyalali recalled. "With some of the other members of the bench, I thought we should call up the record and quash the proceedings, so that the judgment would not stand." Nyalali added, "The sense of justice is universal. It must have reminded the farmers of the colonial days."[1]

Crisis often provides openings. The situation in Tanzania looked bad, not only to the judges and magistrates and to members of the public, but also to the outside world. The prognosis in Uganda and Malawi seemed similarly bleak. Zimbabwe was in the midst of civil war. The struggle had intensified in South Africa. Yet the turmoil eventually would produce changes in attitudes and ideas and create opportunities.

---

[1] Francis L. Nyalali, interview with author, March 21, 1996.

PROFESSIONAL RESPONSIBILITIES

As circumstances grew very difficult, judges confronted the decision of whether to resign. What should a judge do when there was an extralegal change of government, serious erosion of judicial independence, or laws that offended the sense of justice? In Zimbabwe and South Africa, racial discrimination and minority rule also challenged the legal profession, provoking judges and advocates to ask whether they could continue to serve the bench or the bar when public policies conflicted with fundamental values regarding equality before the law. There were no easy answers.

The question arose in Zimbabwe in the 1960s, when justices Robert Tredgold, John Fieldsend, and J. R. Dendy-Young left their posts—Tredgold and Fieldsend in protest over the passage of the Law and Order (Maintenance) Act and Dendy-Young after the unilateral declaration of independence and the establishment of white minority rule in 1965. Fieldsend later returned to serve as chief justice under the new majority government in the early 1980s. Dendy-Young went on to serve as chief justice of Botswana. But Fieldsend's successor, Enoch Dumbutshena, lamented that while the jurists' actions were commendable, the judiciary grew more subservient in their absence.[2] Similarly, Justice Richard Goldstone of South Africa once observed that in his country, judges who spoke out against unjust laws in legal and academic settings, or to policy makers, "tended to preserve the integrity of the South African Bench."[3] Under Chief Justice Michael Corbett, the South African courts had succeeded in curbing some of the worst aspects of apartheid, for a time. Debate about this dilemma surfaced in South Africa's law journals.[4]

In search of guidance, Dumbutshena offered that "the overriding consideration is whether one can still do justice to all manner of people without fear or favour. If one cannot, then the best thing to do is to resign or to retire conveniently."[5] South African scholar Stephen Ellmann offered a different analysis

---

[2] Enoch Dumbutshena, "The Judiciary, the Executive, and the Law," Speech delivered at the National University of Lesotho, November 29, 1987, as reprinted in *Lesotho Law Journal*, 3, 2 (1987), p. 238.

[3] Richard Goldstone, "Do Judges Speak Out?" *South African Law Journal*, 111 (1994), p. 266.

[4] See the debate between Raymond Wacks and John Dugard, for example. Raymond Wacks, "Judges and Injustice," *South African Law Journal*, 101 (1984): 266–285; and John Dugard, "Should Judges Resign?—A Reply to Professor Wacks," *South African Law Journal*, 101 (1984): 286–294.

[5] Enoch Dumbutshena, "How the Judiciary Should React to Violent Changes of Government and de Facto Regimes," Paper presented at the annual meeting of the International Commission of Jurists, Caracas, Venezuela, January 16–20, 1989, as quoted in *Commonwealth Law Bulletin*, 15, 2 (1989), p. 640.

based largely on the consequences of a judge's actions and more consistent with Dumbutshena's observations about his own predecessors on the bench. Ellmann identified three factors he thought should impinge on the judge's calculus: the extent of the taint, or how dirty the judge's hands get if he or she remains on the bench; how much good the judge can do; and how much harm will result if staying appears to legitimize the behavior or statutes that offend deep principles of the rule of law.[6] But none of these approaches yielded neat answers.

Nyalali decided to leave the Tanzanian judiciary shortly after his appointment to the High Court in Arusha. "It was a nasty period. I was not happy with the Chief Justice's leadership of the court. I was outspoken, and some of my comments had appeared in the newspapers." Shortly thereafter, the court announced Nyalali would be reposted from Arusha to Mtwara. Arusha was a prized post. By contrast, Mtwara was known among the judges as a punishing station, remote and difficult. Nyalali would be in good company at Mtwara; his predecessor in the job was Justice Robert Kisanga, whom Nyalali described as "a brilliant judge." Although too inexperienced at the time of Chief Justice Georges's departure, Kisanga had been among the men Georges hoped would succeed him.

Nyalali had grown disillusioned and decided to leave the bench. "It was 1977. The International Labor Organization (ILO) was establishing its first office for Africa and it spotted me."[7] The four years as chair of the Permanent Labor Tribunal had paid off. "The government agreed to release me." Nyalali flew to Geneva with his wife, Loyce. "We looked for a house and bought winter clothes," Loyce remembered. She was excited. "The job seemed a way to escape all the dangerous things happening in Tanzania. My husband would get some rest, and the schools would be good. I really wanted to go."[8] They returned and started to prepare for the move. Nyalali had already started to draft the budget for the new ILO office.

Three days after the couple returned to Arusha, a call came late at night. It was the attorney general. The attorney general said he could not say anything on the telephone. He remarked only, "I think the president has some little job he wants you to do before you leave," and told Nyalali to go with the people who would come to pick him up. Loyce was worried. Nyalali recalled, "The next thing I knew we were at the airport; there was a military plane to pick me up. I think I said, 'Gosh! This can't be a little assignment!' The pilot and his colleagues said, 'Judge, we don't know whether to wish you well or not. Usually we pick up people about to be appointed or about to be fired.'" Nyalali's mind raced. "I knew the law and I knew the president could not fire a judge. I knew Mwalimu would

[6] Stephen Ellmann, "What Role Should Morality Play in Judging?: To Resign or Not to Resign?" *Cardozo Law Review*, 19 (1997): 1047–1059.
[7] Francis L. Nyalali, interview with author, March 21, 1996.
[8] Loyce Phares, interview with author, Dar es Salaam, Tanzania, May 29, 1996.

not do that. He would go through the machinery of the constitution. A higher post was also a problem because I was already on my way to Geneva. I just figured it must be urgent, and that was why he had sent the plane."[9]

The attorney general was waiting at the airport when the plane arrived. He was a friend. Nyalali pushed him for information. He refused to divulge anything. Nyalali objected, "But it's unfair to keep me in suspense!" The attorney general replied, "Well, as a friend, I'm prepared to tell you. But I am attorney general and I can't violate the Secrets Act. It seems the head of state wants to make you a chief commander!" "A chief commander of what?" asked Nyalali.[10] Mentally, he tried to test that title with the name of every institution he knew and he came up dry. At the time there was no Court of Appeal. There was a chief justice already; that post was filled. And anyway he was eleventh in seniority on the court.

Nyalali went to stay with the family of the governor of the central bank, a friend. "I'll telephone you there to tell you when the president wants to see you," said the attorney general. Just as Nyalali was unpacking his clothes, the call came. The attorney general was on the line. He said he had spoken with the president and the president asked, "Where have you left him?" "He says you have kept him in suspense. A car is coming to pick you up."[11]

"I went to the president's residence and he seemed pleased to meet me. I was relieved." The president told Nyalali he was going to make some changes. The country was in a crisis. The current chief justice had agreed to retire. He had considered a number of people who might serve in the office. He knew Nyalali and knew that he had authorized his going to work in Geneva at a much higher salary than the chief justice earned. Loyce recalled that as her husband had explained it, "The president said, 'I have selected you for Geneva. I have selected you for chief justice. You choose.'"[12]

Nyalali paused, torn. He was young, only forty-two, and he should spend this part of his career helping to build his own country. That was what he had wanted to do as a university student. At the same time, the job would be extraordinarily difficult. There were other judges who rightly deserved to have been appointed to the post. They would think he could not do the job. And the conditions in the country were worrisome.

These were also times of significant change in the structure of the courts. Until 1977, the East African Court of Appeal, created before independence, continued in tandem with the new economic arrangements under the Treaty for East African Cooperation, but relationships between the participant coun-

[9] Francis L. Nyalali, interview with author, March 21, 1996.
[10] Ibid.
[11] Ibid.
[12] Ibid.

tries frayed during the 1970s. Uganda no longer played an active part after the assumption of power by Idi Amin. Tanzania and Kenya clashed over ideology and policies. And in 1977, the East African Community collapsed. Although it would be another two years before Tanzania created its own Court of Appeal,[13] Nyalali would be taking on a role different from that of his predecessors.

Nyalali decided to accept the post. It was an honor. It also promised difficult times ahead. Loyce remembered being terribly disappointed. "I was sorry. I had wanted to go to Geneva. It was my first chance to live abroad. The children were miserable; they had wanted to go too. But I thought, 'If God has chosen, that is what we should do.'"[14]

Ordinarily, a new chief justice would have had considerable preparation. He would have served as a principal judge at some stage in his career, or as a judge in charge or deputy chief justice. That background would have provided him with some management experience. Chairing the Permanent Labour Tribunal had provided Nyalali only a partial introduction. A new chief justice also would have spent many years on the country's highest bench. Nyalali had served only a little over two years as a High Court judge. He had no years of service on the Court of Appeal. Five years before when Chief Justice Georges advised the president about the choice of his successor, Nyalali had not been on the list of possible candidates; he was simply not far enough along in his career at the time.

The president's decision to appoint a new chief justice was part of a package of reforms. Nyerere surveyed the landscape and expressed grave disappointment about what he saw happening around him. In a famous pamphlet, he decried the party members and neighborhood leaders who demanded to be paid for work that was supposed to be voluntary. He attacked corruption, theft, and the abuse of public office as the major challenges facing the country. He observed that civil servants and communities sat around waiting for money before they would take the initiative, and that development stagnated in consequence. He deplored the fact that many *ujamaa* villages whose members had borrowed money failed to repay their debts. He proclaimed his dismay about finding that new factories operated at no more than 50 percent of their capacity.[15]

Nyerere's reflection on the Arusha Declaration, ten years after its articulation, was interesting not only for what it said about the state of affairs in the country, but also for the president's new thoughts on the rule of law. Nyerere explained that political leaders and civil servants should accept criticism and

[13] For a detailed discussion of the new court, see G. M. Fimbo, *Constitution Making and Courts in Tanzania* (Dar es Salaam, Tanzania: Faculty of Law, University of Dar es Salaam, 1992), pp. 71–76.

[14] Loyce Phares, interview with author, May 29, 1996.

[15] Julius K. Nyerere, *The Arusha Declaration Ten Years After* (Dar es Salaam, Tanzania: Republic of Tanzania Government Printer, 1977).

understand that their actions were not always correct. "Leadership by intimidation is not leadership," he wrote. "Detention of critics is not the answer; an Area or Regional Secretary who responds to a problem by detaining people—even within his legal powers—is almost always demonstrating his incapacity for leadership."[16] He also expressed concern that temporary "drives" to round up loiterers and criminals and to urge people to work hard had "become a disease," with little to show and much harm done.[17] He took to task the local leaders who tried to make people believe that their projects and whims were law. "[Committee] proceedings and announcements should be of interest as a contribution to public discussion, but they do not constitute law."[18] Finally, he announced that those who manned the machinery of government should give more attention to the practicality of the laws they prepared. "We should give all legislation and rules more careful consideration through the machinery laid down," he wrote.[19]

Clearly perturbed, the president chose to rethink his policies and bring new people into the ranks of the leadership. The year 1977 brought the biggest governmental reshuffling in the country's history. The ruling party and its counterpart in Zanzibar merged to constitute Chama cha Mapinduzi, the party of the revolution. A second shake-up would come in 1982–85, a few years later. A third took place in 1992–93. There was still a lack of ease with some of the principles of the rule of law on the part of the president and his successors, but space opened up for institution building in the judiciary.[20]

In 1977, Nyalali still had a lot to learn and many alliances to build. At the second crisis point, he was prepared to move the court in a new direction. Along with counterparts throughout the region, the Tanzanian courts entered a period in which the relationship between the branches of government would undergo renegotiation. For different reasons in different countries, executive branch officials found it convenient to promote the separation of powers. In 1983, Tanzania would be one of the first to begin this redefinition.

---

[16] Ibid., p. 44.
[17] Ibid., p. 47.
[18] Ibid., p. 48.
[19] Ibid.
[20] Chris Maina Peter has noted that President Nyerere's commitment to the principles of the rule of law was unsteady. Contrast the text in *The Arusha Declaration Ten Years After* with the text of Nyerere's New Year's message in 1982, in which the president stated to Tanzanian citizens, "You will already have heard of new taxes which come into force tomorrow, the first January, 1983. These tax measures will be debated in parliament in its next sitting, but in the meantime they have to be paid by everyone." See Chris Maina Peter, *Human Rights in Tanzania: Selected Cases and Materials* (Köln: Rüdiger Köppe Verlag, 1997), p. 9.

TIME

The stereotypical image of a court usually depicts judges as having no agency outside of the decisions they write. A judge might persuade through the logic laid out in a decision. At the higher levels, the decision and its reasoning will bind the lower levels of the court, increasing the judge's influence. The teaching in most law schools is fixed firmly on this concept of the judicial enterprise. There is little discussion of bargaining between judges on the bench or of negotiation to shape the relationship between the branches of government.

But the requirement that judges be nonpartisan does not mean the exclusion of institutional politics, as some might call it. Judges at the higher levels typically engage in a variety of activities that shape the status of the court. For example, they seek to enhance public knowledge of the way the courts work and explain decisions they think important. At the same time, they shape the administration of the court, the levels of funding the judiciary receives, and other matters. They are strategic actors.

Time is one of the essential elements of successful judicial strategy. A successful chief justice must command a detailed knowledge of the court, gather resources and a reservoir of esteem to help win support, and possess a feel for the public temper. Thus, skill is aided by years of observation along with the opportunity to build a rapport with others and to amass a "credit" in the accounting of favors. Moreover, it usually is necessary to tackle only a few issues at once. And it is often important to wait for the "right moment" to try to advance especially important objectives. A long time horizon permits planning and negotiation. In theory, chief justices with longer tenure in office should be able to build their institutions more effectively than those who last only a few years.

The experiences of courts in eastern and southern Africa would eventually reveal that having time to put policies into place and to choose propitious moments to introduce new procedures was neither a necessary nor a sufficient condition for the development of an independent judiciary. Looking back from the end of the century on the period of 1972–98 revealed a variety of experiences. Tanzania had the fewest chief justices and the longest average length of service. But Botswana, reputed to be one of the most independent of the courts, had the largest number of chief justices (seven), a distinction it shared with Nigeria, as well as the shortest average tenure (3.6 years). Excluding Botswana from the picture, there was a moderate correlation between low independence and decreasing length of tenure in office, as one might anticipate. The comparisons merely pointed up the fact that predisposition, talent, and the behavior of the other branches could overwhelm the importance of having enough time to negotiate reform. Duration in office was significant only if the office holder had the will to build institutional independence, the skills to do so, and opportunity.

Time, or finding "the right time," strongly affected the actions the new Chief Justice Nyalali took upon assuming office. Later legal scholars thought the chief justice had moved too slowly to embark on reform. In a short study Nyalali read with interest, sociologist Sufian Hemed Bukurura puzzled about what he considered Nyalali's lack of progress between 1977 and 1983. In *The Judiciary and Good Governance in Contemporary Tanzania*, produced for the Christien Michelsen Institute, a Norwegian foundation, Bukurura suggested that there was "a difference in Nyalali before 1984 and Nyalali post 1984." He speculated that the change in persona had to do with a change in ideas. Before 1984, legislators were sincerely committed to a nonliberal, nondemocratic ideology. After 1984, the court grew to understand that popular aspirations were fundamentally liberal and democratic after all.[21] Why hadn't that happened sooner?

The chief justice thought Bukurura's wide-ranging book was a useful statement of the problems facing the judiciary, but he took issue with the analysis of the early years of his own career. "There were other reasons for the change in my style of action," he said. "When I was appointed chief justice, I was eleventh in the order of seniority, so there was a commotion. There were people who deserved the job. I was young, and they thought I would repeat the mistakes of my predecessor, with potentially disastrous consequences for the institution." At first, cooperation was forthcoming mainly from those who were contemporaries, or those who were appointed after Nyalali started in the job. "That was understandable. I asked myself how I would have felt in their position." It seemed best not to react, to pretend opposition did not exist. "This kind of problem exists everywhere—in Uganda, in Washington."[22]

The delicate negotiation of age differences slowed progress in the first years. It also encouraged Nyalali's sympathetic interest in the career of John Marshall, who was also younger than most of his fellow justices when he became the fourth chief justice of the United States.[23] Just as Marshall had remarked with respect to his own career, Nyalali commented that he was "determined to say less and act more. I would succeed on merit," Nyalali remembered. One of the first steps was to try to build support within the court itself. He started to redeploy the limited resources at his disposal. "I sent people abroad to conferences, while I did not travel," he recalled.[24] He also set to work to convince the president that it was essential to improve terms of service within the judiciary. He knew the other judges were concerned that he would not be able to look out for them, so an improvement in conditions would help reassure them.

[21] Sufian Hemed Bukurura, *The Judiciary and Good Governance in Contemporary Tanzania: Problems and Prospects* (Bergen, Norway: Christien Michelsen Institute, Development of Human Rights Studies, September 1995), p. 17.

[22] Francis L. Nyalali, interviews with author, March 21, 1996, and May 30, 1996.

[23] Jean Edward Smith, *John Marshall: Definer of a Nation* (New York: Henry Holt, 1996), p. 287.

[24] Francis L. Nyalali, interview with author, March 17, 1996.

Moreover, "to win the internalization or acceptance of an institution, it was important to have certain status symbols," he thought. People took their cues about a person's importance from how well they were treated and how well they could look after others. Part of winning public support was to convince people that the courts could perform their jobs fairly and efficiently, but there was little doubt that aesthetics mattered too, at least initially, before people understood the judicial process better. At the time, prison officials and police commanders had transportation, while the judges walked to work. Deputy ministers had benefits like a car, a house, and water service. Nyalali wondered why they should be entitled to these things while judges were not. "The judiciary was the third branch of government. It should not be treated differently. I took the case to the president. He was ready to listen to most of the problems I brought to his attention and this was one of them."[25] After a year, the terms of service changed, and relationships on the court eased.

"I realized that if I made a mistake many of the judges would organize against me. I also realized I knew nothing about the office."[26] There should have been a system, some routines to help guide a new chief justice, but there appeared to be none. "The administrative practices were ill-defined when I took over. Everything was concentrated in the chief justice's office, even decisions about scheduling cases for hearings. My predecessor did not brief me, for obvious reasons. I did not even have a key to the cabinet where court papers were kept." Nyalali relied on his secretary for help, and thankfully, she rose to the occasion.

There were some missteps in these early years. The new chief justice himself was embroiled in one controversy, when he allegedly requisitioned a case file from a High Court judge under pressure from the president. Whatever the facts of the situation or the merits of the charge, the early impression that the young Nyalali was weak in the face of executive branch pressure appeared to hurt his endeavor to build support among fellow judges.[27]

Nyalali commented that it took him some time to learn his way around the one-party state. The Permanent Constitution of 1977 provided only slightly more resources for a new institution builder to rely on than its predecessor, the Interim Constitution of 1965. Article 3 of the Interim Constitution of 1965 had subordinated all organs of government to the ruling party, and it was still unclear whether that provision carried forward to the 1977 Permanent Constitution, which declared the country a one-party state. The revised constitution of 1977 did offer slightly enlarged protections to safeguard the indepen-

---

[25] Francis L. Nyalali, interview with author, March 21, 1996.
[26] Francis L. Nyalali, interview with author, March 21, 1996.
[27] For a brief reference to this incident, see Peter, *Human Rights in Tanzania: Selected Cases and Materials*, p. 490.

dence of senior judicial officers. New provisions said that the executive or legislature could not abolish the office of a judge of the High Court or a justice of appeal, something governments in other countries had been tempted to do when they could not dismiss the holder of the office himself. Although the 1965 constitution had provided that the salaries and emoluments of senior judges could not be reduced, the country's 1977 constitution took that provision a step further by stipulating that judges were to be paid out of the Consolidated Fund. That meant that the funds to support the judiciary would come out of monies appropriated by a parliamentary act and not out of resources that could be switched to other purposes on the whim of executive branch officials.[28]

The new chief justice also lacked some of the resources and influence typically available to his counterparts in other systems. Most African courts had little administrative support. It was hard for a chief justice to spend the time necessary to deal effectively with the other branches of government. In the United States, Congress had created the Administrative Office for the federal courts in 1939. In 1948, it launched the Judicial Conference to help improve communication within the federal courts and between the branches. Created by statute, the committee of twenty-seven federal judges, including the chief justice, met semiannually to consider policy issues that affected the courts, to make recommendations to the legislatures, and to address administrative problems. In 1967, Congress expanded the court's capacities further by constituting the Federal Judicial Center, a body designed to carry out research and education for the Conference. Tanzania and its neighbors had no real equivalent of this kind of administrative capacity, even on a small scale. The Ministry of Justice, headed by a political appointee, typically was charged with some of the same functions, but the court officials had few ways to confer with each other and could not make their pitch directly to the legislature. Developing an effective working relationship was more difficult, as a result.

Nyalali initiated some changes in management, although later it would be apparent that these did not go far enough. Decentralization seemed imperative. There were too many decisions concentrated in the main office, and that led both to slowness and to misallocation of a chief justice's time. Delegating some authority to High Court zones was one solution. It also offered other benefits. "It enabled judges to participate more in decision making. I knew this was important in order to get a few key people committed." And it provided reassurance. "I felt safer if there were more people involved. This system saved me

[28] Before 1787, English public budgeting practices did not provide parliament with full control over revenues, and it was possible to divert funds to many purposes. To check fraud, the government instituted the idea of a general budget or Consolidated Fund. All revenues flow into this budget and all expenditures come from these resources.

from making mistakes." In short order, the court established a schedule of duties for everyone.

From 1976 through the early 1980s, challenges to judicial independence continued apace. In the late 1970s, as Nyalali assumed office, several cases came before the courts in which judicial independence was explicitly at issue. The rulings of the judges gave a feel for the temper of the times. For example, the government appealed one dispute in which a magistrate had stood firm in the face of executive pressure. While waiting for the appeal to be heard, it rearrested the defendant whom the court had released. Judge Buxton Chipeta, the High Court judge who handled the matter, supported the decision of the lower court. The language of the judgment stated in no uncertain terms that

> . . . the Judiciary is supposed to be an independent institution—independent in the sense that those who are entrusted by the Constitution to decide the rights and liabilities or the guilt or innocence of people must be free from all kinds of pressures, regardless of the corners from which those pressures come. . . . the hope of those that cherish the Rule of Law [is] . . . that such flagrant interference with the independence of the Judiciary will not recur, and that when it does, it will receive the appropriate condemnation by the authorities concerned, for if such interference is ignored or allowed to continue, the freedom of the individual, whose last bastion is an independent Judiciary, will be imperiled.[29]

CRISIS

Time was important for building alliances. But time mattered in a second sense as well. Choosing "the right moment" to initiate change was also critical in the bargaining with the other branches of government.

Nyalali and his counterparts on other courts searched for openings. The judges quickly discovered that these opportunities came in several forms. Problems of corruption within the ranks of the ruling party or of government provided one common starting point for negotiating a new relationship between the branches. To save resources and political capital, party leaders sometimes delegated to the courts the responsibility for making decisions about who was guilty of corrupt practices and who was not. The desire of a new head of state to distinguish himself from his predecessors could be another powerful motive for delegating authority to independent courts. And in some cases, judges thought they could appeal to the head of state to consider his historical image or global reputation. Did leaders want to go down in the history books among those who established the rule of law or among those who extinguished it?

[29] *Republic v. Iddi Mtegule*, High Court of Tanzania at Dodoma, Criminal Revision No. 1 of 1979.

In Tanzania, the "right moment" grew out of a crisis. By the early 1980s, the country's economy was in a desperate state. One reason was that earlier policies had caused enormous dislocation. Although the legislature repealed the *ujamaa* villages program in 1982, the effects of the policies were difficult to repair. A second factor was the Arab oil embargoes of 1973 and 1978, which hit African countries hard. Fuel costs soared and slowed economic growth throughout the region. Third, in 1978, President Nyerere had authorized the Tanzanian armed forces to enter Uganda to displace Idi Amin. Amin's troops had held Ugandans hostage to military rule and excess since 1971. Early in 1978, they had crossed into Tanzania. Fearing disorder, Nyerere decided to march on Kampala, the Ugandan capital, and install another head of state. The campaign drained the Tanzanian treasury. Thus, by 1982–83, the need to rejuvenate the economy had grown urgent.

Corruption had always attracted attention and annoyance, but by the early 1980s, it was widely perceived to have run wild and to have aggravated underlying economic woes. Popular dissatisfaction and resentment of corrupt practices were intense. The government was no longer able to implement its own policies effectively. The leadership worried that scarce resources were disappearing unaccountably, that some of the party faithful and those who did business with the government were looting the public treasury.

A commercial risk assessment service that served foreign investors polled the opinions of business leaders and country "experts" and asked for estimates of the extent to which it was necessary to pay bribes to obtain information or service from government offices. The numbers had to be taken with considerable caution, given their "quick and dirty" character. In 1983, the first year for which data were available, Tanzania ranked "1" on a scale of 0 to 7, with 7 signifying "clean" government. But by 1985, when the index expanded to include a significant number of countries, Tanzania's ranking had improved to a "3," about average for the region, but considerably worse than ratings for many other parts of the world.[30]

In the memories of those who lived through it, the period was worse than the numbers suggested. Reflecting on the subject many years later, Nyalali observed that corruption took hold when the sense of being members of a close community disappeared and reputation no longer mattered to people—at least in the part of their lives they led outside their families. "Corruption by its very nature thrives in transactions involving persons perceived to be outsiders,"[31] he once told his listeners at a seminar. "[D]uring the early days of political independence . . . when the people of the country genuinely perceived themselves

---

[30] Data from *International Country Risk Guide (ICRG)* (East Syracuse, NY: The PRS Group, 1998).

[31] Francis L. Nyalali, "Speech on Corruption Delivered at the Opening of a Seminar Organized by the Danish Association for International Cooperation (MS-TCDC) at Mwengo," Usa-River, Arusha, Tanzania, November 14, 1995.

to be *ndugu* [that is, brothers and sisters] . . . there was hardly any corrupt transaction between them." Why did the problem reappear in the 1970s? One reason was the decision to turn merchants into outsiders. The commercial life of the country depended on these people, yet public policy aimed to eliminate them. Their positions grew insecure. This situation created ideal conditions for the resurgence of corrupt practices, as the merchants sought to maintain their livelihoods and as policy gave party activists a lever to pursue extortion. The trouble came from both sides.

"The second explanation is to be found in the monopolistic system of power that came into existence . . . in the early 1970s," the chief justice continued. The Tanzania African National Union (TANU) underwent a transformation from a mass movement into an elite party. "Thereafter, it was no longer sufficient to be a peasant or worker in order to be a member of the ruling party. One had to successfully undergo a course of ideological training in order to qualify for membership of the ruling party. This had the inevitable effect of creating another . . . group of insiders and outsiders."[32] The chief justice then reached for a literary allusion. "Although theoretically all Tanzania workers and peasants were 'Ndugus' [citizens], some of us had become more so than others (to paraphrase George Orwell)." The same kinds of distinctions appeared in other dealings too.

The government had long experimented with systems for controlling corruption. It had introduced anticorruption legislation in the early 1970s. It had created an ombudsman. It had introduced a leadership code. This time it responded with great severity. In April and May 1983, over a thousand people were arrested as "suspected saboteurs," most of them businessmen. The legislature passed an Economic Sabotage Act that had retrospective effect. The statute authorized vigilante searches and seizure of property, the creation of a special economic crimes tribunal removed from the supervision of the judiciary, and penalties widely described as "draconian." The activities labeled illegal were already so under existing legislation, and the main change wrought was the ouster of the jurisdiction of the courts. The new tribunal was not bound by the rules of evidence and procedure that prevailed in the country's High Court. Someone accused under the act would have "no right to bail, no right of legal representation, and no right of appeal," Appellate Court Justice Robert Kisanga lamented.[33]

In 1981–82, the use of preventive detention laws to arrest and incarcerate over a hundred people suspected of economic crimes had attracted criticism.[34] Observers suggested that the aim of the 1983 legislation was "to avoid extended use of preventive detention on a large scale against economic threats." But the

[32] Ibid.
[33] Robert H. Kisanga, "Independence of the Judiciary in Tanzania," *Indian Bar Review*, 11, 2 (1984), p. 144.
[34] *Africa Contemporary Record, Annual Survey and Documents* (New York: Holmes & Meier/Africana Publishing, 1983), p. B 281.

new act was an invitation to settle grudges and to undermine the rule of law further. It elicited protest—from the Law Society, from aid donors, and from the courts.[35]

The act differed from "economic crimes and corruption" bills introduced in other countries. Elsewhere, proposals usually called for the creation of special investigative units, often with expansive powers, but crimes uncovered were prosecuted in the common law courts, not in a special tribunal. Therefore, there was no ouster of a court's jurisdiction. Even in these circumstances, the legislation often attracted concern from human rights groups. For example, later, in the mid-1990s, when the Botswana government introduced legislation to establish a strong anticorruption unit based on the Hong Kong model, the country's newspapers and voluntary associations immediately responded with criticism. At the center of attention were powers that appeared to allow arrest without a warrant as well as investigation merely on the grounds that a person was living beyond his or her means.[36] International observers considered that the main defect was that the unit was "legalistic," complicated to manage, and therefore unlikely to work well.[37] In the late 1990s, South Africa sought to avert similar criticism by organizing a special investigative unit that could help bring civil complaints, instead of criminal cases, against those suspected of corrupt practices.

The Tanzanian judges felt a bold stand was required. Looking backward, Nyalali observed, "Timing is very important. There are times when one can't speak out against authority. But the 1980s was a time to speak out. The war with Uganda was over. The economy was in critical shape as a result of the war. The government was taking extreme measures to deal with the problem and people were wondering whether it was right to become more authoritarian."[38] There was a lot of extralegal activity. In announcing the new legislation, the president said something to the effect that, "'I hope the judges and lawyers will forgive me; this time I am going to deal with these people outside the courts.'" Nyalali continued, "The legislation came as a shock. We had admired President Nyerere's intellect and courage. It had really been his influence that had made me choose to enter law. Suddenly I had to ask myself whether I should continue as chief justice or resign. How could I continue to preside over the courts when it was declared a matter of policy to bypass the judiciary?"

[35] Issa G. Shivji, "The Rule of Law and Ujamaa: The Ideological Formation of Tanzania," *Social and Legal Studies*, 4, 2 (June 1995), p. 163.
[36] "Ditshwanelo Queries Corruption and Economic Crime Bill," *Botswana Gazette*, July 27, 1994, p. 6.
[37] For a general discussion, see Jeremy Pope, ed., *National Integrity Systems: The TI Source Book* (Bonn: Transparency International, 1995); and World Bank, "Helping Countries Combat Corruption: The Role of the World Bank," PREM Working Paper (Washington, D.C.: World Bank, September 1997).
[38] Francis L. Nyalali, interview with author, March 21, 1996.

The judges of the court deliberated about what to do. Nyalali remembered, "The judges based in Dar es Salaam expressed their anxieties and concerns whenever we met at coffee or tea breaks at the court." The general mood was clear. "I understood the judges expected some firm leadership action from me. I knew we had arrived at a turning point, as indeed it proved to be."

Nyalali would face a severe test. The chief justice's first move was to go to speak with the president. He expressed his concerns and the difficult position in which the new legislation placed him. "We spoke at length and he came to see my point of view. I suggested the country was going down the wrong path. The nation could not survive without the rule of law. This new act was a bad precedent. Other presidents would also oust the jurisdiction of the courts, for reasons less noble, and they would cite President Nyerere's example to justify their actions."

The politics were difficult. During the past decade, members of the public had grown attuned to the attack against privilege. The drumbeat against those who appeared wealthier or different or worked in unpopular trades had become an unreflective mantra in some quarters. The people most affected were merchants, whose services in conveying commodities to people met with official scorn. Marketers and retailers were "parasites." In the party, this mood extended as well to those who had university educations. "Being known as an intellectual in the 1970s and early 1980s was almost equated with being unpatriotic," Nyalali recalled.[39] "It implied one could not be trusted. The country was officially declared a country of workers and peasants. In the Soviet Union, at least in the later period, intellectuals had a recognized role. In Tanzania, they had no role." The university faculty fell under the pall cast by the public mood; so did the lawyers and the judges.

President Nyerere had to move carefully. "There was a danger of a backlash from some of the politicians if he stood up and said, 'The chief justice has urged. . . .' He could not appear to support the court's view in the face of the hostility which existed, or at least without the participation of those who represented other perspectives." The president, who also chaired the political party, suggested to Nyalali that he speak directly with the party politburo. "About a week after my meeting with Mwalimu, I received an invitation. It asked whether I would appear and explain the concerns I had expressed. I was both surprised and concerned. I knew the membership and thought to myself that I stood no chance."

Nyalali sat down to write his first paper in his role as chief justice. It was in Kiswahili. "It was not very long, but it was quite pithy. I allowed other judges to see it in advance. Mr. Justice Kisanga read it and said, 'Don't change a word.'"

The chief justice went off to Dodoma, the country's official capital, a small

---

[39] Ibid.

town in the middle of the country. "I asked Judge Lugakingira to come with me. He was a brilliant judge who played an important part in changing the legal order in the country. He said to me that the attorney general was also going to the meeting and wanted to see the paper in advance, if possible. 'An order?' I wondered. Lugakingira took him a copy, but he came back shaken. He said, 'The attorney general advises we should not deliver the paper. He thinks it will send the wrong signal. He thinks it will boomerang. He thinks the tone is wrong; it is like lecturing to schoolboys.' 'But you read this paper,' I said. 'Did you feel the same way?' 'No,' said Lugakingira. 'Justice Kisanga also read it and he told me not to change a single word. I am going to go ahead.' "[40]

The attorney general said, "CJ, I hear you are determined to go ahead. I just advise you to watch the way you present the paper. You should not lecture. Your voice should be the voice of a pleader." In the end, the attorney general assisted Nyalali in changing his tone, but the words remained untouched.

The speech's point of departure was the general problem of lawlessness in the country.[41] Nyalali remarked that the tendency to disregard the laws was very dangerous for the nation, or for any nation. But the chief justice rapidly turned to parliament's role. He explained that interpretation of laws and regulations was a challenge. Whether they expressed permissions, prohibitions, duties and obligations, or rights, laws required careful interpretation in order to preserve the intention of the legislature. He explained that there were rules that judges and magistrates were required to follow in understanding the meaning of a law. These rules were designed to help draftsmen prepare bills whose meaning judges and magistrates could easily understand. They were also supposed to help limit disputes about the meaning of words and phrases. The chief justice alluded to the consequences of not having such rules: "History has shown the many differences that have occurred in the translation of the Holy Bible and the Holy Koran." Implicit was the image of the wars those disputes about interpretation had brought on.

Nyalali gently observed that parliament had an important role to play in making sure that laws faithfully expressed the members' intentions. The members and ministers must indicate their meaning clearly to the Parliamentary draftsman. They must also pay careful attention to the language the draftsman returns to them. "[I]f members of parliament do not analyze well the arrangement of the bill of law due to lack of time or for any other reasons before discussing it, a law can be drafted that will be different than the intended meaning of the bill."

The legislation in question was an instance of having moved too quickly and

---

[40] Ibid.
[41] Francis L. Nyalali, "Address to the Central Committee of the National Executive Council of the Chama Cha Mapinduzi," Dodoma, Tanzania, May 17, 1984.

having given insufficient consideration to the choice of words. The office of the attorney general had not been fully involved, Nyalali observed. "[T]he law was drafted in a rush and it did not follow the process that was put there to make sure that the law is equal to the intentions and the meaning it was created for. In a situation like this, it is understandable why some of us were sad . . . when we heard a lot of people saying that the President's pronouncement had been deliberately twisted by the lawyers. . . ."

The speech then turned to the administration of justice. In making and enforcing laws, every person and institution had a duty to do justice, Nyalali stated. But there were rules about how the administration of justice was to take place, he continued. "When injury or harm occurs caused by a person or persons, the community . . . has methods or laws for granting relief to the harmed person. In order to avoid further conflict, the injured person and the one who caused the injury were not left to resolve the conflict among themselves." He reiterated the point, "There are methods or laws for dividing rights and duties instead of leaving the concerned parties to fight." Then he explained, "The court has been given the role of administering justice according to those laws. It has happened before . . . that other institutions that are not part of our justice system have made themselves courts without permission from the regulations or the laws of the land, but according to their own wishes. . . . If things like this continue or increase they can disrupt our nation."

Nyalali went on to consider additional sources of lawlessness. He drew attention to the problem of ignorance of the laws. "[T]here are many leaders of the party and the government who do not know even the basic regulations and laws of the land," he observed to the Central Committee. "It is very rare to find a copy of the Constitution in party and government offices. In the few offices that have a copy of the Constitution and books on the constitution, many times those books are full of cobwebs and dust, which is an indication that they have not been used." He suggested that there might be need for the party and the government to establish a program to educate high-ranking leaders on the constitution and the laws. He also urged the party and government to make greater use of the office of the attorney general so that new laws and regulations would be consistent with the constitution and the existing legal framework.

Nyalali drew attention to the plight of the institutions that heard disputes and enforced the country's laws. He noted that the police were understaffed and lacked transportation. The prisons were overcrowded. And in a point that had to be made many times over in future years, he noted that there was delay in the courts as a result of a shortage of paper. Those who prepared the budget had to understand that because the courts had to write down the proceedings of every case, their need for paper was greater than that of other government offices. He pleaded for paper. Without paper, the courts could not hear cases.

The chief justice concluded his remarks with a further caution about ignoring or disregarding the law. He pointed to the everyday consequences. "One of the results of the disregard and disrespect for the law is that citizens become uncertain about their lives, their properties, and their endeavors. They do not know what is prohibited and what is permitted. And if they know, then they are not certain if this situation will continue tomorrow and the day after tomorrow. This situation impedes the lives and the development of the people." He went on to invoke the image of neighboring Uganda, which was then considered an exemplar of the worst of the ills that beset the continent. "During the era of the evil Idi Amin in Uganda, it is said the Ugandans reached a point of not being certain if they would live another day or not. For that reason they tried to fulfill all their life's requirements here on earth in one day. The result was a lot of confusion and the loss of humanity." In his last lines, he appealed to the politicians to set an example to others.

The speech had the tone people would eventually come to expect from Nyalali. It was even-handed and clear—never fiery, never rhetorically elaborate. Yet to a greater degree than many of the later addresses, it explicitly pointed out what was wrong. Portions of the text enumerated the actions the judiciary considered objectionable, including the decision of regional Security and Defence Committees to nationalize peoples' properties unlawfully and the decision to use the Preventive Detention Act to combat lawbreaking, instead of restricting its use to threats to national security. It explained that villagization had no basis in law because the legislature had not passed statutes to implement the policy. It also observed that the neighborhood vigilante groups whose expansion the government and party had encouraged were against the constitution, which barred any person or group except the government from establishing an army in the country.

The chief justice waited for a reaction from the assembled party leaders. The response was far beyond what he had hoped for. "There were some half-hearted attempts to rebut the argument but Mwalimu squashed those. Everyone accepted that what the legislature had done was wrong. Then the question was what to do. They turned the table on the attorney general and said he had not provided them with proper legal counsel. I then understood the reasons for the AG's apprehensiveness. The politicians could not demolish my argument, but they could find an escape route."[42]

The members of the bench returned to the court and held a quiet celebration of their own. "The judges almost emptied a whole crate of beer!," the chief justice recalled.

Two weeks later, the telephone rang with a call from the party's administrative secretary. The officer thanked the chief justice for his speech. He used the

[42] Francis L. Nyalali, interview with author, March 21, 1996.

traditional expression: "I am instructed by the elders to express their appreciation." He said they would pass a resolution on the rule of law. Then he continued, "They thought the speech was so impressive that you should prepare another paper for the larger, national body."[43]

Nyalali grew concerned. "I had thought the matter was over, but it was not. I knew I had the Central Committee on my side, but I was still worried. Most of the people hostile to the courts would be on the National Executive Committee, not on the Central Committee."[44] This time he asked all the judges of the Court of Appeal to escort him, and he invited the chief justice of Zanzibar too. He tried to use the same tone he had used before.

"Something happened," he thought, at the conclusion of his speech. "I could see from the faces of the membership that it was as if I had committed an unmentionable offense. 'You upstart!' the expression seemed to say." He tried to clarify himself by saying that Mwalimu would retire the next year and that it was important to set the tone for future leaders. "I then tried to reiterate one of my central points, 'No one, however high or however low, is above the law.' "[45] That appeared to be sacrilege. "Some of the committee members were lawyers, but they seemed to think of themselves as politicians first and lawyers last on that occasion. I felt betrayed by them." They turned to the president and said it was inconceivable that the chief justice would say these things — that the chief justice was telling the president that he was not above the law. They called the members of the Court of Appeal "stooges of imperialism."

Mwalimu simply listened. "There was an adjournment between sessions. All I could think of was that in the first session there had not been a single voice in support of us," Nyalali remembered.

"When we resumed, Mwalimu was the first to speak. He addressed our opponents. He said he would never dream of living in a country where a person was above the law. We knew he was retiring. Had he not made this statement, he would have left his country with the wrong impression. This was an important statement. After his departure, it would have been total chaos if he had not said these words. You could hear a pin drop, it was so quiet."[46]

The Economic Crimes bill was revised. "The prime minister asked us to appoint a judge to help with revisions," Nyalali remembered. "It was clear the bill would not be repealed in its entirety, but we thought we could get rid of its worst aspects. The revisions were undertaken by Justice Mwakesendo." The amendments reinstated the jurisdiction of the common law courts. The jurisdiction of the new Economic Crimes Court was vested in the High Court. When sitting as an Economic Crimes Court, the court was to consist of a High

[43] Ibid.
[44] Ibid.
[45] Ibid.
[46] Ibid.

Court judge and two lay members. Prosecutions under the new act required the consent of the director of public prosecutions, who could direct that an offense under the act be tried in a resident magistrate's court, under the penal code, which covered many of the same crimes. Although the arrangement still ran against the general proviso in legal circles that a normal criminal offense be tried in the ordinary courts, using the same procedures that applied in all other cases, it was an enormous improvement on its predecessor. By the mid-1990s, the Economic Crimes Court had fallen into disuse; the government had decided to prosecute such cases in the resident magistrate's courts.[47]

The party passed a resolution on the rule of law, as promised, and the newspapers published the text. The radio also announced the party's statement that "no one however high or low is above the law." "That solved the psychological problems," the chief justice observed. "In practice, the story was different. It has taken many years to reach where we are now."[48]

The episode helped give the young chief justice some of the authority he had lacked. "The former chief justice took orders from the ministers," commented one distinguished lawyer years later. "Nyalali put away all that rubbish, even when his judges didn't support him."[49]

OPENINGS

In Tanzania, a confluence of several circumstances created an opening for the judges to renegotiate the relationship between the branches and to engage in institution building. One was the political leaders' perception of a loss of control within the party ranks, in government, and in the society at large. A second was the extremely serious condition of the economy and the pressure foreign aid agencies and financial institutions had quietly brought on the leadership to effect change. A third was the president's imminent retirement, the importance to him of having his own image associated with the good that had happened during his time in office and not the bad.

Slowly the chief justice assembled support for change. The challenge of the coming years would be to broaden and deepen understanding of the importance of an independent judiciary and to create institutional safeguards. That meant he had to make the desirability of an independent court part of the "common sense" of politicians and civil servants. He had to strengthen the professionalism of the judges and magistrates. He had to find enduring allies. And to do these things, he had to show that the courts could do their job effectively.

---

[47] United Republic of Tanzania, Tanzania Financial and Legal Management Upgrading Project (FILMUP), "The Legal Sector in Tanzania: Interim Report of the Legal Task Force," Unpublished report, Dar es Salaam, Tanzania, June 1995, pp. 14–15.
[48] Ibid.
[49] Mohammed Ismael, interview with author, Dar es Salaam, Tanzania, May 22, 1996.

In other countries, comparable "openings" or opportunities to build judicial legitimacy appeared for different reasons. Sometimes judges personally played slightly less central roles in influencing the attitudes of the executive and the legislature. At other times, they were front and center.

In Uganda, the judiciary's fortunes experienced a similar change only two or three years after the Tanzanian initiative. In 1985, Yoweri Museveni, once one of the radical student leaders who had made such an impression at the University of Dar es Salaam, won a slow rebel struggle to displace the second government of Milton Obote from power. A decade before, Idi Amin's government had killed a chief justice. But lawless behavior on the part of government officials had not ended with Amin's overthrow by Tanzanian forces. The man the Tanzanians had installed had quickly fallen to other strongmen. Milton Obote's second government was, if anything, worse than that of Idi Amin. A main reason for Museveni's appeal and his success was the promise to restore respect for justice, even though the new leader was also a sharp critic of the courts. The openness of his National Resistance Movement to the idea of judicial independence was part of creating a new political base, a grounds for differentiating itself from previous regimes.

Moreover, the Museveni government's interest in promoting commercial activity and investment made it easier for some of the judges, the solicitor general, and others to appeal for separation of powers, as well as increased financial resources for the courts. They argued that effective dispute resolution services were essential to attract investors. They built on the president's exhortations that Uganda would have to be able to make a stronger pitch to investors than its neighbors did—that it would have to be very efficient—because it had a bad reputation. It had a bloody past and it was landlocked.[50] As part of a campaign to build confidence, the reformers would have to address the problems of the judiciary.

The judicial system required considerable rebuilding. At the urging of advisers, Museveni started to reassemble the courts. His minister of justice, Abu Mayanja, had a personal interest in seeing the restoration of the rule of law. Many years before, Mayanja had written one of the letters to the editor of *Transition*, rebutting an attack on the concept of judicial independence. He had been jailed over the matter. The courts had dismissed the charges against him, to the great displeasure of the government. Likewise, Museveni called former Chief Justice Samson Wako Wambuzi back from exile and reinstalled him. Wambuzi then reached out to the ranks of the private lawyers and recruited a new deputy chief justice from that quarter. He heard that Justice John Ntagoba, also in exile after threats of violence, had taken a job with the World Intellectual Property Organization office in Harare, Zimbabwe. He sent the minister of justice to Harare to ask Ntagoba to

[50] Justice Harold G. Platt, interview with author, Kampala, Uganda, November 9, 1995.

return as principal judge and to win Ntagoba's release from his contract.

The new justice team began to build a coalition. "We avoided being too ambitious at first," said Peter Kabatsi, the solicitor general, and one of the reformers. "We began with small matters which would not prove too controversial. We persuaded people that changes would help make their work easier."[51] The reformers reached out to National Resistance Council members who were lawyers. "We appealed to their sense of professionalism. We said we needed the justice system to work so that it would be remunerative to practice law again. Traditionally the Law Society of Uganda and the Ministry had not been on good terms. We felt they should get together and we arranged opportunities."

The Ugandan reformers lobbied hard for appointments of lawyers to the posts that would be important to their efforts and built on the increasing presence of fellow law graduates in other agencies. By the mid-1990s, several senior army officers had law degrees, the head of the country's intelligence organization was a lawyer, and the Criminal Investigation Department (CID) and Special Branch had professional law men as directors. "These are young people," Kabatsi remarked. "They respect the courts."

The coalition building had to include the highest levels of the government as well. "We had to persuade the president, too," said Kabatsi. "The president started his own education in law at Dar es Salaam, but he felt too straightjacketed. He went for economics, instead. He had a general appreciation of the rule of law, but we had to persuade him that he too would be subject to the rules. He couldn't go out and disparage decisions."[52] Kabatsi considered the president remarkable in his willingness to ask questions and solicit opinions. His economic advisers built on that. So did the justice reformers.

"Openings" were delicate negotiations. "The political atmosphere is very, very important," commented one Ugandan reformer. "In the past, the judiciary was neglected. There was no sense that the government was interested in what the judges were doing. Now the government complains bitterly about the courts, but it is willing to facilitate change. The president has insulted everybody, but he also said he was willing to help."[53]

In Malawi, a similar juncture would take place only in the mid-1990s. The government of independence leader Hastings Kamuza Banda kept a strong hold on public affairs until the early 1990s, when popular anger against political repression and pressure from aid donors began to force change. Objections to ousting the jurisdiction of the courts or to taking cases to traditional courts that lacked protection from partisan interference figured in the platforms of

---

[51] Peter Kabatsi, solicitor general, interview with author, Kampala, Uganda, November 8, 1995.
[52] Ibid.
[53] Richard Buteere, interview with author, Kampala, Uganda, November 9, 1995.

new opposition leaders. Constitutional provisions developed later would reflect this concern. Banda was voted out of office in 1994, and his successor faced the need to distinguish himself from the past by permitting the courts to develop greater independence.

In Kenya, where judicial independence appeared to suffer in the 1990s, no crisis yet impelled the other branches of government to invest in building a capacity for impartial dispute resolution. By contrast with the situation in Tanzania in the mid-1980s, there was still a sense that the rule of law had not broken down severely with respect to the kinds of everyday transactions ordinary people cared about. Although the country possessed an able and articulate bar, many of whose members defended the need for impartial courts, the executive branch felt secure enough in its power to resist the calls.

The Zambian situation remained ambiguous. The ideas of opposition leaders did not embrace judicial independence as firmly as they did in Malawi. Nor did proximity to states with strongly performing judiciaries—Botswana and Zimbabwe—lead governments to copy those models.

Times were changing. During the mid-1980s, eastern and southern Africa approached a critical juncture, a point when hard experience suddenly made people more open to ideas they had rejected earlier, to new views, and to advocates of change. In several countries, there was suddenly political space to negotiate a new relationship between the branches.

The Rights Revival

THE CHANGING CIRCUMSTANCES of the mid- to late 1980s created opportunities for renegotiating the relationship between the branches of government in many countries. But the capacity to use this new political space to build stronger judicial institutions was intricately bound up with the character of the substantive law. Courts could function effectively and independently but still fail to win the public affection that is important as a long-term protection against encroachment. Enforcing harsh laws was not a ticket to winning future support. In particular, an inability to hear complaints about rights violations was a source of discomfiture. Bills of rights weighted down with limitations clauses or the absence of provisions that would allow the courts to entertain rights cases interfered with institution building. The content or substance of the law, as well as the interpretive strategies judges employed in their work, could enhance or impede the bid to invigorate the separation of powers.

The circumstances that created an opening for Chief Justice Nyalali and the Tanzanian court to champion the rule of law also rejuvenated talk of the need to protect fundamental rights. In the 1950s, the platform of the country's nationalist movement had emphasized equal protection under the law and the guarantee of basic rights. But paradoxically, along with countries like Ghana and Pakistan, Tanzania initially rejected the need to enshrine these guarantees in its independence constitution. Pakistan gained its independence in 1947, three years before the European Convention on Human Rights won adoption. Ghana won independence in 1957, also ahead of the human rights groundswell. The Tanzanian exception lay in an explicit rejection of the need for such guarantees. But by the mid-1980s, the hard experience of the first twenty-five years had started to change minds. In 1984, the same year that

Nyalali made his important address on the rule of law to political party leaders, pressure from state attorneys and the larger legal community, as well as from senior officials, finally pushed the Tanzanian government to reconsider.

The first signs of change came years before empirical studies showed a link between civil and political liberties, on the one hand, and economic development, on the other. A few years later, Nobel Prize winner Amartya Sen suggested that political rights had a major role to play in promoting development, partly by providing incentives for people to exchange information important in solving problems and partly by creating the opportunity to identify and debate needs. For example, he observed, famines did not take place in democracies where political and civil liberties were observed. Why? Because protection of the right to free speech helped ensure that news organizations would publicize such problems and protection of the right to vote would provide members of parliament with an incentive to champion timely redress.[1]

The new frame of mind also emerged years before the countries that provided development aid began to link grants and loans to human rights performance. In the mid-1980s, most bilateral aid donors remained preoccupied with traditional forms of economic assistance, such as macroeconomic policy, infrastructure, and enterprise promotion. Public objections to human rights abuses committed by recipients of American aid in Latin America had placed civil and political liberties on the agenda, but mainly in the negative sense of denying support to violators. U.S. President Jimmy Carter provided additional impetus for a new, global interest in human rights in the mid-1970s, but in Africa that effort died on the sands of the Ogaden, the contested territory between Ethiopia and Somalia, when Soviet material support of the government of Mengistu Haile Mariam in Ethiopia appeared to give new life to Western fears of Soviet expansion. Explicit assistance to nongovernmental, nonpartisan activities in support of rights was a very small part of foreign assistance. Only later, in the 1990s, would rights and "democracy" acquire significant stature for donors.

The early interest in rights was mainly home grown, the result of many thoughtful people taking the measure of their own experience and that of their neighbors. For the courts, the restiveness presented both opportunities and challenges. Some chief justices saw in the changes new ways to strengthen the perceived independence of the judiciary from the other branches of government and to enhance the legitimacy of the courts as institutions, while others thought a bill of rights portended a future of intense and debilitating struggle between the branches of government. Those on the one side reasoned that people would not perceive the courts as either independent or legitimate if

---

[1] For a simple version of the thesis, see Amartya Sen, "Freedoms and Needs: An Argument for the Primacy of Political Rights," *New Republic*, January 10–17, 1994, pp. 31–36, 38.

they could not hold government responsible for violations of rights people considered fundamental to human dignity, such as incarceration without a fair hearing. The ability to grant relief for state violations of these norms would foster respect for the services courts provided and help signal that the courts were independent of the politicians, a potential check on their power. Coupled with powers of judicial review that allowed courts to nullify laws that were in conflict with constitutional provisions, written bills of rights could help limit the ability of politicians to give repressive measures a legal veneer and thereby protect the legitimacy of the courts from severe erosion. As one South African legal scholar said in reference to his own country, "Any judicial reputation for impartiality will be harmed through the courts being constantly required to implement harsh, unpopular and unjust legal rules."[2]

But the desirability of bills of rights was still hotly contested within most African societies, even as evidence mounted pointing to the advantages civil and political liberties could bring. Because these matters were sensitive to new governments, most judges conceded that the risk of backlash was also high. They could point to evidence. In 1950, India became one of the first Commonwealth countries to adopt a bill of rights, and the government and the courts had clashed frequently and bitterly for several years thereafter.[3] That fact was well known to many African leaders. Governments could simply ignore court rulings, reverse decisions by amending the constitution, or retaliate against judges perceived to be unsympathetic to ruling party interests.

Both the language and what judges made of the language mattered. Where judges employed canons of constitutional interpretation to offer firm judicial protection of core liberties, the reputation of the courts among legal professionals for institutional integrity improved. Reportedly the court's popular following also expanded, although the evidence was anecdotal and the trend might have been attributable to other changes too.

BILLS OF RIGHTS

The debate about the importance of justiciable civil and political liberties that spread across many African countries in the mid-1980s had a precursor. In independence negotiations, the same subject had arisen, although the discussion then had focused mainly on whether to have written bills of rights.

Even among judges and lawyers in Africa there were people who doubted

---

[2] Hugh Corder, "Crowbars and Cobwebs: Executive Autocracy and the Law in South Africa," Inaugural Lecture, New Series No. 137 (Cape Town: University of Cape Town October 5, 1988), p. 9.

[3] James S. Read, "Bills of Rights in the 'Third World': Some Commonwealth Experiences," *Verfassung und Recht in Übersee*, 6, 1 (1973), p. 23.

that without "development" first, people would lack the skills to use their civil and political liberties. Moreover, they were concerned that under the conditions that currently prevailed in much of rural Africa, individual rights would prove destabilizing, by allowing extremists to flourish and to erode the rule of law. Where national security, even the unity of states, was under threat there could be no justice at all. Perhaps it was better to proceed slowly, borrowing a few of the elements of a bill of rights, but not the whole. These arguments often surfaced, but they were by far the least compelling of those made against the adoption of strong bills of rights. They also stood the test of time very poorly.[4]

The more thoughtful critics of bills of rights advanced other reasons for their positions. First, they said it was not obvious that written rights provisions were essential for the courts to enforce respect for such principles. It was commonplace to point out that England had no written constitution at all, and individual rights had fared reasonably well there. That England had roughly equivalent historical documents that set forth rights and had adopted a rights document when it signed the European Convention was often overlooked in these political debates.[5] The first application for a hearing under the European Convention was against England over the behavior of colonial officials in Cyprus. And few remarked on England's obligation to adhere to the Universal Declaration of Human Rights in its administration of trusteeship territories in the 1950s. Nyalali recalled the temper of the times. "In my education, I was much influenced by the English tradition, in which there is no written constitution. As a result, I used to believe that there was no need for a written bill of rights. I am now convinced I was quite wrong!"[6]

---

[4] In later years, the people who hawked bills of rights drew attention to the fact that initial conditions in their home countries had seemed inhospitable too. At an exchange held a decade later, American judges urged African counterparts not to assume that all the conditions touted as "prerequisites" for the exercise of rights had existed historically in the United States either. They pointed out that the U.S. Bill of Rights was a document drafted by an elite minority at a time when conditions in the United States had much in common with those in many African countries today. The economy was largely agricultural. Those without land were not asked their opinions, and women and many others could not vote. The early leaders were divided over the advisability of having political parties (the two-party system that prevails in the United States was not part of the Constitution). Some of the original states, such as Georgia, were penal colonies, settled by convicts who could scarcely be considered strong supporters of the rule of law. Although it was important not to borrow things that are wholly alien and presuppose a context that does not exist, judges and lawyers should not have to reinvent the wheel, either. After all, the American founders stole their ideas from France and England.

[5] The courts of Mauritius, Botswana, Namibia, Zimbabwe, and South Africa referred to the Convention in later years. See Christof Heyns, "African Human Rights Law and the European Convention," *South African Journal on Human Rights*, 11, 2 (1995), pp. 252–263.

[6] Francis L. Nyalali, discussion at the U.S.-Africa Judicial Exchange, Washington, D.C., Superior Court of the District of Columbia, American Bar Association, and the National Judicial College, April 1995.

Many African nationalist leaders also considered a written document a poor vehicle for winning adherence of governments to human rights standards. After all, colonial administrators had violated rights norms, despite the importance they accorded the standards. People, not pieces of paper, were what made the difference.

In Tanzania, as elsewhere, although few would admit as much out loud, some officials surely must have grown anxious that they might be sued in court for violations of rights by subordinates over whom they could exercise little control. In other parts of the world, citizens sometimes filed complaints against local governments or senior officials liable for actions taken by employees under their supervision, on the grounds that the implicit policies or management practices of the organizations promoted a violation of a citizen's rights. Relationships between managers and their subordinates always created control issues. In many parts of Africa, supervisors might not communicate with their field staff for long stretches of time, for lack of fuel, want of a functioning vehicle, or poor telephone service. To the extent that there were management guidelines or administrative policies, only rarely was there paper on which to write them. Thus, there was a high risk that one might be embarrassed by actions of "agents" or employees only nominally subject to one's supervision. Governments worried that they would have to pay out large sums in damages or settlements.

Opponents of strengthened political and civil liberties also worried that bills of rights privileged some kinds of individual interests over others. Protection of people accused of committing crimes was usually the focus of such concerns. For example, in phrases familiar to people in many parts of the world, one army representative at a seminar on the administration of justice in Uganda remarked,

> . . . when you look at the constitution of Uganda, the fundamental rights it talks about [are] . . . actually the fundamental rights of . . . individuals. And yet, . . . I hope you will well appreciate, that society also has got rights . . . not enshrined in the Constitution. As a result, we end up having individuals invoking the Constitution . . . they . . . use technicalities of the law and get away with it protected by those constitutional guarantees. . . .[7]

A related issue was whether written bills of rights would allow wealthy minorities to frustrate the will of the majority. Bills of rights protected minority views and interests and easily seemed to controvert the principles of democracy, often equated with majority rule. In countries where Europeans had settled on the

---

[7] Mr. Kaihura, National Resistance Army, as quoted in the Proceedings of the Seminar on Administration of Justice held at the International Conference Center, Kampala, Uganda, January 12–16, 1987, photocopy, p. 61.

land, bills of rights looked as though they might privilege the interests of those who were the agents of colonial power.

There was a parallel fear that judges, who were mainly expatriate at the time of independence, would use the provisions in the bills of rights to prevent new governments from adopting broad social and economic programs.[8] For many years after independence, in most countries, the judges of the higher courts came on contract from other parts of the Commonwealth—England, Ireland, Australia, Ghana, Trinidad, Nigeria, India. There was deep suspicion that these judges would protect the rights of property owners in ways that would frustrate economic development projects.

Concern about cost did not enter scholarly debates about rights in an explicit fashion until the mid-1980s, but there was little doubt that the provisions in a bill of rights could have economic consequences.[9] By contrast with "negative liberties" that specified rights not to be interfered with, some kinds of rights created "positive duties" of governments to provide services to citizens. Certainly there was an element of "positive duty" even in the standard "first-generation" civil and political liberties; the government had to enforce these protections, after all. But rights to education, housing, or health care, for example, went a step farther; they could drain the treasury if fully enforced in some countries. Further, the "horizontal" application of rights, or the ability of private individuals to sue each other in court for violations of rights, inevitably would increase the costs of the judicial system, compared to "vertical" application that limited claims under the bill of rights to actions against governments or against others acting on behalf of the state. And rules concerning standing to sue could affect the cost of rights too, by enlarging or shrinking the set of people who could come before the court. Allowing only injured parties to sue limited litigation, while allowing third parties with no direct connection to the injury to file a complaint potentially expanded the burden on the courts. These issues played no role in discussions at the time of independence and only gradually made an appearance years later, not as arguments against individual rights per se but as arguments about the form those rights should take in "transition" countries that were fiscally strapped.

Those who advocated stronger protection of basic rights placed another set of considerations on the negotiating table. Abuse of power by government officers or party members was often a source of insecurity. Moral outrage inspired by

---

[8] Chris Maina Peter, "Enforcement of Fundamental Rights and Freedoms: The Case of Tanzania," in *African Yearbook of International Law* (Dordrecht: Martinus Nijhoff, 1996), p. 85.

[9] There is a small but growing literature on the costs of rights. For example, see the controversial essay by Richard Posner, "The Costs of Enforcing Legal Rights," *East European Constitutional Review*, 4, 3 (Summer 1995), pp. 71–83; and Stephen Holmes and Cass R. Sunstein, *The Cost of Rights: Why Liberty Depends on Taxes* (New York: W. W. Norton, 1999).

false imprisonment, extortion by members of security forces, labor exactions, or the loss of family farms knew no cultural boundaries. A bill of rights could help reassure people that they would be able to realize a return on investments they made. It could also help reduce the fear of government felt by people who held minority points of view or came from minority ethnic or religious groups. Bills of rights could be conducive to growth and to nation building.

Moreover, a bill of rights had an important expressive function. Africa was at a turning point. The scale of life had changed. It was no longer as strongly tied to the village or the clan as it had once been. People were highly mobile. What the new society lacked, some reasoned, was a set of norms appropriate to the new circumstances in which people found themselves. Enshrining the most basic of those standards in a written bill of rights had an educational purpose.

Finally, without protection of political and civil liberties, it was hard to hold governments accountable for their actions. Without freedom of speech or expression, it was impossible to talk to civil servants and comment about whether the services they delivered met local needs well or poorly. People had to be able to speak their minds. To effect the removal of someone who abused power or performed poorly in a job, people also needed to have the ability to join with others, to associate with each other.

The debate about these pros and cons had its first airing in the late 1950s. In 1953, the European Convention was extended to most of the colonial territories with the understanding that it would lapse upon independence and give way to bills of rights in new constitutions. In 1959–60, Nigeria adopted a bill modeled on the Convention.[10] Uganda followed suit, and other countries such as Botswana, Zambia, and Kenya decided to move in the same direction. The contents of the rights provisions they initially entrenched were very similar, as if cut out according to the same template, right down to the rather lavish use of limitations clauses. But along with Ghana, Liberia, Ethiopia, and Malawi, Tanzania decided not to adopt a bill of rights at all.[11]

The 1964 union of Tanganyika and Zanzibar to form Tanzania provided an opportunity for political leaders to reconsider the matter carefully. President Julius Nyerere established a special commission for this purpose. Zanzibar, which merged with Tanganyika in 1964, had a bill of rights in its constitution in the early 1960s, but the new union constitution had not appropriated that language. The constitution of the political party also contained a declaration of rights. The commissioners debated whether the country's constitution should contain similar language and in the end decided against making any serious changes.

---

[10] Read, "Bills of Rights in 'The Third World': Some Commonwealth Experiences," p. 23.
[11] Simbi Mubako, "Fundamental Rights and Judicial Review: The Zambian Experience," *Zimbabwe Law Review*, 1–2 (1983–84), pp. 97–100.

Akinola Aguda, a distinguished Ghanaian jurist who served on several African courts, recalled that the commissioners worried that a bill of rights would "[require] the courts to stand in judgment over the legislature" and "the judiciary would be drawn into the arena of political controversy. This would make it more difficult, so argued the Commission, for the courts to administer laws impartially."[12] The commission acknowledged concern about governmental abuse of power, but it recommended establishment of a permanent body outside the courts with the responsibility to inquire into any allegations that might arise and report the results of its investigation to the office of the president. It also pointed to the "National Ethic" the party had promulgated and said citizens could have faith that government officers would act according to the moral obligations the "National Ethic" contained.[13]

The commissioners wrote a mention of fundamental rights into the preamble of the 1965 Interim Constitution. That passage read:

> Whereas TANU [the ruling party] believes: (a) that all human beings are equal; (b) that every individual has a right to dignity and respect . . . ; (d) that every citizen has the right to freedom of expression, of movement, of religious belief and of association within the context of law. . . . Now, therefore, the principal aims and objects of TANU shall be as follows: . . . (b) to safeguard the inherent dignity of the individual in accordance with the Universal Declaration of Human Rights.[14]

But a court could not enforce a preamble. The rules of interpretation do not treat the preamble as part of the constitution.

For a brief period, people who considered that their fundamental rights were violated could use a loophole to take their complaints to the courts. The drafters of the 1965 Interim Constitution had appended the constitution of the Tanzania African National Union (TANU), the ruling party, to the main document. The party constitution contained some protections of fundamental rights. Because it appeared as a "schedule," it was legally enforceable. As law faculty member Chris Maina Peter related, "The TANU Constitution contained beliefs and guarantees similar to those found in the Preamble and in most Bills of Rights. According to the law, the schedule, unlike the Preamble, is part of the Constitution. The schedule could therefore be used to deal with

[12] Akinola Aguda, "The Judiciary in a Developing Country," in M. L. Marasinghe and William Conklin, eds., Essays on Third World Perspectives in Jurisprudence (Singapore: Malayan Law Journal, 1984), pp. 163–164.
[13] J. T. Mwaikusa, "Genesis of the Bill of Rights in Tanzania," African Journal of International and Comparative Law, 3 (1991), p. 681.
[14] As quoted in James S. Read, "Human Rights in Tanzania," in Colin Legum and Geoffrey Mmari, eds., Mwalimu: The Influence of Nyerere (London: James Currey, 1995), p. 127.

issues relating to assertion and enforcement of fundamental rights and free-doms. . . ."[15] The legal community made sparing use of this strategy, but judges showed themselves willing to go along. The legislature eventually closed the loophole. In 1977, just as lawyers started to take the initiative, it replaced the Interim Constitution with a new, permanent document to which the party constitution was not appended, cutting off this avenue.

As in the West, the original bills of rights had focused mainly on political and civil liberties, or "first-generation rights." They were vertical rather than horizontal in application—that is, they applied to governments, not to the behavior of private individuals toward one another.[16] Generally they were "negative," not "positive," in that they created only minimal positive duties governments had to fulfill. The more expansive economic and social rights and the substantial duties they created were creatures of a later time. Individuals who claimed to suffer personal injury as a result of a violation of their rights had *locus standi*, or standing to sue, but many African jurisdictions did not provide for class actions or for representative suits filed on behalf of an injured party or class by someone unaffected. The original bills of rights also shared with Western constitutions the restriction that a government sued for violation of an individual's rights had to grant permission for a case to go forward (Western countries often enacted statutes to make this grant of permission fairly automatic).

One point of difference with Western constitutions lay in the limitations clauses that accompanied the rights provisions. These clauses restricted the applicability of rights. Eventually this practice won frowns from the international legal community, which sought to constrain the kinds of limitations that could be considered "necessary" to those set out in the International Covenant on Civil and Political Rights, and then only when the need was pressing, the aim pursued was legitimate, and the restriction imposed was proportionate to the aim.[17] The interpretation of what was necessary, legitimate, reasonable, and proportionate was supposed to be "objective," not based on the subjective perception of a political leader. Vague or overly broad limitations were frowned on. And there was a frank admonition not to use limitations clauses to silence criticism.

Limitations clauses proved important obstacles to enforcement of rights by the courts in some of the countries that had bills of rights. Years later, Chief

---

[15] Peter, "Enforcement of Fundamental Rights and Freedoms," p. 88.

[16] As in the United States, legislatures could enact statutes to provide for the application of the principles in the bill of rights to disputes between private individuals. People then could file complaints alleging violation of due process in employment decisions, violations of property rights or civil liberties, etc. under statute.

[17] Siracusa Principles on the Limitation and Derogation Provisions in the International Covenant on Civil and Political Rights, reproduced in *Human Rights Quarterly*, 7, 1 (1985), pp. 1–14.

Justice Annel Silungwe of Zambia observed that no matter how independent the court, judges are constrained in their handling of rights cases by the language the drafters used. "As it has . . . been pointed out," he noted, "the majority of human rights cases . . . have been decided in favour of the Government [in Zambia]." One reason is that "the burden of proof of an alleged human rights violation is normally on the applicant for he who asserts must prove the assertion." But, "there are too many exceptions and limitations on the guaranteed rights and freedoms in the name of the public interest."[18]

Another difference between the original constitutions of many developing countries and those of many Western countries lay in the principles of derogation. A country may suspend or "derogate from" a right under conditions specified in a constitution. Because the scale of the derogations permissible in some documents could render rights meaningless, the international legal community gradually evolved standards to govern these too. Certain rights were considered nonderogable "under any conditions even for the asserted purpose of preserving the life of the nation." These included freedom from torture; freedom from cruel, inhuman, or degrading punishment and from medical or scientific experimentation without free consent; freedom from slavery or involuntary servitude; the right not to be imprisoned for contractual debt; the right not to be convicted or sentenced to a heavier penalty by virtue of retroactive criminal legislation; the right to recognition as a person before the law; and freedom of thought, conscience, and religion.[19]

FIRST SIGNS OF RENEWAL

Paradoxically, in Tanzania the first signs of renewed focus on rights standards came from the person who earlier had rejected the need for a bill of rights, Julius Nyerere. The motivation was a neighbor, Idi Amin Dada, in Uganda. Amin's human rights abuses in his own country were well publicized. Tanzania also had suffered from Uganda's invasion of its borders in 1971–72. Amin had showered insults on the Tanzanian president. When the Organization of African Unity (OAU) declared that it would hold its annual summit meeting in Kampala, Uganda, in 1975, apparently oblivious to the these problems, Julius Nyerere announced that Tanzania would boycott. Botswana and Zambia joined him. The Tanzanian government issued a statement that said, "When massacres, oppres-

[18] Annel Silungwe, "The Judiciary and Human Rights: The Zambian Experience," Proceedings of the "American Dialogue," Makerere University, Kampala, Uganda, PP/246, Makerere University Human Rights and Peace Center (HURIPEC) Archive, Rampala, Uganda, 1994, no page.
[19] Siracusa Principles on the Limitation and Derogation Provisions in the International covenant on Civil and Political Rights, pp. 1–14.

sion and tortures are used by Africans in independent States of Africa there is no protest anywhere in Africa. . . . We are convinced that the Organization of African Unity will deserve condemnation of the world as an organization of hypocrites if it . . . appears to acquiesce in the murders and massacres which have been perpetuated by the present Ugandan Government."[20]

Having long rejected a bill of rights itself, the government of Tanzania began to push for a regional human rights organization. In its own preamble, the charter of the OAU mentioned that parties to the charter affirmed their adherence to the Universal Declaration of Human Rights.[21] But that was insufficient authority for enforcement. The organization had to create its own document, along the lines of the European Convention, and establish a body to hear complaints brought under its terms. Earlier efforts to do so had borne no fruit. But Nyerere's call mobilized others, and in 1978, Léopold Sédar Senghor, the president of Senegal, in West Africa, hosted a meeting to discuss a human rights instrument for the OAU. Other gatherings followed in Kigali, Monrovia, and Banjul.

Senghor admonished the drafters that "Europe and America have construed their systems of rights and liberties with reference to a common civilization, to respective peoples and to some specific aspirations. It is not for us Africans either to copy them or to seek originality for originality's sake. It is for us to manifest both imagination and skill. Those of our traditions that are beautiful and positive may inspire us. You should . . . constantly keep in mind our values and the real needs of Africa."[22]

The final product, the African Charter of Human and Peoples' Rights, also known as the Banjul Charter, reflected much of the ambiguity of African officialdom on the subject of rights.[23] Keba M'baye, a judge on the International

---

[20] As quoted in Costa Ricky Mahalu, "Africa and Human Rights," in Philip Kunig, Wolfgang Benedek, and Costa R. Mahalu, eds., *Regional Protection of Human Rights by International Law: The Emerging African System* (Baden-Baden: Nomos Verlagsgesellschaft, 1985), p. 15.

[21] B. Obinna Okere, "The Protection of Human Rights in Africa and the African Charter on Human and People's Rights: A Comparative Analysis with the European and American Systems," *Human Rights Quarterly*, 6, 2 (1984), p. 142.

[22] Léopold Sédar Senghor as quoted in Evelyn A. Ankumah, *The African Commission on Human and Peoples' Rights: Practice and Procedures* (The Hague: Martinus Nijhoff, 1996). The original quote comes from Senghor's keynote address at the Dakar drafting conference on November 28, 1979. Senghor said, "Il ne s'agira, pour nous Africains, ni de copier, ni de rechercher l'originalité pour l'originalité. Il nous faudra faire preuve, en meme temps, d'imagination et d'efficacité. Celles de nos traditions qui sont belles et positives pourront nous inspirer. Vous devrez donc avoir constamment a l'ésprit nos valeurs de civilisation et les besoins réels de l'Afrique." The quote appears in Emmanuel Bellow and Prince Bola A. Ajibola, eds., *Essays in Honour of Judge Taslim Olawale Elias* (Dordrecht: Martinus Nijhoff, 1992), p. 437.

[23] The description offered here draws on accounts by Lone Lindholt, *Questioning the Universality of Human Rights: The African Charter on Human and Peoples' Rights in Botswana, Malawi, and Mozambique* (Aldershot, England: Dartmouth/Ashgate, 1997); Ankumah, *The African Commission on Human and Peoples' Rights*; Rosalyn Higgins, "Africa and the Covenant on Civil and Political Rights during the First Five Years of the Journal:

Court of Justice and president of the Supreme Court of Senegal, led the experts on the drafting team. He recognized that many political leaders were deeply ambivalent about the venture. "The reality . . . [is that Africa is] more concerned with achieving economic and social development and maintaining stability of its governments than with recognizing and promoting rights and freedoms."[24] In tune with his times, the judge encouraged his fellow drafters to make the document reflect "a distinctively African conception of human rights."

M'baye's original draft protected freedom of expression, the right to a fair trial, freedom of movement, and several other important basic civil and political rights too. The authors also tried to act on Senghor's advice. In the view of legal scholar Obinna Okere, that ambition suffused the document in four ways, although it gave considerable latitude to gender discriminatory practices in the areas of family and personal law. First, pride of place went to the principle of nondiscrimination or equal protection. Second, the drafters recognized a duty of solidarity among sovereign states in the struggle against foreign domination. Third, every right corresponded with a duty of the individual to the community. And, fourth, the proposed document recognized a "right to development," an idea floated only a few years before in connection with discussions of a new relationship between industrial countries and less industrial countries, the "North" and "the South."[25]

The principle of nondiscrimination was familiar in Western constitutions; the other three concerns, less so. The language of duty could be found in basic human rights documents, such as the Declaration of the Rights and Duties of Man (1948) and the American Declaration of Rights and Duties, but it rarely won the emphasis it received in the commission's draft. It was not clear whether the provisions were supposed to be enforceable or simply hortatory. The "right to development" had no body of doctrine behind it, and the ability of an individual, group, or state to bring such a claim in a court also remained illusory.

The document underwent a transformation when it moved to the ministers of member states for approval. The ministers immediately reached for their red

Some Facts and Some Thoughts," *African Journal of International and Comparative Law,* 5, 1 (March 1993), pp. 55–66; Okere, "The Protection of Human Rights in Africa and the African Charter on Human and Peoples' Rights," pp. 141–159; Richard Gittelman, "The African Charter on Human and Peoples' Rights: A Legal Analysis," *Virginia Journal of International Law,* 22, 4 (1982), pp. 667–714; Rachel Murray, "Decisions by the African Commission on Individual Communications under the African Charter on Human and Peoples' Rights," *International and Comparative Law Quarterly,* 46 (April 1997), pp. 412–434; Edward Kannyo, "The Banjul Charter on Human and Peoples' Rights: Genesis and Political Background," in Claude Welch, Jr., and Ronald I. Meltzer, eds., *Human Rights and Development in Africa* (Albany: State University of New York Press, 1984), pp. 128–151.
[24] As quoted in Okere, "The Protection of Human Rights in Africa and the African Charter on Human and Peoples' Rights," p. 143.
[25] Ibid., passim.

pens. They introduced "clawback clauses" restricting rights the draft granted. They offered few guidelines about the reasons and conditions under which these limitations should apply. One scholar offered as an example that "[u]nder Article 6 of the Charter, '[e]very individual shall have the right to liberty and of the security of his person,'" and "[f]urthermore, 'no one may be arbitrarily arrested or detained.' Yet the charter qualified these guarantees with a clawback clause: '[n]o one may be deprived of his freedom except for reasons and conditions previously laid down by law.' "[26]

Article 10.2 of the draft provided for an unconditional right to freedom of association. Yet, as another scholar pointed out, the final text limited this right subject to "the individual's 'duties of solidarity,' in effect making article 10.2 without any legal content, since the duties are formulated so broadly that they cover almost any given situation."[27] Rights to a public hearing and to a fair trial were not guaranteed, as they were in other regional human rights documents. The ministers appeared determined to restrict the scope of government liability, at the risk of losing an important means for controlling arbitrariness on the part of officials.

The points at which observers anticipated carefully grounded, "distinctively African," innovations also disappointed. Lawyer Richard Kiwanuka observed that even the protection of "peoples' rights" that figured prominently in the document would be exceedingly difficult to secure in practice. He noted, "[T]he timorous approach to the protection of individual rights (or, indeed, any rights claimable against a state party) does not offer much hope for . . . [people's rights] to be significantly asserted."[28] The vaunted attempt to incorporate a notion of duties produced mainly vague phrases. Human rights leader Peter Takirambudde summed up the views of many when he bluntly pronounced the whole "a comparatively weak declaratory regime exacerbated by potential or actual normative incoherence."[29]

It would be wrong to characterize the reception of the charter by the growing human rights community as one of complete displeasure, however. The commission the charter created had several distinguished jurists as members, and there was every reason to believe that the members would gradually fill the gaps, clarify the ambiguities, and interpret the terms in a manner consistent with the broad aims of the initiative. And the charter proved useful, its short-

[26] Gittelman, "The African Charter on Human and Peoples' Rights," p. 692.
[27] Lindholt, *Questioning the Universality of Human Rights*, p. 78.
[28] Richard N. Kiwanuka, "The Meaning of 'People' in the African Charter on Human and Peoples' Rights," *American Journal of International Law*, 82 (1988), p. 100. For more on this subject, see H. W. O. Okoth-Ogendo, "Human and Peoples' Rights: What Point Is Africa Trying to Make?" in Ronald Cohen, Goran Hyden, and Winston P. Nagan, *Human Rights and Governance in Africa* (Gainesville, FL: University of Florida Press, 1983), pp. 74–86.
[29] Peter Takirambudde, "Six Years of the African Charter on Human and Peoples' Rights: An Assessment," *Lesotho Law Journal*, 7, 2 (1991), p. 48.

comings notwithstanding. For example, some Nigerian judges found the document a convenient way to preserve the ability to hear rights cases when military governments suspended domestic rights provisions.[30]

Political leaders also greeted the adoption of the charter with varying degrees of enthusiasm. Julius Nyerere hailed the document and the creation of a commission to hear complaints brought under it. These new contributions enabled people "sometimes to attack [human rights abuse] . . . when it is committed by Black Governments against their own people, whereas before it was regarded as heresy even to speak about such things. . . . These are new developments within the OAU and are not yet strongly entrenched. But Tanzania welcomes them just as we welcomed during 1979 the fall of Amin, and Nguema, and Bokassa. . . ."[31]

It was evident that times were changing. In the late 1950s, the age of empire was "out." It was no longer normatively acceptable to rule by occupation. And in the early post-colonial era, sovereignty first appeared to rest on grounds that were purely "juridical." That is, it rested on recognition of legal boundaries. What governments did within those borders, or whether they really exercised control at all, did not matter much in the international system. But the mid-1980s marked the hazy beginnings of a yet another concept of sovereignty. Sudanese scholar Francis Deng later coined the term "sovereignty as responsibility." Capturing some of the same ideas behind Nyerere's objections to the behavior of his neighbors, Deng and others later began to equate sovereignty with the ability of governments to respect human rights and respond to their citizens' most basic needs.[32]

Of course, Tanzania could scarcely have stood still amid these developments. Adopted in 1981, the African charter would come into force in 1986, and Tanzania had to show that it was on board. It had to reconsider the independence-era decision not to have a bill of rights. International entanglements helped produce domestic change.

The reconsideration was a product of domestic influences as well as of Nyerere's foreign policy. The union with Zanzibar remained delicate. The Zanzibaris were especially adamant that the time had come for a declaration of fundamental rights.[33] The country's dismal economic situation may have contributed to the perception that a new domestic initiative was important too. To restart economic growth, the government had to find a way to reassure farmers and businessmen that they would be able to realize a return on investments

---

[30] Frans Viljoen, "Application of the African Charter on Human and Peoples' Rights by Domestic Courts in Africa," *Journal of African Law*, 43, 1 (1999), pp. 1–17.

[31] Julius Nyerere as quoted in *Africa Contemporary Record*, 1980–81, p. B334–335.

[32] Francis Deng, Sudikiel Kimaro, Terrence Lyons, Donald Rothchild, and I. William Zartman, *Sovereignty as Responsibility* (Washington, D.C.: Brookings Institution, 1996).

[33] Mwaikusa, "Genesis of the Bill of Rights in Tanzania," p. 680; and John Kabudi Palamagamba, "The Directive Principles of State Policy versus Duties of the Individual in East African Constitutions," *Verfassung und Recht in Übersee*, 28, 3 (1995), p. 274.

they made. Tanzanian legal scholar Jani Mwaikusa noted that to reassure people that their property would not be taken in the aftermath of *ujamaa*, some of the country's leaders began to see the utility of a strong show of commitment to individual rights, including the right to property. The language of rights appeared at the same time as a shift in the colloquial terms for local traders and businessmen. Once derided, the entrepreneurs suddenly acquired the nickname, "countrymen with viable capacities," or *wananchi wenye uwezo.*[34]

The national executive committee of the ruling party initiated a nine-month public discussion about whether to adopt a bill of rights and, if so, what to include. Both the legal community and the courts played an active role in the hearings. Published in Kiswahili, the official language, the text that finally emerged in 1984 reflected the influence of the African charter and the intellectual currents of its time. "Rights of equality" featured prominently in the list of Basic Rights and Duties, which included an antidiscrimination or equal protection clause, although in common with several other African countries it left out "gender" in its enumeration of prohibited bases of discrimination. The Bill of Rights and Duties recognized the right to life; to freedom from torture and inhuman or degrading treatment; to the presumption of innocence; to a fair hearing by a court of law or other body; to freedom of speech, religion, and association; to acquire and own property; to participate in national public affairs; and to privacy. It also contained the language of duties, although it was more specific in its handling of these than the charter was.

The document subjected rights to limitations. For example, the bill of rights qualified the freedom of movement, making it subject to "any lawful act or law made for the purpose of . . . imposing restrictions on the exercise of movement so as to 1) execute a sentence or court order; or 2) to secure the fulfillment of any obligations imposed by law on that person; or 3) to protect the interest of the public in general or any specific public interest of a category of the public. . . ."[35] The provision concluded with the statement, "Such an act or law shall not be or be deemed to be invalid or inconsistent with this section." Several other rights were similarly qualified with the phrase, "subject to the laws of the land." And all were subject to the proviso that they not be exercised "in such a manner as to occasion the infringement or termination of the rights and freedoms of others or the public interest."

In Section 30 (2) the drafters also declared

> that no provision contained in this Part of this Constitution . . . shall be construed as invalidating any existing law or prohibiting the enactment of any law or the doing of any lawful act . . . making provision for:

[34] Mwaikusa, "Genesis of the Bill of Rights in Tanzania," p. 693.
[35] Constitution of the United Republic of Tanzania, 1977, as amended 1984. Unofficial translation, Helen Lwegasila Brahim, September 25, 1995, as reproduced in Chris Maina Peter, *Human Rights in Tanzania: Selected Cases and Materials* (Köln; Rüdiger Köppe Verlag, 1977), passim pp. 875–887.

a) ensuring that the rights and freedoms of others or the public interest are not prejudiced by the misuse of the individual rights and freedoms;

b) ensuring the interests of defence, public order, public morality, public health, rural and urban development planning, the development and utilization of mineral resources or the development or utilization of any other property in such manner as to promote the public benefit; . . .

f) enabling any other thing to be done which promotes, enhances or protects the national interest generally.

On its face, the language appeared to erase the guarantees set out in the document. But the actual impact would depend on how judges interpreted this language in the context of the document as a whole.

The list of duties of the individual to society included four items. The first was the duty to work, because "labour alone creates the material wealth of human society, and is the source of the well-being of the people and the measure of human dignity." The second was the duty to abide by the law. The third was the duty to safeguard public property, on which subject the bill of rights and duties said:

Article 27 (2) All persons shall be by law required to safeguard State and communal property, to combat all forms of misappropriation and wastage and to run the economy of the nation assiduously, with the attitude of people who are masters of the fate of their own nation.

The fourth duty was to defend, protect, and promote national independence.

The Tanzanian Bill of Rights and Duties was adopted as the Fifth Amendment to the country's constitution. It was a product of its times. Some elements would weather well. Others would attract increasing criticism as the continent's human rights landscape changed yet again. Soon, neighboring countries also adopted strengthened rights provisions, as new constitutions materialized in Namibia (1990), Zambia (1991), Lesotho (1993), South Africa (1994), Malawi (1995), and Uganda (1995).

UNIVERSALISTS VERSUS RELATIVISTS

Although pressure for recognition of fundamental rights started to show results in the mid-1980s, the arguments were far from over. Outside the legal profession, discussions about the scope of individual rights often collapsed into a sterile debate between "cultural relativists," on the one hand, and "universalists," on the other. Those who were wary of strengthened human rights protection tended to argue that culture was what leant validity to moral norms. Civil and political liberties were "Western" and had no roots in African cultural traditions. Therefore, they were inappropriate, or at the very least, they needed to take more account of duties of the individual toward the community, economic and social rights, and people's rights. Asian leaders resorted to this language more often and with greater vehemence than African leaders did, but the language invaded conversations in most parts of the world to some degree.

In rejoinder, universalists argued that across the globe people placed a high premium on human dignity. Individual rights were derived from this call for equal respect. They were essential concomitants to recognizing another as a human being. Moreover, they argued, the relativist conception would never work. Identifying the person or people who could speak authoritatively for a culture was problematical even when a community had long maintained its heritage. And in most parts of Africa, people had diverse lifestyles, points of view, and senses of what their "cultural traditions" included. Moreover, societies were always in a state of change, and the protections afforded those in traditional communities had broken down in most parts of Africa already. They had grown ineffective. Finally, traditional norms provided no intellectual resources for making the modern state accountable.[36] They were not designed for such a purpose.

This false dichotomy reached extremes. The tendency for Western diplomats and consultants to market prepackaged constitutional provisions abroad without listening carefully to the needs and concerns of others unwittingly leant credibility to the thesis that the movement had imperial motives.[37] Along these lines, the 1993 Bangkok Declaration announced that the concern for human rights was all part of a project to assert Western global hegemony.[38]

This way of framing differences of opinion made it harder, not easier, to think constructively about appropriate responses. One could stake out a third, contextualist approach that better captured the outlook of jurists in many parts of the world. Contextualism recognized moral universals but suggested that how they apply is importantly dependent on the facts at hand. There was certainly nothing timeless or sacred about the reigning interpretation of the U.S.

---

[36] For an introduction to the abundant writing on this topic, see Makau wa Mutua, "The Banjul Charter and the African Cultural Fingerprint: An Evaluation of the Language of Duties," *Virginia Journal of International Law*, 35 (Winter 1995), pp. 339–380; Josiah A. M. Cobbah, "African Values and the Human Rights Debate: An African Perspective," *Human Rights Quarterly*, 9 (1987), pp. 309–331; and Jack Donnelly, "Cultural Relativism and Universal Human Rights," *Human Rights Quarterly*, 6, 2 (1984), pp. 400–419; and K. Ginther and W. Benedek, eds., *New Perspectives and Conceptions of International Law: An Afro-European Dialogue* (Vienna: Springer-Verlag, 1983).

[37] For a balanced view, see William Twining, "Constitutions, Constitutionalism and Constitution Mongering," in Irwin Stotzky, ed., *The Transition to Democracy in Latin America: The Role of the Judiciary* (Boulder, CO: Westview, 1993), pp. 383–394.

[38] For a description and criticism of this view, see Yash P. Ghai, "Asian Perspectives on Human Rights," in James T. H. Tang, ed., *Human Rights and International Relations in the Asia-Pacific Region* (New York: Pinter/St. Martin's, 1995), p. 56.

Bill of Rights. As the American central government grew larger and more powerful, and as economic conditions and technology altered, the way rights were defined and enforced shifted too, to take account of new challenges. The fact of constant change meant that it was just as silly to insist that there was an equally timeless, distinctively African notion of rights and duties.

Among the chief justices of the region, as among most of those in the legal profession, there was little disagreement about this contextualist view. There were differences of opinion about the scope of some of the rights. For example, there was variation in what kinds of speech "freedom of expression" protected. But there was also basic agreement on core issues. Enoch Dumbutshena, who once fled southern Rhodesia as a dissident and later returned to a newly independent Zimbabwe as chief justice, observed that the "universality [of fundamental human rights] can be judged from the fact that no human being wants to be killed. We all want to live. We resent torture and enslavement. We like to be free and not to be imprisoned or detained. We all like to have a say in the governing of our various countries."[39]

Although he paid greater heed than many of his counterparts to the anxieties political leaders expressed about rights, Nyalali shared Dumbutshena's views. In later years he would challenge his fellow Tanzanians on this score. He chided those who insisted that countries must attain a certain level of material well-being before safeguarding political and civil liberties. "[T]he argument concerning the subordination of human rights to the basic needs for food, shelter and clothing . . . is . . . flawed," he stated. "We can all remember that argument as first put forth by colonialists to counter the demands for political independence. The colonialists told us to seek economic development first before demanding political independence."[40] In another exchange, he fell into the pithy speech common in his parts, and remarked, "I would have thought that it is better to be recognized as a human being, however poor, than to be treated like a well fed dog, which is well housed and generally well looked after by its master." As time passed, he warmed more strongly to this view.

"DOUBTS AND DARKNESS"

Although Tanzania's new constitutional amendment was an important step for the country, its language left no doubt that political leaders continued to harbor reservations about a written bill of rights, even as they acknowledged the

[39] Enoch Dumbutshena, "Role of the Judge in Advancing Human Rights," *Commonwealth Law Bulletin*, 18, 4 (October 1992), p. 1300.
[40] Francis L. Nyalali, "Speech Delivered by the Honorable Chief Justice Francis L. Nyalali at the Closing Ceremonies of a Workshop on the Bill of Rights," East African Law Society, Arusha International Conference Centre, Arusha, Tanzania, January 13, 1996.

need to offer such reassurances. The document immediately provoked debate. In short order, the law faculty at the University of Dar es Salaam asked Nyalali to offer his comments. They extended the invitation with the request that the chief justice "clear us of any doubts and darkness surrounding the whole issue of the applicability of the Bill of Rights in the country."[41] They well knew that it was the task of the courts to infuse words and phrases with meaning when those words appeared vague or contradictory, or when they left a gap.

Nyalali labored over the speech. The constraints his role placed on him limited what he could say about how the courts would look upon particular rights provisions. He had to be careful not to appear to favor some parties over others a priori, and he knew it was risky to offer interpretations in the abstract, when the particular facts of a case could alter the court's perspective in unanticipated ways. The customs of the profession made judges wary of offering these kinds of remarks. And even if he elected to break these time-honored rules, he did not really know where his fellow judges stood on these matters themselves. But to the intent listener, the speech also provided some tantalizing hints of strategies lawyers might consider when bringing cases under the new provisions.

The chief justice began by acknowledging what was most surely the sentiment of the audience. He alluded to the terms of the invitation the law faculty had sent him. The invitation had asked him to rid his audience of "doubts and darkness" about the bill of rights. He remarked that his host had chosen this language diplomatically. "What . . . he really means is that the students and members of staff of the Faculty of Law are clear and certain in their minds that the Bill of Rights will either be not applied at all or applied ineffectively in our country. So I propose to tackle today's topic in that light."[42]

In neutral language he acknowledged the difficulty the limitations clauses posed. He noted that in the Bill of Rights and Duties, "it is recognized that whenever conflict arises between the basic rights or duties of the individual on the one hand, and the rights or duties of the community on the other, the latter prevails."

> This position is reflected in the provisions of Article 17(2) (b) (i) and (iii), which restricts the basic right of freedom of movement for the purpose of enforcement of court decisions or the protection of the public interest; and Article 25 (3) (a), (b), (c) and (d) which exempts from the general prohibition against compulsory labour, any labour required in consequence of the sentence or order of a court or any labour required of members of the armed forces . . . or any labour required of any person which is reasonably necessary in the event of a state of emergency or calamity threatening the survival or well-being of the community, and any labour which forms part of normal

---

[41] From Francis L. Nyalali, "The Bill of Rights in Tanzania," Lecture presented at the Faculty of Law, University of Dar es Salaam, Dar es Salaam, Tanzania, September 5, 1985.
[42] Ibid.

communal obligations for the well-being of the community or compulsory nation-building activities according to law. . . .

It is also reflected in the provisions of Article 30 (2) (a), (b), (c), (d), (e) and (f) which exempt from the general prohibition against violation of basic rights and duties, any legislations or actions which seek to protect communal rights to security, peace, morality, health, development and progress. . . .

The justification for this paramountcy of rights and duties of the community over rights and duties of the individual flows from this premise—that a community in danger or need puts everybody in danger or need, whereas an individual in danger or need is alone in danger or need.[43]

But then he observed that the scope of the limitations was not necessarily as great as a quick reading implied.

"This overriding of rights and duties of the individual by rights and duties of the community does not however entail arbitrary action on the part of the community or its institutions," Nyalali commented, ". . . it has to be done according to law." He explained, "In other words, no rights or duties of an individual can be taken away except under existing law." Although this provision left great room for limitation of fundamental rights, Nyalali argued that it ruled out acceptance of ex post facto laws and administrative actions not carried out in conformity with procedures stated in the law, the locus of many of the rights violations in developing countries. He continued, "There is also a logical and commonsense qualification to the overriding nature of communal rights and duties. A basic right or duty of the individual stipulated under the Constitution cannot be overridden by a non-constitutional right or duty of the community. . . ."[44] The clarity with which "community rights" and duties were spelled out and the legal meaning judges would give those provisions would shape the impact of the new bill.

Nyalali then turned to the construction of the document as a whole, and here he proceeded cautiously.

> [R]eliable sources who took part in the formulation of the Bill of Rights in its present form [suggest] that there are still some genuine fears that the adoption of the entire Universal Declaration of Human Rights in a Bill of Rights . . . at this stage in our national history could lead to frequent conflicts which could undermine national stability. Such fears arise from a realization, which is not entirely unfounded, that our nation is still young and without firm traditions and institutions which can easily contain and neutralize constitutional conflicts and shocks. I think these fears tend to be overexaggerated.

The chief justice expanded on the last point, noting that "[r]ecent events concerning political turbulence in Zanzibar followed by peaceful change in politi-

---

[43] Ibid.
[44] Ibid.

cal leadership indicate that this nation of ours is maturing quickly, and is in a position to withstand and resolve its constitutional shocks constructively and peacefully. . . ."[45]

The speech then turned to the degree of congruence between the bill's provisions and the Universal Declaration of Human Rights and the way in which the court might construe the relationship between the Universal Declaration and the new document. Nyalali noted that the language was influenced partly by "a realization that a correct and fruitful enjoyment of basic rights or the proper performance of basic duties under the constitution is possible only if the spirit of the constitution is made to speak loudly and clearly in the provisions." The court would look to the provisions in the document as a whole.

> . . . Under the provisions of sub-Article (2) of Article 7 of the Constitution, these guiding principles which include the Universal Declaration of Human Rights are made not justiciable in court. However, sub-Article (1) of the same Article provides in effect that notwithstanding the provisions of sub-Article (2) the guiding principles are to be taken into account and implemented by all state organs, including those responsible for the administration of justice. . . .
>
> The role of these principles in our constitution is similar to that of the "Directive Principles of State Policy" contained in Part IV of the Indian Constitution. Article 37 of the Indian Constitution states in respect of the Directive Principles of State Policy that "The provisions contained in this Part shall not be enforceable by any court, but the principles therein laid down are nevertheless fundamental in the government of the country and it shall be the duty of the state to apply these principles in making laws."

Nyalali then presented the interpretation the Indian courts had accorded the role of the Directive Principles of State Policy in the Indian constitution. He began by quoting the chief justice of India, who had said that the Indian constitution aimed to bring about a synthesis between "Fundamental Rights" and the "Directive Principles of State Policy," " 'by giving to the former a pride of place and to the latter a place of permanence. Together, not individually, they form the core of the constitution. Together, not individually, they constitute its true conscience.' " Nyalali told his audience, "These views of the Supreme Court of India can be applied *mutatis mutandis* to our Fundamental Goals and Operative Principles of State Policy in conjunction with our Bill of Rights."

The chief justice spoke about the implication of this interpretive move. "It follows," he concluded, "that the provisions of the Universal Declaration of Human Rights, which is one of the Fundamental Goals and Operative Principles of State Policy under our constitution, are a required guide and motivation for all the activities of organs of state, including the courts. . . . I have no doubt that the courts are required to be guided by it in applying and

[45] Ibid.

interpreting the enforceable provisions of the Bill of Rights as well as the other provisions of the Constitution and all other laws."[46]

Toward the end of the talk, Nyalali drew attention to the vital role of the bar in helping to develop new human rights law in the country. Unless lawyers filed briefs that raised claims under the new amendment, the court could not infuse the piece of paper with life. "This willingness and readiness of the courts to apply the Bill of Rights can however be utilized only in appropriate cases brought before the courts," Nyalali explained. "There is no other way because the courts cannot initiate cases. A great deal therefore depends on the vigilance of advocates and state attorneys." Pushing home his point, he observed, "In the final analysis, it all depends on the quality of the law graduates from the Faculty of Law of this University."

Years later, in 1998, the chief justice reiterated these points when he launched a book on Tanzanian human rights law by Professor Chris Maina Peter, a member of the law faculty at the University of Dar es Salaam. In that speech, the chief justice focused on the role of Tanzanian advocates. The Tanzanian courts, like their American counterparts and most other common law courts, exercise powers of judicial review only when live cases or controversies come before them and the matters truly require a decision regarding the interpretation of the constitution. The chief justice pointed out that the principle of impartiality "does not allow a judge or magistrate to institute or frame a complaint before him or her."[47] Lawyers played a central role in animating bills of rights by helping ordinary people bring live controversies before the court. Only in this way could judges help bring laws and practices into conformity with the principles.

Nyalali emphasized that in a country where the majority of citizens were quite poor and lived in rural areas, legal aid would play a vital role. This assistance was essential for people to have their cases heard. And legal aid, advocates unfamiliar with the ins-and-outs of handling constitutional cases should reach out to fellow lawyers with more experience to act as *amici curiae*, or friends of the court. "It is common knowledge," Nyalali remarked, "that many important issues are never raised or never sufficiently argued in court resulting in judicial decisions which disappoint not only the legal fraternity but the public as well." He emphasized the element of partnership between the bench and the bar, commenting, "I think it is fair to say that the quality of judicial decisions in Tanzania and elsewhere depends upon the quality of adjudicators and the quality of legal representation."[48]

---

[46] Ibid.
[47] Francis L. Nyalali, "The Social Context of Judicial Decision Making," Paper presented at a workshop on the state of human rights in Tanzania, British Council Hall, Dar es Salaam, Tanzania, July 3, 1998.
[48] Ibid.

The speech to the law faculty should have helped make partners out of the professors assembled. However, what some of those present remembered most was Nyalali's firm statement that the freedom of association in the new rights provisions did not make opposition political parties automatically legal, a point of view unpopular with those in the audience. The first stirrings of a demand for multiparty politics had started to be heard in Dar es Salaam. To some in the room, the chief justice's words seemed to quash the prospect that the court would support a bid to alter the party system itself. Yet had Nyalali spoken differently, a government, many of whose members were still deeply suspicious of the new amendment and of the courts, might well have gone into open revolt, upsetting two hard years of progress in building the rule of law. Nyalali felt a decision about regime change—about the very form of government itself—was more appropriately a choice for the community to make, not the judges. No one anticipated that less than a decade later Nyalali himself would chair the commission that helped produce the very outcome the critics in the audience desired.

Politics and Interpretive Strategy

THE REFERENCE TO "darkness and doubt" in the university's invitation to the chief justice pointed up the lack of continent-wide consensus among the political elite on the subject of rights in the 1980s. Politicians, policy makers, and community leaders were still divided about the desirability of a written bill of rights and the appropriate scope of any rights conferred. Judges would have to decide whether and how this discord would affect their interpretation of some of the ambiguous terms in amendments and new constitutions. As Nigeria's eminence grise, B. O. Nwabueze wrote in his book, *Judicialism in Commonwealth Africa*, the "problem . . . calls for a sensitive balancing of society's most crucial values—the liberty of the individual and the right of the state to preserve itself."[1]

Throughout much of eastern and southern Africa, the mid-1980s and the 1990s marked the beginnings of a new era in jurisprudence. Members of the bench began to think more carefully and creatively about the methods of interpretation they used in construing the language of constitutions and of statutes. The guidelines they used would help shape acceptance of the judiciary among members of the public, whose support the courts badly wanted and needed, and among the politicians and civil servants who wielded the financial and executive power to render the courts ineffective.

In these uncertain years, Chief Justice Nyalali had to navigate these intellectual currents with special care. Whatever his own personal belief in the importance of the kinds of civil and political liberties in the Universal Declaration of Human Rights and other international conventions, he had to help his court

---

[1] B. O. Nwabueze, *Judicialism in Commonwealth Africa* (London: C. Hurst & Co., 1977), p. 298.

fashion a new jurisprudence that took account of the sharp divisions of opinion that existed in his country and allowed the court to build institutional legitimacy.

The chief justice operated under several constraints. First, there was no way for a court to reach out and decide a matter that looked as though it would enable judges to help infuse the Bill of Rights and Duties with meaning. The court had to wait until someone brought a live controversy before it. There was very little control over the timing of the issues before the court or the kinds of matters brought up. As Nyalali pointed out in his speech to the law faculty, that was the responsibility of individuals and their lawyers.

Moreover the judges held a range of views themselves, as judges did everywhere. They would take different stances, and if the parties to cases did not appeal, inconsistencies would remain. The public would be able to discern trends in the court's reasoning only after considerable time had elapsed.

INTERPRETATION AND LEGITIMACY

Because the country had no justiciable bill of rights for a long time, many of its judges had not invested heavily in thinking about their own philosophies of constitutional interpretation. Even in neighboring countries that had acquired a bill of rights at the time of independence, the judges' training reflected a British tradition of restraint. The courts adhered closely to the plain meaning of the words and to precedent. If restraint was familiar, it was also prudential. Zambian activist Rodger Chongwe observed that over the years judges had "striven hard to preserve the belief that they are not overriding executive powers, but merely coordinating them in accordance with legislative intentions." In his view, "[j]udges everywhere must take care to exercise judicial restraint in order to preserve their independent existence" and "judges in young African nations must be especially careful."[2] Of the small community of judicial "activists" outside of South Africa before the mid-1980s, few had fared well. Even in Botswana, with its reputation for relative effectiveness and independence, there was a widely shared sense that activist chief justices had not lasted long, although no one really knew why they had not stayed on.[3]

[2] Rodger M. A. Chongwe, "Limitations on the Principles of Natural Justice: An African Perspective," Paper prepared for the International Bar Association, *Commonwealth Law Bulletin*, 15, 2 (April 1989), p. 624.
[3] Bojosi Otlhogile, Faculty of Law, University of Botswana, Gaborone, interview with author, March 4, 1996; A. J. G. M. Sanders, "Constitutionalism in Botswana: A Valiant Attempt at Judicial Activism," *Comparative and International Law Journal of Southern Africa*, 16, 3 (November 1983), pp. 350–373; and Adrienne van Blerk, "The Botswana Court of Appeal: A Policy of Avoidance?" *Comparative and International Law Journal of Southern Africa*, 18, 2 (July 1985), pp. 385–395.

In Tanzania and in other parts of the region, neither plain meaning nor precedent necessarily served very well. Precedents came from settings that were sometimes far different from those in which judges had to apply the law. Under these circumstances, restraint could inflict its own forms of unfairness. Wrote a former chief justice of the Gambia, "Unless the judge in Commonwealth Africa realises and accepts that even when he adheres to the precedent of the common law, time uses him as an instrument of innovation, he may be innovative with adverse results. To apply a set of rules in situations, social or economic, different from that in which they evolved is a form of rigid adherence to precedent that puts a gulf between the law applied and the spirit of the people."[4]

When the words were ambiguous or contexts had changed, judges had to use their interpretive skills. In some common law countries, such as the United States, they would first turn to the intention of the drafters, the objectives of the legislature or constituent assembly. But this approach was unusual in most of common law Africa. The older British tradition did not allow judges to look to the record of parliamentary debates or writings that would bear on the way legislators understood the purpose or scope of ordinary legislation. In England itself, this limitation was lifted only in 1993 in the case of *Pepper v. Hart.*[5] The ruling brought English law into conformity with the general practice of the European Community. Judges in common law Africa watched English practice carefully. *Pepper v. Hart* enlarged the space for African courts to consider legislative intent in interpreting a written constitution as well as statute.

Often legislative intent did not suffice for interpretive purposes. Intent was not always easy to discern. One of the lessons political science imparted was that decisions emanating from constituent assemblies or legislatures were almost always complicated "deals" or bargains that made intent difficult to decipher. Some elected officials would take the lead in preparing or championing a bill. Others would agree to support the legislation, not because they shared the objectives of the drafters but because they wanted to trade their votes for the support of others on their own bills later. Arguably by casting a favorable vote on a bill, an elected official signaled that what the drafters said was acceptable enough, given the relative importance of the legislation in question and the time available, to represent his or her "intent" too. But judges often had to reconcile a wide range of views when they looked at the record.

In South Africa, the distinguished lawyer John Dugard expressed a different concern. He considered the method of looking to legislative intent for clarifica-

---

[4] E. O. Ayoola, "Progress and Failure of Localisation of the Common Law by Legislative and Judicial Powers in Common Law Africa," Paper presented at the Second Commonwealth Judicial Conference, Arusha, Tanzania, August 8–12, 1988, photocopy, p. 10.
[5] *Pepper v. Hart* (1993), AC 593.

tion about the meaning of a law "patently incorrect," at least if taken as the sole consideration. "In drafting a statute the government draftsmen cannot possibly foresee all the problems likely to arise in connection with that statute." He added, "Frequently the court is called upon to 'discover' the intention of the legislature on a subject in respect of which the legislature clearly had no intention at all, on a subject the legislature could not possibly have considered."[6] This problem plagued legislatures and courts around the world. It was a good reason for using intent in tandem with other canons of construction.

Nyalali commented, "If the law is to have roots in the hearts and minds of the people of our country, we must articulate it upon principles which have been tested or enunciated in our own history."[7] In interpretation, the intent of the people who had drafted the constitution and the intent of those who had prepared the legislation were sometimes ambiguous. Their words had to be read in the context of the time they were uttered. In trying to interpret the scope of the rights in the Fifth Amendment, Nyalali spent his few private hours rereading the history of the nationalist movement for the views leaders had expressed twenty-five years earlier. This became a personal project. It helped him reassure others that rights were not foreign or Western but had an important place in the aspirations of Africans.

In later years, Nyalali spoke with great enthusiasm on this project, as in a speech to fellow judges at a 1995 seminar in Arusha. "It is apparent that the principles and values which underlie the constitutional and democratic order which is in the process of being built in Tanzania and in other similar countries, are not new to us," he reminded his audience. "These principles and values were articulated on African soil by the great leaders of modern Africa. They are the principles and values which underlay the African liberation struggle and gave birth to our nationhood."[8]

The chief justice then recited the remarks of several important leaders. Although they had not always adhered to the values they articulated, Nyalali wanted to point to their unrealized aspirations. For example, he quoted Kwame Nkrumah, speaking as prime minister in the National Assembly of his country, Ghana, in November 1956. Nkrumah said, "Let me come to the general principles which, I hope, will govern the country's future Constitution. First and foremost, the Government should consider that the constitution is based on the principle that all citizens of Ghana are equal and are all entitled to the same rights." Ghana had no bill of rights at the time, but Nkrumah felt it

---

[6] John Dugard, "The Judicial Process, Positivism and Civil Liberty," Inaugural address printed in the *South African Law Journal*, 91 (1971), p. 183.
[7] Francis L. Nyalali, Keynote speech at the opening of conference on constitutionalism and the legal system in a democracy, Arusha International Conference Centre, Arusha, Tanzania, March 28, 1995, pp. 3–4.
[8] Ibid.

important to specify that "[a]llied to minority rights and of equal importance are the rights of individuals." Nkrumah's list of individual rights included freedom from arbitrary arrest, from arbitrary search and seizure, and from restrictions on speech and association. He urged that all parties should have the ability to offer their views on the government broadcasting station. "Above all the Government believe[s] that the courts of law should be absolutely independent of the Executive and should be a bulwark for the defence of the rights of the individual."

Nyalali also spoke of Julius Nyerere, the leader of Tanzania's nationalist movement. He quoted from Nyerere's address at the opening of the Pan-African Freedom Movement of East and Central Africa Conference in September 1959. "We are telling the outside world that we are fighting for our rights as human beings. We gain the sympathy of friends all over the world—in Asia, in Europe, in America—people who recognize the justice of our demand for human rights," Nyerere had said. Nyerere had gone on to speak of Little Rock, Arkansas, in the United States, where black school children had been blocked from attending the same schools as white children until the 1950s. "It doesn't matter whether he is black," Nyerere proclaimed, "we get infuriated when we see that he is not treated as a true and equal American citizen."[9]

Nyerere had challenged his listeners, "Are we going to turn around then, tomorrow after we have achieved Independence and say, 'To hell with all this nonsense about human rights; we were only using that as a tactic to harness the sympathy of the naive?' Human nature is sometimes depraved I know, but I don't believe it is depraved to that extent. I don't believe the leaders of a people are going to behave as hypocrites to gain their ends, and then turn round and do exactly the things which they have been fighting against."

The chief justice drew upon the example of Nelson Mandela too. "The ideological creed of the ANC [African National Congress] is, and always has been, the creed of African Nationalism," Mandela had said. "It is not the concept of African Nationalism expressed in the cry, 'Drive the White man into the sea.' The African nationalism for which the ANC stands is the concept of freedom and fulfillment for the African people in their own land. The most important document ever adopted by the ANC is the Freedom Charter." Developed in 1955–56 by a coali-

---

[9] As quoted in Ibid. The Pan-African Freedom Movement of East and Central Africa (PAFMECA) started in September 1958 at Mwanza, Tanzania. Julius Nyerere played a central part in organizing this movement against colonial rule, as did Abu Mayanja, later a minister of justice in Uganda under Yoweri Museoeni. Nyerere insisted that PAFMECA be nonracial, by contrast with Nkrumah, who thought Pan-Africanism should be Black. The movement's founding document included an equal protection clause and pledged "uncompromising adherence to the Rule of Law," as well as observance of the Universal Declaration of Human Rights. Richard Cox, *Pan-Africanism in Practice: An East African Study* (London: Oxford University Press, 1964), passim pp. 1–16 and quote, p. 15.

tion of people of all races in South Africa, the Freedom Charter encapsulated the movement's platform. It was based heavily on the Atlantic Charter of 1941, in which Franklin Roosevelt and Winston Churchill set forth basic principles to ensure respect for human dignity in the aftermath of World War II.

Nyalali commented, "In a sense it may therefore be said that the history of countries like Tanzania and other countries of Africa is a history of internalization of the principles and values of a world-wide liberation movement." He then reflected on the reasons why the words of the nationalist leaders often did not match the policies of new governments. He chose his words delicately and charitably, aiming to inspire people to action instead of to lay blame. "[T]he reason why Africa initially failed to build modern nations based on constitutionalism, human rights and democracy after achieving independence," he remarked, "was the absence of a substantial and active minority of people in each country who were as committed as their leaders to the principles and values of the liberation struggle."

Nyalali moved to the implications for judging. "In order for the Courts of law to play their proper role," he concluded, "the judges in those courts have to be fully conscious of the principles and values which motivated the great leaders of the African liberation movement as well as the principles and values which are indigenous to Africa."[10] The views articulated by independence leaders had no binding legal authority, but they could be persuasive, as the *Federalist Papers* were in American constitutional jurisprudence. Unfortunately, the arguments the leaders laid out were less detailed and less sustained than the judges needed in order to obtain more specific guidance.

Plain meaning, legislative intent, and the intent of the founders could all help judges construe ambiguous constitutional provisions, but they were not always sufficient. Additional canons of interpretation usually were necessary. One strategy was to evaluate the meaning of a provision by invoking time-honored common law conventions—principles and presumptions considered so basic that no draftsman could reasonably have had the intention to abrogate them, absent a clear statement to the contrary. South African lawyer John Dugard referred to these conventions as the "jural postulates which form part of our legal heritage."[11] Some of the judges in South African courts had drawn on such principles from the country's Roman-Dutch tradition during the apartheid era, in the absence of a bill of rights. In judicial proceedings, the general effect of such presumptions, when invoked, was to lessen the severity of apartheid legislation. For example, Justice Richard Goldstone noted that these postulates required "a strict interpretation to be placed upon statutory provi-

---

[10] Francis L. Nyalali, Speech at opening of the judicial seminar on constitutionalism and human rights in a democracy, Arusha, Tanzania, June 18–19, 1996.
[11] Dugard, "The Judicial Process, Positivism and Civil Liberty," p. 197.

sions which interfere with elementary rights relating to property, freedom of movement and freedom of speech."[12]

Judges also could consider the meaning of an ambiguous provision in the light of the constitutional document as a whole, instead of focusing only on the language of one provision. American jurists had long used this technique. In his 1984 "darkness and doubt" address to the law faculty, Nyalali had advocated this strategy. He had pointed out that some parts of the constitution incorporated the principles of the Universal Declaration of Human Rights, and although these parts were unenforceable, they nonetheless illuminated the meaning of other, enforceable provisions.

Third, beginning in the late 1980s, judges throughout eastern and southern Africa began to follow the example of some of their South African colleagues by referring to international human rights conventions as well as to customary international law. Drawing international law into common law had a long and distinguished heritage. It was not a novel interpretive move. Blackstone's *Commentaries* had advanced the approach almost three hundred years earlier, and common law courts throughout the world had used it since that time.[13] There were two broad types of international law to which courts referred. One included the terms of treaties or covenants the government had signed. The other was customary international law, a set of rules and practice so broadly shared that they were considered to have the status of law. The rules regulating the authority of these documents varied across countries. Often treaty terms ratified by legislatures were taken to have the force of constitutional provisions. In some countries, the legislative imprimatur was less necessary. Everywhere, rules of customary international law became principles of common law unless they were inconsistent with statutes. And generally courts were required to interpret statutes to avoid conflicts with international law.[14]

Like all interpretive strategies, this approach carried its own distinctive risks. Finding authority in treaties could create a "democratic deficit" of its own, even as it expanded the scope of rights.[15] The constitutionalization of treaty norms would bind a nation to rules developed or agreed to by a few diplomats. Countries whose constitutions required legislative ratification before treaty terms became law suffered less from this deficit, since elected

[12] Richard Goldstone, "The Reception of Dutch-Roman Law in Southern Africa and Sri Lanka, and Its Influence on Civil Liberties," in *Law in Multicultural Societies*, Proceedings of the International Association of Law Libraries Meeting, Jerusalem, July 21–26, 1985 (Jerusalem: B. G. Law Library Center/Hebrew University, 1989), p. 31.

[13] Rosalie P. Schaffer, "The Inter-relationship between Public International Law and the Law of South Africa: An Overview," *International and Comparative Law Quarterly*, 32 (April 1983), p. 283.

[14] Ibid., pp. 285–287.

[15] John H. Jackson, "Status of Treaties in Domestic Legal Systems: A Policy Analysis," *American Journal of International Law*, 86, 310 (1992), pp. 330–331.

officials would have the chance to review agreements and decide whether to assent to the terms.

The use of international law had attracted the attention of judges in South Africa in the apartheid era. Beginning in the early 1970s, South African judges started to appeal to customary international law, where it was not in conflict with statute. However, they found themselves frustrated. It seemed a stretch to consider the provisions embodied in the Universal Declaration as customary international law, and because the government had not signed the main United Nations–sponsored covenants, the treaty-based grounding of fundamental rights was out of reach.[16] In the 1990s, recognition of the utility of international norms in upholding respect for human dignity led the framers of the country's new constitution to acknowledge international norms as a source of law.

Parallel changes in interpretive strategy took place throughout the region, moved forward partly by quiet contacts at judicial conferences. By the mid-1980s, courts in Botswana and Zimbabwe had started to employ international law to help with interpretation of both statutes and constitutional provisions. Slowly, others followed suit. Scholar Tiyanjana Maluwa noted that the constituent assemblies convened to draft new constitutions in Africa in the 1990s created documents that were especially "international law friendly,"[17] opening the prospect of a broader use of international norms into the next century, the drafters thought the benefits outweighed the risk of succumbing to "globalization."

Finally, judges occasionally sought to introduce policy considerations as factors in interpretation too, although African courts tended to do so less explicitly than courts in some other parts of the world. Judges had to tread very carefully if they entered this realm. Some kinds of policy considerations were less controversial than others. For example, judges might construe a right to life or to health care as limited when a country's supply of medical technology was scarce and subject to sharp fiscal constraints, as the South African courts did. Or a court might take into account whether a law or practice respected the relationship between the branches or between the levels of government, as spelled out in the constitution. But policy considerations had to be handled carefully. They could be a conduit for judges' own political points of view, for economic or social fads, or for "executive-mindedness." Further, policy matters usually and most appropriately were left to the political process, at least in countries that had participatory government.

Nyalali suggested that judges should be concerned about the economic impact of their decisions. "Policy" concerns, as they related to economics,

---

[16] John Dugard, "The Role of International Law in Interpreting the Bill of Rights," *South African Journal on Human Rights*, 10, 2 (1995), pp. 208–215.
[17] Tiyanjana Maluwa, "The Role of International Law in the Protection of Human Rights under the Malawian Constitution of 1995," in *African Yearbook of International Law*, vol. 3 (The Hague: Kluwer Law International, 1996), p. 55.

could be brought into the interpretive scheme. He urged the courts to "implement the law of the land not only for the purposes of maintaining peace and security and dispensing justice, but in such a way that the justice dispensed promotes development of the people." What did this mean in practice? The chief justice replied, "[W]here there is more than one possible solution to a legal problem, that which favours or promotes development of the people should always be adopted by the courts."[18] Yet it was often hard to discern what would promote development and what would not.

The bench in eastern and southern Africa included judges who held a wide range of views on these matters. If there was a point of consensus in the mid-1980s, it was that in the future, as canons of interpretation developed, it would be both honest and helpful to spell out clearly the grounds for a decision and the interpretive techniques used. Having to state reasons and relate these to accepted legal values would facilitate law development, help communicate the law, and encourage judges to think about the texts, institutions, and communities to which they were accountable.

DUTIES, THE CONSTITUTION, AND PRIVATE LAW

In the view of many ordinary people, community leaders, and politicians, the continent's real predicament was an excess of a sense of entitlement over a sense of responsibility, not a lack of rights. In a famous lament in the mid-1970s, the Archbishop Kabanga of Lubumbashi, in what was then Zaire, decried the commodification of African societies—the rise of a world where everything was for sale, from health care to justice.[19] The sense of a national community and of the obligations, as well as the rights, that accompanied citizenship seemed to be declining. Younger people and the well-to-do, in particular, seemed to have forgotten about their personal responsibility to improve their lot through hard work, remember their parents and neighbors, pitch in to solve community problems, help in emergencies, overlook small discourtesies, and think twice about saying things that were mean-spirited or likely to cause offense. One heard this same perspective voiced in Western societies, where some people worried that "rights talk"[20] could sometimes lead people to ignore citizenship obligations and erode the civility required for a democracy to func-

---

[18] Francis L. Nyalali, "The Challenge of Development to Law in Developing Countries Viewed from the Perspective of Human Rights, the Rule of Law, and the Role of the Courts in Preserving Freedom," Speech at the First Commonwealth Africa Judicial Conference, Kombo Beach Hotel, Kotu, Gambia, May 5–9, 1986.

[19] Archbishop Kabanga of Lubumbashi, pastoral letter, 1979.

[20] For example, see Mary Ann Glendon, *Rights Talk: The Impoverishment of Political Discourse* (New York: Free Press, 1991).

tion. In countries with few resources, where older family members depended on their children for support instead of on pension systems or bank savings, and where the response to a calamity was usually local, the threat that an ethic of entitlement posed loomed even greater. Nyalali himself thought that "rights talk" in countries like the United States had sometimes become a license for destructiveness, and he expressed particular concern about American tolerance for violence on television and other forms of excess.

This sense was especially acute in Tanzania, perhaps because of the frequent lectures about cooperation and civic spirit President Julius Nyerere offered his countrymen. Unlike other constitutions in the region, Tanzania's declaration of rights was explicitly a bill of rights *and duties*. And Nyalali felt he had to respect the concerns the document reflected. The notion that rights implied correlative duties resonated with principles in Islamic law.[21] It also appeared in many of the basic Western human rights documents, such as the Declaration of the Rights and Duties of Man and the American Declaration of Rights and Duties.

The statements about the duties of the individual toward the community embedded in the Tanzanian constitution had their inspiration in the African Charter of Human and Peoples' Rights, although they were more specific. In most cases they specified no legally cognizable addressee;[22] that is, the duties were owed vaguely to the society but not to a person or body that could file a complaint for a breach. Typically, duties so framed were considered simply declarations. They were legally unenforceable.[23] But in some cases they threatened to undercut rights provisions.

Nyalali mused about more effective ways to promote an ethic of responsibility through the law, without sacrificing the importance of basic rights in the constitution. What really bothered senior leaders and irked ordinary people? One was the private use of public funds. Another was failure to care properly for public property. A third was private profiteering. A fourth was sharp practice, or simple cheating in everyday interactions. These were problems not readily addressed by constitutional provisions. Misuse of public funds was easily prosecuted under laws prohibiting fraud, embezzlement, and other practices. And branches of the private law long deemphasized in Tanzania and other once-socialist countries provided a fairly rich vocabulary for addressing these problems too.

---

[21] See the remark by Keba M'baye: "Par ailleurs, comme en droit islamique des droits de l'homme, les droits subjectifs des uns apparaissent sous la forme des devoirs des autres, ce qui leur attribut une force plus grande et fait apparaitre leur réalité." Keba M'baye, *Les droits de l'homme en Afrique* (Paris: International Commission of Jurists/Éditions A. Pedone, 1992), p. 215.

[22] James W. Nickel, "How Human Rights Generate Duties to Protect and Provide," *Human Rights Quarterly*, 15, 1 (1993), p. 77.

[23] Lone Lindholt, *Questioning the Universality of Human Rights: The African Charter on Human and Peoples' Rights in Botswana, Malawi, and Mozambique* (Aldershot, England: Dartmouth/Ashgate, 1997), p. 238.

Nyalali toyed with the idea of directing the attention of politicians, policy makers, and the bar toward the resources private law offered for strengthening respect for duty. Reintroducing the notion of "unjust enrichment" was one way to promote an ethic of responsibility through the law, the chief justice hinted. The basic idea was that in their dealings, people should not appropriate benefits generated by the labor or material investments of others. If someone knowingly receives a benefit generated by another person's work and keeps that benefit, then he or she has an obligation to provide restitution. There are many circumstances when someone has benefited by accident, by mistake, by compulsion, for a consideration that wholly failed (unwittingly, for example), or as a result of a wrongful action. For example, fiduciaries who abuse trust or who engage in self-dealing have to provide restitution in most parts of the world. The rules that govern restitution in these cases often are considered to have their roots in the principle of unjust enrichment.

In a speech on law and the challenge of development, the chief justice urged lawyers and judges to make greater use of the principle in their reasoning:

> The role of the Court as innovator of legal principles is urgently required in many areas of development activities. There is however one particular area which calls for immediate judicial attention. This concerns the acquisition and distribution of wealth at the expense of others. . . . Jurists should assist through the Courts in checking and controlling this evil by judicious elaboration and application of the principle of Unjust Enrichment. The principle is recognized under American Law, Scots Law, French Law, and Roman-Dutch Law, but its scope requires further elaboration and even extension to adequately deal with this evil in its aggravated modern form, under which developing countries and the individuals therein are subjected to economic looting by a few individuals.[24]

The principle of unjust enrichment might allow people to address some of the problems of profiteering, corruption, and sharp practice.

The doctrine of unjust enrichment had a long history.[25] Its roots lay in continental conceptions of natural justice and equity. The famous English judge, Lord Mansfield, drew these ideas into the common law in several of his decisions in the 1760s. Thereafter, unjust enrichment waxed and waned in popularity. It was replaced for a time by the doctrine of implied contract, when it seemed that some forms of the doctrine had restricted economic growth. The idea won rehabilitation when judges acknowledged that not all cases where moral theories sug-

[24] Nyalali, "The Challenge of Development to Law in Developing Countries," May 5–9, 1986.
[25] For more on unjust enrichment, see Hanoch Dagan, *Unjust Enrichment: A Study of Private Law and Public Values* (Cambridge: Cambridge University Press, 1997), including p. 8 as cited here; and Lord Goff of Chieveley and Gareth Jones, *The Law of Restitution* (4th ed.) (London: Sweet & Maxwell, 1993).

gested restitution was required could fit under the idea of implied contract. In England and many common law countries, excluding the United States, the doctrine of unjust enrichment grew to be a big branch of law by the 1980s.

Nyalali also urged lawyers to make greater use of the principles of equity. "In all my years both in the subordinate and superior courts, only once was a rule of Equity specifically raised by an advocate in a case before me," he observed. "I do not believe that my learned brothers on the Bench have been more fortunate in this regard. I believe that this prevailing silence of Equity accounts for the feeling of injustice that one often hears expressed by litigants in civil cases."

In its early days, the English legal system had permitted people to petition for relief when the application of the laws produced unfair or unusually harsh results. In return, the courts might grant equitable relief, such as an injunction or a requirement that someone carry to completion a task already begun, in lieu of money damages. England bequeathed these principles to other common law jurisdictions. In Africa, courts could apply the doctrines of equity except where legislation or local custom differed from the traditional English rule.[26]

In state courts in common law Africa, people also made relatively little use of tort—the law pertaining to noncontractual liabilities, especially the allocation of the cost of accidents. Tort law was laden with the language of duty. It helped define what constituted "negligent" behavior in a wide variety of contexts. It identified the instances in which special relationships created a special responsibility for others. It pointed to circumstances in which a person or organization would be strictly or automatically liable for accidental injury.

Tort featured prominently in many African customary law systems, but in the decades after independence lawyers made little effort to bring local principles together with ideas from other common law countries to develop appropriate rules.[27] One legal scholar termed the "dearth of 'new' torts" reflecting the kinds of accidents, nuisances, and other problems an "especially striking"[28] lacuna in contemporary African law. Yet in retrospect the gap was not so surprising. Tort law tends to expand where there are parties with deep pockets who can afford to pay substantial damages. There isn't much point in seeking damages from people who can't really pay. Moreover, the large role of government in industry and the service sector meant that damage awards would have to come out of public treasuries, and that was not popular with political leaders, who had other uses for those funds, some good and some bad.[29]

[26] Stephen Cretney, "The Application of Equitable Doctrines by the Courts in East Africa," *Journal of African Law*, 12, 3 (1968), passim, pp. 121–124.
[27] E. Veitch. *East African Cases on the Law of Tort* (London: Sweet & Maxwell, 1972), pp. 2–8.
[28] Jill Cottrell, "The Function of the Law of Torts in Africa," *Journal of African Law*, 31, 1–2 (1988), p. 163.
[29] One of the few exceptions to these general trends was in the law of defamation, which was sometimes popular with political leaders, who used it to protect themselves from criticism. Someone who felt his reputation had been tarnished could sue for defamation and recover

There were other principles that African lawyers and judges could use if people wished to set limits on "sharp practice." By the 1990s, new international covenants on commercial law were beginning to propagate the concepts of "fair dealing" and "good faith." Drawn from continental European legal traditions, these ideas had also gradually worked their way into the United States in more limited ways, through the Uniform Commercial Code. The principles of fair dealing and good faith required that parties involved in a contractual relationship demonstrate faithfulness to agreed common purposes or justified expectations. It was often defined better by what it was not. "Bad faith" failure to cooperate in allowing the other party to perform his end of the deal; "evasion of the spirit of the deal"; "lack of diligence"; intentionally performing most, but not all of the services contracted for; inventing disputes; "asserting an over-reaching . . . interpretation or construction of contract language"; making harassing demands; "wrongfully refusing to accept performance"; failing to mitigate damages; and other sins.[30] Where the parties to a transaction were unequal, and especially where fiduciary relationships existed, many Western courts grew more willing to deviate from the classical "hands-off" attitude toward contract, which treated written terms as definitive. Increasingly, some courts showed themselves willing to consider breaches of good faith or fair dealing in cases where parties were on fairly even footing too. These trends met with criticism from other judges and lawyers, who worried that the standards would give courts too much discretion and introduce unpredictability into the law. Africa would soon begin to confront these choices as international covenants began to diffuse the principles to new parts of the globe.[31]

---

damages. In most common law countries, statements that had a defamatory effect were presumed false unless a defendant showed otherwise. By contrast, to provide a strong defense of free speech, the U.S. Supreme Court granted special protection to statements about public officials and public figures, as well as to statements whose subject matter was of public concern. Plaintiffs had to show that the defendant acted with actual malice, with knowing or reckless falsity, in order to recover damages. As written, the laws in many African countries seemed to invite abuse by officials to harass journalists and critics. Una Ni Raifeartaigh, "Fault Issues and Libel Law—A Comparison between Irish, English, and United States Law," *International and Comparative Law Quarterly*, 40 (October 1991), pp. 768–769; on Africa, see E. Veitch, *East African Cases on the Law of Tort*, p. 11; and on Tanzania, see M. K. B. Wambali, "The Court of Appeal of Tanzania and the Development of the Law of Torts," *Eastern Africa Law Review*, 16, 2 (1989), pp. 213–228.

[30] This list is drawn mainly from Robert S. Summers, "The General Duty of Good Faith—Its Recognition and Conceptualization," *Cornell Law Review*, 67 (1982), p. 813.

[31] For more on these trends, see Boris Kozolchyk, "The UNIDROIT Principles as a Model for the Unification of the Best Contractual Practices in the Americas," *American Journal of Comparative Law*, 46 (1998): 151–179; Michael Joachim Bonell, "The UNIDROIT Principles of International Commercial Contracts: Why? What? How?" *Tulane Law Review*, 69, 5 (1995): 1121–1147; Friedrich K. Juenger, "Listening to Law Professors Talk about Good Faith: Some Afterthoughts," *Tulane Law Review*, 69, 5 (1995): 1254–1257; and Gunther Teubner, "Legal Irritants: Good Faith in British Law or How Unifying Law Ends

By pointing to these ideas in the private law, Nyalali hoped to convince those worried about a flagging sense of public duty that the constitution should not be the exclusive focus of their attention, or even the main vehicle for a conversation about the obligations of individuals toward one another and toward their communities. The kinds of practical problems that inspired many of the calls for inclusion of duties in African constitutions were better handled through statute. Principles that animated the law of restitution, tort, equity, and even "fair dealing" and "good faith" in contract held more promise than constitutionally embedded requirements. Pursuing these ideas was the responsibility of legislators and lawyers. Judges could suggest these options, but they could not write the laws or bring cases raising these issues.

NEGOTIATION

The process of negotiating acceptance of rights was just as important as the substantive legal issues. Political leaders in the other branches of government usually had little time to learn about the law. They worried that the courts might overturn statutes they had drafted, causing them embarrassment. They wanted someone to explain what the court was up to and what they should do. They did not want to be criticized. Obviously some politicians feigned such worries for opportunistic reasons, but for others, the confusion was genuine. To win acceptance of new rights provisions and judicial review, a chief justice needed to practice the four r's: respect, restraint, responsibility, reciprocity.[32]

Chief Justice Nyalali tried to respond within the constraints of his role, bending conventions a bit here and there. For example, he developed a habit of using every encounter with a political leader to make a point about how the courts worked or about law reform priorities. Explanation was a vital task. He once laughed and observed with a bit of embarrassment, "There are a number of photographs of me with political leaders and in nearly all of them I seem to be talking!" He added, "I like these brief meetings to have a point. I try to pretend that it is the last time I will meet with this person."[33]

The drafters of the Bill of Rights and Duties also provided the legislature and the executive branch a three-year grace period before the courts would enforce the new provisions. The purported aim was to "avoid chaos and promote constructive change in the legal sector." In the words of the chief justice, this measure arose from the realization that the country had a "great deal of law . . . inconsistent with the Fifth Constitutional Amendment" that would require

---

up in New Divergences," *Modern Law Review*, 61, 1 (1998): 11–32.
[32] N. Sudarkasa as quoted in Josiah M. Cobbah, "African Values and the Human Rights Debate: An African Perspective," *Human Rights Quarterly*, 9 (1987), p. 320.
[33] Francis L. Nyalali, interview with author, May 29, 1996.

"time to reform or abolish."[34] Lists of these laws were circulated first privately and later publicly.

Still there were problems. Six months after the clock started to run on the government's three-year head start, a worried chief justice noted in a public speech that none of the needed reforms had yet taken place, except in respect of the Preventive Detention Act. "This is too slow a rate and my anxieties are that the Government may not be able to finish in time this crucial reform." As slowness gradually came to be the rule, rather than the exception, Nyalali grew still more concerned. He congratulated the government for inviting the Geneva-based Centre for Human Rights to assist it in reformulating appropriate reforms.[35] Yet five years after the fact, much still remained to be done, and Nyalali warned that if the Law Reform Commission did not act, the court would have to strike down laws because the grace period had elapsed and people had started to file cases that raised issues of constitutional law.

Later, in the mid-1990s, the chief justice tried to look on the bright side. "The list of [unconstitutional] . . . laws is growing smaller because people are taking the cases to court even though the government is not moving to alter them. That may be a better approach in the end. The public internalizes constitutional principles more easily when someone files a complaint and the court offers a reasoned decision than when the legislature simply enacts a change."[36]

The government remained nervous about the court's exercise of its powers of judicial review. In 1994, a decade after the amendment's passage, the legislature enacted the Enforcement of the Bill of Rights Act, which said that when the High Court decided a law was unconstitutional, it could allow Parliament or the executive to correct the defect within a specified period. Objected one member of the law faculty at the University of Dar es Salaam, "This provision is problematic in that it directly interferes with the principle of the separation of powers." He argued, "The principle does not envisage one [branch of government] ordering the other. Under this law, the court, instead of exercising its powers and declaring offending legislation null and void, should instead now give specific instructions either to parliament, the government, or government functionaries."[37]

The chief justice was less concerned. "At the beginning people thought [the Act] . . . was aimed at undermining decisions of the court." But "if you look carefully at the bill you will see that it gives the courts discretion. It gives the

[34] Francis L. Nyalali, "The Bill of Rights in Tanzania," Lecture presented at Faculty of Law, University of Dar es Salaam, Dar es Salaam, Tanzania, September 5, 1985.

[35] Francis L. Nyalali, "Legal Reform for Democracy in Tanzania," *Lawyer* (Journal of the Law Society of Tanganyika) (Dar es Salaam, Tanzania, September–December 1994), p. 5.

[36] Francis L. Nyalali, interview with author, May 29, 1996.

[37] Chris Maina Peter, "Enforcement of Fundamental Rights and Freedoms: The Case of Tanzania," in *African Yearbook of International Law* (Dordrecht: Martinus Nijhoff, 1996), p. 96.

The judges of the Tanzanian Court of Appeal, 1979. Reprinted by permission of the Tanzanian Standard Limited and the Court of Appeal of Tanzania.

President Julius Nyerere swearing in Chief Justice Nyalali, 1977. Reprinted by permission of the Tanzanian Standard Limited and the Court of Appeal of Tanzania.

Primary magistrate's court, Dar es Salaam (after renovation). Courtesy of the author.

Jail, primary magistrate's court, Dar es Salaam. Courtesy of the author.

Meeting with the Canadian high commissioner, who helped finance the renovation of the primary magistrate's court, 1993. Reprinted by permission of the Tanzanian Standard Limited and the Court of Appeal of Tanzania.

Guard of Honor at the opening session of the Court of Appeal, 1986. Reprinted by permission of the Tanzanian Standard Limited and the Court of Appeal of Tanzania.

A show of support for Eusebia Munuo, the first woman appointed to the bench. Reprinted by permission of the High Court and Court of Appeal of Tanzania.

Chief Justice Nyalali in conversation with President Benjamin Mkapa, 1997. Reprinted by permission of the Tanzanian Standard Limited and the Court of Appeal of Tanzania.

government time to rectify the problem at the discretion of the courts."[38] The same situation had arisen in Canada, Nyalali said. The Tanzanian courts later drew on the Canadian example.

The chief justice also tried to ensure that the court did not itself generate challenges to the constitutionality of laws. The courts should not be "ambulance chasers," he said, but instead should decide constitutional questions only if absolutely necessary.[39] The American rules made sense, he thought. American courts decided a constitutional matter only if required to do so. Judges were discouraged from reaching constitutional issues if the matter could be resolved under statute. The reason behind the rule was to limit conflict with the other branches of government to those situations where it was really necessary for the courts to pronounce. Not all African judges and lawyers shared this perspective, but in Nyalali's view, it was an essential tool for stabilizing the relationship between the branches in delicate times.

CONSEQUENCES

In the mid-1980s, some judges worried that the "rights revival" would lead courts to clash with the other branches more than they had in the past, and trigger retaliation. But others held the view that if the bench could not adjudicate disputes about the violation of fundamental rights, judges would never be able to build a reputation for independence and impartiality and they would never secure legitimacy in the eyes of the public. Over the long run, the way courts acquitted themselves in constitutional decisions would shape the strength of the judiciary as an institution.

Nyalali had determined that his earlier belief, as a new magistrate, that a written bill of rights was not essential, was wrong. "We cannot develop a culture supportive of civil rights or human rights unless those rights are recognized by society. The courts can start to articulate and explain those rights, but it is only through rights litigation that we can develop a legal culture that guarantees these."[40] Having a written bill of rights provided a basis on which lawyers can bring such cases.

By the end of the 1980s, there were some hints of things to come. In Tanzania, the introduction of the Bill of Rights and Duties soon led people to challenge the constitutionality of a number of laws, covering everything from land tenure to the assumption of police powers by vigilante groups and the abil-

---

[38] Francis L. Nyalali, interview with the author, May 30, 1996.
[39] Francis L. Nyalali, interview with author, March 17, 1996.
[40] Francis L. Nyalali at a group discussion, U.S.-Africa Judicial Exchange, sponsored by the Superior Court of the District of Columbia, American Bar Association, and National Judicial College, Washington, D.C., April 1995.

ity to discriminate against women under customary law. As in the other parts of common law Africa, and the rest of the Commonwealth, the due process protections in bills of rights generated the most litigation in the early years.[41]

Worrisome problems remained. The ease with which constitutions could be amended to reduce rights protections in many countries topped the list.[42] As it often did, the court of Zimbabwe took the lead in seeking to address this troubling trend. Chief Justice Anthony Gubbay wrote:

> Where a constitution of a country, like that of Zimbabwe, may be amended without difficulty, the provisions of its Declaration of Rights remain ever at risk of being diluted and eroded. The question then is whether it is possible for a judiciary to protect the Declaration of Rights against the passing of such amendments.
>
> The Supreme Court of India has given an affirmative answer. In *Kesavananda Bharati v. State of Kerala* the Court was concerned with a constitutional amendment that empowered the State of Kerala to expropriate land. In *Indira Nehru Gandhi v. Shri Raj Narayan*, the amendment purported to place beyond any form of judicial review or investigation by a court of law, issues relating to the election of a person who is prime minister. The amendments in both cases were held invalid because they were inconsistent with the 'essential features' or 'essential pillars' of the Constitution.[43]

The Zimbabwe court raised the matter in connection with a 1990 amendment to the constitution, which stated that when the government took property it had to offer fair compensation, but then said that the fairness of the compensation could not be challenged in court. Chief Justice Gubbay asked, "Is the right of access to the courts, the right to be heard, an essential feature of the Constitution that embodies legality? It would be wrong of me to venture an answer because conceivably, the validity of the essential features doctrine could be raised at some time before the Zimbabwean courts. I merely indicate that it has not escaped criticism."[44]

Nyalali's preferred strategy was to ease fears, or perhaps to make it awkward for leaders to renege, by recalling the nationalist vision. "[There is] . . . a golden opportunity for us to put right what went wrong at the dawn of the political independence of our countries," he urged. "It is a challenge the people of

---

[41] James S. Read, "Bills of Rights in the 'Third World': Some Commonwealth Experiences," *Verfassung und Recht in Übersee*, 6, 1 (1973), p. 34.

[42] For more, see John Hatchard, "'Perfecting Imperfections': Developing Procedures for Amending Constitutions in Commonwealth Africa," *Journal of Modern African Studies*, 36, 3 (1998), pp. 381–398.

[43] Anthony R. Gubbay, "The Protection and Enforcement of Fundamental Human Rights: The Zimbabwean Experience," *Human Rights Quarterly*, 19 (1997), pp. 251–252.

[44] Ibid., p. 252.

today cannot fail to take up." And he quoted the character Brutus from the play *Julius Caesar* by Shakespeare, whose work Julius Nyerere had once himself translated into Kiswahili:

> There is a tide in the affairs of men,
> Which, taken at the flood, leads on to fortune;
> Omitted, all the voyage of their life
> Is bound in shallows and in miseries.
> On such a full sea are we now afloat.
> And we must take the current when it serves,
> Or lose our ventures.[45]

---

[45] Francis L. Nyalali, Opening address to the First Regional Conference on Law, Politics and Multi-Party Politics in East Africa, Dar es Salaam, Tanzania, October 18–23, 1993. From the speech by Brutus in act IV, scene iii.

Law and Development

BETWEEN 1982 AND 1985, Chief Justice Nyalali's mandate had changed dramatically. The tension in the relationship between the branches had eased, although no one knew how long the changes would last. The new bill of rights opened the way for the courts to use judicial review to check some of the kinds of excess that ordinary Tanzanians had so disliked. Although some thought the exercise of these powers would eventually renew tensions and bring an end to the opening that had so suddenly materialized, for now the judiciary had an opportunity to strengthen itself as an institution. The politicians were briefly and warily giving the judges a chance.

Before long, Uganda and Zambia, and later Malawi, would find themselves at a similar point. Said Peter Kabatsi, later Uganda's solicitor general and a leader in the judicial reform program, at these critical junctures ". . . the biggest problem is not struggling for government support. Instead, it is to create a system that functions."[1]

Nyalali was no novice when it came to institutional reform. He had gotten his feet wet first as a brand-new resident magistrate at Musoma, then at the Institute of Development Management at Mzumbe, and at Bukoba. He had tried out his management ideas during his tenure as chair of the Permanent Labour Tribunal. With the new latitude allowed in the mid-1980s, opportunity for change again presented itself. There was urgency as well; no one knew how long the moderation in the official temper would last.

As always, scarce resources were a problem. Although some of the court's

---

[1] Peter Kabatsi, solicitor general, interview with author, Kampala, Uganda, November 8, 1995.

administrative proposals only entailed a redeployment of time or new ways of operating, judicial coffers were so small in places like Tanzania and Uganda that there was no money to communicate about policy reforms. Unpaid phone bills and the lack of stationery and postage took their toll. Even making lower-court magistrates aware of a change in procedure was sometimes beyond the capacity of the judiciary without assistance from some quarter.

Judiciaries never account for a very large proportion of total government expenditure, anywhere in the world. Effective court systems in industrial countries typically consume about 3 to 4 percent of the national budget, a bit more in some places. In countries with smaller tax bases, one might expect a concentration on core functions such as dispute resolution, policing, primary education, and infrastructure. Theoretically, the share of the national budget the court received would be larger under such circumstances, not smaller. But the experience in eastern and southern Africa showed that politicians thought otherwise. For example, in the mid-1970s, when rule of law had broken down in Uganda, the court received less than 1 percent of the total budget, and the figures were little better in neighboring countries. Substantial increases in the share of the total budget going to the judiciary occurred in countries such as Botswana and Zambia by the 1990s, but others, including Tanzania, continued to lag behind.[2]

National budgets were under constant pressure. In most of the region, governments incurred frequent deficits, and there were always compelling competing uses for the part of the budget the courts received. Although constitutional provisions prevented legislatures from decreasing the salaries of senior judicial officers, any increment in judicial resources was subject to the give-and-take of budget deliberations. The judiciary lacked leverage, partly as a result of budget administrators' unfamiliarity with the judicial process and partly because spending on courts could buy no goodwill from important local leaders who often wanted resources they could dispense as patronage. Where expatriate contract judges had helped staff the upper echelons of the judiciary, they also may have hesitated to push governments for resources, suggested one court registrar, and that left the baseline budgets small.

But, judicial budgets were low for another reason. In most cases, neither the judges nor the ministers of justice, nor attorney generals, had a place in the inner sanctums where the real budget deals were brokered. Nyalali recollected, "The judiciary was not in the kitchen where the resources were cooked; we were waiting at the table!" It took years to find out where the real decisions

---

[2] Comparable figures are difficult to obtain. Some expenditures on courts take place through ministries of justice, whose budgets are separate from the judiciary. Customary court systems and primary courts are financed through ministries of justice or ministries of local government in some instances but not in others.

were made. In the late 1990s, the minister of justice finally managed to get into that group.[3] Even then, problems would remain.

The courts lacked powerful domestic constituents to lobby for more resources and improved operations. The bar was weak or divided in most countries in the region. Private business people in many places were still suspect, partly because of the bad light in which socialist governments had cast them and partly because they were often ethnic minorities. They were vulnerable. Opposition political parties remained illegal, or their powers were sharply circumscribed. Nyalali began to look abroad for help, and chief justices in neighboring jurisdictions did the same.

Initially, some courts made direct overtures to bilateral donors, such as Britain, Ireland, Canada, and the United States. "There was no alternative," Nyalali recalled. "It was the only way to rehabilitate the court. People would require the courts to play the role expected of them, and they would blame the judges if we failed, so I had to solicit funds myself."[4] His own government quickly expressed disquiet about these ventures. "There were raised eyebrows. I got the message to be more careful. I replied, 'If the CJ has good relationships with donors and can secure funds, why not allow him to continue?'" They agreed, cautiously. Some kinds of transfers the courts could handle directly. Others had to go through the treasury.

But money was not the only kind of resource the international community had to offer. Some of the chief justices reasoned that because the courts had little importance or status in the eyes of many government officers, they attracted little respect. Other countries might help change these attitudes through a display of interest. If aid donors showed by their spending that the judiciary mattered, then it would be easier to win domestic support. Moreover, a little international limelight promised greater safety. If the "new deals" of the 1980s and early 1990s turned sour, global networks of lawyers and judges would be able to help communicate information about harassment and other infringements of judicial independence. Their ability to mobilize diplomatic protest would increase the political costs associated with practices that undermined rule of law. As a fallback, but certainly not as a preferred alternative, it also might be possible to enhance the leverage of the courts in negotiations between the branches of government by external pressure, or even by making loans and grants conditional on improvements in the justice sector.

Finally, people in international organizations and in other countries could be sources of ideas. Many other parts of the world shared the common law tradition and had encountered similar problems. Surely there was a way to learn from their experience. Though the judges had little time and few resources to

---

[3] Francis L. Nyalali, interview with author, May 29, 1996.
[4] Francis L. Nyalali, interview with author, July 19, 1997.

distill these lessons, there were already groups, such as the Commonwealth Magistrates' and Judges' Association in London, that had connections and a base of knowledge. Chief justices varied in the degree to which they availed themselves of these resources, or of the ideas and experiences of individual courts and judges in other parts of the world. Nyalali searched aggressively and favored a relatively high level of international engagement.

"By traveling around, I could learn more than by doing research," he commented. "I found I could go to experts and get answers very fast. Everywhere I traveled, I had our problems in mind and asked questions." He continued, "At first I went with trepidation. The chief justices I met at international conferences came from all over. Would we really understand one another? Would there be any common ground?" He discovered that people faced with similar problems usually find that similar solutions work for them. "Everyone had ideas. For example, when I asked about delay, the Americans said, 'Oh yes, we have that problem here—worse than others do!'"[5]

Uganda started to travel a similar route, a bit later. Principal Judge Herbert Ntagoba had studied at the Dar law program many years earlier, and he had stayed in touch with Tanzanian colleagues. He knew what Nyalali was doing and explained the approach to other members of the "reform team" in the court and Ministry of Justice. The Ugandans approached the bilateral aid agencies and succeeded in winning the attention of the Danes and the British. Peter Kabatsi, the solicitor general, remarked that "[t]he World Bank was not interested in the courts at first. When the government turned around economic policy and emphasized privatization, we seized on that opportunity. We said, 'We won't lure investors if we can't resolve disputes more quickly.' Meantime, some of us started to travel to see how others were doing things and how they were solving the problems we also faced."[6] Eventually World Bank support materialized.

By the later part of the decade, the institutional landscape in which the judges worked grew to include a large number of governments, multilateral aid providers, and private foundations. However, the relationships developed were delicate ones. Interests and capabilities were not always fully aligned. The decision to draw on the resources available in the international arena added a whole new level to the negotiations in which the judges were engaged. To work successfully within this second arena, judges had to acquire a sense of the ways history, ideas, and the domestic politics of other countries could affect the alliances they sought to build.

---

[5] Francis L. Nyalali, interview with the author, May 29, 1996.
[6] Peter Kabatsi, solicitor general, interview with author, Kampala, Uganda, November 8, 1995.

LAW AND DEVELOPMENT IN THE 1960s

The new cooperation that grew up in the 1990s took place against the back-drop of an earlier "law and development movement" that had held sway in the 1950s, 1960s and early 1970s. Legal assistance was part of the process of decolonization in much of the world. With the prospect of independence came the need to draft new constitutions, establish bar associations, build courts, and start law schools. The first investments in foreign legal assistance took place in Asia, then shifted to Africa and to Latin America. Private foundations, especially the Ford Foundation in the United States and the Nuffield Foundation in England, took many of the first steps, along with the British and French governments. The U.S. Agency for International Development (USAID) joined, on an experimental basis. The U.S. Congress later provided an umbrella for USAID's efforts when it passed Title IX of the Foreign Assistance Act of 1966 and officially recognized noneconomic forms of support for development.

The momentum for these efforts had many sources. An almost evangelical fervor permeated these early years. William Twining, one of the many distinguished legal scholars who began their careers by teaching in new African law schools, recalled his sympathy with the aspirations of African nationalism, as well as the ferment then taking place at home institutions too. "In the United States 1955–65 was the era of Kennedy and then of Lyndon Johnson's 'Great Society', of the Warren court, BROWN V. The BOARD OF EDUCATION and the War on Poverty—all of which directly affected the ethos, activities, and culture of law schools."[7]

In 1962, Justice William O. Douglas published an article entitled "Lawyers of the Peace Corps." He urged law teachers to go abroad to share the "great capital of knowledge accumulated by our professions" with regions of the world then entering a "long creative period" of legal development.[8] Justice Douglas had long promoted similar involvement of lawyers in solving practical problems in the United States. As a law professor at Columbia University, he had spoken ardently of the need to bridge the gap between "law in books" and "law in action."[9]

The Cold War also encouraged internationalization of the legal profession. On the one hand, the superpowers sought to promote ideas familiar to them; both the United States and the Soviet Union projected their legal ideas abroad. On the other hand, many American lawyers saw rule of law programs as a way

[7] William J. Twining, *Law in Context* (Oxford: Clarendon, 1997), p. 8.
[8] William O. Douglas, "Lawyers of the Peace Corps," *American Bar Association Journal*, 48 (1962), p. 909.
[9] Laura Kalman, *Legal Realism at Yale, 1927–1960* (Chapel Hill: University of North Carolina Press, 1986), op. cit., p. 9.

to promote peace. For example, Charles Rhyne established an active association called World Peace Through Law, later the World Jurists Association, which brought lawyers from different regions together to discuss issues of common interest. The agenda reflected a Western interest in making a world safe for democracy as well as an idealistic involvement in some of the new social challenges of the day. Official minds and idealists saw mostly eye to eye.

Changes in legal thinking also played a role in winning acceptance of law and legal institutions as part of the aid agenda. In the late 1950s, two different views of law contended for preeminence. Early law instruction in the United States as well as in England rested on the view that careful examination of precedent could reveal fundamental legal principles. Through close study of texts, it was possible to discover underlying legal truths with enduring and universal import for human affairs. Legal reasoning was essentially a deductive enterprise, once these principles were known. It simply meant tracing the implications of these basic principles for decisions in particular cases. This "formalist" perspective prevailed both in the United States in the early 1900s and in England well into the 1950s and 1960s.

As the twentieth century progressed, "formalism" came under fire in America. The new "realists" argued that law was about disputes and that the subjects and contexts of dispute change as societies do. Therefore, it was not sensible to think about law as a set of rules about conduct that had a general, transhistorical character. The resolution of conflict did not rest on norms resident in some inner conscience or visible from some special vantage point. Law was merely what judges or officials did about disputes.[10]

As a group, the realists tended to distrust traditional legal rules devised for earlier historical periods and the circumstances of other times and peoples. Instead, their leaders encouraged lawyers to turn to social science, to understand how economic and social change altered the kinds of tasks demanded of the law and to assess the effects of different rules on the behavior of people and organizations. A realist judge might use evidence from such studies as well as social science reasoning as a basis for a decision, in addition to considering precedent. These ideas also prompted the development of textbooks that focused on practical problems, such as bankruptcy, and problem-specific law courses, such as "International Commercial Transactions" or "Poverty Law." This view of the law as malleable—something subject to continuous adaptation as socioeconomic conditions and cultural values change—had clear attractiveness in Africa, where the kinds of disputes were often very different from

---

[10] This description of realism draws heavily on William Twining, *Karl Llewellyn and the Realist Movement* (London: Wiedenfeld and Nicolson, 1973); Laura Kalman, *Legal Realism at Yale 1927–1960*; and Neil Duxbury, *Patterns of American Jurisprudence* (Oxford: Clarendon, 1995).

those that were most common in England. They provided legitimacy for the effort to find and promote rules conducive to economic growth. Realism left its stamp on foreign assistance during the period, although the imprint was less pronounced than critics often claimed.

In the 1960s, international legal assistance to Africa took three main forms. A primary focus was to expand legal education and especially to establish law schools to train African lawyers and judges.[11] A second focus was modernization of law. Speaking at Harvard Law School in the early 1960s, British lawyer James Gower urged that "African states have an especial need . . . for 'law reformers' and 'sophisticated legal planners', and 'most of all perhaps they need constitutional lawyers.' "[12] He emphasized the need to induce "progress,"[13] by contrast with the slightly more modest reform efforts in the United States, which sought mainly to adapt law to social and economic changes. In response to this objective, restatement and adaptation of customary law became an important focal point of foreign legal assistance.[14] The creation of national legal literatures was the third main part of the program.

The first period of foreign legal assistance in Africa was short-lived. By the mid-1970s, aid donors had lost interest and the "law and development movement" had faded. The most serious obstacles to success were political. When the movement had started, as William Twining later observed, "the more virulent critiques of neocolonialism had not yet made themselves felt."[15] By the mid-1970s, a language and outlook critical of the dominant theories and policies had worked its way into popular culture in much of the developing world. Ideas with their origins in Marx, as amended by the Economic Commission for Latin America, challenged the view that economic growth and broad participation in improved standards of living would result from industrialization and expanded participation in the world economy. Relying on foreign private firms to bring investment capital and accepting the priorities aid agencies wanted to advance would contribute instead to stagnation and a growing gap between the rich and the poor. These attitudes had implications for the law. Lawyers and judges were troublesome because they too often appeared to uphold the interests of the haves over the have-nots.[16]

---

[11] See the description in Chapter 2.

[12] As quoted in James C. N. Paul, "American Law Teachers and Africa: Some Historical Observations," *Journal of African Law*, 31, 1–2 (1988), p. 22.

[13] John Merryman describes three types of law reform: tinkering, following, and leading. See John Henry Merryman, "Comparative Law and Social Change: On the Origins, Style, Decline and Revival of the Law and Development Movement," *American Journal of Comparative Law*, 25 (1977), p. 462.

[14] See the description in Chapter 4.

[15] Twining, *Law in Context*, p. 7.

[16] Theories of neocolonialism flourished among many Western scholars who studied Africa as well as among some African academics and politicians in this period. Ghana's first presi-

Much as the chief justices of African courts found this period a difficult one in which to initiate reform, so did aid donors come to question whether the time was appropriate for an investment in law. Intellectual currents, politics, and practical difficulties provoked a crisis within the law and development movement itself. In a famous evaluation of the law and development movement, scholars David Trubek and Marc Galanter warned that the models in the minds of Western lawyers were flawed. The law and development movement rested on the idea that legislation emanated from a pluralist political process which provided broad opportunities for different groups to negotiate with each other. It also assumed that government would treat people as equal before the law, one of the fundamental tenets of many nationalist movements. However, the new governments emerging in many parts of Africa did not mimic the institutions in this liberal paradigm. Centralization of control in the hands of a single party often had replaced multiparty democracy. And to the extent that law remained important, it served the interests of state authorities and social engineers. It had lost its status as a source of norms that could help define appropriate limits on the use of political power.[17] James Gardner, a Ford Foundation program officer active in Latin America in the early years of the movement, drew attention to this shortcoming. With hindsight, Gardner argued "The concept of rule-skeptical, instrumental law tended . . . to undermine the rules and formal entitlements of rule of law, and to have the potential of converting law into an instrument and exercise of repressive policy and power."[18]

Scholars also grew concerned that foreign assistance ignored the distributional implications of law. Although the realists were far more sensitive to the influence of social power on dispute resolution than the formalists, legal assistance often seemed oblivious to the ways the legal system privileged some interests over others. Making use of lawyers and courts took money. Fear that the wealthy might be able to use the system to block programs that served poorer rural majorities engendered malaise both in Africa and among many of the lawyers and scholars who participated as law teachers.[19]

Other difficulties that attended the law modernization initiatives were practical in nature. Robert Seidman, one of the law teachers who first worked in Africa in this period, observed that law reform could scarcely shape behavior in the absence of effective communication. It was one thing for government to

---

dent, Kwame Nkrumah, wrote one of the earliest and pithiest statements in his book, *Neo-Colonialism: The Last Stage of Imperialism* (New York: International Publishers, 1965).

[17] David Trubek and Marc Galanter, "Scholars in Self-Estrangement: Some Reflections on the Crisis in Law and Development Studies in the United States," *Wisconsin Law Review*, 4 (1974), p. 1069.

[18] James A. Gardner, *Legal Imperialism: American Lawyers and Foreign Aid in Latin America* (Madison: University of Wisconsin Press, 1980), p. 5.

[19] Trubek and Galanter, "Scholars in Self-Estrangement," p. 1076.

publish laws, but that step alone would not suffice to reach people without the ability to read or people without the means to acquire the information. Illiteracy, the limited reach of newspapers, the small size of the bar—all impeded awareness of reforms. To the extent that new legislation aimed to influence the activities of ordinary people, it was essential to create ways for people to learn about new rules.[20]

The intermixing of law assistance with Great Power politics also took a toll. The U.S. government's intelligence activities in the Cold War contaminated some of the early law and development efforts. In the 1950s, the Soviet Union had helped create the International Association of Democratic Lawyers. Worried about Moscow's increasing influence in world legal associations, and concerned that the Ford Foundation's choice of projects sometimes benefited interests hostile to the United States, the Central Intelligence Agency countered by providing support to "free world" lawyers. Money passed through a series of dummy foundations in order to disguise its origins, then found its way to legitimate private donors who were unaware of its origins.

The main victim proved to be the venerable International Commission of Jurists. Founded in 1952, the Commission assembled distinguished judges and lawyers to promote understanding of the rule of law. When its unwitting receipt of tainted funds was revealed in 1967, the organization nearly died. The Soviet Union asked for the revocation of its United Nations consultative status, and the Ford Foundation withdrew support. Hard lobbying and financial assistance from European countries saved the organization, but just barely.[21] The episode helped undermine the reputation of legal assistance efforts that involved Americans.

U.S. foreign legal assistance had its longest trial in Latin America, and the experience there helped undermine the programs in Africa. Too often recipients of aid later implicated themselves in human rights abuses on the continent, paying no heed to the advice imparted. U.S. domestic opposition to aid that seemed to go to people involved in death squads grew. Vocal taxpayers did not want their money used for activities that might misfire or appear unsavory.

As if all of these pressures were not enough trouble, the law and development movement also failed to generate the hoped-for social scientific insight. Scholarly inquiry stalled. Part of the problem lay in the difficulty of defining what *development* meant, or whether there might be multiple concepts, each involving normative choices. And the scholars involved often failed to coordinate their work sufficiently to produce cross-national data on questions of common interest.

---

[20] Robert B. Seidman, "The Communication of Law and the Process of Development," *Wisconsin Law Review*, 3 (1972), pp. 689–702.
[21] See the discussion in Howard B. Tolley, Jr., *The International Commission of Jurists: Global Advocates for Human Rights* (Philadelphia: University of Pennsylvania Press, 1994), especially pp. xii and 29.

By 1975, most official foreign legal assistance to Africa had stopped. The United States withdrew. The British government remained active, but it reduced its direct support for judicial training, law reports, and research. The Commonwealth continued to sponsor occasional conferences and official contacts between judges, ministers of justice, and lawyers. The Ford Foundation and the Nuffield Foundation persisted but quietly turned their attention to other aspects, such as the need to build legal literacy and to support African voluntary associations with interests in law and human rights.

THE REVIVAL OF LAW AND DEVELOPMENT

A new law and development movement began in the early 1980s in Latin America and slowly spread to Eastern Europe after the fall of the Berlin Wall. As Nyalali began to face his new institution-building challenges, he could begin to tap the renewed interest, although he was ahead of what one policy maker called the "Rule of Law Revival."[22] Earlier experience shaped the attitudes of some of the donor-country policy makers in the mid-1980s and early 1990s, though for the most part the organizational memories of bureaucratic agencies were short.

Nyalali and other chief justices quietly began to ask for support to train personnel and strengthen institutions. In the United States, the Federal Judicial Center, the administrative arm of the American federal courts, received so many requests for visits and advice from foreign judges that the chief justice of the U.S. Supreme Court directed the center to constitute a special committee to coordinate this new area of activity. Nongovernmental organizations reported that requests for information and advice from developing country lawyers and courts also had increased dramatically.

Courts and legal systems reclaimed a place on the international aid agenda for several reasons. Interest in promoting more accountable government through democratization was a major rationale for this investment. Beginning in the late 1970s and intensifying after the fall of the Berlin Wall, Western aid agencies began to try to bolster "demand" for good government by supporting civic groups that monitored the performance of public institutions and by encouraging multiparty competition for public office. It was increasingly evident that the laws governing fundamental rights, especially speech and association, sharply affected the ability to create a civil society. Although many leaders displayed greater respect for civil and political liberties in the 1990s than they had since independence, the high volatility in the political-liberties ratings countries received from year to year was partly attributable to the ease with

---

[22] Thomas Carothers, "The Rule of Law Revival," *Foreign Affairs*, 77, 2 (1998), pp. 95–106.

which incumbents could clamp down on fledgling political competition by invoking sedition laws or denying registration to voluntary associations and political parties.[23]

The failure of economic reform initiatives in developing countries frustrated donors and the multilateral development agencies and also refocused attention on law. Policy makers had turned their attention to problems of "governance" as paper agreements failed to yield sound macroeconomic policies. Aid monies went astray in many places. Corruption and contract repudiation interfered with prosperity. A World Bank study based on cross-country comparisons pointed to the serious adverse effects of bribery on economies. Bank researchers found that a country that improved its standing on a standard corruption index by two points on a seven-point scale could realize a 4 percentage point increase in its investment rate and a .5 percentage point increase in the growth rate of its annual per capita gross domestic product.[24] Studies began to show that domestic and foreign entrepreneurs in all African subregions cited "crime and violence" among the most serious obstacles to business activity, behind corruption but fairly consistently above foreign currency regulation, policy instability, inadequate infrastructure, and financing problems.[25] Wrote one senior World Bank official, "[S]erious investors look for a legal system where property rights, contractual arrangements and other lawful activities are safeguarded and respected, free from arbitrary governmental action and from pressure by special interest groups or powerful individuals."[26] Law seemed to hold out solutions.

A third source of renewed international donor interest in legal assistance was a breakdown of law and order. A main component of what most people considered rule of law was the level of safety people enjoyed from crime and arbitrary interference in work and family life. Crime had a new and more menacing character. Where once it mainly took the form of stock rustling, petty thefts, and violence between families—crimes that communities could often regulate themselves—increasingly the trouble came from outside the community. There was widespread evidence of involvement of organized, international crime syndicates in vehicle theft, drug dealing, and weapons trades that cross

---

[23] Civil and political liberties ratings are published by Freedom House, a New York–based nongovernmental organization. See *Freedom in the World: The Annual Survey of Political Rights and Civil Liberties* (New York: Freedom House, annual).

[24] Paulo Mauro, "Corruption: Causes, Consequences, and Agenda for Future Research," *Finance & Development*, 35, 1 (1998), p. 12.

[25] Aymo Brunetti, Gregory Kisunko, and Beatrice Weder, "How Businesses See Government," IFC Discussion Paper 33 (Washington, D.C.: IFC/World Bank, 1998).

[26] Ibrahim Shihata, "Judicial Reform in Developing Countries and the Role of the World Bank," in Malcolm Rowat, Waleed Haider Malik, and Maria Dakolias, eds., *Judicial Reform in Latin America and the Caribbean*, World Bank Technical Paper No. 280 (Washington, D.C.: World Bank, April 1995), p. 220.

African borders. In South Africa, the best-studied country, over 480 crime syndicates were active in the mid-1990s. Of these, 187 operated internationally, and 125 had bases in other parts of Africa.[27] Syndicates also flourished in Nigeria, Sierra Leone, Liberia, Côte d'Ivoire, Kenya, Ethiopia, Egypt, and Tanzania.

In the 1990s, responding to both the "pull" of African judges like Nyalali and the "push" of their own policy makers, donor countries gradually began to reallocate assistance to "the legal sector" or "the justice sector." In eastern and southern Africa, the institutional context of foreign legal assistance rapidly became bewilderingly complex. Among the bilateral assistance programs, the Danish aid agency DANIDA was one of the first to become involved, and it maintained one of the largest programs. In financial terms, its assistance to courts, human rights commissions, ombudsmen, auditors, prison reform, and law-related nongovernmental organizations often dwarfed what the Americans or the British provided. The British, Canadian, Swedish, Norwegian, Dutch, and German aid agencies also played significant roles, along with USAID. In most cases, these agencies contracted with private organizations and individuals to supply services. The provision of legal assistance became a hot business that governments and nongovernmental organizations, universities, private firms, and law practices sought to enter, each purveying its own brand of help.

Even a single government's assistance programs were usually fragmented, and one unit often had little idea what the others were doing. For example, U.S. aid was concentrated in the Agency for International Development. But the State Department, which provided small grants to human rights organizations as well as technical support for antidrug activities, also played a role. Although government assistance to foreign police forces was illegal, under U.S. statutes, any consultation and support involving police that did take place through special legislation was managed mainly through the Department of Justice.[28] Even the U.S. Department of Defense provided human rights training and legal education for military lawyers in Africa. Ironically, its programs originally were vested in the Naval Justice School, whose work with landlocked countries eventually grew so substantial that the program had to be renamed the Defense Institute for International Legal Studies.

Multilateral organizations also were involved, and each had its own maze to

---

[27] Greg Mills, *War and Peace in Southern Africa: Crime, Drugs, Armies, and Trade,* World Peace Foundation Report (Cambridge: World Peace Foundation, 1996), p. 2.

[28] In the United States, Section 660 of the Foreign Assistance Act of 1961 prohibited use of funds for police training. An exception, created in 1985 under Section 534(b)(3), included programs to enhance investigative capacities, conducted under judicial or prosecutorial control; assist in developing academic instruction for training law enforcement personnel; or enhance administrative management capabilities of law enforcement agencies, especially with regard to career development, personnel evaluation, and internal disciplinary procedures.

offer. The Commonwealth Secretariat, the executive agency of the Commonwealth, long had a presence in the region as the organizer of periodic consultative meetings and as a source of technical support. The Organization for Economic Cooperation and Development (OECD) and the European Union offered limited support for judicial strengthening and law reform. United Nations organizations that had a long-standing involvement in rule of law expanded their activities under several umbrellas, including those traditionally dedicated to human rights such as the United Nations Human Rights Commission and programs concerned with economic development such as the United Nations Development Program (UNDP) and the United Nations Children's Fund.

The World Bank also found ways to expand its traditional activities to include rule of law. The Bank's Articles of Agreement limited it to financing of projects for productive purposes, that is, programs that would yield increases in rates of economic growth.[29] The new emphasis on law rested more on hunch and anecdote about the impact on prosperity than on systematic evidence. Early policy documents rationalized the need for investment in law and legal systems mainly by general references to the perspectives of business people. "Worldwide experience confirms the importance of rapid and sustainable development of the clarification and protection for property rights, the enforcement of contractual obligations, and the enactment and application of rigorous regulatory regimes," wrote Ibrahim Shihata, the general counsel in the 1990s.[30] Policy proceeded on the basis of theory, not hard empirical research, for the most part, even though recipient countries usually had to repay the assistance out of the higher tax revenues the hoped for prosperity would generate. Gradually, through grant-financed studies and projects, special loans, and components of other loans of broader scope, the World Bank began to support a wide range of investments ranging from law reform to the repair of court buildings.

The new law and development movement differed from its predecessor in several respects. Rule of law concerns were more pronounced in the new law and development era than in the old. Although adaptation of law and legal institutions to facilitate economic growth remained a high priority, there was a simultaneous high-profile investment in strengthening respect for civil and political rights. Second, there was a clearer recognition of the need to consider institutional interrelationships. It was still important to train lawyers, as countries had done during the earlier period, but capable African legal scholars had assumed that role by the second law and development era, lessening the appearance of foreign-ness. In the 1990s, there was greater awareness of the need to strengthen public knowledge of the law, by contrast with lawyer knowl-

---

[29] Shihata, "Judicial Reform in Developing Countries and the Role of the World Bank," p. 230.
[30] Ibid., p. 13.

edge. And there was a slow recognition of the need to build institutional capacity in the judiciary so that the courts might meet the new demands placed on them. The new investments took place at a time when domestic demand for legal change and improved justice systems appeared higher than it had been just after independence.

MANAGING THE RELATIONSHIP

These changes in international relationships did not develop overnight. Nor were they always helpful. African lawyers and judges had to work hard to foster ties that were productive. And that was not always an easy task. Aid agencies displayed a range of sensitivities that complicated negotiations. Donors or the people they hired to provide assistance sometimes were more interested in purveying a set of recipes than engaging the difficult problems on the ground. Moreover, the sheer organizational complexity of the environment generated a steep learning curve and increased the transaction costs in negotiating assistance. Foreign help could also open the courts and law to the appearance of Western-ness.

Law and justice systems were very sensitive politically. The laws on the books in most countries inevitably included some statutes that did not respect international standards or donor-country preferences. And there could be little doubt that at some point a judge would make a decision donor-country officials would not like. Whereas it might be possible to remonstrate with a minister of finance over the appropriateness of a decision, that kind of give-and-take was off limits with respect to the judiciary. Respect for judicial independence meant that donors would have to accept that they had less control over the substantive outcomes of their investments than they might want.

Some policy makers worried about "creating palaces for the application of bad laws" and about assisting courts that were not independent of executive branch influence. Instead they wanted to support "civil society groups" in order to create constituencies for law reform and for improved performance, including greater judicial independence. This approach found favor with those who reasoned that such "demand-side" strategies help ensure that a culture of accountability spread. Others pointed out that this strategy had sharp limitations. If government power could silence private voluntary organizations, or was under no pressure to respond because the groups had little political influence, then a focus on the "demand side" would yield no more than earlier approaches had.

The courts also suffered from a legacy of distrust that had grown up with respect to certain forms of assistance. Most donors disliked investing in buildings or vehicles because funds for these things were often misused. Yet in some countries, civil conflict had wrought such damage that it was no longer possible to function in the physical plant available. One expatriate judge in Uganda offered an example: "The court in Masaka was burned in 1978 during the conflict with Tanzania. It is completely blackened with soot and open to the air, but we still have to use it. The courtrooms in Arua are divided by matting because the walls have collapsed. At Gulu, a tree grows up through the center of the court." The judges drew up a master plan for building and repair. "Then the project slowed down because no one wanted to put money into buildings when there were also high levels of delay in processing cases. They wanted all sorts of studies of these delays, so we took time out to do that." The judge concluded, "Now we are moving on delay and they have re-activated the plan. If they could have seen the vision, we could have started four years ago, and we would almost be finished by now. Under the Marshall Plan, we built buildings. I keep pointing out, this is bomb damage too!"[31] The Ugandan situation was especially bad. Even in the capital, Kampala, infrastructure problems forced four magistrates to hold hearings simultaneously in the same room—one in each corner.[32] But basic building repairs were needed in many of the other countries of the region.

Coordination was a problem everywhere. A project initiated by one agency would interact with another. These "crossover effects" could create severe difficulties. For example, new government spending rules, required under the terms of loans from the international financial institutions, sometimes caused operational problems. Nyalali explained that the multilateral lenders put many countries on a "diet" that made it difficult for the courts to plan. "On a month-to-month basis, the country's expenditure may not exceed its revenue." Although revenue collection improved in the late 1990s, there was still fluctuation. Often it was unclear whether the court would have the resources to carry out its operations in any given month. "It is one thing for parliament to approve funds and another for the Treasury to release the money," Nyalali reflected.[33]

Law was technical. Until the mid-1990s, aid agencies had few trained lawyers on staff in policy positions, even though they had counsel to review contracts their offices issued. New staff members quickly discovered that providing assistance to courts, law reform commissions, and other parts of the justice system required the use of a new vocabulary and specialized knowledge on a par with economics in its complexity. There were no guides to explain how

---

[31] Justice Harold G. Platt, interview with author, Kampala, Uganda, November 9, 1995.

[32] Republic of Uganda, Report of the Commission of Inquiry on Judicial Reform (Kampala, Uganda: Commission of Inquiry on Judicial Reform, 1995), pp. 21–22.

[33] Francis L. Nyalali, interview with author, Dar es Salaam, Tanzania, July 27, 1999. Similarly, poor timing of conferences occasioanlly sent a significant portion of the High Court out of the country at once and contributed to delays in processing cases. And always it seemed that computers or audio equipment purchased for one donor's project proved incompatible with what another had provided.

the judicial branch worked or to outline the range of solutions one might entertain to solve a given problem. Information specific to African common law systems was unavailable in any central location. A field officer with a general social science background and practical experience in economic development activities had every reason to feel overwhelmed. Unfortunately, the donor-country lack of capacity often made sensible reform strategies harder for African jurists to negotiate.

Finally, legislatures in the United States and other Western countries had grown tough in their scrutiny of the benefit derived from expenditures of taxpayer dollars. They insisted that aid agencies report on the measurable benefits their investments had generated. By the end of the 1990s, USAID required quantitatively measurable progress within six months of the start of a project. Although few could quibble with the desirability of seeking to use assistance efficiently, the new regulations reached the point of absurdity. They assumed away many of the real difficulties involved in finding adequate measures, as well as the expense of gathering and analyzing this information once obtained. They were premised on the notion that the only benefits of interest were those in the heads of the designers, ignoring the unintended consequences that often proved the key to success. Moreover, the benefits of many kinds of expenditures often accrued only after a lag, and they interacted with a variety of other circumstances and conditions.[34]

African judges were usually too polite to voice concern. Expatriate judges were more pointed in their criticisms of their compatriots. Said one, "The donors have been a great help, but there are days when they are just a bloody nuisance!"[35]

The complications on the other side were also severe. The chief justices and reformers in the courts had concerns of their own. To begin with, one of their broad goals was to reduce the extent to which the law and the courts were perceived as foreign. Winning support from international sources created a potential vulnerability. An opportunistic critic who considered the judiciary an irritant could point to judges' participation in international programs and receipt of foreign assistance as a sign of "globalization" and loss of sovereignty. Although it was impossible to defuse this kind of objection completely, reformers had to ensure that donors would permit broad domestic participation in choosing and planning activities. They also had to explain cooperative agreements, to ensure that they were understood by politicians and the "interested public" of lawyers, scholars, and community leaders.

---

[34] For a sustained discussion, see Thomas Carothers, *Aiding Democracy Abroad: The Learning Curve* (Washington, D.C.: Carnegie Endowment for International Peace, 1999), Chapters 10 and 11.
[35] Justice David Porter, interview with author, November 1995.

A related concern was whether assistance from abroad might create prob-lems in winning the "institutionalization" of the participation of the courts in the budget process. Foreign contributions were helpful in the early stages of reform, to supplement scarce domestic funds so that the judiciary did not antagonize others who had claims to budget resources. At the same time, it was important that government officials and politicians come to understand the financial needs of the courts and to make it a habit to provide for them rather than rely on outside support.

As time passed, aid agencies introduced periodic consultative group meet-ings in recipient countries to help ease coordination problems. The entry of the World Bank into the field of legal assistance in Africa also made a difference in Tanzania. With the clout that is attached to its relatively greater resources, the World Bank was able to spearhead the creation of Financial and Legal Management Upgrading Projects, nicknamed "FILMUPs," in several coun-tries. In Tanzania, the Ministry of Justice hired someone to direct the program and to coordinate with other donors. This arrangement relieved ministers of justice and chief justices of some of these demands. The Ministry of Justice and courts set their own priorities. They then commissioned assessments or evaluations to help the process along. Afterward, different bilateral donors and international organizations, including the World Bank, decided which parts of the resulting plan they could best help finance or support.

These cooperative programs cut through some of the coordination problems, but they had other unanticipated benefits as well. The Tanzanian judges found that FILMUP helped them explain their budgetary needs more effectively to their own government. "We let the project put us under a microscope, because that gave the government and the donors the ability to hear us. The president was really shocked when he saw the plight of the judiciary. He said he would start to be our 'foremost fund-raiser.'"[36]

Even so, winning and managing international assistance was tremendously time-consuming. In the mid-1990s, a senior Tanzania Law Society official wel-comed Nyalali's integrity and energy, but complained that the chief justice spent too little time attending to the implementation of reforms. "His forum is overseas," the lawyer remarked. "He talks for that audience, like Nyerere. The speeches are good, but he has to do more here. We have pressing problems, and we can't have a chief justice who is abroad all the time."[37] Similar criti-cisms surfaced in other countries as senior judges and "reform teams" tried with only partial success to work with donor countries and shepherd reform at the same time.

But even taking all these problems into consideration, international involve-

---

[36] Francis L. Nyalali, interview with author, May 29, 1996.
[37] Senior Tanganyika Law Society official, interview with author, May 22, 1996.

ment sometimes had the effects Nyalali originally envisioned. He once recalled the great benefit the visit of Mary Robinson, former president of Ireland and later the United Nations High Commissioner for Human Rights, bestowed on the court. "She asked to pay a courtesy call when she visited Tanzania. The judges were amazed and delighted. We asked the government whether they would permit us to play host to President Robinson briefly. They had no objection. We took the step of admitting President Robinson to our bar and made arrangements for her to observe a case in the Court of Appeal. President Robinson entered the courtroom. Then the Justices of Appeal entered and the president bowed. It was very moving for all of us . . . and the case was actually concluded!"[38] The event helped forge solidarity, an important resource in times of stress and change.

[38] Francis L. Nyalali, interview with author, July 19, 1997.

The Quality of Justice

NYALALI HAD SEVERAL broad priorities to pursue in order to preserve the opening the president and the political party handed him in 1983–84. He needed to reduce the number of points at which partisan pressure could influence the judicial process, or he had to improve the flow of information to enhance monitoring, or both. He had to strengthen the importance of professional reputation not only among the judges and magistrates but also among the clerks. Firmness in the face of pressure had to come to mean something. And he sought to develop constituencies or stakeholders, people for whom effective and fair courts were worth protecting. He wanted to enlist public opinion in support of the courts, but he also thought it was important to reach out to people who could affect the relationship between the branches more directly, including the country's political leaders.

The challenges facing other courts in the region were similar. The question before all of them was how to turn these very general ambitions into a concrete program. One cluster of tasks centered on improving the quality and communication of judicial decision making, or what might be called, with some license, "the quality of justice." For courts in a common law system to work, people had to know what judges decided and what reasons they offered. That meant decisions had to be clear and careful, erring on the side of completeness and length when necessary. Another cluster of tasks focused on reducing delay in criminal cases, where potentially innocent defendants risked the loss of liberty. Many of the serious human rights abuses in Africa in this period occurred in the criminal justice system. The perceived integrity of the courts as well as the fairness of the political process demanded that judges try to address these problems within the limitations their roles imposed. A third set of tasks attacked inefficiency in civil proceedings, not only in the kinds of cases that affected entrepreneurial and commercial activity but also in the land disputes and other complaints ordinary people lodged. Measures to curb corruption within the judicial process constituted a fourth sphere of reform, and legal literacy, a fifth.

Most chief justices moved on several fronts at once. But if there was any latitude to approach the tasks of institutional reform sequentially, the problems associated with the quality and communication of judicial decisions probably merited attention first, not necessarily because they were most urgent or most vital but because they were important for transparency and constituency building.

Courts in all common law jurisdictions depended on a very limited repertoire of formal and informal devices to promote clarity and uniformity in the application and development of the law. Doctrines that required respect for precedent—the principle of *stare decisis*—helped ensure predictability and uniformity. Another important mechanism for exercising quality control in these decisions was the appeals process. The prospect of appeal helped instill a fear of reversal, with its attendant humiliation, if the adjudicator did not measure up. Thoughtful criticism, especially from legal scholars, was also important to provide an incentive for careful reasoning.

The scarcity of resources in eastern and southern Africa had weakened all three of these devices for maintaining "the quality of justice." Respect for precedent required knowledge of the decisions of the higher courts. Yet straitened circumstances in many countries after 1982 prevented the courts in most of sub-Saharan Africa from properly recording and disseminating decisions. A shortage of legal materials meant that the best legal minds in the world would have found it difficult to adhere to professional standards of quality in the dispensation of justice. Moreover, most people lacked the financial means to appeal decisions that were flawed. The appeals process could only provide limited protection against inaccuracy or poor reasoning, as a result. The difficulty of securing copies of decisions, coupled with the absence of money for judicial conferences or for meetings with legal scholars and the bar, also limited effective comment from people whose skills best suited them for the role of the constructive critic. All of these problems affected the ability to monitor partisan pressure, to increase the importance of professional reputation, and to explain the law to potential constituents.

Attention to these matters was also politic. It met judges and magistrates on their own ground. It engaged them in thinking about the kinds of ideas and skills that had attracted them to the profession in the first place. Thus, it offered a way to reach out intellectually to judicial personnel and to engage them in the project of reform in a way that delay reduction or anticorruption campaigns could not. To the extent that it involved not only material support but also training, it could create a small stock of valued resources with which a chief justice could reward those who threw themselves energetically into the larger task of institution building.

Such an *esprit de corps* was important. The one matter on which all chief justices agreed was that reform would only succeed if it won the support of judges, magistrates, and other officers of the court. Because most judicial personnel had lifetime security of tenure and could be dismissed only in rare instances, the risk of job loss could not serve as an incentive for good behavior or cooperation. Chief justices had to rely on persuasion, people's concern about their reputations, and a limited ability to dispense perks, such as chances to attend conferences and training workshops. Few people would undertake more work or assume greater risks unless they believed that their efforts would lead to better terms of service or that they might lose opportunities for promotion if they failed to take part.

THE RECORD

The methods for keeping the trial record attracted much grumbling from judges and magistrates, although other reforms were more important and less easy to solve. In the mid-1990s, in most of Africa, the official record of the trial was the judge's longhand notes. Few courts had assistants to keep track of proceedings or stenographers, stenographic machines, or audio recorders, although some of the courts in southern Africa had more experience with these than others did. Typically, the judge recorded the trial as he or she listened, and advocates adjusted the pace at which they delivered their arguments to suit the judge's writing speed. Except at the High Court level, the record was typed only if a party appealed, often at the appellant's expense. Usually it was the practice to transcribe only those portions the appellant requested or that the respondent needed in order to reply.

In surveys conducted a bit later, in the mid-1990s, members of the bar in Uganda, Tanzania, and Botswana suggested that about 15 percent of lawyers thought the record was "often inaccurate" in the courts where they practiced. The surveys were based on random samples of members of the bar in each country. Although based on small numbers—about forty respondents in each case—they provided some evidence of the magnitude of concern about the quality of the record.[1]

The parties to a case could ask to see the notes a judge or magistrate took and they could request corrections, but in practice these rights were rarely invoked. In some countries, such as Kenya, there was no requirement that the advocates be able to review the judge's transcript until the end of the trial, at which point it was difficult for everyone to recall exactly what had transpired. In other countries, such as Tanzania, the rules of procedure required that the

---

[1] Jennifer Widner, Law Society Surveys, 1995–96.

testimony of a witness in the courts below the level of the High Court be recorded by the magistrate or by someone who was under the direction of the magistrate. Then the record was read back to the witness for confirmation. The record had to contain an endorsement by the trial magistrate to the effect that the requirement had been complied with. Nyalali observed that in practice the requirement rarely was fulfilled. "I guess the majority of the magistrates default on this obligation not because of malice," he said, "but because the procedure is time-consuming and inefficient. This is precisely why the procedure does not exist in the higher courts. Moreover, in the higher courts the regular appearance of advocates, who make notes in their own briefs, is a safeguard against improper record keeping by the court."[2]

This system gave rise to a number of other practical concerns beyond accuracy of the record. One was whether note taking by the judge contributed significantly to the slowness of the trial and delay in the justice system. The second was whether trying to keep the record and preside at the trial simultaneously led to inaccuracy. The third was whether the method of keeping the record affected the judge's ability to pay careful attention to facial expressions, gestures, and other evidence that bore on witness credibility.

Solving this problem was not as easy as it might have appeared at first. The question was whether introducing stenographers or audio recording equipment was cost-effective under the conditions that prevailed in eastern and southern Africa. It was all too easy to focus on solutions that would make courts operate more like their counterparts in other parts of the world, while forgetting that judiciaries would have to find ways to support the maintenance or operating costs on their own. Nor did alternative technologies necessarily guarantee an accurate record.

There were three broad approaches to improving court reporting. One was to replace the judge as recorder with a specially trained court reporter who could take shorthand notes. This system allowed the judge to pay more attention to the demeanor of parties and witnesses, and it held out the prospect of a slight increase in the speed with which a trial could be conducted.

A second option was to train and equip a cadre of court reporters who could use specially designed equipment to record proceedings. The reporters would learn their trade in special training programs set up either within each country or regionally. Once a student successfully completed the training, he or she would be allowed to take a "Stentura," a computerized writing machine, to the court. The record collected on the Stentura could then be downloaded to a computer at the court and printed out, almost instantaneously.[3]

---

[2] Francis L. Nyalali, personal communication, October 1998.
[3] Randall A. Czerenda and Alan P. Gross, "Introduction of Computerized Court Reporting in the Gambia," trip memorandum prepared for USAID, Banjul, Gambia, June 20, 1994.

The system had pros and cons. As was true of all of the court reporting systems contemplated, the machinery required electricity to operate. That meant its use was restricted mainly to urban centers. Instability in the electrical supply also meant that purchase of surge protectors and other equipment would have to be factored in. Another problem was the cost of maintaining a well-trained team of reporters. Salaries for judges and magistrates were low in many countries, but wage rates for nonjudicial staff were generally uncompetitive with private sector alternatives. Ministries of justice or courts might spend money to train staff only to find that their reporters left for higher-paying jobs elsewhere as soon as they acquired experience. That meant that courts could be stuck with equipment and no one trained to use it, as well as the bill for the whole venture. Finally, there was no guarantee that court reporters would be immune either from making mistakes or from inducements to alter the record.

The third approach to improving court recording was audio recording of trials and subsequent transcription of the proceedings. In the West this was often a backup system used in conjunction with other methods. In theory, both taping and use of computer-compatible stenographic equipment could cut the demand for paper in the High Court by up to one-half by eliminating the need for written notes by the judge or an assistant. In practice, of course, the judge might wish to keep some notes as the trial progressed, so the savings might be more limited. Although there was less risk of human error in recording testimony, mechanical failure was a concern. Like the Stenturas or other stenographic machines, audio recording required a stable electrical supply. Finally, in some instances it would still be necessary to transcribe the tapes, although the usual practice in the West was not to do so unless a written record was required. Transcription of the tapes required skilled typists and extra time.

Quietly, some of the judges also wondered whether the noise in the courtrooms would affect the quality of the tapes. In most of the countries, court buildings had no air-conditioning, and in the hottest months it was essential to leave the windows open, to catch whatever breeze existed. A significant proportion of the buildings had no glass in the windows in any case, which meant that the noise of the street was fully audible in the courtrooms themselves. Even in some of the high courts it was difficult to hear the judge, counsel, and witnesses above the din from a seat only three rows behind the lawyers' tables. In the wet season, the problem grew still worse, as raindrops drummed on the ubiquitous sheet metal roofing.

Judges also disagreed about the importance of finding new ways to record trial proceedings. Although an instantaneous copy might reduce delay at the High Court level, and a tape would be desirable in politically sensitive, highly visible cases, for much of the run-of-the-mill business of the court the financial outlay seemed greater than need warranted. There were many competing demands for funds. Perhaps it would be better, they suggested, if the courts started slowly by first equipping the clerical staff of the higher courts, whose decisions had precedential value, with computers to speed typing and ease editing. The same computers also could be used to type decisions, which would make law reporting easier. The investment in training and equipment would pay off more handsomely.

NATIONAL LEGAL LITERATURES

Judges are supposed to apply the law to the facts of a case. After the early 1980s, one of the most fundamental problems facing the courts in common law Africa was the sheer difficulty of knowing what the law was. For example, in Tanzania, 64 percent of lawyers surveyed said that they lacked easy access to the country's statutes, while 44 percent said the same in Uganda. Only about a third of the lawyers in the two countries said they had access to judges' decisions, either informally, through other advocates, or through law reports. By contrast, in Botswana, with its long tradition of more effective government, all lawyers said they had easy access to the statutes and two-thirds said they had access to law reports.[4]

By the late 1980s, most countries in the region no longer maintained a current compendium of the statutes, and even when they did, the courts rarely had the money to buy copies. The last time the laws of Uganda were published in one compilation was in 1964. In Tanzania in the mid-1990s, the court could obtain no compilation more recent than 1965. Not even the appellate judges had copies of the laws in their chambers.[5] In many cases, parliaments had not bothered to index legislation, to guide officials or lawyers and judges through the thicket of amendments, deletions, and new bills. And beginning in the early 1980s, most countries halted production of law reports.

Even old research materials had disappeared from many courts. In Uganda, the most severely affected country, law libraries at the court and the university were pilfered or burned during years of conflict. In Tanzania, crumbling typescript copies of High Court and Court of Appeal decisions could be found only in the High Court library in Dar or stacked, uncatalogued, in an upstairs closet at the court. Even in Botswana publication of law reports lagged behind schedule, beginning in the early 1990s..

Procedures inherited from colonial times eased the most immediate problems slightly. "In the former British colonies, a magistrate could ask the High Court about a matter of law," Nyalali advised. "Magistrates' courts were presided over in the early days by district commissioners who exercised judicial

---

[4] Jennifer Widner, Law Society Surveys, 1995–96.
[5] Justice Robert Kisanga, interview with author, Dar es Salaam, Tanzania, May 1996.

powers too. They weren't really lawyers, so when they were uncertain about a point of law, they could ask the High Court, in order to save time and money. We retained that system."[6] If the telephones worked, it was sometimes possible to call the High Court judge assigned to a station or circuit and ask for a verbal summary of the law.

Magistrates and judges coped with the lack of legal materials in other ways too. Many insisted that counsel supply copies of any statutes and decisions to which they referred. Some relied on personal contacts at the High Court to find statutes or typescript decisions and to send a photocopy.[7] But usually, the main source of the law was the notes a judge or magistrate had taken in school. And at the lowest levels of the court, most often magistrates simply followed common sense.

In the years before foreign legal assistance materialized, Nyalali occasionally persuaded the national broadcasting company to allow him air time to discuss important decisions. Magistrates at remote stations commented that these broadcasts were often their only link with other judges for a year or more at a stretch. They found them extremely helpful. The need for radio persisted even after it was possible to publish some of the laws and court decisions, in order to make magistrates aware of changes, and the broadcasts continued.

These coping strategies were better than nothing, but they could have serious consequences. Nyalali observed that very often "judges and magistrates applied old laws. It reached the point where cases were sometimes decided by guesswork. There were lots of inconsistencies in decisions, especially at the primary court level."[8] Magistrates applied land laws inconsistently. And advocates complained that they could not check decisions to acquire an up-to-date knowledge of the law and to "avoid unnecessary reprimand from the courts."[9] Similarly, in Uganda one judge noted, "The farther from the capital the more difficulty the magistrates have. They don't have law books, and the judgments are often odd."[10] Nyalali remarked, "To the public, the inconsistencies signaled corruption, but it was not that."[11] Little was more frustrating and worrying to the courts than the inability to know the law.

Solving the problem posed more challenges than first met the eye. In theory, judges and magistrates in common law systems require a considerable array of legal research materials to do their jobs. In his long engagement with Africa, William Twining, one of the main participants in the first law and develop-

---

[6] Francis L. Nyalali, interview with author, July 19, 1997.

[7] Magistrate, interview with author, Mbarara, Uganda, January 29, 1996.

[8] Francis L. Nyalali, interview with author, July 19, 1997.

[9] A. M. Mapunda, M. C. Mukoyogo, and A. T. Nguluma, "Reflections on Stare Decisis in the Court of Appeal of the United Republic of Tanzania," *Eastern Africa Law Review*, 16, 2 (1989), p. 16.

[10] Justice David Porter, interview with author, Kampala, Uganda, November 1995.

[11] Francis L. Nyalali, interview with author, July 19, 1997.

ment movement, worked to identify basic needs. His list of fundamentals for a national legal literature had several components:

1. Primary sources
    a. A statute book that is up-to-date, flexible, and convenient to use
    b. A system of amendment that suits the convenience of the main users
    c. A regular and comprehensive indexing service
    d. A comprehensive interpretation act

2. Law reporting
    a. A system of reporting decisions of courts and other important tribunals
    b. Law reporting that takes account of the need for consistency and public information about lower tribunals, consistency, and equity in sentencing

3. An efficient system of supplementary intraprofessional communication— judicial circulars, magisterial circulars, practice directions, sentencing guidelines, and court handbooks, for example

4. A national legal archive

5. Secondary literature for legal education: a body of reference works, legal bibliography, and some form of regular bibliographic service[12]

Slightly farther down the list were other important items. Where a constitution or law required that the courts consider decisions from other countries, as in postapartheid South Africa, or where it was considered desirable that judges and lawyers do so, the needs were greater still. Subscriptions to law reports from other jurisdictions were essential.

Ideally, each judge or magistrate should have access to copies of these materials at a local court library. Similar collections should be available to members of the attorney general's chambers, parliamentary draftsmen, and the law faculty and students. But these ideals proved well out of reach.

Some of the tasks of building a legal literature did not properly belong to the court, and judiciaries had to wait for action by the other branches of government. For example, one of the first steps in rebuilding was to produce an index of the laws and a consolidated version of the statutes, which incorporated all changes in one place—a process called *law revision*. Normally parliamentary draftsman and the ministry of justice handled these functions, or private practitioners, who believed they could market the publication and cover their costs, accomplished the task. Members of law faculties sometimes developed their

---

[12] List paraphrased from study by William Twining and Jenny Uglow, eds., *Legal Literature in Small Jurisdictions* (London: Commonwealth Secretariat, 1981), pp. 18–19.

own indexes so they could teach effectively, and they were often a repository of skill and energy. In Tanzania, a young law faculty member named Ibrahim Juma prepared an index on his own, contained on thirteen computer diskettes, with no financial assistance. When the attorney general's office, which received millions of dollars from foreign donors to accomplish the same task, discovered it had competition, it announced that Juma's index was illegal, although, as Juma pointed out, "[T]hey could never identify the statute which made it so."[13] Americans financed the publication of Juma's index, while the attorney general's office continued to develop its own. In the end, the initial antagonisms passed and the courts finally acquired at least one of the documents essential to their work.

Law reporting was an equally important, much-needed tool to enhance the quality of justice. In the common law tradition, the law includes rules enunciated in court decisions in addition to the statutes and the doctrines of equity. For this reason, it was vital for judges and magistrates to have access to the upper-court decisions that were binding on the lower courts and which embodied the precedents fellow members of the High Court and Court of Appeal were enjoined to respect. Moreover, knowing that decisions would be available for all to peruse would theoretically lead judges to pay more attention to their reputations for clear reasoning.

Law reporting had started to wane in many countries at independence. To help new national courts, Alan Milner, based at Oxford, oversaw the development of the African Law Reports (ALR). The ALR was a two-part series designed to make judicial decisions publicly available. One part was organized according to substantive areas of law and brought together important decisions from the seventeen countries included in the program. The other was organized on a country basis. British and American financial support also helped develop a training program to expand the pool of law reporters in Africa.[14]

In the 1970s, foreign financing of the ALR ended.[15] The expectation was that African lawyers and governments would assume responsibility. Reporting endured for varying periods and by various means. In Uganda, inexpensive privately produced reports appeared from time to time, but no official series existed. In Kenya, Chief Justice A. R. W. Hancox worked hard to maintain a law reports series through the mid-1980s and took on the task as a personal project when no other support was forthcoming. No one assumed responsibility after he left. The Zimbabwe reports terminated at about the same time. In Malawi and Botswana, reports persisted until 1989, then production slowed or halted.

---

[13] Ibrahim Juma, interview with author, Dar es Salaam, Tanzania, March 23, 1999.

[14] John Seaman Bainbridge, *The Study and Teaching of Law in Africa* (Hackensack, NJ: Fred B. Rothman & Co., 1972), pp. 137–138.

[15] E. Koffi Tetteh, "Law Reporting in Anglophone Africa," *International and Comparative Law Quarterly*, 20 (January 1971), p. 94.

The Tanzanian legal community tried to sustain law reporting, but it did not succeed. The law faculty attempted to produce its own informal "Law Reports of Tanzania," but this effort fell apart. In 1980, the chief justice's office tried to work with the Ministry of Justice and the law faculty at Dar to produce a new set of reports. An editorial team set out the criteria that would guide selection of the cases to be reported.[16] But progress halted after 1982. The law faculty complained that not all the members of the bench cooperated. Nyalali remembered that "the exercise was bogged down by printing constraints within the country." A shortage of foreign exchange meant that the problem could not be solved by looking for printing capacity outside the country, either. "The editorial board, though downhearted, soldiered on with its task of selecting judgments, hoping for a rainy day when the local printing capacity would improve," Nyalali related. "This resulted in a huge backlog which progressively required larger sums of money to print and publish. Thus when the local printing capacity improved in consequence of the economic policy of liberalization . . . commencing in the mid-1980s, the judiciary department found itself without the financial capacity both to fund the printing of the backlog and assist the editorial board to keep up-to-date with its publication."[17]

Gaining access to decisions from other jurisdictions and to books that explained international trends in important fields of law was also difficult for judges in most countries. For the first twenty years after independence, it was relatively common to find copies of law reports and other materials from Britain, Canada, Australia, India, and the Commonwealth. These countries provided copies to the law libraries at court headquarters, and often to law reform commissions. The United States swapped its reports for copies of local laws or decisions. Justice Vincent Crabbe, who served on several courts in Africa, remembered: "There used to be a program with the Library of Congress in the United States. If you sent the Library books or pamphlets, they would send you the same number in return. So if you sent twelve books, they would send you twelve. When I was in Ghana, we sent the Ghana Official Gazette and the Library of Congress sent us law books. We equipped the attorney general's office that way."[18] Anecdotal evidence suggested that providing law

---

[16] These criteria were (1) cases that stated a new rule of law or restated in modern terms an old rule of law or principle, or modified a rule of the common law; (2) cases that declared, extended, qualified, or distinguished an existing rule of law; (3) cases that interpreted a clause commonly found in contracts, wills, etc.; (4) cases that clarified a law for the benefit of a lower court; (5) cases in which the judge instructed on points of practice or procedure; and (6) cases dealing with quantum of damages, to help produce uniformity. The criteria appear in Mapunda, Mukoyogo, and Nguluma, "Reflections on Stare Decisis in the Court of Appeal of the United Republic of Tanzania," p. 14.

[17] Francis L. Nyalali, interview with author, May 29, 1996.

[18] Justice Vincent Crabbe, interview with author, April 24, 1998.

reports increased the tendency of judges to cite decisions from the donor country as persuasive authority in their own rulings.

In the 1980s, greater austerity worldwide brought an end to most of these exchange programs. It was often even more difficult to obtain judgments and laws from neighboring African jurisdictions than from India or Europe. The Commonwealth Law Books program cut back on its provision of materials through Book Aid International, a remarkable British charity that shipped books to Africa beginning in the mid-1950s. What little arrived from other sources, although appreciated, was usually piecemeal, often orchestrated by nonlawyers from donor-country aid agencies who had little sense of the kinds of materials that would be important.

The results of this gap for jurisprudence were especially poignant. As the South Africans realized in preparing their new constitution, requiring reference to decisions elsewhere could help ensure that a country's jurisprudence took account of other views in the region and around the globe. It could help broaden the familiarity with the reasoning their counterparts used in other countries and push judges to argue cogently why external precedents did or did not make sense in the local context. Further, it could lead to the development of a distinctive regional jurisprudence, as courts in countries similarly situated came to grips with shared problems. Finally, it could spark ideas and show judges ways out of particularly difficult or complex problems.

In the late 1980s and early 1990s there were already calls for exchanges between African legal scholars to promote development of a comparative legal literature for this purpose. The former dean of the University of Nairobi law faculty, Kivutha Kibwana, promoted this idea as his personal project. He called for an Association of African Law Teachers, urged that African comparative law be included in law school curricula, and championed the exchange of law reviews and other publications. He admonished his fellow scholars, "We must learn to take sabbatical leave within Africa even if it is not financially rewarding."[19] But a more powerful tool for accomplishing a similar end was to make law reports from different countries available again.

Nyalali recalled an example of the importance of this kind of access. His office had just acquired its first fax machine when the court had to decide whether it had the inherent power to review its own decisions. "The courts must have the inherent power to review their own decisions, I argued. I was opposed on this matter by the other seven judges of appeal." He confided, "The weak spot of judges is authority; they have to know what grants them authority

---

[19] Kivutha Kibwana, "Enhancing Cooperation among African Law Schools," in *Proceedings of the Fourth Annual Conference of the African Society of International and Comparative Law, Dakar,* Senegal, April 10–13, 1992 (London: African Society of International and Comparative Law, 1992), pp. 293–299.

to make a decision!" He went on: "I had to find an enabling rule that would permit us to review our own decisions in case of fraud or misrepresentation. I sent faxes to CJs in Zimbabwe, South Africa, Australia, New Zealand, Canada, the United Kingdom, and Uganda. I asked whether they had encountered such an issue, and if so how had they decided the matter. In response, they sent photocopies of articles, book chapters, and statutes. My fax machine also worked overtime. My colleagues came round. 'Oh, CJ, you must be right!' they said. They had deep respect for precedent, and now they could see the precedents from other countries. As a result, we determined that the court may review itself using its inherent powers if there is fraud."[20] The fax was a useful solution in a pinch, but it only highlighted the need for access to legal literature.

In the mid-1990s, foreign legal assistance helped rejuvenate law reporting in some places. For example, in Zimbabwe, the Canadian government worked with the courts and the Legal Resources Foundation, a local nongovernmental organization, to produce a multivolume paperback set of reports covering the period 1985 through 1995. Britain and the United States helped finance some of the volumes too. In Uganda, where law reporting was vested by statute in the Law Development Centre, the World Bank provided funds and consultants to develop reports for the Ugandan appellate courts going back to 1958. Similarly, in Tanzania, donors supported the production of law reports for the period 1982–94.

The expense of producing documents could be defrayed partly through commercial sales to lawyers and to universities and organizations. For example, in 1991, when the Ugandans moved to replace the statute books burned during the long civil conflict, it found that several members of the bar wanted copies too and that they were willing to pay for the photocopied sets of laws. In Zimbabwe, where the court had teamed up with a nongovernmental organization to produce law reports, it succeeded in selling copies to foreign law schools. Tanzania was able to publish reports for 1983–92 with the assistance of the World Bank and then found ways to work with a commercial publisher to provide annual updates.

Private initiatives sometimes produced results more rapidly than did the lumbering official process. For example, Professor Chris Maina Peter at the University of Dar es Salaam worked to compile selected human rights cases. Judge Kahwa Lugakingira carefully read the manuscript and offered comments, in a display of cooperation between the bench and the university. Peter then persuaded a German publisher to produce the volume, which appeared late in 1997.[21]

Gradually a regional commercial response developed. The mid- to late 1990s were a period of expansion for many South African enterprises. Juta &

---

[20] Francis L. Nyalali, interview with author, March 21, 1996.
[21] Chris Maina Peter, *Human Rights in Tanzania: Selected Cases and Materials* (Köln: Rüdiger Köppe Verlag, 1997).

Co., which had built a base in publishing both popular and scholarly legal materials in South Africa, saw an opportunity to develop a network throughout the continent, building on its existing strengths. It teamed up with local publishers to take over the entire process of collating, editing, printing, publishing, and distributing law reports for several countries, including Tanzania, Botswana, Zambia, and Malawi.

There were also some items that any judge or magistrate needed as personal tools. In Uganda, the British helped the court publish an abridged set of statutes for distribution to lower-court magistrates as a quick way to remedy some of the deficiencies in the system. Similarly, in Tanzania, donors helped finance a "Manual for Primary Courts," which contained parts of the updated statutes on civil procedure and criminal procedure, customary law, evidence, the magistrates courts, and minimum sentences, as well as selected parts of the law on marriage.

No effort to improve the availability of legal literature absolved magistrates and judges of the need to keep their own notebooks of materials they found useful. In the days before copies of laws and judgments were conveniently available in the United States, Chief Justice John Marshall, Nyalali's role model, had maintained a "commonplace book." His own law teacher, George Wythe, had insisted that his students create such notebooks in which they would record laws and precedents they used in practice. Marshall relied heavily on his and added to it throughout his life. It was one of the few documents he kept.[22] On visits to American courts, Nyalali observed the same practice still in use, despite the vast array of material at the fingertips of judges in the computer age. One of his close American friends observed that she maintained several notebooks with observations about laws, precedents, arguments she liked, and solutions to problems of interpretation. She too relied heavily on these. The "commonplace book" was an important tool across time and across societies, and it required no extra money to maintain.

LEGAL REASONING

Neither legal education nor judicial training had kept pace with changing social, economic, and political conditions. The 1960s and 1970s, when many judges received their law degrees and joined the bench, were the heydays of single-party rule and heavy government involvement in markets. By contrast, the late 1980s and 1990s brought new relationships and unfamiliar issues, which judges often felt they were ill-equipped to address.

One of the areas in which knowledge lagged was human rights. New bills of rights and new constitutions promised an increase in rights cases brought to the

[22] Jean Edward Smith, *John Marshall: Definer of a Nation* (New York: Henry Holt, 1996), p. 80.

courts, yet few judges had much familiarity with the subject. Nyalali's colleague, Justice Robert Kisanga, a member of the African Commission on Human Rights, commented, "When I went to the university, the study of human rights was not part of the curriculum. Now it is gaining ground. The judges of my generation on the Court of Appeal are not conversant with the subject, however."[23]

Some suggested that a new style of decision was required. In developing areas of law, where precedent was less available, judges needed to place a premium on clear explanation of their own reasoning. "The new situation . . . demands a return to the Grand Style decisions" common in American constitutional law, urged one distinguished lawyer-scholar many years before the new law and development movement began to take hold. "In a period of rapid social, political and economic change . . . what is required is . . . substantively rational law-making, rather than legalism."[24] That meant judges needed to broaden the range of interpretive techniques they used and to write out their reasons in a language the educated public could understand.

Another weak spot was commercial law. In a 1995 report, a distinguished member of the Ugandan court had taken the Makerere Law School to task for being "rather narrow and unduly concerned with traditional subjects which were fashionable more than 25 years ago in English law schools,"[25] and he extended his criticism to the Law Development Centre, the one-year practical program required for entrance to the bar. "The training emphasizes litigation at the expense of non-contentious practice or solicitors' work," he wrote.[26] The main focus of his criticism was the shortage of courses related to the law important for the kinds of economic problems public and private sector institutions faced. The judges' preparation was similarly inadequate, suggested several members of the bench, in Uganda and in other countries. Developing familiarity with the newer aspects of international business transactions, joint ventures, and related subjects would be especially important for processing complicated commercial cases more quickly.

The lag in knowledge was one problem. However, both on the court and outside there was also quiet concern about the need to refresh more basic skills. Mohammed Ismael, president of the Tanganyika Law Society in the mid-1990s, commented, "My generation of lawyers and judges have had a hard time. Chief Justice Georges once said to me, 'I pity you young fellows.' The

[23] Justice Robert Kisanga, interview with author, Dar es Salaam, Tanzania, May 31, 1996.
[24] Robert B. Seidman, "Judicial Review and Fundamental Freedoms in Anglophonic Independent Africa," *Ohio State Law Journal*, 35 (1974), p. 844.
[25] Republic of Uganda, "Draft Report of the Committee on Legal Education, Training, and Accreditation in Uganda," Justice Benjamin Odoki, Chair, Committee on Legal Education, Uganda Institutional Capacity-Building Project (Kampala, Uganda: Ministry of Justice and Constitutional Affairs, July 7, 1995), p. 6.
[26] Ibid., p. 8.

best lawyers had left the country, and there were hardly any models for us—no one to learn from. The judges were just as young as we were, except the expats—but they left by 1975."[27] Others worried that low pay in the judiciary in the preceding decades had led many of the best-trained lawyers to enter private practice. They expressed their dismay with "mediocrity" and "timidity" on the bench and asked why judgments were not as well reasoned as they often were in South Africa or Zimbabwe. A better grasp of the law, greater clarity in the opinions drafted, and more familiarity with trends in legal reasoning were necessary. Although they rarely expressed such sentiments so forcefully, the chief justices grew interested in ways to improve judicial writing.

Finally, critics suggested that the recruitment of judges and magistrates who had no practical experience at the bar sometimes meant that judgments fell prey to lawyers' tactics. As one judge observed, "In general, cases decide themselves, but there are always a few where the talent of the lawyers makes a difference. Experience at the bar may turn the scales one way or another. It is important to have practical experience to know the games lawyers play."[28]

It was possible to begin to address some of these problems through judicial training. In the West, judges and lawyers often had to participate in continuing education programs in order to remain in their jobs. In eastern and central Africa, both advocates and judges had long lacked equivalent opportunities, although several courts tried to convene judicial conferences when finances permitted and these facilitated exchange of information. In Tanzania, the country's first chief justice, Telford Georges, organized several such events. Later, Nyalali tried to rejuvenate the program, but it struggled for lack of money. When foreign legal assistance funds became available in the late 1980s and then, more abundantly, in the 1990s, Nyalali and his fellow chief justices accorded priority to judicial and legal training, alongside measures to reduce delay in the courts.

Choosing how best to meet training needs posed at least as many questions as deciding how to rebuild national legal literatures and improve recording systems. One of the first was whether the training should take place locally or abroad. Was it more cost-effective to bring people from other countries to provide instruction, or was it more sensible to send the judges to places that had teachers who could cover a wide range of subjects? Were judges more likely to learn when they were removed from the pressures of the office and able to see different court systems in action, or would they gain in stature locally if judges from other countries visited to provide instruction and the occasion could be used as a "media event"?

Frequent trips abroad attracted criticism at home, and Western hosts often

---

[27] Mohammed Ismael, interview with author, Dar es Salaam, Tanzania, May 22, 1996.
[28] Justice Vincent Crabbe, interview with author, Washington, D. C., April 24, 1998.

had little knowledge of the real problems their African counterparts faced on the ground. But in the early years, when judges felt isolated from the profession and struggled to make ends meet on low salaries, the opportunity to travel improved morale and helped build alliances. Chief justices had to search for a mix that would balance objectives effectively.

There were notable successes. There were also notable failures. Over the first ten years, rules of thumb gradually evolved to help improve the match between needs and assistance. One was that for most courses of instruction, practitioners usually communicated more effectively than professional teachers. Judiciaries were specialized and hierarchical. Judges usually learned best from other judges, or from mixed groups of judges and lawyers who had shared similar problems in their jobs. Status and experience were important to effectiveness. Another was that cultural arrogance could be a problem in international exchanges. The programs that worked best were those in which visitors learned about the systems in which they were teaching, recognized that their own courts were not perfect, and succeeded in establishing a conversation, not a pulpit. Highly substantive, hands-on training, not judicial safaris, were what made the arduous travel worthwhile. A third was that Westerners often made unwarranted assumptions about the availability of equipment and resources, forgetting that in many places electrical supplies were undependable, video formats were different, and photocopiers or computer printers were in short supply.

A fourth, especially important rule of thumb was that programs worked best when instructors included professionals from the region as well as from the West. As time went on, it proved possible to tap expertise in courts and organizations in South Africa, Zimbabwe, and other countries with similar legal heritages and closely related problems. The programs that did so won kudos from the participants, who were eager to build networks with neighbors.

In Tanzania, as in other countries, the lowest level of the court had lacked legal materials for so long and was so demoralized that Nyalali thought it imperative to create a continuing legal education program specially targeted to its needs. After long negotiation, he persuaded the Americans and the British to join with two private foundations, the Ford Foundation and the Konrad Adenauer Foundation, to support a series of three-week seminars, and by the end of June 1998, most primary court magistrates received a chance to upgrade their skills. The program was an experiment, however, and the aim was to find a way to help it endure.

Most important, the bar, as well as the bench, needed to participate in many training programs. In common law systems, the advocates, not the judges, define the issues of the case. Their briefs help shape what the judge takes into account in the decision handed down. As a result, providing assistance only to judges would not necessarily improve the quality of justice. Conversely, neglecting judicial training would only increase the frustration of the bar with a bench it considered out of touch with important trends in the law. In past years, contact between the two groups had declined, and communication had diminished as a result. Although at first some of the judges were nervous about holding joint sessions, after the fact these meetings usually won praise from all sides. One advocate pointed out that joint workshops that included the bench and the bar would make reputation matter to a judge. "If judges and lawyers go on study tours together, then it would be possible to say, 'Hey, you learned about that. What are you doing about it?' "[29]

Justice officials also worked with the government and the bar to consider ways to provide continuing education opportunities directed to the needs of lawyers. In the mid-1980s, Ibrahim Shihata, then director general of the OPEC (Organization of Petroleum Exporting Countries) Fund for International Development, and later general counsel to the World Bank, persuaded bilateral donors and foundations to support an international organization to train developing-country lawyers in foreign investment, international trade, and development assistance. The International Development Law Institute, based in Rome, helped government lawyers acquire skills in negotiation, legal drafting, international contracting, and law reform.[30] But by the late 1990s, only Uganda approached the challenge of continuing legal education among its private lawyers comprehensively. Under the umbrella of the country's institutional capacity building program, the government contracted with the International Law Institute in Washington to develop a sixteen-month continuing education program based in Kampala. Within the first year, over 50 percent of the bar participated in courses on topics in commercial law, including capital markets, joint ventures, privatization, international business transactions, arbitration, lending and loan renegotiation, and international trade. The Ugandans hoped eventually to open the Kampala program to regional participation.

PROFESSIONALISM

All of these changes unfolded slowly between the mid-1980s and the late 1990s, gradually picking up speed. Inevitably progress was uneven, as the effort to solve one problem revealed others that had to be attacked before the courts would see any results. Sometimes the problems were remarkably mundane, a tribute to the similarity of human nature around the world. For example, in several courts judges hoped to restart law reporting and speed the production of trial proceedings by introducing word processors to the High Court secretarial service. Once in electronic form, decisions could be indexed quickly and made available for printing without the need for retyping. But in one court, clerical staff rebelled,

---

[29] Mohammed Ismael, interview with author, May 22, 1996.
[30] L. Michael Hager, "Training Lawyers for Development: The IDLI Experience," *Third World Legal Studies*, 1986 (1986), p. 58.

arguing that they were being asked to do more work for the same pay. The judges pointed out that the computers simply made the work faster and easier and that producing more typed pages did not mean they had worked any harder than before. These interpersonal and management problems had to be solved before programs could proceed. Like challenges existed in other courts.

Most frustrating to reform-minded chief justices and their main allies was the slowness with which a spirit of reform and a renewed sense of professionalism set in. The chief justices hoped to use programs aimed at improving the quality of justice partly to build an *esprit de corps*. If judges and magistrates, or judges and lawyers, saw one another more often, they reasoned, individuals might use their imaginations and energies to help solve the problems the courts faced. "Our first step was to popularize the importance of the rule of law," said Peter Kabatsi, Uganda's solicitor general. "The British and Americans were helpful. We brought in people from outside and used them to help set standards. We hoped people would be inspired by the efforts to help them do their jobs better."[31] Enthusiasm might prove contagious. At the very least, they would become more concerned about what they said and did. They would have to be concerned about what colleagues might ask them and what they would say in return.

It proved harder to build such an *esprit* than anticipated. One reason was that judicial conferences, seminars, and continuing education workshops were sporadic and generally involved relatively few people at any given time. Although the judges of the Tanzanian High Court and Court of Appeal met once a week over tea to discuss court business, judicial personnel complained that there was not enough contact among members of the justice system generally to allow a spirit of change to develop. Nyalali's trusted colleague, Justice Robert Kisanga, commented, "More departmental meetings would help. It is vital to have these because the performance of the court depends heavily on self-criticism. Reputations matter only if people meet each other. If an officer is corrupt, but never has to confront others, then there is no cost to continuing the behavior."[32] The same sentiment was echoed by judges and magistrates at all levels of the courts in other countries of the region, including Botswana.

Although law faculties and law societies experienced rejuvenation in this period, it was still difficult to consider the law as a profession that could speak as a body on institutional matters. Asked whether any colleagues stood out as leaders in the law and the courts, one Ugandan lawyer interviewed in the mid-1990s replied, "Leaders in the legal profession? I am not aware of any. It is hard to get to know people unless one attends seminars and workshops."[33]

Another obstacle to creating a spirit of reform was the legacy of the past. Said

[31] Peter Kabatsi, solicitor general, interview with author, Kampala, Uganda, November 8, 1995.
[32] Justice Robert Kisanga, interview with author, Dar es Salaam, Tanzania, May 31, 1996.
[33] Jane Mwsoke, International Federation of Women Lawyers (FIDA), interview with author, Mbarara, Uganda, January 29, 1996.

one judge, "The slowness of change now is a function of history. In the colonial period, judges could not question colonial legitimacy and they adopted a strong philosophy of judicial restraint. Although that attitude applied to decisions, not to court administration, no one questioned it after independence and it began to affect other aspects of the way we did our jobs too. We fell into the habit of not questioning things, even in our own operations."[34] "People are afraid of losing a job, so they don't make a fuss," said another. "Pride is the problem. There isn't pride in the place. We need to build pride."[35]

Said Uganda's principal judge, "There is still not much agreement within the court, but there are signs of a reawakening."[36] In Uganda, by chance, the judges had stumbled on one way to try to oust the legacy. The government appointed two expatriate judges to chair commissions of inquiry into the judiciary and into other rule of law issues, including corruption. The judges and their Ugandan colleagues conducted investigations and hearings, some of which were reported in the newspapers. "The Commissions had a salutary effect," commented one judge. "They showed where the errors were. Then people went back and changed their routines, so that when the reports came out, they could say they had addressed the problems already."[37]

Finally, momentum was critical. Said one judge, "It is important to keep moving forward, even at the expense of an occasional mistake. The judges have to get used to the idea that they are in charge."[38]

[34] Justice Frederick Egonda-Ntende, interview with author, Kampala, Uganda, February 14, 1996.
[35] Justice David Porter, interview with author, Kampala, Uganda, November 1995.
[36] Justice Jeremiah Herbert Ntagoba, interview with author, Kampala, Uganda, February 1996.
[37] Justice David Porter, interview with author, Kampala, Uganda, November 1995.
[38] Justice Harold G. Platt, interview with author, Kampala, Uganda, November 9, 1995.

Under Remand

TURNING BROAD OBJECTIVES into a concrete plan of action required attention to other problems that were far more difficult to solve than records and law reports. One of the most urgent was delay, and in particular delay on the criminal side of the courts.

All over the world, the adage in legal circles is that "justice delayed is justice denied." Delay affects the fairness of both criminal and civil proceedings. As time passes and cases await trial, the memories of witnesses fade, and delay becomes the enemy of finding the truth. When there are delays in the enforcement of rights, individual protection from arbitrary use of government power is diminished. Slowness in civil litigation often costs money, and where inflation rates are high, some litigants may lose financially as time passes, while others gain dramatically. Because courts in many countries are responsible for maintaining the formal record of legal status (as in adoptions, divorces, etc.), delay impairs the ability of people to move forward with their lives. In extreme cases, when courts do not operate efficiently, people may choose to resolve their differences by other means and the rule of law breaks down.

In Africa, delay put the legitimacy of fledgling courts at risk. It undermined popular support and weakened the protection favorable public opinion offered. On the criminal side, it jeopardized the independence of the judicial process more directly by creating opportunities for interference and abuse. For example, the fact of delay meant that corrupt police officers had a tool they could use to threaten residents and extract money. So certain was the prospect of prolonged detention, and so awful were prison conditions, that anyone who could do so paid the requested bribe to stay out of jail.[1] And where statutes lowered the requirements for a show of evidence at preliminary hearings, governments were able to persecute critics by arresting them and holding them until just before the trial was due to start. At the last minute, the prosecutor would then announce that there was insufficient evidence to proceed. The reputation of the courts suffered.

The Tanzanian case pointed up these kinds of difficulties. Popular frustration with delay in the courts in Tanzania had long been a source of trouble. In the late 1960s, the country's first chief justice, Telford Georges, dispatched then-Magistrate Nyalali to try to reduce delay in the court at Bukoba. When Augustine Saidi replaced Georges, in the 1970s, official distress about the slowness of the courts inspired a new procedure that required every magistrate to provide a detailed report on all criminal cases not concluded within sixty days of the accused person's first appearance in court. The reports were supposed to be prepared in triplicate, and copies went to both the prime minister and the chief justice. After consulting with the chief justice, the prime minister, or another minister designated by him, could take "such action against the public officer who appears to him to have been responsible for occasioning the delay, or against the magistrate . . . as he may consider desirable in the public interest."[2] The policy signified the intensity of public concern about a problem that had expanded dramatically. But severe problems of delay persisted into the 1980s and 1990s.

"Delay in bringing people to trial caused a big outcry in Tanzania," Nyalali observed. "A person served the sentence before being tried! We had to move quickly to solve the problem."[3] Nyalali knew that delay was an especially difficult challenge, because it was not a matter completely under the control of the judiciary. Courts are part of a "justice system," which includes the police, the prisons, prosecutors, and the bar. Delay had its origins partly in poor relationships between these institutions. Moreover, even though each organization complained bitterly about the slowness of criminal or civil proceedings, at one time or another people in all parts of the justice system found delay individually useful. It was up to the judges to play an active role in attacking the problem, but that meant the courts had to engage other parts of government in the process of reform without compromising the separation of powers and jeopardizing the appearance of impartiality.

In some countries, the problem was worse. In 1991, the Ugandan court's discovery that there were 5,400 remand prisoners awaiting trial in the High Court

---

[1] See protest against this practice by the Uganda Law Society, Memorandum, "Observation of Law, Courts, and the Prison Services in Uganda," Law Society, Kampala, Uganda, August 30, 1992, photocopy.
[2] Neville Rubin and Eugene Cotran, eds., *Annual Survey of African Law*, 7, 1973 (London: Rex Collings, 1977), p. 143.
[3] Francis L. Nyalali, interview with author, May 29, 1996.

shocked people into action. Justice David Porter, an expatriate judge who served on the High Court, chaired the Commission of Inquiry into the Management of Criminal Cases, which reported in 1994. Porter was determined to find out how many people were in Uganda's prisons, and how long they had been there, so that "forgotten souls" could finally receive justice. The problem was a tough one. Many of the prisons were administered locally and did not report to the central government. To the extent that any of the prisons kept records, they did so on scraps of paper and had no system for getting the paper to other offices that needed the information. There were court records, but the court records often did not match the police records or the limited information available from the prisons. Porter organized a small team to go to all of the country's prisons. The team would systematically identify all of the people incarcerated and then try to match the names with court records. He programmed Texas Instrument laptop computers to create specialized databases. The Texas Instrument laptops were vital, he said. There was rarely an electrical supply where the team traveled, and it was possible to power them from a Land Rover battery instead.

Chief justices labored under no illusions about the delicacy of the task of reform on the criminal side of the courts. Governments that used delay to their advantage in order to rid themselves of political opponents could make the price of court intervention very high. In Uganda, after Chief Justice Benedicto Kiwanuka took the oath of office, he pushed hard to reduce the time people were under remand and released people who had spent long periods in prison awaiting trial. In *Kulanima v. Uganda*,[4] he ruled that delay was an "exceptional circumstance" in which the courts could grant bail.[5] The ruling—and the judge—met with the displeasure of those in power. Under the government of Idi Amin, Kiwanuka was killed for having protested.

However, in the mid-1980s, times seemed to be changing. Nyalali decided to attack the problem anew. He knew other courts must have experimented with solutions. If some of the problems African courts faced were exotic, delay was not. Courts all over the world had dealt with the same problem. The question was whether it was possible to borrow outside solutions successfully under the conditions that prevailed in the region. How should the courts reform practices, procedures, and organization to make a difference? What could they do with little money?

[4] 1971 High Court Bulletin, 210, 211.
[5] Benjamin J. Odoki, "Reducing Delay in the Administration of Justice: The Case of Uganda," *Criminal Law Forum*, 5, 1 (1994), p. 78.

INSTITUTIONAL CONTEXT

In eastern and southern Africa, the length of pretrial delays in criminal cases varied across countries. In Zambia, for example, by the mid-1990s, most criminal cases were tried within six months of the date on which charges were filed. By contrast, Ugandan police statistics suggested that in 1990, over 4,500 people had been under remand for over 480 days and over 50 percent of the prison population had been under remand for over one year.[6] The Commission of Inquiry on Judicial Reform that convened in 1994–95 heard reports of people held four years or more while awaiting trial.[7] It also found that there were still people incarcerated years before in rural areas who had never been committed for trial and whose names were unknown to the court. One judge related a question he received from a prisoner in 1995: "We may not be very nice people, but don't you think we ought to be tried?"[8]

Some of the problems were located in the court. In countries such as Uganda, there were no permanent High Court stations in rural areas. That meant that criminal cases committed to the High Court outside the capital had to be heard by a circuit judge. If there was no money to pay for fuel or for the judge's temporary accommodation, the circuit would be called off or delayed. Those under remand would remain in jail months longer as a result. Nor did courts always inform counsel or state attorneys of hearing dates. That meant that when the case was called, the accused might be present, but no prosecutor would appear. The judge then adjourned the case for a later date.

Other institutions involved in the justice system bore responsibility as well, and that fact complicated the challenge of reform. Everywhere, police investigations were a source of difficulty. Police forces were generally poorly trained and badly equipped. Abuses of power often stemmed from organizational weakness, not ill intent. The police were easily overwhelmed, and members of the public sometimes expressed sympathy for them with comments that "they do the best they can under the circumstances." When asked about the quality of police protection, villagers in one Ugandan community laughed, pointing out that only the previous week, bandits had routed the police from their compound and taken what little they could find there.[9] In several countries, the 1970s also had seen an expansion of bribery-induced delay: It was possible to "lose files" or win adjournments by paying a little money to an officer.[10]

---

[6] Ibid.

[7] Republic of Uganda, Report of the Commission of Inquiry on Judicial Reform (Kampala, Uganda: Commission of Inquiry on Judicial Reform, 1995), p. 17.

[8] Justice Rajanatham Rajasingham, interview with author, Kampala, Uganda, February 1996.

[9] Jennifer Widner, field notes, Bujuta B, Uganda, 1995.

[10] Widely noted. See, for example, Sufian Hemed Bukurura, *The Judiciary and Good*

These problems of police capacity had a long history in Tanzania. At the time of the country's first major investigation into the collapse of the "rule of law," a commission of inquiry reported that "people cited lax, corrupt, and dishonest and partial investigators; they cited collusion by investigators with criminal and suspicious characters, and they said that many investigators mistreat complainants by either ignoring their complaints or harassing them unnecessarily."

> [T]he people said that CID [Criminal Investigations Department] manpower was insufficient and that most of the investigators were either untrained in the science of investigation, or were inadequately trained in that behalf. In either case, the people said, investigations were not likely to be swiftly and successfully conducted. They also said that the police authorities did not equip investigators with facilities necessary for investigation.

In its conclusions, the commission wrote: "Owing to the historically unfavorable image which the police force has in the eyes of the public . . . people told the commission, the police, and police investigators in particular, do not get sufficient co-operation from the public."[11]

Police relationships with prosecutors were often poor too. A Ugandan commission of inquiry found that "[o]ften police did not trust the prosecutor and wouldn't give the prosecutor's office the material. We tried to change this on a pilot basis by making sure that state attorneys received a copy of the police report, but the police were very annoyed. The procedures didn't support what the police had been doing. If they were told to lose a file, they did so. Retribution was sometimes violent if they didn't." Sometimes the police would prosecute a case without letting the state attorneys know. "People would be charged on the basis of insufficient evidence, and when the case was dismissed, the prosecutors would bear the blame."[12] In the mid-1990s, the courts took the initiative and told magistrates not to accept files unless they bore the prosecutor's signature. But getting police to turn over evidence remained a problem, often because police wanted to maintain control over the prosecution of a matter that was not genuine and knew the state attorneys would throw out the case.[13]

At times, police also seemed to wish to assert authority over the courts. Nyalali observed that in Tanzania, "[t]here have been numerous instances

---

Governance in Contemporary Tanzania (Bergen, Norway: Christien Michelsen Institute, Development and Human Rights Studies, September 1995), p. 13.

[11] United Republic of Tanzania, Judicial System Review Commission, *Report of the Judicial System Review Commission* (Msekwa Report) (Dar es Salaam, Tanzania, Judicial System Review Commission, 1977), pp. 25–26.

[12] Richard Buteere, interview with author, Kampala, Uganda, November 9, 1995.

[13] Ibid.

where the accused, after being discharged in court, has been re-arrested by the police immediately after he ventured out of the court. There has even been an instance where the police after thus re-arresting the accused, filed a new charge before the same trial magistrate who had shortly before made the order of discharge, apparently purely to demonstrate that the police had the last word at that stage of the proceedings."[14] This kind of conduct was an abuse of court process. He suggested that the court could plausibly issue a prerogative order to quash the proceedings under those circumstances.

In neighboring Uganda, Chief Justice Samson Wako Wambuzi also took issue with police behavior. Reported one newspaper, "Justice Wambuzi said some policemen only listen to 'mere statements of complaint' and arrest people before making investigations. Our courts are crowded; prisons are crowded because many people who should not be there are there."[15]

Addressing delay caused by poor police training promised to be a long-term endeavor. Botswana recognized the problem earlier than some of the other countries and used some of its resources to send police for university degrees in law. Uganda began to move law graduates into senior positions in the police and the Criminal Investigations Department (CID), but rapid change at the lowest levels, where the problems were often worst, was not likely to materialize.

Prosecutors themselves also could be a source of trouble. Although in some countries, such as Uganda and Botswana, the majority of criminal cases were prosecuted by the police, in most places state attorneys handled larger matters. Often the state attorneys were roving prosecutors who did not have offices. They traveled and they did not get files on time because the police could not figure out where to send them.[16] And state attorneys were sometimes just plain inefficient. In Uganda, all a state attorney had to do to commit someone to court was to write a one-page note, but in many instances no one would file the document for seventeen months or more.[17] Nor would state attorneys push the police to deliver the investigation reports, so that even three years after a case was committed to court, they would still say the police file was missing. "They did not want to force others to move out of their old pace," suggested one judge.[18] Prosecutors' offices everywhere were notoriously understaffed and were manned mainly by junior lawyers who lacked experience.

The prisons were part of the picture too. Often there were no resources for managing prisons in accordance with international human rights standards. During the 1980s and 1990s, in most African countries, prison conditions fell

[14] Francis L. Nyalali, "Paper on Case Management," Presented at a seminar of judges, Arusha, Tanzania, April 19–23, 1993.
[15] "Police Accused," *New Vision* (Uganda), January 26, 1996.
[16] Republic of Uganda, Report of the Commission of Inquiry on Judicial Reform, p. 23.
[17] Justice David Porter, interview with author, Kampala, Uganda, November 1995.
[18] Justice Harold G. Platt, interview with author, Kampala, Uganda, November 9, 1995.

below acceptable levels and "life-threatening" or "very poor" conditions prevailed in at least 40 percent.[19] Those incarcerated usually received only one meal a day, and that practice offended human rights norms, even though it was sometimes the case that an average person in many of the same countries rarely had the land or money to obtain much more than that. In many places, effective responsibility for providing food, clothing, and bedding lay with the family of the person incarcerated, not with the state. Prison officials lacked the training to maintain records and the resources to get defendants to trial on time.

These problems were less severe in some countries than in others. One judge in Botswana explained that "the relationship between the police, the prisons, the prosecutors, and the courts is not a big issue for us. The prisons receive advance lists of which cases are on. They have transport. If there is a problem, we have telephones and they work."[20] Moreover, chief justices in Botswana had long insisted that magistrates make prison visits, and the magistrates themselves attributed Botswana's comparative success in part to this practice.

Once delays set in, the problem built on itself. People came to expect that the courts would adjourn cases frequently, for lack of the defendant, counsel, prosecutors, or some bit of evidence. That sometimes made people unwilling to testify. In rural areas, witnesses had to leave their work and travel considerable distances to courtrooms, often uncompensated. If word got out that the judge might not hear the case after someone had traveled so far, people would grow unwilling to appear. Said one magistrate, "Testifying is a real burden. Witnesses get tired of coming to court. Sometimes they are forgotten, move on, or die."[21] In 1995, the Ugandan commission of inquiry remarked that prosecutors and police sometimes had difficulty locating witnesses and transporting them to the courts where trials were in progress. "In one case only one witness was heard a year," the commission reported, "so that after three years the case was still only partly heard."[22]

For years no person or organization asserted authority to improve communication and coordination. "The Magistrates did not know how to cure the defects in the system," stated one report, and they did not provide "proper information" about the severity of the situation to the High Court.[23] One Ugandan judge observed, "Judges and magistrates said they didn't have a role because there was no enabling law. We have attacked that severely. The court has all the powers any court has to assure there are no abuses of court process and human rights. English courts have for a long time made it known that if people

---

[19] Analysis based on author's coding of U.S. Department of State, *Human Rights Reports* (Washington, D.C.: U.S. Government Printing Office, multiple years).
[20] Justice J. C. Barrington-Jones, interview with author, Lobatse, Botswana, April 12, 1996.
[21] Chief Magistrate, interview with author, Jinja, Uganda, November 22, 1995.
[22] Republic of Uganda, Report of the Commission of Inquiry on Judicial Reform, p. 17.
[23] Ibid., p. 20.

are not allowed to go to trial quickly, that interferes with their defense, and courts can use their inherent powers to ask about lost files, delays, and inappropriate actions."[24]

FIRST STEPS AND MISSTEPS

To protect innocent people from being held on frivolous criminal charges, justice systems typically required that someone who was arrested quickly be brought before a judge for a preliminary hearing to decide whether there was sufficient evidence to send the case to trial. A magistrate or judge heard a summary of the prosecution's evidence and some of the points the accused wished to raise in rebuttal. In some cases witnesses could be called.

Beginning in the late 1960s, legislatures in some countries decided to lower protection of individual rights in criminal proceedings on the grounds that such a step was needed to reduce time to trial and save money. For example, in 1967, Uganda replaced the preliminary inquiry with "committal proceedings." The prosecutor was allowed to provide a summary of evidence so that the person accused would have some basis for preparing his or her defense, but the accused was then automatically committed for trial and remanded into custody.[25] Looking back on this change thirty years later, Justice Benjamin Odoki, a leader in the Ugandan court, observed that "the summary of evidence procedure changed drastically the nature and purpose of preliminary proceedings." He commented, "[A] magistrate . . . no longer had authority to discharge the accused, although it was held that it was the magistrate's duty to refuse to commit to trial if the prosecution failed to comply with the requirements of the law." Essentially, "the responsibility for determining whether there was sufficient evidence to proceed to trial was left solely to the Director of Public Prosecutions."[26]

Later, the Ugandan legislature altered the procedure further to eliminate even the need for a summary of the evidence. All the prosecutor had to offer was enough information for the accused to know the crime with which he or she was charged. There was no summary of the evidence. This modification was designed to save time because it often took the prosecutor as long as two years to assemble evidence from investigations conducted in remote parts of the country. Purportedly, it was also a response to the shortage of paper. Police and prosecutors often lacked stationery on which to write the summaries of evidence.[27]

---

[24] Justice Harold G. Platt, interview with author, Kampala, Uganda, November 9, 1995.
[25] Odoki, "Reducing Delay in the Administration of Justice," pp. 68–69.
[26] Ibid.
[27] Ibid.

Tanzania followed a similar route. At one point the legislature decided that a magistrate merely be required to inform anyone brought before the court that he or she would be committed for trial. The change allowed the magistrate no discretion to determine whether there was a prima facie case against the person.[28]

During the 1990s, the judges encouraged legislatures to reconsider these changes. In Uganda, for example, they called on the politicians to revive the practice of providing a summary of the evidence and of the state's case.[29]

BAIL

Judges grew increasingly disturbed by the injustice of holding people in remand for long periods of time, and granting bail was one way they could respond.

Acknowledging the terrible burdens that loss of liberty imposes, in industrial countries, bail, or pretrial release, usually was granted as long as there were reasonable grounds to think that the defendant would appear before the court when required and would not jeopardize the safety of another person or the community. In making this decision, the magistrate typically considered the seriousness of the offense, the weight of the evidence, and a number of personal characteristics likely to affect the degree to which the defendant posed a threat. Physical and mental condition, a prior criminal record, and whether the person had a steady job and family ties would all come under consideration.

Bail was deeply unpopular with police, prosecutors, and many members of the public in eastern and southern Africa. Explanations for this antipathy varied. Certainly it interfered with the ability of errant officials to "shake down" members of the community by threatening to arrest and hold them in remand indefinitely. But observers offered other explanations too. Some said that people in rural areas, far from the reach of police, resolved most conflicts on their own and only asked for an arrest if someone was a known troublemaker. They felt bail would allow the person to abscond, or return to cause more havoc. Said one African justice, "Generally people in our societies think there is 'no smoke without fire.' If someone is arrested by the police, they think the person probably did something that damaged the community. Sometimes when we release people pending trial, the local communities send them back to us." Another justice amplified this point, saying, "Small communities tend to know who the troublemakers are. The person may not have committed the offense

---

[28] United Republic of Tanzania, Tanzania Financial and Legal Management Upgrading Project (FILMUP), "The Legal Sector in Tanzania: Interim Report of Legal Task Force," Unpublished report, Dar es Salaam, Tanzania, June 1995.

[29] Republic of Uganda, Report of the Commission of Inquiry on Judicial Reform, p. 33.

with which he or she was charged, but the neighbors often consider the accused a problem nonetheless."[30]

Another magistrate suggested that the antipathy toward bail had its roots in contemporary beliefs about the value of punishment, or retributive justice. "Keeping people in prison is not a good way to handle crime," he remarked. "Yet here, people believe in punishment, not rehabilitation. That's wrong. They are eager to see someone receive two to three years in prison for stealing a soda."

Other people thought bail was really an opportunity for the judge or magistrate to solicit a bribe. One exasperated Ugandan magistrate told the newspapers "that *wananchi* [people] believe that whenever a magistrate asks an accused to apply for bail, the Magistrate is seeking for *'chai'* [literally, "tea;" figuratively, a bribe]. It is one of the most unfortunate aspects of our society," he said.[31]

Surety was also a problem. Traditionally, in England as in Africa, families and elders provided a guarantee to ensure that defendants would appear in court on the trial date. An accused person could be released only on his or her own recognizance or on the recognizance of relatives and elders. Bail was granted on an undertaking to pay money, and an actual deposit or a bond was not required. In the absence of such surety, accused persons were held in jail until the trial date. But in the context of an increasingly mobile society, where social systems were changing rapidly, families and elders were not always willing to play this role. And increasingly people accused of crimes came from outside the community and had no relatives who could stand for them.

The American system of commercial bond as a form of surety had not spread to Africa, or indeed to nearly anywhere outside of the Philippines. Yet it had arisen in response to just the kinds of problems that African societies faced. In the 1820s and 1830s, the United States had an expanding frontier, and neither personal recognizance nor the family provided adequate surety. A system of commercial bail bond provided a solution. In a commercial bond system, if a judge decided to set bail, a bail bondsman could appear before the court to supply a guarantee that the defendant would return. The bondsman usually charged the accused 10 percent of the face value of the bond and required some kind of collateral. If the bondsman could not find the defendant and the defendant failed to appear on the appropriate day, then the bondsman (or his insurance company) paid the court the face value of the bond. The money lost in such instances provided a powerful incentive to monitor the accused's whereabouts and induce him or her to return to court on schedule.

The law in most other common law countries regarded this system as an

[30] Group discussion, reported in Jennifer A. Widner, "The Quality of Justice: Report on the U.S.-Africa Judicial Exchange," Prepared for the U.S. Information Agency (Washington, D.C.: Superior Court of the District of Columbia, American Bar Association, and National Judicial College, July 1995), mimeograph.

[31] Yorakamu Bamwine as quoted in the *Daily Topic* (Uganda), February 3, 1994, p. 1.

attempt to obstruct justice. The belief was that a commercial bondsman was not at risk to the same degree as parties or their relatives and would have less incentive to exercise adequate surveillance. The defendant's own sense of the moral imperative to appear before the court on the date required would also diminish. The focus would shift from the amount of danger an individual posed to society if released on his or her own recognizance to whether the defendant or his or her relatives could put up the necessary collateral to employ the services of a bondsman. Society would be placed at greater risk under a commercial system, as a result.[32]

In Africa, the increasing use of bail by the courts elicited a counterreaction. Legislatures responded by expressly limiting the grounds on which bail could be granted. In Uganda, for instance, the Trial on Indictments (Amendment) Act of 1985 denied the courts the power to grant bail under most conditions, although it did state that among the few exceptional circumstances in which bail was warranted was remand for a period longer than fifteen months before a person was committed for trial.[33] Provisions of penal codes in other countries prohibited granting of bail for serious offenses and often for "economic crimes" or "economic sabotage." And in Botswana, legislators attempted to build support for a law that would ban both bail and the counsel of lawyers for people accused of stealing cars.[34]

The bail issue provoked such a furor in official circles in Uganda that it became a subject of discussion at a special seminar on the administration of justice. The judiciary organized the meeting and invited the president along with representatives of the different groups involved in the legal process. Chief Justice Samson Wako Wambuzi, known for his caution, opened the session with a short speech that went directly to the point. He quoted a letter from the minister of justice, who observed that "[t]here is currently an atmosphere of apparent mutual misunderstanding between law enforcement agencies of the state and the judiciary. This is particularly with regard to criminal cases that go to the courts and the accused are released on bail or acquitted. In some cases the law enforcement agencies get the impression that the law or the judiciary tend to favor the perpetrators of crime and consequently frustrate efforts to fight crime." Wambuzi said that the view was clearly erroneous and "efforts ought to be made to clear the atmosphere."[35]

Lawyers and judges countered by challenging the constitutionality of the

---

[32] Francis Edward Devine, "Outlawing Commercial Bail Bonding: A Comparative Perspective," *Anglo-American Law Review*, 17 (1988), passim, pp. 66–77.

[33] Odoki, "Reducing Delay in the Administration of Justice," p. 79.

[34] As reported in the *Botswana Guardian*, August 18, 1995, p. 2.

[35] Samson Wambuzi, speech as reproduced in Proceedings of the Seminar on Administration of Justice held at the International Conference Center, Kampala, January 12–16, 1987 (Kampala, Uganda: Ministry of Justice, 1987), p. 3.

new laws. In Kenya, the High Court ruled in 1986 that a provision of the Criminal Procedure Code that prohibited bail for serious crimes was inconsistent with a constitutional right to a trial within a reasonable time.[36] And in 1991, *Director of Public Prosecutions v. Daudi s/o Pete*, the first case brought under Tanzania's 1984 bill of rights, similarly challenged the constitutionality of a law that required the courts to deny bail to people accused of committing robbery with violence.[37]

Daudi s/o Pete attracted considerable attention both because of the importance of the rights at stake and because it was unclear how the court would interpret the distinctive wording of the country's constitution. Daudi was an ordinary Tanzanian, who lived near Musoma, in the northern part of Tanzania very near where Nyalali had served in his first judicial post. The area had long had a problem with livestock theft. Daudi said he had seized some cows that were trampling his *shamba*, his crops, so that he could take them to the ten-cell leader, a figure like the leader of the local "neighborhood watch," to obtain compensation. His neighbor kept the cattle for a brother, who worked in the regional commissioner's office. Daudi said that while he was on his way to see the ten-cell leader, he was arrested for cattle theft, but when the police investigated they found no offense and released him. A short time later, charges of robbery with violence, then a nonbailable offense, were instated against him. The prosecutor and the lower-court magistrate said the offense was nonbailable and that they could not release Daudi before a trial, even though they thought his account of events was credible.

Daudi reaffirmed his innocence and protested the decision not to grant bail. He also asked whether there was a constitutional issue at stake. "I am wondering as to whether such cause of action is constitutional," he inquired. "I understand that our Bill of Rights has come into operation. What of it? I thought that we oppressed citizens would be saved by it [the constitution]. If section 148(5) . . . condones denying liberty to a citizen for mere vindictiveness then I am afraid the Bill of Rights is not worth the paper it is written on."[38] No constitutional claim appeared in the initial pleadings, but Daudi's new counsel, Professor Mgongo Fimbo, a member of the law faculty, argued that the constitutional issue was implicit.

The lower court proceeded to hear the criminal case, while the constitu-

---

[36] *Ngui v. Republic of Kenya*, 1986 LRC (Const), 308.

[37] *Director of Public Prosecutions v. Daudi s/o Pete*, Criminal Appeal No. 28 of 1990 (Court of Appeal of Tanzania, May 16, 1991). Commentary on this case appears in John Quigley, "The Tanzanian Constitution and the Right to a Bail Hearing," *African Journal of International and Comparative Law*, 4 (1992), pp. 168–181; and Chris Maina Peter, "Enforcement of Fundamental Rights And Freedoms: The Case of Tanzania," in *African Yearbook of International Law* (Dordrecht: Martinus Nijhoff, 1996), pp. 81–98.

[38] *Director of Public Prosecutions v. Daudi s/o Pete*, Criminal Appeal No. 28 of 1990.

tional question was appealed to the High Court, as required under the Fifth Amendment. While the appeal was pending, the trial in the lower court proceeded and Daudi was acquitted. Daudi then went about his business and put the courts out of his mind. Mgongo Fimbo, acting as *amicus curiae*, carried the matter forward. By contrast with the United States, in parts of common law Africa, an *amicus curiae* could continue an appeal

The case came before Judge James Mwalusanya, then stationed at the Mwanza High Court. Mwalusanya, who had once served as registrar of the court, had worked as part of Nyalali's "team." He had developed a deep interest in methods of constitutional interpretation and believed in putting aside deference to the legislature when a fundamental right was at stake. Legislatures often performed poorly in safeguarding the rights of minorities or of people accused of crimes, he argued, and in these kinds of cases courts had a special role to play. Professor Fimbo saw a golden opportunity to put the country's new Bill of Rights and Duties to the test.

Mwalusanya issued a lengthy and erudite opinion. He held that bail was a right, not a privilege. He determined that the passage of the Criminal Procedure Act that had made the offense unbailable violated the constitutionally enshrined presumption of innocence and violated the separation of powers by denying the judiciary the ability to grant bail. He also said that objections to bail had to be supported by clear reasons and evidence, not by general suspicions or fears.[39]

The office of the Director of Public Prosecutions appealed the judgment. The prosecutor put forward several grounds. He argued that nothing in the pleadings raised the issue of the constitutionality of the section of the Criminal Procedure Act, and he suggested that the provision in question was an acceptable limitation or derogation from a basic right. The language of Article 15 of the constitution, the part of the document on which Judge Mwalusanya had focused, did not deny the legislature the ability to ban bail for serious crimes, the prosecutor argued. Article 15 read, "(2) For the purpose of protecting the right to personal freedom, no person shall be subject to arrest, restriction, detention, exile, or deprivation of his liberty in any other manner save in the following cases: a) in certain circumstances, and subject to a procedure, prescribed by law. . . ." The prosecutor argued that the requirement that there be a "procedure, prescribed by law" was satisfied.

The government also invoked the limitations clause in the bill of rights. The prosecutor said that the limitations clause exempted from constitutional challenge laws that had the purpose of "ensuring the interest of defense, public safety, public order, public morality, public health, rural and urban development planning, the development and utilisation of mineral resources or the

---

[39] The High Court decision appears in Chris Maina Peter, *Human Rights in Tanzania: Selected Cases and Materials* (Köln: Rüdiger Köppe Verlag, 1997), pp. 532–556.

development or utilisation of any other property in such manner as to promote the public benefit."

The Court of Appeal upheld the lower-court verdict, although it disagreed with some of Mwalusanya's reasoning.[40] The three-judge appellate panel ruled that the automatic denial of bail to people accused of particular offenses violated Article 15 of the constitution, which was intended to provide more specific protections of personal liberty. The Fifth Amendment of the Tanzanian constitution permitted limitations on the right to liberty "in certain circumstances, and subject to a procedure, prescribed by law." The court then looked at the procedures used for denying bail. The court noted that a subarticle stated that the aim of the limitation was to protect the right to personal freedom. Thus, the reason it required a "procedure" was to establish a safeguard. Quoting the Indian Supreme Court, Nyalali observed, "Obviously procedure cannot be arbitrary, unfair, or unreasonable." Were the procedures actually in place meaningful? Did they establish a safeguard? Or was the accused "bound to be denied bail whatever he may say on his behalf"? If the latter, then the procedure had no substance and could not serve to limit a liberty. The court found that the legislation Daudi challenged provided no procedure at all.

The ruling also said that legislation that did not permit the court to determine whether defense, public safety, or public order were endangered in any given case was unacceptably broad in its reach. It ousted judicial discretion and thereby violated the doctrine of the separation of powers.

In general, the decision met with an enthusiastic reception. Some said it was overly cautious, since other provisions of the same part of the legal code, vulnerable on the same grounds, were left untouched. Still, it sent a signal and gave the government a chance to take the initiative and bring the other subsections into line with the constitution of its own accord. American legal scholar John Quigley, who had watched the case unfold in Tanzania, observed that the international covenants "did not establish an absolute right of a detainee to release." They required a procedure to determine whether a person should be held. The courts were left to determine what kinds of procedures satisfied that requirement.[41] Nyalali's court had started to do so.

TRIAL IN A REASONABLE TIME

Judges also began to consider dismissing criminal cases in which delays were exceptionally long. A series of constitutional decisions began to lay the groundwork. For example, the Supreme Court of Zimbabwe was clear and emphatic

---

[40] *Director of Public Prosecutions v. Daudi s/o Pete*, Criminal Appeal No. 28 of 1990 (Court of Appeal at Dar es Salaam).
[41] Quigley, "The Tanzanian Constitution and the Right to a Bail Hearing," pp. 178–180.

in stating its position. In *re Mlambo,*[42] the court carefully analyzed the meaning of rights provisions which stipulated that a person "be afforded a fair hearing within a reasonable time."[43] Mr. Mlambo was arrested in 1986 on charges of fraud. He was kept in prison for four and a half years before coming to trial because the state said on twelve separate occasions that it was unprepared to proceed. He applied to the court to dismiss the case against him on the grounds that the delay violated his right to a trial within a reasonable time.

Writing for the court, Chief Justice Anthony Gubbay explained the reasons for the constitutional right in question. Delay gave rise to "restrictions on liberty, inconveniences, social stigma and pressures detrimental to the mental and physical health of the individual. In addition, the unreasonable delay may impair the ability of the individual to present a full and fair defense to the charge." Chief Justice Gubbay found the U.S. Supreme Court case, *Barker v. Wingo,* persuasive.[44] There, Justice Powell had set forth a four-part test to evaluate the meaning of "reasonable time." The test required judges to consider the actual length of the delay, the reasons the government offers for the delay, whether the accused asserted his right to a speedy trial, and the extent to which delay prejudiced the accused's case.

This decision and others emboldened judges in the region. In 1994, Justice Frederick Egonde-Ntende, then a rising star recruited into the Ugandan judiciary from private practice, attracted press attention by taking prosecutors to task. Egonde-Ntende dismissed a case against three people held eight years on remand when prosecutors failed to present witnesses. The press reported approvingly that "[t]he judge was correctly disturbed by the fact that after the case had been pending for as long as eight years, the Prosecuting Attorney had the audacity to apply for an adjournment on account of the absence of prosecution witnesses. As if that was not bad enough, the State Attorney claimed he had only received the case file that morning and needed time to study it."[45]

PLEA BARGAINING

Yet another option was to introduce plea bargaining to speed criminal proceedings, as the Americans had. Plea bargaining allowed the prosecutor to press for

[42] *re Mlambo,* 1991(2) ZLR (Sup. Ct.), 1992(4), 1992(2).
[43] Gino J. Naldi, "The Supreme Court of Zimbabwe Defines the Constitutional Right to a 'Fair Hearing Within a Reasonable Time,'" *African Journal of International and Comparative Law,* 5 (1993), p. 182; and Anthony R. Gubbay, "The Protection and Enforcement of Fundamental Human Rights: The Zimbabwean Experience," *Human Rights Quarterly,* 19 (1997), pp. 247–248.
[44] 407 U.S. 514, 519 (1972).
[45] *New Vision* (Uganda), March 7, 1994, p. 3; and Editorial, "Spare the Judges over Prosecution Failures," *Weekly Topic,* March 11, 1994, p. 3.

lesser charges, fewer charges, or a lighter sentence in exchange for the defendant lodging a plea of "guilty." It was helpful where there was some evidence that the accused person was guilty but where a full investigation would take considerable time and resources. If the accused preferred, he or she could let the investigation continue and if found guilty, serve a long prison sentence. Alternatively, he or she could plead guilty to the more minor offenses for which police had adequate evidence at the time of arrest and spend less time under incarceration.

The judge's role was to make sure that the plea was legal, that the defendant knew his or her rights, that no pressure was applied, and that the defendant accepted the bargain voluntarily. There had to be a factual basis for the plea as well. The judge asked a litany of questions in open court to determine whether the standards of legality were met. However, the judge did not become involved in the discussion between the defendant and the prosecutor and was not bound by agreements between the defendant and the prosecutor about sentencing.

The practice had an especially long history in the United States, where it began to flourish in the late 1800s and was officially recognized later. George Fisher, an American legal scholar, commented that the practice took root in the United States for three main reasons.[46] First, large and growing caseloads made plea bargaining attractive to prosecutors and judges. Second, the allocation of power and responsibility within the justice system was such that prosecutors had the power to bargain. That was not the case historically in England, where until recent times only the attorney general or solicitor general could enter a *nolle prosequi* and end prosecution. Finally, important elements of the concept had already won general acceptance. Plea bargaining had an analogue in the "indeterminate sentence," historically another common practice in the United States, which allowed judges to set minimum and maximum prison terms and let wardens choose release dates. Although the indeterminate sentence was eventually abandoned, its earlier adoption and popularity helped make plea bargaining acceptable. By contrast, in many other parts of the world, judges viewed plea bargaining as an encroachment on the function of the judiciary.

But plea bargaining was not a uniquely American phenomenon. In many civil law jurisdictions, or where there is no such thing as a guilty plea or a "no contest" plea (as in most African countries), comparable negotiations often took place between the police and the person charged, instead of between the prosecutor and the defendant. One Tanzanian justice said he had observed this practice in murder cases in his jurisdiction, although it was not institutionalized or understood in quite the same way. He said it had more the flavor of a "pretrial discussion." Ugandan justices concurred that something like this practice existed where they worked too.

[46] George Fisher, "Plea Bargaining's Triumph," *Yale Law Journal*, 109, 5 (2000), passim, pp. 868–1086.

But many European and African jurists found aspects of plea bargaining objectionable. Some of their concerns centered on the feelings and rights of the victims of crime. For example, they worried that there was no apparent parallel concern for the victims during the bargaining over the charges and sentences that offenders would receive. That meant people might decide to take the law into their own hands. In discussions with their African counterparts on this subject, U.S. judges and prosecutors commented that many Americans felt the same way and saw plea bargaining as a way of setting criminals free before they have paid for their crimes. They said that pressures from victims' rights organizations, as well as sensitivity of prosecutors to public opinion, tended to make this problem less severe in practice than one might expect.[47]

African jurists said they also thought that there was something fundamentally wrong about bargaining over innocence and guilt. American jurists suggested that there was always uncertainty surrounding a trial. Procedural safeguards did not guarantee right outcomes. Even in the best of circumstances, innocent people sometimes were convicted. In giving a defendant advice about whether to bargain, it was important to evaluate the case and consider the quality of the evidence, the possible penalties—even the judge's own history of handling similar cases.

Finally, both American and African jurists expressed concern about the ways in which government may abuse plea bargaining. The system could provide an incentive for prosecutors to overcharge. Knowing that many cases would end in guilty pleas, prosecutors might be tempted to give themselves negotiating room by bringing larger numbers of charges or more serious charges. That practice seemed to contain an element of coercion.

Although plea bargaining won few African converts, there was some cultural basis for limiting the use of incarceration, relieving overburdened resources and consequent delay by placing increased emphasis on the use of compensation and reconciliation in criminal cases. Historically, in resource-scarce societies, those who committed serious offenses against the community were either banished or required to pay damages in money or money equivalents. Only more recently had incarceration been adopted as an alternative.[48]

---

[47] Group discussion, reported in Widner, "The Quality of Justice: Report on the U.S.-Africa Judicial Exchange."

[48] For more on this subject, see James S. Read, "Crime and Punishment in East Africa: The Twilight of Customary Law," *Howard Law Journal*, 10 (1964), pp. 164–186; and the record of the Conference on Penal Problems in East Africa, January 1966, as reproduced in *East African Law Journal*, 2, 1 (1966).

ORGANIZATIONAL SOLUTIONS

Nyalali felt that the courts had to get at the heart of the problem. They had to address the reasons why the delays were occurring. The initial responses of the Tanzanian court paralleled many of the same kinds of reforms with which Nyalali had experimented as a young magistrate. For example, one way to reduce delay was to institute case-flow management committees. The committees grew out of the recognition that adjournments caused by missing defendants, witnesses, or prosecutors or by misplaced paperwork could be alleviated through better communication between the institutions involved. Nyalali decided to convene regular meetings of judicial personnel, the police and CID, state attorneys, and prison authorities to promote cooperation. At the meetings, participants could talk about delayed cases, scheduling, and foreseeable difficulties in transporting people on certain dates or in conveying papers. One court registrar gave an example of the function the committees served. "When we meet as a group each person has to respond. I say, 'This case was adjourned ten times and the judicial officer says he doesn't have the files. What is the problem?' The other people have to discuss the matter. The committee has done a lot to reduce the backlog, here. The registrar has to take the initiative to assemble everyone, however."[49] In 1988, the committees were established on mainland Tanzania at three levels—zones, regions, and districts—in a series of case-flow management circulars.[50]

Evaluations of effectiveness varied. Judge John Mwipopo, who had served as director of public prosecutions at the time of the chief justice's initiative, commented that the committees were very helpful. "Now, I can't imagine how we would work without them. Before, courtroom etiquette was so strict there was no room for dialogue. In the case-flow management committee, there is more flexibility."[51] But the new system did not solve the problem. An outside review conducted in 1994–95 in preparation for the Financial and Legal Management Upgrading Project (FILMUP) noted improvements in the speed with which the court handled criminal cases as a result of the committees. But it also sounded a note of caution. "We agree that these committees have had an impact on the early disposal of criminal cases," the authors wrote. "However, there are some weaknesses which tend to make them less effective. For example, representatives of the Police and Prisons do not always attend meetings . . . and when they do their representatives are normally junior staff members who have no authority." The FILMUP assessment team also expressed concern that the committees were powerless to enforce cooperation. "[A]ll they can do is to submit a report to the Chief Justice who, in turn, may ask the appropriate authority to take the

---

[49] Registrar and magistrate, interviews with author, Arusha, Tanzania, May 24, 1996.
[50] High Court and Court of Appeal, Annual Report, 1985–88 (Dar es Salaam, Tanzania: High Court and Court of Appeal, 1989).
[51] Judge John Mwipopo, interview with author, Mbeya, Tanzania, May 16, 1996.

necessary action."[52] The report recommended amendment of the Criminal Procedure Act to establish the committees formally and to require the police and the prisons to send senior officers to represent them.

In some of the other countries where reformers were trying to decide whether to emulate the Tanzanian example, judges also voiced concern that the committees might give the public the impression that the courts and the executive branch conspired together. Said one judge in neighboring Uganda, "The security people, the courts, and the other services sit down to talk and that looks bad. It looks like the courts lack independence. But it is a good thing for Uganda."[53] He commented that a senior-level case-flow management committee had started to meet in Kampala in June 1995. The first meeting took place in the country's main prison. Participants soon discovered that many problems stemmed from lack of knowledge, not from differences in interests or from duplicity. They quickly recommended copying the committee at lower levels, along the lines of the Tanzanian example.

The case-flow management committees remained a partial solution. In Tanzania, the court worried that lack of resources often meant that prisons could not transport inmates to magistrates in order to sign and file affidavits for bail and other documents that were supposed to be handled in the magistrate's view, away from the specter of coercion by police or prison officers. Said Judge Mwipopo, "The practice was for the prisoner to sign the document in prison before a prison officer, and later the magistrate would sign. That was wrong. The law said these documents had to be signed by the prisoner in the presence of a magistrate. We convened a meeting with the advocates, police, and prisons and asked whether the magistrates should use their responsibility to visit the prisons as an opportunity to carry out some of these functions too. There were objections. Some thought it might look like the magistrate was influenced by the prisons and police, they said. But we asked, 'If the prisoners have to walk to court because there is not transport, what about the dangerous ones who would escape?' That had happened at least once in the area where I worked. Eventually we decided that a magistrate should visit the prisons two or three times a week."[54]

During the apartheid era in South Africa, Justice Richard Goldstone had made unannounced visits to detainees, and he too felt that the practice "made an enormous difference," but for a slightly different reason. He commented "[p]rison officials knew that what we observed would be public and they knew they had to change. They did not want deaths in custody as a result of abusive police interrogations. Prison authorities began to deny police permission to

[52] United Republic of Tanzania, "The Legal Sector in Tanzania: Interim Report of the Legal Task Force," p. 19.
[53] Justice David Porter, interview with author, Kampala, Uganda, November 1995.
[54] Judge John Mwipopo, interview with author, Mbeya, Tanzania, May 16, 1996.

question suspects on their premises, as a result."[55] South Africa also had a High Court circuit, and when the judges traveled they would go to the prisons too. "That has proven very important. That's the separation of powers working," Goldstone observed. "Judges should get out of the ivory tower."

Reformers knew they had few resources to supervise the judicial process carefully, especially at the lower levels. Once someone was in jail, he or she too often became invisible. That placed a premium on changes that could help people bring problems to the attention of the upper levels or prevent people from being imprisoned in the first place. The judges entertained a number of solutions, although not all won immediate implementation. One challenge was to undermine incentives for police shakedowns. In the West, they found a possible model in the post of the "emergency judge" on twenty-four-hour call. The judge would have the power to consider the sufficiency of the evidence and to grant bail, thereby limiting the ability of police to incarcerate innocent people who did not buy them off. Another possibility, raised by the Uganda Law Society, was to establish district committees to which ordinary people could complain about police behavior. "Something must be done or else there may never be genuine peace and tranquility for ordinary Ugandans," read one Law Society memo. "A committee should be set up in every district composed of Uganda Law Society, religious organizations, resistance councillors [elected District Council representatives], and Police. All complaints by *wananchi* [people] of unfair treatment . . . [should] be reported to the committee."[56]

Judges in several countries floated the idea of running an information service for prisoners. In Uganda, Justice David Porter advocated this strategy. "Except in the most serious cases, someone under remand should be out after 240 days, but neither the prison officials nor the prisoners know the rule, so they don't apply it," he observed. "Somebody has to say no to the practices of the state attorneys."[57] An information service for prisoners run by a nongovernmental organization was his favored response. A similar idea attracted the attention of the Botswana bar, one of whose members had spoken out about the need for a "prisoners' friends" movement.[58] In South Africa, just such a prisoners' friends association started in 1910, led by judges, who gave it "respectability." Justice Richard Goldstone later headed the organization and used his role to visit prisons during the states of emergency. Since the end of apartheid, the organization had grown enormously.[59]

[55] Justice Richard Goldstone, interview with author, University of Michigan, Ann Arbor, October 1998.
[56] Uganda Law Society memorandum, "Observation of Law, Courts, and Prison Services in Uganda," Law Society, Kampala, Uganda, August 30, 1992.
[57] Justice David Porter, interview with author, Kampala, Uganda, November 1995.
[58] Richard Lyons, as reported in *Guardian* (Botswana), February 7, 1992, p. 5.
[59] Justice Richard Goldstone, interview with author, University of Michigan, Ann Arbor, October 1998.

NEW BEGINNINGS

In the late 1980s, Chief Justice Nyalali traveled to other courts to look for additional solutions. In Eastern Europe he found that there was "a time limit for processing criminal cases, and I was attracted by that." He obtained copies of the statutes and brought them back to Dar. Then he spoke with the president and suggested that Tanzania emulate the example of the systems in Eastern Europe. "A case would have to take off within sixty days, with few exceptions. The executive branch was reluctant to make the restriction so tight, because it wanted more time to investigate in complicated cases."

The changes introduced by the judges slowly began to affect the disposition of criminal cases. In 1994, Chief Justice Nyalali noted that "[w]hereas before 1985, it took an average of four years to conclude a criminal case through the courts, it now takes an average of two years to do so."[60] But Nyalali observed, "The practice is still problematical. I am not yet satisfied with the criminal side and we will have to go back to that."[61]

[60] Francis L. Nyalali, Speech at the Opening of the Tanzanian Judiciary's Training Program in Alternative Dispute Resolution, Presented at the High Court of Tanzania, Dar es Salaam, Tanzania, August 2, 1995.
[61] Francis L. Nyalali, interview with author, May 29, 1996.

Civil Delay

THE SEVERITY OF delay in criminal cases began to diminish in Tanzania by the 1990s, though there were continuing complaints. "Then members of the public began to demand similar action on civil cases," Nyalali said. Slow disposition of land disputes, matrimonial issues, and commercial matters made it difficult to improve public satisfaction with the judiciary and to build a constituency. This problem also needed attention.

The institutional context that surrounded the handling of civil cases was simpler than for criminal cases. There were no police, prisons, or prosecutors involved. The struggle for control of the schedule was mainly between the courts and the advocates. But that did not mean the problem was easier to solve. Nyalali had to search for new answers. His quest led to the United States, to the Superior Court of the District of Columbia, and to the kind of international partnership the Tanzanian judiciary was able to establish in other domains with counterparts in Ireland, Canada, Denmark, and Germany.

Civil delay caused injustice, even if it did not deprive people of their liberty. One judge explained that in his district, people used the courts strategically in commercial cases. He asserted that businessmen "borrow billions of shillings. If the creditor wants to execute the loan, then the businessmen try to use the courts to delay credit liability. They know the courts are slow and they can delay having to pay back the loan if the case goes to court. If the case goes to different magistrates, then they can play this game for years."[1] Prolonged uncertainty about the outcome of a dispute could lead to economic loss by interfering with the ability to make improvements or invest in business expansion.

[1] Judge John Mwipopo, interview with author, Mbeya, Tanzania, May 1996.

The costs of resolving disputes also increased with delay. When witnesses or foreign counsel had to travel to participate in a trial, the costs of adjournments to clients also could become very high. One Tanzanian advocate told the story of a British lawyer with a case in the High Court. Because of delays, the lawyer had to fly from London to Dar es Salaam repeatedly. "The cost to the client was enormous," he said.[2]

Delays in handling land disputes could impose special hardship in a world where most ordinary people continued to subsist, in part, on what they could grow on their garden plots. Access to land directly affected the ability to put food on the table. Delays in hearing land cases could deny a family a livelihood.

Divorces and domestic abuse cases had to be heard quickly too, in order to remove people from danger. By law, in Tanzania, and by convention in most countries of the region, the first line of recourse in a domestic dispute was to ask family leaders or clan elders to help effect a reconciliation. Tanzania designated a variety of associations, church groups, and government bodies, such as Ward Tribunals, to serve as conciliation boards. To take a case to the courts, the parties had to bring a certificate indicating that conciliation efforts had failed. By the time the case reached a magistrate, the situation was usually tense and urgent.

Nyalali noted the vehemence of popular dissatisfaction with civil delay. "I believe some of you might have seen the cartoon in one of our local newspapers depicting a slow moving tortoise with the remark that it cared only for law," he noted at a meeting of journalists. "The message of that cartoon is loud and clear. . . . The message is this. The courts are too slow and have in a number of cases enforced or administered law at the expense of justice. Is this a valid criticism? I think so."[3]

There was a perennial tussle between judges and advocates about responsibility for delay in civil cases. Each accused the other. Advocates argued that judges and magistrates sat on the bench for too few hours. For rural magistrates, a full day of hearing cases generally meant sitting from 9:00 until noon. In the capital, advocates complained that judges did not arrive until 10:00 and then quit at 12:00, although the judges disputed the allegation. Similar complaints could be heard in neighboring countries. Sometimes they were well founded. At other times, they were not. In Botswana, magistrates said they sat all morning, through lunch; resumed sessions from 4:00 until 6:00 or 7:00; and sometimes worked weekends—"for free," said one, with a tone of dismay in his voice.

The judges countered that the lawyers did not prepare adequately, or on time, and they caused frequent adjournments. In anticipation of adjournments

[2] Members of the Tanzanian bar, group interview, March 12, 1996.
[3] Francis L. Nyalali, "The Challenge of the Private Mass Media in the Wake of Multi-Partism," Address to a dinner hosted by the *Express* and *Mwananchi*, Kilimanjaro Hotel, Dar es Salaam, Tanzania, May 21, 1993, pp. 3–4.

and postponements, counsel sometimes scheduled hearings in two or more courts at once. Because the overwhelming majority of the advocates were solo practitioners, there was no partner or associate to help shoulder the burden if two cases were called at the same time. Although the practice annoyed everyone, including members of the bar, no one intervened to put a stop to it. Said one magistrate who observed that the court had started to recruit judges from the private bar instead of promoting through the ranks, "I don't want to bark at advocates. One may be a judge someday!"

Periodically, the judiciary tried to take control, but the initiatives usually failed. In Tanzania, the Advocates Ordinance of 1990 gave judges the power to suspend lawyers who caused delays in proceedings. The Law Society vigorously protested the proposed legislation, and the measure became a source of tension between the bench and the bar.[4] Some advocates contended that in this new era of interest in law and development, judges spent so much time traveling that they had become an important source of delay themselves.[5] One advocate suggested that there also should be a body to which advocates could complain if a judge adjourned a case. Law Society officers urged that every time a case was continued, the reasons should be put in writing.[6] There was already a requirement that judges do so, but the rule was imperfectly observed.

Members of the bench in other countries were also unsparing. For example, the judges who sat on the Uganda Commission of Inquiry on Judicial Reform criticized the advocates' double booking of appointments as a "waste of time" and a source of "loss to parties and witnesses." "The advocates should be heavily penalized," wrote the authors. "This is the practice in England. The Commission thinks that the law in Uganda should be amended. In a civil case, the advocate himself should pay the opposite side all its costs occasioned by the adjournment at once, as well as double the fees of the case, and costs thrown away."[7]

The observations of one distinguished Tanzanian lawyer, Mohammed Ismael, who served as president of the Tanzania Law Society, mirrored what many advocates felt but rarely stated publicly. "The judges aren't serious and we aren't either. We are all apathetic. No one moves to do things immediately, even when they could do so. There is no urgency about anything. In the judiciary, this attitude has enormous ramifications. They have to assert control."[8] He observed that the advocates' behavior created the delay, but it was up to the judges not to let them get away with it. "If the judges were better, we wouldn't

---

[4] Sufian Hemed Bukurura, *Judiciary and Good Governance in Contemporary Tanzania* (Bergen, Norway: Christien Michelsen Institute, Development and Human Rights Studies, September 1995), p. 21.
[5] Members of the Tanzanian bar, group interview, March 11, 1996.
[6] Members of the Tanzanian bar, group interview, March 12, 1996.
[7] Republic of Uganda, *Report of the Commission of Inquiry on Judicial Reform* (Kampala, Uganda: Commission of Inquiry on Judicial Reform, 1995), p. 31.
[8] Mohammed Ismael, interview with author, May 22, 1996.

be so bad." Some of the judges succeeded. "John Mroso was very good—one of the best. When Mroso was here, you couldn't adjourn a case before him. You can't say that for most of them."

For all of their evident frustration with the bar, the judges knew that Mohammed Ismael was right. They reasoned that either the judge takes control of a case or the lawyers do. When the lawyers are able to control the case, efficiency and expeditiousness may suffer. Lawyers handle many cases, and some are worth more money than others. For economic reasons, they may let some cases wait. They have little individual incentive to work quickly and little control over the other members of their profession. The court is in the best position to remedy the problem of delay, not the lawyers.

As one who had seen both sides in Uganda, Justice Frederick Egonde-Ntende described his experience after he left private practice and and joined the bench. "When I came in 1991, the court was grappling with the issue of delay. Everybody was complaining," he began. The president had taken the courts to task, and the judiciary itself had awoken to the size of the backlog on the criminal side. "My first six months I hardly handled any cases. Cases were being adjourned all the time. A lot of judge time was wasted. I had a lot of experience dealing with delay from the advocates' end and knew the courts were not strong enough." Egonde-Ntende wrote a letter to the principal judge indicating what he thought was wrong. "I compared our court to Zimbabwe, where I traveled. I set out what I thought was wrong with the system and said that if the rules of civil procedure were followed, we could reduce these problems."[9] The paper was discussed briefly, but then it was set aside and nothing happened for more than a year.

In 1993, President Yoweri Museveni started to castigate the courts as enemies of investment, and the court renewed its search for a solution. Egonde-Ntende persuaded the other judges to let him run a "civil session" according to the plan he had proposed, to see whether it made a difference. Sure enough, he found he could dispose of more cases in a shorter amount of time.

COURTROOM POKER

Civil delay is a problem that no court ever solves once and for all. It poses as many difficulties in the litigious societies of the West as it did, and does, in Africa. As one judge in Botswana commented of his court, "There are too many cases chasing too few judges, but the delay level isn't all that bad; it is no worse than the European standard." Outside of Botswana and Zimbabwe, both of which had succeeded in reducing delay, the picture was not quite so happy. Record-keeping

---

[9] Justice Frederick Egonde-Ntende, interview with author, Kampala, Uganda, February 14, 1996.

problems in some countries made it difficult to ascertain and report the time between the filing of the complaint to the time of trial or other disposition. But African judges from the region estimated that the time to trial for civil cases in their countries averaged about four years—a little less in some places, a little more in others.[10] A few years later, an American lawyer working in Uganda observed, "The time from filing a civil suit to the day of trial is not that different in Uganda than in the federal courts in the United States. However, in Uganda, receiving a trial date, and in fact commencing a trial, does not necessarily mean that the case will proceed to a verdict in any set period of time."[11]

Although there were important similarities in the problems courts faced in civil cases around the world, fewer resources, an especially challenging context, and less opportunity to share ideas meant that judiciaries in eastern and southern Africa encountered greater obstacles in their search for solutions than did their counterparts abroad.

There were early antecedents to the reforms judges contemplated in the 1990s. An International Commission of Jurists committee had broached the problem in the late 1970s, and its diagnosis and recommendations were similar to those on which courts fastened later. J. V. R. Lewis reported the main points of the study in the *Zimbabwe Law Journal*:

1. It depends almost entirely on party prosecution; that is, the prosecution of the case is largely in the hands of the parties' representatives from its initiation until the trial itself, and the court has no real power to intervene in the interests of justice to control the progress of the litigation.
2. It is insufficiently open; that is, the system is designed rather like a game of poker, so each party is largely kept in the dark as to the nature and strength of his opponent's case until the "showdown" at the trial.
3. . . . the system depends too heavily on the all-embracing trial itself to secure the doing of justice between the parties.
4. There is a tendency to too much formalism in the system at the expense of common sense.[12]

The article contrasted the "closed systems" of common law Africa with a more open American system in which the rules of civil procedure pushed parties to help each other and to speed the trial process.

In the late 1980s and the 1990s, one task judiciaries faced was to allocate

---

[10] Jennifer Widner, record of group discussion, U.S.-Africa Judicial Exchange, phase I, April–May 1995.

[11] "Litigation Realities in Uganda," International Law Institute, Uganda Office, Kampala, Uganda, n.d., mimeograph in author's files.

[12] J. V. R. Lewis, "Saving of Time and Costs in Civil Litigation," *Zimbabwe Law Journal*, 19, 1 (1979), p. 21.

caseloads more rationally. Throughout the region, legislatures had imposed statutory limits on the monetary value of the civil cases each level of a court could hear. The aim was to ensure that petty cases, such as the theft of a cow, would be brought to the lowest levels, where customary rules were usually observed, and that judges in the higher courts had adequate time to hear complicated cases involving large amounts of money. Legislators, who rarely had training in economics, neglected to consider what would happen over time as inflation took its toll. As the years passed, matters that belonged at the lowest levels began to find their way into the upper courts simply because the purchasing power of the shilling, the *kwacha*, or the *Zim* dollar had declined. The jurisdictional limits were left unrevised, and court dockets once again grew congested.

Nyalali described the situation in Tanzania: "There was a time in this country, when one head of cattle was worth one hundred shillings. That was the normal value of cattle used in payment of bride price under customary marriage. So primary courts had jurisdiction to entertain suits for recovery of cattle. But as time passed, the value of money plummeted so much that currently one would be lucky to get a head of cattle worth under ten thousand shillings."[13] More and more "small" cases landed in the higher courts because the cost of a cow had exceeded the pecuniary limits on the jurisdiction of the primary courts. "In that process, the High Court got congested and bogged down by a case load it could not handle expeditiously." Nyalali persuaded the legislature to revise the limits in 1992, but he was aware that the revision would not solve the problem for very long. He urged, "A formula ought to be found which could have the effect of permanently stopping the undesirable migration of cases from the lower courts to the High Court."

Other increases in the loads of upper courts were less easy to address. Magistrates in several countries offered a particularly poignant proposal. They observed that legislation, customary practices, and public health problems had conspired to produce a sharp increase in defilement cases, which crowded High Court dockets. Defilement was a capital offense and therefore had to be heard by the High Court. Legislators in several countries had increased the age below which sexual intercourse was considered defilement. But the statutory definition conflicted with marriage customs in some communities. The result was a sudden surge in the number of defilement cases on court's docket. The human immunodeficiency virus (HIV) epidemic aggravated the situation further: Frightened, men thought younger women safer partners and entered into relationships with them, unaware that the law prohibited such liaisons. Sometimes community members thought the crime did not merit the death penalty and tried to remove the cases from the judicial system altogether by

---

[13] Francis L. Nyalali, "Paper on Case Management," Paper presented at a seminar of judges, Arusha, Tanzania, April 19–23, 1993, p. 7.

convincing the village courts to hear the matters. Village court officers were not supposed to permit this kind of action, but some did. Magistrates reasoned that it was possible to get these cases into the courts of general jurisdiction, where they belonged, and reduce the delays people encountered in the high courts, by dropping the requirement that the crime carry a death sentence.

Nyalali knew that jurisdictional changes would not get at the real problem, however. He returned to the kinds of suggestions Lewis had offered in his earlier article and looked abroad for others who had faced the same problem and dealt with it effectively. In mid-1992, on his way home from a meeting in Canada, he decided to fly by way of Washington, D.C. There he telephoned the Superior Court of the District of Columbia, the trial court that served the American capital. He had heard that the court was piloting a new approach to civil delay reduction in response to its own very serious difficulties. He hoped Tanzania might learn from the superior court's experience. He met with Judge Nan Huhn, who presided over the court's civil division. The two talked for several hours and began to establish the kind of relationship that exemplified the linkages that the Tanzanian court created in many different parts of the world.

The superior court had much to share, Nyalali learned. At the end of 1988, the court had 37,969 civil cases pending. There were 5,778 civil cases at issue with all complaints, cross-complaints, and counterclaims answered. The first available trial date for these cases was three years in the future. Ten percent of all civil cases on the docket had awaited disposition for more than four years. To Nyalali, the story sounded very familiar.

The superior court had instituted successful reforms from 1989 to 1992 to reduce its own congestion problem. Fourteen months after implementing changes in the calendar and trial management practices, as well as other procedures, the court had reduced its backlog by 50 percent. By 1995, 94 percent of civil cases would reach disposition within eighteen months, despite the court's very high case volume. At the time Nyalali first met with Judge Huhn, some of the successes were evident, while others would unfold only later.

The chief justice wasted no time. Upon his return, he requested that Judge Huhn and her husband, Judge Robert A. Shuker, also of the superior court, visit to examine the applicability of its delay reduction plan to the Tanzanian courts. In April 1993, Shuker and Huhn flew to Tanzania at Nyalali's request to study the country's judicial system and to recommend policies and procedures that would help reduce delay. In their report, the judges commented on a wide range of matters.

The two judges quickly came to occupy an important place in the pantheon of characters who leant a hand to courts all over Africa. Their relationship with the Tanzanian court went beyond the usual in-and-out technical assistance package and blossomed into a working partnership, a continuing friendship, and a source of long-distance advice. Robert Shuker's pedigree resembled the backgrounds of the lawyers active in the law and development movement of the 1960s, except that he had devoted his particular energies to poorer communities in the United States. He was a 1966 graduate of the University of Chicago Law School. He had stayed on in Chicago as trial attorney for the Ford Foundation's Chicago Lawyer Project, which provided counsel to poor youth, then moved on to Washington to work as a prosecutor with the U.S. attorney's office. He had joined the superior court in 1977. Nan Huhn, later Nan Shuker, had worked her way through law school at American University, helped run one of the first programs for battered women and abused children in the District of Columbia, and served as a prosecutor, before joining the bench. She had served on the superior court's Civil Delay Reduction Task Force. Her interest in every last detail and her willingness to throw herself into her work with extraordinary enthusiasm endeared her to her African counterparts, just as it sometimes daunted her colleagues at home.

Both judges commanded respect from the court and community for their contributions, and both won friends on the Tanzanian court in short order. When Robert Shuker died of a sudden heart attack in June 1993, Nan Shuker decided to continue the work they had started together and rallied others to the cause, even persuading high-priced members of the Washington, D.C., bar, including one of its Lawyers of the Year, Harlow Case, to help out.

On their visit to Tanzania in 1993, the Shukers explained the main elements of the superior court reforms to their counterparts in Dar and asked whether they thought there was anything the Tanzanian court might want to borrow. If there was, then the judges said they would provide more information and work with the court to translate the proposals to suit local conditions. They presented a picture of their own problems and the seven parts of their own program of delay reduction: (1) early court intervention, (2) time goals, (3) a strict adjournment policy, (4) a date certain for trial, (5) an aggressive alternative dispute resolution (ADR) program, (6) use of individual calendars, and (7) development of a good working relationship between the bench and the bar.

After the visit of the Shukers in 1993, Nyalali appointed a three-judge committee headed by John Mroso, a High Court judge held in high esteem by the bench and the bar, to recommend measures to reduce civil delay. The Mroso committee came out strongly in favor of three proposals. One was to introduce an "individual calendar system" or "individual diary." The second was to create standards or guidelines for the duration of each aspect of the trial process. The third was to integrate ADR into the Tanzanian courts. The recommendations drew on the superior court's experience, but they were consistent with parallel proposals announced in *Access to Justice*, a review of the English court system that Lord Woolf, the lord chancellor, proposed a year later, in 1994.[14]

[14] Right Honourable the Lord Woolf, *Access to Justice* (Final Report) (London: Her Majesty's Stationery Office, 1996).

EXPERIMENTS

The choice of calendar system affected control over case flow. In an open calendar or master calendar system, long the norm, all cases came to one central place and remained there until ready for trial. Different judges of the court handled discovery problems and the motions that lawyers brought, as the need arose. They were usually unable to develop much familiarity with any given case and could not easily tell when too much latitude had been given to a particular lawyer. When compared to alternative approaches, this system correlated with longer delays.

In an individual calendar system, such as the one adopted by the superior court as part of its reform program, each case stayed with a single judge. As a result, the judge was better able to monitor the case. The judge drew up an order that explained in considerable detail what procedures had to be completed. This order made it very difficult for the lawyers to win repeated continuances or adjournments because the judge to whom the case was assigned knew the full history of the matter. Placing a case under the control of a single judge also assisted the court in monitoring the performance of the judges and identifying who handled cases expeditiously and who needed help. Because of their sheer numbers—or because of special characteristics they displayed, not all types of cases could be managed through an individual calendar. However, in most instances, the system appeared to reduce delay considerably.

The general order the judge issued upon the filing of a complaint included a lot of information useful to the parties and their lawyers. It detailed the obligations of the parties. It told litigants what the procedural requirements were, where to find the rules of evidence, and other important information. It explained how to communicate with the judge's chambers and identified people to contact about specific problems. It described the discovery process and made clear the limits on interrogation. The document was helpful in reducing delays caused by inadequate knowledge of how judicial proceedings work. When parties were unrepresented by counsel, or *pro se*, the order the judge drew up provided the necessary instruction. Where there was concern about the adequacy of counsel's preparedness, the order also helped improve communication. By publishing copies of the general order, law students, new advocates, and members of the public also could see what was expected.

Nyalali thought the individual calendar system and the general order made good sense for Tanzania. In his own address to judges and magistrates during a visit by the American judges, he related the worrying findings of the court's own investigations earlier that year. His office had introduced a new administrative procedure so that all courts would take stock of their cases every quarter. Court administrators had to compare the information on their registers with what the case files said. The first such exercise had revealed a situation in the High Court and Court of Appeal that Nyalali called "critical and alarming."[15] In the High Court, 442 civil cases, including probate and miscellaneous civil causes, were pending over three years. The oldest of these cases had occupied a place on the docket for sixteen years. In 50 cases, files were missing. At the Court of Appeal, 166 cases were pending for over three years. The oldest had been on the docket for twelve years. And in 10 cases, files were missing. Although the absolute numbers were small by comparison with the busiest Western courts, these cases represented a significant proportion of the Tanzanian docket.

Nyalali pointed to an especially desperate situation in which a probate and estate administration case, filed originally in 1964, remained unconcluded, having passed through the hands of nearly every judge who had served on the court. He observed, "The record shows that the hearing of the case has been adjourned or postponed thirteen times by consent of the parties, eight times on the ground that the parties or one of them . . . was not ready to proceed . . . five times for no stated reason, four times for non-appearance by one of the parties who was served with a notice to appear and twice on the ground that the parties were negotiating for a settlement."[16]

The chief justice used the findings of this first stocktaking, and the visit of the two American judges, as an opportunity to turn the court's attention to the need for reform. He suggested that the situation pointed to several conclusions. The first was the need to alter the calendar system. "What is operating in the High Court is a general or open calendar, under which a case is fixed for hearing on particular dates, but without assigning a specific judge to hear it. Under such a system the court often finds itself with a heavy case load fixed for hearing, but without the judicial manpower to hear all the cases. In such a situation, many of the cases fixed for hearing have to be adjourned, regardless of the presence of witnesses and the parties. The practice undoubtedly gives the court a bad name in the eyes of the public and the parties."[17] He pointed to the success of some American courts in reducing delay by introducing a "single judge calendar" or individual calendar system.

In late 1994, the chief justice introduced amendments to the court rules to introduce delay reduction principles—specifically, the individual calendar system and several other aspects of the District of Columbia's reform program. On the civil side, the new rules meant that after the registrar determined that a complaint was legally sufficient and calculated the court fees applicable, and after the plaintiff paid the fees, the case was sent to the judge in charge or mag-

[15] Nyalali, "Paper on Case Management," pp. 13–15.
[16] Ibid., p. 17.
[17] Ibid., p. 16.

istrate in charge, who was required to assign it to an individual calendar within four days. The file was then given to a court clerk who handled all the files for that judge or magistrate.

The new rules produced a mixed reaction. One group of registrars and magistrates explained, "The individual calendar system helped us. Before, files were always moving and we could not always find them. Now the files are with one judge and there is more individual responsibility. The judges can be held accountable. They complained at first. They didn't like the idea of being responsible for so many files, and they said they needed facilities in chambers because there was no place to keep the files. Now that they are used to it, they say it is hard to remember why they didn't like the idea. People in this area are increasingly litigious, and without this system we would be overwhelmed."[18]

But there was also hesitation and confusion. The practice of frequent adjournments persisted, and courtrooms continued to fall silent. Placing responsibility in the hands of an individual judge did not automatically translate into fewer adjournments. Judges and magistrates had to learn to play a tougher role. They had to be firm and deny requests from advocates who were used to having things their way. Nyalali viewed these difficulties as "transitory," but they persisted for some time.

At Nyalali's request, a superior court team intensified its cooperation with the Tanzanian court the following year. Two Tanzanian judges traveled with Nyalali to the United States to study delay reduction and other topics in greater detail. Then the American judges and the clerk of the superior court traveled to Tanzania to broker additional discussions with members of the bar as well as the bench. They spoke with similar groups in Uganda, Malawi, and Zambia.

Duane Delaney, the clerk of the Superior Court of the District of Columbia, the counterpart of a registrar in African courts, tried to figure out why adjournments remained a problem. He explained his own approach to a Tanzanian audience. "Caseflow management connotes supervision of the time and events involved in the movement of cases through a court system from the point of initiation to disposition," he began. "By managing the time between events so that the occurrence of the scheduled activity becomes predictable and certain, a court encourages timely preparation by attorneys, increasing the probability of an early and fair disposition of the case. Caseflow management programs must establish time intervals long enough to allow adequate preparation but short enough to encourage that preparation."[19]

[18] U.S.-Africa Judicial Exchange, group interview with author, Arusha, Tanzania, May 24, 1996.
[19] Duane B. Delaney, "Robert A. Shuker U.S.-Africa Judicial Exchange Program Phase II Report," Prepared for the U.S. Information Agency (Washington, D.C.: Superior Court of the District of Columbia, the American Bar Association, and the National Judicial College, September 15, 1995), mimeograph.

In the experience of the superior court reform program, early intervention by the judge in civil cases reduced delay, both because it ensured that important documents were filed in timely fashion and because scheduled contact between the lawyers for the two parties could increase chances of settlement. To accomplish this objective, a judge ordered a scheduling conference within 90 to 120 days of filing. At that conference, a scheduling order was drawn up, setting forth deadlines for discovery and motions, as well as time limits. The scheduling order specified a time for a pretrial conference. One week before that conference, the parties provided a jointly written statement of the issues, and the attorneys were supposed to be ready to try the case. At the pretrial conference itself, the judge made one final effort to settle the case. If that failed, the judge clarified how the trial would proceed.

MAKING THE RULES WORK

The initial effort to enlist the help of judges and magistrates to put such a system into effect in Tanzania had ambiguous results. Some of the lawyers claimed, "The scheduling orders are in the files, but the meetings that were supposed to generate them don't take place."[20] The lawyers sometimes did not see the orders and could not plan accordingly. There was a tendency to forget to call pretrial conferences.

The Washington, D.C., team pointed out that making these changes required considerable work with the bar. Controlling the docket meant changing an aspect of legal culture. It was important for judges who want to initiate such changes to persuade the members of the bar that these reforms made sense. The attorneys must buy into the new rules. That might take time, but it was an investment the judges thought worthwhile. The superior court had included representatives of the bar on the committee that planned and managed the reforms in its system. "Would a similar arrangement help in Tanzania?" they asked.

Another explanation for the hesitation and confusion had deeper roots. The new experiments took place in a context where the civil procedure code was slightly different. For example, the rules of discovery varied. In common law Africa, discovery rules remained as they had been in the middle part of the century. That is, parties did not have to exchange information before trial. Plaintiffs had to include in their complaints copies of documents on which they planned to rely. But defendants had no reciprocal obligation. Civil procedure rules permitted use of interrogatories—written questions put to the other

---

[20] Members of the Tanzanian bar, group interview with author, Dar es Salaam, Tanzania, March 11, 1996.

side in advance of the trial—and document requests, with the permission of the court. But each party could serve only one set of each on the opposing side. And in neighboring Uganda, a visiting lawyer found that "[i]n a group of twenty-five experienced practitioners, not a single attorney had ever used either discovery tool."[21] The rules did not provide for depositions, a common way to obtain information before trial in the West.

The rules promoted "trial by ambush." One American lawyer working in Uganda observed, "[T]rial by ambush is currently the preferred tactic. This is one reason why judges are so willing to grant adjournments—they realize that generally, neither party has seen their opponent's evidence until they reach the courtroom, and thus neither party has had the opportunity to gather evidence which rebuts or responds to that proffered by the opposing side."[22]

One of the possible explanations for the success of the individual calendar system in the District of Columbia was that rules of discovery were different. In the United States, and some of the other countries involved in providing foreign legal assistance, court rules were revised earlier in the twentieth century to permit "liberalized discovery." Under the new rules of civil procedure, parties were required to respond to each others' requests for evidence relevant to the complaint before the trial. Judges were empowered to impose sanctions on litigants who did not respond to requests for information from the other side or who abused the process. The change in the rules was supposed to improve the ability to decide cases on their merits, speed the trial process, and increase the chances of settlement before a case came to trial. But there was little doubt that it also could create an incentive for one party to escalate the costs of litigation by demanding numerous documents and asking numerous questions, thereby forcing the other to settle or to drop its claim.

One judge on the Ugandan High Court commented, "We must have liberalized discovery." "That's central. Without that, a trial can go on for ages!"[23] The Ugandan Law Reform Commission decided to take the subject under consideration. But the system did not meet with universal acceptance. In Uganda, one foreign lawyer observed, "Not only is there no rule requiring the parties to exchange witness lists prior to trial, most practitioners expressed dismay at having to do so. They asserted the belief that many of their opponents would not be beyond tampering with a witness's testimony, should the name of the witness be turned over prior to trial. Most attorneys also noted that witnesses were always very willing to 'change their story' for whichever side offered the best compensation."[24] These observations drove home the point

---

[21] "Litigation Realities in Uganda," p. 2.
[22] Ibid.
[23] Justice Harold G. Platt, interview with author, Kampala, Uganda, November 9, 1995.
[24] "Litigation Realities in Uganda," p. 2.

that judicial independence and the rule of law required discipline from ordinary citizens too.

Other challenges gradually came to light. One was service of process. Court rules generally stipulated that complaints had to be served on the parties to a case within fourteen days of filing, and replies or answers had to be sent within twenty-one days of receipt of the complaint. In most parts of Africa, the courts retained responsibility for serving documents, while their Western counterparts allowed counsel to retain someone to carry out this task. Although a few courts used personnel attached to the police to help contact parties, for the most part process servers were court employees. Providing them with transport was also the court's job.

Outside capital cities, service of process was "a terrible problem," lawyers in some countries reported. Service could take two months in rural areas where roads were impassable.[25] Austerity and poor management meant that court vehicles often fell into disrepair or fuel budgets were slashed, limiting travel. Moreover, process servers were sometimes corrupt. Some asked advocates for money to carry out the task, and the requests came even if the advocate had no need of assistance. The implied threat was that if the lawyer did not pay, the next time he or she needed service of process, it would not materialize.[26]

If the court could not manage the function effectively, maybe the lawyers could do better, some argued. A few years later, the Tanzanian court adopted private service on an experimental basis in handling election petitions. "We are considering private service of process as a cost-saving measure," Nyalali commented at the time. "We decided to try it out with the election cases. There was argument about what record you should put in the court to say that process had been served. We decided that, for election cases, an attested, signed copy of the document would suffice. We think we will extend the practice to all cases."[27] The judges took the privatization of service of process a step further toward the end of 1997, when new court rules empowered court bailiffs or brokers to effect service on payment of fees by the party on whose behalf process was issued.

There were pros and cons associated with adopting private service of process. Many litigants were unrepresented by counsel and did not understand what was required of them. One question, then, was whether parties who were unrepresented by counsel would be able to understand the rules for service of process. The judges were especially concerned about this risk, as well as another: whether private service would aggravate conflict, leading to arguments on the spot. And in a world of limited transportation, poor mail service, and

[25] Members of the Mwanza bar, group interview with author, Mwanza, Tanzania, March 14, 1996.
[26] Members of the Tanzanian bar, group interview with author, Dar es Salaam, Tanzania, March 12, 1996.
[27] Francis L. Nyalali, interview with author, March 21, 1996.

high distrust, everyone worried how it would be possible to know whether—and when—someone had actually received the documents.

ALTERNATIVE DISPUTE RESOLUTION

Nyalali was much taken with another aspect of the superior court delay reduction program: the use of ADR. The American judges knew that in their court, the overwhelming majority of civil cases, about 90 percent, settled before they reached trial. By institutionalizing opportunities to pursue mediation, arbitration, or neutral case evaluation, they thought it would be possible to increase the speed with which parties come to agreement and remove their cases from the docket. A typical settlement discussion took two to four hours, while a trial could take much longer. In consultation with the bar, the American court modified its procedures to require that the parties in most civil cases try to settle the case before coming to trial. The court would facilitate this process by stipulating the point at which the parties would have to meet and by providing a "neutral" mediator who would try to bring the two sides together. If the parties could not agree, the case would go to trial.

ADR had grown in popularity in U.S. legal circles, and it was attracting interest in England, where the Woolf report, *Access to Justice*, had explored its use. In a trial someone would win and the other person would lose, while in ADR it was possible to apportion gains and losses differently. Trials cost money, while in some cases, ADR was financially sensible because it took less time and in some cases less preparation. ADR also provided the parties both flexibility and some measure of control over the process of resolving the dispute. The parties were often able to negotiate some of the rules that would guide the discussion and help choose the neutral facilitator. By contrast, in a trial, they had no say in either. Further, ADR was confidential, whereas trials were public. Court proceedings were open to media scrutiny, while settlement discussions were not. The neutral facilitator could not be called as a witness in any subsequent trial, should the parties fail to agree. The notes from a mediation were destroyed. Finally, where preserving relationships was important, as it usually was in commerce or in small communities, ADR was often more appropriate than the forced adversarial relationship courtroom procedures inspire.

ADR was not appropriate in all situations, and the superior court program allowed judges to send such cases to trial without trying to obtain settlement first. For example, where there was a clear question of law at stake, instead of a dispute about facts, then a case belonged in the courts so that the precedent could contribute to the development of the law. Or where there was great disparity in the parties, the trial process may be more effective in protecting the rights of the less powerful.

Nyalali liked the approach. It resonated well with tradition. Historically, many African communities had preferred reconciliation to judgment in which one party "won" and another "lost." The spirit of that tradition seemed to have faded over the decades, to Nyalali's dismay. In a speech to an international conference of fellow chief justices, he had urged the legal community to reconsider:

> Principles of great vitality and utility for modern Africa and the world at large can be unearthed and developed from the indigenous inclination for compromise and reconciliation in the settlement of disputes and conflicts. The common law approach of winner-gets-all and loser-misses-all is not ideal for establishing durable harmony in society. In most cases decided by the courts in Common Law countries, rights and wrongs exist on both sides of each case and it is quite unfortunate that at the end of the case, one side comes out with all the rights, and the other side, with all the wrongs.[28]

The Mroso committee, formed to plan reform in the court's handling of civil cases, had also supported the adoption of ADR, partly on the grounds that the principle of amicable settlement resonated strongly with African traditions.

The Tanzanian court decided to implement a system similar to the one at the superior court in Washington, D.C., on an experimental basis. The pilot projects would depart from the superior court model in some respects. For example, the mediators who facilitated settlement would be specially trained magistrates and judges, not members of the bar. In Washington, with access to a large bar, many of whose members were skilled in effecting settlements, it was easier for lawyers to perform that role. Even though the superior court could afford to pay only a very small stipend, the lawyers usually performed the service *pro bono*. If they were very successful in effecting settlements, their reputations would afford them entree into a flourishing new subfield of law. Lawyers often earned significant compensation as arbitrators and mediators. But in Africa, lawyers were fewer, and the economics of the profession were different.

A series of demonstrations, joint efforts by Tanzanian-American teams to mediate live cases, met with an enthusiastic response. People's interests were surprisingly similar across national boundaries, as were their beliefs about the general shape of a fair result. In the demonstration sessions, almost as high a proportion of cases settled as did in Washington. A few did not and were put down for trial.

Potentially, ADR could help the courts address another problem. Reducing

---

[28] Francis L. Nyalali, "The Challenge of Development to Law in Developing Countries Viewed from the Perspective of Human Rights, Rule of Law, and the Role of the Courts in Preserving Freedom," Address at First Commonwealth Africa Judicial Conference, Kombo Beach Hotel, Kotu, Gambia, May 5–9, 1986, p. 13.

the amount of time that elapsed between filing and the disposition of a case was one part of the challenge the courts confronted. Eliminating the backlog was another. Somehow, it was necessary to carry out both tasks at once with the same personnel, since it was hard for courts to employ extra hands on a temporary basis. The superior court faced the backlog problem on a grand scale. The judges in Washington confronted the need to dispose of thousands of cases. They knew that going to trial in all instances would take too much time for them to make a real difference. Instead, the court decided to set aside occasional periods for settlement, suspending other activities. The judges identified the oldest cases on the docket and notified the litigants that the judges and volunteer mediators from the Washington, D.C., bar would meet with the parties to try to reach a settlement. This approach led to the disposal of over half of the backlog within a short period.

As the partnership between the Tanzanian court and the superior court progressed, the ADR demonstrations yielded to "settlement weeks" to reduce the number of cases on the dockets of selected courts. Regular operations were suspended. Instead, Tanzanian magistrates and judges worked with their District of Columbia counterparts to mediate the oldest disputes. The success rate was 70 percent—better than the normal rate for similar programs in the United States.

The experiments were not trouble free. It was "taking time for ADR to take root," commented some of the advocates.[29] There were initial organizational problems. For example, counsel were not always contacted about mediation dates on time. Registrars did not always know which notices to prepare or send. Many lawyers and magistrates had not read the "orange book" of mediation rules that was supposed to guide the process, and advocates were sometimes unaware they had to bring their clients to the sessions, or that they had to have authority to negotiate on their clients' behalf. And while the potentially beneficial effects of ADR and settlement weeks materialized at some pilot sites, at others backlogs grew worse. For example, at the Kisutu Court in Dar es Salaam, court records showed that although the numbers of cases filed had declined slightly in the late 1990s, the number of cases pending had increased sharply.

Some members of the bar remained skeptical. A few cited financial reasons. Potential barriers to the use of ADR were the systems for paying court fees and remunerating advocates. Advocates paid court fees in advance. Having paid, a client might want to see the case litigated to the bitter end. Reformers urged their colleagues to consider refunding part of these payments to parties whose cases settled.[30] But not everyone was attracted by this idea.

---

[29] Tanzania advocates, group interview with author, Mwanza, Tanzania, March 14, 1995.
[30] See, for example, the recommendations of the Republic of Uganda, *Report of the Commission of Inquiry on Judicial Reform*, p. 7.

Deeper criticisms focused on the implications of context for the effectiveness of ADR. Lawyers commented that their clients had usually exhausted mediation within the community before seeking legal help. Taking a case to court only happened when elders or community leaders had already failed to negotiate a settlement. For this reason, clients might well oppose the process. They conceded, however, that they had not yet worked out a way to explain the system to their clients, and that the public in general was unaware of what was involved. And, yes, it was true that the parties to cases settled in the demonstration programs seemed genuinely pleased by the process and the results.

An officer of the Tanganyika Law Society observed that mediation would not be useful in some of the cases that commonly came to court in the country. "ADR won't work in resolving disputes with parastatals [public enterprises]," he argued. "First, their representatives are not allowed to negotiate. They have to go back to their directors and boards to get their agreement every time they want to [settle]. Second, their representatives aren't loyal to them. Even if they have permission, they won't negotiate hard. Instead, they'll take a kick-back from the other party's lawyer."[31]

European observers were often critical. Said one adviser, "ADR doesn't transport well because the conditions that support it don't exist anywhere except in the U.S." He suggested that the success of mediation was related to three distinctively American phenomena. One was the ability of lawyers to take plaintiffs' cases on contingency, paying their costs and fees out of the proceeds from successful cases. He argued that contingency fees tended to lead people to push for higher damage awards, and the risk of having to pay such awards brought defendants to the mediation table. The ability to pursue class action suits had a similar effect. But class actions were not permitted under the laws of most African countries. Finally, litigiousness in the United States created heavy burdens on the courts and gave judges a stake in making the system work.[32]

But there were strong voices on the other side too. Judge John Mwipopo, a former director of public prosecution, observed that the training and the experiments were changing the outlook of the judges. "The advantage of ADR to judges especially is that they stop thinking in old ways," he said. "It is a more open-minded approach. Settlement is an option. The trial is not just a contest. . . . It was the influence of the ADR training which made me think that way."[33] As a remedy for a court often perceived as distant from the lives and thinking of ordinary people, ADR could prove useful.

---

[31] Officer of the Law Society, personal communication, March 11, 1996.
[32] Marcus Murphy, interview with author, March 1996.
[33] Judge John Mwipopo, interview with author, May 16, 1996.

This view attracted considerable support, not least from Nyalali, who considered the innovation a "tremendous success."[34] Even members of the bar began to think that the practice "should be stepped up a bit."[35]

UNANTICIPATED CONSEQUENCES

Whatever their eventual effects on delay reduction, the programs Nyalali initiated had a number of unanticipated consequences. One was that the exposure to a foreign judicial system had led judges to rethink their own approaches to their roles and helped to foster a new engagement with the profession. They did not have to accept what they were offered, either in whole or in part. But the experience did lead them to think about what they did and about standards of practice. It engaged advocates similarly. As the exchange with the superior court proceeded, the judges, magistrates, and other court personnel began to think, "This could actually be fun!"—not a term often used in the region.[36]

Nyalali observed a second "unanticipated consequence." The visits of the American judges provided an occasion for public ceremony and for open discussion. The chief justice took time to invite members of the press to visit the court, learn about the delay reduction program, and meet with the American visitors. The newspapers carried stories the next day, and journalists followed aspects of the new court program. "We carried out reforms on [the] civil side in public view," Nyalali commented, and that "contributed to educating the public about the courts."[37] It was another step toward increasing familiarity with the institution and toward building the legitimacy of the courts in the public eye.

Other courts in the region stepped up their efforts to address civil delay at roughly the same time Nyalali did, but the example of an adventurous neighbor helped. In 1995, Uganda's chief justice, Samson Wambuzi, observed, "I recently visited Tanzania. I liked what I saw. I hope we do the same or better here."[38]

---

[34] Francis L. Nyalali, interview with author, July 27, 1999.
[35] Southern African Human Rights Network lawyers, interview with author, Dar es Salaam, Tanzania, July 28, 1999.
[36] Tanzanian advocates, group interview with author, March 14, 1995.
[37] Francis L. Nyalali, interview with author, May 29, 1996.
[38] Samson Wambuzi, comment to visiting delegation of American judges, August 21, 1995.

Corruption

NYALALI'S EFFORTS TO build the Tanzanian justice system had to deal with another troubling problem: corruption within the judiciary itself. Nothing was more debilitating to institutional legitimacy than suspicion that magistrates, judges, or other court personnel might be "on the take" and therefore partial.

Between the early 1970s and the end of the century, many judges in Africa found themselves in circumstances that challenged professionalism. Judges were paid poorly, sometimes too poorly to support a family. Social pressures sometimes meant that judges and magistrates who declined to take bribes were at once esteemed, for the model they set, and chastised, for their inability to do better by their households and communities. Public attitudes were ambivalent. Observed Tanzanian Judge William Maina, who had experienced the problem himself, "Magistrates were blamed if they did not engage in corruption. People would say, 'He is a foolish person because he has not used his position.'"[1] At the same time, they felt the behavior was wrong when it meant they had to "pay extra." Some courts were better able than others to monitor behavior and to build a culture that provided little harbor for those who participated in corruption.

In Tanzania, the chief justice was determined to build public understanding and support for the courts and for the law. If ordinary people believed that justice was for sale, they would hardly think the courts were helpful, and they would not stand up for the judges and magistrates in difficult times. The perception that private citizens could influence court personnel sent a signal that judges and administrators would surely lack the resolve to stand up to politicians. Members of the public considered that the primary court magistrates

[1] Judge William Maina, interview with author, Dar es Salaam, Tanzania, May 22, 1996.

were often in cahoots with the village power structures, as well as with local officials.[2] As one lawyer observed, corruption had created a system that "reeks of inconsistent decisions because they are not principled, but are anchored on expediency and size of the purse."[3]

Yet solutions were difficult to identify. It was hard to push members of the judiciary to take action. No one liked to say no to a colleague or staff member—or worse still, lay someone off in a world where jobs were scarce. Reporting bad behavior, "blowing the whistle," was awkward because it threatened working relationships. There were real dangers too. Although there was widespread popular dissatisfaction with corruption, plenty of people had a stake in preserving the practice of paying to delay a case, lose evidence, or alter a decision. Those who tried to make the system work according to the rules could find themselves or their families in danger.

During a visit to help with the Tanzanian civil delay reduction program, Duane Delaney, clerk for the Superior Court of the District of Columbia, brought home the universality of the problem and the firmness it required. Two judges of the High Court approached Delaney in the hallway outside of Chief Justice Nyalali's office one afternoon. In hushed tones and with evident embarrassment, they said, "You know we have a terrible problem here. Sometimes our clerks tell people they can get the judge to change a ruling or that they can lose a file in return for money. The people pay what they are asked and the clerks alter the record. We take the blame. What can we do to stop this?" Without a pause, Delaney replied, "Oh, we have that problem too! One time someone even tried to alter a guilty verdict. I fired the clerk. That is the only way to deal with these problems. You have to get rid of the people who do these things to send a clear signal to others."[4]

THE FACE OF CORRUPTION

Hard measures of the severity of the problem were very difficult to obtain. But perceptions often mattered more than realities, and there was no doubt that in many countries, Botswana excepted, the lower courts had bad reputations. In Uganda, President Yoweri Museveni had made his displeasure with judicial corruption well known. Summarized one judge, "The president is fed up. He

---

[2] Group conversation with journalists in Mbeya, Tanzania, May 1996.
[3] R. N. Ben Lobulu, "Corruption and the Administration of Justice," in *The National Integrity System in Tanzania*, Proceedings of a workshop on fighting corruption facilitated by Transparency International and the Economic Development Institute of the World Bank, August 10–12, 1995 (Dar es Salaam, Tanzania: Prevention of Corruption Bureau, 1995, distributed by the World Bank), p. 89.
[4] Author's observation, High Court of Dar es Salaam, Tanzania, August 1995.

is really angered. In 1991, he told us, 'You are corrupt and you should not be complacent.'"[5]

In Tanzania, the hew and cry over corruption dated back to independence. Retired Judge William Maina, whose reputation as a "straight" judge later endowed him with the chairmanship of an anticorruption program, described corruption in the judiciary as "a phenomenon of the 1970s and 1980s," when rule of law had broken down. "Magistrates would physically go and find cases in the registry from which they could make money," he recalled. "When I went on leave, villagers would tell me that they could not win a case unless they paid. Magistrates would adjourn cases to leave time for litigants to get money to pay them off."[6]

A survey carried out in the mid-1990s suggested that about 30 percent of the people who used the courts "paid extra" for service — that is, paid money for which they received no receipt. A comparable proportion reported doing the same in dealings with the police, the revenue service, and the lands service.[7] There was sharp regional variation, with only 8 percent of users reporting the payment of bribes in Dar es Salaam, the capital, compared to a high of 62 percent in Mbeya, in the southwest of the country. The median payment was ten thousand shillings, or about ten dollars, and the average was about twenty-nine thousand shillings. Despite the remark of one respondent to the effect that, "if you pay 'chai' your case is dealt with quickly," the bribes usually correlated with longer waits and more return visits.[8] Those interviewed thought the payments were wrong, "a bad thing," and that the practice was not justified by the low salaries court personnel received.

For Uganda, the other country for which systematic information was available in this period, the figures were slightly worse. In a survey of over eighteen thousand households conducted in 1998, 50 percent of those who had contact with the courts reported paying a bribe, and 63 percent of those who had contact with the police said they had paid money.[9] While some of the payments to courts may well have been user fees charged to respondents who expected free services, the police figures could not be explained away in this fashion, and the taint the police incurred easily affected the perception of the justice system as a whole. About half of those who said they paid bribes for court services paid $32 or less, while the average payment was about $65. Payments to police were

[5] Justice Harold G. Platt, interview with author, November 9, 1995.
[6] Judge William Maina, interview with author, May 1996.
[7] United Republic of Tanzania, Presidential Commission of Inquiry against Corruption, "Service Delivery Survey: Corruption in the Police, Judiciary, Revenue and Lands Service" (Dar es Salaam, Tanzania: Presidential Commission of Inquiry Against Corruption, July 1996), p. 19.
[8] Ibid., p. 20.
[9] Republic of Uganda, "Uganda National Integrity Survey 1998: Final Report," Paper prepared by CIET International for the Inspectorate of Government (Kampala, Uganda: Inspectorate of Government, August 1998), p. 15.

about $32 on average, out of a gross domestic product per capita (a rough approximation of average income) of about $1,160.

Throughout the region, the upper levels of the courts were generally perceived as less prone to corruption, although there were incidents at these higher levels too. Tanzanian Justice Robert Kisanga remarked, "One judge in the High Court asked for a million shillings!" The judge was no longer on the court. But the popular impression that it cost a lot to buy a judge persisted because clerks and support staff who operated their own rackets would go out and say, "If you want a favor of a judge, you must offer a figure commensurate with his stature. . . ."[10]

In Tanzania, as elsewhere, citizen complaints focused on bribery, but people also reported extensive abuses of other kinds. An investigation in the mid-1990s found examples of magistrates in conspiracy with the police. For example, police would falsely arrest a person and receive a kickback from the magistrate when the man or woman paid to win release. Other magistrates denied rights to appeal cases or wrote judgments without holding a hearing until compensated.[11]

The problem was not limited to the magistrates. In some instances, clerks were the main source of trouble. One common ploy was for the clerk to see a decision in advance of its announcement, then to "sell" the judgment to the winning party, claiming that the judge or magistrate was still undecided. The person who paid for the service would then hear the judgment read in court and assume his or her money had helped secure the result, even if the magistrate or judge knew nothing about the transaction. Some magistrates did agree to participate in the scam. "People claim they have paid for a decision if they have paid a clerk. The clerks have 'a system.' They ask new magistrates whether they want to be part of it."[12]

One of the most commonly cited forms of interference with the lower levels of the judiciary was payment to clerks for losing files, or temporarily misplacing files. Strategic delay could lead to longer incarceration of accused persons, or shift economic burdens in a civil case. One Uganda Law Society memorandum complained that "[W]hen prisoners are taken . . . before Magistrates, files 'develop feet' or are 'misplaced' and therefore not available. This is one of the tricks used to make a prisoner pay some money to . . . law enforcing officials: the Prison Officer; the Court Police Prosecutor, and allegedly the Magistrate. After payment of a bribe, the file is easily found."[13]

---

[10] Justice Robert Kisanga, interview with author, Dar es Salaam, Tanzania, May 31, 1996.
[11] United Republic of Tanzania, Presidential Commission of Inquiry against Corruption, *Report on the Commission on Corruption* (Warioba Report), vol. 1 (Dar es Salaam, Tanzania: Presidential Commission of Inquiry against Corruption, November 1996), p. 174.
[12] Magistrate, interview with author, Mbarara, Uganda, January 29, 1996.
[13] Uganda Law Society memorandum, "Observation of Law, Courts, and Prison Services in Uganda," Law Society, Kampala, Uganda, August 30, 1992, mimeograph.

Self-employed officials, such as court brokers or auctioneers and court-appointed administrators of estates, were among the most difficult people to manage. Chief Justice Nyalali recalled that in the 1970s, "the execution of court decrees by court brokers mushroomed into a profiteering and fraudulent business. . . ."

> It was the order of the day for court brokers to attach property in execution of a court decree, but keep it under their custody for an inordinate period so as to increase their storage charges. Under this practice, when the attached property was eventually sold in execution of a court decree, practically all the proceeds of sale went to pay the court broker's storage charges. The decree holder was only partly paid. This led to a fresh attachment of a judgment debtor's property and, so on and so on until the judgment debtor was bankrupted, not by payment to the decree holder, but by payment of the storage charges of the court broker![14]

Eventually the president issued a directive stopping the use of court brokers and required use of executive branch officials. Nyalali observed, "The decree was a violation of the law but it was welcomed." Nonetheless, in the mid-1990s, the court still struggled with similar problems, including irregular attachment of property by auctioneers and collusion between auctioneers and magistrates to sell the property of losing parties.[15]

Upstanding magistrates and court clerks sometimes unwittingly found themselves compromised. By creating the appearance of wrong-doing, ill-intentioned members of the community could extort benefits for themselves. For example, journalists in one Tanzanian town told the story of a magistrate who refused to take a bribe from some Asian businessmen. The magistrate was armed and told the businessmen he would shoot unless they took the money off the table. The businessmen said they knew the magistrate would not shoot them, and they left the money. The man was stuck with the appearance of dishonesty. He was vulnerable from that point forward. The businessmen could always threaten to turn him over to the authorities.[16] Other people related stories about a magistrate who landed in jail, his pockets stuffed with money by those who had arrested him.

Direct threats of retaliation or violence were uncommon, said most magistrates, but they did happen from time to time. In the 1990s, litigants who couldn't buy a verdict occasionally burned the office of the magistrate, includ-

[14] Francis L. Nyalali, "Paper on Court Administration in Tanzania," Paper presented at the seminar of judges of the High Court and Court of Appeal of Tanzania, Dar es Salaam, Tanzania, April 19–23, 1993, p. 23.
[15] United Republic of Tanzania, Presidential Commission of Inquiry against Corruption, *Report on the Commission on Corruption*, p. 177.
[16] Meeting with journalists, Mbeya, Tanzania, May 16, 1996.

ing all of the case files. In an earlier era, judicial officers sometimes had their houses surrounded by armed men who wanted to intimidate. These techniques were not unknown in industrial countries either, as the judges who ordered desegregation of schools in parts of the American South knew all too well. The problem was that in rural Africa there was often no one to turn to for help.

Poor finances and financial systems created an extra source of trouble. Sometimes when clerks and magistrates lacked paper or transportation, they would say that the court could hear a case if the defendant or the litigant was willing to pay for the cost of these supplies or services directly. In some cases, the requests were made of everyone, and the court offered a receipt for the payment. Essentially they asked citizens to pay a user's fee, albeit a somewhat irregular one. When the choice was between waiting a year for the court to receive a supply of stationery or a fuel allowance, or paying extra for the materials, then many litigants preferred to pay.

The problem was that the lack of finance could serve as a pretext for court personnel to take money for themselves. Payments for paper were fungible. They sometimes made their way into private pockets. When budget shortfalls meant that the courts lacked receipt books, the ability to monitor the distinction between "legitimate" payments and illegitimate payments faded almost completely.

Throughout the region, people grappled with this kind of problem. In Uganda, the Commission of Inquiry on Judicial Reform reported, "We have been told of the public paying the charges of the secretaries for typing delayed records; for obtaining action by officials, such as the inclusion of cases in hearing lists. There are the usual accusations of corruption. All this money should be the revenue of the State and implies that fees [on the official schedules] should be raised."[17]

Inconsistent decisions, or unhappiness with outcomes of cases, could lead to frivolous corruption allegations. Said Justice J. K. Mnzavas, "I was Jaji Kiongozi (Principal Judge) for ten years before I was elevated to the Court of Appeal. I was frequently confronted with charges against magistrates. Often the corruption charges arose because the judgments given were unpopular."[18]

MAKING STANDARDS CLEAR

Nyalali was well aware of corruption in the courts when he took office. In 1977, a Judicial Service Review Commission led by Pius Msekwa, the chief executive secretary of Chama Cha Mapinduzi, the ruling party, had reported many of the difficulties people faced in using the courts. However, only in 1984 did Nyalali feel that he had sufficient backing from his fellow judges to begin to address a

---

[17] Republic of Uganda, *Report of the Commission of Inquiry on Judicial Reform* (Kampala, Uganda: Commission of Inquiry on Judicial Reform, 1995), p. 8.
[18] J. K. Mnzavas, interview with author, Dar es Salaam, Tanzania, May 31, 1996.

challenge so difficult. Even then, the ability to act appeared to demand more high-level human resources than the court had at its disposal, and progress was slow and halting. In the mid-1990s, Nyalali remarked, "We still haven't addressed the problem of misconduct very effectively. There are constraints. The chief justice is involved in the entire system, including prison conditions. That is a large number of people. We have tried to proceed methodically."[19]

Nyalali had to be fair to the personnel in his charge as well as to other citizens. The situation was delicate, and good solutions were few. "We started first with basics," the chief justice noted. "We had to make sure that people had a clear understanding of what was proper conduct. Many were vaguely aware of the standards, but some aspects were hazy. We needed to draft a code." It was a basic principle of fairness that people be informed of the rules or standards to which they were expected to adhere, and for that reason the senior judges considered publication of the code essential. Nyalali felt that very often people simply did not know what was expected of them in what was, after all, an unfamiliar institutional context. The magistrate training programs had no "ethics" component in their curricula.

Nyalali sent Justice Barnabas Samatta in search of models. As a former member of the commission that investigated judicial corruption in the mid-1970s, Samatta was well acquainted with the kinds of problems the judiciary faced. Neither Britain nor Canada had a written code of judicial ethics, although the civil service did. "We said, for us, the code has to be written. We have no tradition that would automatically inform people what was expected of them," Nyalali recalled.[20] Written standards provided a way to communicate with magistrates who worked in remote areas. When Samatta traveled to the United States, he called the chief justice to say that he had found something that would work. The American Bar Association (ABA) had first convened lawyers and judges to produce Canons of Judicial Ethics in 1924. It produced a Model Code of Judicial Conduct in 1972, and it revised the code in 1990 and again in 1997. With some slight modifications, Samatta thought the 1972 code would serve Tanzania's purposes well.

Justice Samatta took the ABA Model Code of Judicial Conduct back to Tanzania and said the United States was far ahead of other countries in thinking about the problem. "I was impressed too," Nyalali recalled. "We convened a meeting of all of the judges and magistrates in Arusha. We discussed and adopted the code and made some very slight variations only. It was testimony to the universality of the principles!" The judiciary persuaded the legislature to give the code constitutional backing. "We asked for an amendment to recognize the code of conduct established by the judiciary. Now the constitution reads, 'A judge can be removed if he violates the code established by the judiciary.'"

---

[19] Francis L. Nyalali, interview with author, May 29, 1996.
[20] Francis L. Nyalali, interview with author, May 29, 1996.

Nyalali felt it was important to use the code to educate judicial personnel, and he himself became an avid reader of literature on judicial ethics. He obtained copies of subsequent editions of the ABA model standards, as well as the extensive commentaries on the rules set out there, and quoted from the latter in public speeches. In communicating with other members of the judiciary, he drew attention to other articulations of the same kinds of principles. A devout Catholic, he was fond of quoting Deuteronomy 16:19: "[G]ifts blind the eyes of the wise and change the words of the just." And occasionally he reached to the words of John Marshall, the man he so admired, who said, "I have always thought . . . that the greatest scourge an angry Heaven ever inflicted upon an ungrateful and sinning people, was an ignorant, a corrupt, or a dependent judiciary."[21]

Other courts in the region proceeded in similar fashion. The South African courts also made reference to the ABA Model Code from time to time, and in the 1990s, other judiciaries gravitated to it. One group of judges commented that the pamphlet was the single most important document they acquired during a visit to the United States.[22]

Often what lower-court personnel wanted was not just a code of judicial conduct but a set of scripts a magistrate might use to extract himself or herself from trying situations. The most common bit of such advice shared among magistrates was "just say no." People respected those who stood firm. Said one Ugandan magistrate, "Yes, the 'big men' call, but if the magistrate says 'no' they won't continue to ask. Here [in the president's home district], people try to get Statehouse to intervene. But the president's office refuses, and they stop."[23] Signs of weakness would invite a shower of requests for favors and offers of bribes. The requests for intervention were most common when a magistrate first arrived in an area. A strong will usually led to a gradual decline in the numbers of requests for favors; a weak will led to escalation.

Senior magistrates developed maxims or homilies they tried to pass on to those who were just joining the service. One chief magistrate in Uganda told his younger staff:

1. Patience is needed. If you lose your temper quickly you will make the wrong decision.

---

[21] The quote comes from John Marshall's summation before the Virginia Constitutional Convention in January 1830. See Hugh Blair Grigsby, *The Virginia Convention of 1829–1830*, reprint edition (New York: Da Capo Press, 1969), p. 619.

[22] As noted in Jennifer Widner, "The Quality of Justice: Report on the U.S.-Africa Judicial Exchange," Prepared for the U.S. Information Agency (Washington, D.C.: Superior Court of the District of Columbia, American Bar Association, and the National Judicial College, July 1995), mimeograph. The judges came from Tanzania, Uganda, Zambia, and Malawi.

[23] Magistrate, interview with author, Mbarara, Uganda, January 29, 1996.

2. Be ready to listen and expect criticisms. One party will inevitably lose. Losing parties will not be happy.
3. Guard against the temptations of corruption. There is a tendency in the population, especially among the land grabbers, to think people can use money to influence a magistrate. Don't succumb, or you will be reversed on appeal.
4. Aim at survival. Don't aim to be very rich. A magistrate's life is supposed to be a model to others. Serve as an example to the community.
5. Avoid social drinking.

These simple rules could make an enormous difference in the kinds of difficult situations that developed, the chief magistrate commented, "yet we have examples of magistrates who violate these rules, especially at the lower levels."[24]

A code had to be backed by the ability to investigate suspected violations and to take steps to discipline those who broke the rules. In the 1980s, such actions were undertaken by the country's Judicial Service Commission, but the commission had not been as effective as hoped. In 1991, the legislature altered the arrangements. But Nyalali was uncomfortable with the new system, which effectively made the chief justice the investigator, prosecutor, and adjudicator. Unaware that it was the legislature, not the courts, that had enacted these measures, critics took the chief justice to task for rushing in with a solution that would prove inappropriate.[25] In the late 1990s, the legislature changed the law again, easing this awkward situation. The process was revamped to ensure that the chief justice was not involved in investigating or prosecuting ethics violations. "Those functions have been vested in the Judges in Charge of the High Court zones," Nyalali explained. "The changes were in line with our efforts to decentralize the administration of the Judiciary Department."[26]

Dismissing judicial personnel for violations took a toll on the size of the bench during the 1990s. "If there are public complaints, we follow up," Nyalali remarked. "The Judicial Service Commission takes appropriate action. Twenty of the primary court magistrates are dismissed every year, on average. Punitive action is not the best approach, though. We need corrective action. The dismissal rate of primary court magistrates, combined with retirement, means there is a deficit of primary court magistrates."[27] In the mid-1990s, only about half of the primary court posts were filled. Elderly traditional court holders had died, low salaries made it hard to attract people, and there were few facilities for training.

[24] Chief Magistrate, interview with author, Jinja, Uganda, November 22, 1995.
[25] Sufian Hemed Bukurura, *Judiciary and Good Governance in Contemporary Tanzania* (Bergen, Norway: Christien Michelsen Institute, Development and Human Rights Studies, September 1995), p. 41.
[26] Francis L. Nyalali, personal communication, October 1998.
[27] Francis L. Nyalali, interview with author, May 29, 1996.

That much was true, said Nyalali, but another important reason for the deficit was the dismissal of a high proportion of magistrates on disciplinary grounds.[28]

Firing clerks and other nonjudicial staff who engaged in corrupt practices was another matter. In many countries, nonjudicial personnel came under the purview of the public service commission, not the courts, and employment rules often made it very difficult to dismiss someone who had lost files or altered judgments.[29] Throughout most of the 1970s, 1980s, and early 1990s, public service rules also made it hard to link performance to pay or promotion.

ACCOUNTING AND CONTROL

Across countries, successive commissions of inquiry called for better management of the lowest courts by chief justices and principal judges. Chief justices understood the task but often found it difficult to respond. In Tanzania, Nyalali commented, "Supervision is our great weakness. We have had inadequate resources to supervise magistrates. So the magistrates are small emperors without fear that someone from above will come down on them."[30]

Conventional wisdom in economics held that reducing the numbers of required permissions or other papers was the best way to reduce official corruption. Every need for a service, a signature, or a ruling on a motion created opportunities for pursuit of personal gain—for using position to exact payment. Yet in the context of the courts, there were sharp limits on the ability to streamline procedures without jeopardizing fairness in other ways. It was possible to eliminate "mention hearings" and replace these with fixed schedules advocates had to respect, as some of the civil delay reduction measures did. But generally there were few analogues to the "free market" solutions championed in other domains.

The introduction of alternative dispute resolution (ADR) was the closest equivalent, and it appeared to have a beneficial effect, in the chief justice's view. Under the procedure, it is not the judge or magistrate who decides the case, but the parties themselves. "There is no room for lost case files, evidence tampering, or a decision improperly obtained. My colleagues and I have no doubt whatsoever that ADR is going to be the most effective tool for combating corruption in the Tanzanian courts. Members of the public are already aware of the potential."[31] The advocates were far less optimistic that ADR would solve the problem, however.

Increasing the transparency of proceedings was another broad line of attack.

---

[28] Francis L. Nyalali, "Paper on Court Administration in Tanzania," p. 9.
[29] Magistrate, interview with author, Mbarara, Uganda, January 29, 1996.
[30] Francis L. Nyalali, interview with author, May 29, 1996.
[31] Francis L. Nyalali, personal communication, October 1998.

For example, it was important to ensure that decisions were public. Complained members of the Tanzania bar, "High Court judges often meet in their chambers, not in the courtrooms. Why? Is it that chambers are quieter and cooler, so that it is easier to follow proceedings, or is it that bribes can pass unnoticed? Or is there less public exposure and less risk of embarrassment?"[32]

A third possibility was to assign the most delicate cases or those involving large sums of money to the most upstanding judicial staff. Resident magistrates, who had supervisory powers, had experimented with various strategies themselves. One tactic was to allow a respected senior magistrate to assign cases to those whom he believed had no conflicts of interest, instead of relying on the magistrates to recuse themselves or face reversal on appeal. Said one higher-level magistrate, "One gets adept at shifting cases to magistrates who have no social ties to the parties, so they can't easily be subject to interference."[33] Of course, this practice only worked if the judge in charge was "clean." It also contravened the rule of thumb that to prevent forum shopping, cases should be assigned randomly to adjudicators. And it sometimes meant that a few good people got stuck with all the hard, and sometimes dangerous, cases. Nonetheless, it attracted support from many members of the judiciary.

Magistrates and judges also had thoughts about how to control the behavior of clerks. One tactic was to keep decisions under lock and key where clerks could not reach them. One Ugandan magistrate offered a story, by way of illustration. "When I was just starting out, there were attempts to bribe me. At my first post, I couldn't speak the local language. I left a file out, where a clerk could see it. The clerk stole the judgment and read it. Then he went to the winning party and told him to bring a goat if he wished the magistrate to decide in his favor. The man arrived when the clerk was out of the office, and he explained that the goat was in return for the decision. He tethered the goat by a tree. The chief magistrate was furious. He called me to account, and I said I didn't know anything about a goat. Now we lock decisions away, and if there are missing files, we close court until the missing papers can be found."[34]

Not all lower courts had the resources even to buy locks. In one burnt-out courthouse, a magistrate pioneered a creative line of attack. He was distraught when he learned that a clerk read his decisions, then tried to "sell" the verdicts to the winners. The magistrate left a fake decision in full view of the staff. But when the time came to read the verdict, he pulled out the real text and awarded the decision to the opposing side. The faces of those who thought they had purchased the outcome fell. So did the clerk's stock. However, the tactic was scarcely one that others could borrow on a large scale.

---

[32] Members of the Tanzanian bar, group interview with author, March 12, 1996.
[33] Chief Magistrate, interview with author, Masaka, Uganda, February 6, 1996.
[34] Ibid.

TERMS OF SERVICE

Low remuneration was a partial cause of judicial corruption, although it was by no means the only one, or even the main one. Those who fared worst were the lower-level magistrates and the court staff. Justice Robert Kisanga, one of Nyalali's close colleagues, commented that "corruption is a corollary of the resource problems in the court. We hear a lot about corruption in the lower cadre. Those people are lowest paid and the cases we hear about are of people soliciting bribes of three thousand to ten thousand shillings [three to ten dollars]. They are very small. It is clear the magistrates are trying to make ends meet. These are the typical cases."[35] The same was true of the courts in neighboring countries.

Early in his career as chief justice, Nyalali succeeded in winning transportation for the judges, and that gesture helped his colleagues see him as an ally. But inflation so eroded pay levels during the early part of his tenure that circumstances remained very difficult through most of the 1990s. Although Tanzanian judges received other benefits or "allowances," which meant their effective rates of pay were higher than they seemed if one looked at the pay stub, there was no question that they were poorly compensated even by regional standards: the equivalent of sixty dollars per month, plus car and gas, house and utilities, and two people to provide household help. When they retired, they lost the allowances, so even if it was possible to feed a family, buy clothes, and pay for their children's education on these meager salaries, they had to find some way to save for their old age.[36] Even at the upper levels, compensation for judges in Tanzania was so low that it was imperative to have a farm or business on the side, although ethics rules restricted the kinds of activities the judges could undertake.[37]

To reduce the temptation to take "extra" payments to supplement incomes, chief justices and aid donors argued that substantial increases in judicial

---

[35] Justice Robert Kisanga, interview with author, Dar es Salaam, Tanzania, May 31, 1996.
[36] In 1994–95, Uganda and the Seychelles upgraded judicial salaries, but Tanzania lagged far behind.
[37]   SOME COMPARATIVE MONTHLY SALARIES

	Tanzania	Uganda	Zimbabwe	Seychelles
Chief Justice	$233	$1,433	NA	$4,481
Appellate Judge	$214	$1,043	$952	NA
High Court Judge	$197	$853	$878	$3,595

Source: United Republic of Tanzania, Tanzania Financial and Legal Management Upgrading Project (FILMUP), "The Legal Sector in Tanzania, Interim Report of the Legal Task Force," Unpublished report, Dar es Salaam, Tanzania, June 1995, p. 11. The Uganda figures reflect an increase in pay scales and the monetization of benefits or allowances not reflected in the Tanzania data.

salaries were essential. Judges and magistrates should be removed from the civil service pay scale and placed on a higher one—a treatment governments increasingly accorded other personnel whose effectiveness and impartiality were vital to the smooth functioning of the economy. Revenue collectors and the staff of investment authorities benefited from such treatment, and senior figures in the treasury or Ministry of Finance sometimes had their salaries "topped up" by contributions from multilateral agencies too.

Aid donors often insisted on "monetization" of benefits as well. Instead of receiving in-kind allowances for housing, utilities, and transportation, judges would see the money equivalent of these in their paychecks. The argument was that individual choices made in the marketplace would lead to more satisfactory living conditions, from the point of view of the judges, and relieve the courts of the burden of managing housing and extra transportation.

In Tanzania, where judges were especially poorly paid, Nyalali found himself among those in the "cautious" camp whose members wanted to retain allowances and perks, while other judges looked forward to the higher salaries. Although the housing stock for the judges did require maintenance and repair, the value of the housing allowance effectively adjusted automatically for inflation, while the real value of salaries could erode unless legislatures took action to adjust them frequently. In Nyalali's experience, the legislature had rarely done so, and unless the new terms of service contained a legal requirement to adjust salaries for inflation, in the future the judiciary could find itself facing tough times once again.

The effort to give people choice of private alternatives in the housing market and get the courts out of the business of managing property sounded fine on paper, said some judges. But the shortage of housing in many areas was such that personnel had little real choice and would necessarily depend on the good offices of one or two local leaders to find them a place to live, creating a potential conflict of interest. Monetization where there were no competitive housing markets and where transport options were still limited could aggravate the problems the judiciary faced. It would also increase the amount of time required for rotations and transfers to take effect, because it would mean that judicial staff would have to take time to "shop" for accommodation.

The proposed changes won a mixed reception from members of the public and judicial personnel. Uganda was one of the first to implement the new idea. Salaries improved dramatically, and housing was eliminated. In Kampala, the capital, a newspaper captured the ambivalent impressions the measure created on the street. Its coverage of the announcement of the new terms of service began, "It was heartwarming over the weekend to see President Museveni and the High Court judges on TV chatting in a very relaxed atmosphere."

One cannot help to recall that the judges just secured their *abyaffe* the other day. They are probably the only public servants, besides the URA [Uganda

Revenue Authority] and UIA [Uganda Investment Authority] staff, who do not have to steal to survive.

We do not know exactly how they secured their living wage from the cash-strapped state. Could be that their limited numbers made it easier. But one thing is certain, government was losing a lot by underpaying the judiciary.

Not only was the administration of justice botched up, but the state was losing too many cases. Those that involved heavy claims against government were drawing the treasury so much that in the end, it makes more sense to spend a little more in salaries and save a lot on unjustifiably fat claims against the state.

. . . Let us hope the happy judges will now dispense justice without fear or favour. And above all, let it not only be the state that has rewarded them whose interests they will watch out for, but all tax payers and residents of this country.[38]

MAKING REPUTATIONS MATTER

It was also vital to make reputations matter. Corruption would not diminish unless the people who staffed the courts, whatever their role, were convinced that how they behaved would have an impact on the esteem in which they were held and on their ability to rise within the service or retain their jobs. Several things were essential to make that happen. One was a bold gesture to signal a break with the past. Another was to create a flow of accurate information about performance. A third was to develop promotion scales for nonjudicial staff and lower-level magistrates, and to make criteria for advancement clear.

Public criticism of judicial corruption had long been "in the air," but it was often difficult to convince people to speak on the record or point to those whom they suspected so that the Judicial Service Commission and disciplinary boards could act. Wrote Ben Lobulu, a Tanzanian lawyer, "The Bar is aware of the tremendous powers that a judge has over a practising advocate. To antagonise a judge attracts the risk of dire consequences in case of a slip. This has inhibited advocates from coming out and telling what ails the judiciary. A judge would use the occasion of writing judgments to demolish the reputation of a critical advocate."[39]

Under pressure from foreign partners to clean up corruption in government, Tanzanian President Benjamin Mkapa, Chief Justice Nyalali, and other leaders turned to a special program being pioneered by a nongovernmental organization called Transparency International and to the World Bank's Economic Development Institute (EDI). Founded in 1955 to conduct interactive training

---

[38] Editorial, *Daily Topic* (Uganda), August 29, 1994, p. 3.
[39] Lobulu, "Corruption and the Administration of Justice," p. 89.

programs for developing-country officials, EDI operated very differently from the rest of the World Bank, with a heavy emphasis on participation from ordinary citizens.[40] Bank President James Wolfensohn had made taking aim at corruption one focus of EDI activity, while Transparency International helped pool ideas about how to combat the problem.

Together, the two organizations proposed an ambitious program of "National Integrity Workshops" and the development of a "National Integrity System."[41] The aim was to transform corruption into a "high-risk, low-return" undertaking through increased monitoring by a variety of groups, including the media, while placing integrity on the agenda of public sector leaders. It was important that people not rely on foreigners for solutions, the designers believed. Instead, nongovernmental associations, including members of the professions, should assume major responsibility for monitoring corrupt practices and for generating ideas about how to overcome them.

At the request of citizens and public officials in a country, EDI and Transparency International said they would facilitate the development of country-specific national integrity systems. Although the form of intervention varied slightly across countries, it typically began with a large-scale social survey to evaluate the extent and magnitude of corruption in the different branches and services of government. Typically carried out under the direction of international research teams working with local officials, the studies included interviews with thousands of respondents—far more than the average sample survey in the United States. The information the survey produced gave citizens a way to assess the forms and magnitude of corruption, district by district, within a country. It provided a way to confront officials with evidence that could not be dismissed as anecdotal or made up.

Next the program addressed itself to the "eight pillars" of the community: senior political leadership, "watchdog" agencies, parliament, civic groups, the judiciary, the media, the private sector, and administrative reform programs. Representatives of each "pillar" developed a paper on the problem of corruption and the role it could play in devising a solution. The papers and survey information were then discussed in a public forum, covered by the press. For the media, the event was an occasion to develop skills for reporting on governance in general and corruption problems in particular. A commission of local officials developed a final report and a publicly aired action plan. In Tanzania, these documents became known as the "Warioba Report,"[42] named after the commission head, Joseph Warioba, who delivered a document Transparency

[40] The EDI later became the World Bank Institute (WBI).
[41] For more information, see Petter Langseth and Rick Stapenhurst, "National Integrity System Country Studies," EDI Working Paper (Washington, D.C.: World Bank, 1997).
[42] United Republic of Tanzania, Presidential Commission of Inquiry against Corruption, *Report on the Commission on Corruption.*

International officials described as "a report the likes of which few countries have ever seen." They recalled, "It lambasted the country's institutions and their leaders, without exception, for the parlous state the country was in."[43]

Public officials were made accountable in several ways. In the late 1990s, World Bank loan agreements were conditional on action to reduce corruption, and the proposals citizens and officials offered at the integrity workshops provided locally devised plans whose pursuit World Bank officials would approve. Training of journalists to cover problems of corruption often continued after the initial burst of activity, to help develop solid investigative reporting skills and a cadre of corruption monitors.

It took courage to agree to support an integrity system. Both the surveys and the public discussions put reputations on the line. People often mentioned offenders or suspected offenders by name, and these allegations were passed on to disciplinary bodies for further investigation. The judiciary and other government bodies had to come up with proposals that sounded as though they would have an impact and be realistic, given the resources available for carrying them out.

Trust in the foreign personnel who worked on the projects was critical too. Judges cited the influence of Transparency International Director Jeremy Pope, a New Zealander who had worked with courts as director of the Law Department of the Commonwealth for over seventeen years. Pope had the confidence of many people and knew the issues well.

During the mid- to late 1990s, National Integrity Workshops were launched in Tanzania, Uganda, Zimbabwe, and Namibia, with varying degrees of success. Chief Justice Nyalali won accolades from program personnel for the "enlightened" way he addressed problems and for his concern to make the process work. He suspended two officials for misconduct and turned the cases over to the Judicial Service Commission. And within two years, the judiciary had established committees charged with supervising the conduct of judges and magistrates at regional, zonal, and national levels. But the program also created some awkward situations. For example, the attorney general's office attracted criticism when, for insufficient evidence, it failed to prosecute some of the civil servants the exercise fingered for corruption. The public appetite for action did not always sit happily with the need to respect the requirements of the law.

Although the judges as a group proved less enthusiastic about participating in Uganda, where the eminent Justice Benjamin Odoki had stood out as a strong advocate of the program, observers considered that overall the process worked better there than in Tanzania and other places. The judiciary gradually came around. The workshops were well received, and the inspector general of government started to carry out the action plan, which was extended to include

---

[43] Peter Eigen, "Overview," in Transparency International, Annual Report for 1997, http://www.transparency.de/introducing_ti/an_report97.html, accessed May 1998.

a parliamentary retreat on corruption, a regional conference on good government and private sector development, as well as training to help journalists develop investigative reporting skills. The Ministry of Justice and attorney general aided the program.

The National Integrity Workshops were one way to increase the importance of reputation in the battle against corruption. They helped enlist journalists in the acquisition and dissemination of information. They helped encourage people to use the complaints processes in place. They put the issue on the agendas of senior decision makers. What they did not do was address the problem of making individual reputations matter within the judiciary itself.

Another way to wean people away from corrupt practices was to make performance matter for salary increases and advancement within the profession. This was difficult when resources often did not exist to grant pay raises and when the numbers of senior posts were limited. In several common law African countries, magistrates said that they were unaware of the criteria used in promotions or found the little information they were provided confusing. Lack of a clear career path made many magistrates think they would inevitably remain where they were, in low-wage positions and often in remote communities. Said one, "The corruption of Grade I magistrates is because they cannot rise unless they get a degree and a diploma. Because they can't rise, reputation doesn't mean anything."[44] A Botswana magistrate similarly complained that the decision of the chief justice in his country to decline to support additional education for magistrates produced demoralization. It seemed to cut off the ability to rise within the ranks. A Ugandan magistrate remarked, "The criteria for advancement within the judiciary are unclear. It is very difficult for magistrates to rise right now. Promotions to the High Court go to the advocates."[45]

CHARACTER

Like civil delay, corruption was a problem that required vigilance on the part of court administrators everywhere in the world. Some aspects of human nature varied little across societies. The inclination to use public office for private gain knew no national boundaries. Yet differences in norms, in the risks of punishment, and in the importance of reputation produced wide disparities in the degree to which this kind of self-interested behavior could flourish.[46]

---

[44] Magistrate, interview with author, Masaka, Uganda, February 6, 1996.
[45] Magistrate, interview with author, Mbarara, Uganda, January 29, 1996.
[46] For an interesting overview of the general issues, see Paul Collier, "How to Reduce Corruption," Paper presented to the Conference on Good Governance and Sustainable Development, Abidjan, Côte d'Ivoire, November 22–24, 1999, World Bank, Washington, D.C., November 1999.

In Tanzania, as in much of Africa in this period, street talk often accorded greater importance to the quality of the person as a source of good or bad behavior, than to institutional design. It was popular to think that finding the right people, men and women of good character, was what mattered. These views surfaced in the country's National Integrity Workshops. The Warioba Report noted, "One citizen who met the Commission expressed concern regarding the dispensation of justice by the High Court after the present Judges retire. He said that, although there is corruption in the High Court, it is only a few Judges who are involved. Many are diligent and faithful. His concern was that should the present Judges, upon retirement, be replaced by others nominated from amongst serving Resident Magistrates, corruption will flourish in the High Court."[47] In the citizen's view, individual example could help mold the judiciary as well as popular expectations about the rule of law. In a world in which personal connections still shaped resources and advancement, the persona of leaders exercised a powerful effect on confidence in government.

There could be little doubt that character was centrally important. Yet at the same time, the diagnosis of corruption laid out in successive investigations by the commissions of inquiry suggested that even the best men and women could be placed in circumstances where the pressures to deviate from ethics rules were enormous. To rely on "finding good people" as a solution diverted attention from the need to think creatively about ways to redesign organizations. The court had to work to reduce the numbers of points at which influence could be brought to bear. It had to pay attention to the wage issue. At the same time it had to raise the risks that corrupt behavior would be caught and punished.

[47] United Republic of Tanzania, Presidential Commission of Inquiry against Corruption, *Report on the Commission on Corruption*, p. 176.

CHAPTER FIFTEEN

The Democratic Gamble

DURING THE LATE 1980s and early 1990s, the Tanzanian court had entered into a delicate entente with the legislature and the executive. Nyalali tried to use this space to launch a wide range of reforms. He reached out to the international community for help. Chief justices of most other courts in the region did the same. Nevertheless, Nyalali was worried. The improvements he sought would take time to materialize. Each effort to change an aspect of organization or practice had revealed more problems.

The question in the back of the chief justice's mind was whether there might be some other way to help ensure that the opening created in the mid-1980s would endure. Finding domestic constituents or stakeholders, people with an interest in an independent and effective court system, was important. His thoughts turned to the structure of the political system. What would make it in the interests of the politicians to support an independent judiciary?

Nyalali had little doubt that a multiparty system would work to the advantage of his institution. If a party and its leaders thought there was some uncertainty about whether it would win a majority in the next election, an independent and effective judiciary would look more attractive. A politician could never know for certain what an opposition party might do to its critics if it came to power. In too many countries, those who harbored different ideas found themselves in jail. While judges could not prevent bad laws from winning adoption, they could strike down provisions that were inconsistent with the meaning of the constitution, deny them the force of law, and ensure that jailed opponents received a fair hearing. Nyalali also felt that "[c]ourage among judicial officers is easier to nurture and develop in a multiparty democracy than under a one-party regime."[1] Institutions could shape character, and vice versa.

As the 1990s began, Tanzania had a single-party system of government. Then in an unusual turn of events, Nyalali's wish began to come true. In 1991, the chief justice received a call from the president, Ali Hassan Mwinyi. Although he had retained chairmanship of the ruling party, "Mwalimu" Julius Nyerere had stepped down as president in 1986. The party leadership had settled on Mwinyi as his successor. Now Mwinyi asked to meet. "I thought it must be a case of delay the president was worried about. I was very surprised when instead he spoke about his decision to appoint a commission to consider the advisability of a multiparty system! I was even more surprised when he said he thought I would be the right person to chair the commission."[2] Nyalali had reservations, but the president went on to explain further. "He said that the commission would be of unique and exceptional importance. It was a delicate exercise. It required a person who was highly respected and that as far as he knew I fit that description. The commission would be made up of a disparate group of people, and it was essential to have someone who could manage contending views."

COMMISSIONS AND JUDICIAL INDEPENDENCE

Nyalali agonzied about the decision. The president's request raised complicated issues about the ability of judges to offer "advisory opinions" or to sit on commissions. These actions themselves could place the independence of the judiciary at risk.

Within the common law tradition, national courts divided over these matters. The American federal courts anchored one end of the spectrum. All judges had to be careful that their actions did not appear to make them creatures of the legislature or the executive branch, and providing abstract advice could convey the wrong impression.[3] Moreover, abstract opinions could never anticipate all of the circumstances that might affect the application of a law to a concrete set of facts. The adversarial process inevitably placed more information and more argument on the table for consideration. Therefore, deciding matters of interpretation in the context of live cases and controversies would

---

[1] Francis L. Nyalali, Keynote speech delivered at a seminar organized by the Commonwealth Judicial Education Institute for judges in East and Central Africa, Sheraton Hotel, Kampala, Uganda, February 26, 1996.
[2] Francis L. Nyalali, interview with author, May 29, 1996.
[3] There were occasional departures from this view. For example, John Marshall served as a delegate to the Virginia Constitutional Convention, Abe Fortas wrote letters to the president, and Earl Warren chaired the inquiry into the Kennedy assassination. But for the most part, judges in the federal courts steered clear of this kind of interaction.

yield a more incremental but more sensible development of the law. And finally, the prestige of the courts and the law could suffer if decisions in real controversies did not mimic the general advice judges offered.

Service on commissions was also suspect. Judges had specialized knowledge of the legal system, and their advice on legal issues could be helpful.[4] But service on commissions dealing with other sorts of matters could jeopardize the appearance of impartiality. If a judge was associated with a position or group of people as a result of participation in a commission, there was always a risk that someone might consider him or her predisposed toward a particular outcome. Worse, the image of the court might be tainted.

The English and Canadian courts were more open to the idea of judges providing advice and sitting on commissions. It was a duty of early English judges to offer answers to legal questions posed by the executive branch. Although this practice diminished after the 1700s, it did not disappear. Likewise, the Canadian Supreme Court offered general opinions referred by legislatures on the grounds that this practice was consistent with the text of the Canadian constitution (the British North America Act). After World War II, civil law systems in continental Europe, as well as the International Court of Justice, also permitted advisory opinions, at least with respect to constitutional issues.[5]

President Mwinyi's request put the chief justice in an awkward spot. If he accepted, Nyalali would incur the attendant risks that chairing commissions could create for a court. Moreover, the task of this particular body would almost certainly require Nyalali to offer advisory opinions.

Nyalali thought about the difficulties at the time. "The exercise involved a lot of risk to the judiciary. Such reports on controversial matters were known to have been rejected and even condemned in the past." People would have a hard time separating Nyalali the individual from Nyalali the head of the court.

---

[4] E. Wayne Thode, *Reporter's Notes to Code of Judicial Conduct* (Chicago: American Bar Association, 1973), p. 26; and Lisa L. Milord, *The Development of the ABA Judicial Code* (Chicago: American Bar Association, 1992), p. 33.

[5] For more on the debate about advisory opinions and service on commissions, see Stewart Jay, *Most Humble Servants: The Advisory Role of Early Judges* (New Haven: Yale University Press, 1997); James L. Huffman and MardiLyn Saathoff, "Advisory Opinions and Canadian Constitutional Development: The Supreme Court's Reference Jurisdiction," *Minnesota Law Review*, 74 (1990), pp. 1251–1336; William M. Landes and Richard A. Posner, "The Economics of Anticipatory Adjudication," *Journal of Legal Studies*, 23 (June 1994), pp. 683–719; Louis Favoreu, "American and European Models of Constitutional Jurisprudence," in David Clark, ed., *Comparative and International Law: Essays in Honor of John Henry Merryman* (Berlin: Duncker & Humbolt, 1990), pp. 105–120; Kenneth James Keith, *The Extent of the Advisory Jurisdiction of the International Court of Justice* (Leyden: A. W. Sijthoff, 1971); Joseph Jaconelli, "Note: Hypothetical Disputes, Moot Points of Law, and Advisory Opinions," *Law Quarterly Review*, 101 (October 1985), pp. 587–626; and A. W. Brian Simpson, "The Judges and the Vigilant State," *The Denning Law Journal*, 1989 (1989), pp. 145–167.

"I knew if the commission failed, people would not see differences between me and the judiciary. They would condemn the judiciary. But if we succeeded, the image of the judiciary would be greatly improved. Putting the judiciary at the heart of the process could have a positive effect, too."[6]

The decision Nyalali faced was one that judges in other countries in the region would encounter, in various forms, as well. In Uganda at about the same time, Justice Benjamin Odoki was asked to chair a commission to prepare a new draft constitution. In South Africa, judges were drawn into the consultations about the country's new constitution. Justice Richard Goldstone, by then an international figure, deliberated about the dilemmas in print and concluded there was no simple yes or no about what a judge should do. He decided that "particularly when the Constitution is in flux and fundamental legal rights are being debated by the nation the judges have a duty to join the debate. They are clearly well-qualified to do so. If they enter that debate in a non-partisan manner they can hardly be accused with any justification of displaying bias or interfering with their independence or that of their colleagues."[7] The words were similar to those Nyalali used to describe his own reasoning, when he made his decision to accept the president's assignment.

CONSULTATION

It was no surprise that Tanzania's leaders decided to consider adoption of a multiparty system in this period. During the previous two years, Africa had started to experience what some called a "second liberation." Beginning with the small country of Benin, in West Africa, one government after another had responded to mounting popular anger about economic mismanagement, corruption, and other matters by taking steps to expand opportunities for participation in political life. Some had paused after lifting the severest restrictions on the freedom of the press and the freedom of association. Others had legalized opposition parties and sponsored multiparty elections. The wave of change had started slightly earlier in Francophone countries, where a series of national conferences to redraft constitutions took place. Zambia was the first of the Anglophone countries to follow suit.

The changes had several sources.[8] Economics mattered. During the 1970s

---

[6] Francis L. Nyalali, interview with author, May 29, 1996.
[7] Richard Goldstone, "Do Judges Speak Out?" *South African Law Journal*, 111 (1994), p. 268.
[8] For analysis of these changes, see Jennifer Widner, ed., *Economic Change and Political Liberalization in Sub-Saharan Africa* (Baltimore: Johns Hopkins University Press, 1994); Celestin Monga, *The Anthropology of Anger* (Boulder, CO: Lynne Rienner, 1996); Michael Bratton and Nicolas van de Walle, *Democratic Experiments in Africa: Regime Transitions in Comparative Perspective* (Cambridge: Cambridge University Press, 1997); and Pearl

and early 1980s, a nearly continent-wide trend toward declining rates of per capita growth in gross domestic product sparked growing popular anger. In the mid-1980s, these problems led many governments to adopt structural adjustment programs in exchange for support from international financial institutions. The programs usually entailed cutbacks, an end to government intervention in many different aspects of economic life, and sales of public companies. To reduce deficits, political leaders usually had to lay off civil servants. It grew harder to purchase the loyalty of citizens, as opportunities for patronage declined.

In the late 1980s, models from afar helped crystallize the calls for change ringing in the streets. The "CNN effect" was potent. BBC and CNN news reports about the fall of the Berlin Wall, new multiparty systems in Eastern and Central Europe, and the movement toward majority rule in South Africa provided a vocabulary and a method. As parallel changes started in Africa, the residents of one country could also use the radio to learn from the experiences of neighbors. The spirit was contagious.

Aggrieved publics had to organize to convince ruling parties to yield. Nearly everywhere, lawyers played important roles in the leadership of new "prodemocracy" movements. They formed opposition parties, lobbied for the lifting of restrictions on speech and association, hammered out drafts of new constitutions, argued cases before the courts, and ran workshops to explain "democracy" to people less well off. They were not always successful. They often landed in jail themselves. The organizations and parties they founded often broke down amid internecine conflict. Too often, they found it difficult to reach out beyond capitals to the countryside, where the majority of people lived. But they were important figures in the process of change.

The period of "the second liberation" had its awful sides as well. In a few places, heightened competition for political power proved the spark that ignited powder kegs. Two of Tanzania's neighbors, Rwanda and Burundi, as well as the Republic of the Congo (known as Congo-Brazzaville) and the Democratic Republic of the Congo (formerly Zaire) entered a period of ghastly civil strife. The twin of expanded political freedom too often appeared to be the collapse of order and a descent into violence.

In the mid-1980s, Botswana was the only significant multiparty system in Africa, outside of the small island nation of Mauritius and single party-dominant Senegal.[9] During this period, its own elections became more competitive, especially at the local level. Most of the other countries of common law eastern and southern Africa responded cautiously to the new democratic trend. In 1991,

---

Robinson, "The National Conference Phenomenon in Francophone Africa," *Comparative Studies in Society and History*, 36, 3 (1994): 575–610.

[9] Zimbabwe was nominally multiparty, but violence against opposition parties persisted.

when the president approached Chief Justice Nyalali to preside over the commission, the governments of Kenya, Uganda, Tanzania, Zimbabwe, and Malawi still groped for a way to respond to internal and external pressures for change.

In Tanzania, as in several other countries, distinguished leaders took steps to meet democracy activists halfway. In 1990, former President Julius Nyerere shocked many of his countrymen by casually announcing at a press conference that the events in Eastern Europe would soon affect Tanzanians too. He urged Chama Cha Mapinduzi, the ruling political party—then the only political party—to consider initiating political reform on its own. "The one party is not Tanzania's ideology; having one party is not God's will. One party has its own limitations," he explained to his listeners, "It tends to go to sleep."[10] He launched the debate on political change by stating that it would no longer be treasonable to talk about opposition parties.[11] The rumor in the streets was that the former president had "toured the country in 1986 and 1987 to 'dynamise' the party [and] . . . what he saw shocked him because as president he had been shielded from the rot."[12]

By the time of the controversial press conference, there were already signs that opposition parties had started to form behind the scenes, although they remained loose alliances of lawyers, clergy, and academics. Tanzanian political scientist Mwesiga Baregu described what happened next. "For a while, CCM [Chama Cha Mapinduzi] was in disarray; leaders contradicted each other and sometimes themselves. Secretary General Rashidi Kawawa denied any connection between Eastern European socialism and Tanzania's *ujamaa*. President Mwinyi, the party's vice-chairman, argued that multipartyism was diversionary and potentially divisive. He raised the spectre of tribalism and the possibility of national disintegration. . . ."[13] Nyerere repeated his challenge a short time later, and by September 1990, President Mwinyi had moderated his stance and indicated that the country could move toward a multiparty system if there was popular support for doing so.

It was in this context that the president approached Nyalali to chair the commission on whether Tanzania should have "one party or many." On March 5, 1991, he officially launched the Presidential Commission on Political Change. The chief justice would serve as chairman and Abdulwahid M. Borafia, deputy

---

[10] As quoted in Mwesiga Baregu, "The Rise and Fall of the One-Party State in Tanzania," in Jennifer A. Widner, ed., *Economic Change and Political Liberalization in Sub-Saharan Africa* (Baltimore: Johns Hopkins University Press, 1994), p. 169.

[11] United Republic of Tanzania, Presidential Commission on Single Party or Multiparty System in Tanzania, *Report and Recommendations of the Commission on the Democratic System in Tanzania* (Nyalali Report), vol. 1 (Dar es Salaam, Tanzania: Presidential Commission on Single Party or Multiparty System in Tanzania, 1991, English edition 1992), p. 67.

[12] K. I. Tambila, "The Transition to Multiparty Democracy in Tanzania: Some History and Missed Opportunities," *Verfassung und Recht im Übersee*, 28, 4 (1995), pp. 475–476.

[13] Baregu, "The Rise and Fall of the One-Party State in Tanzania," p. 169.

chairman. Julius Sepeku was secretary to the commission. The remaining twenty members were drawn ten each from the mainland and Zanzibar. They spanned the political spectrum, including "one person who, I was told, was a self-described anarchist," Nyalali said.

The executive summary of the final report reflected on the reasons for constituting the commission. The country had plunged into a deep economic crisis during the 1980s, the authors noted. Central planning had crippled the economy, and people were beginning to question the decisions of the policy makers in Dodoma and Dar. They associated the policies with the single-party system. Moreover, growing differences in standards of living and life opportunities had started to breed greater pluralism in political points of view. Finally, during the late 1980s, the ruling party, Chama Cha Mapinduzi, had lost much of its vigor. As Nyerere had remarked, "the Party had failed to control leaders who embezzled public property and those who had formed the habit of intimidating people."[14]

The position of Zanzibar vis-à-vis the mainland was also a growing focus of concern and attention. The decision to consider a shift to multiparty rule was seen by some as a way to defuse tensions between the island and the rest of the country.

Nyalali explained to the members and to the public that the commission's terms of reference were to "find out what the people of Tanzania want." "Let's start with their views," he exhorted his team. "Let us find out the real state of affairs."[15] The commission would need to reach out to Tanzanians from all walks of life and all regions, and its members would need to listen carefully to the views of thousands of people.

The commission members discussed ways to organize the task of canvassing opinion. Many years before, Pius Msekwa, one of the commission members, had led a special inquiry into the collapse of the rule of law. Although the legislature had not acted on most of his committee's recommendations, the report was held in esteem and it continued to provide a benchmark, twenty years later. The investigation he had led was broadly consultative and included meetings with many ordinary citizens. The methodology of the Msekwa Report provided one model.[16] Next door in Uganda a similar enterprise was also under way. In 1989, Justice Benjamin Odoki accepted the chairmanship of the Uganda Constitutional Commission, with a mandate to seek general agreement on the ideals the country's new constitution should include. Commission

---

[14] United Republic of Tanzania, Presidential Commission on Single Party or Multiparty System in Tanzania, *Report and Recommendations*, p. 67.
[15] As recounted in Francis L. Nyalali, interview with author, May 29, 1996.
[16] United Republic of Tanzania, Judicial System Review Commission, *Report of the Judicial System Review Commission* (Msekwa Report) (Dar es Salaam, Tanzania: Judicial System Review Commission, 1977).

members had fanned out across the country to explain their task and to obtain views from a broad cross section of society through seminars and debates.[17] In South Africa, the constitution-making process also invited public comment and contributions.

In Tanzania, the commission members decided to collect opinions in six main ways. They would sponsor a series of public meetings across the country, where people could express their views in informal hearings. They would ask for research papers and offer people from different walks of life an opportunity to draft memoranda on any of the subjects that were part of the commission's investigation. The staff would monitor views expressed in the newspapers, which by this time included several lively Kiswahili papers under private ownership. Evidence from a questionnaire, or survey, would yield additional information from people the commission might not reach at hearings. Finally, a few of the commission members would travel abroad to see how multiparty systems worked in similar countries and to learn about the difficulties that attended the transition from one-party rule.

To work efficiently, the members divided into seven subcommittees. Nyalali recalled that "the fear of failure was very high. We therefore established a methodology and a pace never seen here before."[18] The members made an elaborate chart so that each working committee knew when it had to start and complete each task. "It was like a jigsaw puzzle. Each step had to be carried out according to the schedule. Everyone knew that a delay in one of the subcommittees would mean a delay in all of them, because of the way we organized the tasks."

Great fanfare accompanied the beginning of the commission's work. Because members had a responsibility to sample public opinion on a wide range of issues, the publicity was a way to prepare communities for the visits they would receive. Shortly after the first meeting, the chief justice spoke on Radio Tanzania and explained the job of the commission. The radio also rebroadcast coverage of retired President Julius Nyerere's farewell speech of the year before, along with excerpts from the other 1990 speeches in which Nyerere urged people to think about the political choices they faced. Radio on the mainland and in Zanzibar, as well as Zanzibar television, produced special programs on the choice between a single-party system and a multiparty system.

---

[17] Benjamin J. Odoki, "Writing of a Democratic Constitution," *East African Journal of Peace and Human Rights*, 1, 2 (1993), p. 201. See also Oliver Furley and James Katalikawe, "Constitutional Reform in Uganda: The New Approach," *African Affairs*, 96 (1997), pp. 243–260; on the general trend in a West African context, Victor T. Le Vine, "The Fall and Rise of Constitutionalism in West Africa," *Journal of Modern African Studies*, 35, 2 (1997), pp. 181–206; and on the details of the South African case, Heinz Klug, "Participation in the Design: Constitution-Making in South Africa," *Review of Constitutional Studies*, 3, 1 (1996), pp. 18–59.
[18] Francis L. Nyalali, interview with author, May 29, 1996.

"We feared there would be a tendency not to publish news about the commission," Nyalali said. "We impressed on the president that we wanted the report to be public. He made that commitment, and the newspapers reported it. Later, when some officials expressed reservations about publishing the recommendations, we were able to overcome the resistance by referring to that earlier commitment."[19]

The commission members traveled throughout the country, holding 1,016 private and public meetings with citizens. An estimated 36,299 people participated in these. The exercise took place in two periods of two months each, the first beginning in early May 1991 and the second in early July. It was designed to tap popular opinion, not the views of the country's political elite. Therefore, the commission did not meet with members of the armed forces or the government, except for the retired president of Zanzibar, Aboud Jumbe, and the retired president of the Republic, Julius Nyerere. To further inform its deliberations, the commission drew on research papers, newspaper articles, over a thousand memoranda submitted by individuals and private groups, and 16,348 questionnaires.

"Our system worked so well that we started to beat our schedule," Nyalali remembered. "A meeting that was supposed to last for two days would take five hours."[20] The pace proved too rough at times. The deputy chair and another member suffered strokes during the months of the commission's work, and Nyalali himself fell ill from fatigue at one point and had to take a brief break. Loyce commented that her husband was often immersed in his work at night, but he became especially so during this period. "Sometimes he did not even hear us, he was so involved with what he was reading or writing. I would go work in the garden. Eventually he would come out to see me in the flowers, and we would chat or go for a walk with the children."[21]

"With our disparate group it was important to go through this exercise," Nyalali commented. "The only way to find common ground was to collect evidence of public opinion and use it to help focus the discussion on real interests." Otherwise, it would have been too easy for commission members to fall into disagreement about abstract principles. The difference between "real interests" and "abstract positions" was not necessarily as great as Nyalali's distinction suggested, but the kinds of concerns embodied in the statements of ordinary people about what they valued most helped ground the high-flung vocabulary the political activists used. Often what ordinary citizens wanted could be achieved in a way the politicians had not envisioned.

In drafting the final recommendations, the members only disagreed about whether the country should have a federal system or not. "We ended up being

[19] Francis L. Nyalali, interview with author, May 29, 1996.
[20] Ibid.
[21] Loyce Phares, interview with author, May 29, 1996.

so closely knit that when we had a final party here at the house, commission members shed tears. We had grown into a friendly, close, personal group. After that, we always addressed one another in a special way when we met."[22]

"In a way," Nyalali commented, "my judicial experience on the bench made a difference to the work of the commission. We saw our task as involving a resolution or decision of a controversy or dispute between two sides or parties — those who did not want change and those who did." He remarked, "As in a courtroom case, there was bound to be an area of common ground or consensus between the contending parties and another area [in which] . . . matters [remained in hot dispute]. . . . Our job was to identify these two areas with clarity and then to proceed to resolve the controversy in a manner which was consistent with the established consensus." The chief justice observed that this approach usually led to agreement. People would be persuaded. "I was thus not surprised when the report prevailed even upon those who had strongly opposed even the very idea of appointing the commission."[23]

THE NYALALI REPORT

In preparing its recommendations, the commission found itself confronted with a delicate task. The members perceived tension between people's straightforward answers to close-ended questions on the surveys, on the one hand, and their comments in open-ended discussions. The information the committee gathered contained seeming contradictions and would require interpretation.

When asked straight-out whether they favored a one-party system or a multiparty system, without necessarily thinking about the implications of their choices, most people cast their votes for the status quo. As measured through the written questionnaires, public opinion on the Tanzanian mainland was 79.7 percent in favor of continuing the single-party system, while a slimmer majority of Zanzibaris polled similarly. The open discussions with the subcommittees yielded much the same result. The champions of the single-party system argued that those who supported legalization of opposition parties were just hungry for power. Some thought political pluralism would create irreconcilable divisions. Others said allowing political competition would increase inequality, "enhance neocolonialism," and make it easier for other countries to recolonize Tanzania. Still others believed multipartyism to be an alien idea, either because it "comes from outside" or because it finds support mostly among the educated and privileged.[24] "The most cynical question repeatedly raised at the commission's hear-

---

[22] Francis L. Nyalali, interview with author, May 29, 1996.
[23] Francis L. Nyalali, personal communication, October 1998.
[24] United Republic of Tanzania, Presidential Commission on Single Party or Multiparty System in Tanzania, *Report and Recommendations*, p. 78.

ings," wrote political scientist Mwesiga Baregu, "was: If one CCM is such a burden in terms of extracting resources [such as] . . . taxes, sundry contributions, chickens, etc . . . what will life under many CCMs be like?"[25]

Opinion polls are not always the best way to discover what people really believe, just as the first statement from a witness, plaintiff, or defendant does not necessarily provide a reliable indication of what happened in an incident. Usually polls allow no room for nuanced answers, for considering how context might affect preferences, or for deliberation. In Uganda, Justice Odoki had rejected the idea of administering a survey as a way to assess views. He defended his stance. "It has . . . been claimed that the [Uganda] Commission was using an unscientific methodology because it did not circulate a questionnaire as a means of collecting views. The Commission is not carrying out social research, but inquiring about the constitutional views of the people of Uganda. This cannot be expressed in questionnaires." Odoki expanded, "We decided against administering a questionnaire because of their vulnerability at the grassroots level. The process could have been rigged by unscrupulous and opportunistic elements of society. Moreover, such questionnaires are difficult to complete by the masses. The commission would have needed extensive resources to administer such questionnaires."[26] Odoki said his commission thought that open-ended questions, which people could answer or not as they wished, would yield more detailed information than a standard survey.

In Tanzania, Nyalali decided not to take the results of the questionnaires and the meetings as final. Rather, he sought to probe, to arrive at an accurate interpretation of what they meant. He began by asking under what conditions people had offered their views. The commission's report remarked that "[s]ome districts in Tanzania form [a] geographical border with countries which are experiencing political turmoil. These districts have been receiving refugees from neighbouring countries quite regularly. . . . [Many of these refugees] have associated war and civil strife with political pluralism. . . . [Residents' views were therefore] influenced by the belief that a single party political system is a prerequisite for peace and tranquillity."[27] The commission also considered the effect of low educational standards. It commented that "[i]n rural areas, especially, people did not seem to be conversant with the concept of [a] political system [or] the advantages and disadvantages of a particular system. . . . Many . . . spent a lot of time contradicting themselves."[28]

Second, the commission noted that both advocates of the single-party system and those who favored legalizing opposition parties shared many points of view. Both sides wanted reform. There was basic agreement on the need for "more

[25] Baregu, "The Rise and Fall of the One-Party State in Tanzania," p. 171.
[26] Odoki, "Writing of a Democratic Constitution," p. 222.
[27] United Republic of Tanzania, Presidential Commission on Single Party or Multiparty System in Tanzania, *Report and Recommendations*, p. 69.
[28] Ibid.

democracy," in the sense of expanding freedom of association. People did not believe that civic associations should have to be part of the ruling party. There was also common ground that more than one candidate ought to be allowed to contest the presidency, so that voters could cast more than a yes or no vote. Majorities in both groups said they believed the National Assembly/House of Representatives, not the ruling party, should be supreme. There were many other points on which the two sides concurred, including the need to distinguish the roles of the party and the civil service, the desire to make politicians more accountable to the people and to prevent them from using political activity to enrich themselves, the importance of term limits for elected office holders, and equality of opportunity to contest elections.

The commission concluded that ". . . many of the people who prefer the continuation of the single-party political system want certain changes to be made in the current system. However, an in-depth study of some of the changes being demanded in regard to the inadequacies of democracy in the single-party system cannot be effected but in political pluralism."[29] As in many of his speeches, in a talk two years later Nyalali underscored the contribution of multipartyism to accountability. Referring to the commission's exercise, he observed that "[t]here is consensus among the people that Tanzanian leadership at all levels is remote in the sense of being unrepresentative of and unaccountable to the people; and that appropriate change is required so as to establish leadership which represents the interests of and is accountable to the people. . . ."[30]

The report also contained a number of asides that perhaps reveal the commissioners' own sense of what was right for the country and of what entered the calculus. For example, one part addressed itself to the problem of making leaders accountable. It expounded:

> Accountability of leadership very much depends on the nature of a political system. In a system which constitutionally provides for one party, where the sole Party exercises monopoly in politics and the economy, the leadership very often becomes more accountable to the party leadership rather than the people. It is evident that mono-party politics in Tanzania displays many defects in regard to political and economic monopolisation. Below we mention some of these defects:
>   1) The concept of party supremacy, which is enshrined in both the Constitutions of the United Republic of Tanzania and the Revolutionary Government of Zanzibar, means that the three constituent organs of the

---

[29] Ibid., p. 123.

[30] Francis L. Nyalali, "Intervention on Democratization," Unpublished speech to the annual seminar of DANIDA (Danish Development Cooperation) advisers in Tanzania, Dar es Salaam, Tanzania, April 22–23, 1994.

State, namely the Executive, the Legislature, and the Judiciary, are first and foremost accountable to the Party. This system had rendered the performance of the organs of the State ineffective.

2) The Constitution requires that aspirants for parliamentary elections must be members of Chama Cha Mapinduzi. This system results in having representatives who are more accountable to the Party rather than the electorate. . . .

The passage concluded, "Both government and elected leaders would be more accountable to the population under the multiparty system."[31]

The commission also recognized the limits of what a change in the rules of political life could accomplish. The members carefully reviewed the experiences of Botswana, Mauritius, Nigeria, and Senegal in an effort to distill the lessons these countries offered. Although much taken with the example of stability amid serious political competition in Mauritius, they pointed to weaknesses in the other countries—weaknesses Tanzania would need to avoid. For example, they noted that although opposition political parties were gaining strength in Botswana, one-party dominance was promoted by the ability of the minister of local government, lands, and housing to nominate additional members of urban councils, and the absence of any subventions to help political parties enter the arena. The Senegalese example was less helpful, in their view, again partly because of the limits the government set on right of association and its recourse to preventive detention laws. The commission members concluded that "Senegal is an illustration of political pluralism without the expansion of democracy."[32]

The commission drew several lessons from the experiences of these other African countries.

(1) There is a greater chance for human rights to be protected under multi-party political systems than would be the case under a [single] party;

(2) Political pluralism provides a wider opportunity for people to participate in making decisions that affect them through their own representatives;

(3) In countries in which political pluralism has been successfully practised for a long time, [a] democratic culture . . . has been established among the people. This is a formidable protection against reversion to mono-partism.

---

[31] United Republic of Tanzania, Presidential Commission on Single Party or Multiparty System in Tanzania, *Report and Recommendations*, pp. 59–60.
[32] Ibid., p. 65.

(4) In some countries, like Nigeria and Ghana, it has been easier to re-establish military rule because a democratic multi-party political culture has not taken root among the people; and

(5) We have also learned that political pluralism is not a sufficient condition for democracy. It is quite possible for [a] multi-party system to go hand in hand with violation of human rights. Senegal is a case in point.[33]

Finally, the commissioners tried to reply to the concerns they had heard. They acknowledged that political pluralism was potentially destabilizing. It was certainly possible for parties to organize along ethnic or religious lines, for example. It was also likely that on occasion, supporters of one side or another would become vengeful, breaking the bounds of civility and causing disruption in parts of the country, just as occasionally happened in the single-party system. Further, if political groupings paralleled divisions between mainlanders and Zanzibaris, trouble might ensue. The commissioners also noted that although foreign interference was possible under any system, where there were poorly funded opposition parties seeking to gain a voice, the prospect of striking deals to secure financial support from abroad would be very tempting.

But the advantages outweighed the disadvantages. The commissioners placed a high premium on preserving human rights, and they argued that only a multi-party system permitted the latitude of choice prescribed in documents such as the Universal Declaration of Human Rights. Further, they suggested that under one-party government a substantial proportion of the population of voting age was effectively without the franchise. Those who were not members of the ruling party were simply denied the opportunity to participate in political life.

> . . . there are also some people who simply may not feel like joining any party at all. All that they want to see is a stable government which caters for their wishes. We are saying that political pluralism does not necessarily mean that every adult Tanzanian will join a political party. But this will be upon the individual's free will to decide.
>
> The important thing is that every (Tanzanian) person will be free to join a political party of his choice.[34]

A multiparty system could also ease the problems of political succession, the commission argued. The opposition would keep a "shadow cabinet" ready and waiting so that when an incumbent government failed to live up to expectations, an alternative was available. Above all, the threat of loss at the ballot box

---

[33] Ibid., p. 66.
[34] Ibid., p. 129.

will make leaders more accountable to the voting public and thereby counteract self-aggrandizement. Balancing the weight of the evidence, then, the commissioners concluded that Tanzania was best served by a transition to a multiparty system.

The report's authors sought to minimize the risks of a transition by extending their recommendations in several ways. They were concerned that absent a political culture supportive of multiparty competition, the first elections could prove destabilizing. Thus, they proposed a transition that would take place over three years, during which people would be given an opportunity to discuss the plans and to learn about the process, with the aim of building "a new political culture of competition without resorting to violence."[35] Even more important, they proposed that the legislation regarding political parties require that all parties be national in character and have substantial numbers of members from both the mainland and Zanzibar, to dampen incentives for secession or division. They also suggested that the union be reconfigured to establish a federal system, with a union government, a Zanzibar government, and a mainland government.

After dispatching their main task, Nyalali and his fellow commission members took the occasion to explain that if the country adopted a multiparty system, a number of other changes in constitutional provisions, laws, and institutions would prove essential. It was a fine opportunity to communicate, in a neutral way, some of the court's concerns about the need for law reform.

The authors were especially critical of passages in the constitution on human rights, redrafted only a few years before. "The Constitution should be written in such a way that it does not allow these rights to be given by one hand and taken away by another,"[36] the authors stated emphatically. The commissioners urged that the human rights as stipulated in the Universal Declaration of Human Rights should feature prominently in the constitution. Drafters should avoid imposing limitations on these rights, although they conceded that limitations "accepted in international covenants" were reasonable—for example, limitations to protect the rights of others, to control and prevent the spreading of diseases, to prevent or combat disasters, and to maintain peace and security. In conformity with international standards, however, certain rights, such as equality before the law, the right to participate in national public affairs, and the right of an individual not to be prosecuted for criminal offenses committed prior to the enactment of an appropriate law, should never be subject to limitation.[37]

Finally, at the end of their report and recommendations, the commission

[35] Ibid., p. 133.
[36] Ibid., p. 106.
[37] Ibid., p. 145–146.

members set forth a list of laws that required revision or reform. Courts must enforce the laws on the books. With the proposed changes in the constitution, some laws or acts of parliament would become unconstitutional, while others would be "bad law," which the courts nonetheless would have to enforce, at the peril of their own legitimacy in the eyes of the public. The commissioners urged the government to change these laws of its own accord and not wait for the courts to strike down offending provisions. "We recommend that certain laws should be amended because they either deny or constrain the rights and freedoms of the people. . . . [M]any . . . are antiquated or have become out of date and should not be on our statute books. Some should be repealed and others should be amended . . . either by the office of the Attorney General or the Law Reform Commission."[38] The commission prepared a separate volume of its report to detail the legislation in question and the modifications required. The targets included the Preventive Detention Act, 1962—the legislation that had caused such trouble in the 1970s.

In May 1992, the legislature passed a bill to adopt a multiparty system. The bill amended the constitution to provide for the change. Tanzania began to join the ranks of the countries that were part of the new wave of political change spreading across the continent.

But public optimism was tempered the next day. Only twenty-four hours later, the parliament passed a Political Parties Bill to provide for the registration of political parties and spell out a number of related changes in procedure. Although the first bill largely conformed with the suggestions in the report, the second proved deficient in a number of ways. Harrison Mwakyembe, a prominent lawyer and scholar, observed that the second bill had "dashed the hopes of members of the opposition and many expectant Tanzanians who had thought that the multi-party system in the country would be ushered in on a clean slate or at least adhere to the recommendations of the Nyalali Commission to the letter."[39]

The situation became slightly awkward for Nyalali. Nascent opposition parties were irate about the limitations the bill appeared to impose on their activities, and they called on the ruling party to yield to a caretaker government presided over by the chief justice. The esteem in which the public held the chief justice and the court had evidently risen. That part of the gamble had worked. But in the search for someone whom they believed they could trust, the opposition had proposed to breach the separation of powers by vesting the senior judicial officer with executive authority.

---

[38] Ibid., pp. 165–166.
[39] Harrison George Mwakyembe, *Tanzania's Eighth Constitutional Amendment and Its Implications on Constitutionalism, Democracy and the Union Question*, Juristische Schriftenreihe 58 (Hamburg: Die Deutsche Bibliothek/Deutschen Akademischen Austaushdienstes, 1998), pp. 162–163.

MULTIPARTY POLITICS AND THE JUDICIARY

The chief justice had agreed to chair the Presidential Commission on Political Change partly out of a hope that his involvement would help people become better acquainted with the judiciary. He believed the occasion would allow the image of the judges and the courts to become associated in people's minds with universal principles of fairness and with some of the fundamental rights in the international covenants. He also anticipated that the exercise would increase the perception of the law as the important "glue" that held democratic communities together.

Multiparty politics and judicial independence reinforced one another, he believed. When a people decided to regulate its affairs through the interaction in elections and markets, it was important to have rules to ensure fair competition and freedom of choice, as well as an impartial umpire to enforce them. In an article in the *Lawyer*, the journal of the Tanzanian bar, he wrote that "under a multiparty democracy, law and government must replace political party ideology and organisation as the fundamental bonds which hold people together in the nation state. There can be no doubt that, without establishing law and government as such new bonds, the process of change from a one party state to a multi-party state could lead to the disintegration of society."[40] If democracies and market systems depended on law and courts to function effectively, however, so might the judiciary find that it benefited from the new incentives politicians faced. The relationship was symbiotic. "Big things start in small ways," Nyalali said to a group of visitors some years later. "The changes in the legal system that are beginning to happen are very much a part of the process of democratization."[41]

The commission report had dealt at length with the judiciary. The members seized the opportunity to explain the judicial role and to highlight the need for independence. In its recommendations, the commission noted that the judiciary was the third branch of government, separate from but as important as the executive and the parliament or legislature. The opening passages also laid out a broad role for the courts as defenders of human rights. "The Judiciary should ensure that Parliament does not enact any law which contravenes the Constitution. Also, the Judiciary should be empowered to scrutinise the activities of the Executive to make sure that it does not violate the basic Human Rights provided for in the Constitution,"[42] wrote the commissioners.

---

[40] Francis L. Nyalali, "Legal Reform for Democracy in Tanzania," *Lawyer* (Journal of the Law Society of Tanganyika) (September–October 1994), p. 6.

[41] Francis L. Nyalali, group conversation, March 11, 1996.

[42] United Republic of Tanzania, Presidential Commission on Single Party or Multiparty System in Tanzania, *Report and Recommendations*, p. 106.

It takes time for all of the implications of new institutional arrangements to sink in. In 1995, three years after the Nyalali Commission report appeared, the country's first multiparty elections would again place the chief justice in an awkward spot. As political parties searched for presidential candidates to run in the election, the major parties inquired whether Nyalali would be interested in serving as a candidate. "I had to refuse! I had strong reasons, and I gave them. The first was that my candidacy would have undermined the credibility of the Nyalali Report. People would have thought I had chaired the Commission just to prepare my own way! They would have considered it a Machiavellian device to serve my self-interest." The chief justice said the party leaders were always surprised when he made this observation to them. They said they had not seen it that way.

"Second, I believed then and still believe that what we had been trying to do to win acceptance of the law and the courts, the measures we had taken—these were about to take off. There were signs that people were listening to the judges," Nyalali said. "I felt it was the wrong time for me to vacate the office of chief justice. I had a feeling the party leaders understood and respected my stand."[43] Nyalali and the courts had to be very careful not to show favoritism or appear to become involved. Despite their best efforts, a cartoon in the *East African*, a new regional newspaper, showed the Tanzanian judiciary on the side of the opposition.[44]

The career of Enoch Dumbutshena, former chief justice of Zimbabwe, was instructive. Just shortly before these events, Dumbutshena had resigned from the judiciary and formed a political party of his own. An activist in his early years, he sought to offer people an alternative to the old-style patronage politics of Robert Mugabe. Dumbutshena lost the vote, but the mere fact of his involvement added tension to the relationship between the courts and the executive branch. The conventional wisdom among judges and lawyers in the region was that the judiciary should not be a springboard into partisan politics.[45] Institutional integrity was at stake.

The challenges the elections posed would be great enough without such complications. Thirteen political parties contested the first election under Tanzania's new system. Four sponsored presidential candidates. In the presidential race, the incumbent political party, the Chama Cha Mapinduzi, and its candidate, Benjamin Mkapa, captured 61.8 percent of the vote, according to official statistics. Augustino Mrema, a former Chama Cha Mapinduzi minister who switched his candidacy to the National Committee for Construction and

[43] Francis L. Nyalali, interview with author, May 30, 1996.
[44] As cited in Sufian Hemed Bukurura, *The Judiciary and Good Governance in Contemporary Tanzania: Problems and Prospects* (Bergen, Norway: Christien Michelsen Institute, Development and Human Rights Studies, September 1995).
[45] John Dugard, conversation with author, Harare, Zimbabwe, July 1999.

Reform, came in second, with 27.8 percent of the votes cast. In the elections for parliament, the Chama Cha Mapinduzi won 80 percent of the 232 seats, and the main opposition parties divided the remainder among them.

The election was not perfect. Observers and opposition political parties considered several aspects of the electoral process flawed. Some of the problems stemmed from the election acts themselves, which included contradictory language and at least one conflict with the terms of the constitution. On the mainland, there were irregularities here and there, in addition to complaints about unfair campaign practices. Polls often opened late. But, it was the Zanzibar election that proved the source of great dismay. Last-minute changes of procedure, including a shift in poll opening and closing times, created confusion. More seriously, observers discovered that in some cases there were discrepancies between the numbers of votes cast and registration figures and between the numbers of ballots counted at polling stations and the official results.

For the courts, a new crisis loomed. Nyalali had spotted it before the elections and had tried to act quickly to forestall trouble. Election administration did not stop after the ballots were counted. There were always accusations of unfair campaign practices, and the High Court had to decide these. Even in the days of one-party rule, election petitions had been common. The first multiparty election was bound to continue the trend. Nyalali estimated that about 150 petitions would be filed in the weeks after the election.

As in the other countries of the region, the courts had considerable responsibility for resolving election disputes. Decisions by the Electoral Commission about the validity of a candidate's nomination could not be appealed to the courts, under Tanzanian law—nor could decisions of the registrar of political parties about party registration. The courts had no power to declare a presidential election null and void. But complaints about manipulation of voter registration could be brought in a magistrate's court, and complaints about unfair campaign practices fell under the jurisdiction of the High Court.[46]

The problem was that the government had made no provision for this part of the electoral process. "Parliament had already been dissolved, and therefore it could not vote to release funds." In budgetary straits, the government was using donor funds to support the administration of the election, but it had not thought ahead to what it would have to do in the aftermath of the poll results. "No funds had been set aside for us to hear the petitions. It was quite a shock to discover this problem. If the disputes could not be heard and resolved, the democratic process would be discredited."[47]

---

[46] Pamela Reeves and Keith Klein, "Republic in Transition: 1995 Elections in Tanzania and Zanzibar," International Foundation for Electoral Systems Observation Report (Washington, D.C.: International Foundation for Electoral Systems, December 1995), p. 19.
[47] Francis L. Nyalali, interview with author, May 30, 1996.

Hearing the petitions would cost the courts heavily. The High Court judges were already spread thin, and they were trying to reduce the backlog on the dockets. An influx of election petitions, which had to be heard with due speed, would displace all other court business for several months. It might be possible to bring retired judges back to help handle the load, and the court could temporarily upgrade the jurisdiction of some of the more experienced resident magistrates so that they could hear cases that would otherwise have come before the High Court. "We asked for—and received—an amendment in the law so an experienced magistrate could be authorized to exercise jurisdiction of the High Court. This relieved the burdens the elections placed on the administration of justice for [the] general public," said Nyalali. In order to increase speed and ensure that there was an accurate record, since these cases were always sensitive, audio recorders would be helpful. The court had none. Finally, there was the persistent matter of paper. There was never enough paper.

The president and the chief justice spoke. Nyalali asked permission to consult the donors, again. He met with the ambassadors of several countries. "They saw the problem immediately," he said. The government of Canada provided stationery. The Nordic countries and the European Union provided photocopiers, as well as fuel and lodging allowances for judges who went on circuit to hear the cases in rural areas. They also helped automate recording in one courtroom at each of the High Court centers. "Our requests were to serve temporary needs, but I thought it was important that they serve long-term goals too. The equipment was something we could build on." The donors made it a condition that the government contribute 20 percent of the cost. "Unfortunately, the government contribution was never forthcoming, but we economized and stretched the resources to make them work."

Within two weeks of the elections, ninety petitions were filed. That number climbed to 134. As the court prepared to hear the complaints and candidates learned all that was involved in making a successful argument, some of the plaintiffs dropped their cases. Some withdrew after settling with their opponents. A little over forty cases solidified. But all of the petitions the judges heard attracted public interest. "In some places, we had to set up loudspeakers outside the courtroom, in trees, because there was not enough space in the courtrooms for all the people who wanted to attend," Nyalali commented. The court had become a center for deliberation and public education about democratic norms. It had also found a new set of constituents in the men and women who sought to run for office on fair terms.

Legal Literacy

ALTHOUGH THE TEMPO of judicial reform in Tanzania had accelerated by the late 1990s, Nyalali continued to worry about the future of the courts and the rule of law. Theoretically, the shift to competitive multiparty systems gave politicians a material stake in an impartial, well-functioning judiciary. But this logic was not yet apparent to the politicians themselves. And the statesmen of Nyalali's generation knew only too well how fragile the new arrangements could be. Within a few years of independence, the Westminster parliamentary model had collapsed almost everywhere in Africa. Now, in the 1990s, it was unclear whether the prospects were really much better.

Nyalali did not wish to stake the future of his institution on the behavior of a single set of constituents. He aimed to reach farther and to create a base of support among members of the general public. He hoped that if people learned how to use the courts and took disputes there, they would begin to appreciate the judiciary and put themselves out a bit to save it when it was threatened. But for this logic to play out, people had to perceive the courts as institutions open to them. Nyalali commented, "Today the issue is basically the question of awareness of the law."[1]

Nyalali's concern to cultivate public acceptance of the courts as protection against overly zealous officials caught outsiders by surprise. The conventional social science wisdom was that public opinion often did not matter much. There was an adage among social scientists that it takes more than an aggrieved citizenry to affect policy or government performance. Anger must translate into organized or collective action. And where the benefit sought would be avail-

---

[1] Francis L. Nyalali, interview with author, May 29, 1996.

able to everyone if the effort succeeded, as in the defense of an independent judiciary, it was unlikely people would join together to do something. Instead, they would hope their neighbors would sustain the costs inevitably incurred in trying to bring influence to bear. In American parlance, "they would free-ride." Moreover, even if people did get out in the streets or organize, their actions did not ensure that anything would happen. Plenty of leaders were strong enough or clever enough to weather the storm without bending to popular demands. In the context of Africa, where low literacy rates and limited communications technology seemed to make it especially difficult to speak of "public opinion," the idea that popular support mattered could easily seem far-fetched.

Were the theories of the political scientists wrong? Nyalali believed that public opinion was important for judicial independence and accounted for his own long tenure. Although the constitution gave security of tenure to the other members of the court, it did not extend that portion to the chief justice. Nyalali suggested that on three occasions, the question of his removal had arisen, once during the presidency of Mwalimu Julius Nyerere, once under Ali Hassan Mwinyi, and once under Benjamin Mkapa. In each case, the prospect of unfavorable public opinion saved him.

The first incident occurred not long after Nyalali's initial appointment. Nyalali was relatively junior and his colleagues were skeptical of him. "The situation was so serious that Mwalimu [Julius Nyerere] began to doubt his own wisdom. He thought about reversing his decision."[2] Long after the incident, a friend in the administration told Nyalali that the president had weighed whether he should remove someone for what his colleagues said or whether he should remove someone only for what that person did. He settled on the second view. He said Nyalali had violated no norms of good behavior, and the public would not understand his action if he removed the chief justice for other reasons.

The second occasion was in Mwinyi's presidency. A question arose in connection with a controversial speech. "I had spoken against an action of the government that undermined the independence of the judiciary and the rule of law," Nyalali related.[3] "I made the remarks during the opening of the new primary courts that the Canadian High Commission had helped rehabilitate." The government had refused to repair the buildings, and Nyalali had worked hard to win outside assistance. "I had taken the High Commissioner on a visit and then made my speech. My words were tough but true." Even the high commissioner was unnerved and asked how Nyalali would get away with the statement. "I said it was my responsibility to speak out." The remarks disturbed officials in the executive branch, and the chief justice was later told there was some discussion of his removal at high levels. The feeling was that his criticism

---

[2] Francis L. Nyalali, interview with author, July 27, 1999.
[3] Ibid.

had gone too far. Nyalali's confidant said that the hesitation came when someone asked, "But what shall we tell the public?" The public would demand to know the reasons, and there was nothing wrong in the conduct.

The third instance occurred when his Makerere school friend, President Benjamin Mkapa, was abroad. The *Business Times*, part of the country's new press, sponsored a conference on constitutional reform. Nyalali spoke up about the problem of underfunding the judiciary. "One inference that could be drawn from my remarks was that the government had set out to undermine the judiciary," Nyalali recalled. "Extra funding had been diverted from the court to the police and security forces during the late 1980s. What other conclusion could one draw but that the aim was to weaken the court?" Mkapa was very disturbed. He called Nyalali and expressed his dismay. As Nyalali related the story, Mkapa said, "Chief Justice, my quarrel is not with the content of your remarks but with the timing. We have already launched a task force on the judiciary, and here you say that we do not have an independent judiciary." Nyalali replied, "My belief was that many of the issues the task force was going to look into had already been reviewed by the Nyalali Commission, and the government had done little about the recommendations." And Mkapa rejoined, "But when you speak, people listen."

Nyalali drew conclusions from these encounters. "We don't want to rely on the constitution alone. We need to pay attention to the way the institution serves or fails to serve the public. We need to make people aware of what the courts should do and of why they can't do their jobs. I survived not because of the constitution but because of the public."

There were other examples of the importance of public opinion too. For instance, during the campaigns against corruption, officials had not always followed regulations. A primary court magistrate in a southern part of the country was on circuit between the villages in his area. The regional commissioner thought he was away from his post and up to no good. He suspended the magistrate. There was a sensation in the press. "The Regional Commissioner had no power to suspend the magistrate but he thought that because of the campaign against corruption, people would support him," Nyalali said. A judge intervened and said the action was unacceptable.

"I was then in Arusha presiding over the Court of Appeal. I asked colleagues what to do. I felt I should intervene to support the judge in charge." Nyalali asked his colleagues whether he should call a press conference. "Two of the judges of appeal disagreed. Another said, 'the public expects you to say something.'" Nyalali met the press and the newspapers covered the story. The magistrate reported to work the next day. "I received a message from a minister. He asked to convey the cabinet's support of my position. He wanted to remove any doubts."[4]

[4] Ibid.

Lawyers and activists also cautioned that it was wrong to underestimate the ordinary person's understanding. For example, Chris Mulei, a distinguished Kenyan lawyer, remarked that it was unfortunate that many urban people denigrated the views of rural relatives. "People know the issues!" he declared. "I am always being stopped in the market by people to answer questions. The Catholic church in my area asked me to address the congregation after Mass, and that drew the largest crowd the church had ever seen. People are interested. . . ." Mulei cautioned that the emerging middle class and foreign donors should not equate illiteracy with lack of sophistication. "In my village over 70 percent of people are illiterate, but no chief can misbehave. These people are no fools."[5]

OPINION AND COMMUNICATION OF THE LAW

Legal literacy, a general sense of the principles in the law, was important for building an opinion supportive of the courts. First, in most common law systems, judges could only decide matters brought before them by people who had suffered an injury for which the law offered a remedy. There had to be an actual "case or controversy." The courts could do nothing to clarify ambiguities in statutes or to decide the constitutionality of a law or practice unless someone with standing filed a complaint. And people would only do so if they had a general sense of the kinds of issues the courts would agree to hear and knew that they could avail themselves of the services courts provided.

"The greatest danger to the rule of law was public ignorance of rights and the means to enforce those rights," Nyalali remarked.[6] "People don't know how to use the courts. And judges spend a lot of time giving advice, sometimes coming dangerously close to being counsel for the litigants."[7] Justice Robert Kisanga, who often served as chief justice in Nyalali's absence, expressed similar concerns and became a force in championing civic education. "The courts will play their role effectively if the people know their fundamental rights and freedoms as enshrined in the constitution or as secured by the ordinary legislation, and if they also know the procedures laid down for vindicating them in case of violations," he commented. "However, the bulk of the people in East and Central Africa, especially in the rural areas, are largely ignorant of these rights." Kisanga worried particularly about the lack of awareness of criminal procedure. "The Criminal Procedure Act makes fairly elaborate provisions designed to safeguard the rights of suspects," he remarked. But "the vast major-

---

[5] Chris Mulei, interview with author, Nairobi, Kenya, September 1995.
[6] Francis L. Nyalali, interview with author, May 29, 1996.
[7] Ibid.

ity of the suspects who are arrested daily by the police do not know these rights. The result is that such violations do not reach the courts for adjudication and redress."[8]

Finally, in areas of "settled law," where there were few ambiguities for the courts to address, legal literacy could help people resolve disputes on their own. If there were greater popular knowledge of how the courts had decided like cases, people could "bargain in the shadow of the law," settling their differences among themselves, on the basis of what a court was likely to say if the case went to trial. Sometimes people developed their own conventions for handling routine problems. But popular awareness of the new legal norms could help people decide what such informal rules ought to be. The better the flow of information about the law, the more people could maintain the "rule of law" informally.

The chief justice often seemed to place the need to build a legal culture ahead of many other aspects of reform. He spoke of it constantly. It weighed more heavily on his mind than many of the procedural changes he had initiated to improve institutional performance. He was not alone. Legal scholar Robert Seidman, who had served in Ghana and later in eastern and southern Africa, had once drawn attention to the limited utility of law reform where legal literacy was low and communication was poor. In the industrial democracies with common law systems, the courts generally took only minimal steps to communicate. That is, they sought to make the decisions available to interested citizens in the form of law reports but did no more than that. "Conforming to notions of laissez-faire," Seidman wrote, "citizens retain the burden of learning the law, while the state accepts responsibility to make the law available."[9] This division of labor assumed that private actors—not just bar associations but also welfare and rights organizations or civil rights groups such as the National Association for the Advancement of Colored People (NAACP) in the United States—would help spread the word. But in late-twentieth-century Africa, communications networks were rarely adequate to the task. Linguistic diversity, the limited size and scope of the free press, urban-rural divisions that concentrated information in the capital—all these conditions militated against the kind of communication that underpinned common law systems in industrial countries.[10]

Responding to these observations, Tanzania's judges embarked on what Justice Lameck Mfalila of the Court of Appeal dubbed "extrajudicial activism."

[8] Robert H. Kisanga, "The Protection of Civil and Political Human Rights in the Societal Realities of East and Central Africa," Paper presented at the Conference on Constitutionalism and the Legal System in a Democracy, Arusha, Tanzania, March 28–29, 1995.

[9] Robert B. Seidman, "The Communication of Law and the Process of Development," *Wisconsin Law Review*, 1972, 3 (1972), p. 690.

[10] On this subject, see O. K. Mutungi, "The Communication of the Law under Conditions of Development: The Kenya Case," *East African Law Journal*, 9, 1 (1973): 11–42.

They launched workshops on a variety of legal topics, including gender issues and labor laws. They started a newspaper column on the courts to explain decisions, and the chief justice took to the radio waves. Several judges wrote pamphlets on the courts and the law, and Justice Mfalila chaired a committee to help the Ministry of Education develop a civics and law unit for use in schools. In most countries, these tasks fell more often to nongovernmental organizations, and eventually these kinds of groups took a larger role in Tanzania too. By the end of the 1990s, artists and journalists were putting law on center stage in many African countries.

ATTENTIVE PUBLICS

It is hard to imagine a country, or even a neighborhood, where every member is deeply interested in a wide range of policy matters and seeks to influence decisions about these by writing letters, attending meetings, contacting public officials, or organizing lobbies or protests. Most citizens have neither time nor money to do so. Except when a matter is of critical importance, most people pay only passing attention and invest little energy. Even when the issue affects their lives, they may do nothing in the hope that others, better situated, will take the initiative. For this reason, it is common to accord special importance to the ideas and beliefs of the "attentive public" or "issue public"—the subset of people whose livelihoods are affected by the problem, whether because of its impact on their sources of income or because they are paid to pay attention.

The major "attentive public" was the bar. In theory, the lawyers had a special stake in the impartiality and effectiveness of the courts because of the degree to which their livelihoods depended on being able to plead a case successfully on its merits. But the evidence did not always support this expectation. Although everyone complained about delay, ineffectiveness, or corruption, in most countries there was no concerted bar effort to urge redress, and there was quiet acknowledgment that the deficiencies of the system were convenient on occasion. Moreover, there was broad agreement across countries that bar associations were more likely to follow than to lead when it came to pressure for improvement in the laws, respect for rights, and administration of justice. The exception to the generalization was the Kenyan bar. But its members, many of whom had lobbied on behalf of human rights, soon found their ranks divided on partisan grounds. In other countries where the rule of law had collapsed earlier, law societies moved quickly to reassert themselves after these initial openings, but they felt themselves powerless to affect government behavior, especially in bad times.[11]

[11] Jennifer Widner, Law Society Surveys, 1995–96.

In per capita terms, the Tanzanian bar was one of the smallest in Africa in the mid-1990s. The economic policies of the 1960s and 1970s had left little scope for private firms to operate, and the private demand for legal services was correspondingly small. By 1993, when judicial reform began in earnest, mainland Tanzania and Zanzibar together had no more that 179 practicing lawyers. Of those, 30 worked for the Tanzania Legal Corporation. A report prepared for one donor aid agency noted, "With a total population of about 26 million there is only one lawyer per 145,000 inhabitants. In comparison, the number is one lawyer per 25,000 in both Senegal and Zimbabwe."[12]

But if Tanzania had a smaller, less powerful bar than some of the countries in the region, it was more fortunate than its neighbors in the new character of student politics. University students in the region were prone to the quixotic temper of their counterparts in other parts of the world. Demonstrations could materialize over matters from the noble to the mundane. What distinguished the students at the University of Dar es Salaam from others was their increasing resort to the courts as a forum for sorting out their differences with the administration and the government. The cases they brought attracted publicity and helped promote law as a way of handling conflict.

Costa Mahalu, who served on the law faculty before entering his country's diplomatic service, observed, "University students, wherever they are, have always taken pride in being anti-establishment."[13] Before the 1990s, the students took their grievances to the streets and considered the judiciary as an institution which "meted out punishment to anti-establishment interests." But a change took place in the 1990s. "They started seeing and probably believing in the doctrine of the separation of powers and therefore the independence of the judiciary."

> Early in the 1990s, students from the Dar es Salaam Technical College filed suit against their institution and against the Government for an illegal expulsion of students. They won their case and the students were reinstated. . . . Since then there have been several cases filed by students . . . as well as universities against their immediate authorities and the relevant ministries.[14]

The experience showed that universities could become an important base for promoting the rule of law.

---

[12] Republic of Tanzania. Tanzania Financial and Legal Management Upgrading Project. "Report on the Dissemination of Legal Information and Legal Aid," Unpublished report prepared by Frigo Consult with the support of the Danish Development Corporation (DANIDA), Dar es Salaam, Tannzania (May 1994), p. 44.

[13] Costa Mahalu, personal communication, September 24, 1998.

[14] Ibid.

SHAPING LEGAL CULTURES

Promoting legal literacy in the larger community posed a greater challenge. In the industrial democracies, knowledge about how to participate in politics, about the law, and about the courts passed between people in many different ways. Civics classes in schools supplemented knowledge transmitted through the family. Broadcast news programs, newspaper columns, and popular "court TV" provided additional vehicles. Voluntary associations, such as the NAACP and the League of Women Voters in the United States, played a role. Government itself was rarely involved in these efforts, although judges sometimes visited schools to talk about their jobs and schoolchildren took field trips to visit the court.

Equivalent kinds of voluntary organizations and activities had languished, then disappeared in most of Africa between the mid-1960s and the early 1980s. However, local innovation, later bolstered by a worldwide social movement to promote "civil society," caused a resurgence of associational life to appear again by the mid-1980s. Even the numbers of international nongovernmental organizations with branches in African countries rose sharply. In South Africa, there was a roughly fourfold increase in international nongovernmental organizations between the mid-1960s and the later 1990s. In other countries of the region, the increase was over tenfold. In most instances, the major part of the change came in the 1990s.[15] By the end of the century, civic education, including legal literacy, had become a veritable industry.[16] Said one Tanzanian activist, "There is a perception among people that human rights are rising and attracting more attention. That triggers more organizations."[17]

Immediately the people who initiated these efforts confronted questions about the appropriate subject matter and medium. What would attract popular interest? How did people learn best? Were there any lessons about "what not to do"?

The programs had to contend with the distinctive features of the social landscape that then prevailed in Africa. The urban-based character of many voluntary associations and the media in the legal sector created a potential clash of

[15] Although data on numbers of purely domestic voluntary associations in the countries of eastern and southern Africa are unavailable, it is possible to assess the numbers of international nongovernmental associations. The trends are sharply upward in the 1990s. See Union of International Associations, *Yearbook of International Organizations* (Munich: K. G. Saur, 1997/98), p. 1746.

[16] For a sustained discussion of human rights programs pursued by the new voluntary associations, see Claude E. Welch, Jr., *Protecting Human Rights in Africa: Strategies and Roles of Non-governmental Organizations* (Philadelphia: University of Pennsylvania Press, 1995) as well as Mary McClymont and Stephen Golub, eds., *Many Roads to Justice: The Law-Related Work of Ford-Foundation Grantees around the World* (New York: Ford Foundation, 2000).

[17] Southern Africa Human Rights Network, Tanzania chapter, group interview with author, Dar es Salaam, Tanzania, July 28, 1999.

cultures that threatened communication within predominantly rural countries. Kenyan lawyer Chris Mulei held up the model of the Pope, who had visited his country in 1995. "The people who provide civic education must try to blend in with those with whom they wish to communicate," he remarked. "They should follow the example of the Pope, who donned robes made of African cloth and used local languages and idioms during his visit. A woman struggling to support her children in rural Kenya is not going to listen to the city lady wearing Cutex [nail polish]. She is going to think, 'How could I possibly pay to have my children wear Cutex on their nails?' and turn away."[18]

Wisdom accumulated gradually within the region. Alfred Ndambiri, of the Legal Resources Foundation in Nairobi, Kenya, explained that civic education and legal literacy programs created special challenges in rural areas. "It is often difficult to get the same group of people to come repeatedly to workshops, to expand their knowledge, because people have to attend to their farms and other affairs. They do not have much time to spare."[19]

The subject matter had to be practical. Kenyan lawyer Jane Weru commented that legal literacy programs worked best when promoters first tried to discover what community members considered important. "Start with land rights, sanitation problems, education, and health, then move to the implications of the law or the constitution for these," she observed. Addressing concrete problems gradually made it possible to move to more abstract concerns.[20]

Botswana's Molokomme and her colleague in Uganda, Florence Butegwa, drew additional lessons from experience with particular reference to women. Although women's groups were among the associations most actively engaged in legal education, gender complicated rural legal literacy initiatives. She observed that women were often socialized to handle problems in a patient, private manner and were reluctant to take advantage of the resources law offered, even if they knew what the law was. They feared losing social support. They pointed out that men should attend the same meetings their wives do, so that they can hear the information for themselves. But at the same time, they acknowledged that women whose relatives were in the audience often feel unable to participate in the discussions.[21]

Legal literacy campaigns began to use more unusual media. In his book, *The Anthropology of Anger*, Cameroonian author Celestin Monga remarked that

[18] Chris Mulei and staff, interview with author, Nairobi, Kenya, September 1995.

[19] Alfred Ndambiri, Legal Resources Foundation, Nairobi, Kenya, interview with author, Nairobi, Kenya, October 1995.

[20] Jane Weru, Kituo cha Sheria, interview with author, Nairobi, Kenya, October 1995.

[21] Athaliah Molokomme, "Disseminating Family Law Reforms: Some Lessons from Botswana," *Journal of Legal Pluralism and Unofficial Law*, 30–31 (1990–91), pp. 303–329; and Florence Butegwa, "Challenges of Promoting Legal Literacy among Women in Uganda," in Margaret Schuler and Sakantala Kadirgmar-Rajasingham, eds., *Legal Literacy: A Tool for Women's Empowerment* (New York: United Nations Development Fund for Women, UNIFEM WIDBOOKS, 1992).

the arts were especially important vehicles for political communication in Africa, a sentiment shared by the Legal Resource Foundation directors. Historically, people had voiced protest through music and theater in troubled years, and again in the prodemocracy movements of the late 1980s.[22] Popular musicians such as Francis Bebey channeled expression through African parables and allegories, while Fela Ransome Kuti, Alpha Blondy, and others turned to new and borrowed musical forms to get political messages across.

Most practitioners agreed with Ndambiri's parallel observation that "when people are caught in a cocoon of apathy,"[23] the method or medium must provide an element of engagement and theater. And a partial solution to the time problem and to apathy lay in making legal literacy a dialogue. "Trainers should not assume they know what people think," commented legal scholar Kivutha Kibwana, in this connection.[24] Building legal literacy meant engaging citizens in a conversation.

The more creative nongovernmental organizations began to build on this insight. Launched in 1973, Kituo cha Sheria, one of the oldest such efforts in Africa, provided a good illustration. A purely Kenyan organization, which received outside assistance only beginning in 1988, Kituo provided paralegal services to people in poorer communities. By the mid-1990s, it served about two thousand clients per year. On the side, it developed a number of legal literacy programs. Where people could not read or write, the organization moved to the use of theater and video. Kituo asked churches to identify theater groups in communities. It then provided the groups with materials and ideas and asked them to develop a script and act out a play. Church halls provided a venue for many of the plays, as well as sites for showing filmed versions of some of the productions.

Other organizations followed suit. The Kenyan Legal Resources Foundation produced a series of plays called *You, the Judge.* These dramatized court cases and invited audience participation. Local troupes and amateurs performed in several languages. In Botswana, schools near the capital city held a "Human Rights Day" that included role playing, a mock trial, and a letter-writing campaign on behalf of people in different countries imprisoned illegally or subject to human rights abuse. Amnesty International materials played an important role in the development of the day's activities.[25]

Radio also proved a convenient medium for legal literacy programs in other countries. In South Africa, Bush Radio, part of a growing group of independent community broadcasters, added legal reporting to its offerings. A condition of the community radio licenses, first issued in South Africa in 1993, was that

[22] Celestin Monga, *The Anthropology of Anger* (Boulder, CO: Lynne Rienner, 1996), p. 98.
[23] Alfred Ndambiri, Legal Resources Foundation, Nairobi, Kenya, interview with author, Nairobi, Kenya, October 1995.
[24] Kivutha Kibwana, interview with author, Nairobi, Kenya, October 1995.
[25] "Amnesty International Clubs in Schools," *Mwegi* (Botswana), April 14–30, 1995, p. 12.

broadcast schedules include news, public affairs, and civic education. The regular programs soon began to incorporate third- and fourth-year law students who talked to listeners about their rights under the new constitution. It added commentary on the cases before the Truth and Reconciliation Commission, provided by a member of the commission.

Foreign visitors to the region also heard familiar voices. In the late 1990s, the popular American program, "Judge Judy," began to air in Tanzania. Judge Judith Scheindlin, known for dispensing "justice with an attitude," heard real disputes about rent payments, loud music, and other everyday matters in her television courtroom. Her no-nonsense style and her crisp statements of basic principles of law began to waft across African airwaves.

Television broadcasting was less accessible than radio to most people, but it was the rare small town that did not have a bar where people could watch.

JUDICIAL INITIATIVES

Although these trends made themselves felt, Tanzania had fewer local nongovernmental organizations in the 1980s and 1990s than its neighbors did.[26] Lawyers attributed the difference in numbers to government intolerance during the first part of the postindependence period. Women's organizations entered the field first, and other groups followed. The Women's Legal Aid Centre offered workshops and legal services. It also produced a radio program that aired 139 broadcasts in 1998 alone on topics ranging from inheritance law and land tenure to the constitution. Word got out. In 1989, ninety-three people applied for help; by 1998, the center's lawyers handled 3,412 cases. The Legal Aid Committee at the university revived too. In addition to providing legal assistance, the group of seven faculty members who ran the Committee sponsored a Thursday radio program on legal affairs and answered about one hundred letters from around the country each month.

But in the early years, the relative scarcity of "legal sector" voluntary associations in Tanzania pushed the court itself to consider a larger role in promoting legal literacy. In the late 1980s, judges began to volunteer to go to rural areas to teach because there were few attorneys and people were bringing lots of cases, often without much sense of what the law said or how the courts worked. In 1992, the court formalized these initiatives and launched a legal education program.[27]

---

[26] University of Minnesota Human Rights Library, http://sunsite.wits.ac.za/law/humanrts/africa/tanzania.htm, accessed May 1998.

[27] In most industrial democracies, courts sponsor educational outreach programs too. For example, in the United States the Federal Judicial Center provides classroom materials on judicial independence on its Web site, http://www.uscourts.gov/outreach/judindepcur.html, accessed July 2000.

"We set up a management committee to run a literacy program," Nyalali stated. "We turned courtrooms into classrooms in many places. But we weren't good teachers. We did not choose practical material. We thought people would be interested in the rules of court."[28] The judges wanted to develop a leaflet that explained how to use the courts, because they found that when people came to court, they didn't know the procedures. However, for the judges, "how to use the courts" meant "rules of evidence" and the result was "The Theory of the Rules of Evidence" in English—a project the judges themselves later viewed with some chagrin! Judge James Mwalusanya also drafted several short Kiswahili publications on law and the courts for public distribution. Ten thousand copies were printed, but the Ministry of Education, which was charged with distributing them, allowed them to sit in a warehouse instead, apparently for lack of transport.[29] Similar implementation problems plagued efforts elsewhere.

The Tanzanian court also began to use radio as a medium. It developed a broadcast called "*Ijue Mahakama Yako*/Know Your Court," which aired every Wednesday afternoon. The programs tried to explain points of law and introduce the court, ironically proving especially useful as a way to communicate within the judiciary itself. Without resources for travel and telephone, it was often very difficult for magistrates to know of new rules laid down in the decisions of the Court of Appeal or the High Court. The broadcasts helped ease this problem.

Eventually an experiment in the United States caught the attention of the Tanzanian judges. One of the more successful American efforts to promote legal literacy started as a program to reach high school students in poverty-ridden urban areas. In the United States in the 1970s, public confidence in the legal system was low. Experimentally, a group of students at Georgetown University started a project to teach "practical law" in local schools. The high school students wanted to call what they were learning "street law" and the label stuck. The local program turned national, and communities in almost all of the states founded their own organizations, each of which was self-supporting. The National Institute for Citizen Education in the Law (NICEL) became the home base. The key to the approach's popularity was a combination of content and strategy—teach practical law to ordinary citizens in a highly interactive way, said the organization's founders.[30]

"As long as the instruction is practical and people can relate it to their lives, they will get excited about it, they'll want to learn and it will help them," observed the organization's co-director, Ed O'Brien. The participatory methods

[28] Francis L. Nyalali, interview with author, May 29, 1996.

[29] Republic of Tanzania, Financial and Legal Management Upgrading Project, "Dissemination of Legal Information and Legal Aid," pp. 88–89.

[30] This section is based on coverage of NICEL's Africa activities on the U.S. Information Service Web page, http://www.usinfo.state.gov, accessed May 1997; and on Mary Larkin, interview with author, August 27, 1997.

of teaching involved debates, role playing, mock trials—in other words, student-centered learning that exercised the imagination. "It is important to get people 'fired up' or energized, so they'll make a contribution instead of just sitting back and listening to a lecture," O'Brien commented.[31]

On a U.S. study tour in the 1980s, James McQuoid-Mason, the dean of a South African law school, visited the Street Law program. He convinced the codirector to start a similar project in South Africa during the apartheid era, thinking that if more people knew the legal system, it would be easier to bring down apartheid. He hoped this initiative might eventually result in both greater awareness of law and rights among youth and the adaptation of the NAACP's litigation strategy to African circumstances. Street Law, South Africa, grew out of the effort, sponsored by the Association of Law Societies in 1987.[32]

In South Africa, NICEL's U.S. Street Law text was adapted to create booklets on criminal, consumer, family, housing, and employment law. Along with *Human Rights for All*, a book jointly developed by NICEL and Lawyers for Human Rights in South Africa, these shorter texts, usually rich in cartoons, found their way into secondary schools and adult education programs. So did an interactive style of teaching. The NICEL/Georgetown University model, in which law students receive academic credit for teaching in the high schools, won adoption in several of the twelve South African law schools. The program developed a television show starring Max Mboya, the African "Street Lawyer," as well as a national magazine aimed at teenagers. Rural South Africans received human rights instruction from NICEL-trained paralegals who used simplified materials on the Universal Declaration of Human Rights. A South African nongovernmental organization, Democracy for All, grew out of the Street Law project and addressed itself more broadly to literacy about government. It began to help the government fulfill its pledge to incorporate civic education in all high schools by the year 2005.

Slowly, and in more limited form, the program spread to Kenya, Uganda, Malawi, and Tanzania. The Tanzanian aim was to develop a curriculum for the schools, but NICEL started with the court's leaflet titled "The Rules of Evidence." "We suggested they get an ordinary citizen to read the leaflet," said a NICEL staff member. "They found out that ordinary citizens could not use the manual."[33] With the financial assistance of a Dutch association, NICEL helped the court to

---

[31] Ed O'Brien, conversation with judges in U.S.-Africa Judicial Exchange, Proceedings summarized in Jennifer A. Widner, "The Quality of Justice: Report of the U.S. Africa Judicial Exchange," Prepared for the U.S. Information Agency (Washington, D.C.: Superior Court of the District of Columbia American Bar Association, and the National Judicial College, July 1995), mimeograph.

[32] D. J. McQuoid-Mason, "Street Law Education for South African School Children and the Protection of Human Rights in Criminal Justice Proceedings," in M. Cheriff Bassiouni and Ziyad Motala, eds., *The Protection of Human Rights in African Criminal Proceedings* (Dordrecht: Martinus Nijhoff/Kluwer, 1995), pp. 331–350, here at p. 332.

[33] Mary Larkin, interview with author, Washington, D.C., August 27, 1997.

look at experiences in other countries, to explore what worked in similar contexts. A court teacher-trainer went to South Africa to observe Street Law there. Then a team composed of representatives of the courts and the Ministry of Education collaborated to produce the basic text and ideas for a legal component of the school civics curriculum.

Except in South Africa, the initial drafts reflected considerable caution. The writers emphasized what citizens should expect of government and tied "good government" to the realization of economic and social rights. Political and civil rights received less attention. Curriculum development emphasized topics that were not threatening to incumbent governments, since politicians would have to endorse the use of the materials. Even in Kenya, the Legal Resources Foundation, which was often bold, chose partly to concentrate its attention on materials useful in everyday life. "The curricula are not threatening," said Mburu Gitu and Alfred Ndambiri, two of the organization's leaders. "They focus on matters of practical importance, such as succession and inheritance. The meaning of the laws and the constitution arises within the discussion of problems that have more immediate relevance."[34]

THE COURTS AND THE PRESS

Reformers throughout the region thought the press played a critical role in building legal literacy and in monitoring the behavior of the courts. Said Peter Kabatsi, solicitor general in Uganda, "We need the press especially, in order to help preserve the rule of law. The average person knows if a judgment is excessive and journalists can smell it."[35] Nyalali also felt that the newspapers were vital for communicating the law, monitoring the courts, and providing a way for citizens to communicate with each other about the moral issues that undergirded the law itself.

The press was essential for creating a public. "It is through the mass media that a nation communes with itself and with other nations beyond," Nyalali told the Tanzania Journalists' Association in 1992.[36] "It is in that way that the authorities within a nation, such as the Legislature, Executive, and the Judiciary, sense the problems and aspirations of the people they are established

[34] Mburu Gitu and Alfred Ndambiri, Legal Resources Foundation, Nairobi, Kenya, interview with author, Nairobi, Kenya, October 1995.
[35] Peter Kabatsi, interview with author, Kampala, Uganda, February 1996.
[36] Francis L. Nyalali, "Speech on Mass Media Ethics and Law in a Changing Political Order," Delivered to the Tanzania Journalists' Association, Dar es Salaam, Tanzania, September 14, 1992.

to serve. Conversely, it is through the same channel that the people sense the capacity and policies of those authorities."

But the formation of public opinion proper also required forums in which people could exchange views and deliberate. Nyalali was insistent on this point. "In the heydays of apartheid in South Africa," he remarked, "there was no South African public as such, because the individual members of South African society could not commune with one another on the basis of their membership of South African society." Nyalali observed, "Without a public, South Africa was predictably both mindless and heartless. It had neither a collective conscience nor a collective consciousness of itself. In the absence of a South African public, the massacres of Soweto were inevitable."[37] The absence of freedom of speech and assembly had "excluded the existence of a public in communist Eastern Europe and the Soviet Union, as well as in all one party political regimes."

There were several possible ways to increase opportunity for public deliberation. "To some limited extent newspapers provide such fora in their limited columns of letters to the editor," Nyalali suggested. "In a multi-party democracy one expects to find more concrete fora in the form of more '*Jangwanis*' and more '*Mnazi mmojas*' in every town and city in the country—that is, open air spaces where people may assemble and be truly public. There was a time in our towns and cities when the greatest concern of informed people was to ensure the availability of adequate and safe open spaces where adults may freely discuss matters brought to their attention by the mass media. . . ."[38] These spaces had disappeared in the 1970s and 1980s. But the courts themselves constituted yet another forum. A public tribunal is "a mechanism for the presentation of contending matters for opinion by the public," Nyalali believed. The courtroom in a common law system allowed each party to set out its case in a sustained fashion and provided a generally accepted set of rules for interrogation and for evaluating the merits of the arguments laid out.

Throughout the region, the press was eager to play a role in transmitting information about public policy in general but especially on covering controversies as they were set before the courts. By the mid-1990s, coverage of legal disputes, law reform, and change in the judiciary was a mainstay in the daily reporting of the region's major newspapers. There was a happy convergence of interest. People found stories about legal disputes interesting. The journalists appreciated the relative ease with which it was possible to cover a legal dispute, where both the record and the courtroom were open to inspection, by contrast

---

[37] Francis L. Nyalali, "The Challenge of the Private Mass Media in the Wake of Multi-Partism," Address to a dinner hosted by the *Express* and *Mwananchi*, Kilimanjaro Hotel, Dar es Salaam, Tanzania, May 21, 1993, p. 2.
[38] Ibid.

to most government offices. In the mid-1990s, when asked what they most wanted to do to develop their skills, journalists and would-be reporters throughout Tanzania ranked instruction in legal reporting at the top of their "wish lists," along with obtaining copies of the country's constitution.[39]

At least five local newspapers, including the Kiswahili press, carried legal columns. Evaluators attached to the Financial and Legal Management Upgrading Project interviewed editors and learned that the columns provoked considerable interest in the Kiswahili language editions. "There was a big difference between the effect of the columns in English and those in Kiswahili. The editors of the Sunday News and the Express received little or no feedback from their readers and were not even sure how effective the columns were. By contrast, the editors of *Mzalendo* and *Mwananchi* received a great deal of feedback in the form of letters congratulating the column, requesting further information, raising new points of law, etc. In addition, people actually came to the office requesting specific articles of law which they had heard about but had been unable to obtain."[40]

Judges throughout the region worried about the quality of the new journalism. The articles sometimes sacrificed accuracy for sensationalism, and few editors had any legal knowledge on which they could draw to ensure the quality of what they printed. Symptomatic of the level of concern, the subject of the press came up during international exchanges and workshops. For example, during a discussion in Kampala, Uganda, a group of judges asked an official from the Superior Court of the District of Columbia how it was possible to eliminate errors in the press. The American responded, "In court, we issue a written order about what has happened and our court administrator gets a copy. He uses that to answer inquiries. We also issue written statements in response to questions. The reporters don't like this. Sometimes they still deviate, but at least we have protected ourselves and the court." He said that the court had also tried to establish better relations with the press: "Every time the court starts a new program we invite journalists so people know about it. We try to put the best foot forward. This is especially important because most people don't come before a court willingly."[41]

Initially, the judges of the Tanzanian Court of Appeal sought to write legal columns for some of the papers and said they could find funding to support such contributions. They thought the accuracy of the legal information important, so why not offer accounts of major decisions themselves? However, the

---

[39] Drawn from written evaluations and survey forms collected after each of six journalism workshops on covering "good government," Jennifer Widner, on behalf of the United States Information Service, Dar es Salaam, Tanzania, May 1996.

[40] United Republic of Tanzania, Tanzania Financial and Legal Management Upgrading Project (FILMUP), "Report on the Dissemination of Legal Information," Unpublished report, Dar es Salaam, Tanzania, 1995, p. 92.

[41] Judge Richard Levie, workshop, Kampala, Uganda, August 1995.

editor of *Mwananchi* reported that he had declined to accept the offer to subsidize the columns. He believed the subject so important that the judges deserved free space.[42]

Eventually journalists assumed responsibility for reporting, as the judges' time was required for other matters. Nyalali began to promote professional standards that would help increase accuracy and reduce sensationalism. "The public is entitled to be kept informed by the mass media about the restoration of public controversies submitted to the courts. Such transmission is essential for the Rule of Law and for multiparty democracy. To be able to discharge this function properly, the mass media needs to ensure that the journalists who are assigned to cover court cases are reasonably conversant with the law of the land."[43] Nyalali added, in an aside, "At the moment, I venture to say that the reporting of football matches is better done than that of court cases." He volunteered the help of the court in teaching journalists the rudiments of the law. "I am sure the judges and magistrates would be willing, if invited, to teach elementary law at the school of journalism in Dar es Salaam," he offered.[44]

Some chief justices were more pleased with press coverage than others. Enoch Dumbutshena, a former chief justice of Zimbabwe, related the ways the court had handled an especially difficult situation.

The Supreme Court of Zimbabwe had occasion to entertain an appeal from Ian Smith, a former Prime Minister of Rhodesia. He was, in the eyes of most Africans, a thoroughly bad man. He believed and practised apartheid. He detained, for long periods, African leaders. He publicly declared that there would be no majority rule 'in a thousand years.' He fought a civil war in order to deny Africans majority rule.

At independence in 1980 he was elected to Parliament and again in 1985. The ruling party did not like Smith. Parliament suspended him from service of the House of Assembly for twelve months. It denied him his salary and allowances. He applied to the High Court for an order declaring the non-payment of his salary and allowances illegal. The application was dismissed. He appealed to the Supreme Court. The appeal was allowed.

The Speaker of the House of Assembly called a press conference and said Parliament would not comply with the Supreme Court judgment. Then he described what kind of a person Smith was.

Because the case was a very sensitive one . . . the Supreme Court issued a press statement of its own which stated in simple terms the separation of powers and the duty of the Court to interpret laws made by Parliament. It was a public relations exercise. The President and the Executive issued a press statement of their own. They supported the Supreme Court. . . .

---

[42] United Republic of Tanzania, Tanzania Financial and Legal Management Upgrading Project, "Report on the Dissemination of Legal Information," p. 92.
[43] Francis L. Nyalali, "Challenge of the Private Mass Media in the Wake of Multi-Partisim."
[44] Ibid.

. . . . it was unusual for the Courts in Zimbabwe to deal with the press. But this was an extraordinary case. . . . It was necessary for the judiciary to react in the manner they did. It paid. The independence of the judiciary was emphasised. The public accepted that Smith's past had nothing to do with the justice of his case. . . .[45]

Dumbutshena must have struggled emotionally with this decision. As an activist in the struggle against white minority rule, he himself had been the target of Ian Smith's security forces.

Yet some of his fellow judges began to think that less publicity was better than more. The standoff between the courts and the executive at the century's end, over the arrest and imprisonment of journalists by the army, might not have materialized had the matter been handled quietly, behind the scenes, some whispered. The man who was then chief justice, Anthony Gubbay, was away when the troubles broke out. He preferred a less public approach.

In Kenya, where times were tense, rights activists also argued from time to time that less publicity was a good thing. As a litigator, Oki Ooko-Ombaka, director of the Public Law Institute in Kenya, commented that it was generally a mistake to attract publicity. "Publicity causes the government to lose face. It is currently possible to get away with more than used to be the case, provided one doesn't go to the press."[46] At the same time, he acknowledged, people were often unaware that they could take a dispute to the courts, and press coverage could help alter perspectives.

The relationship between the press and the judiciary would probably always remain a source of debate. Nyalali developed into an important defender of a role for the media in a part of the world where tradition might have pushed him to hold the opposite view. "I am aware of the doubts and unease felt by some judges and magistrates not only in Tanzania, but worldwide, about the role of the public media in the court room," he commented. "I am, however, one of those who firmly believe that the benefits of allowing the public media into the courtroom outweigh the disadvantages that may occur from time to time. In any case, the so-called excesses of the public media in reporting court proceedings can be minimized under a mutual arrangement by which court journalists are better informed about the nature of court process and proceedings, and the judges and magistrates are similarly better informed about the practice and ethics of journalism."[47]

---

[45] Enoch Dumbutshena, "Role of the Judge in Advancing Human Rights," *Commonwealth Law Bulletin*, 18, 4 (October 1992), pp. 1304–1305.
[46] Oki Ooko-Ombaka, interview with author, Nairobi, Kenya, October 1995.
[47] Francis L. Nyalali, "The Social Context of Judicial Decision Making," Paper presented at a workshop on the state of human rights in Tanzania, British Council Hall, Dar es Salaam, Tanzania, July 3, 1998.

LAW DAY

The search for additional ways to build a new legal culture continued. For all their importance, workshops, print media, new school curricula, theater, and even radio had limited reach. The farther from the capital, or an important town, and the poorer the person, the lower the chances that the legal literacy campaigns would find an audience. Yet it was vitally important that the effort to build a new social movement in support of constitutionalism and rule of law extend throughout the society.

Nyalali's religious devotion inspired him to experiment in ways other chief justices had not. Vatican II had made a difference in his life, as in the lives of other African Catholics. Before Vatican II, the Catholic church was the clergy, the hierarchy. After Vatican II, the Catholic church was the clergy in the laity. "One could even see the difference in the arrangement of the church service," Nyalali remarked. "Before Vatican II, the altar was in front, and everyone was behind it. The priest appeared to lead his flock, but the flock was often left behind! After Vatican II, the altar was placed in the center, facing the congregation. It is in the middle, surrounded. The priest and the church are closer to ordinary followers."[48] The church's membership and influence in Africa started to expand dramatically.

Nyalali hit on an idea that drew on his belief in the importance of religious faith as well as legal tradition. What better way to reach people in remote areas and to instill a sense of the principles that governed the courts than to enlist the help of the churches? The only organizations consistently able to reach out into rural areas and into all corners of the society were religious groups. The bigger, more established churches, especially the Catholic church, the Anglicans, and the Presbyterians, had elaborate networks in the countryside. At this time, religious leaders almost always respected the same values the courts considered important. They were also fellow arbiters of value and thus occupied a status related to that of the courts in people's minds. They were effective communicators. And governments in most countries had respected their independence and left them alone even when ruling parties had absorbed other associations. Why not invite religious leaders to participate in the annual Law Day ceremonies that opened the legal year?

Law Day provided a tremendous opportunity. Usually the president attended the festivities, and all the judges and advocates appeared in their formal robes. The press covered the event and the speeches. If religious leaders attended and walked with the judges and if they could be convinced to ask their congregations to pray for the wisdom of the judges and the independence of the courts, then people would begin to understand. They would draw an analogy between

[48] Francis L. Nyalali, interview with author, July 27, 1997.

religion and the work of the courts. They would listen to the appeals. "Best of all, it will not cost anything!" Nyalali confided.

The courts went to religious leaders and asked that they help start a Law Day and hold prayers for the judges' impartial and thoughtful decision making. In this special ceremony the religious figures would also ask people to pray for the lawyers. The response was overwhelming in the first year. The most moving event was in Arusha, where it was agreed that all religious groups would congregate in front of the court with the judges. Thereafter, the judges entered the court to go to work, and the religious leaders observed the proceedings. In other places, there were special seminars on the administration of justice.

The celebrations were "a pleasant surprise for most people," according to the chief justice. They were colorful. The representatives from all three branches were present so that people could see the three branches of government personified. Religious leaders—Moslem and Christian—gave sermons and cautioned judges and lawyers to act against corruption. The program was broadcast on the radio.[49] Nyalali argued that this kind of effort was at least as important as others in winning the internalization of the legal system.

In neighboring Kenya, there was casual evidence that Chief Justice Nyalali had an idea that was useful for the times. Several churches in Kenya had actively championed greater respect for basic human rights in earlier years. In 1997, an informal national poll of two hundred people carried out by journalists suggested that if people believed that established institutions worked in the interest of Kenyans at all, they considered the churches far more sympathetic to their concerns than the three branches of government. Although the poll could not be taken as a wholly accurate reflection of public attitudes, given the small size (and uncertain design) of the sample, the results were suggestive. Wrote one of the men involved in the study,

> The data might depress the Chief Justice, but here it is. Only 2 per cent of those interviewed had any confidence that the Judiciary is working in the interests of Kenyans. The rating for the Judiciary compared, sadly, with that for the police (1 per cent) and, not surprisingly, for the Electoral Commission (3 per cent). A whopping 63 per cent had no confidence whatsoever in any of these institutions. And just in case it is said that this data is manufactured to further a partisan agenda, only 2 per cent had any confidence in political parties, including the Opposition. Contrast that with the Church. Fifty-three per cent said they had a lot of confidence in religious groups, churches and mosques included. The data has a moral. Respect and confidence are earned, not enforced.[50]

[49] Francis L. Nyalali, interview with author, July 19, 1997.
[50] Wachira Maina, "Protecting Free Speech," *Sunday Nation*, Nairobi, Kenya, April 13, 1997, p. 5.

The strategy also harbored potential dangers. One worry was that religious groups might someday step over a boundary and informally seek to trade their participation in the ceremonies for an emphasis on specific values in substantive court decisions. Such pressure would compromise the impartiality of the court. At that point the relationship would have to come to an end. Another danger was that the ceremonies would cease to focus on general principles, as they did in Tanzania, and instead become an opportunity to air a court's own internal struggles. Such a misstep in Uganda, in the late 1990s, had harmed the reputation of the court, instead of improved it.

RULES OF PROCEDURE AND CONSTITUENCY BUILDING

The Tanzanian judges had taken steps to enter into a dialogue not only with the "attentive public" but also with mass attitudes. They sought to forge a new legal culture by teaching, persuading, and helping to foster a social movement. But several concerns remained. One was that the nongovernmental organizations were not always independent. In some cases, government leaders began to create their own front organizations. Judges in Zimbabwe worried that these groups had started to snipe at the judiciary, as part of the struggle between the courts and the executive to work out an appropriate relationship. And in other countries, as former nongovernmental organization leaders began to enter politics, they sometimes failed to let go of their ties. Speaking of South Africa, anti-apartheid activist John Dugard commented, "NGOs [nongovernmental organizations] aren't as powerful as they used to be. Their leaders were appointed to government and they don't necessarily see that the organizations they left need to be independent."[51]

The judges also worried about reaping a backlash of disappointment if people inspired by a new social movement lacked the resources to use the courts. People might feel aggrieved, know where to take their complaints, and understand the basic principles behind the law but be unable to mobilize the skills and the money to go forward. As a result, there was growing casual interest in Africa not only in legal aid, which had started to expand, but also in the changes taking place in India's legal scene, then a site of considerable experimentation.

Many African judges were aware of the public interest litigation movement, or social action litigation, that flourished in South Asia. Gradually, popular organizations such as labor and peasants' groups had started to use the language of law to secure their protection as individuals and communities.[52]

[51] John Dugard, interview with author, Harare, Zimbabwe, August 1999.
[52] Clarence J. Dias, "The Impact of Social Activism and Movements for Legal Reform in

Action by supreme courts in the region proved instrumental in launching this trend. Ordinarily, the only people who had standing before the court were those who had suffered personal injury. South Asian courts took issue with that bequest from the English legal system. They expanded standing to include public-spirited individuals and voluntary associations who brought complaints on behalf of segments of the population who were unable to use the courts. The people they represented could not take their cases to be heard for financial reasons, or because they could not read or felt they suffered a stigma.[53] The third parties who brought the complaints did not have to include a member of the injured class among their own number, as they did in the United States and many other common law jurisdictions.

A former attorney general for India, Soli Sorabjee, explained the liberalization of *locus standi* this way. "The major concern . . . is that if the doors of the Court are closed to a party who, though not personally affected, is espousing a genuine cause and has drawn the Court's attention to a breach of constitutional obligations, governmental agencies would be left free to violate the law. This is detrimental to the public interest. It also subverts the rule of law."[54]

The doctrine surrounding *locus standi* was not the only thing that changed. In India, the Supreme Court began to accept letters addressed to the court as formal complaints. In actions that suggested a very significant departure in the traditional role of the judge in the common law systems, it also began to appoint commissions to investigate and collect facts when a group alleged that a fundamental right was infringed. Parties would be allowed to dispute the facts in a commission's report. The court would then act on the evidence collected.

These trends inspired both support and criticism. Adulation came from those who emphasized improvement in access to justice and judicial development of law in a way that was theoretically less skewed toward the needs of the wealthy. Criticism came from those who felt that the new trend placed too much power in the hands of judges. The controversy remained, as African courts began to consider adopting the practice.

The interest in these ideas remained only that. In Africa, building awareness of the law was still a tall order, and most courts lacked the capacity to handle the increased caseload the Indian experiment implied. The influence of new

---

South Asia," in Sara Hossain, Shahdeen Malik, and Bushra Musa, eds., *Public Interest Litigation in South Asia: Rights in Search of Remedies* (Dhaka, Bangladesh: University Press Limited, 1997), pp. 3–16; and McClymont and Golub, *Many Roads to Justice.*

[53] Justice D. A. Desai, "The Jurisprudential Basis of Public Interest Litigation," in Sara Hossain, Shahdeen Malik, and Bushra Musa, eds., *Public Interest Litigation in South Asia: Rights in Search of Remedies* (Dhaka, Bangladesh: University Press Limited, 1997), pp. 20–21.

[54] Soli J. Sorabjee, "Protection of Fundamental Rights by Public Interest Litigation," in Sara Hossain, Shahdeen Malik, and Bushra Musa, eds., *Public Interest Litigation in South Asia: Rights in Search of Remedies* (Dhaka, Bangladesh: University Press Limited, 1997), p. 30.

curricula, plays, radio broadcasts, and paralegal services on popular legal literacy was still hard to assess. Lawyers and judges thought they saw changes in ideas begin to take place. In Botswana, they observed, with some chagrin, people seemed to believe that to be heard one had to go to the courts, especially when dealing with government departments, even if the matter could be settled more easily in other ways. Litigiousness loomed on the horizon.

GAPS

The efforts to build constituencies through legal literacy programs continued on the basis of faith, more than on hard empirical evidence. But one of the most striking testaments that the efforts were beginning to take effect was the increasing assumption that judicial independence should be respected. In a sign of the times, the editors of the Uganda *Daily Topic* exclaimed, "Independence of the judiciary is an indispensable component of the internationally revered rule of law, which is firmly hinged to the principles of natural justice. This might explain why any apparent infringement . . . precipitates a seemingly spontaneous hullabaloo."[55] The comment was a far cry from the debates in *Transition* about judicial independence twenty-five years earlier that had landed so many Ugandan lawyers and judges in trouble during the early days of Idi Amin.

The courts had a harder time building a rapport with the other branches of government than with the public because of the constraints imposed by their institutional position. Legislators and administrators made financial decisions that affect the strength of the courts. They passed new laws that affected the jurisdiction of the courts, the number of judges, and even rules of procedure. Nyalali attributed many problems, including the jurisdictional disputes between lower-court magistrates and district officials, to lack of knowledge. "People often behave contrary to directives just because they don't know better."[56]

However, the need to preserve separation of powers made it difficult for the courts to work closely with the other branches of government to enhance legal literacy. It was important to preserve both impartiality and the appearance of impartiality. Direct communication with members of the other branches could compromise the separation of powers. As a result, enhancing legal literacy in the other branches of government was largely left to donors and nongovernmental organizations. Serious efforts to meet the need for understanding and information within government were few and far between, and most programs focused on law reform, not on the courts or the relationship between the branches. There were some exceptions. The Institute for a Democratic

---

[55] Editorial, *Daily Topic* (Uganda), January 18, 1994, p. 3.
[56] Francis L. Nyalali, interview with author, July 19, 1997.

Alternative in South Africa (IDASA), South Africa's largest voluntary association, developed a Parliamentary Information and Monitoring Service, which included in its activities publication of a weekly newspaper called the *Parliamentary Whip*. The newspaper was designed to inform people about decisions the legislature had taken, or planned to take, and it included serious discussion of legal issues, although the courts were not a focus of reporting. In Kenya, another nongovernmental organization, the Centre for Governance and Development, sponsored a "Bills Digest" with similar aims and occasional pamphlets on other legal topics. "Our MPs [Members of Parliament] hardly read the bills coming before them," commented the center's director. "The language is often arcane. We want to simplify and highlight the underlying social and economic issues for them."[57] Print runs for some editions of the digests sold out, so popular did the series become. But one of the frontiers in the effort to build new legal cultures and institutional arrangements continued to lie within governments themselves.

[57] Chris Mulei and staff, interview with author, September 1995.

Custom, the Constitution, and the Common Law

WOMEN WERE AMONG the people Nyalali most hoped would turn to the courts for help in resolving conflicts. In his view, there was no better way to draw African principles into the common law and to begin to build an understanding of constitutional norms than to support judicial development of family law. Ordinary people usually had little sympathy for those suspected of theft, murder, or treason. By contrast, matters concerning personal status, the family, succession, and inheritance occupied center stage in most people's lives and engaged people's attention. When these kinds of disputes landed in court, judges had an opportunity to communicate the principles embodied in the new constitutions and bills of rights and to integrate them with custom. Gradually they could make the law more uniform and less foreign. As they did so, they hoped that people would accord increasing value to state law and to impartial adjudication in independent courts.

Some day, judges and lawyers might look back on the end of the twentieth century and say that the cases that had contributed most to law development in this period were not those that concerned political liberties but those that were about gender and family. The "personal is political," a catch phrase of the 1990s, provided one of the best epigrams for this period.[1]

In English and American universities, family law often seemed unglamorous. Along with trusts and wills, it was a bread-and-butter subject. It was possible to earn a living as a lawyer handling divorce, child custody, and inheritance cases.

---

[1] Joe Oloka-Onyango and Sylvia Tamale, "'The Personal Is Political,' or Why Women's Rights Are Indeed Human Rights: An African Perspective on International Feminism," *Human Rights Quarterly*, 17 (1995), pp. 691–731.

With a few exceptions, however, these were areas of relatively settled law. They rarely gave rise to riveting arguments before the highest court. But in eastern and southern Africa, the reality of the 1980s and 1990s was quite different.

The prominence of family law was partly attributable to social and economic change. Although rural dwellers were still in the majority, African countries had long had the highest rates of urbanization in the world. The influx of people into cities did not mean that kin ties disappeared. Hard times often meant that connections between the city and the countryside remained very important. People who moved to the capital or to a town maintained their relationships with the people back home not only out of affection but also out of necessity. The farm at one's place of birth was still an important source of food when prices rose in the city or when shortages struck. Rural social networks were an important form of insurance, and urban folk invested in their communities out of prudence if not out of love.

But for a growing number of people in the east and the south, the "balance of trade" within these rural-urban networks had started to change. Some people, men and women, had grown moderately prosperous and lived a different lifestyle from friends and family at their birthplaces. Others sought to protect their hard-earned assets for their childrens' education instead of the maintenance of the extended kin group. Trips home were less frequent. Ceremonies passed unobserved. Children attended urban schools and lost the ways of the community. Land registration policies diminished group control of land.[2] Tensions between clan and individual, rural life and urban, the old ways and the new began to manifest themselves in disputes about schooling, burial, and inheritance. Some of these ended up in court.

Although these cases were about the allocation of rights and responsibilities among kin in general, they affected relationships between men and women most strongly. Women often assumed the responsibilities of the head of household in the absence of a husband who had gone to look for work in town or in another country and not returned. Deaths due to acquired immunodeficiency syndrome (AIDS) or civil conflict similarly scrambled the conventional division of labor, as well as norms governing succession and inheritance. Yet women's participation in the family, community, and economy was often restricted in ways that impeded adaptation to changed new circumstances.

Customary rules frequently denied women equal rights with men in important spheres of activity. Typically, under customary law women lacked full capacity to make decisions in matters that concerned them. In Botswana, for example, legal scholar Athaliah Molokomme recalled the Tswana aphorism,

---

[2] See comment by a past chairman of the Kenya Law Society in Ahmed I. Salim, "Conflict between Common Law and Customary Law in Kenya: Regarding Burial Rights," in Jamil M. Abun-Nasr, Ulrich Spellenberg, and Ulrike Wanitzek, eds., *Law, Society, and National Identity in Africa* (Hamburg: Helmut Buske Verlag, 1990), p. 138.

mosadi ke ngwana wa monna, or "a woman is the child of a man." The practical implication of the phrase was that women always had to have guardians.[3] In
marriage, the husband acted in this capacity, with final say in many household
decisions. Women could not bring suits in the customary court but had to
depend on men to do so on their behalf.[4] In many communities throughout
eastern and southern Africa, this minor status meant that women could not
enter into contracts and therefore found their ability to provide for themselves
and their households sharply restricted. For example, often women could not
dispose of clan land, although men could. These limitations often appeared
flexible on the ground, but rules could be bent both ways: both to provide for
women and in other cases, to deny obligations toward wives and sisters.[5]

From the 1960s through the 1980s, the effect of courts on the character of
customary law provisions regarding women had varied, both across countries
and across levels of the court. In Tanzania, there was scattered evidence that
the common law courts were "biased against the customary law."[6] University of
Dar law faculty member Akilagpa Sawyerr analyzed cases from the 1960s and
early 1970s and suggested that the courts privileged a notion of the family as
the nuclear family—husband, wife, and children—over the customary idea
that "family" included a larger group of kin.[7] He found that judges did not treat
kinship as automatic grounds for entitlement to the property of the nuclear
family, as many customary systems did.[8] Fifteen years later, his colleague on
the law faculty, Barthazar Rwezaura, reported that judges had also limited the
rights of parents by taking the welfare of the child into account, again something that customary laws did not do explicitly.[9]

The law sometimes varied across levels of a national court system too. In

---

[3] Athaliah Molokomme, "Women's Law in Botswana: Law and Research Needs," in Julie
Stewart and Alice Armstrong, eds., *The Legal Situation of Women in Southern Africa,*
Women and Law in Southern Africa, vol. 2 (Harare: University of Zimbabwe Publications,
1990), p. 13.
[4] Ibid., pp. 15–16.
[5] Ibid.
[6] Akilagpa Sawyerr, "Judicial Manipulation of Customary Family Law in Tanzania," in
Simon Roberts, ed., *Law and the Family in Africa,* Seminar on New Directions in Family
Law, Leyden, 1974 (The Hague: Mouton, 1977), p. 115.
[7] Ibid.
[8] For example, in *Loijurusi v. Ndiinga* (1971 TZ HCD 331), Sawyerr wrote that "the respondent took his sister and her children away from her husband, the appellant, 'in order to exact
payment of bride price'. . . . This was rejected by the Primary Court, but upheld by the
District Court as being in accord with Masai customary law. In the High Court the respondent's action was condemned as 'clearly inequitable and contrary to public policy'. . . . Not
even the wider family was to be allowed to interfere with [the nuclear family] . . . , which
[the court] . . . described as 'the fabric of the entire society.'" Sawyerr, "Judicial
Manipulation of Customary Family Law in Tanzania," p. 124.
[9] Barthazar Rwezaura, "The Integration of Marriage Laws in Africa with Special Reference
to Tanzania," in Jamil M. Abun-Nasr, Ulrich Spellenberg, and Ulrike Wanitzek, eds., *Law,
Society, and National Identity in Africa* (Hamburg: Helmut Buske Verlag, 1990), p. 149.

Tanzania, the primary courts often applied old law or the law of the communities they served. They had not always kept up with the reasoning and rules established by the High Court and Court of Appeal.[10] Even when the High Court explicitly changed a rule, the primary courts would often continue to apply the old version. For instance, although empowered to do so, magistrates rarely asked questions about how proposals for division of assets, custody of children, and other important matters affected the ability of women to maintain themselves, although the higher courts did so.[11]

From the mid-1980s onward, the expansion of organized women's groups and paralegal services in most parts of eastern and southern Africa helped channel much of the debate about gender relationships into the courts, instead of the legislature, where men dominated. Although only a small minority of women challenged their unequal status, those who felt aggrieved were more likely to find direction and help in obtaining redress or relief than during any earlier decade. In Zimbabwe, women succeeded in winning the passage of an age of majority act that limited the ability of fathers and husbands to monopolize decision-making power over many spheres of activity. In Botswana, they challenged the constitutionality of a discriminatory provision in the country's citizenship law and won. In another sign of the times, one Ugandan judge who was asked about legal literacy programs laughed and exclaimed, "Those are fighting words! To the rural people in my community, that means 'the women are waging war!' The men all think the women are out to upset things."[12]

In the cases they brought to the courts, women appealed to principles in the common law or to the antidiscrimination clauses in new constitutions and international covenants. The latter had the status of law in some countries and provided persuasive authority in others. Most of the countries in the region were signatories to the Convention on the Elimination of All Forms of Discrimination Against Women (CEDAW), which required parties to take corrective and affirmative actions to improve the status of women. It was generally conceded that the principle of nondiscrimination had acquired the status of customary international law.[13]

There was no doubt that court adjudication of these matters could aggravate tensions within communities. Just as there were advocates for change in the

[10] Ibid., p. 152.
[11] Ulrike Wanitzek, "Legally Unrepresented Women Petitioners in the Lower Courts of Tanzania: A Case of Justice Denied," in Jamil M. Abun-Nasr, Ulrich Spellenberg, and Ulrike Wanitzek, eds., Law, Society, and National Identity in Africa (Hamburg: Helmut Buske Verlag, 1990), p. 191.
[12] Justice Frederick Egonda-Ntende, interview with author, Kampala, Uganda, August 1995.
[13] For example, see Tiyanjana Maluwa, "Changing Power Relations between Men and Women in Southern Africa: Some Recent Legal Developments," Working Paper No. 28 prepared for the workshop "Transformations of Power and Culture in Africa," University of Michigan, Ann Arbor, November 18, 1996, p. 13.

direction of equality for women, so were there articulate voices forecasting that integration of new norms would result in the collapse of the family, problems with a new generation of youth unfamiliar with the norms of their communities, and a descent into lawlessness.

Moreover, the interpretative tasks these clashes created for the courts were challenging. Most of the constitutions in the region required respect for customary law at the same time they prohibited practices that discriminated on the basis of gender, ethnic background, race, or religion. On the one hand, the Banjul Charter, the African Charter on Human and People's Rights, pledged commitment to the family as "custodian of morals and traditional values recognised by the community" and seemed to leave room for gender-based inequalities. On the other hand, it followed this statement with the stipulation that member states should ensure the elimination of discrimination against women, it made no attempt to explain how the two clauses could be made consistent.[14]

WOMEN AND THE COURTS

The judges who presided over cases about customary law and gender in the high courts or courts of appeal lived lives that were different from those of many of their countrymen and women. Although many maintained farms to support their families or to retire to later, most spent their time in urban settings. They traveled. They had access to books and read broadly. Their spouses worked outside the home. In short, they were cosmopolitan. There was always a risk of "losing touch" with the communities they served.

Chief Justice Nyalali was very much a family man. His official residence in Dar es Salaam was a simple but gracious house on a close near the Indian Ocean. On the bright blue walls of the living room, above shelves filled with old editions of the *Harvard Law Review* and copies of the country's National Integrity Study, were many pictures of family members. Among them was a framed homily, "A Man's Success Is Not How Much Money He Has Made But What Kind of Family He Has Brought Up."

The decor reflected the people who lived in the house. The apparent looseness of family ties in the United States, the high incidence of divorce and of "living together," distressed Nyalali. He disapproved vigorously. Loyce observed that her husband gave more time to the family than she had anticipated when she married—more than was usual for a Tanzanian man and more than one

---

[14] For a commentary on this subject, see Christina Murray, "Democracy, the Family and the African Charter on Human and People's Rights," in *Proceedings of the Fourth Annual Conference of the African Society of International and Comparative Law*, Dakar, April 10–13, 1992 (London: African Society of International and Comparative Law, 1992), pp. 187–197.

might have thought possible under the pressures of his job. "He is really devoted to the family and to God," she remarked.[15] The couple was building a house to which they could retire. The foundation was already dug near the international school, where Loyce had once taught in order to supplement the family income and to pursue her own professional career. The plan was for the house to have the shape of a cross, the four points representing the family's four children.

Sitting in the living room, surrounded by these pictures, the chief justice recalled with obvious pain a day in 1986 when Loyce and the children were traveling to Mbeya to visit a relative. He had seen his family off early in the morning at the airport. Later that day, as he was working, came the news that the plane in which they were traveling had crashed. The engines had failed. Many people were killed. He thought he had lost any reason to go on living. "I felt I was going to collapse, but I thought 'I must give my family a decent burial first,' then I could do so." After several hours, information arrived that miraculously his wife and children had survived after all. The chief justice later remarked that the incident had put life in perspective and given him new faith and new resolve. A photograph of his family standing near the wreckage of the plane hung in the entrance hallway to the house, as a reminder.

In his professional life, Nyalali early on had taken a different stance on the position of women than many other judges and magistrates. For example, in 1983, he delivered a judgment in the case of *Bi. Hawa Mohamed v. Ally Sefu* in which he recognized a wife's domestic services as a contribution that entitled her to a share of matrimonial property. The issue was whether, under the Law of Marriage Act of 1971, Bi. Hawa Mohamed was entitled to share in the proceeds from the sale of a house upon the dissolution of her marriage by divorce. Did family chores constitute "work"? The lower courts said the woman was not entitled to a share. As one assessor remarked, "She was only a mere wife, and the house was bought by the husband with his own money."[16] Nyalali disagreed. He looked to the intention of the legislature in enacting the Law of Marriage Act of 1971 and suggested that the mischief that statute sought to cure was the exploitation of married women. "Guided by this objective of the Act," he wrote, "we are satisfied that the words 'their joint efforts' and 'work towards the acquiring of the assets' have to be construed as embracing the domestic 'efforts' or 'work' of husband and wife." The judgment was binding on the lower courts and helped alter the country's legal landscape.[17]

[15] Loyce Phares, interview with author, Dar es Salaam, Tanzania, May 29, 1996.
[16] *Bi. Hawa Mohamed v. Ally Sefu*, Court of Appeal of Tanzania, Civil Appeal No. 9 of 1983.
[17] By contrast with Tanzania, Uganda's laws long required proof of a monetary contribution by the wife before the woman could receive a share of the assets in a divorce. The Ugandan courts made little effort to enlarge the notion of proof to recognize in-kind earnings that helped support the family or to attach monetary values to the services the woman provided.

In its early years, the courts over which Nyalali and his predecessors presided had few women on the bench. Although the country won an early reputation for being more responsive to the problems of women than other countries in the region through the passage of the groundbreaking Law of Marriage Act of 1971,[18] most of those who heard cases about personal status, marriage, or inheritance were men. The first woman to join the Tanzanian judiciary was Eusebia Munuo. Munuo had graduated with a bachelor of laws degree from the new program at the University of Dar es Salaam in 1970. She was determined to join the bench but knew that no woman had served in the judiciary before. A new graduate normally would have spent time as an intern in the attorney general's office, but the young Munuo was determined to embark on the course she had planned for herself, and she summoned her courage and went to see Chief Justice Telford Georges, who then ran the courts. The chief justice listened and asked her whether she thought she could try a murder case. "We talked, then he told me if I could win a release from the attorney general's office, he would take me. Fortunately, the attorney general was interested in the idea, and the next day he provided a letter to the chief justice. I went back to the judiciary and was immediately sworn in."[19]

Munuo spent a year and a half as a magistrate in Dar and then was posted to Mwanza and later, Morogoro, to the Mzumbe Institute of Development Management, to train primary court magistrates. "I was sent there to encourage women to go into the judiciary. Quite a number of women joined. My presence did get more women appointed," Munuo reflected. In April 1987, after eighteen years as a magistrate, Munuo was appointed a High Court judge. In 1991, when the legislature passed a law which said that a spouse could not sell property without the consent of his partner, Munuo handled a landmark case brought under the new statute. "Women feel encouraged to come to court when they see that result. A few successes like that can make a big difference."[20]

By the 1990s, there were more women on the bench, and in some important law schools in Africa over 45 percent of the students were women. Associations of women judges and magistrates began to organize in each country, after an international body formed in 1991. In Uganda, members of the women judges

---

Similarly, the law required that a wife's name appear on the title to a piece of land if she was to have standing in a land dispute. "Sometimes a sympathetic judge would say that the wife was implicitly a signatory," commented one member of the bench, but usually that was not the case. Justice Lititia Mukasa-Kikonyogo, interview with author, Kampala, Uganda, February 1996.

[18] This law supplanted customary laws in the area of marriage and provided women with considerably more rights than they had earlier.

[19] Eusebia Munuo, interview with author, Arusha, Tanzania, May 24, 1996.

[20] Ibid.

association visited the United States to observe equivalent groups, and returned to pursue a set of objectives they framed on the basis of what they had seen. They decided to broaden their original focus on domestic violence, arguing that there was no culture of rights on which to build. "People step all over each other," one founder commented. "People don't enforce rights here, even among the men, so we decided to try to become active in promoting human rights generally."[21] The group also focused on gender sensitization in the courts and on the recruitment of more women to the judiciary. They maintained elements of their original objective, by deciding to encourage law reform in the area of domestic violence and by trying to write a book on the subject.

At least as important as having more women on the bench was having more women members of the bar, or at least promoting a "gender-sensitive" legal imagination. The briefs submitted to the judge in a case defined the issues in contention and the arguments to be considered. To integrate the customary law and the common law in a way that responded to changing social conditions required the skills of those who understood the pressures families faced, could identify restrictions that required amendment, and knew how to argue effectively in court. Paralegal organizations, legal trusts, and public law institutes staffed by dynamic women lawyers arose to do just that.

Especially in southern Africa, a lively network of women lawyers and paralegals, some Western trained and some who acquired their skills closer to home, tried to respond to what they perceived as the needs of other women less well off. They undertook grassroots training and "consciousness raising," but they often concentrated their efforts on conducting research and publicizing their results, lobbying for legislative change, or taking important cases to court.

Women in Law and Democracy in Africa (WILDAF) was an example. Beginning in 1990, WILDAF provided training and assistance for legal literacy, law reform, and human rights monitoring. Based in Harare, the network had 150 member organizations throughout Africa. Among its main objectives were strengthening legal rights programs for women, providing training to groups for development of legal literacy, and coordinating activities with other related organizations such as Women and Law in Southern Africa (WLSA), an especially important research organization. The group established an emergency response system to help publicize serious abuse or violation of women's rights. It produced a quarterly newsletter to help link its member organizations in different countries.

New personnel could only bring about change if there was opportunity. This time, opportunity existed too. New rights provisions came into force in Tanzania, Zambia, Namibia, Lesotho, Malawi, South Africa, and Uganda in the late 1980s and early 1990s. General antidiscrimination or equality clauses often were included. Some of the new constitutions also included language

---

[21] Justice Lititia Mukasa-Kikonyogo, interview with author, Kampala, Uganda, February 1996.

that made it easier for courts to apply international law or find persuasive authority in international standards.

Courts began to take sides in what seemed to some a political battle between proponents of "traditional" and "modern" gender relations. Critics said judges had no business doing so, that policy calculations were better left to legislatures. But others said that limits on gender equality did not constitute an ordinary policy matter. They weren't entirely a matter for legislatures to decide.

BLOOD VERSUS LIFESTYLE

The outlines of a new jurisprudence began to emerge in the late 1980s and 1990s. Courts confronted three broad types of cases. One type focused on choice of law. The second related to conflicts between constitutional principles and customary norms that were embedded in state law. The third concerned clashes between customary practices and constitutional principles.

One important issue for both men and women in late-twentieth-century Africa was whether one could elect to abide by the norms of a kinship group or whether one was obliged to live under the law of the community into which one was born. As rural folk perceived their urban relatives and younger people withdrawing from community affairs, they worried. They grew concerned partly because of the financial implications. Households often pursued occupational diversification as a hedge against risk. Some family members found salaried jobs in the city, others worked in the fields, several might hawk vegetables or make simple furniture and utensils, and a few went abroad. If the urban-based members cut themselves off from rural relatives, the insurance system would collapse. Those who pulled away and led "modern," urban lifestyles threatened the livelihoods of others, differently situated.

Moreover, preserving generational ties among kin was vital for older people in a world where few banks extended services to rural areas and the banking system as a whole operated poorly. In the West it was possible to save for one's old age in many different ways—by having the government deduct Social Security taxes from money wages and pay back that money later in the form of a pension, by depositing a share of earnings in a savings account at the bank, and by participating in a variety of private pension systems and investment programs. Where none of these possibilities existed, one's younger relatives played an equivalent role. They provided labor, food, and other forms of support. Although they still did so to some degree in the West, their function and the system of obligations that supported it were much more important in African contexts.[22]

---

[22] Paul Collier, Director, Centre for the Study of African Economies and Director of Research, World Bank, conversation with author, October 1995.

Rural people also were concerned about identity. If people did not respect their obligations to the clan and observe its rituals, then what would happen to the principles one had come to accept in everyday life, the common sense that freed one from having to make hundreds of calculations about what to do? The prospect of losing one's reference points, of being cut adrift, was as unsettling in the village as it was anywhere. A weakening of the attachment to clan identities would force people to make choices, and choice was a source of anxiety in most parts of the world, not just in Africa.

From the perspective of rural members, it was important to bind the kin group together at a time when there were many forces pulling people apart. Life ceremonies, especially burials, became important points of contact, reaffirmation, and financial exchange. Ceremonies often commemorated the good deeds of the deceased and encouraged those left behind to follow the examples set.

Burial societies were the main voluntary associations in most parts of rural Africa at this time. They helped people bear the expense and work involved in funerals by allowing them to make small regular payments to an insurance fund. The fund would cover the cost of a funeral out of the mutual savings, and members would help mourn the departed. In parts of western Africa, ceremonies were often lavish and required substantial contributions from relatives and friends. Competition developed among urban elites to see who had offered most or looked after rural kin best. In Ghana, even the construction of coffins acquired the status of an art form. Magnificent caskets in the image of cocoa pods, Mercedes cars, taxis, ships, and fish were paraded through villages, as relatives sought to bury loved ones in a style that captured their occupations in life.[23]

Disputes about the rules that would govern burials often landed in the courts. And for the judges the issue was which "linking factors" the court should use to determine whether a person should be buried according to custom or according to the preferences of the deceased and his or her spouse. These decisions affected women because they often pitted the claims of a widow against the claims of a clan and opened the possibility that customary norms of succession and inheritance would apply, along with customary burial rules.

One of the cases that received the greatest public attention was *Virginia Edith Wambui* [Wamboi] *Otieno v. Joash Ochieng Ougo and Omolo Siranga,* an appeal from the High Court of Kenya to the Kenyan Court of Appeal in 1987.[24] The case concerned the burial of S. M. Otieno, a Kenyan criminal lawyer well respected in his profession and his urban community in Nairobi, the capital. By birth, Otieno was a Luo from the western part of the country. He left his home, studied law in India, and joined the bar. He married Virginia Edith Wambui, who was from the Kikuyu community just north of Nairobi,

---

[23] Thierry Secretan, *Going into Darkness* (London: Thames & Hudson, 1995).
[24] Civil Appeal 31 of 1987 1 KAR (1982–88) at 1049.

the daughter of a distinguished doctor and politician. The couple had raised a family in the suburbs of the capital, joined a church, and spent evenings with friends, mostly professionals, at a pub where S. M. Otieno was famed for his recitations from Shakespeare. Wambui was a member of national women's organizations and had taken the daring step of running for parliament. In 1985, S. M., as he was known, died suddenly, without a will. The question was which rules would govern his burial.

As Wambui made plans to bury her husband on a plot of land they had bought in the Ngong Hills, outside of Nairobi, S. M.'s brother, Joash Ochieng' Ougo, a foreman with the national railway, asserted that the body ought to be buried according to Luo custom at S. M.'s birthplace. Joash Ochieng' Ougo assembled a committee of the clan to plan the ceremony. The national radio station announced both burials in its broadcasts, piquing public curiosity.

At Wambui's request, a court granted an injunction to block the ceremonies until the dispute could be resolved. Wambui then sought a declaratory judgment that she could carry out the burial of her husband. She said that her husband's lifestyle indicated that matters arising from his death should be handled under the common law, not under Luo customary law. Counsel pointed out that S. M. had entered into marriage with a woman of a different cultural heritage; that he and Wambui jointly owned property; that the couple had baptized their children in church and spoke English at home; that in life, S. M. was a member of many national professional societies, while he had visited his birthplace only six times and had disregarded many important Luo conventions; and finally, that he had a prodigious grasp of Shakespeare. The judge found that S. M. was "a metropolitan and a cosmopolitan" not subject to customary law, and as a matter of law, under Section 160 of the Succession Act, he granted an *ex parte* judgment to Wambui.

The clan took the matter to the Court of Appeal. On review, a three-judge panel ruled that the High Court judge should have heard the other side and considered whether Luo customary law could have applied. The appellants had introduced evidence which suggested that S. M. had wished to be buried at his Luo home. There were also points of law in question. What was the status of the customary rules in matters of succession? Under Kenyan law, responsibility for burial typically lay with a group, not with a nuclear family or a spouse.

The case was remanded to a different judge of the High Court, who decided in favor of the clan. Wambui appealed.

The Court of Appeal upheld the judgment that gave control of the burial to the clan. The country's Judicature Act stated, "[T]he common law, doctrines of equity and the statutes of general application shall apply so far only as the circumstances of Kenya and its inhabitants permit." Section 3, subsection 2 further read, "The High Court, Court of Appeal and all subordinate courts shall be guided by African customary law in civil cases in which one or more of the parties is subject to it or affected by it, so far as it is applicable and is not repugnant to justice and morality or inconsistent with any written law, and shall decide all such cases according to substantial justice without undue regard to technicalities of procedure and without undue delay."[25]

These passages and like provisions in the judicature acts of other countries in the region were taken to mean that the courts should take customary law as guidance, but what did guidance mean? The court found that in Kenya the legislature had decided to give customary laws primacy in matters concerning the family, marriage, divorce, and succession. Although the assembly had since passed statutes to govern succession, the court considered that these were "supplementary" to the customary law.

The court also said that although the Law of Succession Act provided for a married woman to take up the administration of her husband's estate, to do so, Wambui would have had to apply for letters of administration. At the time of the case, she had not done so. Her application had been contested. The court decided that Wambui thus had no case under the common law or under the statute. "While she may be the preferred choice in s 66 of the Law of Succession Act she had not yet received her grant and cannot lawfully act in that predicament."

The court made several additional points. It judged consistent with principles of justice and morality and written law the customary provision that "a man cannot change his tribal origin." It said that Luo customary law prescribed a particular procedure to be followed if a clan member wished to establish a home in another location and limit his ties with his community. S. M. had moved away, but he had not followed the procedure. Finally, it found that the constitution of Kenya allowed for discriminatory rules respecting burial and let stand the Luo rule that the wife was bound by the law of her husband's community, irrespective of lifestyle.

The case and the decision riveted the Kenyan public.[26] It was covered in the newspapers and on radio, and it became the topic for discussion in schools and on buses. The story attracted many interpretations. Some saw it as a victory for customary law in the courts and decided to pay a little more attention to their kin back home.[27] To others, it had a political resonance. The president had commented on the dispute while the case was *sub judice*, and his remarks had favored the clan. At the same time, an important senior Luo political leader,

---

[25] Ibid.

[26] The S. M. Otieno case spawned many commentaries. One perspective, by two nonlawyers who reported extensively on popular reaction, appears in David William Cohen and E. S. Atieno Odhiambo, *Burying S. M.: The Politics of Knowledge and Social Power in Africa* (Portsmouth: Heinemann, 1992). A more lawyerly treatment is Salim, "Conflict between Common Law and Customary Law in Kenya," pp. 133–138.

[27] Cohen and Odhiambo, *Burying S. M.*, p. 14.

many of Wambui's Kikuyu kinsmen, and women's groups, none on friendly terms with the leaders of the executive branch, had backed Wambui. Women's organizations and the country's legal scholars called for revision of the Law of Succession Act.

Kenyan legal scholar Jackton Ojwang was among the few to suggest that maybe the outcome was not really a victory for customary law. In its decision, the court had made itself the main interpreter of customary rules and practices.[28] It had also pointed to the fact that a change in the statutes concerning the law of succession might well have led a court to a different decision.

In many respects, the decision in *Otieno* ran counter to the trend in eastern and southern Africa. In Tanzania, Nyalali observed that the case would have had completely the opposite outcome in his country. "In Kenya, once a tribesman, always a tribesman. In Tanzania, we took the contrary view." A person could escape the environment of the customary law into which he was born. "As someone moves, he can choose the law that he wishes to apply. That's why Tanzania is non-tribal. A person can change his status and community."[29]

The chief justice related a parallel case his court had handled:

A man died intestate. He was from the south of Tanzania where the society was matrilineal. He was married to a Chagga, and the Chagga were patrilineal. The customary law applied. In the south, the deceased's uncle or someone who stands in the shoes of the uncle inherits both the property and the children. The Chagga community was different. So there was a conflict of the customary laws. The woman argued against the application of customary law. The courts applied the common law, ruling in favor of the widow.

Our position was the reverse of the one taken by the Kenyan courts. The position was consistent with building a national consciousness. Tanzanian courts have held that customary law is part of the law of Tanzania and applies to a person who belongs to the relevant community. The customary law statutes[30] apply to every person who has accepted to belong. But one can opt out of the community too. . . .

The widow succeeded because her late husband had a university education. In life he rarely visited his region in the south. He only went once on leave with his children, except in emergencies. The way he conducted his life was not consistent with normal tribal behavior. He had ceased to be a tribesman, in our view.

I believe our law is more consistent with tradition than the Kenyan decision

[28] Jackton B. Ojwang, "The Meaning, Content and Significance of Tribal Law in an Emergent Nation: The Kenya Case," in *Law and Anthropology*, International Yearbook for Legal Anthropology, vol. 4 (Vienna: VGO, 1989), p. 139.

[29] Francis L. Nyalali, interview with author, Lushoto, Tanzania, March 1996.

[30] By contrast with Botswana and several other countries in the region, Tanzania had tried to codify customary laws, and the codifications were enacted as statutes.

was. Earlier in our history, one could be adopted into a tribe. By interpreting this practice, the courts held that if one could be adopted, one could also opt out.[31]

Differences in statutes and in techniques of interpretation produced significant cross-national variation in outcomes. In some countries, statutes provided individuals the opportunity to remove themselves from the application of particular customary laws. In Botswana, for example, a man or a woman could say under which legal system they wish to marry, and when they did so, they accepted the rules associated with the system they indicated. That was in theory, of course. Research by legal scholar Athaliah Molokomme suggested that many people were unaware of these options, "couched as they are in language which lay persons do not understand. Since matters of private law are close to a people's way of life, it is largely according to customary law that most people conduct their private affairs."[32]

Always, these situations were sources of strain. Philosopher Anthony Appiah, who was at the center of a dispute about the burial of his father, eloquently recalled the turbulence surrounding these events in the epilogue to *In My Father's House: Africa in the Philosophy of Culture*, an award-winning reflection on identity and race. Joe Appiah was the head of an Ashanti matriclan, but he was educated abroad and married in England. He had led a distinguished career as a lawyer and member of parliament. With his wife, Peggy, of English descent, he had raised a brood of children who became scholars and writers, citizens of the world who lived scattered across the globe. He had asked his son to draft a codicil to his will, stipulating that his church and his wife, Peggy, carry out the rites associated with the funeral.[33] In writing elsewhere, he had announced his preference for a simple church ceremony, without a public viewing, and with his family in white, instead of the brown and black he associated with the gloom of funerals. The clan did not approve. Appiah wrote, ". . . [I]n the midst of it—when partisans of our side were beaten up in my father's church, when sheep were slaughtered to cast powerful spells against us, . . . it seemed that every attempt to understand what was happening took me further back into family history and the history of Asante; further away from abstractions . . . further into what would probably seem to a European or American as an almost fairytale world of witchcraft and wicked aunts and wise old men and women."[34] The funeral did take place in the church, but with considerable fanfare and a huge crowd that included the unannounced presence of the head of state, Jerry Rawlings.

---

[31] Francis L. Nyalali, interview with author, July 19, 1996.
[32] Molokomme, "Women's Law in Botswana," p. 12.
[33] Kwame Anthony Appiah, *In My Father's House: Africa in the Philosophy of Culture* (New York: Oxford University Press, 1992), p. 183.
[34] Ibid., p. 181.

CUSTOM AND THE CONSTITUTION

A second type of clash concerned not choice of law, but the constitutionality of statutes that condoned unequal treatment. The question was whether discriminatory laws enacted by democratically elected legislatures, whose members reflected customary beliefs that women were less competent decision makers than men, could withstand scrutiny under constitutionally enshrined antidiscrimination clauses. Beginning in the mid-1980s, women in southern Africa began to challenge these laws, and courts in eastern Africa watched with interest.

The landmark case for the region was *Attorney General of the Republic of Botswana v. Unity Dow*,[35] better known as "The Citizenship Case." Unity Dow was a Botswana citizen, a lawyer by training. She had three children with her husband, Peter Dow, who had resided in Botswana for fourteen years but remained a citizen of the United States. In 1990, she challenged the constitutionality of the Citizenship Act of 1984, which stipulated that a child born to a Motswana[36] man was automatically a citizen of Botswana, whether his wife was from Botswana or from another country. A child born out of wedlock to a Motswana woman and a foreign man could be a citizen. A child born of a marriage between a Motswana woman and a foreign man would not have citizenship. Dow argued that the provisions of the law were in conflict with Section 3 of the country's constitution, read in conjunction with Sections 5, 7, 14, and 15. Section 3 guaranteed the fundamental rights and freedoms of the individual "whatever his race, place of origin, political opinions, colour, creed or sex." Section 14 guaranteed freedom of movement. Section 15 was an antidiscrimination clause.

Related legislation existed in other countries in the region. For example, in Kenya, under Section 91 of the constitution, a Kenyan man who married a foreign woman could pass his citizenship to his children, while a Kenyan woman who married a foreigner could not.[37] Nearly identical provisions existed in Uganda, Zambia, Swaziland, Lesotho, and a number of other countries.

The attorney general argued that Dow had no *locus standi* (standing to sue) because her own rights were not affected. Dow's counsel, Julian Browde, replied that it was artificial to treat Dow as an individual without consideration of her family environment. Her own right not to be deprived of freedom of

---

[35] Civil Appeal No. 4 of 1991, Botswana. There is an exposition of the case in Michael P. Seng, "In a Conflict between Equal Rights for Women and Customary Law, the Botswana Court of Appeal Chooses Equality," *University of Toledo Law Review*, 24 (Spring 1993), pp. 543–582.

[36] In many African languages, the prefix *Ba*, *Wa*, or *Ga* indicates people, plural. Thus, in Setswana, *Motswana* means a single individual, while *Batswana* means more than one person.

[37] Kivutha Kibwana, "Women and the Constitution in Kenya," *Verfassung und Recht Übersee*, 25, 1 (1992), p. 10.

movement and her own protection from expulsion would be meaningless if her husband and children had no such guarantees.

The attorney general also argued that the constitution permitted unequal treatment based on gender. He noted that in Section 15 (3), the constitution's antidiscrimination clause, sex was not mentioned. The country had a number of statutes that treated women differently from men. Moreover, the customary laws of the country, the Roman-Dutch law still part of Botswana's legal tradition, and the common law all were discriminatory in various ways, and a large part of the country's law would be liable to be struck down by a finding that the Citizenship Act was in conflict with antidiscrimination provisions in the constitution. He observed, "The whole fabric of the Customary Law in Botswana . . . is based upon a patrilineal society, which is gender-discriminatory in its nature. . . . It is not unfair to say that if gender discrimination were outlawed in customary law, very little of customary law would be left at all."[38] He also pointed to a report prepared by the Law Reform Commission, which had canvassed people's views and found that those interviewed supported the existing citizenship legislation.

High Court Judge Morton Horwitz listened to the arguments of both sides and ruled in favor of Dow. He decided to take a "generous" approach to interpreting the constitution, considering the document as a whole, instead of the specific passages cited, only. He found that Dow had *locus standi* as a result of the adverse impact of the Citizenship Act on her own freedom of movement. He further found that the Citizenship Act abrogated the fundamental liberties and protections laid out in the constitution. He conceded that "sex" was not in the list of attributes expressly stated in the antidiscrimination clause but found that the phrasing of the clause was at odds with the phrasing of other sections, and he suggested that the meaning of the clause had to be construed in the light of the rest of the document. He also pointed to the fact that Botswana had signed the Organization of African Unity (OAU) Convention on Non-Discrimination and the United Nations CEDAW as evidence that the exclusion had no significance. Finally, he pointed to persuasive precedents from other countries, including a 1975 judgment by Lord Denning in a case about a nearly identical statute in Mauritius.[39]

The government appealed the judgment. It argued that Horwitz was generally correct to claim that in interpreting a constitution, a judge should be less concerned about the words themselves and consider the document as a whole in an effort to discern meaning. However, in Botswana, the constitution itself adopted as the rules for its own interpretation the country's Interpretation Act,

---

[38] Attorney general's heads of argument as reproduced in Unity Dow, ed., *The Citizenship Case: The Attorney General of the Republic of Botswana vs. Unity Dow, Court Documents, Judgements, Cases and Materials* (Gaborone, Botswana: Lentswe La Lesedi Pty, 1995), p. 20.
[39] *R. vs. Secretary of State for Home Affairs and Another*, 1975 (2) ALL E.R. 1081.

which required the court to pay attention to the actual language used and to the traditions and usages that gave meaning to the language. The High Court had overstepped its bounds.

The government reasserted the claim that Dow had no *locus standi* because her own rights were not threatened. Second, it said the constitution made provision for preserving the customary law along with the common law and statute law in force at its inception. Third, an important government objective was served by the act. "The acquisition of citizenship through the father would appear to be a reflection of the fact that the wife and children of a man, as head of the family, are more likely to settle in the country of which he is a citizen and thereby acquire a genuine link with that country," wrote the attorney general.[40]

The government also suggested that a constitutional ban on gender discrimination was far from clear. Section 3 established entitlement to certain individual rights but it did not stipulate that there should be equal protection, the attorney general argued. The pertinent part of the constitution was really Section 15, the antidiscrimination clause. Section 15 left out gender as a protected category, and the High Court was wrong to say that gender was implicitly included in the list.[41] The Interpretation Act required the application of the *inclusio unius exclusio alterius* rule (that which is not expressly included is excluded). Finally, the treaties against discrimination the country had signed had not been ratified and did not have the status of law.

Justices Amissah, Aguda, and Bizos of the Court of Appeal upheld the High Court's decision and presented concurring opinions. Justices Schreiner and Pukrin dissented. All of the judges were "contract judges." Justices Amissah and Aguda were from western Africa and were longtime leaders on the African judicial scene. Justices Bizos and Schreiner were from South Africa.

On the question of the appropriate way to interpret a constitution, the major-

[40] Appellant's heads of argument, as quoted in Dow, *The Citizenship Case*, p. 70.
[41] The constitutions of other countries in the region, including Tanzania, contained the same kind of discrepancy. The Tanzanian constitution read:

Part III . . .
    13. (1) All persons are equal before the law and are entitled, without any discrimination, to equal opportunity before and protection of the law.
    (2) No legislative authority in the United Republic shall make any provision in any law that is discriminatory either of itself on in its effect. . . .
    (4) No person shall be treated in a discriminatory manner by any person acting by virtue of any law or in the discharge of the functions of any State office.
    (5) For the purposes of this section the expression discriminatory means affording different treatment to different persons attributable only or mainly to their respective descriptions by nationality, tribe, place of origin, political opinions, colour, creed or occupation whereby persons of such description are subjected to disabilities or restrictions to which persons of another such description are not made subject or are accorded privileges or advantages which are not accorded to persons of another such description.

ity pointed out that the Interpretation Act stipulated "such fair and liberal construction as will best attain its object according to its true intent and spirit." That left a lot of space, and over the years many judges helped develop principles and rules to resolve the ambiguity. They pointed to decisions from Botswana and from other countries to support the position that a constitution is a special enactment that is not easily or often amended. Wrote Justice Amissah, "The object it is designed to achieve evolves with the . . . development and aspirations of its people."[42] He reviewed the precedents and commented, "The lessons they teach are that the very nature of a constitution requires that a broad and generous approach be adopted in the interpretation of its provisions." The principles of interpretation included "that all relevant provisions bearing on the subject for interpretation be considered together as a whole in order to effect the objective of the constitution; and that where rights and freedoms are conferred . . . derogations from such rights and freedoms should be narrowly and strictly construed."

Under these rules of interpretation, the antidiscrimination clause, Section 15, did not stand alone. It had to be read in the context of the constitution as a whole. Reaching to the experience of other countries, Justice Amissah pointed out that

> [t]he United States constitution makes no specific reference to discrimination as such. Yet several statutes have been held to be in contravention of the Constitution on the ground of discrimination. These cases have been decided on the basis of the 14th Amendment . . . which forbids any State to 'deny to any person within its jurisdiction the equal protection of the laws'. . . . In Botswana, when the Constitution, in section 3, provides that 'every person . . . is entitled to the fundamental rights and freedoms of the individual,' and counts among these rights and freedoms 'the protection of the law', that fact must mean that, with all enjoying the rights and freedoms, the protection of the law given by the Constitution must be equal protection.[43]

Because the constitution contained no specific derogations from fundamental rights on the basis of gender, the court could not read such limitations into the text. The application of the *expressio unius* rule was incorrect. If the drafters had wanted to exclude women in Section 15, then they would have done so explicitly, as they had with reference to matters other than gender elsewhere in the document.[44] Moreover, there were other groups not listed in the section to whom the authors had almost certainly wanted to extend the rights in question, such as the disabled.

The court respected the constitutional requirement that legislative powers

[42] Dow, The Citizenship Case, p. 128.
[43] Judgment of Justice Amissah as reported in Dow, *The Citizenship Case*, p. 133.
[44] Ibid., p. 142.

resided with parliament, but it noted that the separation of powers did not mean that elected officials were entitled to enact any and every law they wished. It noted that Section 86 of the constitution said that the power of parliament "to make laws for the peace, order and good government of Botswana" was "subject to the provisions of the Constitution."

On the matter of whether the lower court's ruling was consistent with the customs that informed the perspectives of those who drafted the constitution and legislation, the court commented:

> Our attention has been drawn to the patrilineal customs and traditions of the Botswana people to show . . . that it was proper for Parliament to legislate to preserve or advance such customs and traditions. Custom and tradition have never been static . . . [and] they have always yielded to express legislation. . . . [T]he custom will as far as possible be read so as to conform with the Constitution. But where this is impossible, it is custom not the Constitution which must go.[45]

The court found the evidence of people's opinions embodied in the Report of the Law Reform Committee unconvincing. Wrote Justice Amissah, "It is noticed . . . from the report itself that the expression of the people was made in the form of answers to questions. The manner in which those questions were put does not appear in the report. Neither do we know the explanations made to the people before they came out with the recorded answers. . . . For this reason, the report loses much of its value as an expression of the people."

Throughout the judgment and concurring opinions were frequent references to international trends in legal thinking about discrimination and citizenship. The court recognized that international treaties, unless ratified, were not law, but it pointed out that they were nonetheless persuasive for the purposes of interpretation. Justice Aguda announced that he wished to take judicial notice of the fact that Botswana was one of the few countries in Africa where liberal democracy had taken root. He wrote, "It seems clear . . . that all three arms of the government—the Legislative, the Executive and the Judiciary—must strive to make it remain so except to any extent as may be prohibited by the Constitution in clear terms. . . . [W]e cannot afford to be immune from the progressive movements going on around us in other liberal and not so liberal democracies such movements manifesting themselves in international agreements, treaties, resolutions, protocols, and other similar understandings as well as in the respectable and respected voices of our other learned brethren in the performance of their adjudicatory roles. . . ."[46]

On the matter of whether Dow had standing, Justice Amissah rejected the

[45] Ibid., p. 135.
[46] Judgment of Justice Aguda as reported in Dow, *The Citizenship Case*, p. 166.

state's argument that Dow had no *locus standi* by way of her children. In Botswana, it is the guardian who has responsibility for children, under the law, and the guardian the law recognized was the father. But the constitution recognized the legal authority of a parent as well as a guardian, and a parent could be a mother.

> The mother's concern for permission for her children to stay cannot be lightly dismissed on the ground that it was no business of hers, the responsibility being the children's father's. Well-knit families do not compartmentalise responsibilities that way. As long as the discretion lies with the government authorities to decide whether or not to extend further the residence permit of the husband, on whose stay in Botswana the stay of the respondent's children depend, the likelihood of the children's sudden exhaustion of their welcome in the country of their mother's birth and citizenship is real. . . . [W]ere they refused continued stay, not only the children's position but the mother's enjoyment of life and her freedom of movement would be prejudiced.[47]

The dissenting opinions focused on the methods of constitutional interpretation and suggested that the court should pay more attention to the intent of the framers and the wording of specific provisions.

The case attracted considerable discussion outside the court, and people took sides. Parliament and the House of Chiefs were both deeply skeptical of the court's decision. Anticipating opposition, the government dragged its heels in bringing a bill to amend the Citizenship Act to make the law conform with the constitution. After two years of inaction, the failure to amend the statute became an embarrassment to the government, which encountered considerable criticism from the legal profession and from abroad. Eventually it organized a joint caucus of the two main political parties, to help pass the legislation. When it brought the proposal to the floor in 1995, the debate was lively. The amendments passed, but many felt their hands had been forced.

Conveying a sentiment broadly shared, one member of parliament argued, "Whilst we agree that the Act is *ultra vires* the constitution, I wonder if I would be wrong to say the Constitution is also *ultra vires* our culture. . . ."[48] In words reminiscent of similar debates in other parts of the world, including the United States, he continued:

> Mr. Speaker, our judiciary is free and independent and whatever it takes, we must accept. But we are worried that there might be a tendency of some of

---

[47] Judgment of Justice Amissah as reported in Dow, *The Citizenship Case*, p. 157.
[48] Mr. Maruatona as quoted in Hansard 118, August 7–10, 1995, debate on Citizenship (Amendment) Act, p. 10.

our women "recruiting" some men into this country. I strongly believe that this is the unfolding scenario. . . . [W]e might find ourselves in trouble because they might bring undesirable people into this country.

In most cases Setswana names have meanings. . . . We are now going to have names with no meaning at all. Some of our children would be van de Merwes, Bandas, and all the like. That means our culture would soon be the endangered species.[49]

Added another member, after a very deferential statement of respect for the court and the rule of law, "We are making a mockery of our democracy if we believe that [the people] . . . can vote each and every one of us into this House but we do not trust them to . . . approve a legislation that goes to the roots of the people of this country and how they are constituted as a people."[50] He averred, "We are proud that this case did go before the court because it is the same court that we have protected when other people did not believe that we could have a free judiciary." He then expressed his support for constitutional change, saying, "I believe that we should fully understand that two of the judges dissented. . . . We should not try to underplay this issue, many democracies including the United States and other countries, have gone through referendums on the basis that a Court of Appeal had made a decision that they felt . . . was not on all fours with culture and the interests of the people."

Support for amendment of the act was also forthcoming. One member made a bold defense of Dow and a plea for conformity with international standards. He also noted that Botswana was multicultural and that it was therefore dangerous and difficult to privilege one culture in legislation. A woman member of parliament observed to her colleagues, "Like a constitution, custom is not static. Custom is dynamic, it changes with the people, it grows, and this amendment is an indication of the change in our way of life."[51] She argued that discrimination impeded economic growth and improvement in standards of living. "When you discriminate in any community, the community is going to suffer politically, economically, socially, and its development is going to be retarded. . . . If we did empower all members of the community equally, . . . every member of the community would be more productive." Finally, she suggested that additional sections of the act were problematical because they made specific references to some tribes, while they made no reference to people of other backgrounds.

There was no denying the fears of customary authorities that regional and

[49] Ibid.
[50] Mr. Robi as quoted in Hansard 118, August 7–10, 1995, debate on Citizenship (Amendment) Act, p. 25.
[51] Mrs. Phumaphi as quoted in Hansard 118, August 7–10, 1995, debate on Citizenship (Amendment) Act, p. 30.

international women's groups had a hand in some of the legal challenges that seemed to restrict the application of customary law or be at odds with the spirit of those laws. Certainly, from the perspective of Botswana's House of Chiefs and many members of Parliament, *Unity Dow* bore the imprint of foreign meddling. Women and law in Southern Africa and the Swedish International Development Authority helped raise funds to help Dow pursue the case. The International Women's Rights Action Watch in Minnesota provided guidance. The Urban Morgan Institute of Human Rights in Cincinnati helped conduct legal research and find decisions unavailable in Gaborone. Among the many friends who provided support was Lady Ruth Khama, the widow of the country's first president, whose interracial, cross-national marriage had attracted both scandal and adulation in the 1950s and resulted in her husband's losing his hereditary claim to a Tswana kingship.

Yet there was also evidence that the case was very much a reflection of the temper of the times in Botswana. In the acknowledgments to her book, Unity Dow thanked her parents, who taught "fairness and equality between the sexes."[52] As many Batswana, her parents had chosen to support the education and aspirations of their daughters, as well as their sons. Unusual in many respects, the country was one of the few in the world that could claim to educate a higher proportion of its women than its men. The judges might well have taken those statistics as evidence of popular aspirations quite different from those advanced by the *kgosi*, or chiefs, and the politicians.

The "new Botswana" evident in the debate over the case won recognition a few years later. In January 1998, Unity Dow was the first woman appointed to the High Court of Botswana. The invitation caught her by surprise. She commented that her initial reaction was, "That's not me. I'm an activist. If I take this position, what am I losing and what am I gaining?"[53] She accepted, believing that her new judicial position would allow her to gain a new voice, even if she would have to abide by certain restrictions.

Like cases began to come to court throughout the region and sometimes met with an even stronger reaction than the Botswana Parliament and House of Chiefs had offered. In Zimbabwe, the Immigration Service refused to grant permanent residence to the foreign husbands of Zimbabwe citizens, although it permitted foreign-born wives of Zimbabwe men to stay. The court struck down the practice as unconstitutional in two decisions that appeared in 1994.[54] Two years later, a constitutional amendment altered the law by denying both foreign wives and foreign husbands permanent rights of residency by virtue of marriage.

---

[52] Dow, *The Citizenship Case*, p. vi.
[53] Tim Ledwith, "The Journey of Unity Dow," *Amnesty Action* (Winter 1999), pp. 6–7.
[54] *Rattigan v. Chief Immigration Officer* (1995 (2) SA 182, Zimbabwe) and *Salem v. CIO* (1995 (4) SA 280, Zimbabwe). See Anthony R. Gubbay, "The Protection and Enforcement of Fundamental Human Rights: The Zimbabwean Experience," *Human Rights Quarterly*, 19 (1997), pp. 227–254.

African lawyers anticipated that many more suits about when laws providing unequal treatment were permissible would soon materialize. South African legal scholars and lawyers often looked to Canadian examples because the drafters of the rights and limitations clauses of the new South African constitution had looked very closely at the Canadian Charter of Rights and Freedoms and borrowed extensively from it.[55] The South Africans referred to the Canadian decision in R. v. *Oakes*,[56] a case about the limitations the state could place on a fundamental right. In *Oakes*, the Canadian court laid out the grounds on which deviation from fundamental rights would be tolerated. The court said of the application of the limitation clause:

> To establish that a limit is reasonable and demonstrably justified in a free and democratic society, two central criteria must be satisfied. First, the objective, which the measures responsible for a limit on a Charter right or freedom are designed to serve, must be 'of sufficient importance to warrant overriding a constitutionally protected right or freedom'. . . . The standard must be high in order to ensure that objectives which are trivial or discordant with the principles integral to a free and democratic society do not gain . . . protection. It is necessary, at a minimum, that an objective relates to concerns which are pressing and substantial in a free and democratic society before it can be characterised as sufficiently important.
>
> Secondly, once a sufficiently significant objective is recognised, then the party invoking . . . must show that the means chosen are reasonable and demonstrably justified. This involves 'a form of proportionality test'. . . . Although the nature of the proportionality test will vary depending on the circumstances, in each case courts will be required to balance the interests of society with those of individuals and groups. There are, in my view, three important components of the proportionality test. First, the measures adopted must be carefully designed to achieve the objective in question. They must not be arbitrary, unfair or based on irrational considerations. In short, they must be rationally connected to the objective. Secondly, the means, even if rationally connected to the objective in the first sense, should impair 'as little as possible' the right or freedom in question. . . . Thirdly, there must be proportionality between the effects of the measures which are responsible for limiting the Charter right or freedom, and the objective which has been identified as of 'sufficient importance.'[57]

The American courts, whose decisions peppered Dow's legal briefs, similarly permitted laws or government practices that granted unequal treatment on the

---

[55] Azhar Cachalia, Halton Cheadle, Dennis Davis, Nicholas Hayson, Penuell Maduna, and Gilbert Marcus, *Fundamental Rights in the New Constitution* (Kenwyn, South Africa: Juta & Co., 1994), pp. 5–7.

[56] Canada, YR 26 DLR 4th 200.

[57] As quoted in Cachalia, *Fundamental Rights in the New Constitution*, pp. 6–7.

basis of gender only when there was an important government purpose served and the measures were narrowly tailored. Further, the basis for differential treatment had to be "real" and not based on a stereotype about the capacities or behavior of a group.[58]

EQUALITY CLAUSES, BILLS OF RIGHTS, AND CUSTOMARY LAW

Some of the most difficult cases concerned clashes not between statutes and constitutions but between widespread social practices or rules enforceable under customary law and the antidiscrimination provisions in constitutions. Some of these customary norms explicitly deprived women of the capacity to make decisions about their own lives. These included provisions that accorded married women the status of minors and made their husbands their guardians. Other practices, such as bridewealth, created a potential for abuse but also might have had beneficial effects.

These cases were especially challenging. Often they addressed intimate aspects of people's lives. In other parts of the world, governments had moved to consider aspects of family relationships proper subjects of government concern, but the development of these areas of law was almost always greeted with strong resentment against the intrusion of the state in private matters where religious preferences were often important.

Where constitutions and bills of rights applied only "vertically" to government bodies or to those who had assumed state powers, and not "horizontally" to individuals' treatment of each other, there was little occasion to bring constitutional challenges against unequal treatment within the family to court. In the United States, for example, a court could hear a challenge to a law or government policy that discriminated. But it could not apply the constitution to the decisions of private parties, unless the constitutional principles were embodied in statute that regulated the activities in question. If a family or a religious community wished to make women subordinate decision makers, as members of the American-based Southern Baptist Convention decided in 1998, they could do so provided they violated no statutes.

By contrast, in much of Africa the statutory recognition of customary law meant that it was possible to adjudicate practices that were generally outside the purview of the courts in the West. Headmen, elders, and other "traditional

---

[58] By contrast with many industrial countries, the United States and Canada had experience with deep legal pluralism too. An American case, *Martinez v. Santa Clara Pueblo* (540 F2d 1039, 10th Circuit, 1976), pointed up some important differences in the handling of a very similar dispute. The case was a near mirror image of *Unity Dow*, except that the law complained of was not a state law but a rule of the Pueblo Indian tribe. The Supreme Court dismissed the suit before reaching the merits. (*Santa Clara Pueblo et. al. v. Martinez*, 426 U.S. 49; 98S.CT.1670)

authorities" had special status in most places, and the rules they administered were recognized as law in the courts. They wielded governmental power, even if they were not administrative entities like districts, counties, or states.

In Tanzania, customary practices and the constitution came into conflict in several spheres, but especially with respect to women's control of land. In many of the country's communities, clan land could be held only by men. The men were supposed to hold the land in trust for future members of the group, and until the colonial period ownership was vested in the clan. The decision to transfer or sell the land did not belong exclusively to an individual member until changes in land tenure systems were introduced later. Wives could use the land to produce food for the household, but women's labor did not generate proprietary rights. Women could not inherit, sell, or pass on the title. Although the role of the clan in land allocation changed over time, women often continued to be excluded.[59]

In 1986, the Tanzanian Court of Appeal ruled that unequal treatment of women under customary land laws was unconstitutional. At the time, it had no power to command the legislature to revise the rule, which was enshrined in the country's customary law code. The three-year "grace period" after the adoption of the Fifth Amendment containing the bill of rights was still in effect. In *Rukuba Nteme v. Bi. Jalia Hassan and Gervas Baruti*,[60] Rukuba Nteme sued a former ward, Bi. Jalia Hassan, who had sold a parcel of land to someone outside the clan. Bi. Jalia Hassan, a woman, had received the land from Rukuba Nteme, a cousin, who had held it in trust for her after her father's death, when she was only a child. Rukuba Nteme initially had refused to hand the land over when Bi. Jalia Hassan reached the age of majority. Bi. Jalia Hassan sued him and was successful. After the court case, she sold her cousin part of the land and farmed the rest herself. Twelve years later she decided to sell the rest of the parcel to a third party, Gervas Baruti, and she used the proceeds to buy another plot in another part of the village. After numerous suits and countersuits, Rukuba Nteme applied to the Court of Appeal for certification on a point of law, which was "whether a female under Haya Customary Law can dispose of clan land to a stranger."

The advocate for the appellant, Rukuba Ntema, argued that under the Local Customary Law Declaration No. 4 Order, 1963, women in the Bahaya community have no right to sell clan land. They were allowed only to use the land for life. The advocate for Bi. Jalia Hassan countered with the argument that the customary law had changed. The recognition of new rules was evident in the

---

[59] Useful discussions of this issue appear in Rose Mtengeti-Migiro, "Legal Developments on Women's Rights to Inherit Land under Customary Law in Tanzania," 24, 4, *Verfassung und Recht im Übersee* (1991), pp. 362–371; and Gita Gopal and Maryam Salim, *Gender and Law: Eastern Africa Speaks*, World Bank Directions in Development Series (Washington, D.C.: World Bank, 1998).

[60] Civil Appeal 19 of 1986, Court of Appeal at Mwanza, Tanzania.

fact that clan elders had witnessed and accepted the second transaction, the sale to an outsider. Further, he argued that the custom, which treated men and women differently, was unconstitutional.

The Court of Appeal decided the matter in favor of the appellant, but the judgment was based on technical grounds and did not reach the clash of principles between the customary law and the country's new constitution. In his opinion, Nyalali wrote that the arguments of Bi. Jalia Hassan's counsel were intriguing but that the court was not yet able to decide matters brought under the new Bill of Rights and Duties because the three-year grace period before enforcement was still in effect. He merely pointed out that people ought to be aware of the court's earlier decision in *Naagwi Kimito v. Gibeno Werema*,[61] in which it determined that customary law had no exceptional status. Wrote Chief Justice Nyalali, ". . . [c]ustomary law in this country has the same status as any other law." The court therefore would have no difficulty considering its congruence with constitutional principles.

In other countries, such as Zimbabwe and South Africa, customary practices such as bridewealth or *lobola* were contested in law reform commission proceedings and occasionally in court. In most parts of Africa, to marry a woman a man had to offer a payment or gift, called bridewealth, to the woman's parents. The form varied. In many places, it took the form of livestock. In others, it included money. Sometimes it was a token payment; at others, it involved a substantial transfer of wealth.

These cases were difficult. Although a clear instance of different treatment, there were arguments on both sides about the injuries and protections the practice created. Moreover, bridewealth was subject to many variations, some of which appeared to have little ill effect on the status of women, while others opened the potential for abuse. And the practice was generally popular.

But many African feminist lawyers and scholars in the 1990s argued that bridewealth contributed to the subordination of women and ought to be abolished.[62] In Botswana, the payment was considered to allow a man to "chastise his wife more freely," a euphemism for corporal punishment or beating, and it limited the rights of the woman over custody of children in the event of death or divorce.[63] In parts of Zimbabwe, payment of *lobola* was typically in two parts, the first of which entitled the husband to the woman's labor and the second, entitlement to children as well as exclusive right to dissolve the marriage.[64] In Uganda, the bridewealth a family received for a daughter sometimes

[61] Civil Appeal No. 20 of 1984 (unreported).
[62] See, for example, Angeline Shenje-Peyton, "Balancing Gender, Equality, and Cultural Identity: Marriage Payments in Post-Colonial Zimbabwe," *Harvard Human Rights Journal*, 9 (Spring 1996), pp. 105–144.
[63] Molokomme, "Women's Law in Botswana," p. 16.
[64] Shenje-Peyton, "Balancing Gender, Equality, and Cultural Identity," p. 106.

became the basis for the brideprice her brothers paid to obtain wives of their own, researchers suggested.[65] This use of the payment potentially placed great pressure on a young woman to make a match when she was too young to consider her interests or when she felt she had to sacrifice her interests to those of the family. Elsewhere there were reports of women who encountered resistance to divorce from an abusive spouse on the grounds that the family could not afford to refund the bridewealth.

By the end of the century, these cases were beginning to come before courts in various parts of the region. For example, the Zimbabwe court interpreted the Age of Majority Act and several other reforms in a way that made it possible for women to marry without the payment of *lobola*. And in Kenya, women's groups praised the actions of a man who sued his brother to block the brother's marriage of his nine-year-old daughter to a man three times her age. Upon overhearing the news of her betrothal, the child fled to a boarding school, which had taken in several runaway girls from her community. In *Ololouaya v. Ololouaya*, the girl's uncle argued that his brother shortsightedly sought the bridewealth the marriage would bring, in order to provide for other members of the family.[66]

LEGAL INTEGRATION

Nyalali considered legal integration important for the institutional status of the courts. Only when the customary laws, state laws, and constitution shared the same principles would people orient themselves toward the courts as authoritative arbiters of value in the civic realm. Yet it was clearly difficult to effect this integration of the laws, and nowhere more so than with respect to family law or the law of personal status. If the procedures chosen to accomplish the task produced a big divergence between popular practice and preferences on the one hand, and an official fantasy on the other, the legitimacy of the courts would suffer too.

This issue had arisen in South Africa and Mauritius, where commissions had deliberated about how to handle *shari'a*, Islamic law, within constitutional frameworks that contained antidiscrimination clauses. Citizens who practiced Islam had two options. They could ask to have *shari'a* recognized as official law, just as customary law could be recognized in statute. They would then

[65] Florence Butegwa, "Challenges of Promoting Legal Literacy Among Women in Uganda," in Margaret Schuler and Sakuntala Kadirgmar-Rajasingham, *Legal Literacy: A Tool for Women's Empowerment, United Nations Development Fund for Women* (New York: UNIFEM WIDBOOKS, 1992), p. 139.

[66] Unreported. See report on CARE: Info Center: Newsroom, June 1998 News Archives, http://www.care.org/info-center/newsroom/1998/bride.html, accessed April 2000.

have to accept to reform *shari'a* to make it compatible with the constitution, either through codification or through a slower process of harmonization by the courts. Or they could follow the route of many religious groups in the United States, accepting that religious law would receive no recognition by government and would be unenforceable in court but would also be free from state pressure for reform.[67]

By contrast with *shari'a*, customary laws in many parts of Africa already had state recognition and were enforceable through the courts. Unless people voted to alter that status, the question was which approach—codification and reform by the legislature or slow adjustment by the courts—would prove the best route for bringing about gradual convergence. Nyalali thought the former was more consistent with democracy. He suggested that at some point the law reform commission should initiate a countrywide discussion. It should survey customary norms and consult people about the best way to reconcile the general principles of customary law with constitutional provisions, he thought. A consultative process would improve communication of the law and consensus building. But Nyalali also recognized that the slow adjustment and flexibility possible through piecemeal review in the courts also had advantages.

Issa Shivji, a longtime observer of Tanzanian legal affairs, concurred and expanded on the second view. In reference specifically to land issues, he expressed hope that three things would happen. There should be an effort to pick out the principles of customary law and use them in the reasoning of cases, he said. In addition, he added, there should be an effort to give customary forums a more democratic content. The public continued to place trust in elders and village assemblies, he noted. It should be possible to build on that and work to include women in these assemblies. Finally, he suggested that the courts meet in the villages more often. "That would help build up a body of principles of fairness and justice in these cases. The magistrates could spot the trends in the way communities handled these cases and try to develop these."[68] This practice would put them in a better position to help integrate local custom with constitutional principles.

---

[67] Abdullahi Ahmed An-Na'im, personal communication to author at seminar organized by the World Bank, Washington, D.C., April 2000.
[68] Issa Shivji, interview with author, Dar es Salaam, Tanzania, May 1996.

Trouble Spots

AS A "SECOND LIBERATION" swept much of Africa in the 1990s, so did the collapse of order and the spread of severe civil conflict in places like Somalia, Liberia, Sierra Leone, and Rwanda. At the same time that political openings took place in much of common law Africa, the countries bordering the eastern and southern regions succumbed to factional feuding, often with an ethnic tinge. Internal wars sent refugees spilling over boundaries and turned countries such as Malawi, Tanzania, and Kenya into hosts of some of the largest refugee populations in the world. In the late 1990s, there were over twice as many refugees temporarily settled in eastern Africa as in the United States.[1] Tanzania provided haven to 558,000 in 1998.

At the same time that judges, lawyers, and nongovernmental organizations struggled to build a new legal culture, so too did the challenges increase. Across the region, judges recalled those same phrases from Learned Hand's "Spirit of Liberty" taped above the desk of a Ugandan administrative assistant: "Liberty lies in the hearts of men and women; when it dies there, no constitution, no law, no court can save it; no constitution, no law, no court can even do much to help it."[2] The spirit of moderation and tolerance that characterized most of the continent's early independence movements had frayed in many places. Under these conditions, efforts to build could easily seem sadly beside the point.

[1] United Nations High Commission for Refugees, http://www.unhcr.ch/statist/98oview/tab1_1.htm, accessed July 2000.
[2] The quotation is from Learned Hand's speech on May 21, 1944, at a ceremony in Central Park, New York City, to swear in 150,000 naturalized citizens.

There were many dangers. Courts were reactive instead of proactive, and it was impossible for them to intervene in a conflict unless they were brought in by one of the parties or by the police. Yet when resources were scarce, taking a dispute to a judge could easily loom too expensive and too slow to be useful. Where people felt their person and property immediately threatened, they might turn to self-help instead of to the judicial system. A sharp increase in the sense of danger or insecurity could lead people away from established institutions to remedies of their own. They suspended many of the normal protections accorded individual rights. They put the judges in a weaker position to defend separation of powers and to uphold fundamental rights.

Was there any role for the courts to play in dampening severe conflict or reducing the perceived need for self-help, such as vigilantism? Could courts fend off tempestuous times or limit the damage that occurred? Many people in the international community hoped so. And even if judges often shared Learned Hand's perspective, there could be little doubt that some of the disputes ordinary people brought to the courts provided an opportunity for legal minds to influence the way people thought about the region's growing security problems, even if they could not address the root causes.

STRAINS

Angola, Somalia, Liberia, Chad, Rwanda, Burundi, Sierra Leone, the Democratic Republic of the Congo, the Sudan, Guinea-Bissau, Nigeria—in the 1990s, these names and others fueled the image of a region on the verge of anarchy. To predict a common fate for an entire region was wrong. Conditions varied across countries. Men and women of good will sought to intervene and to forestall the train of events that produced devastation in neighbors. Political leaders could learn. The fate was not inevitable. Yet it was hard not to concede that worrisome strains and stresses had developed nearly everywhere.

Although reliable information on crime for Africa was scant, and often difficult to interpret, the available evidence suggested that crime was an increasing problem. In southern Africa, the subject attracted particular attention. A 1996 survey reported in the *Financial Mail* found that 45 percent of South Africans surveyed called crime the country's biggest problem. Although unemployment rates were high, only 18 percent considered unemployment as serious a problem as crime.[3] Similarly, surveys of rural residents in Botswana in the same period found that a majority of people interviewed considered that the crime situation had changed for the worse during the past five years.[4]

---

[3] As cited in Greg Mills, *War and Peace in Southern Africa: Crime, Drugs, Armies, and Trade,* World Peace Foundation Report (Cambridge: World Peace Foundation, 1996), p. 1.
[4] Jennifer Widner, Public Attitudes Surveys, 1995–96.

Street crime was one problem. Even in Botswana, with a history of growth and stability, people worried about lawlessness among younger people. Nearly all parents sent their children to primary school and another third to secondary education, but that was not enough to prevent disorderliness, locally termed *Bo-bashi*. Elected officials sometimes noted the decline of discipline.[5] Said one minister, "The Setswana tradition has disappeared. In the past everybody took responsibility for any child. Today if a parent corrected somebody else's child, this parent could be prosecuted. As a result of this there is lawlessness among the children. Children abandon their homes and roam the streets in towns. . . . One hears of people looking for cattle over the radio but nothing about their missing children."[6]

The Botswana House of Chiefs laid the matter even more clearly at the door of the courts and the law. Chief Seepapitso IV commented, "We appear to be ashamed of our nationhood to such an extent that we practice other nations' traditions and customs. This is why we have no control of our children. Batswana believe that a cane does not 'kill' a child. The cane is a corrective. . . . [D]iscipline has disappeared among our youth due to the modernisation of our culture and values. We should annul the Penal Code and revert to our own customs. . . . We recruit foreigners to be our judges and they regard judgment of juvenile culprits to be barbaric. . . . Imagine that, and yet these people were employed by us. They defied Parliament which is the highest authority in the country. . . . The law administering strokes with a cane was enacted by Parliament."[7]

Similar sentiments could be heard throughout the region. By contrast with the rest of the world, Africa was home to populations over half of whose members were below the age of twenty-five. Even in remote parts of the continent, there was usually a way to connect car batteries to power a video cassette recorder, and the imagery and language of *Rambo*, *Bruce Lee*, and other action films captured young imaginations. Parents, community leaders, chiefs, and elected representatives argued about "the youth problem" and the collapse of morals everywhere.

Governments or their agents were often the main sources of insecurity. A serious barrier to trade in some parts of the region was "the illegal roadblock" created by gendarmes, customs officials, forest police, and others in order to extract money from truckers, bus passengers, and private car owners. The proportion of countries in which roadblocks occurred increased sharply from the end of the 1980s, when informal toll collection plagued about half of the countries of sub-Saharan Africa, to over 70 percent through most of the 1990s.[8] Governments reasoned, with some justification, that if they removed security personnel, private extortionists would take their place.

---

[5] See for example, Botswana, House of Chiefs, *Official Report* (Gaborone, Botswana: House of Chiefs, October 14–25, 1991).
[6] Ibid., p. 38.
[7] Ibid., pp. 41–42.
[8] Analysis based on author's coding of U.S. Department of State, *Human Rights Reports* (Washington, D.C.: U.S. Government Printing Office, multiple years).

Even if people trusted police, there were fewer authorities to whom they could turn for help. Nyalali cited statistics. "In the United Kingdom there were 132,100 police officers for a population of about 56.6 million people in 1985," he wrote. "This comes to about one police officer for every 406 people. In the Federal Republic of Germany with a population of 61,000,200 in 1982 there were 192,771 police officers, that is, one police officer for every 316 people. As to judicial officers, there were about 17,000, that is, one judicial officer per 359 people." The comparable figures in the United States were 418 people per police officer and about 8,000 people per judge. By contrast, said the chief justice, "In Tanzania with an estimated population of 23 million people in 1987 there were about 23,000 police officers, that is one police officer per 1,000. As to judicial officers, there were 1,379 judges and magistrates of all descriptions, that is one judicial officer per 17,000 people."[9]

Growing crime pushed some governments to engage in practices that bred popular discontent and placed them on a collision course with courts. For example, as crime increased, some observers noticed a tendency for governments to implicitly condone torture of suspects.[10] There were reports of torture in custody from Botswana, Lesotho, and Zambia, for example, and such practices were likely to be at least as widespread elsewhere. In Zimbabwe, legislation was enacted to prohibit the ombudsman from examining police conduct, and in Zambia the government announced a police "shoot to kill" policy to deter crime. A lower proportion of African countries compared to countries from other regions of the world signed the Convention Against Torture, and only Malawi, Mauritius, and Namibia actually ratified the convention.[11]

A deepening sense of personal insecurity in some parts of the region encouraged resort to self-help. One policy maker whose work at the Global Coalition for Africa gave her a special vantage point commented that crime and public safety were "phenomenally important" in understanding the trends in Africa at the end of the twentieth century. "Crime eats away at communities, like corruption," she commented. "People's sense of self-worth starts to be affected."[12]

---

[9] Francis L. Nyalali, "Structures and Dynamics of Law Enforcement," Keynote address no. 3 in *Report of the Eighth Commonwealth Magistrates' Conference*, Ottawa, September 18–24, 1988 (London: Commonwealth Magistrates' and Judges' Association, 1988), pp. 78–96. The American police figures come from Federal Bureau of Investigation, *Uniform Crime Reports* (Washington, D.C.: U.S. Government Printing Office, 1995). The federal, state, and local figures for judges are drawn from WANT's *Federal-State Court Directory, 2000 edition* (New York: WANT Pub. Co., 2000).

[10] Reports of torture in custody occurred in the majority of African countries throughout the 1990s. These figures do not reflect official approval of the practice. They partly illustrate lack of central control over police forces.

[11] Frans Viljoen, "The Relevance for Africa of the Six Major United Nations Human Rights Treaties and Their Mechanisms," Paper presented at the eleventh annual meeting of the African Society for International and Comparative Law, Harare, Zimbabwe, August 1999.

Nyalali agreed and traced his own country's trajectory to a crime wave that followed the villagization program of the 1970s. "The disruption caused by this move inevitably gave rise to a crime wave in the countryside," he suggested. "The government had no capacity to deal with the crime wave, and a popular vigilante movement emerged. The government had no alternative but to accommodate it."[13]

At the end of the century, any popular tolerance of political corruption that once may have existed had also worn thin. People who had once tolerated inequality and corrupt practices on the part of officials grew less patient. The famous development economist Albert O. Hirschman had forecast this change in mood, though his comments were not about Africa per se. He argued that tolerance of inequality was "like a credit that falls due at a certain date." A "tunnel effect" causes people to see others' improving fortunes favorably as long as they can eventually expect to benefit. However, at some point, if benefits have not materialized, inequality is met with fury. Where a country experienced negligible economic growth or a general decline in the standard of living, a dangerous "institutionalized envy" could become the norm, because under such conditions inequality may signal "anticipation of absolute deprivation."[14] The credit was beginning to fall due in much of Africa. Corruption and the inequalities it created no longer bought the loyalty of ordinary people. Instead, it had become the mortar that cemented the privilege of a new upper class.

LAND AND NATIONHOOD

In Africa, growing competition for land was an important source of violence at the end of the twentieth century. Especially in areas of high-density settlement and on the outskirts of cities, both lawlessness and litigiousness were associated with disputes about ownership of plots or farms. Although land boards handled many of the disagreements, the busiest courts were generally those in areas subject to land shortages. When it came to these matters, men and women, especially women, usually considered the judiciary fairer than local or customary assemblies[15] and fairer than many of the land boards.

---

[12] Aileen Marshall, Global Coalition for Africa (GCA), Washington, D.C., interview with author, May 1998. The GCA facilitates quiet, high-level discussion of serious policy problems between leaders in the region.

[13] Francis L. Nyalali, personal communication, March 1999.

[14] Albert O. Hirschman and Michael Rothschild, "The Changing Tolerance for Income Inequality in the Course of Economic Development," *Quarterly Journal of Economics*, 87, 4 (November 1973), passim, pp. 544–566.

[15] Jennifer Widner, Public Attitudes Survey, 1995–96, survey data and open-ended interviews;

Historically, most parts of Africa had a surplus of land to labor. That is, people—not acreage—were the scarce factor of production. Most agriculture remained low intensity and depended on long fallow periods to rejuvenate soil fertility, by contrast with the intensive cultivation that technological improvements like irrigation and fertilizers made possible in other places. This situation was the reverse of the case in Europe during much of the period of the Middle Ages. Indeed, one of the common explanations for the rarity of anything resembling feudalism in Africa was that with an abundance of land, a chief or king could not use control over access to farm plots as an incentive to win men's service as warriors or administrators. Kingships based on control over access to land, accompanied by something like the institution of serfdom, appeared only in a few parts of Ethiopia, Uganda, Rwanda, and Burundi and the northwest tip of Tanzania—the area known as the "Great Lakes Region." But as the twentieth century drew to a close, the relationship of land to labor was changing. It was probably no coincidence that repeated episodes of massive civil strife erupted in Rwanda and Burundi, where population densities exceeded those in the rest of Africa.

Under these conditions, the absence of clear land law became a source of dispute. Through much of the 1980s and into the 1990s, several countries in the region lacked statutes regarding the ownership and transfer of land. In Uganda, the Amin-era land laws were in abeyance in the early 1990s, and the Law Reform Commission was slow to develop replacement legislation. Similarly, in Tanzania, the villagization policies in the 1970s had no basis in law. No statute had motivated them. Land rights were a volatile political issue in Zimbabwe, where veteran liberation fighters sought space claimed by white-owned commercial farms, and in South Africa and Namibia, where people displaced from their land under white minority rule could claim restitution under terms partly spelled out in new constitutions and partly developed by the courts. In Kenya, the appearance of illegal purchases of public land by high officials elicited public outrage and violence.

For the courts, the absence of clear land law posed difficult decisions about the appropriate role judges and magistrates should play. De facto, where there was no land law, magistrates acted as mediators and used common sense to help resolve disputes. This role was not always easy to fulfill. One magistrate in Uganda described the situation where he worked. "Here [in much of the central and south central part of the country], there is a different land tenure system, called *mailo*," he explained.[16] *Mailo* land, from the word "mile," had its

---

and Lynn Khadiagala, "Seeking Justice in Uganda: The Adjudication of Women's Property Rights and the Failure of Popular Justice," Paper prepared for the American Political Science Association annual meeting, Boston, MA, September 3–6, 1998.

[16] Chief Magistrate, interview with author, Mukono, Uganda, November 21, 1995.

roots in an agreement between the king of Buganda and the British government in the early 1900s. "The Kabaka [king of Buganda] was given control over land and he gave plots to his chiefs. There were already people cultivating the land, and they became tenants." Under this system, by contrast with the principles embodied in most African customary tenure law, one person could "own" more than three hundred to five hundred acres. The *mailo* owner possessed a certificate granting title to the land, even though he himself did not occupy the land. For a long period, the customary tenants, "*Kibanja* holders," simply went about their affairs undisturbed.

The magistrate explained that with the end of the civil war in Uganda, the demand for agricultural products had increased and the value of land had risen. The *mailo* owners decided they wanted to develop or sell their acreage. "The owner can't get a loan from bankers to invest unless the land is clear, and purchasers don't want to negotiate with tenants. For us, the problem comes when customary tenants are evicted—when the *mailo* owner wants to develop or sell—and the tenants bring the case to court." Without any clear law, the magistrates "try to find a way to get people to coexist." "It is very difficult. We consider whether the owner has provided any compensation for improvements or permanent crops the tenant may have planted. We try to consider the alternatives available to the tenants and encourage the *mailo* owners to show some compassion."

In Tanzania, the situation was a little different. The villagization policies of the 1970s had no legal underpinning; they were simply policies of the government. With the passage of the Bill of Rights and Duties in the mid-1980s and popular perception of a more open political climate, people began to bring cases to court challenging the government's earlier seizure of lands they had held under customary law. Describing the context, Judge Eusebia Munuo explained, "A lot of people were displaced by villagization and others were forced to leave the land entirely. At the time, if a person challenged the changes, he would be held under the Preventive Detention Act." Since that time, the problem had simmered underground. "After the enactment of Bill of Rights, all these people gathered the courage to come to the courts. We saw a lot of cases."[17]

The legislature first responded by trying to extinguish customary rights in land, by way of a government notice.[18] Chaos ensued, and the president appointed a commission, chaired by Professor Issa Shivji, on the Faculty of Law at Dar, to investigate what should be done. The Shivji Commission offered three broad recommendations that aimed at a pragmatic resolution of the coun-

---

[17] Eusebia Munuo, interview with author, Arusha, Tanzania, March 1996.
[18] Simon Coldham, "Land Tenure Reform in Tanzania: Legal Problems and Perspectives," *Journal of Modern African Studies*, 33, 2 (1995), passim, pp. 227–242.

try's land problems: (1) preexisting customary rights should be extinguished if affected by villagization but saved if not; (2) land rights created during the program should be validated; and (3) "redress should be provided for those who lost their land rights as long as the deprivation was 'grossly unjust and unfair and contrary to the then prevailing policies, practices, and principles of villagisation.'" As one observer pointed out, "The first two recommendations recognise that as a matter of practical politics it would be impossible to reverse the process that created over 8000 sizeable villages since the late 1960s."[19]

Within days of the submission of the Shivji Commission's report, however—well before anyone could have considered the contents closely—the government won passage of new legislation that aimed to preserve the status quo and to remove land cases from the jurisdiction of the courts. Munuo commented, "The government grew worried and enacted a law that said no claims could be contested. The courts' jurisdiction was ousted. People would have to take their disputes to land tribunals in the political wards. The decisions would be political, then."[20]

Action began to unfold in Arusha, where land claims were hotly disputed, and challenges to the law materialized. The key case found its way to the courtroom over which Judge Munuo presided. The men behind the test case were Lohay Akonaay and Joseph Lohay, father and son. In 1987, they sued to recover land the government had taken from them. They had held the land under customary law since colonial days. They had lost it during Operation Vijiji, the villagization program the government had sponsored in the 1970s. The court recognized the mens' claim to the land and ordered the government to return the parcel to them, and the government appealed.

In 1992, while the appeal was pending, the new law, the Regulation of Land Tenure (Established Villages) Act of 1992, extinguished customary rights in land in areas subject to villagization during the 1970s. The law also stipulated that the government would not compensate people whose customary title was extinguished, and it ousted the jurisdiction of the courts. Lohay Akonaay and Joseph Lohay went to court again, challenging the constitutionality of the new statute. Munuo granted their petition and declared the new law null and void.

The case, *Attorney-General v. Lohay Akonaay and Another*,[21] landed in the Court of Appeal, with the government's case argued by Augustine Mrema, the deputy attorney general, later a candidate for the presidency in the 1995 elections. The deputy attorney general argued that customary land was not "property" in the same sense as other land. The owner could not exclude all others, because under law all land was vested in the president of the republic and

---

[19] Coldham, "Land Tenure Reform in Tanzania: Legal Problems and Perspectives," p. 237.
[20] Eusebia Munuo, interview with author, Arusha, Tanzania, March 1996.
[21] Civil Appeal No. 31 of 1994, reported in 1995 LRC 399.

could not be transferred without the consent of the president. The government also argued that there was no legal basis for the court to require compensation for unexhausted improvements, that the constitution permitted the ouster of the court's jurisdiction in land cases, that there was no element of discrimination in the provisions of the new law that reallocated land between people, and that Judge Munuo had erred in striking down the whole land act.

Writing for a three-judge panel of the Court of Appeal, Nyalali took up these issues one at a time. On the status of customary land rights, the chief justice observed that "[i]f the Attorney General is correct, then most of the inhabitants of Tanzania mainland are no better than squatters in their own country." He noted that under the mandate of the League of Nations and its later obligations to the Trusteeship Council, Britain was supposed to safeguard the land for its indigenous inhabitants, not extinguish those rights. These background understandings informed the constitution's provisions on land. Eventually this principle was formalized in an ordinance that declared all land public, vested in the governing authority on trust for the benefit of the indigenous inhabitants of the country. The operative phrase was "on trust." Although people could be deprived of land through procedures consonant with constitutional principles, there was no basis for the government's claim that inhabitants had to have obtained prior consent from the government in order for their claims to constitute a property right.

Having established that customary rights in land were real property rights, the court then went on to say that compensation was due when someone was deprived of land and that what was fair compensation would depend on the circumstances of each case. Compensation was due whenever there was any value added to the land—for example, through clearing, planting, or other investments of labor as well as unexhausted improvements. The court cited the supremacy of constitutional provisions over statute and noted that the constitutional provisions were in line with the policies the country's first president, Julius Nyerere, had articulated many years before.

Finally, Nyalali concurred with the opinion of the High Court that the parts of the act that ousted the jurisdiction of the courts were unconstitutional. They were at odds with the provisions regarding the separation of powers.

In a move that should have mollified government authorities, however, the Court of Appeal went on to say that the practical effect of the judgment was limited, because the ruling did not extend to the many cases where customary rights had been extinguished in accordance with law during the 1970s, prior to the enactment of the Bill of Rights and Duties. Thus, the court's ruling would not produce instability in landholding in most of the country. And in other land judgments at about the same time, Judge Munuo commented that the courts also upheld the statute of limitations. "A lot of claims would be barred after 12 years. So if someone was deprived of land without compensation in

1974, he should have filed a case by 1986." Munuo amplified, "The Court of Appeal used the principle of acquiescence. . . . If people have occupied land for more than 22 years they can't go back now and dispute a claim. So although courts can now hear land cases, these two principles mean that most people are barred from filing." She added, for many people, "There is no real relief in law, but at least the moral claim was recognized and policy makers and politicians have to be more careful."[22]

Lohay Akonaay was not the only type of challenging land issue to reach the Court of Appeal. One of the most delicate problems facing many African countries was to decide how to handle claims to land by pastoral communities and other itinerant groups displaced by public programs.

In 1952 in Tanzania, the colonial government established the Mkomazi Game Reserve in the northeastern part of the country. The area bordered the Tsavo National Park in Kenya, with which it formed an ecological continuum, a home to herds of elephant and other wild animals. Early German explorers had documented the presence of Maasai pastoralists in the area in the late 1800s. Members of the community moved in and out of the reserve in search of water for their cattle herds. And after the creation of the park, the Maasai who were born in the reserve were allowed to remain. The British authorities recorded the names of the inhabitants. These lists were updated periodically after independence to ensure that only those born in the reserve took up residence there.

In the Serengeti and other national parks, where it was felt that pastoralism, ecological management, and tourism were incompatible, customary rights were extinguished by legal means. Pastoralists received compensation, and they moved or were relocated. In reserves the policy was different. In Mkomazi the government allowed grazing and some other types of uses. As monitoring broke down and the entry of pastoralists from other areas resulted in overuse, officials initiated a series of meetings and discussions to resettle people elsewhere, but no effort was made to move people out of the reserve.

In the late 1980s, the ministry decided to revoke all residence permits and to require the pastoralists to leave the reserve. The exact reasons were unclear. Some suggested that pastoralism and game management were no longer fully compatible uses. Others hinted that public policy had grown to favor uses that generated taxable revenue. In 1988, game scouts evicted the Maasai from Mkomazi, in some cases with considerable force, burning homes and assaulting residents. No provision was made for resettlement.

Seeking redress, the pastoralists first petitioned the Office of the President, the prime minister, the minister for home affairs, the Office of the Attorney General, and the then ruling party. "They found no sympathy," advocate

---

[22] Eusebia Munuo, interview with author, Arusha, Tanzania, May 1996.

Ibrahim Juma related. "The prevailing view was that the pastoralists were endangering the Game Reserve. Their way of life was regarded as incompatible with the liberal economy Tanzania was trying to build."[23]

The pastoralists then went to the Legal Aid Committee at the University of Dar es Salaam in 1993, five years after their eviction. Recent court decisions had given new meaning to land rights and had accorded customary claims the status of "property" under state law. Advocates S. E. Mchome and Ibrahim Juma of the university's Legal Aid Committee filed two cases on behalf of fifty-three Maasai against the Minister for Tourism, Natural Resources, and Environment and others.

The counsel for the pastoralists set forth four claims. First they wanted the court to declare that "the customary land rights of the pastoralists residing in Mkomazi were not subordinate and inimical to the wildlife conservation in the Reserve." Second, they argued that the eviction of the residents of Mkomazi was not done in accordance with the laws of Tanzania. Third, they asked the court to state that the laws that established the reserve "did not expressly or by implication extinguish the customary land rights of the Kwavi Maasai residing in Mkomazi." Finally, they complained that the exorbitant fines imposed on the evicted pastoral Maasai by the game scouts were unlawful.

The Maasai had mixed success at the High Court level, where Judge Eusebia Munuo presided. The judge recognized that individuals had customary rights to land in one part of the reserve but did not recognize the claim to the whole area through which the Maasai moved to herd and hunt. And while she recognized the plaintiffs' customary rights to land, she denied restitution, arguing that restitution was no longer practicable. Instead she ordered that the defendants pay monetary compensation and relocate the plaintiffs to another area with sufficient suitable grazing land. To the disappointment of the Maasai, the judge did not allow the plaintiffs to represent their whole community.

The Maasai appealed, hoping in part to obtain the recognition of their ancestral title to the whole reserve, restitution instead of compensation, and redress for the community, not just for the individuals who had brought the complaint.

Nyalali presided over the three-judge panel of the Court of Appeal that heard the case. The decision in *Lekengere Faru Parutu Kamunyu*[24] came as a disap-

---

[23] Ibrahim Juma, "Wildlife Conservation versus Customary Land-Use: Lessons Drawn from Mkomazi Game Reserve Case," Paper presented at the Law and Development Seminar, University of Michigan, Ann Arbor, March 1999, p. 8 and in speech. For more on the rights of pastoralists in wildlife conservation areas, see Issa G. Shivji and Wilbert B. Kapinga, *Maasai Rights in Ngorogora, Tanzania* (London: International Institute for Environment and Development/Hakiardhi, 1998).
[24] Court of Appeal of Tanzania, *Lekengere Faru Parutu Kamunyu and 52 Others v. Minister for Tourism, Natural Resources, and Environment,* Civil Appeal No. 53 of 1998 from Consolidated Civil Case No. 33 of 1994.

pointment to the Maasai and to champions of the rights of indigenous communities, who had followed the case closely. But others felt that it served the interests of the nation as a whole. The Court of Appeal failed to find ancestral title, saying that the record showed early habitation by pastoral communities, but that the Maasai seemed to have joined these groups mid-century and could not be deemed the original claimants. There were disagreements about the interpretation of the evidence. Counsel for the appellants thought the court had gotten it wrong. In Tanzania, as in other countries, figuring out which communities constituted the original inhabitants was a tricky business. Ethnic group boundaries were fluid, and documentation was often poor or nonexistent.

The judges also observed that the law created two sets of rights, not one. Maasai ordinarily resident in the area at the time the reserve was established, as well as their direct descendants, had a continued right of residence. However, that right was separate from the right to graze livestock. To graze cattle or goats required a permit, and an official could revoke a permit. That left the Maasai who lived in the reserve legitimately with the prospect that they might lose their livelihood at any time. Effectively, it meant that the right of residence was tenuous at best. The court noted this problem: "The twenty-seven successful appellants are pastoralists. It is pointless for them to claim restitution of their residence in Mkomazi Game Reserve without the Director's permit to graze their cattle. . . ."

The court then considered the implication of this situation for the form of redress available to the Maasai. It found restitution inappropriate, because of the uncertainty that those allowed to return would also receive grazing permits. Instead, it upheld the High Court opinion that monetary compensation and resettlement offered the better option. It added only that the government should play a more central role in relocation than the High Court had prescribed. It ordered the government to find alternative grazing land comparable to the land provided to other pastoralists in the country within six months of the judgment.

Nyalali later commented that the case was well researched. He was impressed that the advocates for the Maasai had gone back to the German period in assembling their case. But he professed his private concern about the public policy issues involved. He worried that recognition of ancestral claims could mean that 125 tribes could claim land and "what is left is Tanzania." That would endanger the sense of nationhood. "Ethnicity is frowned upon and feared here," he commented. "We accept that a person can change his tribe. Our policy on this subject developed over years of national struggle. The nationalist struggle was a vote against sectarianism."[25] A different decision would have unlocked Pandora's box, he felt.

[25] Francis L. Nyalali, interview with author, Dar es Salaam, Tanzania, July 27, 1999.

Lekengere was interesting in two respects. It showed the increasing popular use of the courts to try to solve very difficult social problems. People were beginning to orient themselves toward the judiciary as an important forum for resolving disputes. At the same time it pointed up the magnitude of the dislocation and the need that lay behind many of the new cases coming before courts throughout the region. Absent alternative ways to earn an income and put food in the mouths of family members, land was becoming a flashpoint. Courts in countries like Tanzania with less concentrated, more equal landholding had an easier time building acceptance than did courts in countries where much of the arable land was in the hands of a few, as it was in Zimbabwe. It would take clever and careful government policy to ensure that mounting desperation did not overwhelm the ability of even the most measured and thoughtful court to help resolve disputes peacefully.

VIGILANTISM

Courts became players in another deeply troubling problem too. Throughout the region, rising crime had promoted a resort to "self-help" or vigilantism and mob justice. Although governmental respect for civil liberties increased in the 1990s in most African countries, mob violence or vigilantism persisted and in some countries appeared to be on the rise. The proportion of countries in Africa with at least one serious outbreak of vigilantism during a year increased from about 19 percent in 1991 to at least 35 percent, and possibly as high as 58 percent, in 1997, although there was considerable year-to-year fluctuation around the general trend.[26]

Modern-day vigilantism had several sources. In rural areas, it was often a response to the lack of an effective government presence. Police had few resources, and crime victims often had to pay for transportation of police to their communities. Under these circumstances, it often seemed better for a community to pursue law and order on its own. Uganda institutionalized such arrangements by granting official recognition to village-based Local Defense Units, to whom the central government provided limited training. Botswana's unarmed tribal police served a similar function. Other countries were concerned about the potential for abuse and were more reticent about granting recognition to such groups. Whatever the policy, there was little doubt that vigilantism in rural areas was often a way to make up for the limited ability of government to respond to an important problem.

Some vigilantism had other roots, however. Especially around election time,

[26] Analysis based on author's coding of the U.S. Department of State, *Human Rights Reports* (Washington, D.C.: U.S. Government Printing Office, multiple years).

political parties themselves sometimes proved a source of mob violence. Many African political parties mobilized "youth wings" prior to elections, and in some cases, these units simply served as standing committees with a more permanent paramilitary character. In Kenya, they often harassed political opponents, pursued critics, and extorted money from vulnerable market women and businessmen, inspiring fear and intolerance. They elicited criticism from religious and community leaders, who called on politicians to assert control over their activities. Similarly, some vigilantism was simply gang activity in disguise.

In Tanzania, vigilantism came to the center of public attention earlier than it did in many countries, and people drew the courts into the picture by bringing suits against neighbors who took the law into their own hands. The origins of vigilantism lay not in the machinations of politicians or local thugs but in a real need for defense. In the late 1970s and early 1980s, the incidence of cattle rustling and related crime rose sharply in the areas of Tanzania near the Kenyan border and around Lake Victoria. People often considered the police ill-prepared to track the rustlers.[27] As in many parts of Africa, young people had traditionally formed self-help groups to supply community services. These groups often helped to meet peak labor demands during planting or harvesting or to take care of other community needs. Among the WaSukuma, the people who shared Chief Justice Nyalali's cultural heritage, the groups gradually acquired a role in defending communities against marauders and especially against the rustlers.[28] They organized forces called *sungusungu*, the local name for the black ants that aggressively defended their anthills. Other communities launched analogous groups.

Government officials gradually began to give these organizations encouragement. They had little alternative, given their own limited capacities. Parliament enacted the People's Militia Act, 1975, which helped it to enroll thousands of young men in a national effort to stop economic sabotage. *Sungusungu* groups began to proliferate at the ward and district levels.[29] The organizations spread to twelve of the country's twenty mainland regions. Local party officials had drawn up guidelines for the *sungusungu* they promoted. The guidelines listed several offenses armies should handle including cattle rustling and the theft of other movable property, smuggling and poaching, manufacture and possession of illegal liquor and bhang (a drug that is smoked), failure of children to attend school, failure to take part in communal work projects, and

---

[27] Sufian Hemed Bukurura, "The Maintenance of Order in Rural Tanzania: The Case of Sungusungu," *Journal of Legal Pluralism and Unofficial Law*, 34 (1994), pp. 10–11.
[28] J. T. Mwaikusa, "Maintaining Law and Order in Tanzania: The Role of Sungusungu Defence Groups," in Joseph Semboja and Ole Therkildsen, eds., *Service Provision under Stress in East Africa: The State, NGOs, and People's Organizations in Kenya, Tanzania, and Uganda* (Copenhagen: Centre for Development Research, 1995), pp. 166–167.
[29] Bukurura, "The Maintenance of Order in Rural Tanzania," p. 7.

sale of goods at illegal prices or by illegal businesses. The government had told the *sungusungu* they could punish those who committed such offenses and send people they believed had committed other crimes to the police.

But complaints also mounted. The voluntary character of the organizations began to disappear. Members often took part of the property they seized to compensate themselves for their effort.[30] Some of the groups violated laws and pursued innocent people. They punished traders or farmers for charging "too much" for the wares and produce they sold, beating the "perpetrators" and taking their cattle. Citizens voiced anger about threats of violence to extract confessions, disappearances of cattle the groups wrongly assumed belonged to others, accusations of witchcraft, return of women to spouses they had fled, and punishment of officials believed to be corrupt. Communities requested police intervention to curb abuses, and cases involving the *sungusungu* began to appear in court.

Nyalali early on had grown worried about the organizations. Certainly he recognized the difficulties that rural communities faced, remote from an effective police force. Yet he was also well aware of the dangers that private enforcement could pose to the rule of law. He had warned the leadership of the political party Chama Cha Mapinduzi of precisely that problem in 1984.

Lawyers also expressed their concern about the *sungusungu* phenomenon. Jani Mwaikusa, from the University of Dar es Salaam Faculty of Law, suggested that if the organizations had limited themselves to mediating civil disputes, no one would have had much argument with them. The problem lay with the assumption of authority in criminal matters. In Tanzania, customary criminal law had long been abolished. Further, the constitution did not permit the creation of paramilitary units outside the ambit of the army.

In 1987, three years after Nyalali's initial expression of concern to political leaders about vigilante violations, complaints began to reach the highest levels of the court. In three cases,[31] High Court Judge James Mwalusanya determined that the *sungusungu* were unconstitutional and operated outside the law. In short order, other people filed civil complaints in the Mwanza High Court station on Lake Victoria where Mwalusanya then worked.

The ruling in *Ngegwe s/o Sangija*[32] set out the main elements of the court's approach to the problem of vigilantism. The case concerned the activities of a

---

[30] Mwaikusa, "Maintaining Law and Order in Tanzania," p. 175.
[31] *Charles Charari Maitari v. Matiko Chacha Cheti and Four Others*, High Court of Tanzania at Mwanza, Civil Case No. 15 of 1987; *Ngegwe s/o Sangija and Three Others v. Republic*, High Court of Tanzania at Mwanza, Criminal Appeal No. 72 of 1987; and *Misperesi K. Maingu v. Hamisis Mtongori and Nine Others*, High Court of Tanzania at Mwanza, Civil Case No. 16 of 1988.
[32] *Ngegwe s/o Sangija and Three Others v. Republic*, High Court of Tanzania at Mwanza, Criminal Appeal No. 72 of 1987.

traditional army known as the Yowe Committee for Peace and Order, which operated in the Mara region near the border with Kenya. Cattle rustling plagued communities in the area. Police had earlier arrested a villager, Malongete Maduhu, on suspicion of cattle rustling, but the court had acquitted the man. The man's community banished him despite the court's decision. When the man did not move out of his dwellings quickly enough, the Yowe committee moved in, destroyed the man's eight huts, and took the household furnishings. They then beat Malongete Maduhu. The police later arrested the Yowe committee members and charged them with malicious damage to property under the appropriate provisions of the country's penal code. The trial court convicted and the members appealed the judgment.

Mwalusanya upheld the lower-court decision. In dicta, he made a number of broad observations about the constitutionality of traditional armies. First, he noted that the *sungusungu* sought to arrest and punish people for offenses spelled out under existing statutes. "Trying to deal with any crime which is covered under the law of our land" in any way other than that provided for under law "is a punishable offence called misprision of offenders" under the country's penal code.[33] Moreover, another section of the penal code "provided an additional offence for any one trying to deal with offenders outside the legal framework": false assumption of the authority of a judicial officer.

Mwalusanya then reached to the recently enacted bill of rights not yet in effect. He noted that Article 15 of the bill of rights, the right to liberty, stated that "[n]o one may be deprived of his freedom or in any way be arbitrarily arrested or detained or deported except a) in accordance with the law; b) when so detained by a court of law in a court case or when sentenced after a criminal trial."[34] Moreover, Article 16, the right to privacy and security of person, also contained language that rendered the traditional armies unconstitutional. Section 2 of Article 16 stipulated that the government "will not in any way infringe or take away that basic right" to privacy and security of person. It permitted some interference with the right, but only provided the limitation took place through "properly enacted law and rules of procedure."[35]

Also in dicta Mwalusanya pondered the implications of his decision for traditional armies and community law enforcement. Under law, powers of citizen arrest existed, but people who tried to arrest lawbreakers were then required to turn their suspects over to the authorities. The *sungusungu* had reached for much more extensive authority, and the law could condone this broader grant of authority only under very limited conditions. Mwalusanya first imagined a much more limited role for the *sungusungu*, mainly as investigators and media-

[33] Ibid.
[34] Ibid.
[35] Ibid.

tors in petty civil disputes. That approach would be unsatisfactory to many community members, he thought. "I understand that if the traditional army is left to operate on this limited scale," he wrote, "it will not be of much use and cost effective. It will be a bulldog without teeth." He then remarked that where law and order had truly broken down as appeared to be the case in Mara, communities could request that the president declare a state of emergency. In a state of emergency, properly declared, the regional commissioner or district commissioner could recruit the traditional armies to help out with law enforcement. But no states of emergency had been declared.

The import of these decisions took time to sink in. The bill of rights remained in abeyance, still in its transition period. Parliament had to decide whether to take the judgments as the basis for changing the law or wait until another constitutional challenge materialized and the court struck down the laws that empowered the *sungusungu*. Legislators debated the matter in the aftermath of Judge Mwalusanya's decision. Perhaps for want of a better alternative or inspired by the possibilities the groups provided for asserting authority, political leaders continued to condone the *sungusungu*, apparently oblivious to the views judges expressed in court. In 1989, the office of the president granted an amnesty to all *sungusungu* members arrested on suspicion of having committed crimes, as well as those already convicted and in prison.[36] Parliament passed legislation to transform the groups into a People's Militia whose members had powers of arrest identical to that of the police. An official championed the *sungusungu* as "young CCM [Chama Cha Mapinduzi] members who are fulfilling the party's call for mass action to maintain security."[37] And in 1990, then minister for home affairs, Augustine Mrema, announced that he would encourage the expansion of the *sungusungu* to urban areas and insist that every man participate.[38] When one group exceeded its mandate the following year and removed a magistrate from the bench while court was in session, the president ordered the charges brought against the group dropped.[39]

Parliament passed new enactments aimed at harmonizing the role of the vigilante groups and the police, but the actions did little to solve the more fundamental problems. Nyalali gradually and quietly asserted his views in the effort to develop a workable solution. In a letter to the president, he proposed alternative wording of new legislation, which would make existing laws consistent with the constitution and, he argued, promote the rule of law. He followed the suggestion with a memorandum when the government failed to act. But in 1999, he noted that the challenge of harmonizing the village teams with the

---

[36] Mwaikusa, "Maintaining Law and Order in Tanzania," p. 172.
[37] Chama Cha Mapinduzi Chief Secretary Rashidi Kawawa as quoted in Ray Abrahams, "Sungusungu: Village Vigilante Groups in Tanzania," *African Affairs*, 86 (1987), p. 190.
[38] Mwaikusa, "Maintaining Law and Order in Tanzania," p. 170.
[39] Ibid., pp. 172–173.

official state police functions continued. He commented, "In my opinion, without harmonization, the government machinery will fall apart."[40]

Tanzania's *sungusungu* cases exemplified the difficult issues courts faced throughout the region. There was no doubt that the traditional armies' mode of behavior in the late 1980s and early 1990s violated a widely shared sense of the rule of law both as respect for rules and as respect for a right to due process in the deprivation of liberty or property. The armies' mode of action posed a challenge to the very institution of the law and of the court. They also struck many ordinary citizens as unfair, if the number of cases brought by victims in the aftermath of Mwalusanya's decision was any indication. At the same time, there was equally little doubt that the government had minimal ability to respond to the security needs of rural communities—especially those along borders. Those whose property police could not protect would cry that they received no help from government and that the rule of law was therefore irrelevant.

WITCHCRAFT

Citizens asked courts to adjudicate disputes about another vexing challenge, a perceived upsurge in witchcraft accusations and murders in many communities. Witchcraft beliefs embraced a wide range of ideas, practices, and motivations, but in their various forms they usually shared the idea that the power to inflict injury and benefit could be exercised through unobservable, supernatural means. Further, so great was the danger witches appeared to pose that people who were believed to have participated in witchcraft could be subject to harassment, maiming, or murder.

The absence of a fair hearing and reliance on spectral evidence or no evidence at all, coupled with the magnitude of the injuries accusers inflicted, seemed to violate the basic tenets of the rule of law. To the extent that the rule of law embodies a belief in due process—that anyone accused of an offense should have a fair hearing before an impartial judge—then witch murders and vigilantism posed a problem. There was no impartial third party involved in vigilante justice or in the passion-driven witch murder.

Witchcraft accusations appeared to increase in many parts of Africa during the late 1980s and 1990s. No systematic data will ever be available to confirm whether the perceived trend was real or not, but newspaper reports and editorials, coupled with the impressions of lawyers and judges, leant some credibility to the anecdotes people told. In Tanzania, Ministry of Home Affairs statistics reported that in the fourteen years between 1970 and 1984, there were 3,333

---

[40] Francis L. Nyalali, personal communication, March 1999.

reported witchcraft-related incidents in which 3,692 people died.[41] These "base rate" figures most surely underreported the extent of the beliefs and accusations. And the beliefs did not disappear with the passage of time. In the late 1990s, Tanzanian legal scholar Chris Maina Peter observed with obvious frustration that "[e]ducation on the part of our people seems not to be of assistance . . . as thirty years after independence, the belief in witchcraft seems to be getting stronger. . . ."[42] There were outbreaks in many different settings, from Cameroon to Tanzania and Zimbabwe, and even to the antiapartheid movement in South Africa.

Early anthropologists had reasoned that witchcraft was a way to maintain equilibrium when communities endured rapid economic and social change. It deterred people from transgressing local norms and helped ensure higher levels of equality and order. Fear of accusation and death led people to conform with local conventions, reduce displays of difference, and otherwise watch their steps during difficult times. In this vein, one rural woman in Uganda observed, "Our village council tries to scare people by saying there are witches in the area. It makes us behave ourselves. We fear what people might say and do."[43] The beliefs helped uphold the moral system by creating suspicion of behavior "thought to be rude, mean, or snatching."[44] In the 1980s and 1990s, witchcraft beliefs appeared in a wide variety of contexts, however. The functional analysis could not accout for the range of forms or the highly local character of many of the outbreaks.

In some instances witchcraft provided an explanation for social calamities that were hard to understand. Witchcraft accusations sometimes appeared in instances when the hidden mental illness of a community member wrought havoc. Devastating to people who depend on thatched roofs over their heads, arson could easily elicit specific or general accusations. One society's pyromaniac is another's witch.[45] Similarly, people sometimes attributed epidemics to the influence of witches. For example, in Ghana, in 1996, elderly women were killed by several youths who had accused them of causing cerebral-spinal meningitis.[46]

---

[41] Simeon Mesaki, "Witch-Killing in Sukumaland," in Ray Abrahams, ed., *Witchcraft in Contemporary Tanzania* (Cambridge: African Studies Center, University of Cambridge, 1994), p. 52.

[42] Chris Maina Peter, *Human Rights in Tanzania: Selected Cases and Materials* (Köln: Rüdiger Köppe Verlag, 1997) p. 135.

[43] Survey respondent, Political Attitudes Surveys, 1995–96, open-ended interview with author, Mbarara District, Uganda, February 1996.

[44] As paraphrased in Mary Douglas, "Introduction: Thirty Years after Witchcraft, Oracles, and Magic," in Mary Douglas, ed., *Witchcraft Confessions and Accusations* (London: Tavistock, 1970), p. xviii–xix.

[45] Jennifer Widner, Public Attitudes Surveys, 1995–96.

[46] Edward Ameyibor, "Witches Refuse to Go Home," http://www.ipshre@harare.iafrica.com, accessed July 14, 1998.

In other instances jealousy seemed to motivate accusations. The aim was to "level" inequalities in status and wealth, bringing down the successful innovators as well as those whose gains were ill-gotten. Often such accusations were linked to growing disparities in access to land or to differences in the success or failure of new cropping techniques. The accusations seemed to come from people who were concerned that some of their kin or neighbors were getting ahead. Certainly, jealousy was widely perceived by ordinary people to be a widespread problem. "Jealousy is what stands in the way of development in our communities," said one survey respondent, in a comment echoed by others.[47] Looking back on research conducted during the 1930s, scholar Martin Chanock recalled, similarly, the views expressed to him: "'What our parents used to say to us was 'Pride'. If a man is proud and is not sociable with his neighbours; if he boasts . . . he is a witch!' Also mentioned were 'hoeing a very large field'; or 'Being more wealthy'; or 'Eating fine food alone.' "[48] In Nyalali's Tanzania, witchcraft outbreaks sometimes had a similar character. Wrote one researcher of the community she studied, "[T]he better off . . . are accused of witchcraft because getting ahead is felt to be at the expense of social obligations to both kin and neighbours."[49] In Cameroon, new owners of larger cocoa plots found themselves accused of turning their victims into zombies who worked on their plantations, invisibly.[50]

Yet there was also evidence that wealthier people mobilized the language of witchcraft to their own ends too. Denunciations could be used to move people off of land, for example. The vocabulary could be turned to retaliate against those perceived to stand in the way of the newly rich or the newly empowered. There were reports of urban people who accused rural kin of bewitching their work and their families.[51]

Young men and women, those theoretically more attuned to new intellectual currents, were often the accusers. For example, in South Africa, notorious outbreaks of witchcraft during the 1980s and early 1990s appeared to have their roots among youthful antiapartheid activists. Some of the protesters organized themselves as vigilantes, committed abuses in the course of their activities, and

---

[47] Jennifer Widner, Botswana and Uganda Local Government Satisfaction Surveys, 1995–96.

[48] Martin Chanock, *Law, Custom and Social Order* (Cambridge: Cambridge University Press, 1985), p. 101 in reference to a study by Monica Wilson.

[49] Maia Green, "Shaving Witchcraft in Ulanga," in Ray Abrahams, ed., *Witchcraft in Contemporary Tanzania* (Cambridge: African Studies Center, University of Cambridge, 1994), p. 29.

[50] Peter Geschiere, "Globalization and the Power of Indeterminate Meaning: Witchcraft and Spirit Cults in Africa and East Asia," *Development and Change*, 29 (1998), p. 822.

[51] Ralph A. Austen, "The Moral Economy of Witchcraft," in Jean Comaroff and John Comaroff, eds., *Modernity and Its Malcontents* (Chicago: University of Chicago Press, 1993), pp. 90 and 92.

then resorted to witchcraft denunciations as a justification, when confronted by community members. Similarly, the *sungusungu* vigilante groups originally organized to respond to cattle rustling and other concerns sometimes turned the language of witchcraft against marginal members of their own communities, possibly also to provide a justification for their own excesses. Their actions could easily have attracted some support from parents or relatives, not out of shared belief, but from a desire to protect their families' reputations, to "cover up" their childrens' misdeeds. Yet although this kind of explanation accorded reasonably well with the known facts, it flies in the face of evidence from South Africa that youthful activists also killed the daughters of suspected witches on the grounds that the trait could be inherited.[52] Beliefs appeared to matter.

All of the kinds of problems associated with witchcraft outbreaks increased during the late 1980s and 1990s. Economic crises of various sorts and political liberalization altered the playing field. Peter Geschiere, a scholar with long experience in the study of witchcraft beliefs, suggested that the inequalities that arose in Africa during the 1980s and 1990s were unsettling. "New forms of power and wealth seem to rupture old domestic solidarities. That is why they evoke strong sentiments of jealousy and therefore hidden aggression."[53] These changes created fertile ground for witchcraft beliefs where there were few ideological competitors.

Most common law countries still had laws on the books that technically permitted prosecution for witchcraft. Witchcraft proclamations originally enacted in the colonial period and retained by independent governments enabled people to prosecute witches in court, under certain narrowly defined circumstances, although they forbade witchcraft and witchcraft allegations in most situations. For example, the Ugandan Witchcraft Act made it illegal to threaten another with death by witchcraft, to cause injury by witchcraft, to practice witchcraft, to claim to be a witch, or to hire another to perform witchcraft. But in a 1973 case, *Uganda v. Fenekansi Oyuko*, the court ruled that the evidence required to establish whether someone is engaged in witchcraft must go beyond rumor to "acknowledgment, conduct and life."[54] Spectral evidence was unacceptable.

More often, courts saw parties present witchcraft as a defense to a criminal charge or as grounds for mitigation. Members of a family or community would

---

[52] Peter Delius, *A Lion Amongst the Cattle* (Portsmouth: Heinemann, 1996), pp. 191–196.

[53] Geschiere, "Globalization and the Power of Indeterminate Meaning," p. 10.

[54] Daniel D. N. Nsereko, "Witchcraft as a Criminal Defence, from Uganda to Canada and Back," *Manitoba Law Journal*, 24, 1 (Fall 1996), pp. 38–39. See also T. W. Bennett and W. M. Scholtz, "Witchcraft: A Problem of Fault and Causation," *Comparative and International Law of Southern Africa* (CILSA), XII (1979), pp. 288–301; and K. O. Mutungi, *The Legal Aspects of Witchcraft in East Africa* (Nairobi, Kenya: East African Literature Bureau, 1977).

fetch the police in the aftermath of a killing, maiming, or property damage. Then the accused would offer a defense claiming the act was excused either because the victim's acts, words, or reputation constituted provocation or because the belief in witchcraft was so strong that fear could drive a person into a condition tantamount to insanity. Counsel raised belief in witchcraft as grounds for mitigation, as they did in South Africa when those accused of murdering witches and their daughters were brought to trial.[55] Provocation or insanity could lead to reclassification of murder as manslaughter because it negates the required *mens rea* for murder.

Eastern African precedent typically held that witchcraft was not available to mitigate a crime if there is no immediate attack that provoked the infliction of injury.[56] The familiar requirements used in "fighting words" defenses in other common law systems applied. For example, as legal scholar Daniel Nsereko observed, the Ugandan code insisted that those accused of injuring an alleged witch must have acted under "sudden provocation," arising out of a "wrongful act or insult," and "before there is time for . . . passion to cool."[57] Because these elements were not present in most cases, witchcraft defenses tended to fail.

The Tanzanian court was part of the general trend in its handling of witchcraft. In 1988, in *Malando Malinganya and Mzalendo Malinganya v. The Republic*, the Court of Appeal reiterated the rules that governed. Most of the facts in the case were not in dispute. Two youths from neighboring families, Swale Kizinza and Kalwinzi Malinganya, had quarreled while drawing water from a well. In the words that followed the youths exchanged accusations of witchcraft. According to Kalwinzi Malinganya, Swale Kizinza asserted that his grandmother had witchcraft powers, had caused the death of Kalwinzi Malinganya's father earlier, and would soon bewitch three more members of his family. According to Swale Kizinza, it was Kalwinzi who had accused his family of practicing witchcraft.

Kalwinzi Malinganya reported the information he claimed to have received to his brothers and other family members. The Malinganya family then summoned the ten-cell leader and the branch secretary of the party, who in turn organized a village meeting to discuss the problem. Shortly thereafter three members of the Malinganya family fell ill and were taken to the hospital. One of the women died.

After the burial, Kalwinzi Malinganya's two brothers found Swale Kizinza's grandmother and great aunt tending vegetables in a field, attacked them with bush knives, and left them to die. They then reported their actions to their own household, the mourners at their homestead, and the village leaders, who put them in the village lockup. The defense counsel argued that the initial assertion of

[55] Delius, *A Lion Amongst the Cattle*, p. 204.
[56] *Eria Galikuwa v. Republic*, 18 Eastern African Court of Appeal 175.
[57] Nsereko, "Witchcraft as a Criminal Defence, from Uganda to Canada and Back," pp. 50–51.

witchcraft, followed by the death of the wife of one of the accused, "was so frightening that the appellants were provoked into killing the two elderly women."[58]

In the proceedings of the trial court, the two assessors sitting with the trial judge had urged acquittal on the grounds that witchcraft allegations constituted provocation. The trial judge disagreed. The defendants appealed the trial judge's decision on multiple grounds.

Writing for a three-judge panel, Nyalali held that the defense of provocation was not available to the defendants.

> It seems to us that the difference of views between the gentlemen assessors and the learned trial judge is attributable to the difference between the ordinary meaning of provocation, and the legal meaning of provocation. Provocation in the ordinary meaning does not afford a defence to a charge of murder. Only provocation in the legal sense amounts to a defence as stated and defined under sections 201 and 202 of the Penal Code.
>
> We note that similar provisions have existed throughout East Africa for a considerable period of time, and for that reason the case law concerning provocation based on witchcraft was collated by the Court of Appeal for Eastern Africa in the landmark case of *Eria Galikuwa vs. R.* . . . . In that case the circumstances of provocation by witchcraft were summarized as follows:

> '(1) The act causing death must be proved to be done in the heat of passion, i.e. in anger; fear of immediate death is not sufficient.
> (2) If the facts establish that the deceased was performing some act in the presence of the accused which he believed, and an ordinary person of his community would genuinely believe, was an act of witchcraft against him and the accused was so angered as to be deprived of his self-control, the defence of grave and sudden provocation was open to the accused.
> (3) A belief in witchcraft per se did not constitute a circumstance of excuse or mitigation for killing a person believed to be a witch or wizard when there is no immediate provocative act.
> (4) The provocative act must amount to a criminal offence under the criminal law.
> (5) The provocation must be not only grave but sudden and the killing have been done in the heat of passion.
> (6) The provocative act might indicate a future intention on the part of the doer and might therefore be of such a nature as to come within the definition of legal provocation.'[59]

The court suggested that there was no sudden provocation. Moreover, the killing was premeditated.

---

[58] *Malando Malinganya and Mzalendo Malinganya v. The Republic,* Criminal Appeal No. 87 of 1988, Court of Appeal of Tanzania at Mwanza.
[59] Ibid.

Yet within the legal sector there was considerable internal debate about these matters, and courts sometimes diverged in the strategies they supported. Judges typically acknowledged that in not recognizing suspicion of witchcraft as reasonable provocation, they imposed stiff sentences on people who genuinely may have believed they faced a dire threat. At the same time, they argued that court decisions had an expressive function and that by taking a strong stand against witchcraft beliefs they could generate a change in legal culture more supportive of the rule of law. Historically, in much of eastern Africa, judges tended to convict, then offer a recommendation for executive clemency.[60] In Uganda, occasionally courts dealt with the tension between community norms and broader legal principles by accepting more liberal interpretations of the insanity defense.[61]

The stances courts took did appear to affect the incidence and character of witchcraft accusations and practices. If the casual perception was of a general trend toward increased indulgence in witchcraft beliefs during the last years of the twentieth century, nonetheless the problem acquired much larger proportions in some places compared to others. In Cameroon, where the legal system placed fewer restrictions on the kinds of evidence acceptable in witchcraft cases, there was a significant increase in the number of incidents and an expansion of the forms witches were believed to assume. Although earlier state courts adhered to contemporary common law trends and refused to convict for witchcraft or accept witchcraft as a defense, in the mid-1970s, the legal community did an about-face.[62] Restrictions on reputational evidence, and implicitly on the use of spectral evidence, were relaxed. Witch doctors were allowed to appear in court as witnesses. One judge even permitted a witch doctor to sue an individual for damages on the grounds that the person, an alleged witch, had interfered with his investigation.[63] New forms of witchcraft, including one that affected only boys, appeared. And politicians mobilized the occult to their own purposes.[64] A market for the services of witch doctors developed, as new urban elites were prepared to pay handsomely for assistance in combating witchcraft accusations, keeping allegations out of court, and ensuring that court action was taken against those who accused those who were better off.[65]

The pattern bore striking parallels to patterns in early modern Europe and the United States. There, even where witchcraft beliefs were strong, accusa-

[60] Robert B. Seidman, "Witch Murder and Mens Rea: A Problem of Society under Radical Social Change," *Modern Law Review*, 28 (1965), p. 49.

[61] Nsereko, "Witchcraft as a Criminal Defence, from Uganda to Canada and Back," p. 59.

[62] Cyprian F. Fisiy and Peter Geschiere, "Judges and Witches, or How Is the State to Deal with Witchcraft?" *Cahiers d'études africaines*, 118, XXX-2 (1990), pp. 135–156.

[63] Ibid., pp. 144–145.

[64] Ibid.

[65] Ibid., p. 151.

tions against witches were restrained so long as an authoritative institution could offer ritual protection, as the medieval church once did.[66]

The Salem witch trials in the early history of the United States echoed the arguments of African lawyers for firm court intervention and adherence to standard evidence law.[67] In that instance, and in many of the African outbreaks, the accusations had multiple sources. Young girls caught doing things they weren't supposed to do blamed their behavior on witchcraft by marginal members of the community. Parents came to their defense, taking up their charges. Religious leaders fueled the ensuing witch hunt in an effort to build a base of support for themselves and permanent homes among people who had tossed out their predecessors. Then the less landed and less entrepreneurial leveled accusations against the more "modern" and successful. The many motives fed on each other in the absence of a government, which could provide an accepted, routinized way to resolve disagreements. Those accused landed in prison without a trial until a special tribunal formed and sent several women to their death. Only after nineteen people were hanged did religious leader Increase Mather intervene and insist that the courts abjure the use of spectral evidence of the sort the tribunal had accepted. When they did so, the accusations stopped.

CREATING AN OPEN DOOR

As Learned Hand had observed, the judiciary by itself could not prevent intolerance from polarizing the communities the courts served. Yet courts in Africa, as in the United States, searched for ways to help ease tensions.

The Tanzanian court found ideas in Washington, D.C., at the Superior Court of the District of Columbia. The superior court had helped train Tanzanian magistrates in the techniques of alternative dispute resolution, as part of an effort to reduce delay. But the magistrates also visited a superior court program that put those same skills to work in an effort to help people mediate disputes between neighbors. The superior court's "Multi-Door Division" ran an unusual "Citizens' Intake Program" that tried to help community members solve problems without filing lawsuits or taking their disagreements to the street. The program worked with nongovernmental organizations to build a network of mediators familiar with the law. When a group of neighbors brought a problem to the program's attention, the superior court helped them find peo-

---

[66] See Mary Douglas's paraphrase of Keith Thomas's long book in Mary Douglas, ed., *Witchcraft Confessions and Accusations* (London: Tavistock, 1970), p. 73. The Thomas book is *Religion and the Decline of Magic* (New York: Charles Scribner's Sons, 1971).
[67] Paul S. Boyer and Stephen Nissenbaum, *Salem Possessed: The Social Origins of Witchcraft* (Cambridge, MA: Harvard University Press, 1974).

ple who could sit down with them, listen, talk about how they might solve the problem creatively, and help structure a settlement.

This innovation attracted the attention of visiting African jurists, who thought it could be a useful adjunct to the court's services at the lower levels. One of the Tanzanian judges who had visited the superior court returned home and promptly tried out the idea. Stationed in Arusha, the capital of land litigation in Tanzania, Judge John Mroso had just arrived back from the United States when community members brought him an especially intractable conflict that neither elders nor religious leaders had succeeded in resolving. The people involved thought that their communities would certainly clash violently if the problem could not be resolved quickly. They were angry. Mroso sat down with them and found that before too long it was possible to work out a basis for agreement and for a cessation of hostilities. He smiled, looking pleased but a bit weary, "The people said they were so pleased that they would start to bring all of their problems to the court!"[68]

[68] John Mroso, interview with author, August 1995.

Taking Stock

IT WAS HARD for the chief justice to find time for reflection. During the early 1990s, Nyalali sometimes slipped away to spend a day or two at a favorite retreat. In spite of the effort to decentralize authority within the courts, the press of business made it hard to find the peace to think about institutional goals and strategy, or to write an especially difficult opinion.

The chief justice's favorite haven was a place called Lushoto. The small town had taken root on the slopes of the Usambara Mountains in Northern Tanzania. In the days of the single-party state, the government had maintained a political party training center there, and a small campus of low, white-washed buildings remained: a very simple dormitory, a mess hall, a few classrooms, some guestrooms. There were no frills. The atmosphere was austere.

To get to Lushoto, one took the Moshi-Arusha road north out of Dar. On the drive, the humidity of the Indian Ocean coast gradually gave way. And eventually the wetter, hilly landscape of the eastern part of the country began to flatten into the savannas of the northern plains, pierced here and there by steep mountains. At a lively spot-in-the-tarmac called Mombo, a still narrower road turned off and wound upward, with many hairpin turns, through scenery reminiscent of parts of the American Southwest or of Greece. Streams gushed over rocks and down a deep ravine, intermittently visible through gaps in the eucalyptus. Villagers had cleared the ridges as well as the land below, revealing rust-red clay, the distinctive laterite soil of Africa. From time to time, it was possible to glimpse some of the long vistas for which the eastern and southern parts of the continent were famous.

If Nyalali coveted anything, he coveted this place for the judiciary. He wanted an institute to train court administrators, magistrates, and judges—a place of simplicity and dignity, not far removed from the lives ordinary people live. He wanted a meeting place for courts throughout this part of Africa. People argued with him that the location was a little too out-of-the-way, well over two hours' drive from Arusha, where the nearest airport was located. The faint of heart also observed that the access road could handle only one car in either direction at any given time, and at most points the road edge dropped off into the ravine, allowing no room for carelessness. Nonetheless, its location and austerity made the campus relatively inexpensive to own and operate. And given his belief in a symbiosis between democracy and the rule of law, Nyalali may also have felt that there was something symbolically appropriate about inhabiting a place that had formerly served as a leadership training camp in the single-party era.

When time permitted, Nyalali devoted himself to the Lushoto project. By 1996, he had won an agreement to turn the campus into a center to train registrars and clerks about how to run the country's courts. Administrative reform had been a central theme in his own career, from his early initiatives in Musoma and Bukoba to his introduction of new calendar systems, case-flow management techniques, and alternative dispute resolution. Improving effectiveness had also played a central role in his relationship with the Superior Court of the District of Columbia and other groups in the United States. The Republic of Ireland had assisted greatly with a judicial training course, and the Tanzanians felt a special kinship with the Irish, whom they perceived to have a more recent history of colonial subjugation. But the Americans had approached management problems creatively in Nyalali's view.

In March 1996, Nyalali opened the new Lushoto Institute for Judicial Administration to train the clerks and registrars who played a central role in making the courts work. He dedicated the main lecture hall to the memory of Robert Shuker, who had started the deep friendship with the judges of the superior court, a friendship carried forward vigorously by Judge Nan Shuker. A bronze plaque outside the hall bore Robert Shuker's name. In his dedication speech, Nyalali noted that although Lushoto was originally designed to be an institute for training judges and magistrates, "we have decided that at this stage in our history, a main purpose of the institute should be to train court administrators. One of the subjects new court administrators will study is case-flow management—a subject about which our friends on the District of Columbia Superior Court have had much practical wisdom to impart."[1]

Nyalali explained, "Before, the courts took people straight from secondary school into the system. They were trained at the level of a certificate in law. At Lushoto, the first class will be selected from the supporting staff already in the

---

[1] Francis L. Nyalali, Lushoto Institute for Judicial Administration dedication speech, author's notes, March 1996.

judiciary. Later it will be open to others and the courts will place ads in the press so that people can apply for these posts. The aim is to begin to create a career structure—a hierarchy or promotion ladder."

THE LONG VIEW

Although Lushoto came to emphasize court administration, it was also, as Nyalali suggested, a good place to reflect on the broader changes taking place in the judicial world throughout the region. Nyalali's tenure as chief justice was long—longer than that of any other chief justice of his time. When he stepped down in February 2000, he had served over twenty-four years. He turned the court over to Barnabas Samatta, who had served as deputy chief justice, the *jaji kiongozi*, and attracted considerable respect in that role.

Nyalali's twenty-plus years in the post had seen deep changes in Africa. There were more people. They were more mobile. They were young. And their activities increasingly impinged on one another. With less space per capita and new technologies that made the world a smaller place, private activities imposed costs on others in ways they had not before. As the scale of life changed, the skills of neighbors and elders sometimes proved inadequate to resolve disputes.

Even more pressing was the need to restrain that new creature, the modern state. As in other parts of the world, what really bothered people—what had provoked a *volte-face* in the early 1980s in Tanzania, for example—was arbitrariness on the part of those empowered by new institutions. Law and courts could be harnessed to help to establish a system of checks and balances—a sober second thought to help prevent abuse of public trust. They provided a mechanism for building accountability. But the courts had no inherent legitimacy, and unless people were willing to use them and accept them, it would be too easy for an unsympathetic head of state to undermine their very basis without so much as modest protest from anyone.

Independence from partisan influence in particular cases, the kind of independence rooted in the separation of powers, helped foster the qualities essential to effective performance of these roles. This kind of autonomy might not have been so necessary in community forums, where people had plenty of opportunity to assess the integrity and fair-mindedness of the chief or elders as well as the insight of leaders into local affairs. But in a large nation-state, where people could not study the character of those who presided over dispute resolution and applied the law, this kind of independence contributed importantly to the willingness to use the courts and respect their decisions.

How was it possible to create this sort of independence? Appropriately, in his role as a sitting chief justice, Nyalali was too reserved to summarize his own thinking about institution building out loud. But his actions during preceding years, taken together with insights gleaned from experience in other parts of the region, suggested a way to think about the task. It was possible to offer some general observations about the enterprise, as well as some practical rules of thumb.

The general observations came first. Policy makers and social scientists often sought formulas or covering laws they could use to provide quick understanding in unfamiliar settings. Nyalali and other chief justices thought this a vain ambition, with respect to building independent courts. It was true that some things, like economic growth or participation, could be understood as a function of higher incomes, more exposure to news, an increase in the number of decision makers, and other discrete factors. But many of the institutions that governed social life had a different character. They were "made, not born." They were crafted through a process of bargaining and negotiation. Instead of looking for a formula, people needed to recognize that the smartest strategy for building an independent judiciary would always depend on the behavior of many people, outside the courts as well as inside. There was no single best route.

A second general observation, linked to the first, was that not all historical periods presented equally auspicious points of departure for institutional change. In the case of Africa, the 1990s created better opportunities for the emergence of independent courts than had the first decades after colonial rule. The international political climate was more conducive, and the public temper was more favorably disposed in the 1990s than in the 1960s and 1970s. Conditions didn't determine whether independent courts could emerge, but they did affect the probabilities of success. Even short-term shifts in regional circumstances could alter ideas and incentives in ways that made it easier for a court to embark on reform later in a wave of change rather than earlier.

Resource scarcity was another general factor that shaped bargaining between institutions. Bad telephone service, shortages of paper, failure to publish law reports, no money to pay witnesses, poor training of police, economies that meant judges worked out of prosecutors' offices—all of these circumstances made it harder to build effectiveness and independence. Yet these things did not dictate outcomes. The existence of considerable variation in trends across countries that were similarly situated pointed to the recognition that institutional relationships were the product of negotiation and that organizational leaders had some space to shape results even if poverty created special obstacles.

A fourth important point was that the substantive law mattered. A body of rules, procedures, constitutional principles, international standards, and professional conventions shaped what judges could and could not do in their efforts to increase the capacity and independence of their institutions. A realistic understanding of the options available and acceptable means of pursuing them depended on knowledge of the law, and not just of one country's law but of the range of possibility presented by similar kinds of systems in other parts of the world.

New, justiciable bills of rights could enhance the appearance of fairness by giving the courts the ability to take up cases where an ordinary person complained the government or a politician had violated a basic entitlement. Earlier, some courts in the region were unable to hear such matters, and judges worried people would conclude that the judiciary served only those in power. The occasional rights case resolved against a government officer could send a powerful signal about impartiality to the larger community. The substantive law and methods of interpretation mattered for building bridges. So did efforts to communicate in ways ordinary people could understand.

Finally, under these circumstances, the best advice one court could give another was to point out some of the mechanisms of change, the properties of different structures and arrangements, and experiences with local experiments. The "rules of thumb" Nyalali and others might have offered had mainly to do with these sorts of matters.

RULES OF THUMB

Most judges started with the observation that without the power of the purse or the army behind it, as had the legislature and the executive, the judiciary initially found itself at the mercy of the other branches. Therefore, in the first instance, independence usually resulted from the desire of the legislature or the executive to delegate authority to an impartial body. The motives for this grant of autonomy varied in the early years. They were idiosyncratic. Personal experience prompted some heads of state, such as Seretse Khama in Botswana, to take for granted that independent courts were important. Both the bench and the bar circulated across borders in southern Africa, and the presence of so many antiapartheid judges, lawyers, and activists helped make judicial independence part of common sense in policy circles. In other countries, opportunities to develop judicial independence arose as leaders grew concerned about corruption within the ranks of the ruling parties or with arbitrariness and excess on the part of lower officials whose actions they could not supervise directly. The ability of private parties or prosecutors to bring complaints against wayward civil servants and party members in independent courts helped reduce the need for senior politicians to monitor and cajole. Tanzania exemplified this model. In still other places, as in Uganda, a new government had defined itself in opposition to the abuses of power committed under its predecessors. One of those abuses had been the infringement of judicial independence, including the assassination of a chief justice. To make good on its own claims to legitimacy, the government had to give the courts latitude.

But if independence often had its roots in a delegation of authority by the executive or the legislature, that is not where the story ended. This grant of power could easily prove ephemeral. There was little to prevent a change of heart among a country's political leaders or a shift in the attitudes of legislators. Nor was there any guarantee that either could control the behavior of supporters or local strongmen. To secure an independent judiciary, to make it last, it was vital to find more permanent allies.

In other parts of the world, independent national courts had grown up slowly and haltingly, often in tandem with the expansion of competitive markets and democracy. The elements of this trio had rarely appeared all at once, but each tended to reinforce the others by creating mutually supportive constituencies. Over time, the judges argued, opposition political party leaders would find independent judiciaries useful to safeguard civil and political liberties and to ensure impartial adjudication of election disputes. Similarly, when eventually exhausted by the practice of paying for judgments or resorting to self-help, entrepreneurs in competitive market systems would come to believe that their fortunes were tied at least partly to impartial enforcement of rules that preserved competition and protected contracts. And economically powerful interest groups outside government wanted to ensure impartial resolution of disputes or help prevent each new legislative session from overturning the laws its predecessor had enacted.[2]

It was surely significant that the effort to build judicial independence in eastern and southern Africa corresponded with greater interest in markets and democracy. As Nyalali had said in his speeches, law was the glue that held these systems together—that helped make them work—and vice versa. In Tanzania, Uganda, and South Africa, judges were important in making some of these broad changes in the character of political and economic life happen, although they acted in a nonjudicial capacity when they did so. Nyalali had helped lead the commission that recommended adoption of a multiparty system of government. Justice Benjamin Odoki had overseen the drafting of a new constitution in Uganda. In South Africa, judges were heavily consulted in the design of the country's new constitutional framework.

But it takes time for people to develop maxims about where their interests lie in new contexts. The incentives institutional changes create in theory do not always match the reality. There is a learning curve. For some time to come, the courts would be unable to rely on private actors or political party leaders as steady constituents. Moreover, they themselves had to make their usefulness apparent before they would win allegiance from these potential clienteles.

As a temporary measure, cultivating international interest in judicial institutions could help. To build popular acceptance, courts needed to perform better, and that took both ideas and money. The financial situations of countries

---

[2] William M. Landes and Richard A. Posner, "The Independent Judiciary in an Interest Group Perspective," *Journal of Law and Economics*, 18, 3 (December 1975), passim, pp. 875–901.

throughout the region in the late 1980s were such that the judiciary faced tough competition for scarce funds. Therefore, linkages across borders were important. They could generate ideas. They could yield support and enhance the courts' leverage in negotiations with the other branches. Moreover, greater international involvement could provide protection from egregious infringement of judicial independence by placing the courts "in the limelight," making them highly visible to outsiders.

The bilateral and multilateral aid donors were generally receptive. Development policy had started to shift in the late 1980s, as economists realized that the competitiveness of markets depended on an array of laws and institutions. Young technocrats in ministries of finance had started to think about law reform and judicial capacity building as important elements of policy. In some countries, they allied with reformers in ministries of justice and in the courts. Nyalali pursued international relationships aggressively, acquiring financial assistance, friends, and ideas.

These linkages carried risks. A constant worry was that the courts would appear "foreign." Some courts still employed contract judges in their upper tiers. Even where the ranks were entirely local the procedures courts used and the precedents to which they reached were unfamiliar to the average citizen. It was important for African courts not to aggravate the perception unduly. Going abroad for assistance had to be a temporary measure to help with the first stages of reform.

Sustaining and strengthening the independence that the openings of the 1980s and 1990s had made possible required several types of investments. One was to reduce the vulnerability of court procedures to interference. To this end, successful courts worked to limit the number of points at which administrative discretion created an avenue for partisan influence. They sought to enhance the flow of information and to create a voice for people who might be victims of delay or abuse. They tried to increase the salience of reputations for impartiality and effectiveness in the promotion of judges, magistrates, and nonjudicial personnel.

A second important area of investment was to encourage the appointment of people with legal training to positions where their knowledge could help inexperienced civil servants and police avoid actions that put the separation of powers at risk. Having a network of lawyers in the upper ranks of the ministries of justice, the law reform commission, the parliamentary draftsman's office, the police and security forces, the prisons, and the office of the president could help reduce misunderstandings, catch problems before they passed the point of no return, and generate a policy community sensitive to the importance of the rule of law, though it offered no guarantees.

The other critical investment was to create a broad base of support among the public at large. From a pragmatic, institutional point of view, it was helpful to be able to mobilize the specter of public outrage as a deterrent against infringement of judicial independence. If people felt they were served well by the courts, they might come to the aid of the judiciary in troubled times. Of course, building a rapport with ordinary people was important for bigger, moral reasons too. Chief Justice Nyalali held strong convictions that the legal process should be accessible to everyone and that the concerns of the farmer should weigh as heavily as those of the businessman in the capital city.

Judges could not handle these tasks by themselves. Their roles, as well as the press of business, prevented them from pursuing extensive involvement in legal literacy initiatives and law reform. Moreover, where institution building remained highly concentrated in the hands of the chief justice and a few of his fellow judges, as it did in Tanzania, effectiveness could suffer from the difficulty of managing many projects simultaneously. Even among Nyalali's close associates on the court there were some who worried that the chief justice had so much to do that he did not take time to consult adequately. Others acknowledged the problem but argued that there were few alternatives. Commented Judge William Maina, "It may sound like a one-man show but it may have to be that way. The situation as [the chief justice] . . . found it when he took over required a strong hand. There still needs to be more consultation. The CJ has good ideas but they are spread too thin. He has to supervise but he also has to hear cases. The president of the Court of Appeal is not the CJ in Kenya and that's a better arrangement."[3] It would take not just a remarkable person but a remarkable group of people to craft a new institutional arrangement.

REGIONALISM AND AFRICAN ROOTS

At the same time that Nyalali was trying to build Lushoto into a center that could serve the judiciary, he committed himself to work more closely with other courts in the region. At the time of independence, regional courts of appeal had existed in eastern Africa and for Botswana, Swaziland, and Lesotho. This arrangement meant that in the early years, judges in these countries had shared bodies of precedent. Because the judges on the regional courts of appeal were mainly on contract from other parts of the Commonwealth, the decisions too easily could be labeled "foreign." But by the mid-1990s, the idea of reviving regional interaction among members of the bench and the bar appealed to the chief justice.

Of course, there was a prudential reason for building greater interaction among courts and within the legal profession. The circulation of people improved the flow of information. If problems developed in one country, one's

[3] Judge William Maina, interview with author, Dar es Salaam, Tanzania, May 1996.

new colleagues in neighboring jurisdictions could then speak up and help draw regional or international attention to transgressions. Knowing of this possibility, political leaders would be more reticent to try to bring influence to bear in a particular case, to harass officers of the court, or to oust the jurisdiction of the courts altogether. The "limelight" effect that operated in the international arena could work at the regional level too, with less risk that the courts would be perceived as subject to global or Western influences. Lawyers commented that national governments perceived the regional discussions as less threatening than the same kinds of conversations held within their own borders, perhaps because the idea of regional meetings contained an implicit acknowledgment that problems were not specific to any one government or place.[4]

But this rationale was not clearly uppermost in Nyalali's mind. What seemed as important to him were the twin possibilities of fashioning a distinctively African or regional jurisprudence and a body of lore or wisdom about court administration tailored to the local context. The schedule and the character of the cases before the Court of Appeal had allowed Nyalali relatively little opportunity to pursue these ideas. He was not alone in this ambition. A decade earlier, judges and lawyers from all over Africa had formed the African Society of International and Comparative Law. The first conference had taken place in 1989, in Lusaka, Zambia, and the organization had started to publish its own review.[5]

In the mid-1990s, the courts were still relatively remote from each other. Said one justice in Botswana, "Judicial Africa is very insular. That has a lot to do with funding. There is little exchange with other countries, and almost nothing to do with Zimbabwe, even though their decisions are very good. We have a lot of respect for their CJ."[6]

Many judges regarded the new South African constitution as the likely instigation of a new era in African legal thought. That constitution said that the courts may have regard for foreign case law in interpreting the bill of rights, including the decisions offered by judges in neighboring African countries, although these would in no way be binding. Before judges assembled for a seminar in Arusha in June 1996, Nyalali stated,

> The process of internalization involves a synthesis between what is derived from the outside and what exists inside. . . . there must be a synthesis in Africa between the worldwide principles and values and indigenous principles and values. This phenomenon is . . . apparent in the South African Constitution

[4] For example, see Oki Ooko-Ombaka, director of the Public Law Institute, Kenya, interview with the author, October 1995.

[5] Note, *Commonwealth Law Bulletin*, 15, 1 (1989), p. 315.

[6] Justice J. C. Barrington Jones, interview with author, Lobatse, Botswana, April 12, 1996.

where the principle of UBUNTU is recognized and has been articulated by the Constitutional Court of South Africa, Langa, J., in the case of *S. v. Makwanyane and Another* (1995). . . . I believe here lies the key to the success of Africa's efforts to build modern societies on the basis of constitutionalism, human rights and democracy.[7]

Nyalali was eager that Lushoto eventually become a place where judges could discuss the interpretation of constitutions and discuss their own decisions.

In 1995, lawyers formed a regional bar association, the East African Law Society. Wrote the officers of the Uganda Law Society on the creation of the new organization, "To practice law in East Africa today is to be an East African. Daily it entails looking up the law in the law reports which contain the judgments of courts of the three countries and in such law journals as the *East African Law Journal* and the *East African Law Review* which are no longer published. It also entails studying the statutes of each country to see how one country has solved a problem another country is favoring."[8] In addition to sharing information and training opportunities, the new society agreed to send observers to all major trials in the region.

The courts followed suit in short order.[9] They began with a series of regional seminars and then initiated some common projects. For example, to maximize the use of limited resources for continuing legal and judicial education for judges and magistrates, the chief justices of Kenya, Uganda, and Tanzania agreed in 1996 to establish an East African program managed by a regional committee. The committee comprised three senior-ranking judicial officers from each country. Nyalali was especially pleased, because the committee said it intended to deliver its services through the recently established Lushoto Institute of Judicial Administration.[10]

THE MAN AND THE INSTITUTION

The search for general insight could not obscure the fact that individual personal qualities mattered for institution building. Try though they may to develop general theorems, policy makers and social scientists ultimately had to

---

[7] Francis L. Nyalali, Speech at opening of the judicial seminar on constitutionalism and human rights in a democracy, Arusha, Tanzania, June 18–19, 1996. *Ubuntu* roughly translates as "shared values" that are distinctively African.

[8] Official statement of the Uganda Law Society on the creation of the East African Law Society, November 1995, in archives of the Uganda Law Society, Kampala, Uganda.

[9] The Commission for East African Cooperation was reinstated at about the same time. In 1996, Uganda, Kenya, and Tanzania inaugurated a secretariat to revive economic cooperation.

[10] Francis L. Nyalali, personal communication, October 1998.

concede that at critical junctures—moments of rapid change—thoughtfulness, endurance, fortitude, and other traits could affect outcomes. Not everyone was personally suited to every task. Some chief justices, like Anthony Gubbay in Zimbabwe and his counterparts in South Africa, crafted especially eloquent decisions. Others, like Nyalali, had an unusual ability to communicate with a wide range of people, to experiment, and to reach beyond the usual constraints on role, without injuring the office.

Nyalali's tenure spanned a shift in the possibilities for change, and it is a measure of the man that he recognized the character of the period in which he lived. He accepted Tanzania's senior judicial post in 1976, when rule of law and respect for the courts were at a low ebb. The country was then engaged in a social experiment, which fired imaginations but proved too generous in its estimate of the human capacity for cooperation and insufficiently mindful of the determination of individuals, everywhere, to chart their own courses, the exhortations of their leaders aside. Six years later, with the help of other members of the court, he began to respond to a change in the public temper and to demands to revive the rule of law.

Between 1976 and 1998, Nyalali's career embraced an array of important contributions, not all of them perhaps fully appreciated at the time they occurred. As a young chief justice, with uncertain backing from older members of his court, he went before the leadership of the ruling party and successfully urged the repeal of legislation that threatened to undermine the rule of law. Some said he was too slow to address the executive and the legislature about the dangers the courts and the country faced from official arbitrariness. But it is difficult to second-guess judgments about timing. There was a high penalty to be paid for not choosing the right moment—the risk of losing the president's support, the likely effects of persistent confrontation on the attitudes of the party faithful, and the demoralization of the court that would result from failure. And building a coalition within the judiciary remained his first priority.

Shortly after his effort to persuade the ruling party of the need to respect the independence of the judiciary, Nyalali was called to help shape the court's interpretation of a new, challengingly drafted Bill of Rights and Duties. He broke with the methods of interpretation inspired by his own training and common among judges on African courts at the time. Instead, he directed attention to the special difficulties of reading a constitution and invoked approaches used more commonly in Canada, the United States, and India than in England. He suggested that people look beyond the words to the structure of the document, the broad purposes of the drafters, and the intentions of the nationalist leaders whose aims and spirit Africa needed to rekindle, as well as to international law. A few chief justices in other parts of the region were beginning to do the same, but Nyalali was at the forefront with them, no laggard, and his speeches to legal scholars and lawyers should have left little doubt about the exciting era of

African jurisprudence to come. At the same time, Nyalali called for his countrymen to activate the language of duties in the new bill by reaching to familiar branches of private law that had received little use in African legal systems.

It was a disappointment to some that the many demands the chief justice faced restricted the time he had to devote to using these new methods of interpretation. Slowly, more eloquent decisions began to issue from the High Court, which had original jurisdiction in constitutional cases. The Court of Appeal had the opportunity to review some of these judgments, but the numbers of constitutional claims were still quite limited and the time available to think and write was sharply constrained by the press of judicial business. As a result of these two circumstances, Nyalali found it hard to contribute as much as he hoped to the development of the new jurisprudence he had helped launch.

Nonetheless, Nyalali crafted some important and very distinctive opinions. In an era when women's positions at home and in society were usually strikingly inferior to those of men, Nyalali wrote a judgment that counted a spouse's domestic services—cooking, cleaning, and caring for children—as contributions to the assets of a married couple and therefore as claims on those assets upon the dissolution of a marriage. The precedent bound the lower courts and changed the treatment many women received in the judicial system. Similarly, the chief justice leant his support to a lower-court judgment that said customary law could not discriminate against women by giving men and women different capacities to inherit, hold, and transfer land, even clan land.

Building on his early experiments as a magistrate, Nyalali tried to enhance the performance of the courts and the quality of justice ordinary people received. Improving court administration was a tall order, and the challenge would long continue. It had only just begun. But under Nyalali's direction, the Tanzanian courts experimented with a wide variety of innovations, some home grown and others brought from courts with similar problems overseas.

In an unusual set of circumstances, the chief justice presided over a major change in his country's political system, a distinction only a few other judges could share. He supervised the commission that recommended adoption of multiparty democracy. During the long hearings and investigation, he used his judicial skills to weigh and balance testimony. Many people in like circumstances might have been content with a superficial reading of survey results and cast their votes for the single-party status quo. Nyalali read the figures carefully and thought about their context, as well as about what people said they wanted in response to open-ended questions. He concluded that only a multiparty system could deliver what people desired from government. In 1995, the country held its first elections under the new system the Nyalali Commission helped inaugurate.

More visible than many chief justices in the region, Nyalali attracted considerable public respect. For one so centrally concerned with institution building, the question was whether this personal popularity could be used to help ensure that the court emerged from these years strengthened, understood, and accepted. By the mid-1990s, there were positive signs that people thought of the court as an entity and not as an extension of Nyalali himself. When the executive branch needed to reassure people that a delicate task would be handled with integrity, it reached to the judiciary. For example, Judge William Maina retired from the court to take over corruption investigations in the Permanent Commission of Inquiry. And when one of the country's public ferries sank in Lake Victoria, drowning more than nine hundred people, Justice Robert Kisanga was appointed to the commission that probed the causes of the accident. Times were changing.

Personal example was important, even if the objective was to build an institution. The chief justice was long concerned that the courts be a means to an end. That end was the rule of law, not in the sense of a "law of rules," but in the appropriation of certain basic principles, such as entitlement to a fair hearing, as part of the common sense people used in negotiating everyday life. Disputes arose all the time in people's lives. When they did so, Nyalali hoped the parties would handle their differences in ways that mirrored the values courts sought to embody. Those values or principles included things like the belief in the right to an impartial hearing, the presumption of innocence, the right to offer a defense of one's actions, the right to have the counsel of others, and protection from the retrospective application of a new rule. In a speech on the challenge of economic development to law, Nyalali argued that "the dispensation of justice according to law and order is not a monopoly of the Courts—it happens every minute in the multifarious interactions between individual persons every day of the week. That is why people have a concept of the just and upright man in the community." The kind of persona or citizenship Nyalali hoped to encourage was much like the individual he had tried to be. "He is the person who does justice not only through the courts, but in his everyday life."[11]

---

[11] Francis L. Nyalali, "The Challenge of Development to Law in Developing Countries Viewed from the Perspective of Human Rights, the Rule of Law and the Role of the Courts in Preserving Freedom," First Commonwealth Africa Judicial Conference, Kombo Beach Hotel, Kotu, Gambia, May 5–9, 1986, p. 23

Glossary of Foreign Terms and Specialized Vocabulary

LEGAL TERMINOLOGY

There are differences in the vocabulary that lawyers use in the countries that figure in this book, as well as in the spellings of words. I have adopted American English spellings, except in titles, organization names, and quoted material, where I have retained British usage. The book uses both *advocate* and *lawyer* to mean someone who practices law. The definitions are drawn from *Black's Law Dictionary*, 1991.

adjournment (Eng.)	a continuance or postponement (American)
advocate (Eng.)	a lawyer
amicus curiae	friend of the court; a party with strong interest in or views on the subject matter of an action
barrister (Eng.)	a lawyer admitted to plead at the bar or argue before the court
delict (Roman-Dutch)	tort, or noncontractual liability
dicta	opinions of a judge that go beyond the facts of the particular case before the court
expressio unius exclusio alterius	the expression of one thing means the exclusion of the other
inclusio unius exclusio alterius	the inclusion of one thing means the exclusion of the other
locus standi	right to be heard before a court of justice on a given question
mens rea	an element of criminal responsibility: a guilty mind; a criminal intent
mutatis mutandis	the necessary changes having been made; substituting new terms

nolle prosequi	a formal entry upon the record, by the plaintiff in a civil suit or by a prosecuting attorney in a criminal action, of an intent not to continue to prosecute a case
pro bono	work or services done or performed free of charge
pro se	without employing the advice of counsel; representing oneself
ratio decidendi	the ground or reasons of a decision
registrar (Eng.)	a clerk of court (American)
stare decisis	policy of abiding by decided cases; doctrine that when a court has set out a principle in a decision, it will apply it in all future cases where the facts are substantially the same
sub judice	being under the consideration of the court
tort	noncontractual liability, the law of accidents
ultra vires	performed without any authority

SELECTED FOREIGN WORDS

wananchi	common people (Kiswahili)
jaji	judge (Kiswahili)
jaji kiongozi	deputy chief justice (Kiswahili)
jaji mkuu	chief justice (Kiswahili)
mahakama	judiciary, courts (Kiswahili)
mwalimu	teacher, an honorific as used with the name of the president (Kiswahili)
ujamaa	relating to the family; also the name of a government policy that encouraged communal farming (Kiswahili)
shamba	a farm plot (Kiswahili)
kgosi	a chief (Setswana)
ubuntu	shared values that are distinctly African
lobola	bridewealth (southern African term for a general practice)

Bibliography

WORKS AND SPEECHES BY FRANCIS L. NYALALI

Nyalali, Francis L. "Address to the Central Committee of the National Executive Council of the Chama Cha Mapinduzi," Dodoma, Tanzania, May 17, 1984.

Nyalali, Francis L. *Aspects of Industrial Conflict: A Case Study of Trade Disputes in Tanzania, 1967–1973.* Dar es Salaam, Tanzania: East African Literature Bureau, 1975.

Nyalali, Francis L. "The Bill of Rights in Tanzania." Lecture presented at Faculty of Law, the University of Dar es Salaam, Dar es Salaam, Tanzania, September 5, 1985.

Nyalali, Francis L. "The Challenge of Development to Law in Developing Countries Viewed from the Perspective of Human Rights, the Rule of Law, and the Role of the Courts in Preserving Freedom," First Commonwealth Africa Judicial Conference, Kombo Beach Hotel, Kotu, Gambia, May 5–9, 1986.

Nyalali, Francis L. "The Challenge of the Private Mass Media in the Wake of Multi-Partism." Address to a dinner hosted by the *Express* and *Mwananchi*, Kilimanjaro Hotel, Dar es Salaam, Tanzania, May 21, 1993.

Nyalali, Francis L. "The Changing Role of the Tanzanian Bar," *Lawyer* (Journal of the Law Society of Tanganyika), (1994): 3–5.

Nyalali, Francis L. "Cross-cultural Perspectives of the Proof Process: The Tanzanian Experience." Paper presented at the annual meeting of the Society for the Reform of Criminal Law, Vancouver, Canada, August 3–7, 1992.

Nyalali, Francis L. "A Discourse on the Relationship between the Judicature and the Government Presented by the Honorable Mr. Justice F. L. Nyalali, Chief Justice of Tanzania at the Third Commonwealth Africa Judicial Conference at Livingstone, Zambia, on the 6th April, 1990."

Nyalali, Francis L. "A Good Will Message from Chief Justice F. L. Nyalali, Former Chairman of the Presidential Commission on a One Party or Multi-Party

Political System in Tanzania, to the Seminar on Transition to Multi-Party Democracy in Tanzania, 19th November, 1992 at Dar es Salaam."

Nyalali, Francis L. "International Co-operation in Criminal Matters in Eastern Africa," pp. 294–303, in Eser Albin and Otto Lagodny, eds., *Principles and Procedures of a New Transnational Criminal Law.* Documentation of an International Workshop 1991. Freiburg, Germany: Society for the Reform of Criminal Law and Max Planck Institute for Foreign and Criminal Law, 1992.

Nyalali, Francis L. "Intervention on democratization." Unpublished speech to the annual seminar for DANIDA (Danish Development Cooperation) advisers in Tanzania, Dar es Salaam, Tanzania, April 22–23, 1994.

Nyalali, Francis L. Keynote speech delivered at opening of conference on Constitutionalism and the Legal System in a Democracy, Arusha International Conference Centre, Arusha, Tanzania, March 28, 1995.

Nyalali, Francis L. Keynote speech delivered at a seminar organized by the Commonwealth Judicial Education Institute for judges in East and Central Africa, Sheraton Hotel, Kampala, Uganda, February 26, 1996.

Nyalali, Francis L. "Legal Reform for Democracy in Tanzania," *Lawyer* (Journal of the Law Society of Tanganyika), (September–December 1994): 6–7, 5.

Nyalali, Francis L. "Mada ya Jaji Mkuu F. L. Nyalali Kwenye Semina Kwa Wabunge, Tarehe 29 Januaru 1991-Dodoma, Kuhusa Kazi Na Wajibu wa Bunge Katika Kutunga Sheria."

Nyalali, Francis L. "A Message to the Tanganyika Law Society," *Lawyer* (Journal of the Law Society of Tanganyika), (Special issue 1995), (1995): 3–4.

Nyalali, Francis L. Opening address to the First Regional Conference on Law, Politics, and Multi-Party Politics in East Africa, Dar es Salaam, Tanzania, October 18–23, 1993.

Nyalali, Francis L. "Paper on Case Management." Presented at a seminar of judges, Arusha, Tanzania, April 19–23, 1993.

Nyalali, Francis L. "Paper on Court Administration in Tanzania." Paper presented at the seminar of judges of the High Court and Court of Appeal of Tanzania, Dar es Salaam, Tanzania, April 19–23, 1993.

Nyalali, Francis L. "Paper on the Role of the Judge in the Protection of Human Rights Delivered by Honorable Francis L. Nyalali, Chief Justice of Tanzania at the Seventh Appellate Judges Conference at Abuja, Nigeria, 7th–10th September 1992."

Nyalali, Francis L. "The Social Context of Judicial Decision Making." Paper presented at a workshop on the state of human rights in Tanzania, British Council Hall, Dar es Salaam, Tanzania, July 3, 1998.

Nyalali, Francis L. Speech at opening of the judicial seminar on constitutionalism and human rights in a democracy, Arusha, Tanzania, June 18–19, 1996.

Nyalali, Francis L. "Speech Delivered by the Honorable Chief Justice Francis L. Nyalali at Closing Ceremonies of a Workshop on Bill of Rights." East African Law Society, Arusha International Conference Centre, Arusha, Tanzania, January 13, 1996.

Nyalali, Francis L. Speech at the Opening of the Tanzanian Judiciary's Training

Programme in Alternative Dispute Resolution presented at the High Court of Tanzania, Dar es Salaam, Tanzania, August 2, 1995.

Nyalali, Francis L. "Speech of Honorable Francis L. Nyalali Given at Tanganyika Law Society Dinner, 13th August 1994, Kilimanjaro Hotel, Dar es Salaam," Tanzania.

Nyalali, Francis L. "Speech on Corruption Delivered at the Opening of a Seminar Organized by the Danish Association for International Cooperation (MS-TCDC) at Mwengo." Usa-River, Arusha, Tanzania, November 14, 1995.

Nyalali, Francis L. "Speech on Legal Reform for Democracy in Tanzania." Delivered at the Centre of African Studies, School of Oriental and African Studies, University of London, London, England, October 5, 1994.

Nyalali, Francis L. "Speech on Mass Media Ethics and Law in a Changing Political Order." Delivered to the Tanzania Journalists' Association, Dar es Salaam, Tanzania, September 14, 1992.

Nyalali, Francis L. "Speech to Open Seminar on Children's Rights Organized by the Tanganyika Law Society on 16th June 1994 at Dar es Salaam," Tanzania.

Nyalali, Francis L. "Structures and Dynamics of Law Enforcement." Keynote address no. 3, pp. 78–96, in *Report of the Eighth Commonwealth Magistrates' Conference, Ottawa, 18–24 September, 1988.* London: Commonwealth Magistrates' and Judges' Association, 1988.

GOVERNMENT DOCUMENTS

Namibia, Republic of. Law Reform and Development Commission. *The Ascertainment of Customary Law and the Methodological Aspects of Research into Customary Law: Proceedings of a Workshop.* Windhoek, Namibia: Law Reform and Development Commission, February/March 1995.

Tanzania, United Republic of. *Report of the Presidential Commission of Inquiry into Land Matters* (Shivji Commission), vol. 1, *Land Policy and Land Tenure Structure.* Uppsala, Sweden: Scandinavian Institute of African Studies and Ministry of Lands, Housing, and Urban Development, United Republic of Tanzania, 1994.

Tanzania, United Republic of. High Court and Court of Appeal. *Annual Report, 1985–1988.* Dar es Salaam, Tanzania: High Court and Court of Appeal, 1989.

Tanzania, United Republic of. Judicial System Review Commission. *Report of the Judicial System Review Commission* (Msekwa Report). Dar es Salaam, Tanzania: Judicial System Review Commission, 1977.

Tanzania, United Republic of. Presidential Commission of Inquiry against Corruption. *Report on the Commission on Corruption* (Warioba Report), 2 vols. Dar es Salaam, Tanzania: Presidential Commission of Inquiry against Corruption, November 1996.

Tanzania, United Republic of. Presidential Commission of Inquiry against Corruption. "Service Delivery Survey: Corruption in the Police, Revenue and

Lands Service." Survey financed by the World Bank and carried out by CIET International on behalf of the Commission. Dar es Salaam, Tanzania: Presidential Commission on Corruption, July 1996.

Tanzania, United Republic of. Presidential Commission on Single Party or Multiparty System in Tanzania, *Report and Recommendations of the Commission on the Democratic System in Tanzania* (Nyalali Report), vol. 1. Dar es Salaam, Tanzania: Presidential Commission on Single Party or Multiparty System in Tanzania, English edition 1992.

Tanzania, United Republic of. Tanzania Financial and Legal Management Upgrading Project (FILMUP). "Final Report on the Attorney-General's Chambers and Other Government Legal Offices." Dar es Salaam, Tanzania: Financial and Legal Management Upgrading Project, 1995.

Tanzania, United Republic of. Tanzania Financial and Legal Management Upgrading Project (FILMUP). "The Legal Sector in Tanzania: Interim Report of the Legal Task Force." Unpublished report, Dar es Salaam, Tanzania, June 1995.

Tanzania, United Republic of. Tanzania Financial and Legal Management Upgrading Project (FILMUP). "Report on the Dissemination of Legal Information." Unpublished report, Dar es Salaam, Tanzania, 1995.

Tanzania, Republic of. Tanzania Financial and Legal Management Upgrading Project (FILMUP). "Report on the Dissemination of Legal Information and Legal Aid." Unpublished report prepared by Frigo Consult with the support of the Danish Development Corporation (DANIDA), Dar es Salaam, Tanzania, May 1994.

Uganda, Republic of. "Draft Report of the Committee on Legal Education, Training, and Accreditation in Uganda, Justice Benjamin Odoki, Chair, Committee on Legal Eucation, Uganda Institutional Capacity-Building Project" (Kampala, Uganda: Ministry of Justice and Constitutional Affairs, July 7, 1995).

Uganda, Republic of. "Proceedings of the Seminar on Administration of Justice." International Conference Center, Kampala, Uganda, January 12–16, 1987. Photocopy.

Uganda, Republic of. *Report of the Commission of Inquiry on Judicial Reform.* Kampala, Uganda: Commission of Inquiry on Judicial Reform, 1995.

Uganda, Republic of. "Uganda National Integrity Survey 1998: Final Report." Paper prepared by CIET International for the Inspectorate of Government. Kampala, Uganda: Inspectorate of Government, August 1998.

United Kingdom (Great Britain). Lord High Chancellor's Office. *Report of the Committee on Legal Education for Students from Africa.* London: Her Majesty's Stationery Office, January 1961.

United Kingdom (Great Britain). Overseas Development Administration. "Draft Report on the Tanzanian Judiciary." Report of a commission chaired by Mark Bomani. London: Overseas Development Administration, 1994.

U.S. Department of State. *Human Rights Reports.* Washington, D.C.: U.S. Government Printing Office, annual series, multiple years.

ADDITIONAL SOURCES

Abdullahi Ahmed An-Na'im and Francis Deng, eds. *Human Rights in Africa: Cross-Cutting Perspectives*. Washington, D.C.: Brookings Institution, 1990.

Abel, Richard L. *Politics by Other Means: Law in the Struggle Against Apartheid, 1980–1994*. New York: Routledge, 1995.

Abrahams, Ray. "Law and Order and the State in the Nyamwezi and Sukuma Area of Tanzania," *Africa*, 59, 3 (1989): 356–370.

Abrahams, Ray. "Sungusungu: Village Vigilante Groups in Tanzania," *African Affairs*, 86 (1987): 179–196.

Abrahams, Ray, ed. *Witchcraft in Contemporary Tanzania*. Cambridge: African Studies Center, University of Cambridge, 1994.

Acharyya, Bijay Kisor. *Codification in British India*. Tagore Law Lectures, 1912. Calcutta: Banerji & Sons, 1914.

Acheampong, Kenneth Asamoa. "The African Charter and the Equalization of Human Rights," *Lesotho Law Journal*, 7, 2 (1991): 21–34.

Adelman, Sammy, and Abdul Paliwala. *Law and Crisis in the Third World*. London: Hans Zell, 1993.

Africa Contemporary Record, Annual Survey and Documents. New York: Holmes & Meier/Africana Publishing, 1983.

African Conference on Local Courts and Customary Law. *Record of the Proceedings of the Conference on African Courts and Customary Law*, Dar es Salaam, Tanzania, September 8–18, 1963. Dar es Salaam: Faculty of Law, University of Dar es Salaam, 1964.

Aguda, Akinola. "The Judiciary in a Developing Country," pp. 137–166 in M. L. Marasinghe and William Conklin, eds., *Essays on Third World Perspectives in Jurisprudence*. Singapore: Malayan Law Journal, 1984.

Agyemang, Augustus A. "African Courts, the Settlement of Investment Disputes and the Enforcement of Awards," *Journal of African Law*, 33, 1 (1989): 31–44.

Aihe, D. O. "Neo-Nigerian Human Rights in Zambia," *Zambia Law Journal*, 3–4 (1971–72): 43–63.

Ali, Picho. "Ideological Commitment and the Judiciary," *Transition*, 7, 36 (1968): 47–49.

Ali, Picho. "The 1967 Republican Constitution of Uganda," *Transition*, 7, 34 (1968): 11–12.

Allen, Thomas. "Constitutional Interpretation and the Opening Provisions of Bills of Rights in African Commonwealth Countries," pp. 321–340 in *Proceedings of the Fifth Annual Conference of the African Society of International and Comparative Law*, Accra, Ghana, September 20–24, 1993. London: African Society of International and Comparative Law, 1993.

Allott, Anthony N. "The Authority of English Decisions in Colonial Courts," *Journal of African Law*, 1, 1 (Spring 1957): 23–39.

Allott, Anthony N. "The Independence of the Judiciary in Commonwealth Countries: Problems and Provisions," pp. 71–99 in *Report of the Tenth*

Commonwealth Magistrates' and Judges' Conference, Victoria Falls, Zimbabwe, August 22–26, 1994. London: Commonwealth Magistrates' and Judges' Association, 1994.

Allott, Anthony N. "International Developments in Customary Law—The Restatement of African Law and Thereafter," in Republic of Namibia, Law Reform and Development Commission, *The Ascertainment of Customary Law and the Methodological Aspects of Research into Customary Law. Proceedings of a Workshop*. Windhoek, Namibia: Law Reform and Development Commission, February/March 1995.

Allott, Anthony N. "Judicial Precedent in Africa Revisited," *Journal of African Law*, 12, 1 (1968): 3–31.

Allott, Anthony N., "Legal Development and Economic Growth in Africa," pp. 194–209 in J. N. D. Anderson, ed., *Changing Law in Developing Countries*. New York: Praeger, 1963.

Allott, Anthony N., and E. Cotran. "A Background Paper on Restatement of Laws in Africa," pp. 18–41 in *Integration of Customary and Modern Legal Systems in Africa*. Proceedings of a Conference on Integration of Customary and Modern Legal Systems in Africa. Ibadan: University of Ife, August 24–29, 1964. New York: Africana Publishing, 1971.

Allott, Anthony N., and Gordon R. Woodman, eds. *People's Law and State Law*. Dordrecht: Foris Publications, 1985.

Amissah, A. D. E. "The Role of the Judiciary in the Governmental Process: Ghana's Experience," *African Law Studies*, 13 (1976): 4–30.

Amoah, P. K. "The Independence of the Judiciary in Botswana, Lesotho, and Swaziland," *CIJL Bulletin*, nos. 19–20 (April–October 1987).

Anderson, J. N. D. *Islamic Law in Africa*. London: Frank Cass, 1955.

Anderson, J. N. D. "The Impact of Islamic Law on Commonwealth Legal Systems," pp. 63–80 in Robert R. Wilson, ed., *International and Comparative Law of the Commonwealth*. Durham, NC: Duke University Press, 1968.

Anderson, J. N. D. "Islamic Law in Africa: Problems of Today and Tomorrow," pp. 164–183 in J. N. D. Anderson, ed., *Changing Law in Developing Countries*. New York: Praeger, 1963.

Andrews, Penelope. "Spectators at the Revolution? Gender Equality and Customary Law in a Post-Apartheid South Africa," pp. 261–286 in *Law and Anthropology*. International Yearbook for Legal Anthropology, vol. 7. London: Martinus Nijhoff/Kluwer, 1994.

Ankumah, Evelyn A. *The African Commission on Human and Peoples' Rights: Practice and Procedures*. The Hague: Martinus Nijhoff, 1996.

Appiah, Kwame Anthony. *In My Father's House: Africa in the Philosophy of Culture*. New York: Oxford University Press, 1992.

Austen, Ralph A. "The Moral Economy of Witchcraft," in Jean Comaroff and John Comaroff, eds., *Modernity and Its Malcontents*. Chicago: University of Chicago Press, 1993.

Austen, Ralph A. *Northwest Tanzania under German and British Rule: Colonial Policy and Tribal Politics, 1889–1939*. New Haven: Yale University Press, 1968.

Ayoola, E. O. "Progress and Failure of Localisation of the Common Law by Legislative and Judicial Powers in Common Law Africa." Paper presented at the Second Commonwealth Judicial Conference, Arusha, Tanzania, August 8–12, 1988. Photocopy.

Bainbridge, John Seaman. *The Study and Teaching of Law in Africa*. Hackensack, NJ: Fred B. Rothman & Co., 1972.

Baregu, Mwesiga. "The Rise and Fall of the One-Party State in Tanzania," pp. 158–181 in Jennifer A. Widner, ed., *Economic Change and Political Liberalization in Sub-Saharan Africa*. Baltimore: Johns Hopkins University Press, 1994.

Barya, John-Jean, and Joe Oloka-Onyanga. "Popular Justice and Resistance Committee Courts in Uganda." Report for the Center for Basic Research and the Friedrich Ebert Foundation. Kampala, Uganda: Center for Basic Research, 1994.

Bassiouni, M. Cheriff, and Ziyad Motala, eds. *The Protection of Human Rights in African Criminal Proceedings*. Boston: Martinus Nijhoff/Kluwer, 1995.

Beckstrom, John B. "Transplantation of Legal Systems: An Early Report on the Reception of Western Laws in Ethiopia," *American Journal of Comparative Law*, 21 (1973): 557–583.

Bellow, Emmanuel, and Prince Bola A. Ajibola, eds. *Essays in Honour of Judge Taslim Olawale Elias*. Dordrecht: Martinus Nijhoff, 1992.

Bennett, T. W. "The Compatibility of African Customary Law and Human Rights," pp. 18–35 in *Acta Juridica*, 1991. Capetown: Juta & Co., for the University of Capetown Faculty of Law, 1991.

Bennett, T. W. "Conflict of Laws—The Application of Customary Law and the Common Law in Zimbabwe," *International and Comparative Law Quarterly*, 30 (January 1981): 59–103.

Bennett, T. W. "The Equality Clause and Customary Law," *South African Journal on Human Rights*, 10, 1 (1994): 122–130.

Bennett, T. W. "The Interpersonal Conflict of Laws: A Technique for Adapting to Social Change in Africa," *Journal of Modern African Studies*, 18, 1 (1980): 127–134.

Bennett, T. W. *A Sourcebook of African Customary Law for Southern Africa*. Cape Town: Juta & Co., 1991.

Bennett, T. W., and W. M. Scholtz. "Witchcraft: A Problem of Fault and Causation," *Comparative and International Law of Southern Africa*, (CILSA), XII (1979): 288–301.

Bennett, T. W., and T. Vermeulen. "Codification of Customary Law," *Journal of African Law*, 24, 2 (1980): 206–219.

Bhagwati, P. N. "The Role of the Judiciary in the Democratic Process: Balancing Activism and Judicial Restraint," *Commonwealth Law Bulletin*, 18, 4 (October 1992): 1262–1267.

Bierwagen, Rainer Michael, and Chris Maina Peter. "Administration of Justice in Tanzania and Zanzibar: A Comparison of Two Judicial Systems in One Country," *International and Comparative Law Quarterly*, 38 (April 1989): 395–412.

Bjornlund, Eric C. "The Devil's Work? Judicial Review under a Bill of Rights in South Africa and Namibia," *Stanford Journal of International Law*, 26 (Spring 1990): 391–434.

Blerk, Adrienne van. "The Botswana Court of Appeal: A Policy of Avoidance?" *Comparative and International Law Journal of Southern Africa*, 18, 2 (July 1985): 385–395.

Bonnell, Michael Joachim. "The UNIDROIT Principles of International Commercial Contracts: Why? What? How?" *Tulane Law Review*, 69, 5 (1995): 1121–1147.

Boucher, Steve, Antonio Francisco, Laurel Rose, Michael Roth, and Fernanda Zaqueu. "Legal Uncertainty and Land Disputes in the Peri-Urban Areas of Mozambique: Land Markets in Transition." Report to U.S. Agency for International Development prepared by Ohio State University and the Wisconsin Land Tenure Center. Washington, D.C.: U.S. Agency for International Development, CID, August 1993.

Bouman, Marlies. "A Note on Chiefly and National Policing in Botswana," *Journal of Legal Pluralism and Unofficial Law*, 25–26 (1987): 275–300.

Boyer, Paul S., and Stephen Nissenbaum. *Salem Possessed: The Social Origins of Witchcraft*. Cambridge, MA: Harvard University Press, 1974.

Bratton, Michael, and Nicolas van de Walle. *Democratic Experiments in Africa: Regime Transitions in Comparative Perspective*. Cambridge: Cambridge University Press, 1997.

Brown, Nathan J. *The Rule of Law in the Arab World: Courts in Egypt and the Gulf*. Cambridge: Cambridge University Press, 1997.

Brownlie, Ian. "The Rights of Peoples in Modern International Law," pp. 1–16 in James Crawford, ed., *The Rights of Peoples*. Oxford: Clarendon, 1988.

Brunetti, Aymo, Gregory Kisunko, and Beatrice Weder. "How Businesses See Government." IFC Discussion Paper 33. Washington, D.C.: IFC/World Bank, 1998.

Bukurura, Sufian Hemed. *The Judiciary and Good Governance in Contemporary Tanzania: Problems and Prospects*. Bergen, Norway: Christien Michelsen Institute, Development and Human Rights Studies, September 1995.

Bukurura, Sufian Hemed. "The Maintenance of Order in Rural Tanzania: The Case of Sungusungu," *Journal of Legal Pluralism and Unofficial Law*, 34 (1994): 1–29.

Burg, Elliot M. "Law and Development: A Review of the Literature and a Critique of 'Scholars in Self-Estrangement,'" *American Journal of Comparative Law*, 25 (1977): 492–530.

Butegwa, Florence. "Challenges of Promoting Legal Literacy among Women in Uganda," pp. 139–159 in Margaret Schuler and Sakuntala Kadirgmar-Rajasingham, eds., *Legal Literacy: A Tool for Women's Empowerment*. New York: United Nations Development Fund for Women, UNIFEM WIDBOOKS, 1992.

Butegwa, Florence. "Kenyan Women's Rights: Report of a Field Study," pp. 53–69 in Mary Adhiambo Mbeo and Oki Ooko-Ombaka, eds., *Women and Law in*

Kenya: Perspectives and Emerging Issues. Nairobi, Kenya: Public Law Institute, 1989.

Cachalia, Azhar, Halton Cheadle, Dennis Davis, Nicholas Haysom, Penuell Maduna, and Gilbert Marcus. *Fundamental Rights in the New Constitution.* Kenwyn, South Africa: Juta & Co., 1994.

Cameron, Edwin. "Judicial Accountability in South Africa," *South African Journal of Human Rights,* 6 (1990): 251–265.

Canter, Richard S. "Family Dispute Settlement and the Zambian Judiciary: Local-level Legal Adaptation," pp. 69–92 in Simon Roberts, ed., *Law and the Family in Africa.* Seminar on New Directions in Family Law, Leyden, 1974. The Hague: Mouton, 1977.

Carothers, Thomas. *Aiding Democracy Abroad: The Learning Curve.* Washington, D.C.: Carnegie Endowment for International Peace, 1999.

Carothers, Thomas. "The Rule of Law Revival," *Foreign Affairs,* 77, 2 (1998): 95–106.

Carpenter, Gretchen. "Constitutional Interpretation by the Existing Judiciary in South Africa—Can New Wine Be Successfully Decanted into Old Bottles?" *Comparative and International Law of Southern Africa,* 28 (1995): 322–337.

Chanock, Martin. *Law, Custom, and Social Order.* Cambridge: Cambridge University Press, 1985.

Chanock, Martin. "The Law Market: The Legal Encounter in British East and Central Africa," pp. 279–305 in W. J. Mommsen and J. A. de Moor, eds., *European Expansion and Law.* New York: Berg/St. Martin's Press, 1992.

Chanock, Martin. "Making Customary Law: Men, Women, and Courts in Colonial Northern Rhodesia," pp. 53–67 in Margaret Jean Hay and Marcia Wright, eds., *African Women and the Law: Historical Perpsectives.* Boston: Boston University African Studies Center, 1982.

Chongwe, Roger M. A. "Limitations on the Principles of Natural Justice: An African Perspective." Paper prepared for the International Bar Association. *Commonwealth Law Bulletin,* 15, 2 (April 1989): 620–626.

Church, W. Lawrence. "The Power of the Courts to Call Witnesses," *Zambia Law Journal,* 3–4, 1–2 (1971–72): 162–168.

Cobbah, Josiah A. M. "African Values and the Human Rights Debate: An African Perspective," *Human Rights Quarterly,* 9 (1987): 309–331.

Cohen, David William, and E. S. Atieno Odhiambo. *Burying S. M.: The Politics of Knowledge and Social Power in Africa.* Portsmouth: Heinemann, 1992.

Coldham, Simon. "Human Rights in Tanzania: Case Notes," *Journal of African Law,* 35, 1–2 (1991): 205–208.

Coldham, Simon. "Land Tenure Reform in Tanzania: Legal Problems and Perspectives," *Journal of Modern African Studies,* 33, 2 (1995): 227–242.

Collier, Paul. "How to Reduce Corruption." Paper presented to the Conference on Good Governance and Sustainable Development, Abidjan, Côte D'Ivoire, November 22–24, 1999. World Bank, Washington, D.C., November 1999.

Comaroff, John L. *Rules and Processes: The Cultural Logic of Dispute in an African Context.* Chicago: University of Chicago Press, 1981.

Corder, Hugh. "Crowbars and Cobwebs: Executive Autocracy and the Law in South Africa." Inaugural Lecture, New Series No. 137, Capetown: University of Capetown, October 5, 1988.

Corder, Hugh. "Establishing the Legitimacy for the Administration of Justice in South Africa," *Stellenbosch Law Review*, 2 (1995): 203–215.

Cory, Hans, and M. M. Hartnoll. *Customary Law of the Haya Tribe*. Cass Library of African Law, No. 7, 1945. Reprint. London: Frank Cass & Co., 1971.

Cotran, Eugene. "The Unification of Laws in East Africa," *Journal of Modern African Studies*, 1, 2 (1963): 209–220.

Cottrell, Jill. "The Function of the Law of Torts in Africa," *Journal of African Law*, 31, 1–2 (1988): 161–184.

Cox, Richard. *Pan-Africanism in Practice: An East African Study*. London: Oxford University Press, 1964.

Crawford, J. R. "The History and Nature of the Judicial System of Botswana, Lesotho, and Swaziland," *South African Law Journal*, 86, 3 (1969): 476–485 and 87, 1 (1970): 76–86.

Cretney, Stephen. "The Application of Equitable Doctrines by the Courts in East Africa," *Journal of African Law*, 12, 3 (1968): 119–145.

Cunningham, Andrew J. "The European Convention on Human Rights, Customary International Law, and the Constitution," *International and Comparative Law Quarterly*, 43 (July 1994): 537–567.

Czerenda, Randall A., and Alan P. Gross, "Introduction of Computerized Court Reporting in the Gambia," trip memorandum prepared for USAID, Banjul, Gambia, June 20, 1994.

Dagan, Hanoch. *Unjust Enrichment: A Study of Private Law and Public Values*. Cambridge: Cambridge University Press, 1997.

Davis, Dennis. "Democracy—Its Influence upon the Process of Constitutional Interpretation," *South African Journal on Human Rights*, 10, 1 (1994): 103–121.

Davis, Dennis M. "Social Power and Civil Rights: Towards a New Jurisprudence for a Future South Africa," *South African Law Journal*, 108, 3 (1991): 453–475.

De Soto, Hernando. *The Other Path*. New York: Harper & Row, 1989.

Delaney, Duane B. "Robert A. Shuker U.S.-Africa Judicial Exchange Program Phase II Report." Prepared for the U.S. Information Agency. Washington, D.C.: Superior Court of the District of Columbia in conjunction with the American Bar Association and the National Judicial College, September 15, 1995. Mimeograph.

Delius, Peter. *A Lion Amongst the Cattle*. Portsmouth: Heinemann, 1996.

Deng, Francis, Sadikiel Kimaro, Terrence Lyons, Donald Rothchild, and I. William Zartman. *Sovereignty as Responsibility*. Washington, D.C.: Brookings Institution, 1996.

Derrett, J. Duncan M. "Justice, Equity and Good Conscience," pp. 114–153 in J. N. D. Anderson, ed., *Changing Law in Developing Countries*. New York: Praeger, 1963.

Desai, Justice D. A. "The Jurisprudential Basis of Public Interest Litigation," pp. 20–21 in Sara Hossain, Shahdeen Malik, and Bushra Musa, eds., *Public Interest*

Litigation in South Asia: Rights in Search of Remedies. Dhaka, Bangladesh: University Press Limited, 1997.

Devine, Dermott J. "The Relationship between International Law and Municipal Law in the Light of the Interim South African Constitution 1993," *International and Comparative Law Quarterly,* 44, 1 (1995): 1–18.

Devine, Francis Edward. "Outlawing Commercial Bail Bonding: A Comparative Perspective," *Anglo-American Law Review,* 17 (1988): 66–77.

Dias, Clarence J. "The Impact of Social Activism and Movements for Legal Reform in South Asia," pp. 3–16 in Sara Hossain, Shahdeen Malik, and Bushra Musa, eds., *Public Interest Litigation in South Asia: Rights in Search of Remedies.* Dhaka, Bangladesh: University Press Limited, 1997.

Donnelly, Jack. "Cultural Relativism and Universal Human Rights," *Human Rights Quarterly,* 6, 2 (1984): 400–419.

Douglas, Mary. "Introduction: Thirty Years after Witchcraft, Oracles, and Magic," pp. xiii–xxxvii in Mary Douglas, ed., *Witchcraft Confessions and Accusations.* London: Tavistock, 1970.

Douglas, William O. "Lawyers of the Peace Corps," *American Bar Association Journal,* 48 (1962): 909–910.

Dow, Unity, ed. *The Citizenship Case: The Attorney General of the Republic of Botswana vs. Unity Dow, Court Documents, Judgements, Cases and Materials.* Gaborone, Botswana: Lentswe La Lesedi Pty, 1995.

Dow, Unity, and Puseletso Kidd. *Women, Marriage, and Inheritance.* Series on Women and Law in Southern Africa. Gaborone, Botswana: Women and Law Southern African Trust, 1994.

D'Sa, Rose M. "Reforming the Right of Silence in Criminal Trials: A Commonwealth Perspective," *African Journal of International and Comparative Law,* 2 (1990): 604–625.

DuBow, Frederic Lee. "Justice for People: Law and Politics in the Lower Courts of Tanzania." Unpublished dissertation, Department of Sociology, University of California at Berkeley, 1973.

DuBow, Frederic Lee. "Language, Law, and Change: Problems in the Development of a National Legal System in Tanzania," pp. 85–98 in William O'Barr and Jean O'Barr, eds., *Language and Politics.* The Hague: Mouton, 1976.

Dugard, John. "International Law and the 'Final' Constitution," *South African Journal on Human Rights,* 11, 2 (1995): 241–251.

Dugard, John. "The Judicial Process, Positivism and Civil Liberty," *South African Law Journal,* 91 (1971): 181–200.

Dugard, John. "The Role of International Law in Interpreting the Bill of Rights," *South African Journal on Human Rights,* 10, 2, (1995): 208–215.

Dugard, John. "Should Judges Resign?—A Reply to Professor Wacks," *South African Law Journal,* 101 (1984): 286–294.

Dumbutshena, Enoch. "How the Judiciary Should React to Violent Changes of Government and de Facto Regimes." Paper presented at the annual meeting of the International Commission of Jurists, Caracas, Venezuela, January 16–20, 1989, and summarized in *Commonwealth Law Bulletin,* 15, 2 (1989): 640–641.

Dumbutshena, Enoch. "The Judiciary, the Executive, and the Law." Speech delivered at the National University of Lesotho, November 29, 1987, as reprinted in *Lesotho Law Journal*, 3, 2 (1987): 237–244.

Dumbutshena, Enoch. "Role of the Judge in Advancing Human Rights," *Commonwealth Law Bulletin*, 18, 4 (October 1992): 1298–1305.

Dumbutshena, Enoch. "The Rule of Law in a Constitutional Democracy with Particular Reference to the Zimbabwean Experience," *South African Journal on Human Rights*, 5, 3 (1990): 311–321.

Dumbutshena, Enoch. *Zimbabwe Tragedy*. Nairobi, Kenya: East African Publishing House, 1975.

Dundes-Renteln, Alison, and Alan Dundes. *Folk Law: Essays in the Theory and Practice of Lex Non Scripta*. 2 vols. Madison: University of Wisconsin Press, 1994.

Duxbury, Neil. *Patterns of American Jurisprudence*. Oxford: Clarendon, 1995.

Elias, T. O. *Judicial Process in the Newer Commonwealth*. Lagos, Nigeria: University of Lagos Press, 1990.

Elias, T. O. "The Problem of Reducing Customary Laws to Writing," pp. 319–330 in Alison Dundes-Renteln and Alan Dundes, eds. *Folk Law: Essays in the Theory and Practice of Lex Non Scripta*. Madison: University of Wisconsin Press, 1994.

Elias, T. O. "The Role of the International Court of Justice in Africa," *African Journal of International and Comparative Law*, 1, 1 (1989): 1–12.

Ellmann, Stephen. "What Role Should Morality Play in Judging?: To Resign or Not to Resign?" *Cardozo Law Review*, 19 (1997): 1047–1059.

Epstein, Lee, and Jack Knight. *The Choices Justices Make*. Washington, D.C.: CQ Press, 1998.

Erasmus, H. J. "Roman Law in South Africa Today," *South African Law Journal*, 106, 4 (1989): 666–677.

Essien, Victor. "Customary Law and Western Legal Influences in Modern-Day Africa (Case Studies from Ghana and Nigeria)," pp. 171–204 in Richard Danner and Marie-Louise H. Bernal, eds., *Introduction to Foreign Legal Systems*. New York: Oceana Publications for American Association of Law Libraries, 1994.

Favoreu, Louis. "American and European Models of Constitutional Jurisprudence," pp. 105–120 in David Clark, ed., *Comparative and Private International Law: Essays in Honor of John Henry Merryman*. Berlin: Duncker & Humbolt, 1990.

Feltoe, G., and P. Lewin. "Remedies for Unlawful Interference with Personal Liberty in Zimbabwe," *Zimbabwe Law Review*, 6 (1987): 26–53.

Fimbo, G. M. *Constitution Making and Courts in Tanzania*. Dar es Salaam, Tanzania: Faculty of Law, University of Dar es Salaam, 1992.

Fimbo, G. M. "Public Participation in Judicial Proceedings in Tanzania," *Eastern Africa Law Review*, 17, 1 (June 1990): 18–33.

Fisher, George. "Plea Bargaining's Triumph," *Yale Law Journal*, 109, 5 (2000): 868–1086.

Fisiy, Cyprian F., and Peter Geschiere. "Judges and Witches, or How Is the State to Deal with Witchcraft?" *Cahiers d'études africaines*, 118, XXX–2 (1990): 135–156.

Fiss, Owen M. "The Limits of Judicial Independence," *University of Miami Inter-American Law Review*, 25 (1993): 57–67.

Fiss, Owen M. "The Right Degree of Independence," pp. 55–72 in Irwin Stotzky, ed., *The Transition to Democracy in Latin America: The Role of the Judiciary*. Boulder, CO: Westview, 1993.

Fletcher, George P. "The Rule of Law," in *Basic Concepts of Legal Thought*. New York: Oxford University Press, 1996.

Franck, Thomas M. "The New Development: Can American Law and Legal Institutions Help Developing Countries?" *Wisconsin Law Review*, 3 (1972): 767–801.

Frank, Bernard. "The Tanzanian Permanent Commission of Inquiry—The Ombudsman," *Journal of International Law and Policy*, 2 (1972): 255–279.

Freedom House. *Freedom in the World: The Annual Survey of Political Rights and Civil Liberties*. New York: Freedom House, annual.

Freeman, Marsha. "Measuring Equality: A Comparative Perspective on Women's Legal Capacity and Constitutional Rights in Five Commonwealth Countries," *Commonwealth Law Bulletin*, 16, 4 (1990): 1418–1443.

Friedman, Lawrence M. "On Legal Development," *Rutgers Law Review*, 24 (1969): 11–64.

Furley, Oliver, and James Katalikawe. "Constitutional Reform in Uganda: The New Approach," *African Affairs*, 96 (1997): 243–260.

Gaer, Felice D. "First Fruits: Reporting by States under the African Charter on Human and Peoples' Rights," *Netherlands Quarterly of Human Rights*, 1 (1992): 29–42.

Gardner, James A. *Legal Imperialism: American Lawyers and Foreign Aid in Latin America*. Madison: University of Wisconsin Press, 1980.

Georges, P. Telford. See James and Kassam below.

Geschiere, Peter. "Globalization and the Power of Indeterminate Meaning: Witchcraft and Spirit Cults in Africa and East Asia," *Development and Change*, 29 (1998): 811–837.

Ghai, Yash P., "Asian Perspectives on Human Rights," pp. 54–70 in James T. H. Tang, ed., *Human Rights and International Relations in the Asia-Pacific Region*. New York: Pinter (St. Martin's), 1995.

Ghai, Yash P. "Constitutions and Governance in Africa: A Prolegomenon," pp. 51–75 in Sammy Adelman and Abdul Paliwala, eds., *Law and Crisis in the Third World*. London: Hans Zell for University of Warwick, 1993.

Ghai, Yash P. "Law and Lawyers in Kenya and Tanzania," pp. 144–176 in Clarence J. Dias, ed., *Lawyers in the Third World: Comparative and Developmental Perspectives*. Uppsala, Sweden: Scandinavian Institute of African Studies, 1981.

Ghai, Yash P. "Law, Development and African Scholarship," *Modern Law Review*, 50 (October 1987): 750–776.

Ghai, Yash P. "Legal Education in Kenya and Tanzania," pp. 261–282 in A.

Bockel, Y. P. Ghai, J. Imbert, et al., *Legal Education in Africa South of the Sahara/La formation juridique en Afrique noire*. Brussels: International Agency of Legal Sciences/Établissements Émile Bruylant, 1979.

Ghai, Yash P. "Legal Radicalism, Professionalism, and Social Action: Reflections on Teaching Law in Dar es Salaam," pp. 26–35 in Issa Shivji, ed., *The Limits of Legal Radicalism: Reflections on Teaching Law at the University of Dar es Salaam*. Dar es Salaam, Tanzania: Faculty of Law, University of Dar es Salaam, 1986.

Ghai, Yash P. "Matovu's Case: Another Comment," *Eastern Africa Law Review*, 1, 1 (April 1968): 68–75.

Ghai, Yash P. *The Rule of Law in Africa*. Bergen, Norway: Christien Michelsen Institute, 1990.

Ghai, Yash, and Patrick McAuslan. *Public Law and Political Change in Kenya*. Nairobi, Kenya: Oxford University Press, 1970.

Gibson, James L., Gregory Caldeira, and Vanessa Baird. "On the Legitimacy of National High Courts," *American Political Science Review*, 92, 2 (June 1998): 343–358.

Ginther, K., and W. Benedek, eds. *New Perspectives and Concepts of International Law: An Afro-European Dialogue*. Vienna: Springer-Verlag, 1983.

Gittelman, Richard. "The African Charter on Human and Peoples' Rights: A Legal Analysis," *Virginia Journal of International Law*, 22, 4 (1982): 667–714.

Glendon, Mary Ann. *Rights Talk: The Impoverishment of Political Discourse*. New York: Free Press, 1991.

Glendon, Mary Ann, Michael Wallace Gordon, and Christopher Osakwe. *Comparative Legal Traditions: Text, Materials, and Cases*. St. Paul, MN: West, 1985.

Goldstone, Richard. "Do Judges Speak Out?" *South African Law Journal*, 111 (1994): 258–269.

Goldstone, Richard. "The Reception of the Dutch-Roman Law in Southern Africa and Sri Lanka, and Its Influence on Civil Liberties," pp. 21–24 in *Law in Multicultural Societies*. Proceedings of the International Association of Law Libraries Meeting, Jerusalem, July 21–26, 1985. Jerusalem: B. G. Law Library Center/Hebrew University, 1989.

Goodrich, Herbert F., and Paul Wolkin. *The Story of the American Law Institute, 1923–1961*. St. Paul, MN: ALI Publishers, 1961.

Gopal, Gita, and Maryam Salim. *Gender and Law: Eastern Africa Speaks*. World Bank Directions in Development Series. Washington, D.C.: World Bank, 1998.

Gordley, James. "Comparative Legal Research: Its Function in the Development of Harmonized Law," *American Journal of Comparative Law*, 45 (1995): 555–567.

Gordley, James. "European Codes and American Restatements: Some Difficulties," *Columbia Law Review*, 81 (1981): 140–157.

Gower, L. C. B. *Independent Africa—The Challenge to the Legal Profession*. Cambridge, MA: Harvard University Press, 1967.

Gray, Sir John. "Opinions of Assessors in Criminal Trials in East Africa as to Native Custom," *Journal of African Law*, 2, 1 (1958): 5–18.

Green, Maia. "Shaving Witchcraft in Ulanga," in Ray Abrahams, ed. *Witchcraft in Contemporary Tanzania*. Cambridge: African Studies Center, University of Cambridge, 1994.

Greer, Stephen. "Preventive Detention and Public Security: Towards a General Model," pp. 23–40 in Andrew Harding and John Hatchard, eds., *Preventive Detention and Security Law: A Comparative Survey*. International Studies in Human Rights. Dordrecht: Martinus Nijhoff, 1993.

Griffiths, Anne. "Legal Duality: Conflict or Concord in Botswana?" *Journal of African Law*, 27, 2 (1983): 150–161.

Griffiths, Anne. "The Problem of Informal Justice: Family Dispute Processing among the Bakwena—A Case Study," *International Journal of the Sociology of Law*, 14, 3–4 (1986): 359–376.

Gubbay, Anthony R. "Human Rights in Criminal Justice Proceedings: The Zimbabwean Experience," pp. 307–321 in Cherif Bassiouni and Ziyad Motala, eds., *The Protection of Human Rights in African Criminal Proceedings*. Dordrecht: Martinus Nijhoff/Kluwer Academic, 1994.

Gubbay, Anthony R. "The Protection and Enforcement of Fundamental Human Rights: The Zimbabwean Experience," *Human Rights Quarterly*, 19 (1997): 227–254.

Guni, Vengai. "The Independence of the Judiciary in Zimbabwe," pp. 127–131 in *Report of the Tenth Commonwealth Magistrates' and Judges' Conference, Commonwealth Magistrates' and Judges' Association, Victoria Falls, Zimbabwe, August 22–26, 1994*. London: Commonwealth Magistrates' and Judges' Association, 1994.

Gye-Wado, Onje. "A Comparative Analysis of the Institutional Framework for the Enforcement of Human Rights in Africa and Western Europe," *African Journal of International and Comparative Law*, 2, 1 (1990): 187–201.

Hager, L. Michael. "Training Lawyers for Development: The IDLI Experience," *Third World Legal Studies*, 1986 (1986): 57–62.

Hannum, Hurst. "The Butare Colloquium on Human Rights and Economic Development in Francophone Africa: A Summary and Analysis," *Universal Human Rights*, 1, 2 (April–June 1979): 63–87.

Harding, Andrew, and John Hatchard. "Introduction," pp. 1–22 in Andrew Harding and John Hatchard, eds., *Preventive Detention and Security Law: A Comparative Survey*. Dordrecht: Martinus Nijhoff, 1993.

Harding, Andrew, and John Hatchard, eds. *Preventive Detention and Security Law: A Comparative Survey*. International Studies in Human Rights. Dordrecht: Martinus Nijhoff, 1993.

Harvey, William Burnett. "The Challenge of the Rule of Law," *Michigan Law Review*, 59 (1961): 603–613.

Harvey, William Burnett. "Ghana: The Curtain Falls." Unpublished manuscript in "A Selection of Lectures and Informal Talks on Law and Universities and the Communities That Usually Tolerate and Sometimes Support Them." Collection of papers in the estate of William Burnett Harvey, Boston, MA, 1999.

Harvey, William Burnett. *An Introduction to the Legal System of East Africa.* Nairobi, Kenya: East African Literature Bureau, 1975.

Harvey, William Burnett. *Law and Social Change in Ghana.* Princeton: Princeton University Press, 1966.

Harvey, William Burnett. "The Rule of Law in Historical Perspective," *Michigan Law Review*, 59 (1961): 487–500.

Harvey, William Burnett. "A Value Analysis of Ghanaian Legal Development since Independence." Unpublished manuscript in "A Selection of Lectures and Informal Talks on Law and Universities and the Communities That Usually Tolerate and Sometimes Support Them." Collection of papers in the estate of William Burnett Harvey, Boston, MA, 1999.

Hatchard, John. *Individual Freedoms and State Security in the African Context: The Case of Zimbabwe.* Athens, OH: Ohio University Press/James Currey/Baobab Books, 1993.

Hatchard, John. "'Perfecting Imperfections': Developing Procedures for Amending Constitutions in Commonwealth Africa," *Journal of Modern African Studies*, 36, 3 (1998): 381–398.

Hatchard, John. "Undermining the Constitution by Constitutional Means: Some Thoughts on the New Constitutions of Southern Africa," *Comparative and International Law Journal of Southern Africa*, 28, 1 (March 1995): 21–35.

Hatchard, John. "Zimbabwe," pp. 293–311 in Andrew Harding and John Hatchard, eds., *Preventive Detention and Security Law: A Comparative Study.* Dordrecht: Martinus Nijhoff, 1993.

Hay, Margaret Jean, and Marcia Wright, eds. *African Women and the Law: Historical Perspectives.* Boston: Boston University African Studies Center, 1982.

Heyns, Christof. "African Human Rights Law and the European Convention," *South African Journal on Human Rights*, 11, 2 (1995): 252–263.

Higgins, Rosalyn. "Africa and the Covenant on Civil and Political Rights during the First Five Years of the Journal: Some Facts and Some Thoughts," *African Journal of International and Comparative Law*, 5, 1 (March 1993): 55–66.

Hirsch, Susan F. *Pronouncing and Persevering: Gender and the Discourse of Disputing in an African Islamic Court.* Chicago: University of Chicago Press, 1998.

Hirschman, Albert O., and Michael Rothschild. "The Changing Tolerance for Income Inequality in the Course of Economic Development," *Quarterly Journal of Economics*, 87, 4 (November 1973): 544–566.

Hlatchwayo, Ben. "Judicial Activism and Development: Warning Signals from Zimbabwe," *Zimbabwe Law Review*, 9–10 (1991–92): 1–13.

Hofstra Law Review. Symposium on the American Law Institute. *Hofstra Law Review*, 26 (Spring 1998).

Holmes, Stephen, and Cass R. Sunstein. *The Cost of Rights: Why Liberty Depends on Taxes.* New York: W. W. Norton, 1999.

Holphe, John. "The Role of Judges in a Transformed South Africa—Problems, Challenges, and Prospects," *South African Law Journal*, 112 (1995): 22–31.

Hossain, Sara, Shahdeen Malik, and Bushra Musa, eds. *Public Interest Litigation in*

South Asia: Rights in Search of Remedies. Dhaka, Bangladesh: University Press Limited, 1997.

Howard, Rhoda. "Evaluating Human Rights in Africa: Some Problems of Implicit Comparisons," *Human Rights Quarterly,* 6, 2 (1984): 160–179.

Howard, Rhoda, "The Full-Belly Thesis: Should Economic Rights Take Priority Over Civil and Political Rights? Evidence from Sub-Saharan Africa," *Human Rights Quarterly* 5, 4 (1983): 467–490.

Huffman, James L., and MardiLyn Saathoff. "Advisory Opinions and Canadian Constitutional Development: The Supreme Court's Reference Jurisdiction," *Minnesota Law Review,* 74 (1990): 1251–1336.

Hutchison, Thomas W. *Africa and Law: Developing Legal Systems in African Commonwealth Nations.* James N. Roethe [and others] of the staff of the Wisconsin Law Review. Introduction by A. Arthur Schiller. Madison: University of Wisconsin Press, 1968.

Ileti, K. F. "Post-Mwongozo Workers' Disputes in Tanzania: Two Case Studies," *Eastern Africa Law Review,* 7, 2 (1974): 157–188.

International Commission of Jurists. "Draft Principles on the Independence of the Judiciary (Siracusa Principles)," *CIJL Bulletin,* 25/26 (April–October 1990): 59–71.

International Congress of Jurists. *The Rule of Law in a Free Society.* A Report of the International Congress of Jurists, New Delhi, January 5–10, 1959. Geneva: International Commission of Jurists, 1959.

Jackson, John H. "Status of Treaties in Domestic Legal Systems: A Policy Analysis," *American Journal of International Law,* 86, 310 (1992): 310–340.

Jackson, Tudor. *Guide to the Legal Profession in East Africa.* London: Sweet & Maxwell, 1970.

Jaconelli, Joseph. "Note: Hypothetical Disputes, Moot Points of Law, and Advisory Opinions," *Law Quarterly Review,* 101 (October 1985): 587–626.

James, R. W., and F. M. Kassam. *Law and Its Administration in a One Party State: Selected Speeches of Telford Georges.* Nairobi, Kenya: East African Literature Bureau, 1973.

Jay, Stewart. *Most Humble Servants: The Advisory Role of Early Judges.* New Haven: Yale University Press, 1997.

Jearey, J. H. "Trial by Jury and Trial with the Aid of Assessors in the Superior Courts of British African Territories," Part I, *Journal of African Law,* 4, 3 (1960): 133–146.

Jeary, J. H. "Trial by Jury and Trial with the Aid of Assessors," Parts II and III, *Journal of African Law,* 5, 1 (1961): 36–47 and 5, 2 (1961): 82–98.

Juenger, Friedrich K. "Listening to Law Professors Talk about Good Faith: Some Afterthoughts," *Tulane Law Review,* 69 (1995): 1254–1257.

Juma, Ibrahim. "Wildlife Conservation versus Customary Land-Use: Lessons Drawn from Mkomazi Game Reserve Case." Paper presented at the Law and Development Seminar, University of Michigan, Ann Arbor, March 1999.

Kadish, Sanford. "The Model Penal Code's Historical Antecedents," *Rutgers Law Journal,* 19 (1988): 521–538.

Kahn, Ellison. "Restore the Jury? Or 'Reform? Reform? Aren't Things Bad Enough Already?'" Multipart article, *South African Law Journal*, 108, 4 (1991): 672–687 through 109 (1992): 321–337.

Kalman, Laura. *Legal Realism at Yale, 1927–1960.* Chapel Hill, NC: University of North Carolina Press, 1986.

Kamau Kuria, Gibson, and Algeisa M. Vasquez. "Judges and Human Rights: The Kenyan Experience," *Journal of African Law*, 35, 1–2 (1991): 142–173.

Kannyo, Edward. "The Banjul Charter on Human and Peoples' Rights: Genesis and Political Background," pp. 128–151 in Claude Welch, Jr., and Ronald I. Meltzer, eds., *Human Rights and Development in Africa.* Albany: State University of New York Press, 1984.

Kanywanyi, J. "Twenty-five Years of Teaching Law in Dar es Salaam," *Zimbabwe Law Review*, 7 (1989–90): 31–56.

Kanywanyi, J. L. "The Struggle to Decolonise and Demystify University Education: Dar's 25 Years Experience Focused on the Faculty of Law," *Eastern Africa Law Review*, 16, 1 (1989): 1–70.

Kapinga, Wilbert B. L. "The Legal Profession and Social Action in the Third World: Reflections on Tanzania and Kenya," *African Journal of International and Comparative Law*, 4, 4 (1992): 874–891.

Kaplan, Robert. "The Coming Anarchy," *Atlantic Monthly*, 273, 2 (February 1994): 44–46, 48–49, 52, 54, 58–60, 62–63, 66, 68–71, 72–76.

Keith, Kenneth James. *The Extent of the Advisory Jurisdiction of the International Court of Justice.* Leyden: A. W. Sijthoff, 1971.

Kerr, A. J. "The Reception and Codification of Systems of Law in Southern Africa," *Journal of African Law*, 2, 2 (1958): 82–100.

Khadiagala, Lynn. "Seeking Justice in Uganda: The Adjudication of Women's Property Rights and the Failure of Popular Justice." Paper prepared for the American Political Science Association annual meeting, Boston, MA, September 3–6, 1998.

Kibwana, Kivutha. "Enhancing Cooperation among African Law Schools," pp. 293–299 in *Proceedings of the Fourth Annual Conference, African Society of International and Comparative Law, Dakar, April 10–13, 1992.* London: African Society of International and Comparative Law, 1992.

Kibwana, Kivutha. *Fundamental Rights and Freedoms in Kenya.* Nairobi, Kenya: Oxford University Press, 1990.

Kibwana, Kivutha, ed. *Law and the Administration of Justice in Kenya.* Nairobi, Kenya: International Commission of Jurists, Kenya Section, 1992.

Kibwana, Kivutha. "Women and the Constitution in Kenya," *Verfassung und Recht Übersee*, 25, 1 (1992): 6–20.

Kibwana, Kivutha, and Kathurima M'Inoti. "Human Rights Issues in the Criminal Justice Systems of Kenya and the African Charter on Human and Peoples' Rights: A Comparative Analysis," pp. 119–130 in Cherif Bassiouni and Ziyad Motala, eds., *The Protection of Human Rights in African Criminal Proceedings.* Dordrecht: Martinus Nijhoff/Kluwer, 1994.

Kigula, John. "Land Disputes in Uganda: An Overview of the Types of Land

Disputes and the Dispute Settlement Fora." Unpublished manuscript, Makerere Institute for Social Research, March 1993.

Kisanga, Robert H. "Independence of the Judiciary in Tanzania," *Indian Bar Review*, 11, 2 (1984): 135–153.

Kisanga, Robert H. "The Legal Profession, Pluralism, and Public Interest Litigation," *Ethnic Studies Report*, 3, 1 (1985): 45–52.

Kisanga, Robert H. "Problems of Administering Justice in Tanzania." Paper presented at the Judge's Seminar at Arusha, Tanzania, 25–26, 1991.

Kisanga, Robert H. "The Protection of Civil and Political Human Rights in the Societal Realities of East and Central Africa." Paper presented at the Conference on Constitutionalism and the Legal System in a Democracy, Arusha, Tanzania, March 28–29, 1995.

Kiwanuka, Richard N. "The Meaning of 'People' in the African Charter on Human and Peoples' Rights," *American Journal of International Law*, 82 (1988): 80–101.

Klug, Heinz. "Participating in the Design: Constitution-Making in South Africa." Special issue on the South African constitution in transition, *Review of Constitutional Studies*, 3,1 (1996): 18–59.

Knox-Mawer, R. "The Jury System in British Colonial Africa," *Journal of African Law*, 2, 3 (1958): 160–163.

Kozolchyk, Boris. "The UNIDROIT Principles as a Model for the Unification of the Best Contractual Practices in the Americas," *American Journal of Comparative Law*, 46 (1998): 151–179.

Kuria, G. K., and J. B. Ojwang. "Judges and the Rule of Law in the Framework of Politics: The Kenyan Case," *Public Law*, (August 1979): 254–281.

Kurland, Philip B. "The Constitution and the Tenure of Federal Judges: Some Notes from History," *University of Chicago Law Review*, 36 (1969): 665–698.

Ladley, Andrew. "Changing the Courts in Zimbabwe: The Customary Law and Primary Courts Act," *Journal of African Law*, 26, 2 (Autumn 1982): 95–114.

Landes, William M., and Richard A. Posner. "The Economics of Anticipatory Adjudication," *Journal of Legal Studies*, 23 (June 1994): 683–719.

Landes, William M., and Richard A. Posner. "The Independent Judiciary in an Interest Group Perspective," *Journal of Law and Economics*, 18, 3 (December 1975): 875–901.

Langbein, John. "Mixed Court and Jury Court: Could the Continental Alternative Fill the American Need?" *American Bar Foundation Research Journal*, 1 (1981): 195–219.

Langseth, Petter, and Rick Stapenhurst. "National Integrity System Country Studies." EDI Working Paper. Washington, D.C.: World Bank, 1997.

Lapidus, Ira M. *A History of Islamic Societies*. Cambridge: Cambridge University Press, 1988.

Larkins, Christopher M. "Judicial Independence and Democratization: A Theoretical and Conceptual Analysis," *American Journal of Comparative Law*, 44, 4 (Fall 1996): 605–626.

Ledwith, Tim. "The Journey of Unity Dow," *Amnesty Action* (Winter 1999): 6–7.

Le Vine, Victor T. "The Fall and Rise of Constitutionalism in West Africa," *Journal of Modern African Studies*, 35, 2 (1997): 181–206.

Lewis, J. V. R. "Saving of Time and Costs in Civil Litigation," *Zimbabwe Law Journal*, 19, 1 (1979): 20–30.

Lindholt, Lone. *Questioning the Universality of Human Rights: The African Charter on Human and Peoples' Rights in Botswana, Malawi, and Mozambique.* Aldershot, England: Dartmouth/Ashgate, 1997.

"Litigation Realities in Uganda." Kampala, Uganda: International Law Institute Uganda Office, n.d. Mimeograph.

Littlewood, Sir Sidney. "The Legal Profession in African Territories," pp. 154–163 in J. N. D. Anderson, ed., *Changing Law in Developing Countries*. New York: Praeger, 1963.

Lobulu, R. N. Ben. "Corruption and the Administration of Justice," pp. 87–93 in *The National Integrity System in Tanzania*. Proceedings of a workshop on fighting corruption facilitated by Transparency International and the Economic Development Institute of the World Bank. Dar es Salaam, Tanzania: Prevention of Corruption Bureau, 1995. Distributed by the World Bank.

Lord Goff of Chieveley and Gareth Jones. *The Law of Restitution* (4th ed.). London: Sweet & Maxwell, 1993.

Lubuva, D. "Reflections on Tanzania's Bill of Rights," *Commonwealth Law Bulletin*, 14, 2 (April 1988): 853–857.

Lugakingira, K. S. K. "Personal Liberty and Judicial Attitude: The Tanzanian Case," *Eastern Africa Law Review*, 17, 1 (1990): 107–133.

Mahalu, Costa Ricky. "Africa and Human Rights," pp. 1–30 in Philip Kunig, Wolfgang Benedek, and Costa R. Mahalu, eds., *Regional Protection of Human Rights by International Law: The Emerging African System*. Baden-Baden: Nomos Verlagsgesellschaft, 1985.

Mahalu, Costa. "Three Decades of the Law in Context Approach," pp. 83–94 in Issa Shivji, ed., *Limits of Legal Radicalism: Reflections on Teaching Law at the University of Dar es Salaam*. Dar es Salaam, Tanzania: Faculty of Law, University of Dar es Salaam, 1986.

Makinson, David. "Rights of Peoples: Point of View of a Logician," pp. 69–92 in James Crawford, ed., *The Rights of Peoples*. Oxford: Clarendon, 1988.

Maluwa, Tiyanjana. "Changing Power Relations between Men and Women in Southern Africa: Some Recent Legal Developments." Working Paper No. 28 prepared for the workshop on "Transformations of Power and Culture in Africa," University of Michigan, Ann Arbor, November 18, 1996.

Maluwa, Tiyanjana. "The Role of International Law in the Protection of Human Rights under the Malawian Constitution of 1995," in *African Yearbook of International Law*, vol. 3. The Hague: Kluwer Law International, 1996.

Manase, Wilson T. "Grassroots Education in Zimbabwe: Successes and Problems Encountered in Implementation by the Legal Resources Foundation of Zimbabwe," *Journal of African Law*, 36, 1 (1992): 11–17.

Mann, Kristin, and Richard Roberts. *Law in Colonial Africa*. Portsmouth: Heinemann/James Currey, 1991.

Mapunda, A. M., M. C. Mukoyogo, and A. T. Nguluma. "Reflections on Stare Decisis in the Court of Appeal of the United Republic of Tanzania," *Eastern Africa Law Review*, 16, 2 (1989): 1–23.

Martin, Robert. "In the Matter of an Application by Michael Matovu," *Eastern Africa Law Review*, 1, 1 (April 1968): 61–67.

Mauro, Paulo. "Corruption: Causes, Consequences, and Agenda for Future Research," *Finance & Development*, 35, 1 (1998): 11–14.

Mayanja, Abu. "Government's Proposal for a New Constitution of Uganda," *Transition*, 6, 32 (1967): 20–25.

Mbao, M. "The Criminal Justice System on Trial in Zambia: A Case Note," *Journal of African Law*, 36, 2 (1992): 175–182.

Mbao, Melvin. "Zambia," pp. 279–292 in Andrew Harding and John Hatchard, eds., *Preventive Detention and Security Law: A Comparative Survey*. Dordrecht: Martinus Nijhoff, 1993.

M'baye, Keba. *Les droits de l'homme en Afrique*. Paris: International Commission of Jurists/Éditions A. Pedone, 1992.

Mbeo, Mary Adhiambo, and Oki Ooko-Ombaka, eds. *Women and Law in Kenya: Perspectives and Emerging Issues*. Nairobi, Kenya: Public Law Institute, 1989.

Mbunda, L. X. "Limitation Clauses and the Bill of Rights in Tanzania," pp. 79–94 in C. K. Mtake and Michael Okema, eds., *Constitutional Reforms and Democratic Governance in Tanzania*. Dar es Salaam, Tanzania: Freidrich-Naumann-Stiftung, 1994.

McClain, William T. "Recent Changes in African Local Courts and Customary Law," *Howard Law Journal*, 10 (1964): 187–226.

McClymont, Mary, and Stephen Golub, eds. *Many Roads to Justice: The Law-Related Work of Ford Foundation Grantees around the World*. New York: Ford Foundation, 2000.

McQuoid-Mason, D. J. "Street Law for South African School Children and the Protection of Human Rights in Criminal Justice Proceedings," pp. 365–358 in M. Cherif Bassiouni and Ziyad Motala, eds., *The Protection of Human Rights in African Criminal Proceedings*. Dordrecht: Martinus Nijhoff/Kluwer Academic, 1994.

Merry, Sally Engle. "Review of Lawrence Rosen's *The Anthropology of Justice*," *Columbia Law Review*, 91 (December 1990): 2311–2327.

Merryman, John Henry. "Comparative Law and Social Change: On the Origins, Style, Decline and Revival of the Law and Development Movement," *American Journal of Comparative Law*, 25 (1977): 457–489.

Mesaki, Simeon. "Witch-Killing in Sukumaland," pp. 47–60 in Ray Abrahams, ed., *Witchcraft in Contemporary Tanzania*. Cambridge: African Studies Center, University of Cambridge, 1994.

Milford, Lisa L. *The Development of the ABA Judicial Code*. Chicago: American Bar Association, 1992.

Mills, Greg. *War and Peace in Southern Africa: Crime, Drugs, Armies, and Trade*. World Peace Foundation Report. Cambridge: World Peace Foundation, 1996.

Mogwe, Alice. "Human Rights in Botswana," *Alternatives* 19, 2 (1994): 189–193.

Moisey, R. W. "The Role of Assessors in the Courts of Tanzania," *East African Law Journal*, 3, 4 (1967): 348–353.

Molokomme, Athaliah. "Customary Law in Botswana: Past, Present, and Future," pp. 347–369 in Sue Brothers, Janet Hermans, and Doreen Nteta, eds., *Botswana in the 21st Century: Proceedings of a Symposium of the Botswana Society.* Gaborone, Botswana: Botswana Society, October 1993.

Molokomme, Athaliah. "Disseminating Family Law Reforms: Some Lessons from Botswana," *Journal of Legal Pluralism and Unofficial Law*, 30–31 (1990–91): 303–329.

Molokomme, Athaliah. "Political Rights in Botswana: Regression or Development?" pp. 163–174 in John Holm and Patrick Molutsi, eds., *Democracy in Botswana*. Gaborone, Botswana: MacMillan Botswana, 1989

Molokomme, Athaliah. "Women's Law in Botswana: Law and Research Needs," pp. 7–46 in Julie Stewart and Alice Armstrong, eds., *The Legal Situation of Women in Southern Africa*. Women and Law in Southern Africa Series, vol. 2. Harare: University of Zimbabwe Publications, 1990.

Monga, Celestin. *The Anthropology of Anger*. Boulder, CO: Lynne Rienner, 1996.

Morris, Henry F. *Evidence Law in East Africa*. Law in Africa Series No. 24. London: Sweet & Maxwell, 1968.

Morris, Henry F. "How Nigeria Got Its Criminal Code," *Journal of African Law*, 14, 3 (1970): 137–154.

Morris, Henry F., and James S. Read. *Indirect Rule and the Search for Justice: Essays in East African Legal History*. Oxford: Clarendon, 1972.

Mtaki, C. K., and Michael Okema, eds., *Constitutional Reforms and Democratic Governance in Tanzania*. Dar es Salaam, Tanzania: Freidrich-Naumann-Stiftung, 1994.

Mtengeti-Migiro, Rose. "Legal Developments on Women's Rights to Inherit Land under Customary Law in Tanzania," 24, 4 *Verfassung und Recht im Übersee* (1991): 362–371.

Mubako, Simbi. "Fundamental Rights and Judicial Review: The Zambian Experience," *Zimbabwe Law Review*, 1–2 (1983–84): 97–132.

Muigai, Githu. "The Judiciary in Kenya and the Search for a Philosophy of Law: The Case of Constitutional Adjudication," *Journal of Human Rights Law and Practice* (Nigeria), 1, 1 (1991): 7–44.

Murray, Christina. "Democracy, the Family and the African Charter on Human and People's Rights," pp. 187–197 in *Proceeedings of the Fourth Annual Conference of the African Society of International and Comparative Law*, Dakar, April 10–13, 1992. London: African Society of International and Comparative Law, 1992.

Murray, Rachel. "Decisions by the African Commission on Individual Communications under the African Charter on Human and Peoples' Rights," *International and Comparative Law Quarterly*, 46 (April 1997): 412–434.

Mutua, Makau wa. "The Banjul Charter and the African Cultural Fingerprint: An Evaluation of the Language of Duties," *Virginia Journal of International Law*, 35 (Winter 1995): 339–380.

Mutungi, O. K. "The Communication of the Law under Conditions of Development: The Kenya Case," *East Africa Law Journal*, 9, 1 (1973): 11–42.

Mutungi, Onesmus K. *The Legal Aspects of Witchcraft in East Africa*. Nairobi, Kenya: East African Literature Bureau, 1977.

Mwaikusa, J. T. "Genesis of the Bill of Rights in Tanzania," *African Journal of International and Comparative Law*, 3 (1991): 680–698.

Mwaikusa, J. T. "Government Powers and Human Rights in Africa: Some Observations from the Tanzanian Experience," *Lesotho Law Journal*, 6, 1 (1990): 75–105.

Mwaikusa, J. T. "The Limits of Judicial Enterprise: Judicial Powers in the Process of Political Change in Tanzania," *Journal of African Law*, 40, 2 (1996): 243–255.

Mwaikusa, J. T. "Maintaining Law and Order in Tanzania: The Role of Sungusungu Defence Groups," pp. 166–178 in Joseph Semboja and Ole Therkildsen, eds., *Service Provision under Stress in East Africa: The State, NGOs, & People's Organizations in Kenya, Tanzania, and Uganda*. Copenhagen: Centre for Development Research, 1995.

Mwaikusa, J. T. "Separation of Powers and the Coming of the Multi-Party Politics," pp. 109–117 in C. K. Mtake and Michael Okema, eds., *Constitutional Reforms and Democratic Governance in Tanzania*. Dar es Salaam, Tanzania: Freidrich-Naumann-Stiftung, 1994.

Mwakyembe, Harrison George. *Tanzania's Eighth Constitutional Amendment and Its Implications on Constitutionalism, Democracy and the Union Question*. Juristische Schriftenreihe 58. Hamburg: Die Deutsche Bibliotek/Deutschen Akademischen Austauschdienstes, 1998.

Mwalusanya, James. "Conditions for Functioning of a Democratic Constitution," pp. 21–36 in C. K. Mtake and Michael Okema, eds., *Constitutional Reforms and Democratic Governance in Tanzania*. Dar es Salaam, Tanzania: Freidrich-Naumann-Stiftung, 1994.

Mwalusanya, James. "The Protection of Human Rights in Criminal Justice Proceedings—The Tanzania Experience," pp. 285–306 in M. Cherif Bassiouni and Ziyad Motala, eds., *The Protection of Human Rights in African Criminal Proceedings*. Dordrecht: Martinus Nijhoff/Kluwer, 1994.

Naldi, Gino J. "Constitutional Developments in Zimbabwe and Their Compatibility with International Human Rights," *African Journal of International and Comparative Law*, 3 (1991): 372–385.

Naldi, Gino J. "The Supreme Court of Zimbabwe Defines the Constitutional Right to a 'Fair Hearing within a Reasonable Time,'" *African Journal of International and Comparative Law*, 5 (1993): 182–205.

Nasir, Jamal J. *The Islamic Law of Personal Status*. London: Graham & Trotman/Kluwer, 1986.

Ndulo, Muna. "Ascertainment of Customary Law: Problems and Perspectives with Special Reference to Zambia," pp. 339–349 in Alison Dundes-Renteln and Alan Dundes, eds., *Folk Law: Essays in the Theory and Practice of Lex Non Scripta*. Madison: University of Wisconsin Press, 1994.

Neff, Stephen C. "Human Rights in Africa: Thoughts on the African Charter of

Human and Peoples' Rights in the Light of Case Law from Botswana, Lesotho and Swaziland," *International and Comparative Law Quarterly*, 33 (1984): 331–347.

Nkrumah, Kwame. "The Future of African Law," *Review of Contemporary Law*, 9 (1962–63): 9–14.

Nkrumah, Kwame. *Neo-Colonialism: The Last Stage of Imperialism.* New York: International Publishers, 1965.

Nickel, James W. "How Human Rights Generate Duties to Protect and Provide," *Human Rights Quarterly*, 15, 1 (1993): 77–86.

Nimitz, August H., Jr. *Islam and Politics in East Africa: The Sufi Order in Tanzania.* Minneapolis: University of Minnesota Press, 1980.

Nsereko, Daniel D. N. "Witchcraft as a Criminal Defence, from Uganda to Canada and Back," *Manitoba Law Journal*, 24, 1 (Fall 1996): 38–59.

Nwabueze, B. O. *Judicialism in Commonwealth Africa.* London: C. Hurst & Co., 1977.

Nwogugu, E. I. "Abolition of Customary Courts—The Nigerian Experiment," *Journal of African Law*, 18 (1974): 1–19.

Nyerere, Julius K. *The Arusha Declaration Ten Years After.* Dar es Salaam, Tanzania: United Republic of Tanzania, Government Printer, 1977.

Nyerere, Julius K. "The Judiciary and the People," pp. 109–114 in *Freedom and Socialism.* Dar es Salaam, Tanzania: Oxford University Press, 1968.

Nyerere, Julius K. "*Ujamaa*—The Basis of African Socialism," pp. 162–171 in *Freedom and Unity: A Selection from Writing and Speeches, 1952–65.* Dar es Salaam, Tanzania: Oxford University Press, 1966.

Nyerere, Julius K. *Ujamaa: Essays on Socialism.* Dar es Salaam, Tanzania: Oxford University Press, 1968.

Odoki, Benjamin J. "Reducing Delay in the Administration of Justice: The Case of Uganda," *Criminal Law Forum*, 5, 1 (1994): 57–90.

Odoki, Benjamin J. "Writing of a Democratic Constitution," *East African Journal of Peace and Human Rights*, 1, 2 (1993): 195–223.

Ojwang, J. B. "Kenya," pp. 105–122 in Andrew Harding and John Hatchard, eds., *Preventive Detention and Security Law: A Comparative Survey.* Dordrecht: Martinus Nijhoff, 1993.

Ojwang, Jackton B. "The Meaning, Content and Significance of Tribal Law in an Emergent Nation: The Kenyan Case," pp. 125–140 in *Law and Anthropology.* International Yearbook for Legal Anthropology, vol. 4. Vienna: VGO, 1989.

Ojwang, J. B., and Phoebe N. Okowa, "The One-Party State and Due Process of Law: The Kenya Case in Comparative Perspective," *African Journal of International and Comparative Law*, 1, 2 (1989): 177–205.

Ojwang, J. B., and J. A. Otieno-Odek, "The Judiciary in Sensitive Areas of Public Law: Emerging Approaches to Human Rights Litigation in Kenya," *Netherlands International Law Review*, 35 (1988): 29–52.

Okema, Michael, and Jwani Mwaikusa, eds. *Constitutions and Opposition in Africa.* Seminar Report. Dar es Salaam, Tanzania: Friedrich Ebert Stiftung Faculty of Law, University of Dar es Salaam, 1992.

Okere, B. Obinna. "The Protection of Human Rights in Africa and the African Charter on Human and People's Rights: A Comparative Analysis with the European and American Systems," *Human Rights Quarterly*, 6, 2 (1984): 141–159.

Okoth-Ogendo, H. W. O. "Human and Peoples' Rights: What Point Is Africa Trying to Make?" pp. 74–86 in Ronald Cohen, Goran Hyden, and Winston P. Nagan, *Human Rights and Governance in Africa*. Gainesville, FL: University of Florida Press, 1983.

Oloka-Onyango, Joe. "Beyond the Rhetoric: Reinvigorating the Struggle for Economic and Social Rights in Africa," *California Western International Law Journal*, 26, 1 (1995): 1–73.

Oloka-Onyango, J. B. "Judicial Power and Constitutionalism in Uganda." Working Paper No. 30. Kampala, Uganda: Centre for Basic Research, January 1993.

Oloka-Onyango, Joe. "Police Powers, Human Rights and the State in Kenya and Uganda: A Comparative Analysis," *Third World Legal Studies*, (1990): 1–36.

Oloka-Onyango, Joe, and Sylvia Tamale. "'The Personal is Political,' or Why Women's Rights Are Indeed Human Rights: An African Perspective on International Feminism," *Human Rights Quarterly*, 17 (1995): 691–731.

Otlhogile, Bojosi. "Criminal Justice and the Problems of a Dual Legal System in Botswana," *Criminal Law Forum*, 4, 3 (1993): 521–533.

Otlhogile, Bojosi. *A History of the Higher Courts of Botswana 1912–1990*. Gaborone, Botswana: Mmegi Publishing House, 1994.

Palamagamba, John Kabudi. "The Directive Principles of State Policy versus Duties of the Individual in East African Constitutions," *Verfassung und Recht in Übersee*, 28, 3 (1995): 272–303.

Palamagamba, John Kabudi. "The United Republic of Tanzania after a Quarter of a Century: A Legal Appraisal of the State of the Union of Tanganyika and Zanzibar," *African Journal of International and Comparative Law*, 5, 2 (June 1993): 310–339.

Palley, Claire. "Rethinking the Judicial Role: The Judiciary and Good Government," *Zambia Law Journal*, 1, 1 (1969): 1–35.

Paul, James C. N. "American Law Teachers and Africa: Some Historical Observations," *Journal of African Law*, 31, 1–2 (1987): 18–28.

Paul, James C. N. "Some Observations on Constitutionalism, Judicial Review and Rule of Law in Africa," *Ohio State Law Journal*, 35 (1974): 851–869.

Penal Problems in East Africa. Record of the Conference on Penal Problems in East Africa. *East African Law Journal*, 2, 1, (1966).

Peter, Chris Maina. "Enforcement of Fundamental Rights and Freedoms: The Case of Tanzania," pp. 81–89 in *African Yearbook of International Law*. Dordrecht: Martinus Nijhoff, 1996.

Peter, Chris Maina. "Five Years of the Bill of Rights in Tanzania: Drawing a Balance Sheet," *African Journal of International and Comparative Law*, 4 (1992): 131–167.

Peter, Chris Maina. "Fundamental Rights and Freedoms in Kenya: A Review Essay," *African Journal of International and Comparative Law*, 2 (1991): 61–98.

Peter, Chris Maina. *Human Rights in Africa: A Comparative Study of the African Human and People's Rights Charter and the New Tanzanian Bill of Rights.* Studies in Human Rights, No. 10. New York: Greenwood Press, 1990.

Peter, Chris Maina. *Human Rights in Tanzania: Selected Cases and Materials.* Köln: Rüdiger Köppe Verlag, 1997.

Peter, Chris Maina. "Incarcerating the Innocent: Preventive Detention in Tanzania," *Human Rights Quarterly,* 19 (1997): 113–135.

Peter, Chris Maina. "Tanzania," pp. 247–257 in Andrew Harding and John Hatchard, eds., *Preventive Detention and Security Law: A Comparative Study.* Dordrecht: Martinus Nijhoff, 1993.

Peter, Chris Maina, and M. K. B. Wamali. "Independence of the Judiciary in Tanzania: A Critique," *Verfassung und Recht in Übersee,* 21, 1 (1998): 72–87.

Pfeiffer, S. B. "Notes on the Role of the Judiciary in the Constitutional Systems of East Africa Since Independence," *Case Western Reserve Journal of International Law,* 10 (1978): 11–53.

Picciotto, Sol. "Law, Life, and Politics," pp. 36–47 in Issa Shivji, ed., *Limits of Legal Radicalism: Reflections on Teaching Law at the University of Dar es Salaam.* Dar es Salaam, Tanzania: Faculty of Law, University of Dar es Salaam, 1986.

Pope, Jeremy, ed. *National Integrity Systems: The TI Source Book.* Berlin: Transparency International, 1995.

Posner, Richard. "The Costs of Enforcing Legal Rights," *East European Constitutional Review,* 4, 3 (Summer 1995): 71–83.

Quansah, E. K. "The Corruption and Economic Crime Act (1994) of Botswana," *Journal of African Law,* 38, 2 (1994): 191–196.

Quashigah, Edward Kofi, and Obiora Chinedu Okafor. *Legitimate Governance in Africa: International and Domestic Legal Perspectives.* The Hague: Kluwer Law International, 1999.

Quigley, John. "The Tanzanian Constitution and the Right to a Bail Hearing," *African Journal of International and Comparative Law,* 4 (1992): 168–182.

Raifeartaigh, Una Ni. "Fault Issues and Libel Law—A Comparison between Irish, English, and United States Law," *International and Comparative Law Quarterly,* 40 (October 1991): 763–783.

Read, James S. "Bills of Rights in the 'Third World': Some Commonwealth Experiences," *Verfassung und Recht in Übersee,* 6, 1 (1973): 21–47.

Read, James S. "Crime and Punishment in East Africa: The Twilight of Customary Law," *Howard Law Journal,* 10 (1964): 164–186.

Read, James S. "Human Rights in Tanzania," pp. 125–145 in Colin Legum and Geoffrey Mmari, eds., *Mwalimu: The Influence of Nyerere.* London: James Currey, 1995.

Read, James S. "Studies in the Making of Colonial Laws," *Journal of African Law,* 23, 1 (1979): 1–9.

Read, James S. "Tony Allott: A Colleague's Tribute," *Journal of African Law,* 31, 1–2 (1988): 3–14.

Redish, Martin H., and Lawrence C. Marshall. "Adjudicatory Independence and the Values of Procedural Due Process," *Yale Law Journal,* 95 (1986): 455–476.

Reeves, Pamela, and Keith Klein. "Republic in Transition: 1995 Elections in Tanzania and Zanzibar." International Foundation for Electoral Systems Observation Report. Washington, D.C.: International Foundation for Electoral Systems, December 1995.

Remington, Frank. "The Future of the Substantive Criminal Law Codification Movement: Theoretical and Practical Concerns," *Rutgers Law Journal*, 19 (1988): 867–895.

Roberts, Simon. "The Survival of the Traditional Tswana Courts in the National Legal System of Botswana," *Journal of African Law*, 16, 2 (1972): 103–128.

Roberts-Wray, Sir Kenneth. *Commonwealth and Colonial Law*. New York: Praeger, 1966.

Roberts-Wray, Sir Kenneth. "The Independence of the Judiciary in Commonwealth Countries," pp. 63–80 in J. N. D. Anderson, ed., *Changing Law in Developing Countries*. New York: Praeger, 1963.

Robinson, Pearl. "The National Conference Phenomenon in Francophone Africa," *Comparative Studies in Society and History*, 36, 3 (1994): 575–610.

Rosberg, James. "The Rise of an Independent Judiciary in Egypt." Ph.D. dissertation, Department of Political Science, Massachusetts Institute of Technology, Cambridge, MA, 1995.

Rosen, Lawrence. *The Anthropology of Justice: Law as Culture in Islamic Society.* Cambridge: Cambridge University Press, 1989.

Rubin, Neville. "The Content and the Methods of Legal Education in Africa," pp. 41–136 in A. Bockel, Y. P. Ghai, J. Imbert, et al., eds., *Legal Education in Africa South of the Sahara/La formation juridique en Afrique noire*. Brussels: International Association of Legal Sciences+Établissements Émile Bruylant, 1979.

Rubin, Neville, and Eugene Cotran, eds. *Annual Survey of African Law*. London: Frank Cass, 1967–1969; London: Rex Collings, 1970 onward.

Rwelamira, Medard R. K. "The Tanzania Legal Internship Program: A New Horizon in Legal Education," *African Law Studies*, 15 (1977): 29–44.

Rwezaura, Barthazar. "The Changing Role of the Extended Family in Providing Economic Support for an Individual in Africa," *Bayreuth African Studies*, 11 (1989): 57–89.

Rwezaura, Barthazar. "Constraining Factors to the Adoption of Kiswahili as a Language of the Law in Tanzania," *Journal of African Law*, 37, 1 (1993): 31–45.

Rwezaura, Barthazar. "The Integration of Personal Laws: Tanzania's Experience," *Zimbabwe Law Review*, 1–2 (1983–84): 85–96.

Rwezaura, Barthazar. "The Integration of Marriage Laws in Africa with Special Reference to Tanzania," pp. 139–162 in Jamil M. Abun-Nasr, Ulrich Spellenberg, and Ulrike Wanitzek, eds., *Law, Society, and National Identity in Africa*. Hamburg: Helmut Buske Verlag, 1990.

Rwezaura, Barthazar. "Reflections on the Relationship between State Law and Customary Law in Contemporary Tanzania," *Tanzania Law Reference Bulletin*, 2, 1 (1988): 3–24.

Rwezaura, Barthazar. *State Law and Customary Law: Reflections on their*

Relationship: Contemporary Tanzania. Saarbrücken, Germany: Europa Institut, 1987.

Sachs, Albie. "Two Dimensions of Socialist Legality: Recent Experience in Mozambique," *International Journal of the Sociology of Law*, 13 (1985): 133–146.

Salacuse, Jezwald W. "Modernization of Law in French-Speaking Africa: Fantasy or Revolution?" *African Law Studies*, Preliminary issue (January 1969): 62–73.

Salim, Ahmed I. "Conflict between Common Law and Customary Law in Kenya: Regarding Burial Rights," pp. 133–138 in Jamil M. Abun-Nasr, Ulrich Spellenberg, and Ulrike Wanitzek, eds., *Law, Society, and National Identity in Africa.* Hamburg: Helmut Buske Verlag, 1990.

Salzberger, Eli M. "A Positive Analysis of the Doctrine of the Separation of Powers, or: Why Do We Have an Independent Judiciary," *International Review of Law and Economics*, 13 (1993): 349–379.

Sanders, A. J. G. M. "Constitutionalism in Botswana: A Valiant Attempt at Judicial Activism," *Comparative and International Law Journal of Southern Africa*, 16, 3 (November 1983): 350–373.

Sarkin-Hughes, J. "South Africa," pp. 209–230 in Andrew Harding and John Hatchard, eds., *Preventive Detention and Security Law: A Comparative Survey.* Dordrecht: Martinus Nijhoff, 1993.

Sawyerr, Akilagpa. "Application of Law in Tanzania: A 'Proper Remedy' Approach to Some Problems of Legal Pluralism," *Eastern Africa Law Review*, 7, 3 (1974): 223–246.

Sawyerr, Akilagpa. "Customary Law in the High Court of Tanzania," *Eastern Africa Law Review*, 6, 3 (1973): 265–284.

Sawyerr, Akilagpa, ed. *East African Law and Social Change.* Proceedings of a Seminar on Law and Social Change in East Africa, University College, Dar es Salaam, Tanzania, 1966. Nairobi, Kenya: East African Publishing House, 1967.

Sawyerr, Akilagpa. "Judicial Manipulation of Customary Family Law in Tanzania," pp. 115–128 in Simon Roberts, ed., *Law and the Family in Africa.* Seminar on New Directions in Family Law, Leyden, 1974. The Hague: Mouton, 1977.

Schaffer, Rosalie P., "The Inter-relationship between Public International Law and the Law of South Africa: An Overview," *International and Comparative Law Quarterly*, 32 (April 1983): 277–315.

Schuler, Margaret, and Sakuntala Kadirgmar-Rajasingham. *Legal Literacy: A Tool for Women's Empowerment.* New York: United Nations Development Fund for Women, UNIFEM WIDBOOKS, 1992.

Schwartz, Alan, and Robert E. Scott. "The Political Economy of Private Legislatures," *University of Pennsylvania Law Review*, 143, 3 (January 1995): 595–654.

Scotton, J. F. "Judicial Independence and Political Expression in East Africa—Two Colonial Legacies," *East African Law Journal*, 6 (March 1970): 1–19.

Secretan, Thierry. *Going into Darkness.* London: Thames & Hudson, 1995.

Seidman, Robert B. "The Communication of Law and the Process of Development," *Wisconsin Law Review*, 1972, 3 (1972): 686–719.

Seidman, Robert B. "Drafting for the Rule of Law," *Yale Journal of International Law*, 12 (1987): 84–120.

Seidman, Robert B. "Judicial Review and Fundamental Freedoms in Anglophonic Independent Africa," *Ohio State Law Journal*, 35 (1974): 820–850.

Seidman, Robert B. "A Note on the Gold Coast Reception Statutes," *Journal of African Law*, 13, 1 (1969): 45–51.

Seidman, Robert B. "The Reception of English Law in Colonial Africa Revisited," *Eastern Africa Law Review*, 2, 1 (1969): 47–86.

Seidman, Robert B. "Rules of Recognition in the Primary Courts of Zimbabwe: On Lawyers' Reasonings and Customary Law," *International and Comparative Law Quarterly*, 32 (October 1983): 871–903.

Seidman, Robert B. *The State, Law, and Development*. London: Croom Helm, 1978.

Seidman, Robert B. "On Teaching Law and Development," *Third World Legal Studies*, (1986): 53–62.

Seidman, Robert B. "Witch Murder and Mens Rea: A Problem of Society under Radical Social Change," *Modern Law Review*, 28 (1965): 46–61.

Sen, Amartya. "Freedoms and Needs: An Argument for the Primacy of Political Rights," *New Republic*, January 10–17, 1994, pp. 31–36, 38.

Seng, Michael P. "In a Conflict between Equal Rights for Women and Customary Law, the Botswana Court of Appeal Chooses Equality," *University of Toledo Law Review*, 24 (Spring 1993): 563–582.

Shaidi, Leonard J. "Crime, Justice and Politics in Contemporary Tanzania: State Power in an Underdeveloped Social Formation," *International Journal of the Sociology of Law*, 17, 3 (1989): 247–271.

Shapiro, Martin. *Courts: A Comparative and Political Analysis*. Chicago: University of Chicago Press, 1987.

Shapiro, Martin. "Islam and Appeal," *California Law Review*, 68, 2 (1980): 350–381.

Shenje-Peyton, Angeline. "Balancing Gender, Equality, and Cultural Identity: Marriage Payments in Post-Colonial Zimbabwe," *Harvard Human Rights Journal*, 9 (Spring 1996): 105–144.

Shihata, Ibrahim. "Judicial Reform in Developing Countries and the Role of the World Bank," in Malcolm Rowat, Waleed Haider Malik, and Maria Dakolias, eds., *Judicial Reform in Latin America and the Caribbean*. World Bank Technical Paper No. 280. Washington, D.C.: World Bank, April 1995.

Shimba, Lawrence. "The Status and Rights of Judges in Commonwealth Africa: Problems and Prospects," *Lesotho Law Journal*, 3, 2 (1987): 1–19.

Shivji, Issa G. *The Concept of Human Rights in Africa*. London: CODESRIA Book Series, 1989.

Shivji, Issa. "Contradictory Developments in the Teaching and Practice of Human Rights Law in Tanzania," *Journal of African Law*, 35, 1–2 (1991): 116–134.

Shivji, Issa, ed. *Limits of Legal Radicalism: Reflections on Teaching Law at the University of Dar es Salaam*. Dar es Salaam, Tanzania: Faculty of Law, University of Dar es Salaam, 1986.

Shivji, Issa G. "The Rule of Law and Ujamaa in the Ideological Formation of Tanzania," *Social and Legal Studies*, 4, 2 (June 1995): 147–174.

Shivji, Issa G., ed. *State and Constitutionalism: An African Debate on Democracy*. Harare, Zimbabwe: SAPES Trust, 1991.

Shivji, Issa G., and Wilbert B. Kapinga. *Maasai Rights in Ngorogoro*, Tanzania. London: International Institute for Environment and Development/Hakiardhi, 1998.

Silungwe, Annel. "The Judiciary and Human Rights: The Zambian Experience." Proceedings of the "American Dialogue," Makerere University, Kampala, Uganda, PP/246. Makerere University Human Rights and Peace Center (HURIPEC) Archive, Kampala, Uganda, 1994.

Simpson, A. W. Brian. "The Common Law and Legal Theory," pp. 119–139 in Alison Dundes-Renteln and Alan Dundes, eds., *Folk Law: Essays in the Theory and Practice of Lex Non Scripta*, 2 vols. Madison: University of Wisconsin Press, 1994.

Simpson, A. W. Brian. *In the Highest Degree Odious: Detention without Trial in Wartime Britain*. Oxford: Clarendon, 1992.

Simpson, A. W. Brian. "The Judges and the Vigilant State," *Denning Law Journal*, 1989 (1989): 145–167.

Simpson, A. W. Brian. "Round Up the Usual Suspects: The Legacy of British Colonialism and the European Convention on Human Rights," *Loyola Law Review*, 41, 2 (1995): 629–711.

Slater, D. R., and J. B. Ojwang. "Law Reform in Africa: A Comparative Study of the Tanzanian and Kenyan Experiments," *Verfassung und Recht in Übersee*, 18, 2 (1985): 123–138.

Smit, Dirk van Zyl, and Norma-May Isakow. "Assessors and Criminal Justice," *South African Journal on Human Rights*, 1, 3 (1985): 218–235.

Smith, David N. "Man and Law in Urban Africa: A Role for Customary Courts in the Urbanization Process," *American Journal of Comparative Law*, 20 (1972): 223–246.

Smith, Jean Edward. *John Marshall: Definer of a Nation*. New York: Henry Holt, 1996.

Sorabjee, Soli J. "Protection of Fundamental Rights by Public Interest Litigation," pp. 27–41 in Sara Hossain, Shahdeen Malik, and Bushra Musa, eds., *Public Interest Litigation in South Asia: Rights in Search of Remedies*. Dhaka, Bangladesh: University Press Limited, 1997.

Southern California Law Review. Special issue on judicial independence. *Southern California Law Review*, 72, 2 (1999).

Stevens, Robert. *The Independence of the Judiciary: The View from the Lord Chancellor's Office*. Oxford: Clarendon, 1993.

Steyler, Nico. "The Judicialization of Namibian Politics," *South African Journal on Human Rights*, 9, 4 (1993): 477–499.

Stokes, Eric. *The English Utilitarians and India*. Oxford: Clarendon, 1959.

Stotzky, Irwin, ed. *The Transition to Democracy in Latin America: The Role of the Judiciary*. Boulder, CO: Westview, 1993.

Summers, Robert S. "The General Duty of Good Faith—Its Recognition and Conceptualization," *Cornell University Law Review*, 67 (1982): 810–839.

Takirambudde, Peter Nanyenya, ed. *The Individual under African Law*. Proceedings of the First All-Africa Conference, October 11–16, 1981. Kwaluseni, Swaziland: University of Swaziland Department of Law, 1982.

Takirambudde, Peter. "Six Years of the African Charter on Human and People's Rights: An Assessment," *Lesotho Law Journal*, 7, 2 (1991): 35–68.

Tambila, K. I. "The Transition to Multiparty Democracy in Tanzania: Some History and Missed Opportunities," *Verfassung und Recht im Übersee*, 28, 4 (1995): 468–488.

Tanner, R. E. S. "The Codification of Customary Law in Tanzania," *East African Law Journal*, 2, 2 (1966): 105–116.

Teitel, Ruti. "Paradoxes in the Revolution of the Rule of Law," *Yale Journal of International Law*, 19 (1994): 239–247.

Tetteh, E. Kofi. "Law Reporting in Anglophone Africa," *International and Comparative Law Quarterly*, 20 (January 1971): 87–98.

Teubner, Gunther. "Legal Irritants: Good Faith in British Law or How Unifying Law Ends up in New Divergences," *Modern Law Review*, 61, 1 (1998): 11–32.

Thode, Wayne E. *Reporter's Notes to Code of Judicial Conduct*. Chicago: American Bar Association, 1973.

Tolley, Howard B., Jr. *The International Commission of Jurists: Global Advocates for Human Rights*. Philadelphia: University of Pennsylvania Press, 1994.

Trubeck, David. "Toward a Social Theory of Law: An Essay on the Study of Law and Development," *Yale Law Journal*, 82, 1 (1972): 1–50.

Trubek, David, and Marc Galanter. "Scholars in Self-Estrangement: Some Reflections on the Crisis in Law and Development Studies in the United States," *Wisconsin Law Review*, 4 (1974): 1062–1104.

Tuchman, Barbara. *Practicing History*. New York: Ballantine Books, 1981.

Twining, William. "Academic Law and Legal Development." Taylor Lectures, 1975. Lagos, Nigeria: Faculty of Law, University of Lagos, 1976.

Twining, William. "The Camel in the Zoo," pp. 15–25 in Issa Shivji, ed., *Limits of Legal Radicalism: Reflections on Teaching Law at the University of Dar es Salaam*. Dar es Salaam, Tanzania: Faculty of Law, University of Dar es Salaam, 1986. Essay reprinted in William Twining, *Law in Context: Enlarging a Discipline*, below.

Twining, William. "The Concept of a National Legal Literature," pp. 7–21 in William Twining and Jenny Uglow, eds., *Legal Literature in Small Jurisdictions*. A Report of a Conference Held at Osgood Hall Law School, York University, Ontario, November 3–5, 1978. London: Commonwealth Secretariat, 1981.

Twining, William. "Constitutions, Constitutionalism and Constitution-Mongering," pp. 383–394 in Irwin Stotzky, ed., *The Transition to Democracy in Latin America: The Role of the Judiciary*. Boulder, CO: Westview, 1993.

Twining, William. *Karl Llewellyn and the Realist Movement*. London: Wiedenfeld and Nicolson, 1973.

Twining, William. *Law in Context: Enlarging a Discipline*. Oxford: Clarendon, 1997.

Twining, William. "The Restatement of African Customary Law: A Comment," *Journal of Modern African Studies*, 1, 2 (1963): 221–228.

Twining, William, and Jenny Uglow, eds. *Legal Literature in Small Jurisdictions*. London: Commonwealth Secretariat, 1981.

Union of International Associations. *Yearbook of International Organizations.* Munich: K. G. Saur, 1997/98.

van Donge, Jan Kees. "The Arbitrary State in the Ulunguru Mountains: Legal Arenas and Land Disputes in Tanzania," *Journal of Modern African Studies,* 31 (1993): 431–448.

Vanderlinden, J. "Civil Law and Common Law Influences on the Developing Law of Ethiopia," *Buffalo Law Review,* 16, 1 (1966): 250–266.

Vanderlinden, J. "The Recording of Customary Law in France during the Fifteenth and Sixteenth Centuries and Recording of African Customary Laws," *Journal of African Law,* 3, 3 (1959): 165–175.

Van Reenen, T. P. "The Relevance of the Roman (-Dutch) Law for Legal Integration in South Africa," *South African Law Journal,* 112, 2 (May 1995): 276–308.

Veitch, E. *East African Cases on the Law of Tort.* London: Sweet & Maxwell, 1972.

Veneklasen, Lisa. "Women's Legal Rights Organizing and Political Participation in Africa," pp. 249–273 in Margaret Schuler and Sakuntala Kadirgmar-Rajasingham, eds., *Legal Literacy: A Tool for Women's Empowerment.* New York: United Nations Development Fund for Women, UNIFEM WIDBOOKS, 1992.

Viljoen, Frans. "Application of the African Charter on Human and Peoples' Rights by Domestic Courts in Africa," *Journal of African Law,* 43, 1 (1999): 1–17.

Viljoen, Frans. "The Relevance for Africa of the Six major United Nations Human Rights Treaties and Their Monitoring Mechanisms." Paper presented at the 11th annual meeting of the African Society of International and Comparative Law, Harare, Zimbabwe, August 1999.

Wacks, Raymond. "Judges and Injustice," *South African Law Journal,* 101 (1984): 266–285.

Waddams, S. M. "Codification, Law Reform, and Judicial Development," *Journal of Contract Law,* 9 (1996): 192–199.

Waldron, Jeremy. *The Law.* London: Routledge, 1990.

Wambali, M. K. B. "The Court of Appeal of Tanzania and the Development of the Law of Torts," *Eastern Africa Law Review,* 16, 2 (1989): 213–228.

Wambali, M. K. B., and C. M. Peter. "The Judiciary in Context: The Case of Tanzania," pp. 213–228 in Neelan Tirachelram and Radhika Coomaraswamy, eds., *The Role of the Judiciary in Plural Societies.* New York: St. Martin's Press, 1987.

Wanda, B. P. "Malawi," pp. 123–130 in Andrew Harding and John Hatchard, eds., *Preventive Detention and Security Law: A Comparative Survey.* Dordrecht: Martinus Nijhoff, 1993.

Wanda, Boyce P. "The Role of Traditional Courts in Malawi," pp. 76–92 in Peter Nanyenya Takirambudde, ed., *The Individual under African Law.* Proceedings of the First All-Africa Conference, October 11–16, 1981. Kwaluseni, Swaziland: University of Swaziland, Department of Law, 1982.

Wanitzek, Ulrike. "Legally Unrepresented Women Petitioners in the Lower Courts of Tanzania: A Case of Justice Denied," pp. 183–198 in Jamil M. Abun-Nasr,

Ulrich Spellenberg, and Ulrike Wanitzek, eds., *Law, Society, and National Identity in Africa*. Hamburg: Helmut Buske Verlag, 1990.

Watson, Alan. *Legal Origins and Legal Change*. London: Hambledon Press, 1991.

Watson, Alan. *Legal Transplants: An Approach to Comparative Law*. Charlottesville: University Press of Virginia, 1974.

Watson, Alan. *Sources of Law, Legal Change, and Ambiguity*. Philadelphia: University of Pennsylvania Press, 1984.

Wechsler, Herbert. "The Challenge of a Model Penal Code," *Harvard Law Review*, 65, 7 (1952): 1097–1133.

Welch, Claude E., Jr. *Protecting Human Rights in Africa: Strategies and Roles of Non-governmental Organizations*. Philadelphia: University of Pennsylvania Press, 1995.

Weston, A. B. "Law in Swahili—Problems in Developing a National Language," *Swahili*, 35, 2 (1965): 2–13.

Widner, Jennifer A., ed. *Economic Change and Political Liberalization in Sub-Saharan Africa*. Baltimore: Johns Hopkins University Press, 1994.

Widner, Jennifer A. "The Quality of Justice: Report on the U.S.-Africa Judicial Exchange." Prepared for the U.S. Information Agency. Washington, D.C.: Superior Court of the District of Columbia in conjunction with the American Bar Association and the National Judicial College, July 1995. Mimeograph.

Williams, David V. "State Coercion against Peasant Farmers: The Tanzanian Case," *Journal of Legal Pluralism*, 20 (1982): 95–127.

Woodman, Gordon. "Customary Law, State Courts, and the Notion of Institutionalization of Norms in Ghana and Nigeria," pp. 143–163 in Anthony Allott and Gordon R. Woodman, eds., *People's Law and State Law*. Dordrecht: Foris Publications, 1985.

Woodman, Gordon. "Some Realism about Customary Law—The West African Experience," pp. 83–110 in Alison Dundes-Renteln and Alan Dundes, eds., *Folk Law: Essays in the Theory and Practice of Lex Non Scripta*. Madison: University of Wisconsin Press, 1994.

Woodman, Gordon. "Unification or Continuing Pluralism in Family Law in Anglophone Africa: Past Experience, Present Realities, and Future Possibilities," *Lesotho Law Journal*, 4, 5 (1988): 33–79.

Woodman, Gordon R. "Legal Pluralism and the Search for Justice," *Journal of African Law*, 40, 2 (1996): 152–167.

Woodman, Gordon R. "The Peculiar Policy of Recognition of Indigenous Laws in British Colonial Africa: A Preliminary Discussion," *Verfassung und Recht in Übersee*, 22, 3 (1989): 273–284.

Woolf, Right Honourable Lord. *Access to Justice* (Final Report). London: Her Majesty's Stationery Office, 1996.

World Bank. "Helping Countries Combat Corruption: The Role of the World Bank." PREM Working Paper. Washington, D.C.: World Bank, September 1997.

Index